THE

HOMES OF THE NEW WORLD;

IMPRESSIONS OF AMERICA.

BY

FREDRIKA BREMER.

TRANSLATED BY MARY HOWITT.

"SING UNTO THE LORD A NEW SONG."—*Psalm* xcvi.

IN TWO VOLUMES.

VOL. II.

NEW YORK:
HARPER & BROTHERS, PUBLISHERS,
329 & 331 PEARL STREET,
FRANKLIN SQUARE.
1853.

THE

HOMES OF THE NEW WORLD.

LETTER XXVI.

On the Mississippi, October 15th.

TOWARD sunset on the most lovely and glorious evening, we came out of the narrow little winding Five River, and entered the grand Mississippi, which flowed broad and clear as a mirror between hills which extended into the distance, and now looked blue beneath the mild, clear blue heavens, in which the new moon and the evening star ascended, becoming brighter as the sun sank lower behind the hills. The pure misty veil of the Indian summer was thrown over the landscape; one might have believed that it was the earth's smoke of sacrifice which arose in the evening toward the gentle heavens. Not a breath of air moved, every thing was silent and still in that grand spectacle; it was indescribably beautiful. Just then a shot was fired; a smoke issued from one of the small green islands, and flocks of ducks and wild geese flew up round about, escaping from the concealed sportsman, who I hope this evening returned without game. All was again silent and still, and the Menomonie advanced with a quiet, steady course up the glorious river.

I stood on the upper deck with the captain, Mr. Smith, and the representative from Minnesota, Mr. Sibley, who, with his wife and child, were returning home from Washington.

Was this, then, indeed, the Mississippi, that wild giant

of nature, which I had imagined would be so powerful, so divine, so terrible? Here its waters were clear, of a fresh, light-green color, and within their beautiful frame of distant violet-blue mountains, they lay like a heavenly mirror, bearing on their bosom verdant, vine-covered islands, like islands of the blessed. The Mississippi was here in its youth, in its state of innocence as yet. It has not as yet advanced very far from its fountains; no crowd of steamboats muddy its waters. The Menomonie and one other, a still smaller boat, are the only ones which ascend the river above Galena; no cities cast into it their pollution; pure rivers only flow into its waters, and aborigines and primeval forests still surround it. Afterward, far below and toward the world's sea, where the Mississippi comes into the life of the states, and becomes a statesman, he has his twelve hundred steamers, and I know not how many thousand sailing-boats, gives himself up to cities and the population of cities, and is married to the Missouri: then it is quite different; then is it all over with the beauty and innocence of the Mississippi.

But now, now it was beautiful, and the whole of that evening on the Mississippi was to me like an enchantment.

The Mississippi, discovered by Europeans, has two epochs, and in each a romance: the one as different to the other as day and night, as the sun-bright idyl to the gloomy tragedy, as the Mississippi here in its youth, and the Mississippi down at St. Louis, as Mississippi-Missouri. The first belongs to the northern district, the second to the southern; the former has its hero, the mild pastor, Father Marquette; the latter the Spanish soldier, Ferdinand de Soto.

France and England, equally jealous competitors for territorial acquisitions, were the first possessors of the land of North America. The French Jesuits were the first who penetrated into the wildernesses of Canada and to the great lakes of the West. Religious enthusiasm planted the Puritan colony on Plymouth Rock; religious enthusiasm planted the cross, together with the lilies of France, on the shores of the St. Lawrence, beside Niagara, and as far as St. Marie, among the wild Indians by Lake Superior. The noble, chivalric Champlain, full of ardor and zeal, said, "The salvation of a soul is worth more than the conquest of a kingdom."

That was at the time when the disciples of Loyola went forth over the world to conquer it as a kingdom for the Prince of Peace, and inscribed the sign of the cross in Japan, in China, in India, in Ethiopia, among the Caffirs, in California, in Paraguay. They invited the barbarian to the civilization of Christianity. The priests who penetrated from Canada to the deserts of Western America were among the noblest of their class.

"They had the faults of ascetic superstition; but the horrors of a Canadian life in the wilderness were resisted by an invincible, passive courage, and a deep internal tranquillity. Away from the amenities of life, away from the opportunities of vain-glory, they became dead to the world, and possessed their souls in unutterable peace. The few who lived to grow old, though bowed by the toils of a long mission, still kindled with the fervor of apostolic zeal. The history of their labors is connected with the origin of every celebrated town in the annals of French America: not a cape was turned, not a river entered, but a Jesuit led the way."

The Jesuits, Bribeuf and Daniel, and the gentle Lallemand, accompanied a party of barefooted Hurons to their country through dangerous forests. They won the regard and the love of the savages.

Bribeuf, who is said to have been the pattern of every religious virtue, lived fifteen years among the Hurons, baptizing them to the religion of Christ, and instructing them in the occupations of peace. Works of love, self-mortification, prayers deep into the night—such was his life. Yet all the more increased his love for the Master whom he served, and his desire to suffer in His service. He thirsted after it as others thirst after the delights of life. He made a vow never to decline the opportunity of martyrdom, and never to receive the death-blow except with joy.

Such was a faith to remove mountains; and it did more, it implanted the vitalizing love of Christ in the blood-thirsty heart of the savage. The great warrior Ahasistari said, "Before you came to this country, where I have incurred the greatest perils, and have alone escaped, have I said to myself, 'Some powerful spirit has the guardianship of my days!'" And he professed his belief in Jesus as the good Genius and Protector, whom he had before unconsciously adored. After trials of his sincerity he was baptized; and enlisting a troop of converts, savages like himself, "Let us strive," he exclaimed, "to make the whole world embrace the faith in Jesus."*

Further and further still advanced the missionaries toward the West; they heard of powerful and warlike Indian races, such as the mighty Sioux, who dwelt by the great River Mississippi, of the Erie, and Chippewas, and Potawatomies, and others who dwelt by the great lakes. Dangers, fatigues, wildernesses, savages, all stood in threatening array before them, but only the more to allure them.

Hostile tribes overcame the Indians who conducted them. The savage Mohawks took the missionary Isaac Jogues prisoner, and with him the noble chief Ahasistari. Ahasistari had succeeded in finding a hiding-place; but when he saw Jogues a captive, he stepped forth to him, saying, "My brother, I made a vow to thee that I would share thy fate, whether life or death—How am I to keep my vow?"

The savages exercised their cruelty upon them for sev-

* Bancroft.

eral days and nights. When Jogues ran the gauntlet, he consoled himself with a vision of the glory of the Queen of Heaven. One evening, after a day of torture, an ear of Indian corn was thrown to the good father, and see! upon the broad leaf there were drops of water, or of dew, sufficient to baptize two captive Christian converts!

Ahasistari and two of his people were burned. He met death with the pride of an Indian and the calmness of a Christian.

Father Jogues had expected the same fate; but his life was spared and his liberty granted to him. Roaming through the magnificent forests of the Mohawk Valley, he wrote the name of Jesus on the bark of trees, graved the cross, and took possession of these countries in the name of God. Often lifting up his voice in thanksgiving, consoling himself in his sorrow with the thought that he alone, in that vast region, adored the true God, the God of heaven and of earth.

He returned safely to his own people in Canada, but merely, two years afterward, to set out once more to seek new perils in the same service. "I shall go, but shall never return," said he, on setting out; and soon afterward was taken prisoner by the Mohawks, who said that he, by his enchantments, had blighted their harvest. Timid by nature, yet courageous through his zeal, he received his death-blow with calmness.

Bribeuf, Anthony, Daniel, and the mild Lallemand, all suffered martyrdom amid such torments as only Indians can devise; suffered it with that pious courage which only the love of Christ can inspire.

The villages and settlements founded by the good fathers were burned, and the Christian converts perished by fire and sword. All the many years' labor of the Jesuits was destroyed, and the wilderness seemed once more to grow over their traces.

Such great adversities might be supposed sufficient to

quench the ardor of the missionaries. Not at all! They pressed forward anew.

While the savage nations were carrying on cruel wars one with another, and converting all the paths through the forest of the West into paths of death, the Bishop of Quebec, Francis de Laval, was animated by the desire of conveying the doctrines of peace to the shores of the Great River. He desired to go himself; but the lot fell on René Mesnard. Every personal consideration seemed to retain him at Quebec, but powerful instincts urged him to risk his life in the enterprise. He was already old when he entered on the path still red with the blood of his predecessors. "In three or four months," wrote he to a friend, on his journey, "and you may add my name to those of the dead."

He went, never again to return. Afar off in the wilderness of the West, while his attendant was one day occupied in the transport of a boat, he entered a forest and was never more seen: his cassock and breviary were long retained as amulets among the Sioux! Another missionary was killed by the arrows of the Indians during a fight between two hostile tribes.

It is a refreshment to turn from these bloody and cruel scenes, which marked the first introduction of Christianity by Europe into the West, to the idyllian and peaceful episode of the Jesuit missionary, Marquette, and his labors amid those savage, warlike Indian tribes. It is like a sunbeam between thunder-clouds.

Already had the indefatigable Father Aloüez visited most of the Indian tribes around Lake Superior, and during two residences among them had taught the Chippewas to chant the Paternoster and Ave Maria, had been invited by the Potawatomies, the worshipers of the sun, to their huts; had smoked the pipe of peace with the Illinois tribes, who told him of their great fields overgrown with tall grass, where troops of wild deer and buffaloes grazed;

he had even met the quarrelsome and mighty Sioux, who lived on wild rice, covered their huts with skins of animals instead of bark, and dwelt upon the prairie near the Great River, which they called Messipi.

Marquette determined to discover and sail down the Great River.

He had gathered around him the remains of the Huron nation, and settled down with them on the shores of Lake Michigan, where there was abundance of fish. There they built themselves huts.

It was from this place that Marquette, accompanied by a Frenchman named Joliet, and a young Indian of the Illinois tribe as guide, set forth on his journey of discovery. The French intendant of Canada, Talon, favored Marquette's enterprise, wishing to ascertain whether the banner of France could be carried down the Great River as far as the Pacific Ocean, or planted side by side with that of Spain on the Gulf of Mexico.

Marquette sought by his journey the honor of a higher master than an earthly sovereign: "I shall gladly lay down my life for the salvation of souls," said he, in answer to a messenger of the Potawatomies, who warned him "that these distant nations never spared strangers; that their mutual wars filled the shores with warriors; and that the Great River abounded with monsters which devoured both men and canoes; and that the excessive heat was mortal." And on hearing his reply, the children of the wilderness united with him in prayer for his preservation.

"At the last village on Fox River ever visited by the French," using the words of Bancroft the historian, for I can not have a better guide, "where Kickapoos, Mascoutins, and Miamis dwelt together on a beautiful hill, in the centre of the prairies and magnificent groves that extended as far as the eye could reach, and where Aloüez had already raised the cross, which the savages ornamented with brilliant skins and crimson belts, a thanksgiving offering to the great Manitou, the ancients assembled in council to receive the pilgrims.

"'My companion,' said Marquette, 'is an envoy of France to discover new countries, and I am embassador from God to enlighten them with the Gospel;' and offering presents, he begged two guides for the morrow. The wild men answered courteously, and gave in return a mat, to serve as a couch during the long voyage.

"Behold then, in 1673, on the 10th of June, the meek, single-hearted, unpretending, illustrious Marquette, with Joliet for his associate, five Frenchmen as his companions, and two Algonquins as guides, lifting their canoes on their backs, and walking across the narrow portage that divides the Fox River from the Wisconsin. They reach the water-shed; uttering a special prayer to the immaculate Virgin, they leave the streams that, flowing onward, could have borne their greetings to the castle of Quebec; already they stand by the Wisconsin. 'The guides returned,' says the gentle Marquette, 'leaving us alone, in this unknown land, in the hands of Providence.'

"France and Christianity stood in the valley of the Mississippi.

"Embarking on the broad Wisconsin, the discoverers as they sailed west went solitarily down the stream, between alternate prairies and hill-sides, beholding neither man nor the wonted beasts of the forests. No sound broke the appalling silence, but the ripple of their canoe and the lowing of the buffalo. In seven days 'they entered happily the Great River with a joy that could not be expressed;' and the two birch-bark canoes, raising their happy sails under new skies and to unknown breezes, floated down the calm magnificence of the ocean stream over the broad, clear sand-bars, the resort of innumerable water-fowl; gliding past islets that swelled from the bosom of the stream, with their tufts of massive thickets, and between the wide plains of Illinois and Iowa, all garlanded with majestic forests, or checkered by island groves and the open vastness of the prairie.

"About sixty leagues below the mouth of the Wisconsin, the western bank of the Mississippi bore on its sands the trail of men; a little foot-path was discerned leading into a beautiful prairie, and, leaving the canoes, Joliet and Marquette resolved alone to brave a meeting with the savages. After walking six miles they beheld a village on the banks of a river, and two others on a slope at a distance of a mile and a half from the first. The river was the Meu-in-gou-e-na, or Moingona, of which we have corrupted the name into Des Moines. Marquette and Joliet were the first white men who trod the soil of Iowa. Commending themselves to God, they uttered a loud cry. The Indians hear; four old men advance slowly to meet them, bearing the peace-pipe, brilliant with many-colored plumes.

"'We are Illinois,' said they; that is, when translated, 'we are men;' and they offered the calumet. An aged chief received them at his cabin with upraised hands, exclaiming, 'How beautiful is the sun, Frenchman, when thou comest to visit us! Our whole village awaits thee; thou shalt enter in peace into all our dwellings.'

"At the great council, Marquette published to them the one true God, their Creator. He spoke also of the great captain of the French, the governor of Canada, who had chastised the Five Nations and commanded peace; and he questioned them respecting the Mississippi, and the tribes that possessed its banks. For the messengers who announced the subjection of the Iroquois, a magnificent festival was prepared of hominy and fish, and the choicest viands from the prairies.

"After six days' festivities among these wild people, the little band proceeded onward. 'I did not fear death,' said Marquette; 'I should have esteemed it the greatest happiness to have died for the glory of God.'

"They passed the perpendicular rocks, which wore the appearance of monsters; they heard at a distance the noise of the waters of the Missouri, known to them by its Algonquin name of Pekitanoni; and when they came to the most beautiful confluence of rivers in the world, where the swifter Missouri rushes like a conqueror into the calmer Mississippi, dragging it, as it were, hastily to the sea, the good Marquette resolved in his heart one day to ascend the mighty river to its source; to cross the ridge that divides the oceans, and, descending a westerly flowing stream, to publish the Gospel to all the people of this New World.

"In a little less than forty leagues the canoes floated past the Ohio, which was then and long afterward called the Wabash. Its banks were tenanted by numerous villages of the peaceful Shawnees, who quailed under the incursions of the Iroquois.

"The thick canes began to appear so close and strong that the buffalo could not break through them, and the insects became intolerable. The prairies vanished, and forests of white wood, admirable for their vastness and height, crowded even to the skirts of the pebbly shore. It was also observed that, in the land of the Chickasaws, the Indians had guns.

"They reached the village of Mitchigamea, in a region which had not been visited by Europeans since the days of De Soto. 'Now,' thought Marquette, 'we must indeed ask the aid of the Virgin. Armed with bows and arrows, with clubs, axes, and bucklers, amid continual whoops, the natives, bent on war, embarked in vast canoes made out of the trunks of hollow trees; but at the sight of the mysterious peace-pipe held aloft, God touched the hearts of the old men, who checked the impetuosity of the young; and, throwing their bows and quivers into the canoes as a token of peace, they prepared a hospitable welcome.'

"Thus had the travelers descended below the entrance of the Arkansas to the genial climes which have scarcely any winter but rains, to the vicinity of the Gulf of Mexico, and to tribes of Indians who had obtained arms by traffic with the Spaniards or with Virginia.

"So, having spoken of God, and the mysteries of the Catholic faith—having become certain that the Father of Rivers went not to the ocean, east of Florida, nor yet to the Gulf of California, Marquette and Joliet left Arkansea and ascended the Mississippi.

"At the thirty-eighth degree of latitude they entered the River Illinois, and discovered a country without its equal for the fertility of its beautiful prairies, covered with buffaloes and stags—for the loveliness of its rivulets, and the prodigal abundance of wild ducks and swans, and of a species of parrot and wild turkeys. The tribe of Indians that tenanted its banks entreated Marquette to come and reside among them. One of their chiefs, with their young men, conducted the party by way of Chicago to Lake Michigan; and before the end of September all were safe in Green Bay.

"Joliet returned to Quebec to announce the discovery, the fame of which, through Talon, quickened the ambition of Colbert. The unaspiring Marquette remained to preach the Gospel to the Miamis, who dwelt in the north of Illinois, round Chicago. Two years afterward, sailing from Chicago to Mackinaw, he entered a little river in Michigan. Erecting an altar, he said mass according to the ritual of the Catholic Church, and then desired the men who had conducted his canoe to leave him alone for half an hour.

"At the end of the time they went to seek him, but he was no more. The good missionary-discoverer of a world had fallen asleep on the margin of the stream that bears his name. Near its mouth the canoe-men dug his grave in the sand. Ever after, the forest-rangers, if in danger on Lake Michigan, would invoke his name. The people of the West will build his monument."

Thus much of Father Marquette; a short human life; but how full, how beautiful, how complete and perfect! Do you not see a ray of heavenly light shine through that misty, blood-stained valley of the Mississippi? Lower down on the Mississippi I shall tell you of Ferdinand de Soto.

Mississippi, October 16th.

Cold and chilly; but those stately hills, which rise higher and higher on each side the river, covered with forests of oak now brilliant in their golden-brown array beneath the autumnal heaven, and those prairies with their infinite stretches of view, afford a spectacle forever changing and forever beautiful. And then all is so young, so new, all as yet virgin soil! Here and there, at the foot of the hills, on the banks of the river, has the settler built his little log-house, plowed up a little field in which he has now just reaped his maize. The air is gray, but altogether calm. We proceed very leisurely, because the water is low at this time of the year, and has many shallows; at times it is narrow, and then again it is of great width, dotted over with many islands, both large and small. These islands are full of wild vines, which have thrown themselves in festoons among the trees, now for the most part leafless, though the wild vines are yet green.

We are sailing between Wisconsin on the right and Iowa on the left. We have just passed the mouth of the Wisconsin River, by which Father Marquette entered the Mississippi. How well I understand his feelings on the discovery of the Great River! I feel myself here, two hundred years later, almost as happy as he was, because I too am alone, and am on a journey of discovery, although of another kind. The Wisconsin flows into the Mississippi between shores overgrown with wood, and presents a beautiful idyllian scene.

We shall to-morrow enter upon a wilder region and among the Indians. If the weather is only not too cold!

Evening. It seems as if it would clear up; the sun has set and the moon risen, and the moon seems to dissipate the clouds. At sunset the Menomonie put to land to take in fuel. It was on the Iowa bank of the river. I went on shore with Mr. Sibley. A newly-erected log-house stood at the foot of the hill, about fifty paces from the river; we went into the house, and were met by a handsome young wife, with a nice little plump lad, a baby, in her arms; her husband was out in the forest. They had been at the place merely a few months, but were satisfied, and hopeful of doing well there. Two fat cows with bells were grazing in the meadow, without any tether. Every thing within the house was neat and in order, and indicated a degree of comfort. I saw some books on a shelf; these were the Bible, prayer-books, and American reading-books, containing selections from English and American literature, both verse and prose. The young wife talked sensibly and calmly about their life and condition as settlers in the West. When we left the house, and I saw her standing in the door-way with her beautiful child in her arms, she presented a picture in the soft glow of the Western heaven, a lovely picture of the new life of the West.

That young, strong, earnest mother, with her child on her arm, that little dwelling, protected by the husband, who cherished in himself the noblest treasures of thought and of love—behold in these the germ which, by degrees, will occupy the wilderness, and cause it to blossom as the rose.

16*th*. A glorious morning, as warm as summer! It rained in the night, but cleared up in the morning; those dense, dark masses of cloud were penetrated, rent asunder by the flashing sunbeams; and bold, abrupt shadows, and heavenly lights played among the yet bolder, more craggy, and more picturesque hills. What an animated scene it was! and I was once more alone with America, with my beloved, my great and beautiful sister, with the sibyl at whose knee I sat listening and glancing up to her with looks full of love. Oh what did she not communicate to me that day, that morning full of inspiration, as amid her tears she drank in the heavenly light, and flung those dark shadows, like a veil, back from her countenance, that it might be only the more fully illumined by the Divine light! Never shall I forget that morning!

They came again and again, during the morning, those dark clouds, spreading night over those deep abysses; but again they yielded, again they gave place to the sun, which finally prevailed, alone, triumphant, and shone over the Mississippi and its world in the most beautiful summer splendor; and the inner light in my soul conversed with the outward light. It was glorious!

The further we advanced, the more strangely and fantastically were the cliffs on the shore splintered and riven, representing the most astonishing imagery. Half way up, probably four or five hundred feet above the river, these hills were covered with wood now golden with the hue of autumn, and above that, rising, as if directly out of it, naked, ruin-like crags, of rich red brown, representing fortifications, towers, half-demolished walls, as of ancient, magnificent strongholds and castles. The castle ruins of the Rhine are small things in comparison with these gigantic remains of primeval ages; when men were not, but the Titans of primeval nature, Megatheriums, Mastodons, and Ichthyosaurians rose up from the waters, and wandered alone over the earth.

It was difficult to persuade one's self that many of these bold pyramids and broken temple-façades had not really been the work of human hands, so symmetrical, so architectural were these colossal erections. I saw in two places human dwellings, built upon a height; they looked like birds'-nests upon a lofty roof; but I was glad to see them, because they predicted that this magnificent region will soon have inhabitants, and this temple of nature worshipers in thankful and intelligent human hearts. The country on the other side of these precipitous crags is highland, glorious country, bordering the prairie-land—land for many millions of human beings! Americans will build upon these hills beautiful, hospitable homes, and will here labor, pray, love, and enjoy. An ennobled humanity will live upon these heights.

Below, in the river, at the feet of the hill-giants, the little green islands become more and more numerous. All were of the same character; all were lovely islands, all one tangle of wild vine. The wild grapes are small and sour, but are said to become sweet after they have been frosted. It is extraordinary that the wild vine is every where indigenous to America. America is of a truth Vineland.

I have heard the prophecy of a time and a land where every man shall sit under his own vine, and none shall make him afraid; when the wolf and the lamb shall sport together, and the desert shall blossom as the rose, and all in the name of the Prince of Peace.

These hills, spite of their varieties of form and of their ruin-like crags, have a general resemblance; they are nearly all of the same height, not exceeding eight or nine hundred feet. Good republicans, every one of them!

Last evening, just at sunset, I saw the first trace of the Indians in an Indian grave. It was a chest of bark laid upon a couple of planks supported by four posts, standing underneath a tree golden with autumnal tints. It is thus that the Indians dispose of their dead, till the flesh is dried off the bones, when these are interred either in the earth or in caves, with funeral rites, dances, and songs. Thus a coffin beneath an autumnal tree, in the light of the pale evening sun, was the first token which I perceived of this poor, decaying people.

Soon after we saw Indian huts on the banks of the river. They are called by themselves "tepees" (dwellings), and by the English "lodges;" they resemble a tent in form, and are covered with buffalo hides, which are wrapped round long stakes, planted in the ground in a circle, and united at the top, where the smoke passes out through an opening something like our Laplander's huts, only on a larger scale. There is a low opening in the form of a door to each hut, and over which a piece of buffalo hide can be let down at pleasure. I saw through the open doors the fire burning on the floor in many of the huts; it had a pleasant, kindly appearance. Little savage children were leaping about the shore. It was the most beautiful moonlight evening.

17*th*. Sunshiny, but cold. We have Indian territory through the whole of our course on the right; it is the territory of Minnesota, and we now see Indians encamped on the banks in larger or smaller numbers. The men, standing or walking, wrapped in their red or yellow-gray blankets; the women, busied at the fires either within or without the tents, or carrying their children on their backs in the yellow blankets in which they themselves are wrapped. All are bareheaded, with their black locks hanging down like horses' tails, or sometimes plaited. A great number of children, boys especially, leap about shouting on the shores. We proceeded very slowly, and stuck fast on the shallows continually as we wound among the islands. In the mean time, little canoes of Indians glided quickly, and, as it were, shyly hither and thither along the shores and the islands, the people seeming to be looking for something among the bushes. They appeared, for the most part, to be women in the boats; but it is not easy to distinguish a man from a woman, as they sit there wrapped in their blankets, with their bare, unkemped hair. They were seeking for wild berries and herbs, which they collect among the bushes. How savage and like wild beasts they looked! And yet it is very entertaining to see human beings so unlike the people one sees every day, so unlike our own selves!

The Indians we see here are of the Sioux or Dacotah nation, still one of the most powerful tribes in the country, and who, together with the Chippewas, inhabit the district around the springs of the Mississippi (Minnesota). Each nation is said to amount to twenty-five thousand souls. The two tribes live in hostility with each other; but have lately held, after some bloody encounters, a peace congress at Fort Snelling, where the American authorities compelled these vengeful people, although unwillingly, to offer each other the hand of reconciliation.

Mr. Sibley, who has lived many years among the Sioux, participating in their hunting and their daily life, has related to me many characteristic traits of this people's life and disposition. There is a certain grandeur about them, but it is founded on immense pride; and their passion for revenge is carried to a savage and cruel extreme. Mr. Sibley is also very fond of the Indians, and is said to be a very great favorite with them. Sometimes, when we sail past Indian villages, he utters a kind of wild cry, which receives an exulting response from the shore.

Sometimes we see a little log-house, with two or three Indian lodges beside it. Such houses belong to half-blood Indians, that is to say, one whose father was a white man and mother an Indian, and these are his relations by the mother's side, or the relatives of his Indian wife, who have come to dwell near him. He is commonly engaged in trade, and is a link between the Indian and European.

We have now also some Indians on board, a family of the Winnebagoes, husband, wife, and daughter, a young girl of seventeen, and two young warriors of the Sioux tribe, adorned with fine feathers, and painted with red and yellow, and all colors, I fancy, so that they are splendid. They remain on the upper deck, where I also remain, on account of the view being so much more extensive. The Winnebago man is also painted, and lies on deck, generally on his stomach, propped on his elbows, and wrapped in his blanket. The wife looks old and worn out, but is cheerful and talkative. The girl is tall and good-looking, but has heavy features, and broad, round shoulders; she is very shy, and turns away if any one looks at her. I saw the three have their dinner: they took a piece of dark-colored meat, which I supposed to have been smoke-dried, out of a bag, and alternately tore a piece from it with their teeth. I offered them cakes and fruit, which I had with me; the wife laughed, and almost snatched them from me. They were well pleased to receive them, but expressed no thanks. The young Sioux warriors look like some kind of great cock. They strut about now and then, and look proud, and then they squat themselves down on their hams, like apes, and chatter away as volubly as any two old gossips ever did. All the men have noses like a hawk's bill, and the corners of their mouths are drawn down, which gives a disagreeable, scornful expression to the countenance. Nothing, however, about them has struck me so much as their eyes, which have a certain hard, inhuman expression. They seem to me like those of wild beasts, cold, clear, with a steady, hard, and almost cruel glance. One could fancy that they had caught sight of some object, some prey a long way off in the forest. The glance is not deficient in intelligence or acuteness, but it is deficient in feeling. There is an immense difference between their eyes and those of the negroes. The former are a cold day, the latter a warm night.

Last night we passed through Lake Pepin in the moonlight. It is an extension of the Mississippi, large enough to constitute a lake, surrounded by magnificent hills, which seem to inclose it with their almost perpendicular cliffs, one among which is particularly prominent, and is called Wenona's Cliff, from a young Indian girl who here sang her death-song and then threw herself into the waters below, preferring death to marriage with a young man whom she did not love.

Late last evening I noticed a tall Indian who was standing with his arms crossed, wrapped in his blanket, under a large tree. He stood as immovable as if he had grown into the tree against the boll of which he leaned. He looked very stately. All at once he gave a leap forward, and, uttering a shrill cry, bounded down to the shore; and then I saw, at no great distance, an encampment of about twenty huts in the forest near the river, where fires were burning, and there seemed to be a throng of people. Along the shore lay a considerable number of small canoes, and I imagined that the warning cry of the man had reference to these, for when our steamer swung past the place, for it was at a bend of the river where the camp stood, it occasioned a sort of earthquake to those little boats, which were hurled like nut-shells one against another, and on toward the shore. The people who were seated in the boats leaped upon the shore, others came running from the huts down to the boats; the whole encampment was in motion; there was a yelling and a barking both of men and dogs, and shrill cries which were heard long after the Menomonie had shot past on her foaming career. The camp, with its fires, its huts, and its people, was a most wild and animated scene.

At another place, during the day, we saw a large, pale red stone standing on a plain near the river. I was told that this stone, and all large stones of this kind, are regarded as sacred by the Indians, who swear by them, and around which they hold their councils, believing that they are the abiding-place of a divinity.

In the afternoon we shall reach St. Paul's, the goal of our journey, and the most northern town on the Mississippi. I am sorry to reach it so soon; I should have liked this voyage up the Mississippi to have lasted eight days at least. It amuses and interests me indescribably. These new shores, so new in every way, with their perpetually varying scenes; that wild people, with their camps, their fires, boats, their peculiar manners and cries—it is a continual refreshment to me. And to this must be added that I am able to enjoy it in peace and freedom, from the excellent arrangement of the American steam-boats for their passengers. They are commonly three-decked—the middle deck being principally occupied by the passengers who like to be comfortable. Round this deck runs a broad gallery or piazza, roofed in by the upper deck, within which are ranged the passengers' cabins, side by side, all round the vessel. Each cabin has a door, in which is a window opening into the gallery, so that one can either enter the gallery this way, or enjoy the scenery of the shore from the cabin itself; it has also another door, which opens into the saloon. The saloon aft is always appropriated to the ladies, and around this are their cabins; the second great saloon also, used for meals, is the assembling-place of the gentlemen. Each little apartment, called a state-room, has commonly two berths in it, the one above the other; but if the steamer is not much crowded, one can easily obtain a cabin entirely to one's self. These apartments are always painted white, and are neat, light, and charming; one could remain in them for days with the utmost pleasure. The table is generally well and amply supplied; and the fares, comparatively speaking, are low. Thus, for instance, I pay for the voyage from Galena to St. Paul's only six dollars, which seems to me quite too little in comparison with all the good things that I enjoy. I have a charming little "state-room" to myself, and the few upper-class passengers are not of the catechising order. One of them, Mr. Sibley, is a clever, kind man, and extremely interesting to me from his knowledge of the people of this region, and their circumstances. There are also some emigrant families who are on their way to settle on the banks of the River St. Croix and Stillwater, who do not belong to what are called the "better class," although they rank with such—a couple of ladies who smoke meerschaum-pipes now and then—and, in particular, there are two half-grown girls, who are considerably in my way sometimes—especially one of them, a tall, awkward girl in a fiery-red, brick-colored dress, with fiery-red hair as rough as a besom, and eyes that squint, and who, when she comes out, sets herself to stare at me with her arms crossed, her mouth and eyes wide open, as if I were some strange Scandinavian animal, and every now and then she rushes up to me with some unnecessary, witless question. I regard these girls as belonging to—the mythological monsters of the Great West, as daughters of its giants, and did not scruple to cut them rather short! Ah! people may come to this hemisphere as democratic as they will, but when they have traveled about a little they will become aristocratic to a certain extent. To a certain extent—but beyond that I shall never go, even though the daughters of the giants become so numerous as to shut out my view. And this brick-colored, foolhardy girl would—of this I am certain—with a few kind and intelligent words, assume a different mode of behavior, and, if I were to be any length of time with her, she and I should become good friends. And there is in one of these emigrant families an old grandmother, and yet not so very old after all, who is so full of anxiety, so quietly active, and so thoughtful for every one who belongs to her, and who is evidently so kind and motherly in disposition, that one must willingly take in good part all her questions and her ignorance of geography, if one has any thing good in one's self. And that one has not when one gets out of temper with the manners of the giants' daughter, and wills to be at peace.

The captain of the steamer, Mr. Smith, is an extremely agreeable and polite man, who is my cavalier on board, and in whose vessel the utmost order prevails.

We see no longer any traces of European cultivation on shore, nothing but Indian huts and encampments. The shores have become flatter since we left Lake Pepin, and the scenery tamer.

LETTER XXVII.

St. Paul's, Minnesotà, October 25th.

At about three miles from St. Paul's we saw a large Indian village, consisting of about twenty hide-covered wigwams, with their ascending columns of smoke. In the midst of these stood a neat log-house. This was the home which a Christian missionary had built for himself among the savages, and here he had established a school for the children. Upon a hill beyond the village, a number of stages were placed in a half circle, upon which rested coffins of bark. Small white flags distinguished those among the departed who had been most recently brought there. The village, which is called Kaposia, and is one of the established Indian villages, looked animated from its women, children, and dogs. We sped rapidly past it, for the Mississippi was here as clear and deep as our own River Götha, and the next moment, taking an abrupt turn to the left, St. Paul's was before us, standing upon a high bluff on the eastern bank of the Mississippi; behind it the blue arch of heaven, and far below it the Great River, and before it, extending right and left, beautiful valleys, with their verdant hill-sides scattered with wood—a really grand and commanding situation—affording the most beautiful views.

We lay to at the lower part of the town, whence the upper is reached by successive flights of steps, exactly as with us on the South Hill by Mose-back in Stockholm. Indians were sitting or walking along the street which runs by the shore. Wrapped in their long blankets, they marched on with a proud step, and were some of them stately figures. Just opposite the steamer, and at the foot of the steps, sat some young Indians, splendidly adorned with feathers and ribbons, and smoking from a long pipe which they handed from one to the other, so that they merely smoked a few whiffs each.

Scarcely had we touched the shore when the governor of Minnesota, Mr. Alexander Ramsay, and his pretty young wife, came on board, and invited me to take up my quarters at their house. And there I am now; happy with these kind people, and with them I make excursions into the neighborhood. The town is one of the youngest infants of the Great West, scarcely eighteen months old, and yet it has in this short time increased to a population of two thousand persons, and in a very few years it will certainly be possessed of twenty-two thousand, for its situation is as remarkable for beauty and healthiness as it is advantageous for trade. Here the Indians come with their furs from that immense country lying between the Mississippi and the Missouri, the western boundary of Minnesota, and the forests still undespoiled of their primeval wealth, and the rivers and lakes abounding in fish, offer their inexhaustible resources, while the great Mississippi offords the means of their conveyance to the commercial markets of the world, flowing, as it does, through the whole of Central America down to New Orleans. Hence it is that several traders here have already acquired considerable wealth, while others are coming hither more and more, and they are building houses as fast as they can.

As yet, however, the town is but in its infancy, and people manage with such dwellings as they can get. The drawing-room at Governor Ramsay's house is also his office, and Indians and work-people, and ladies and gentlemen, are all alike admitted. In the mean time, Mr. Ramsay is building himself a handsome, spacious house, upon a hill, a little out of the city, with beautiful trees around it, and commanding a grand view over the river. If I were to live on the Mississippi, I would live here. It is a hilly region, and on all hands extend beautiful and varying landscapes; and all abounds with such youthful and fresh life.

The city is thronged with Indians. The men, for the most part, go about grandly ornamented, and with naked hatchets, the shafts of which serve them as pipes. They paint themselves so utterly without any taste that it is incredible. Sometimes one half of the countenance will be painted of a cinnamon-red, striped and in blotches, and the other half with yellow ditto, as well as all other sorts of fancies, in green, and blue, and black, without the slightest regard to beauty that I can discover. Here comes an Indian who has painted a great red spot in the middle of his nose; here another who has painted the whole of his forehead in small lines of yellow and black; there a third with coal-black rings round his eyes. All have eagles' or cocks' feathers in their hair, for the most part colored, or with scarlet tassels of worsted at the ends. The hair is cut short on the forehead, and for the rest hangs in elf-locks or in plaits on the shoulders, both of men and women. The women are less painted, and with better taste than the men, generally with merely one deep red little spot in the middle of the cheeks, and the parting of the hair on the forehead is died purple. I like their appearance better than that of the men. They have a kind smile, and often a very kind expression; as well as a something in the glance which is much more human; but they are evidently merely their husbands' beasts of burden. There goes an Indian with his proud step, bearing aloft his plumed head. He carries only his pipe, and when he is on a journey, perhaps a long staff in his hand. After him, with bowed head and stooping shoulders, follows his wife, bending under the burden which she bears on her back, and which a band, passing over the forehead, enables her to support. Above the burden peeps forth a little round-faced child, with beautiful dark eyes: it is her "papoose," as these children are called. Its little body is fastened by swaddling-clothes upon its back on a board, which is to keep its body straight; and it lives, and is fed, and sleeps, and grows, always fastened to the board. When the child can walk it is still carried for a long time on the mother's back in the folds of her blanket. Nearly all the Indians which I have seen are of the Sioux tribe.

Governor Ramsay drove me yesterday to the Falls of St. Anthony. They are some miles from St. Paul's. These falls close the Mississippi to steam-boats and other vessels. From these falls to New Orleans the distance is two thousand two hundred miles. A little above the falls the river is again navigable for two hundred miles, but merely for small vessels, and that not without danger.

The Falls of St. Anthony have no considerable height, and strike me merely as the cascade of a great mill-dam. They fall abruptly over a stratum of a tufa rock, which they sometimes break and wash down in great masses. The country around is neither grand, nor particularly picturesque; yet the river here is very broad, and probably from that cause the fall and the hills appear more inconsiderable. The shore is bordered by a rich luxuriance of trees and shrubs, springing up wildly from among pieces of rock, and the craggy tufa walls with their ruin-like forms, which, however, have nothing grand about them. River, falls, country, views, every thing here has more breadth than grandeur.

It was Father Hennepin, the French Jesuit, who first came to these falls, brought hither captive by the Indians. The Indians called the falls "Irrara," or the Laughing Water; he christened them St. Anthony's. I prefer the first name, as being characteristic of the fall, which has rather a cheerful than a dangerous appearance, and the roar of which has nothing terrific in it. The Mississippi is a river of a joyful temperament. I have a painting of its springs—a present from Mr. Schoolcraft—the little lake, Itaska, in the northern part of Minnesota. The little lake looks like a serene heavenly mirror set in a frame of primeval forest. Northern firs and pines, maples and elms, and other beautiful American trees, surround the waters of this lake like a leafy tabernacle above the cradle of the infant river. Afar up in the distant background lies that elevated range of country, called by the French "Hauteur des terres," resembling a lofty plateau, covered with dense forest, scattered over with blocks of granite, and interspersed with a hundred springs: five of these throw themselves from different heights into the little lake.

When the infant Mississippi springs forth from the bosom of Itaska, it is a rapid and clear little stream, sixteen feet broad, and four inches deep. Leaping forward over stocks and stones, it expands itself ninety miles below its spring into Lake Pemideji—a lake the waters of which are clear as crystal, and which is free from islands. Here it is met by the River La Place, from Assawa Lake. Forty-five miles lower down it pours itself down into Lake Cass, the terminal point of Governor Cass's expedition in 1820. When the Mississippi emerges from this lake, it is one hundred and seventy-two feet broad, and eight feet deep. Thus continues it increasing in width and depth, receiving richer and richer tribute from springs and rivers, now reposing in clear lakes, abounding in innumerable species of fish, then speeding onward, between banks covered with wild roses, elders, hawthorns, wild rice, wild plums, and all kind of wood fruit, strawberries, raspberries, cranberries, through forests of white cedar, pine, birch, and sugar-maple, abounding in game of many kinds, such as bears, elks, foxes, raccoons, martens, beavers, and such like; through the prairie country, the higher and lower full of bubbling fountains—the so-called Undine region; through tracts of country, the fertile soil of which would produce luxuriant harvests of corn, of wheat, potatoes, etc., through an extent of three or four hundred miles, during which it is navigable for a considerable distance, till it reaches St. Anthony. Just above this point, however, it has greatly extended itself, has embraced many greater and smaller islands, overgrown with trees and wild vines. Immediately above the falls, it runs so shallow over a vast level surface of rock that people may cross it in carriages, as we did to my astonishment. At no great distance below the falls the river becomes again navigable, and steamers go up as far as Mendota, a village at the outlet of the St. Peter's River into the Mississippi, somewhat above St. Paul's. From St. Paul's there is a free course down the Mississippi to the Gulf of Mexico. The Falls of St. Anthony are the last youthful adventure of the Mississippi. For nine hundred miles the river flows along the territory of Minnesota, a great part of which is wild and almost unknown country.

But to return to the falls and to the day I spent there.

Immediately below the largest of the falls, and enveloped in its spray, as if by shapes of mist, lies a little island of picturesque, ruin-like masses of stone, crowned with rich wood—the most beautiful and the most striking feature of the whole scene. It is called the Cataract Island of the laughing water-fall. It is also called "Spirit Island," from an incident which occurred here some years since, and which I must relate to you, because it is characteristic of the life of the Indian woman.

"Some years ago, a young hunter, of the Sioux tribe, set up his wigwam on the bank of the Mississippi, a little above St. Anthony's Fall. He had only *one* wife, which is an unusual thing with these gentlemen, who sometimes are possessed of as many as twenty; and she was called Ampato Sapa. They lived happily together for many years, and had two children, who played around their fire, and whom they were glad to call their children.

"The husband was a successful hunter, and many families, by degrees, assembled around him, and erected their wigwams near his. Wishing to become still more closely connected with him, they represented to him that he ought to have several wives, as by that means he would become of more importance, and might, before long, be elected chief of the tribe.

"He was well pleased with this counsel, and privately took a new wife; but, in order to bring her into his wigwam without displeasing his first wife, the mother of his children, he said to her,

"'Thou knowest that I never can love any other woman so tenderly as I love thee; but I have seen that the labor of taking care of me and the children is too great for thee, and I have therefore determined to take another wife, who shall be thy servant; but thou shalt be the principal one in the dwelling.'

"The wife was very much distressed when she heard these words. She prayed him to reflect on their former affection—their happiness during many years—their children. She besought of him not to bring this second wife into their dwelling.

"In vain. The next evening the husband brought the new wife into his wigwam.

"In the early dawn of the following morning a death-song was heard on the Mississippi. A young Indian woman sat in a little canoe with her two small children, and rowed it out into the river in the direction of the falls. It was Ampato Sapa. She sang in lamenting tones the sorrow of her heart, of her husband's infidelity, and her determination to die. Her friends heard the song, and saw her intention, but too late to prevent it.

"Her voice was soon silenced in the roar of the fall. The boat paused for a moment on the brink of the precipice, and the next was carried over it and vanished in the foaming deep. The mother and her children were seen no more."

The Indians still believe that in the early dawn may be heard the lamenting song deploring the infidelity of the husband; and they fancy that at times may be seen the mother, with the children clasped to her breast, in the misty shapes which arise from the fall around the Spirit Island.

This incident is only one among many of the same kind which occur every year among the Indians. Suicide is by no means rare among their women.

A gentleman who wished to contest this point with me, said, that during the two years which he had lived in this region, he had only heard of eleven or twelve such occurrences. And quite enough too, I think! The occasion of suicide is, with the Indian woman generally, either that her father will marry her against her wishes and inclination, or, when she is married, that the husband takes a new wife. Suicide, a fact so opposed to the impulses of a living creature, seems to me to bear strong evidence in favor of the pure feminine nature of these poor women, and shows that they are deserving of a better lot. As young girls, their choice is seldom consulted with regard to marriage. The wooer spreads out before the girl's father his buffalo and beaver skins, he carries to the mother some showy pieces of cloth and trinkets, and the girl is —sold. If she makes any opposition, the father threatens to cut off her ears and her nose; and she, equally obstinate with him, cuts the matter short by—hanging herself; for this is the mode of death which is generally selected. It is true that the desire for revenge may be the mainspring of suicide, and it is well known that the Indian women emulate the men in cruelty to their enemies and war-captives; still, their hard lives as women are not the less to be deplored; and their strength to die, rather than degrade themselves, proves that these children of nature are more high-minded than many a woman in the higher ranks of civilization. The beauties of the forest are prouder and nobler than are frequently they of the saloon. But true it is that their world is a weary one, and affords them nothing but the husband whom they must serve, and the circumscribed dwelling of which he is the master.

We drank tea on a considerable island in the Mississippi, above the falls, at a beautiful home, where I saw comforts and cultivation, where I heard music, saw books and pictures—such life, in short, as might be met with on the banks of the Hudson; and how charming it was to me! Here, too, I found friends in its inhabitants, even as I had there. The dwelling had not been long on the island; and the island, in its autumnal attire, looked like a little paradise, although still in its half-wild state.

As to describing how we traveled about, how we walked over the river on broken trunks of trees which were jammed together by the stream in chaotic masses, how we climbed and clambered up and down, among, over, and upon stocks, and stones, and precipices, and sheer descents—all this I shall not attempt to describe, because it is indescribable. I considered many a passage wholly and altogether impracticable, until my conductors, both gentlemen and ladies, convinced me that it was to them a simple and every-day path. Ugh!

The day was cold and chilly, and for that reason the excursion was more fatiguing to me than pleasant.

I have had several rambles in the immediate neighborhood, sometimes alone and sometimes in company with the agreeable Governor Ramsay, or with a kind clergyman of this place. In this way I have visited several small farmers, most of them French, who have come hither from Canada. They all praise the excellence of the soil and its fertility; they were capital people to talk with, seemed to be in a prosperous condition, had many children, but that neatness and general comfort which distinguish the homes of the Anglo-Americans I did not find in their dwellings, but rather the contrary. On all sides the grass waved over hills and fields, tall and of an autumnal yellow. There are not hands enough here to mow it. The soil is a rich black mould, which is superb for the growth of potatoes and grain, but not so agreeable for pedestrians in white stockings and petticoats. A fine black dust soils every thing. The most lovely little lakes lie among the hills, like clear mirrors in romantic peace and beauty. It is a perfectly Arcadian landscape; but there yet lack the shepherds and shepherdesses. The eastern shore of the Mississippi, within Minnesota only, belongs to the whites, and their number here does not as yet amount to more than seven thousand souls. The whole western portion of Minnesota is still Indian territory, inhabited principally by two great nations, Sioux or Dacotahs, and Chippewas, who live in a continual state of hostility, as well as by some of the lesser Indian tribes. It is said that the government is intending shortly to purchase the whole of this country; and that the Indian tribes are willing to treat, and to withdraw themselves to the other side of the Missouri River, to the steppland of Nebraska and the Rocky Mountains. These Indian tribes have already become so degraded by their intercourse with the whites, that they value money and brandy higher than their native soil, and are ready, like Esau, to sell their birth-right for a mess of pottage. But that cruel race which scalps children and old people, and which degrades women to beasts of burden, may as well move off into the wilderness, and leave room for a nobler race. There is, in reality, only a higher justice in it.

October 26th. I went yesterday with my kind entertainers into the Indian territory, by Fort Snelling, a fortress built by the Americans here, and where military are stationed, both infantry and cavalry, to keep the Indians in check. The Indians are terribly afraid of the Americans, whom they call "the Long Knives," and now the white settlers are no longer in danger. The Indian tribes, spite of the American intervention, continue their bloody and cruel hostilities among themselves. Not long since a number of Sioux warriors surprised a Chippewa village while the men were away on their hunting, and killed and scalped sixteen persons, principally women and children. Governor Ramsay ordered the ringleaders of this attack to be seized and taken to prison. They went with a proud step and the demeanor of martyrs for some noble cause.

I was extremely curious to see the inside of one of those tepees or wigwams, the smoke and fires of which I had so often seen already; and as we chanced to see, soon after entering the Indian territory, four very respectable Indian huts, I hastened to visit them. Governor Ramsay, and an interpreter whose house was just by, accompanied me. I directed my steps to the largest wigwam; to the *opening* of which two lean dogs were fastened with cords. The Indians eat their dogs when other food fails. We opened the curtain of hide which represents a door, but instead of the dirt and poverty which I expected to find, I was greatly surprised to see a kind of rude Oriental luxury and splendor.

The fire burned in the middle of the hut, which was large and well covered with buffalo skins. Two men, whose faces were painted with red stripes and devices, sat by the fire carving pipes from a blood-red kind of stone. Round the walls of the hut sat the women and children, upon cushions very showily embroidered, and laid upon white blankets. Some of them were painted with a brilliant red spot in the middle of their cheeks, the parting of their hair being painted red also. They looked really handsome and full of animation, with their bright black eyes and disheveled hair, thus seen in the light of the flickering fire. Besides this, they were friendly, and seemed amused by my visit. They made room for me to sit down beside them. The old women laughed and chattered, and seemed very much at their ease. The younger ones were more grave and bashful. The men did not look up after their first glance at our entrance, but continued silently to work away at their pipes. A great kettle, suspended by a rope from the poles at the top of the hut, hung over the fire. It was dinner-time. A young woman who sat on my right fed her little papoose, which seemed to be about three years old, and which had also a grand red spot on each of its fat round cheeks.

"Hoxidan?" said I, pointing to the child, that word signifying *boy*.

"Winnona," replied she, in a low, melodious voice, that word signifying *girl*.

And with that my stock of Indian words was exhausted. I requested by signs to taste the soup of which she and the child were eating, and she cheerfully handed to me her bowl and spoon. It was a kind of thin soup, in which beans were boiled, without salt, and without the slightest flavor which I could perceive. She then offered me a cake which was just baked, of a golden brown, and which looked quite delicious. It was, I believe, made of wheaten flour, and without salt also, but very excellent nevertheless.

The interpreter was gone out. Gov. Ramsay had also seated himself. The Indians filed on at their pipes; the flames flickered merrily; the kettle boiled; the women ate or looked at me, half reclining or sitting carelessly by the fire-light. And I—looked at them. With inward wonder I regarded these beings, women like myself, with the spirit and the feelings of women, yet so unlike myself in their purpose of life, in daily life, in the whole of their world!

I thought of hard, gray, domestic life, in the civilized world, a home without love, hedged in by conventional opinion, with social duties, the duty of seeking for the daughters of the family suitable husbands, otherwise they would never leave the family; and with every prospect of independence, liberty, activity, joy closed, more rigidly closed by invisible barriers, than these wigwams by their buffalo hides; a Northern domestic life—such an one as exists in a vast number of Northern homes—and I thought that that Indian hut and that Indian woman's life was better, happier as *earthly life*.

Thus had I thought in the gas-lighted drawing-rooms of New York and Boston, in the heat and the labor of being polite or agreeable; of conversation and congratulation; of endeavoring to look well, to please and to be pleased, and—I thought that the wigwam of an Indian was a better and a happier world than that of the drawing-room. There they sat at their ease, without stays, or the anxiety to charm, without constraint or effort, those daughters of the forest! They knew not the fret and the disquiet, the ennui and the fatigue, which is the consequence of a brief hour's social worry; they knew not the disgust and the bitterness which is produced by little things, little vexations, which one is ashamed to feel, but which one must feel nevertheless. Their world might be monotonous, but in comparison it was calm and fresh within the narrow wigwam, while without there was free space, and the rustling forest open to them with all its fresh winds and odors. Ah!

But again I bethought myself of the Indian women—bethought me of their life and condition; with no other purpose and no other prospect in life than to serve a husband whom they have seldom chosen themselves, who merely regards them as servants, or as a cock regards the hens around him. I saw the wife and the mother humiliated by the entrance of the new wife into the husband's dwelling, and his affection being turned to the stranger in her sight, and in the same home, and in the fire-light of that same hearth which had been kindled on her marriage day, saw her despised or neglected by the man who constituted her whole world. Ah! the wigwam, the free space of the forest, had no longer peace or breathing room for the anguish of such a condition; alleviation of its agony or its misery is found merely in degradation or death. Winnona's death-song on the rock by Lake Pepin; Ampato Sapa's death-song on the waters of the Mississippi, when she and her children sought for the peace of forgetfulness in their foaming depths; and many other of their sisters, who yet to this day prefer death to life, all testify how deeply tragical is the fate of the Indian woman.

And again I bethought myself of love-warmed homes in the cultivated world, in the North as well as in the South; homes such as are frequent, and which become still more and more so among a free and Christian people, where the noble woman is the noble man's equal in every thing, in pleasure and in need; where good parents prepare even the daughters of the house for a life of independent activity and happiness, for the possession of a world, an object which is beyond the circumscribed boundary of the dwelling-house, no longer a buffalo-hide-enveloped wigwam. I bethought me of her right, and the possibility of her acquiring a sphere of action in the intellectual world which would make the torments of civilized life, whether small or great, seem like cloudlets in a heaven otherwise bright; bethought me of my own Swedish home, of my good mother, my quiet room, my peace and freedom there, as on the maternal bosom, with space and view limitless as infinity. And I thanked God for my lot!

But these poor women here! Three families resided in this wigwam; there were only three husbands, but there were certainly twelve or thirteen women. How many bitter, jealous feelings must burn in many a bosom assembled here, day and night, around the same fire, partaking of the same meal, and with the same object in life!

I visited the other wigwams also. Each one presented the same scene with but little variation. Two or three men by the fire, several women sitting or lying upon blankets or embroidered cushions round the walls of the hut, and occupied with nothing for the moment. The men carved red-stone pipes, which they sell to the whites at very high prices; the work, however, in this hard stone is not easy. This red stone is obtained from quarries situated far up the Missouri. I can not but admire the hands of these men; they are remarkably beautiful and well formed, and are evidently, even as regards the nails, kept with great care; they are delicate and slender, resembling rather the hands of women than men.

I saw in one wigwam a young woman, who, as she sat with her rich, unbound hair falling over her shoulders, seemed to me so unusually handsome that I wished to make a sketch of her. I also wished to take the portraits of a couple of Indians, and requested Governor Ramsay to prefer my request. He therefore, by means of the interpreter, Mr. Prescott, stated to an old chief named Mozah-hotah (Gray Iron) that I wished to take the likenesses of all great men in this country, to show to the people on the other side of the great water, and therefore that I requested him to sit to me a short time for that purpose.

The old chief, who is said to be a good and respectable man, looked very grave, listened to the proposal attentively, and gave a sort of grunting assent. He then accompanied us to the house of the interpreter, from the doors and windows of which peeped forth many little faces with their Indian features and complexion, for Mr. Prescott has an Indian wife, and many children by her.

I was soon seated in the house with the old chief before me, who expressed some annoyance because he was not in grand attire, having merely a couple of eagle's feathers in his hair, and not being so splendidly painted as he ought to have been. He wore under his white woolen blanket a blue European surtout, which he appeared anxious to have also included in the portrait. He evidently considered this as something out of the common way. He seemed a little uneasy to sit, and not at all comfortable when the interpreter was out of the room. The Indians universally believe that a likeness on paper takes away from the life of the person represented, and on that account many Indians will not allow their portraits to be taken.

The young Indian woman followed the old chief; she came attired in her wedding-dress of embroidered scarlet woolen stuff, and with actual cascades of silver rings, linked one within another, and hanging in clusters from her ears, round which the whole cluster was fastened; down to her shoulders, her neck and breast were covered with masses of coral, pearls, and other ornaments. The head was bare and devoid of ornament. She was so brilliant and of such unusual beauty that she literally seemed to light up the whole room as she entered. Her shoulders were broad and round, and her carriage drooping, as is usual with Indian women, who are early accustomed to carry burdens on their back; but the beauty of the countenance was so extraordinary that I can not but think that if such a face were to be seen in one of the drawing-rooms of the fashionable world, it would there be regarded as the type of a beauty hitherto unknown. It was the wild beauty of the forest, at the same time melancholy and splendid. The bashful gloom in those large, magnificent eyes, shaded by unusually long, dark eyelashes, can not be described, nor yet the glance, nor the splendid light of the smile which at times lit up the countenance like a flash, showing the loveliest white teeth. She was remarkably light-complexioned for an Indian; the round of the chin was somewhat prominent, which gave rather too much breadth to her face, but her profile was perfect. She was quite young, and had been married two years to a brave young warrior, who, I was told, was so fond of her that he would not take another wife, and that he would not allow her to carry heavy burdens, but always got a horse for her when she went to the town. She is called *Mochpedaga-Wen*, or Feather-cloud-woman. A young Indian girl who came with her was more painted, but not so handsome, and had those heavy features and that heavy expression which characterize the Indian women, at least those of this tribe.

I made a sketch of Mochpedaga-Wen in her bridal attire. She was bashful, with downcast eyes. It was with a pleasure mingled with emotion that I penetrated into the mysteries of this countenance. A whole nocturnal world lay in those eyes, the dark fringes of which cast a shadow upon the cheek. Those eyes glanced downward into a depth, dreamy, calm, without gloom, but at the same time without joy and without a future. The sunlight of the smile was like a sunbeam of a cloudy day. The Feather-cloud had no light within itself. It was lit up from without, and was splendidly tinted only for a moment.

After this gentle and beautiful, but melancholy image, I must introduce to you the brave young warrior, and the great Sprude-bosse, or Dandy—"Skonka Shaw," or "White Dog," the husband of the "Feather-cloud," who entered duly painted and in great pomp of attire, with a huge tuft of feathers helmet-wise falling backward from the head, and with three dark eagles' feathers, with tufts of scarlet wool, stuck aloft in his hair, and with the marks of five green fingers on his cheeks, to indicate that he was a brave warrior and had killed many enemies. He was tall and flexible of form, and he entered with a gay, animated aspect, amid a torrent of words, equally fluent with what I had heard in the House of Representatives at Washington, and of which I understood—about as much. His countenance had the same characteristics that I had already observed among the Indians, the hawk nose, broad at the base, clear, acute, but cold eyes, which opened square, with a wild-beast-like glance; the mouth unpleasing, and for the rest, the features regular and keen. I made a sketch also of him; his countenance was much painted with red, and yellow, and green; there was nothing shy about it, and it looked very warlike. But that which won for him favor in my eyes was that he was a good husband and loved his beautiful Feather-cloud.

Mrs. Ramsay, in the mean time, had gone out with her, and put on her costume. And as she was very pretty—of the pure Quaker style of beauty — she appeared really splendidly handsome in that showy costume, and the Feather-cloud seemed to have great pleasure in seeing her in it. But the handsome young white lady had not, after all, the wonderful, mystic beauty of Feather-cloud. There was between them the difference of the primeval forest and the drawing-room.

I observed in the conversations of these Indians many of those sounds and intonations which struck me as peculiar among the American people; in particular, there were those nasal tones, and that piping, singing, or lamenting sound which has often annoyed me in the ladies Probably these sounds may have been acquired by the earliest colonists during their intercourse with the Indians, and thus have been continued.

While I am with the Indians I must tell you of a custom among them which appears to me singular; it refers to their peculiar names and their mode of acquiring them. When the Indians, either man or woman, arrive at maturity, they go out into some solitary place, and remain there fasting for several days. They believe that the Spirit which has especial guardianship over them will then reveal itself; and that which during these days strongly attracts their sight or affects their imagination, is regarded as the image or token by means of which their guardian angel reveals itself to them, and they adopt a name derived from that object or token. When they have obtained the wished-for revelation, they return to their family, but under a kind of higher guidance, and with a greater right of self-government.

From a list of Indian names I select the following:

Horn-point; Round-wind; Stand-and-look-out; The Cloud-that-goes-aside; Iron-toe; Seek-the-sun; Iron-flash; Red-bottle; White-spindle; Black-dog; Two-feathers-of-honor; Gray-grass; Bushy-tail; Thunder-face; Go-on-the-burning-sod; Spirits-of-the-dead.

And among the female names, these:

Keep-the-fire; Spiritual-woman; Second-daughter-of-the-house; Blue-bird, and so on.

Feather-cloud must have looked especially toward heaven to find her guardian angel. May it conduct her lightly along her earthly pilgrimage, and preserve her from the fate of Winnona and Ampota Sapa! But—those deep eyes, full of the spirit of night, seem to me prophetic of the death-song.

The death-song consists of unmusical tones, almost devoid of melody, by which the Indians, male or female, relate the cause of their death, accuse their enemies, or praise themselves.

They believe that the spirit after death still lingers for a time near those earthly precincts which they have just left, and that they continue to be still, in a certain manner, akin to earth. Therefore are maize and other provisions placed at the foot of the corpse during the time that it lies on its elevated scaffold, exposed to the influence of light and air. The deceased has not as yet entered into the realm of spirits; but when the flesh is withered from the bones, these are buried with songs and dances. Then has the departed spirit arrived in the land of spirits.

"We believe," said a celebrated Indian chief to one of my friends, "that when the soul leaves the body, it lingers for some time before it can be separated from its former circumstances, during which it wanders over vast plains in the clear, cold moonlight. Finally, it arrives at a great chasm in the earth, on the other side of which lies the land of the blessed, where there is eternal spring, and rich hunting-grounds abundantly supplied with game. There is, however, no other means of crossing this gulf excepting by a barked pine-tree, which is smooth and slippery. Over this the spirits must pass if they would reach the land of bliss. Such spirits as have lived purely and well in this world are able to pass this narrow bridge safely, and safely to reach those regions of the blessed. Such, however, as have not done so can not pass over this smooth tree-stem, but lose their footing and fall into the abyss."

This, for savages, is not so very bad an idea of retribution after death. The Indians' estimate, however, of good and evil is, in other respects, very imperfect and circumscribed; and their idea of reward and punishment after death is merely the reflex of their earthly joys and misfortunes.

They believe, as we do, in a Spirit of spirits, a supreme God, who rules over every thing and all things, and the Indians of the Northwest call him the "Great Manitou." He appears to be a power without the peculiar moral attributes. They also believe in a number of lesser Manitous, or divinities, and it seems to me that, as regards their theology, they are rather Pantheists than Monotheists. They behold a transformed divinity in the forest, in stones, in animals, in every thing which lives or which evinces an in-dwelling power. Manitou is in the bear and the beaver, in the stone which emits the spark of fire, but above all, in the forest which whispers and affords protection to man.

It seems to me worthy of observation that these Indians believe that every animal has a great original prototype or type from which it is descended; hence all beavers are descended from the *great beaver*, which lives somewhere forever under the water; all bluebirds from the *great bluebird*, which flies invisibly above the clouds in the immeasurable heights of space. The great beaver is the great brother of all beavers, the great bluebird is the brother and protector of all bluebirds.

They seek to propitiate Manitou by gifts and sacrifices, which are often bloody and cruel. The mediators between themselves and Manitou are their so-called medicine-men; men who, by means of the knowledge of the mysteries of nature and the power of magic, are considered able to invoke spirits, to avert misfortune, to heal sickness, and obtain the fulfillment of human wishes. These men are highly esteemed among the Indians, and are both their priests and physicians.

You behold at the fall of night fires flaming upon the prairie-hills on the banks of the Mississippi, and a crowd of Indians, men and women, assembled around them, making the most extraordinary gestures. Let us approach nearer. Copper-colored men and women, to the number of about one hundred, are dancing around, or rather hopping, with their feet close together and their arms hanging straight down, to the unmelodious music of a couple of small drums and some dried gourds, which, being filled with small stones, make a rattling noise when they are shaken. The musicians are seated upon the green-sward. The dancing men are painted in their grandest, but yet most hideous manner, tawdry and horrible; and several women, also, are plentifully covered with silver rings, and with little silver bells hanging to their ears and to their moccasins, and which they shake with all their might as they hop along.

Every one has a little medicine-bag made of skin.

These are all medicine-men and women; and around them is a ring of spectators, men, women, and children.

After a couple of old men have seated themselves in the ring and talked for a little while, a march commences, in which the whole circle is included, during which first one and then another individual steps out of the procession, and takes his stand a little apart from the circle. A medicine-man then, having blown into his medicine-bag, springs forward with a shrill resounding cry, and holds it before the mouth of one of the patients standing in the outer circle, who on that falls down insensible, and lies on the ground for a time with quivering limbs. Thus falls one after another of the assembly. An old Indian stands smiling with a cunning expression, as if he would say, "They'll not so soon catch me!" At the first application of the medicine-bag, therefore, he merely staggers forward a few paces; after the second, bursts into an hysterical laugh, and it is not until the third mystical draught that he falls down with convulsed limbs. In a little while the fallen again rise and reunite themselves to the procession, which is continued until all its members have gone through the medicine-process, the unmelodious music sounding without intermission. The old men seem more amused by this scene than the young.

The medicine-dance is one of the chief festivities of the Indians of Minnesota, and lasts for several days. They have also other dances, among which the war-dance is most known. Men alone take part in this. They paint their faces and bodies in the most horrible manner, and their dance consists of the wild gestures and threatening demonstrations which they make against each other. I have seen a painting of the scalp-dance of the women, which is danced when the men return from war with the scalps of their enemies. These scalps, being placed on tall poles, are held by women, who, with their female compeers, dance, or rather hop round, very much in the manner of geese with their feet tied, and with about as much grace. The beating of drums, songs, and wild cries accompany the dance. The men stand round with eagles' feathers in their hair contemplating this dance, which is a greater delight, both to their eyes and their ears, than probably any which the genius of Bournonville could create, or the skill of Taglioni or Elsler perform.

But I must yet add a few facts regarding the past and present state of this savage people, which I obtained from trustworthy sources, partly from books, partly from oral communications, as well as from my own observations.

When the Europeans first penetrated that portion of America lying east of the Mississippi, a great deal was said about vast stretches of desolate country; and since a more accurate knowledge has been obtained of the Indian tribes from Canada in the North, to Florida and Louisiana in the South, and their population has been estimated, it appears that the whole Indian race, east of the Great River, amounts to about 180,000 souls. The tribes or families into which they are divided all greatly resemble each other in physiognomy and manners, although some of them are more warlike and cruel, and others more peacefully disposed. The principal tribes have lived, for the most part, in a state of bloody hostility with each other from time immemorial.

Research into the languages of the various Indian tribes has proved that, however numerous the tribes may be, there exist but eight radically distinct languages; and of these five only are now spoken by tribes of eminence, the other three having died out, and the languages of the remainder of the tribes appear to be dialects of some one or other of the principal languages. These languages have a definite form and construction; they are affluent in definitions, and the definitions of individual beings, but are deficient in terms for the general idea. They indicate a popular mind which has not advanced beyond the realm of experience into that of reflection. Thus, for example, they have names for the various kinds of oak, but not for the genus oak; they speak of a *holy man*, but they have no word for *holiness;* they could say our father, mine or thy father, but they have no word for *father*. There is nothing in their language which indicates a higher degree of cultivation among them as a people than they are at present in possession of. They love to speak in a symbolical manner, all their symbols being derived from the realm of nature; and their writings and their art speak also by means of such. I have seen a buffalo-hide covered with figures, in the style of children's drawings, which represented battles, treaties of peace, and other such events; the sun and the moon, trees, and mountains, and rivers, fish and birds, and all kinds of animals, having their part in the delineations; men and horses, however, in the most distorted proportions, being the principal actors. I have also seen Indian songs inscribed upon trees and bark in similar hieroglyphics.

The religious culture of the Indian has adopted the same symbolic characters derived from natural objects. They constitute a living hieroglyphic writing. They have no sense of the worship of God in spirit and in truth, or in the influence of love. But they have many religious festivals; the Indians of Minnesota more than ten, at which they offer sacrifices to the sun and the moon, trees, rivers, stones, serpents—nay, indeed, to all things and all animals, to propitiate their spirits or their divinities. The festival of the sun is celebrated by day, that of the moon by night. One festival is for their weapons of war, which they regard as sacred, or as being possessed of an innate divine power. At all these festivals they have dancing and the beating of drums, as well as singing and many ceremonies. The principal transaction on these occasions, however, seems to be feasting; and as the Indians appear to consider it a duty to eat every thing which is set before them, frequently more than they are able, they are sometimes obliged to take medicine that it may be possible for them to pursue their eating. At the *Feast of the Spirits*, if the guest fails to eat all that is placed before him, he must redeem himself by the forfeit of a buffalo or beaver skin. Great quantities of provisions, especially of venison, are collected for these festivities. In the mean time they are often famished with hunger.

Their medical knowledge, even if classed with superstitious usages, is not to be despised, and they have large acquaintance with healing herbs and the powers of nature. A lady of Philadelphia, who resided many years among the Indians, in order to gain a knowledge of their various remedies, drew up, on her return, an Indian materia-medica, which became much celebrated, and many new curative means have thus enriched the American pharmacopœia. Women are also, among the Indians, esteemed as physicians and interpreters of dreams; and the Winnebago Indians, who dwell by Lake Superior, in the northeastern part of Minnesota, have now, singularly enough, two queens whom they obey—the one for her wisdom, the other for her courage and bravery. Otherwise, women among the Indians are, as is well known, servants who do all the hard work, as well without as within the house. They dig the fields (pieces of land without form or regularity), sow and reap, gather wild rice, berries, roots, and make sugar from the juice of the sugar-maple. When the man kills a deer, he throws it down for the woman, who must prepare it for household use.

"What estimate may be given of the morals and character of the Indian women in this neighborhood?" inquired I from a lady of St. Paul's, who had resided a considerable time at this place.

"Many are immoral, and can not be much commended; but others, again, there are who are as virtuous and blameless as any of us."

I have also heard incidents cited which prove that the Indian woman will sometimes assume, in the wigwam, the privilege of the husband, bring him under the rule of the moccasin, and chastise him soundly if he offend her. He never strikes again, but patiently lets himself be beaten black and blue. He knows, however, that his turn will come, and he knows well enough that he can then have his revenge.

When an Indian dies, the women assemble round the corpse, make a howling lament, tear their hair, and cut themselves with sharp stones. A missionary in Minnesota saw a young Indian woman slash and cut her flesh over her brother's corpse in the most terrific manner, while other women around her sung songs of vengeance against the murderer of the dead. The god of revenge is the ideal of the savage.

The virtues of the Indian man are universally known. His fidelity in keeping a promise, his hospitality, and his strength of mind under sorrow and suffering, have often been praised. It strikes me, however, that these his virtues have their principal root in an immense pride. The virtue of the Indian is selfish. That dignity of which we have heard so much seems to me more like the conceit of a cock than the natural dignity of a noble, manly being. Now they raise themselves up, and stand or walk proudly. Now they squat all in a heap, sitting on their hams like dogs or baboons. Now they talk with proud words and gestures; now prate and jabber like a flock of magpies. There is a deal of parade in their pride and silence. Occasionally beautiful exceptions have been met with, and still exist, where the dignity is genuine, and the nobility genuine also. These exceptions are met with among the old chiefs in particular. But the principal features among the Indians are, after all, idolatry, pride, cruelty, thirst of vengeance, and the degradation of woman.

They have no other government nor governors but through their chiefs and medicine-men. The former have but little power and respect, excepting in their own individual character, and they seem greatly to fear the loss of their popularity in their tribe.

Such, with little variation, are the manners, the faith, and the condition of the North American Indians.

A great deal has been said, and conjectured, and written, and much inquiry has been made on the question of whence came these people? And it now seems to be an established idea that they are of the Mongolian race, from the northern part of Asia, a resemblance having been discovered between them and this people, both in their appearance and mode of life, and also because Asia and America approach each other so nearly at this point, that the passage from one hemisphere to the other does not appear an improbable undertaking for bold coasting voyagers.

The Peruvians of South America, and those noble Aztecs, who possessed a splendid, though short-lived power, and whose noblest ruler spake words as wise and poetry as rich as that of King Solomon; these Indians, and those whose devastated cities have lately been discovered in Central America, were evidently of a higher race than the people of North America, and their remains, as well as all that is known of their manners and customs, prove them to be kindred to the noblest Asiatic races.

The zealous upholders of the doctrine that all mankind have descended from one single human pair, and who placed them in Asia, are reduced to great straits to explain the emigration of these various people from the mother country. I can not understand why each hemisphere should not be considered as the mother country of its own people. The same power of nature, and the same creative power, are able to produce a human pair in more than one place. And when God is the father, and nature the mother, then must indeed, in any case, the whole human race be brethren. And the Adamite pair may very well consider themselves as the elected human pair, sent to instruct and emancipate those young kindred pairs which were still more in bondage than themselves to the life of earth. God forgive us for the manner in which we have most frequently fulfilled our mission.

But North America is not altogether to blame with regard to her Indians. If the Indian had been more susceptible of a higher culture, violence and arms would not have been used against him, as is now the case. And although the earlier missionaries, strong in faith, and filled with zealous ardor, succeeded in gathering around them small, faithful companies of Indian proselytes, yet it was evidently rather through the effect of their individual character than from any inherent power in the doctrines which they preached. When they died their flocks dispersed.

Sometimes white men of peculiar character have taken to themselves Indian wives, and have endeavored to make cultivated women of them; but in vain. The squaw continued to be the squaw; uncleanly, with unkemmed hair, loving the dimness of the kitchen more than the light of the drawing-room, the ample envelopment of the woolen blanket rather than tight lacing and silken garments. The faithful wife and tender mother she may become, steadfast to home and the care of her family as long as her husband lives and the children are small; but when the children are grown up, and if the husband be dead, then will she vanish from her home. When the birds warble of spring and the forest, and the streams murmur of renovated life, she will return to the wigwams of her people in the forest or by the river, to seek by their fires for freedom and peace. This wild life must assuredly have a great fascination.

Of all the tribes of North American Indians now existing, the Cherokees and Choctaws are the only ones which have received Christianity and civilization. When the Europeans first visited these tribes, they were living in small villages in the highland district of Tennessee, Georgia, and Alabama; they were peaceful, and pursued agriculture. They were drawn from their homes by fair means and foul, and obtained land west of the Mississippi, in the western part of the State of Missouri, and there it is said they have become a large and flourishing community, greatly augmenting in number, and assimilating to the manners and customs of Europeans. They are employed in agriculture and the breeding of cattle; they build regular houses, and have of late years reduced their language to writing, and have established a printing-press. I have, among my American curiosities, a Cherokee newspaper, printed in the Cherokee language.

The wild Indians, who for the most part sustain themselves by fishing and hunting, are becoming more and more eradicated, in part by mutual wars, and in part by the small-pox, as well as by brandy, which, adulterated by pernicious inflammatory ingredients, is sold to them by the white traders. The American government has strictly interdicted the sale of spirituous liquors to the Indians, but they are so covetous of intoxicating drinks, and mean souls are every where so covetous of gain, that the prohibition is of very little avail. Spirituous liquors are smuggled in with other merchandise among the Indians of this district. The American government buys land from the Indians, and with the money which is annually distributed among them as payment they purchase "fire-water," as well as the means of life, for which they pay an exorbitant price. Thus they are impoverished by degrees, and fall into utter penury. Thus they become more and more degraded, both morally and physically, nor have their medicine-men either remedy or magic art against the poisoned contact of the whites.

Noble men among the Indians have spoken strong and bitter words against these whites, and against their own people falling under their influence.

"If the Great Spirit," said a Sioux chief to a Christian missionary, "had intended your religion for the red man, he would have given it to him. We do not understand what you tell us; and the light which you wish to give us darkens that clear, straight path upon which our fathers walked!"

As he lay dying he said to his people,

"Dig my grave yourselves, and do not let the white man follow me there!"

Ah! over his grave the white man is advancing in the name of light and civilization, and the "people of the twilight" give way before him, dying away by degrees in the wilderness, and in the shadows of the Rocky Mountains. It can not be otherwise.

And whatever interest I may feel in high-minded characters among the Indians, still I can not possibly wish for a prolonged existence to that people, who reckon cruelty among their virtues, and who reduce the weak to beasts of burden.

The people who subject them, and who deprive them of their native land, are—whatever faults they may have—a nobler and more humane people. They have a higher consciousness of good and evil. They seek after perfection; they wish to cast aside the weapons of barbarism, and not to establish on the new earth any other abiding fortress than that of the Church of Christ, and not to bear any other banner than that of the Prince of Peace. And in latter times especially have they proved, even in their transactions with the Indians, that they are earnest in this desire.

The Indians, like the Greenlanders, look down upon the white race with a proud contempt, at the same time that they fear them; and their legend of what happened at the creation of the various races proves naïvely how they view the relationship between them.

"The first man which Manitou baked," say they, "was not thoroughly done, and he came white out of the oven; the second was overdone, was burned in the baking, and he was black. Manitou now tried a third time, and with much better success; this third man was thoroughly baked, and came out of the oven of a fine red brown—this was the Indian."

The learned of Europe divide the three principal races of the earth into People of the Day—the Whites; People of the Night—the Negroes; and People of the Twilight—the Indians of the Eastern and Western hemispheres.

What the negroes say about themselves and the other races I know not; but this appears to me certain, that they stand in closer proximity to the people of the day than to the people of the twilight in their capacity for spiritual development; that they have a grander future before them than the latter, and less self-love than either.

Fort Snelling lies on the western bank of the Mississippi, where the St. Peter's flows into that river; and at this point the view is glorious over the broad St. Peter's River, called by the Indians the Minnesota, and of the beautiful and extensive valley through which it runs. Further up it flows through a highland district, and amid magnificent scenery inland five hundred miles westward. "There is no doubt," writes a young American, in his travels through Minnesota, "but that these banks of the St. Peter's will some time become the residence of the aristocracy of the country."

This must be a far-sighted glance, one would imagine; but things advance rapidly in this country.

We visited, on our way to Fort Snelling, a waterfall, called the Little Falls. It is small, but so infinitely beautiful that it deserves its own picture, song, and saga. The whitest of foam, the blackest of crags, the most graceful, and, at the same time, wild and gentle fall! Small things may become great through their perfection.

Later. I have to-day visited, in company with a kind young clergyman, the so-called Fountain Cave, at a short distance from the city. It is a subterranean cavern with many passages and halls, similar probably to the celebrated Mammoth Cave of Kentucky. Many such subterranean palaces are said to be found in Minnesota, although they have not yet been explored; neither has this grotto been thoroughly penetrated. I enjoyed myself sitting under its magnificent arched portico, drinking of its crystalline fountain, and listening to the song of its falling water in the far interior of the grotto. The grotto is reached by an abrupt and deep descent, resembling a gigantic pit; within this one finds one's self surrounded by lofty walls of sandstone, one of which expands if tselinto a gigantic portal, and all beyond is dark. The whole circle of the inclosing walls is perforated with innumerable small round holes, in which small birds have their nests.

To reach the grotto, we passed through extensive meadows lying along the Mississippi. The grass stood tall and yellow. The air was as warm as a summer's day. It was the Indian summer. The meadows looked most pleasant, most fertile and inviting. We met a milk-maid also coming with her milk-pails; she was handsome, but had artificial curls, and did not look like a regular milk-maid, not as a true milk-maid in a pastoral ought to look.

But this Minnesota is a glorious country, and just the country for Northern emigrants—just the country for a new Scandinavia. It is four times as large as England; its soil is of the richest description, with extensive wooded tracts; great numbers of rivers and lakes abounding in fish, and a healthy, invigorating climate. The winters are cold and clear; the summers not so hot as in those states lying lower on the Mississippi. The frosts seldom commence before the middle of September.

Lake Itaski, the cradle of the Mississippi, lies one thousand five hundred and seventy-five feet above the Mexican Gulf; and the highland district which surrounds Itaska in a half circle on the north, that gigantic terrace, *Hauteur des terres*, where the springs of those mighty rivers, the Mississippi, the St. Louis, the St. Lawrence, the Red River, and many others have their source, lies still two hundred feet higher. The whole of Minnesota is hilly. Minnesota is bounded on the east by Lake Superior (the Mediterranean Sea of America), and is brought by this into connection with the Eastern States, with the St. Lawrence, and the Hudson, and the Atlantic Ocean. It has Canada on the north, on the west the wild Missouri, navigable through almost the whole of its extent, and flowing at the feet of the Rocky Mountains, rich in metals and precious stones, and with prairies where graze wild herds of buffaloes, elks, and antelopes. On the other side of Missouri lies that mystical Indian Nebraska, where, beyond the Rocky Mountains, and for the most part still unknown, lies Oregon, an immense territory, with immense resources in natural productions, vast stretches of valley and vast rivers, the Columbus and the Oregon, which empty themselves into the Pacific Ocean, and in whose cascades salmon leap in shoals, as in the rapid rivers of Norway and Sweden. On the south of Minnesota lies the fertile Iowa, a young state, with beautiful rivers, the Iowa, Cedar, and Des Moines; extensive stretches of valley and rich pasture-lands; and through the very heart of Minnesota flows that great artery, the Mississippi, the birth of which it witnesses, and upon whose waters it can convey all the produce of the North to the South, and obtain all the produce of the South both for the North and for itself.

What a glorious new Scandinavia might not Minnesota become! Here would the Swede find again his clear, romantic lakes, the plains of Scania rich in corn, and the valleys of Norrland; here would the Norwegian find his rapid rivers, his lofty mountains, for I include the Rocky Mountains and Oregon in the new kingdom; and both nations their hunting-fields and their fisheries. The Danes might here pasture their flocks and herds, and lay out their farms on richer and less misty coasts than those of Denmark. The Rocky Mountains are a new Seveberg with mythological monsters, giants and witches enough to feed the legendary mind and the warlike temperament. The gods must yet combat here with the Hrimthursar and the giants; Balder must have a fresh warfare with Loke, in which Balder will be victorious, and the serpent of Midgaerd be laid at rest in the Pacific Ocean—at least till the great Ragnarok.

Neither would the joys of Valhalla be wanting in the New Vineland of the vine-crowned islands of the Mississippi, and the great divine hog Schrimmer has nowhere such multitudes of descendants as in the New World. But the Scandinavians must not rest satisfied with the heathenish life of festivity. They must seek after nobler enjoyments.

But seriously, Scandinavians who are well off in the Old Country ought not to leave it. But such as are too much contracted at home, and who desire to emigrate, should come to Minnesota. The climate, the situation, the character of the scenery agrees with our people better than that of any other of the American States, and none of them appear to me to have a greater or a more beautiful future before them than Minnesota.

Add to this that the rich soil of Minnesota is not yet bought up by speculators, but may every where be purchased at government prices, one dollar and a quarter per acre. I have been told that the Norwegian pastor in Luther's Dale, Mr. Clausen, is intending to remove hither with a number of Norwegians, in order to establish a settlement. Good. There are here already a considerable number both of Norwegians and Danes. I have become acquainted with a Danish merchant, resident here, who has made a considerable fortune in a few years in the fur trade with the Indians, and who has built himself a large and handsome country house at some little distance from the city. His wife, who is the daughter of an Indian woman by a white man, has the dark Indian eye, and features not unlike those of the Feather-cloud woman, and in other respects is as much like a gentlewoman as any agreeable white lady. I promised this kind Dane, who retains the perfect Danish characteristics in the midst of Americans, that I would, on my return, in passing through Copenhagen, pay a visit to his old mother, and convey to her his greeting.

And here I may as well remark, *en passant*, that the children of Indian women by white men commonly attach themselves to the white race. They are most frequently fine specimens of humanity, although not of a remarkably elevated kind. They are praised for their acuteness of eye, and the keenness of their perceptive faculties generally. I have heard that the greater number of the steersmen of the Mississippi boats belong to this half-blood race.

A young Norwegian woman lives as cook with Governor Ramsay; she is not above twenty, and is not remarkably clever as a cook, and yet she receives eleven dollars per month wages. This is an excellent country for young servants.

I shall to-morrow commence my voyage down the Mississippi as far as Galena; thence to St. Louis, at which place I shall proceed up the Ohio to Cincinnati, and thence to New Orleans, and, advancing onward, shall proceed from some one of the southern sea-port towns to Cuba, where I intend to winter.

I am not quite satisfied about leaving this part of the country. I wish to see more of the Indians and their way of life, and feel something like a hungry person who is obliged to leave a meal which he has just commenced.

I wish to see more of the country and the aborigines, but do not exactly see how and in what manner. Neither roads nor means of conveyance are to be met with here, as in the more cultivated states. Besides which, I must not any longer remain in this family, which has so hospitably provided me a chamber by sending the only child of the family, a beautiful little infant, and its nurse, into a cold room. The child must return into its warm chamber, for the nights are getting cold. I long for the South, and dread these cold nights on the Mississippi; and it is too far, and the roads are too difficult for me to go to another family, residing at some distance, who have kindly invited me to their house, and—the inward light does not afford me any illumination, and the inward voice is silent. I shall therefore commence my journey, but someway I have a presentiment that I shall have to repent it.

I shall part from my cheerful and kind hostess with regret. I shall take with me a pair of Indian moccasins for your little feet, and another pair for Charlotte's, and a bell-purse of Indian work for mamma. The work of the Indian women is ornamental and neat, although deficient in taste and knowledge of design. Scarlet and fine colors predominate in their embroidery as well as in the festal attire of their people. Scarlet seems to be a favorite color with all children of nature.

I have gained some information from the young Presbyterian missionary here regarding the effect of missionary labors among the Indians, which seems to promise a brighter future for them than I had hitherto imagined. Since the Gospels have been translated into the language of the principal tribes and have been studied by them, Christianity has made considerable advances among the savage people, and with each succeeding year have the results of missionary labors been more and more striking.

When, in 1828, "a revival" in the religious life occasioned a reanimation and a new organization of missionary labor, there were only thirty-one missionaries among the Indians, with a revenue of only 2400 dollars for carrying out the work of instruction.

At this time (1850) there are 570 missionaries—more than half of whom are women, among the Indians, with a revenue of 79,000 dollars yearly; to these missionaries must be added 2000 preachers and helpers among the natives themselves. A thousand churches of various Christian denominations have been erected, and the number of professing Christians of the Indian tribes amounts at this time to 40,537. A great number of schools have been established, and are increasing daily, where the Indian children may receive instruction in reading, writing, and arithmetic, as well as in handcraft trades. The women easily acquire these latter. The boys learn to read and write with greater facility than the girls; but it is very difficult to accustom them to order and punctuality. It is not until after religious conversion that it is possible to impart moral and physical cultivation to them, before which they will have nothing to do with it. The number of schools has already increased to between four and five hundred, and the number of scholars, both boys and girls, is more than 30,000. Seminaries for boys and girls have also been established. Printing-presses have been introduced, and printed works in thirty different languages have been produced. Mr. Williamson, the missionary of Kaposia, considers the ignorance of the Indians to be the greatest impediment to their cultivation. The women are the most accessible to religious impressions; the men, in particular those of the warlike tribes, as the Sioux, for instance, are more difficult to influence, and they will not listen to a doctrine which is diametrically opposed to that which constitutes their heathenish virtue and happiness. The missionaries, therefore, have as yet made but little way among the Sioux, nor indeed have they yet advanced among the savage tribes lying between Minnesota and the Rocky Mountains. It will not be long, however, before they do so.

From the annual report of the American Board of Missions for the year 1850, from which I have taken many of the above facts, I extract the following words:

"How long will it be before we establish a synod on the shores of the Pacific Ocean? Already are our missionaries scattered over the whole of the United States east of the Mississippi, with the exception of one little valley in the northeast. They have crossed that river, and are now beginning zealously to occupy that immense country which extends westward of it, from the Mexican Gulf to the British colonies of the North. Nay, more still; they have wandered over the whole continent, and in that new world of the West have begun to found a kingdom of God. What will our progress be ultimately? The spires of our churches along the shores of the Atlantic are illumined by the light of the morning sun. Advancing over the country, it shines upon them through the whole day; and when it sets, its last rays still rest upon these as they rise upward along the shores of the Pacific Ocean. Yes, we have done something, with God's aid; but we have yet infinitely more to do before we have fulfilled the measure of our duty."

That is a good little specimen of the labor and the eloquence of the West.

Thus a little flock even of the red men have on earth entered the kingdom of Christ. And if, out of those 40,000 who publicly acknowledge themselves of the Church of Christ, 10,000 only, nay if only 1000 be really Christians, there is still enough for an infinite future. In those "happy lands" where the red children of God will one day be at home, beyond the dark abyss, will they labor for the liberation of their brethren, "the children of the twilight," who remain in the realm of shadows.

The kingdom of the Savior and the work of salvation

are not circumscribed to this little space and to this short time. Their space and their time are eternal as the heart of God. I know that the missionaries here promulgate another doctrine; and it is incomprehensible how they by that means are able to make any progress, incomprehensible how they can have any satisfaction in so doing. But a light, stronger, mightier, than that of these circumscribed doctrines must proceed from the Word of Christ to the heart of the heathen, and attract it to His cross and His crown, from the hunting-grounds and the wild dances of earth to His heaven. I can not believe otherwise.

It is evening, and the bright glow of fires lights up the western heaven, as it has done every evening since I came here. It is the glow of the Indian prairie fires, which they kindle to compel the deer to assemble at certain points, as it is now their hunting season. In this manner they take a vast number of deer, but at the same time destroy the chase, and by that means occasion still greater want, or are compelled to go still further westward into the wilderness.

But the West is brilliant, and all the saints—St. Peter, St. Paul, St. Charles, a settlement still higher up, St. Anthony, who is beginning to build a city—who have taken up their abode on the Northern Mississippi, and who now are lit up by the fires of the Indians, will give a new dawn to the wilderness and a new light to life.

The West is brilliant from the burning prairies, from the wild chase. I love that glow, because it has a poetical splendor; it shines over the moon-dances, and the councils, and the feasts of the spirits. But it is, after all, rather brightness than light.

When homes such as those of Andrew Downing and Marcus S., and of my good friend Mrs. W. H., which is almost a Swedish home, stand upon the heights of the Mississippi and St. Peter's; when church spires shine out and scalp-dances are no longer danced there; when voices such as those of Channing, and Emerson, and Beecher, and Bellows, lift themselves in the councils, and when Lucretia Motts speak there also for freedom, peace, and the rights of woman; when the Christian Indian States, Nebraska, &c., stand peacefully side by side of Minnesota, then—it may be in a hundred years—then will I return to Minnesota and celebrate a new feast of the spirits; and I will return thither in—the spirit!

LETTER XXVIII.

On the Mississippi, Oct. 24.

FLOATING down the Great River, "the Father of Rivers," between Indian camps, fires, boats, Indians standing or leaping, and shouting, or rather yelling, upon the shores; funeral erections on the heights; between vine-clad islands, and Indian canoes paddling among them! I would yet retain these strange foreign scenes; but I proceed onward, passing them by. We leave this poetical wilderness, the region of the youthful Mississippi, and advance toward that of civilization. The weather is mild, the sun and the shade sport among the mountains—a poetical, romantic life!

Oct. 25th. Sunbright, but cold. The Indians have vanished. We have passed the "*Prairie du Chien;*" the idolstone of the red Indian; the Indian graves under the autumnally yellow trees. The hills shine out, of a splendid yellow-brown. The ruins and the pyramids of primeval ages stand forth gloomy and magnificent amid the brilliant forests. With every bend of the river new and astonishing prospects present themselves. I contemplate them, read Emerson's Essays, and live as at a festival. We approach the commencement of two towns on the shore of Iowa, Gottenborg, a descendant, as I imagine, of our Götheborg, and Dubuque.

Oct. 27th. Again at Galena, among the lead mines, for a couple of days. It is Sunday, and I am returned from church, where I have heard a young Presbyterian minister, of the Presbyterian Church, Mr. Magoon. A true disciple of the Great West! No narrow evangelical views. No, an evangelical consciousness as wide as the Western prairies, as vast as the arch of heaven which spans them, and with breathing-room for the fresh winds of infinity.

The young minister's theme was the relationship which exists between a cultivated and a religious life.

The importance of a true philosophy in the doctrines of religion, in order the better to understand and to develop them.

The importance of the development of physical life in promoting the advance of spiritual life.

God's guiding hand in the awakening of all this, both in society and the Church, was shown by him in an animated and earnest manner.

Job said, "He says to the lightning, go! And it goeth!"

The electric telegraph is the lightning of God's finger, made subservient to man.

Philosophy is God's light in reason, illumining the darkness both of reason and of the Scriptures.

"It is thus that a metaphysical distinction may save a soul."

I could but think, on hearing this, of H. Martensen's dialectical gifts of God!

Lastly; the union of the highest life of the head and the heart, operating in and explanatory of all spheres of life, as they exist in the Church of the Millennium. These were the principal topics in the sermon of this young minister.

An earnest prayer, full of purport, on the prayer "Thy Kingdom Come," completed the whole service; one of the most liberal and comprehensive, one of the freshest and most refreshing which I have heard from the pulpit of any country.

A tirade against Catholicism was the only feature in it to be regretted, because it does not become the Great West to exclude any form of the divine life. And what, indeed, are all the various Christian communities other than various pews in the same church, dividing the whole into groups of families or relations?

The old Pilgrim Church seems to me now to be the one which exhibits most indwelling life, which grows and expands itself to embrace the whole of human life, and to baptize it to the kingdom of God.

Oct. 29th. I have established myself excellently at the American Hotel, and I do not intend, during the few days that I shall remain here, to accept the kind invitation which I have received to a beautiful private home. I have here my nice little Irish maid, Margaret, and have every thing exactly as I wish—among the rest, potatoes, morning, noon, and night, quite as good as our Aersta potatoes. I enjoy my freedom and my solitary rambles over the hills round the town during these fine days.

Yesterday, the agreeable, liberal-minded young minister, Mr. Magoon, drove me and a lady, a friend of his, to a height—Pilot Knob, I think it is called—by the Mississippi, from which we were to see the sun set. Arrived there, we clambered up among bushes, and long grass, and stones—difficult enough; and obtained, when we had gained the summit, one of those ocean-like land views which the Great West only presents. And through that infinite billowy plain rolled the Mississippi, like a vein of silver, far, far away into the immeasurable distance; and over land and river reposed the misty veil of the Indian summer, and its inexpressible, gentle peace. The sun had just set; but a roseate glow lay like a joyful benediction over that vast fertile region. It was indescribably grand and pleasant.

I thought how a year ago, at this season, my spirit had been depressed at New York; how, later, it darkened still more for me at Boston, and how I then thought, "Shall I be able to endure it?" And now I stood serene and vigorous by the Mississippi, with the Great West open before me, with a rich future, and the whole world bright! I thanked God!

On our return to Galena, the carriage broke down. The young clergyman sprang out, pulled forth some rope and a knife, and began to work in good earnest, as he said, merrily,

"You must know, Miss Bremer, that coach-building belongs, here in the West, to our theology."

The emigrants to the West must, to a certain degree, experience the trouble and the renunciation of the early Pilgrim Fathers. And in order to succeed, they require their courage and perseverance.

But people pass through these necessary stages much more quickly now than they did then. The beautiful, excellent American homes, with verandas, and trees, and gardens, which begin to adorn the hills round Five River, prove this. The good home, and the church, and the labors of Christian love, encroach daily more and more upon the fields and the life of heathenism. I do not now mean of the Indian, but of the white man.

I shall to-day go on board the good steam-boat Minnesota, to descend the Mississippi as far as St. Louis. Perhaps I may make a pause by the way, at the town of Rock Island, to visit the Swedish settlement of Eric Jansen, at Bishop's Hill, a few miles from the town.

Among the agreeable memories of my stay at Galena, I shall long retain that of a banker, Mr. H., who showed me so much kindness, such brotherly or fatherly consideration and care for me, that I shall ever think of him and of his city with gratitude.

The newspapers of the West are making themselves merry over the rapturous reception which the people of New York have given Jenny Lind. In one newspaper article I read:

"Our correspondent has been fortunate enough to hear Jenny Lind—sneeze. The first sneezing was a mezzotinto soprano, &c., &c.;" here follow many absurd musical and art terms; "the second was, &c., &c.;" here follow the same; "the third he did not hear, as he fainted."

I can promise the good Western people that they will become as insane with rapture as their brethren of the East, if Jenny Lind should come hither. They now talk like the Fox about the Grapes, but with better temper.

One of the inhabitants of St. Paul's, who had been at New York, returned there before I left. He had some business with Governor Ramsay, but his first words to this gentlemen were, "Governor! I have heard Jenny Lind!"

Jenny Lind, the new Slave Bill, and the protests against it in the North, Eastern, and Western States, are, as well as the Spiritual Rappings or Knockings, the standing topics of the newspapers.

While people in the Northern States hold meetings and agitate against this bill, which allows the recapture of fugitive slaves in the free states, various of the Southern States, especially the Palmetto State and Mississippi, raise an indignant cry against the infringement of the rights of the South, and threaten to dissolve the Union. And the states compliment each other in their newspapers in any thing but a polite manner. A Kentucky journal writes thus of South Carolina:

"Why has she not marched out of the Union before now? The Union would be glad to be rid of such a baggage!"

On the Mississippi, November 2d.

We are lying before Rock Island. Some kind and agreeable gentlemen have just been on board, with a proposal to convey me to the Swedish settlement. I can not be other than grateful to them for their kindness and good-will; but the nights are becoming cold; I am not quite well, and—what should I do there? We, my countrymen and myself, should not understand one another, although we might speak the same language. But I was well pleased to gain intelligence from these gentlemen, merchants of Rock Island, regarding the present condition of the Swedes in the colony.

Since the death of the bishop, as they called Eric Jansen, they have gone on more prosperously. He, however, by his bad management, left them burdened by a large debt of ten or eleven thousand dollars, and some of them are now gone to California to get gold, to endeavor by that means to liquidate it. Some of the Swedes at Bishop's Hill have unremittingly proved themselves to be honest, pious, and industrious people, and as such they have the confidence of the inhabitants of the town (Rock Island), and obtain on credit the goods for which they are at present unable to pay. They have built several handsome brick houses for themselves, and manage their land well. They have begun to grow and to spin flax, and they derive an income from the linen thread they have thus to sell. They continue steadfast in their religious usages, their prayers, and their faith in Eric Jansen, who seems to have had almost a demoniacal power over their minds. When they were ill and did not recover by the remedies and prayers of Eric Jansen, he told them that it was owing to their want of faith in him, and because they were reprobate sinners. Many died victims to the diseases of the climate, and for want of proper care.

The respectable and agreeable man, who was well acquainted with the Swedish colony, would not say any thing decidedly against Eric Jansen, nevertheless he doubted him; on the contrary, he praised Eric Jansen's wife as being very excellent and agreeable. She also had died of one of those fevers which raged in the colony; and four days afterward, Eric Jansen stood up during divine service in the church, and declared that "the Spirit had commanded him to take a new-wife!" And a woman present stood up also and said, that "the Spirit had made known to her that she must become his wife!" This was four days after the death of the first excellent wife. Such a proceeding elucidates the spirit which guided Eric Jansen.

His murderer, the Swede Rooth, will be tried in the morning. It is believed that he will be acquitted, as the occasion of the deed was such as might well drive a man mad. Rooth had married a girl in the Swedish colony, contrary to the wishes of Eric Jansen. Persecuted by the enmity of Jansen, it was Rooth's intention to leave the place, and accordingly he had privately sent off his wife and child, a little boy, in the night. They were pursued by order of Jansen, captured, and conveyed in a boat down the Mississippi, no one knew where; it is said to St. Louis. Captain Schneidan saw Rooth on the very morning when the intelligence of this reached him. He was pale and scarcely in his right senses. In this excited state of mind he hastened to Eric Jansen, whom he met just setting off to church in the midst of his followers. He thus addressed him:

"You have had my wife and child carried off, I know not where. They are perhaps dead, and I may never see them more! I do not care to live any longer myself, but you shall die first!" And, so saying, he drew forth a pistol and shot him in the breast. Eric Jansen died almost in a moment. Rooth made no attempt to fly, but allowed himself to be seized by the exasperated people.

The little colony amounts to between seven and eight hundred persons, and is now under the government of two men whom they have selected, and they continue to hold the same religious faith in freedom from sin as during the life of their first leader. Taken abstractedly, their faith is not erroneous. The new man does not sin; but then they overlook the fact that sin is never perfectly eradicated from the human heart here on earth, and that, therefore, we must always remain sinful creatures till the time of our conversion arrives. The principal error of the Swedish emigrants consists in their faith in the sinner Eric Jansen, and in sinners such as themselves.

The weather is wet and chilly. The scenery of the banks is still of a highland character, but decreases in magnificence and beauty. The hills are broken up, as it were, and lie scattered over the prairies, which terminate with the river. White towns and churches shine out here and there along the shores. We are here on the shore of Illinois. Rock Island is situated at the outlet of the Illinois into the Mississippi. On the opposite side lies the State of Iowa, and there shines out white and lovely the little city of Davenport, which derives its name from its founder, and its celebrity from a horrible murder committed there on the person of an old man, one Sunday morning, by four young men, for his money. It is not long since. Bloody deeds have happened and still happen on the banks of the Mississippi.

November 3*d.* We steam down the Mississippi but slowly. The steamer drags along with her two huge barks or flat-boats, laden probably with lead from Galena, one on each side of the vessel. They say that these are a means of safety in case any accident should befall the steamer, and her passengers thus be in danger; they might then save themselves in the flat-boats. But they make the voyage very slow, and in the night I hear such extraordinary noises, thunderings and grindings in the vessel, as if it were panting, bellowing, and groaning under its heavy labor, and were ready to give up the ghost. These are probably occasioned by its hard work with the flat-boats. But it is not agreeable, and the sound is so dreadful at night that I always lie down dressed, ready to show myself in public in case of an explosion. Such misadventures are of every-day occurrence on the Mississippi, and one hears frequently of such also on other rivers and on the lakes of this country. Several of the passengers on board have with them life-preservers, belts or girdles of caoutchouc, to save them in case of danger. I have none; I have here neither an intimate acquaintance nor friend, who would put forth his hand to me in a moment of danger. But I know not how it is; I feel as if there were no need for fear. Only I am always prepared for a nocturnal "start."

The captain of the steamer is evidently a prudent general, and all goes on calmly and well. The table is abundant and excellent. The only thing that I feel the want of is milk for coffee and tea; cream is a thing not to be thought of, and is seldom met with any where in this country. One must learn to dispense with milk on one's river voyages in the West and South. I can manage to swallow coffee without milk; but it is almost impossible for me to take tea without it. I made a little complaint about it at tea last evening.

"Well!" said a Colonel Baxter, an excellent man, opposite to me, "we frequently did not taste milk for many weeks together during the Mexican war!"

"Oh!" said I, "but then you had glory to console yourselves with. What can not people dispense with when they have that! But here in a steam-boat, without glory and without milk! it is too much!"

They laughed, and this morning we had plenty of milk to breakfast.

The greater number of the attendants are negroes. The stewardess is a mulatto, neither agreeable nor good tempered. There are not many passengers in the better part of the vessel, and by no means disagreeable. The gentlemen's side is rather full; two thirds of these have a somewhat common appearance; they are "business-men" from head to foot.

I spend most of my time in my pleasant little state-room, or in walking backward and forward under the piazza in front of it, where I amuse myself by the spectacle of the river and its shores. The waters of the Mississippi still retain their bright yellow-green color, though they are beginning to be turbid. Three-decked steamers, large and small, with their pair of chimneys, puffing out vehemently under the influence of "high pressure" as they advance up the stream, speed past us; vast timber-floats, upon which people both build and cook, row down the stream with gigantic oars; covered barks, vessels, and boats of every description and size are seen upon the river. It becomes more animated and broader, but still continues to flow on with a majestic calmness.

On our right lies the State of Iowa Illinois on the left. The views are grand and extensive; broad stretches of valley expand; the hills become lower; the land, to a great distance, slopes gradually down to the river in gentle, billowy meadows, with a background of wood. It has a beautiful and fertile appearance, but is not much cultivated. We are now in the corn-regions of the Mississippi Valley; rich in all kinds of grain, but principally in the rich golden-yellow maize.

Along the Mississippi, through its whole extent, from Minnesota to the Gulf of Mexico, lies a pearl-band of states. There are on the eastern side of the river Wisconsin, Illinois, Kentucky, Tennessee, Mississippi, and Louisiana; and on the western side, Iowa, Missouri, Arkansas, and Louisiana, for, like Minnesota, Louisiana embraces both banks of the Mississippi; Minnesota at its commencement among the hills, Louisiana at its outlet into the sea. Between these two states, Minnesota in the north, and Louisiana in the south, flows the Mississippi, through a variety of regions distinguished by dissimilar climates and natural productions. Minnesota is its north, with the pine forests of the North, and Northern winters, with bears and elks, with the wild roses and the berries of the North, with primeval forests and Indians. Wisconsin, Illinois, Kentucky, Tennessee in the east, Iowa and Missouri, and a part of Arkansas in the west, are situated within the temperate zone. Agriculture and civilization are extending there. These states, like their neighboring states in the East, Michigan, Indiana, and Ohio, constitute the great corn magazine of America, and the central portion of the Mississippi Valley. Beyond these, to the east, extend the Alleghany Mountains, and the Eastern or Atlantic States. Beyond the Mississippi States, to the west, extends the Indian wilderness, Nebraska, and the Rocky Mountains. With Tennessee on the east, and Arkansas on the west, we enter the region of cotton; with Louisiana, the region of sugar, the south, and summer life.

Illinois and Iowa are still free states; to the south of these lie the Slave States. In Illinois and Iowa there are Swedish and Norwegian settlements, but further south they have not yet advanced. The central Mississippi States are occupied more by Germans and Irish; and more southern still, by French and Spaniards. All these are governed by the laws and manners of the Anglo-Norman race. It is the same with the Jews, who are very numerous in America, especially in the West. But they also enjoy all civil rights like natives of the country, and are much less distinguished from the European population here than they are in Europe; so little, indeed, that I have scarcely ever thought "that is a Jew," it being hardly possible to distinguish a Jew in this country from a dark-complexioned American.

We are now within sight of Nauvoo, formerly the capital of the Mormon district, and the magnificent ruin of their former temple is seen standing on its elevated site. One of my friends, who some years ago was traveling on the Mississippi, went on shore at Nauvoo, a few days after the Mormon prophet, Joe Smith, was killed by the people of Illinois. He saw the people of the town and the district, a population of about twenty thousand, come forth from their dwellings to the singing of psalms; saw them advance westward into the wilderness to seek there for that promised land which their prophet had foretold to them. After a wandering of three thousand miles through wildernesses, amid manifold dangers and difficulties, and the endurance of much suffering, they arrived at the Great Salt Lake, and its fertile shores. There they have within a few years so greatly increased and multiplied, that they are now in a fair way to become a powerful state. Faith can, even in these days, remove mountains—nay, more, can remove great cities. Nauvoo is now purchased by the French communist, Cabet, who will there establish a society of "*Egalitairé.*"

Yes, in this Great West, on the shores of the Great River, exist very various scenes and peoples. There are Indians; there are squatters; there are Scandinavians, with gentle manners and cheerful songs; there are Mormons, Christian in manners, but fanatics in their faith in one man (and Eric Jansenists are in this respect similar to the Mormons); there are desperate adventurers, with neither faith nor law, excepting in Mammon and club-law; gamblers, murderers, and thieves, who are without conscience, and their number and their exploits increase along the banks of the Mississippi the further we advance south. There are giants, who are neither good nor evil, but who perform great deeds through the force of their will, and their great physical powers, and their passion for enterprise. There are worshipers of freedom and communists; there are slave-owners and slaves. There are communities who build, as bees and beavers do, from instinct and natural necessity. There are also, clear-headed strong, and pious men, worthy to be leaders, who know what they are about, and who have laid their strong hand to the work of cultivation. There are great cities which develop the highest luxury of civilization, and its highest crimes; who build altars to Mammon, and would make the whole world subservient. There are also small communities which possess themselves of land in the power of the peace principle, and in the name of the Prince of Peace. Lydia Maria Child tells us of such an one, either in Indiana or Illinois. It is a short story, and so beautiful that I must repeat it in her own living and earnest words.

"The highest gifts my soul has received, during its wild pilgrimage, have often been bestowed by those who were poor, both in money and intellectual cultivation. Among these donors, I particularly remember a hard-working, uneducated mechanic from Indiana or Illinois. He told me that he was one of the thirty or forty New Englanders who, twelve years before, had gone out to settle in the Western wilderness. They were mostly neighbors, and had been drawn to unite together in emigration from a general unity of opinion on various subjects. For some years previous, they had been in the habit of meeting occasionally at each other's houses to talk over their duties to God and man in all simplicity of heart. Their library was the Gospel, their priesthood the inward light. There were then no anti-slavery societies; but thus taught, and reverently willing to learn, they had no need of such agency to discover that it was wicked to enslave. The efforts of peace societies had reached this secluded band only in broken echoes, and non-resistance societies had no existence. But with the volume of the Prince of Peace, and hearts open to his influence, what need had they of preambles and resolutions?

"Rich in spiritual culture, this little band started for the Far West. Their inward homes were blooming gardens; they made their outward a wilderness. They were industrious and frugal, and all things prospered under their hand. But soon wolves came near the fold, in the shape of reckless, unprincipled adventurers; believers in force and cunning, who acted according to their creed. The colony of practical Christians spoke of their depredations in terms of gentlest remonstrance, and repaid them with unvarying kindness. They went further—they openly announced, 'You may do us what evil you choose, we will return nothing but good.' Lawyers came into the neighborhood, and offered their services to settle disputes. They answered, 'We have no need of you. As neighbors, we receive you in the most friendly spirit; but for us, your occupation has ceased to exist.' 'What will you do if rascals burn your barns and steal your harvests?' 'We will return good for evil. We believe this is the highest truth, therefore the best expediency.'

"When the rascals heard this, they considered it a marvelous good joke, and said and did many provoking things which seemed to them witty. Bars were taken down in the night, and cows let into corn-fields. The Christians repaired the damage as well as they could, put the cows in the barn, and at twilight drove them gently home, saying, 'Neighbor, your cows have been in my field. I have fed them well during the day, but I would not keep them all night, lest the children should suffer for their milk.'

"If this was fun, they who planned the joke had no heart to laugh at it. By degrees, a visible change came over these troublesome neighbors. They ceased to cut off horses' tails, and break the legs of poultry. Brute boys would say to a younger brother, 'Don't throw that stone, Bill! When I killed the chicken last week, didn't they send it to mother, because they thought chicken broth would be good for poor Mary? I should think you'd be ashamed to throw stones at *their* chickens.' Thus was evil overcome with good, till not one was found to do them willful injury. Years passed on, and saw them thriving in worldly substance beyond their neighbors, yet beloved by all. From them the lawyer and the constable obtained no fees. The sheriff stammered and apologized when he took their hard-earned goods in payment for the war-tax. They mildly replied, ''Tis a bad trade, friend. Examine it in the light of conscience, and see if it be not so.' But while they refused to pay such fees and taxes, they were liberal to a proverb in their contributions for all useful and benevolent purposes.

"At the end of ten years, the public lands, which they had chosen for their farms, were advertised for sale by auction. According to custom, those who had settled and cultivated the soil were considered to have a right to bid it in at the government price, which at that time was 1·25 dollars per acre. But the fever of land speculation then chanced to run unusually high. Adventurers from all parts of the country were flocking to the auction; and capitalists in Baltimore, Philadelphia, New York, and Boston were sending agents to buy Western lands. No one supposed that custom or equity would be regarded. The first day's sale showed that speculation ran to the verge of insanity. Land was eagerly bought in at seventeen, twenty-five, and thirty dollars an acre. The Christian colony had small hope of retaining their farms. As first settlers, they had chosen the best land, and persevering industry had brought it into the highest cultivation. Its market value was much greater than the acres already sold at exorbitant prices. In view of these facts, they had prepared their minds for another remove into the wilderness, perhaps to be again ejected by a similar process. But the morning their lot was offered for sale, they observed with grateful surprise that their neighbors were every where busy among the crowd begging and expostulating: 'Don't bid on these lands! these men have been working hard on them for ten years. During all that time, they never did harm to man or brute. They were always ready to do good for evil. They are a blessing to any neighborhood. It would be a sin and shame to bid on *their* lands. Let them go at the government price.' The sale came on; the cultivators of the soil offered 1·25 dollars, intending to bid higher if necessary. But among all that crowd of selfish, reckless speculators, *not one bid over them!* Without an opposing voice, the fair acres returned to them! I do not know a more remarkable instance of evil overcome with good. The wisest political economy lies folded up in the maxims of Christ.

"With delighted reverence I listened to this unlettered backwoodsman, as he explained his philosophy of universal love. 'What would you do,' said I, 'if an idle, thieving vagabond came among you, resolved to stay, but determined not to work?' 'We would give him food when hungry, shelter him when cold, and always treat him as a brother.' 'Would not this process attract such characters? How would you avoid being overrun by them?' 'Such characters would either reform or not remain with us. We should never speak an angry word, or refuse to minister to their necessities, but we should invariably regard them with the deepest sadness, as we would a guilty or beloved son. This is harder for the human soul to bear than whips or prisons. They would not stand it; I am sure they could not. It would either melt them or drive them away. In nine cases out of ten, I believe, it would melt them.'"

Lydia Maria Child adds, "This, the wisest doctrine of political economy, is included in the doctrines of Christ." As for me, these words run in my mind, "Blessed are the peace-makers, for they shall possess the earth." And when I look around me in these regions for that which is the most triumphant and the most overpowering element in the Mississippi States, and among the freebooters of California at the present time, I see clearly that it is the power and dominion of the peace-maker.

On the Mississippi, near the Rapids, November 3d.

We have lain still for several hours. The river has here a dangerous, sharp, rocky bottom, and, as the water is low, the passage is dangerous. They wait for the wind becoming perfectly still, that they may discern the places where the stream is rippled by the rocks. It is already so calm that I can scarcely imagine how it can be calmer. The Mississippi glances like a mirror in the sunshine, merely here and there furrowed by the stream. It is now quite as warm as summer, and I am impatient at lying quiet in the heat and the strong sunshine. The bed of the Mississippi has not been cleared, and it is a sign that the government of the United States has its deficiencies and its shallows, when they can tolerate such impediments on a great river where there is such constant traffic. But it is not agreed as to whether the government or the people ought to do the work, and therefore it remains undone, to the great detriment of the traffic of the river.

I have made two agreeable acquaintances on board, in two gentlemen from Connecticut, strong, downright Yankees; and the young daughter of one, a most charming girl of twenty—a fresh flower, both body and soul—a splendid specimen of the daughters of New England. We have also now a pair of giant women on board, such as belong to the old mythological population of Utgaerd; and I have been particularly amused by the conflict between the wild and the cultivated races in the persons of one of these ladies and my lovely flower of New England. The former, in a steel-gray dress, with a gray, fierce countenance, stiff and middle-aged, sat smoking her pipe in the ladies' saloon when we entered it from the dining-hall in the afternoon. She sat in the middle of the room, and puffed out the smoke vehemently, and looked as if she would set the whole world at defiance. The ladies looked at her, looked at each other, were silent, and endured it for a while; the smoke, however, became at length intolerable, and one whispered to another that something must be done to put a stop to this unallowable smoking.

Miss S. called the stewardess: "You must tell that lady that it is not permitted to smoke in this room."

"I have told her so, Missis, but she takes no notice. It is of no use talking to her."

Again they waited a while to see whether the smoking lady would not pay attention to silent, but very evident signs of displeasure. But no, she sat as unmoved as ever, and filled the room with smoke.

The lovely young Miss S. now summoned courage, advanced toward the smoker, and said, in a very polite, but, at the same time, firm and dignified manner, "I don't know whether you have observed that your cabin has a door which opens on the piazza, and—it would be much more agreeable for you, and for all of us, if you would smoke your pipe there."

"No. I prefer smoking here in this room."

"But it is forbidden to smoke here."

"It is forbidden for gentlemen, but not for ladies."

"*It is forbidden to smoke here*, as well for you as for any one else; and I must beg of you, in the name of all the ladies present, that you will desist from so doing."

This was said with so much earnestness, and so much grace at the same time, that the giant woman seemed struck by it.

"No, well! wait a bit!" said she, angrily; and, after she had vehemently blown out a great puff of tobacco-smoke by way of a parting token, she rose up and went into her own apartment. The power of cultivation had gained the victory over rudeness; the gods had conquered the giants.

We shall now proceed on our way, but by land, and not by water. Our heavily-laden vessel can not pass the shallows. It must be unloaded here. The passengers must proceed by carriages about fifteen or sixteen miles along the Iowa shore to a little city where they may take a fresh steamer, and where there are no longer any impediments in the river. My new friends from Connecticut will take me under their wing.

St. Louis, November 8th.

I am now at St. Louis, on the western bank of the river, deliberating whether or not to go to a bridal party to which I am invited, and where I should see a very lovely bride and "the cream of society" in this great Mississippi city, the second after New Orleans. I saw the bridegroom this forenoon, as well as the bride's mother; he is a very rich planter from Florida, and very much of a gentleman, an agreeable man. The bride's mother is a young-elderly beauty, polite but artificial; somewhat above fifty, with bare neck, bare arms, rouged cheeks, perfumed, and with a fan in her hand; a lady of fashion and French politeness. They have invited me for the evening. An agreeable and kind acquaintance of Mr. Downing's, to whom I had a letter, would conduct me thither in company with his wife, but—but—I have a cold, and I feel myself too old for such festivals, at which I am, besides, half killed with questions; so that the nearer it approaches the hour of dressing, the clearer becomes it to my own mind that I must remain quietly in my own room. I like to see handsome ladies and beautiful toilets, but—I can have sufficient descriptions of these, and I have seen enough of the *beau monde* in the Eastern States to be able to imagine how it is in the West.

I am now at an hotel, but shall remove, either to-morrow or the day after, to the house of Senator Allen, a little way out of the city.

I came here yesterday with my friends from Connecticut. The journey across the Iowa prairie in a half-covered wagon was very pleasant. The weather was as warm as a summer's day, and the sun shone above a fertile, billowy plain, which extended far, far into the distance. Three fourths of the land of Iowa are said to be of this billowy prairie-land. The country did not appear to be cultivated, but looked extremely beautiful and home-like, an immense pasture-meadow. The scenery of the Mississippi is of a bright, cheerful character.

In the afternoon we reached the little town of Keokuk, on a high bank by the river. We ate a good dinner at a good inn; tea was served for soup, which is a general practice at dinners in the Western inns. It was not till late in the evening that the vessel came by which we were to continue our journey, and in the mean time I set off alone on a journey of discovery. I left behind me the young city of the Mississippi, which has a good situation, and followed a path which led up the hill along the river side. The sun was descending, and clouds of a pale crimson tint covered the western heavens. The air was mild and calm, the whole scene expansive, bright, and calm, and idyllian landscape on a large scale.

Small houses, at short distances from each other, studded this hill by the river side; they were neatly built of wood, of good proportions, and with that appropriateness and cleverness which distinguishes the work of the Americans. They were each one like the other, and seemed to be the habitations of work-people. Most of the doors stood open, probably to admit the mild evening air. I availed myself of this circumstance to gain a sight of the interior, and fell into discourse with two of the good women of the houses. They were, as I had imagined, the dwellings of artisans who had work in the town. There was no luxury in these small habitations, but every thing was so neat and orderly, so ornamental, and there was such a holiday calm over every thing, from the mistress of the family down to the very furniture, that it did one good to see it. It was also Sunday evening, and the peace of the Sabbath rested within the home as well as over the country.

When I returned to my herberg in the town it was quite dusk; but it had, in the mean time, been noised abroad that some sort of Scandinavian animal was to be seen at the inn, and it was now requested to come and show itself.

I went down, accordingly, into the large saloon, and found a great number of people there, principally of the male sex, who increased more and more until there was a regular throng, and I had to shake hands with many most extraordinary figures. But one often sees such here in the West. The men work hard, and are careless regarding their toilet; they do not give themselves time to attend to it; but their unkemmed outsides are no type of that which is within, as I frequently observed this evening. I also made a somewhat closer acquaintance, to my real pleasure, with a little company of more refined people; I say *refined* intentionally, not *better*, because those phrases, better and worse, are always indefinite, and less suitable in this country than in any other; I mean well-bred and well-dressed ladies and gentlemen, the aristocracy of Keokuk. Not being myself of a reserved disposition, I like the American open, frank, and friendly manner. It is easy to become acquainted, and it is very soon evident whether there is reciprocity of feeling or not.

We went on board between ten and eleven at night, and the next morning were in the waters of the Missouri, which rush into those of the Mississippi, about eighteen miles north of St. Louis, with such vehemence, and with such a volume of water, that it altogether changes the character of the Mississippi. There is an end now to its calmness and its bright tint. It now flows onward restless and turbid, and stocks and trees, and every kind of lumber which can float, are whirled along upon its waves, all carried hither by the Missouri, which, during its impetuous career of more than three thousand miles through the wilderness of the West, bears along with it every thing which it finds on its way. Missouri is a sort of Xantippe, but Mississippi is no Socrates, because he evidently allows himself to be disturbed by the influence of his ill-tempered spouse.

Opposite St. Louis boys were rowing about in little boats, endeavoring to fish up planks and branches of trees which were floating on the river.

The first view of St. Louis was very peculiar. The city looks as if it were besieged from the side of the river by a number of immense Mississippi beasts, resembling a sort of colossal white sea-bears. And so they were; they were those large, three-decked, white-painted steamers, which lined the shore, lying closely side by side to the number of above a hundred; their streamers, with names from all the countries on the face of the earth, fluttering in the wind above their chimneys, which seemed to me like immense nostrils; for every steam-boat on the Mississippi has two such apparatus, which send forth huge volumes of smoke under the influence of "high pressure."

When we reached St. Louis it was as warm as the middle of summer, and many of the trees in the streets yet bore verdant foliage. I recognize the tree of the South, the "pride of India," which bears clusters of flowers like lilac during the time of flowering, and afterward clusters of red, poisonous berries; and the beautiful acacia, alanthus, and sycamore.

November 7th. Scarcely had I reached St. Louis when I was obliged to take to my bed in consequence of violent headache. My charming young friend from New England attended me as a young sister might have done. When she was obliged to leave me to proceed forward with her father, I found here an Irish servant-girl, who looked after me excellently during my short indisposition. I was better, and then went to pay a morning visit to the bridal pair, who are now residing at the hotel. It was in the forenoon; but the room in which the bride sat was darkened, and was only faintly lighted up by the blaze of the fire. The bride was tall and delicately formed, but too thin, but for all this lovely, and with a blooming complexion. She was quite young, and struck me like a rare hot-house plant, scarcely able to endure the free winds of the open air. Her long, taper fingers played with a number of little valuables fastened to a gold chain, which, hanging round her neck, reached to her waist. Her dress was costly and tasteful. She looked, however, more like an article of luxury than a young woman meant to be the mother of a family. The faint light of the room, the warmth of the fire, the soft, perfumed atmosphere—every thing, in short, around this young bride, seemed to speak of effeminacy. The bridegroom, however, was evidently no effeminate person, but a man and a gentleman. He was apparently very much enamored of his young bride, whom he was now about to take, first to Cincinnati, and then to Florida and its perpetual summer. We were regaled with bride-cake and sweet wine.

When I left that perfumed apartment, with its hot-house atmosphere and its half daylight, in which was carefully tended a beautiful human flower, I was met by a heaven as blue as that of spring, and by a fresh, vernal air, by sunshine and the song of birds among the whispering trees. The contrast was delightful. Ah, said I to myself, this is a different life! After all, it is not good; no, it is not good, it has not the freshness of Nature, that life which so many ladies lead in this country; that life of twilight in comfortable rooms, rocking themselves by the fireside from one year's end to another; that life of effeminate warmth and inactivity, by which means they exclude themselves from the fresh air, from fresh invigorating life! And the physical weakness of the ladies of this country must, in great measure, be ascribed to their effeminate education. It is a sort of harem-life, although with this difference, that they, unlike the Oriental women, are here in the Western country regarded as sultanesses, and the men as their subjects. It has, nevertheless, the tendency to circumscribe their development, and to divert them from their highest and noblest purpose. The harems of the West, no less than those of the East, degrade the life and the consciousness of woman.

After my visit to the bride, I visited various Catholic asylums and religious institutions, under the care of nuns. It was another aspect of female development which I beheld here. I saw, in two large asylums for poor orphan children, and in an institution for the restoration of fallen women (the Good Herder's Asylum), as well as at the hospital for the sick, the women who call themselves "Sisters," living a true and grand life as mothers of the orphan, as sisters and nurses of the fallen and the suffering. That was a refreshing, that was a strengthening sight!

I must observe that Catholicism seems to me at this time to go beyond Protestantism in the living imitation of Christ in good works. The Catholic Church of the New World has commenced a new life. It has cast off the old cloak of superstition and fanaticism, and it steps forth rich in mercy. Convents are established in the New World in a renovated spirit. They are freed from their unmeaning existence, and are effectual in labors of love.

These convents here have large, light halls instead of gloomy cells; they have nothing gloomy or mysterious about them; every thing is calculated to give life and light free course. And how lovely they were, these conventual sisters, in their noble, worthy costume, with their quiet, fresh demeanor and activity! They seemed to me lovelier, fresher, happier, than the greater number of women living in the world whom I have seen. I must also remark that their nuns' costume—in particular the headdress—was, with all its simplicity, remarkably becoming and in good taste; and that gave me much pleasure. I do not know why beauty and piety should not thrive well together. Those horrible bonnets, or poke-caps, which are worn by the Sisters of Mercy in Savannah, would, if I were ill, frighten me from their hospital. On the contrary, the sight of these sisters here would assuredly make a sick person well.

During one of those prophetic visions with which our Geijer closed his earthly career, he remarked, on a visit to me, "Convents must be re-established anew; not in the old form, but as free societies of women and men for the carrying out works of love!" I see them coming into operation in this country. And they must have yet a freer and milder form within the evangelical Church. The deaconess institutions of Europe are their commencement.

The excess in the number of women in all countries on the face of the earth shows that God has an intention in this which man would do well to attend to more and more. The human race needs spiritual mothers and sisters. Women acquire in these holy sisterhoods a power for the accomplishment of such duty, which in their isolated state they could only obtain in exceptional cases. As the brides and handmaidens of Christ, they attain to a higher life, a more expansive consciousness, a greater power. Whether similar religious societies of *men* are alike necessary and natural as those of women, I will not inquire into, but it seems to me that they are not. Men, it appears to me, are called to an activity of another kind, although for the same ultimate object—the extension of the kingdom of God upon earth.

Last evening and the evening before I made my solitary journeys of discovery both within and without the city.

St. Louis is built on a series of wave-like terraces, considerably elevated above the Mississippi. It seems likely to become an immense city, and has begun to build suburbs on the plain at great distances apart; but already roads are formed, and even a rail-road and streets from one place to another. These commencements of suburbs are generally on high ground, which commands glorious views over the river and the country. Thick columns of coal-black smoke ascend, curling upward in the calm air from various distances, betokening the existence of manufactories. It has a fine effect seen against the golden sky of evening, but those black columns send down showers of smuts and ashes over the city, which has not a fine effect. They are building in the city lofty and vast warehouses, immense shops and houses of business. The position of the city near the junction of the Missouri and the Mississippi, its traffic on the former river, with the whole of the Great West, and by the latter with the Northern, Southern, and Eastern States, give to St. Louis the means of an almost unlimited increase. Probably a railroad will connect St. Louis with the Pacific Ocean. It is an undertaking which is warmly promoted by a number of active Western men, and this would give a still higher importance to the city. Emigration hither also increases every year, and especially from Germany. How large this increase is may be shown by the fact that in 1845 its population amounted to thirty-five thousand souls, and that in 1849 it was nearly double that number. The State of Missouri has now about two millions of inhabitants, and is yet, as a state, not above thirty years old.

As I wandered through the streets in the twilight I saw various figures, both of men and animals, which gave me any thing but pleasure. Such I had often seen and grieved over at New York; just such people, with the look half of savageness and half of misery—just such poor worn-out horses. Ah! we need still to pray the Lord of all perfection, "Thy kingdom come!" I returned to my hotel with a melancholy and heavy heart.

One of the peculiarities which I observed was the number of physicians, especially dentists, which seemed to abound. Every third or fourth house had its inscription of "physician." What could be the use of all their remedies here?

Among the persons who have visited me here were some of the so-called "New Church," that is, Swedenborgians, who, in consequence of my confession of Faith in "Morgon Väkter," had the opinion that I belonged to the "New Church." I could not, however, acknowledge that I did belong to the New Church; for I find in the old, in its later development through the great thinkers of Germany and Scandinavia, a richer and a diviner life. Swedenborg's doctrine of the Law of Correspondence has for its foundation the belief and teaching of all profoundly-thinking people, from the Egyptians to the Scandinavians; but Swedenborg's application of his doctrine appears to me not sufficiently grand and spiritual.

Every where in North America one meets with Swedenborgians. That which seems to be most generally accepted among them is the doctrines of Christ's divinity, and of the resemblance which the world of spirits bears to the earth, and its nearness to it.

In their church-yards, one often finds upon a white marble stone beautiful inscriptions, such as,

He (or she) entered the spiritual world on such and such a day.

This is beautiful and true; for I say with Tholuck, "Why say that our form is *dead? Dead!* that word is so heavy, so lifeless, so gloomy, so unmeaning. Say that our friend has departed; that he has left us for a short time. That is better, and more true."

Crystal Springs, Nov. 10.

Since I last wrote I have removed to the beautiful home, and into the beautiful family of Senator A. A pretty young girl, the sister of the master of the house, has given me her room, with its splendid view over the Mississippi and Missouri Valley. But the beautiful weather has now changed into cold and autumnal fog, so that I can see nothing of all the glory. The air is very thick. But such days are of rare occurrence in this sunbright America, and the sun will soon make a way for itself again. Mr. A. has calculated the number of sunny days in a year for three several years, and he has found them to be about three hundred and fifteen; the remainder were thunder-storms and rainy days, and of the latter the number was the smaller.

Mr. A. is an interesting and well-informed young man, well acquainted with every movement in the state, of which he is a senator, as well as an active participator in its development. Thus, during the past summer, he has delivered no less than five hundred "stump-speeches"* (I hope I have not made a mistake of a couple of hundred in the number), traveling about in Missouri advocating the laying down of a rail-way from St. Louis through Missouri to the shores of the Pacific Ocean, and exhorting them to give in their adherence to the scheme. And he has been extremely successful. In St. Louis alone names are given in to the amount of two millions of dollars for the carrying out of the undertaking. It is true that they will have to tunnel through and to blast the solid walls of the Rocky Mountains, but what does that signify to an American?

The city of St. Louis was founded by rich traders. Dealers in furs and Catholic priests were the first who penetrated the wildernesses of the West, and ventured life to win, the former wealth, the latter souls.

Trade and religion are still, at this moment, the pioneers of civilization in the Western country.

One of the most important branches of speculation and

* Such is the name given to occasional speeches, which are delivered with the intention of agitating for or advancing any object, by men who travel about for that purpose, and assemble an audience here and there, often in the fields or the woods, when they mount a tree-stump or any other improvised platform, and thence address the people, the more vehemently the better. Short but highly-seasoned speeches, which go at once to the point in question, have the greatest success. Stump-speeches and stump-orators belong to the characteristic scenes of the Great West.

trade in and around St. Louis is, at the present time, the sale of land. The earlier emigrants hither who purchased land, now sell it by the foot at several thousand dollars a square foot. The exorbitant prices at which I have been told land sells here seem almost incredible to me. Certain it is that many people are now making great fortunes merely by the sale of their plots of ground. One German, formerly in low circumstances, has lately sold his plot, and has now returned to his native land with wealth to the amount of one hundred thousand dollars.

Mr. A., who is one of the "self-made men" of the Great West, and who began his career at Morton by publishing a Penny Magazine, is now a land proprietor, and sells also plots or pieces of ground for large sums. He, like Mr. Downing (with whom he has also, in appearance, a certain resemblance), unite at the same time the practical man and the poetical temperament, in particular for natural objects.

There are a great number of Germans in St. Louis. They have music and dancing parties, which are zealously attended. There are also here both French and Spaniards. At the hotels all is in French style, with French names for dishes and wines. The Irish here, as every where else throughout the United States, constitute the laboring population; excepting negro slaves, the greater portion of servants are Irish.

Spite of the greatly increasing trade of the city, it is still extremely difficult, nay, almost impossible for a young emigrant to obtain a situation in any place of business. If, on the contrary, however, he will begin by doing coarse hand-labor, as a miller's man, for instance, or a worker in a manufactory, he can easily find employment and get good wages. And if he lives carefully, he may soon gain sufficient to undertake higher employment. Better still are his prospects if he can superintend some handcraft trade; he is then in a fair way to become the artificer of his own fortune.

November 11th. Again summer and sunshine, and a glorious view over the Mississippi and the expanse of country! The heavens are light blue, the earth is light green, every thing is bathed in light. I have walked with my young friend over the hills around this place, and Mr. A. has driven me out to see the whole neighborhood. That which always strikes me most in the Great West is the vast extent of landscape. It produces upon me a peculiarly cheerful and expansive feeling. I can not but involuntarily smile as I seem to long to stretch out my arms and fly over the earth. It feels to me very stupid and strange not being able to do so. Mr. A. drove me to part of the neighborhood where the wealthy citizens of St. Louis built their villas. There are already upon the hills (though they can hardly be called hills; but merely terraces or plateaux) and in the valleys whole streets and groups of pretty country houses, many of them really splendid, surrounded by trees, and flowers, and vines, and other creepers. How life increases here, how rapidly and how joyously! But do not tares spring up with the wheat? I have still hope, although I have lost my faith in the Millennium of the Great West.

The State of Missouri seems to be one of the richest states of the Union as regards natural beauty and natural resources, as well as one of the largest. They speak of its northern portion as of the natural garden of the West; it possesses, westward, lofty mountains, rich in metals, interspersed with immense prairies and forest; southward, toward Arkansas, it becomes boggy, and abounds in morasses. To the west of the state lies the Indian Territory, the people of which have embraced Christianity and civilization. The Cherokees are the principal, but many other tribes have united themselves to this in smaller associations, as the family of Choctaws, Chickasaws, Fox, and Sac Indians. Whether this Indian territory stands in the same relationship to the government of the

United States as other territory during its period of gradation and preparation, and whether at some future time it will become an independent Indian state in the great Union, I do not know decidedly, though I regard it as probable.

Missouri is a slave state. But it seems at this moment to maintain the institution of slavery rather out of bravado than from any belief in its necessity. It has no products which might not be cultivated by white laborers, as its climate does not belong to the hot South. Missouri also sells its slaves assiduously "down South."

"Are you a Christian?" inquired I from a young handsome mulatto woman who waited on me here.

"No, Missis, I am not."

"Have you not been baptized? Have you not been taught about Christ?"

"Yes, Missis, I have a godmother, a negro woman, who was very religious, and who instructed me."

"Do you not believe what she told you about Christ?"

"Yes, Missis; but I don't *feel* it here, Missis," and she laid her hand on her breast.

"Where were you brought up?"

"A long way from here, up the Missouri, Missis; a long way off!"

"Were your owners good to you?"

"Yes, Missis; they never gave me a bad word."

"Are you married?"

"Yes, Missis; but my husband is a long way off with his master."

"Have you any children?"

"I have had six, Missis, but have not a single one left. Three are dead, and they have sold the other three away from me. When they took from me the last little girl, oh, I believed I never should have got over it! It almost broke my heart!"

And they were so-called Christians who did that! It

was not wonderful that she, the negro slave, had a difficulty in *feeling* Christianity, that she could not feel herself a Christian. What a life! Bereaved of husband, children, of all that she had, without any prospect of an independent existence; possessed of nothing on the face of the earth; condemned to toil, toil, toil, without hope of reward or day of rest; why should it be strange if she became stupid or indifferent, nay, even hostile and bitter in her feelings toward those in whose power she is—they who call themselves her protectors, and yet who robbed her of her all? Even of that last little girl, that youngest, dearest, only child!

This pagan institution of slavery leads to transactions so inconsistent, so inhuman, that sometimes in this country, this Christian, liberal America, it is a difficult thing for me to believe them possible, difficult to comprehend how it can be a reality, and not a dream! it is so difficult for me to realize it.

The topic of interest at this moment in St. Louis is the return of Senator Benton from Washington, and his great speech in the State House, to give an account of his conduct in Congress as regards the great and momentous question between the Northern and the Southern States. Such speeches, explanatory or in justification of their line of conduct, are customary in all the states on the return of the senator to the state which he represents in Congress. I read Colonel Benton's speech last evening. The bold representative of the slave state, who alike openly vindicated its rights as such, while he condemned slavery, is here also like himself bold, candid, unabashed, half man and half beast of prey, rending to pieces with beak and claws, and full of enjoyment in so doing.

I remember the last words of his speech, which are really manly and excellent.

"I value a *good* popularity, that is to say, the applause of good men. That of all others I shall ever disregard;

and I shall welcome censure which is hurled at me by the illiberal and the mean."

Missouri, as well as Arkansas, has a deal of heathenism, and a deal of wild, uncultivated land still. Civilization is as yet at its commencement in these states, and slavery retards its progress as with strong fetters. Fights and bloody duels are of frequent occurrence among the white population. Bowie-knives and pistols belong to the wardrobe of a man, especially when traveling in the state. Besides, he must be continually prepared to meet with those unprincipled fortune-hunters who hasten from Europe and the Eastern States (the prodigal sons of those countries) into the West to find there a freer scope for their savage passions.

To-morrow, or the day after, I steer my course to Cincinnati, whence I shall write to you again.

LETTER XXIX.

Cincinnati, Nov. 30th.

ONLY a kiss in spirit and a few lines to-day, because I have so many irons in the fire that I am, as it were, a little bewildered in my head, but that is with sweet wine!

I have been located since last Tuesday in the most agreeable and the most kind of homes, where those most agreeable of human beings and married people, Mr. and Mrs. S., middle-aged, that is to say, about fifty, wealthy and without children, find their happiness in gathering around them friends and relations, and in making them happy. I am occupying one of the many guest-chambers of their handsome and spacious house, and am treated with as much kindness as if I were a member of the family. A pale, gentle, and grave young clergyman (a mourning widower), and two unmarried ladies, relations of my entertainers, compose the family. My host, a giant in stature, and his little wife, have a good deal of humor, so that there is no lack of savory salt for the every day meal.

A word now about the journey hither from St. Louis. It was made in six days, by the Asia, safely and quietly, spite of the uneasy companionship of four-and-twenty little children from ten years to a few months old. One could not but think one's self well off if only a third of the number were not crying at once. There were also some passengers of the second or third sort, ladies who smoked their pipes and blew their noses in their fingers, and then came and asked how one liked America. Ugh! There are no greater contrasts than exist between the cultivated and the uncultivated ladies of this country.

One mother with her daughter pleased me, nevertheless, by their appearance and their evident mutual affection. But just as I was about to make some advances to the mother, she began with the question whether the United States answered my expectations. And that operated upon me like a bomb.

I spent my time, for the most part, quietly in my own cabin, finding companionship in my books, and in the spectacle presented by the banks of the river. When evening came, and with it candles, I had the amusement of the children's going to bed in the saloon, for there were not berths for them all. There was among the passengers one young mother, not above thirty years old, with eight children, the youngest still at the breast. She had gone with her husband and children to settle in the Far West, in some one of the Mississippi States, but the husband had fallen ill of cholera on the way, and died within four-and-twenty-hours. And now the young mother is returning with all her fatherless little ones to her paternal home. She is still very pretty, and her figure is delicate. Although now and then a tear may be seen trickling down her cheek as she sits of an evening nursing her little baby, yet she does not seem overcome by her loss, or greatly cast down. Seven of the children, four boys and three girls, are laid each evening in one large bed, made upon a long mattress, exactly in front of my door, without any other bedding than this mattress and a coverlit thrown over them. I have been much amused by a little lad of three years old, a regular Cupid both in head and figure, whose little shirt scarcely reached to his middle. He could not manage to be comfortable in the general bed, and longed probably for the warm mother's bosom; and therefore continually crept out of the former, and stole softly and resolutely, in his Adamic innocence, into the circle of ladies, who were sitting round the room talking or sewing by lamp-light. Here he was snapped up by his mother in his short shirt (much in the same way as our dairy-maids may snap up by their wings a chicken which they will put into a pen, or into the pot), and thus carried through the room back to his bed, where he was thrust in, à la chicken, with a couple of slaps upon that portion of his body which his little shirt did not defend, and then covered in with the quilt. In vain. He was soon seen again, white and round, above the quilt, spite of the hands of brothers and sisters, which let fall upon him a shower of blows: higher and higher he rose, raised himself on hands and feet, and the next minute my curly-headed Cupid stood on his two bare feet, and walked in among the circle of ladies, lovely, determined, and untroubled by the plague of clothes, or by bashfulness, where he was received by a burst of laughter, to be snapped up again by his mother, and again thrust under the quilt with an extra whipping, but too gentle to make any very deep impression. Again the same scene was renewed, to my great amusement, certainly six or seven times during an hour or two each evening. A little crying, it is true, always accompanied it; but the perseverance and the calm good humor of the little Cupid were as remarkable as his beauty, worthy of an Albano's pencil. But pardon me! such tableaux are not exactly of your kind. But this you should have seen!

Now for the scenery by the way. A little below St. Louis, we saw on the Mississippi the magnificent three-decked steamer the St. Louis, run aground in the middle of the river. We steamed past without troubling ourselves about it. It was a beautiful and sunny day. The landscape on the banks presented, for some time, nothing remarkable. Presently, however, on the Missouri bank rose up, close to the river, perpendicular cliffs, the walls of which presented the most remarkable imagery in bass-relief, sometimes also in high relief, of altars, urns, columns and pyramids, porticoes and statues, which it is difficult to persuade one's self are chiseled by the hand of Nature and not of art. These remarkable rocky walls occur at various places, but detached, and only along the Missouri shore.

Thus, still proceeding southward down the Mississippi, we arrived at the embouchure of the Ohio. The scenery here is expansive and flat. The clear blue Ohio, "the beautiful river," flows calmly and confidingly into the turbid Mississippi-Missouri, as the serene soul of one friend into the disquieted mind of another. The banks of both rivers are overgrown with brushwood. The whole region has a mild and cheerful appearance. A little deserted and desolate settlement lay, with its ruinous houses, upon the point between the two rivers. It was called Cairo. It was intended for a great trading town, but had been found so unhealthy that, after several unsuccessful attempts, it had been finally abandoned.

The Asia turned her course majestically eastward, from the Mississippi up the Ohio, between the two states of Ohio and Kentucky. The Ohio River is considerably smaller than the Mississippi; the shores are higher, and more wood-covered. The river is clear and beautiful. One

sees first along the banks trees being felled and log-huts, then come farms, and, lastly, beautiful country houses upon the hills, which increase in height and in degree of cultivation. The trees become tall and beautiful on each side the river, and in their leafy branches may be observed green knots and clusters, which, in the distance, look not unlike birds' nests. These are mistletoe, which here grows luxuriantly. The views now expand, the trees become more scattered, the hills retire backward, and upon the shore of the beautiful Ohio rises, with glittering church-spires, and surrounded by vineyards and ornamental villas, with a background of a semi-circle of two hills, a large city: it is Cincinnati, the Queen of the West.

Sixty years since this city was not in existence. Its first founder was living here only two years since. Now it has one hundred and twenty thousand inhabitants. That one may call *growth*.

Before I leave the Asia, I must cast a parting glance at Mehala, the good old negro woman who was the stewardess of the vessel. She was one of those good-tempered, excellent creatures, which one can not help growing fond of, and with a great deal of that tact and prudence which belong to the negro race. She had had fourteen children, but had lost them all by death and slave-dealing. She knew only for a certainty where three of them were to be found, but that was at a great distance. She spoke sorrowfully, but without bitterness. She now belonged to a German family, who had, at her own desire, hired her out for service on the vessel, "because," she said, "they did not understand how to treat their servants." All her aim and endeavor was to save sufficient to purchase her own freedom; then she could, she knew, go to her married daughter in Kentucky, and there maintain herself by washing. She had already saved a little sum. On taking leave, the excellent old woman embraced me so cordially that it did my very heart good. As a contrast to

this woman was another, the laundress on board, as cross and ill-tempered as the other was amiable.

The Asia had not long reached Cincinnati when a mild, pale gentleman came on board, and conveyed me in a carriage to the new home whither I had been invited. This was the clergyman and friend, the guest of the family, and of whom I have already spoken. When the door of the house opened I was met by a young middle-aged lady, whose charming countenance bore such a speaking impression of goodness and benevolence that I felt myself involuntarily attracted to her, and glad to be in her house; and the attraction and the pleasure have increased ever since.

I have heard Cincinnati variously called "The Queen of the West," "The City of Roses," and "The City of Hogs." It deserves all three names. It is a handsome, nay, a magnificent city, with the most beautiful situation among vineyard-hills, green heights adorned with beautiful villas, and that beautiful river, Ohio, with its rich life and its clear water. It has, in the time of roses, it is said, really an exuberant splendor from these flowers, and I see roses still shining forth pleasantly among the evergreen *arbor vitæ*, on the terraces, before the beautiful houses. But the predominant character at this moment is as "the City of Hogs." This is, namely, the season when the great droves of these respectable four-footed citizens come from the western farms and villages to Cincinnati, there to be slaughtered in a large establishment solely appropriated to this purpose, after which they are salted and sent to the Eastern and Southern States. I have many times met in the streets whole regiments of swine, before which I made a hasty retreat, partly because they entirely fill up the whole street, partly because their stench fills the air and poisons it. I called them respectable (aktinness wârd), because I in every way guard (akta) myself against them. I have a salutary abhorrence of the whole of their race in this country, and if I could but impart the same to many others, then would there be many healthier and happier people than there are. I now see that Mohammed was a much wiser man and legislator than I imagined. If he could come back, be made President of the United States, and prohibit the eating of swine's flesh, and enforce the prohibition, and drive all swine out of the country, then would the Union be saved from the greatest evil after civil war, from—*Dyspepsy!*

But among so much that is beautiful and so much that is good, I ought not any longer to detain myself with pigs!

I have had some beautiful rambles here and there in the neighborhood, and have made many interesting acquaintance also out of the house. Foremost among these must I mention the phrenologist, Dr. Buchanan, an intellectual, eccentric little man, full of life and human love, who greatly interests me by his personal character and by the large views which he takes in his Neurology and Analysis of the human brain, "of the immense possibilities of man," allowing at the same time wide scope to the freedom of the human will. Buchanan is, in a high degree, a spiritualist, and he regards spiritual powers too as the most potent agents of all formation—regards the immaterial life as the determiner of the material. Thus he considers the will in man as determining the inner being, as influencing the development of the ductile brain, for good or for evil, and the ductile brain operates upon, elevates or depresses the skull.

Further, I am cheered in a high degree by the views current here on the subject of slavery and its possible eradication, and in the future of the negroes, as well as of Africa, through its colonization by Christian negroes from America, settled on the coast of Africa, and by the products of free labor in a wholly tropical climate being superior to that of slave labor in a half-tropical climate.

I read in the African Repository, a periodical which is published here by Mr. D. Christy, agent of the Colonization Society in Ohio, some interesting papers on the subject of Liberia and Sierra Leone, and the increase of the colonies on the coast of Africa. The State of Ohio has lately taken a decided step by the purchase of a large district of country on the African coast called Gallinas, several hundred miles in extent, and where the slave-trade was hitherto greatly carried on. Some wealthy men in Cincinnati have appropriated several thousands of dollars to this purpose ; and, in consequence of this circumstance, and the new country being colonized by free negroes from Ohio, it is called Ohio in Africa. An essential barrier has thus been placed against the carrying on of the slave-trade on the African coast.

A State Convention is at the present moment being held here, which consists of one hundred and eight citizens, to change, or, to speak more correctly, to develop the Constitution of the State, which is now probably fifty years old. I was present yesterday at one of the sittings, and shook hands with a considerable number of the wise fathers, most of whom are handsome, middle-aged men, with open countenances, and broad, clever foreheads. A great portion of the members are lawyers; there are, however, several farmers, merchants, and men of different trades. Two only of the members were unmarried men. The object which the Convention has in view is to extend the power of the people, as, for example, in the appointment of judges and other official persons.

Other interesting objects there are, besides, which are refreshing to my inmost being. There is really in Ohio a movement of central life as well in thought as in action, which I have not met with in any other state of America ; and, however it may be, I seem to be living here in the very centre of the New World.

In short, my little heart, I *live*. I embrace in my spirit

the present and the future in various developments, in various parts of the earth, near and afar; and I feel that much is developing itself within my own soul which formerly lay bound, or merely lived with a half existence; and I thank God!

December. I have now resided nearly three weeks in this good home, with these kind and good S.'s, and seen a good deal of people and of the town, as well as of the beautiful region around this place. The country is of the most beautiful and of the most attractive character that any one can imagine; lovely villas are scattered over the fertile hills, and commanding the most glorious views over the river and the whole country. The people—yes, they are even here of all sorts, the good and the bad, the agreeable and the disagreeable; some most amiable, with whom one would wish to remain long, to remain always, and others whom one would wish—where the pepper grows. Yet the greater number whom I have seen belong to the good and charming, and I have enjoyed much happiness with them.

I saw three young brides at a bridal party the other day, all of them very handsome, one remarkably so, for a beautiful soul beamed in her countenance. I said to her with my whole heart, "God bless you!" I saw on this occasion many beautiful toilets and many beautiful faces. The American ladies dress well and with good taste. And here, indeed, one seems to meet nothing but handsome faces, scarcely a countenance which may be called ugly. Yet, nevertheless, I think it would be a refreshment to see such a one, if in it I found that beauty which seems to me generally, not always, to be deficient in these truly lovely human roses, and which I may compare to the dewy rose-bud in its morning hour. There is a deficiency of shadow, of repose, of the mystery of being, of that nameless, innermost depth, which attracts the mind with a silent power in the consciousness of hidden and noble treasure. There is a deficiency of that quiet grace of being, which in itself alone is beauty. Am I unjust? Is it the glitter of the drawing-room and the chandelier which bewilders me?

One observation I considered as well founded. Artifice and vanity exercise no less power over our sex in this country than they do in the great cities of Europe, and far more than in our good Sweden. Some proofs of this fact have almost confounded me. The luxurious habits and passion for pleasure of young married ladies have not unfrequently driven their husbands to despair and to drunkenness. I once heard a young and handsome lady say, "I think that ladies, after they are married, are too little among gentlemen. When I go to a ball I always make it a duty to forget my children."

A scandalous lawsuit is now pending here between a young couple who have been married a few years. It was a most magnificent wedding; the establishment, furniture, every thing, was as expensive and splendid as possible; every thing was silk, and velvet, and jewels. Soon, however, discord arose between the married pair, in consequence, it is said, of the young wife's obstinacy in rouging against the wish of her husband. Her vain and foolish mother appears to have taken the side of the daughter against the husband, and now the two are parted, and a correspondence is published which redounds to the honor of none of the family.

On the other hand, the besetting sins of the men in the Great West are gambling and drunkenness; it may be summed up in that state of feeling which is called recklessness.

"For what do people marry here in the West; for love or for money?" inquired I of an elderly, clever, and intellectual gentleman, one of my friends.

"For money," replied he, shortly.

His wife objected to that severe judgment; but he

would not retract it, and she was obliged to concede that money had a great influence, after all, in the decision of a match.

That marriages, in spite of this, should often turn out happy, must be attributed to our Lord's mercy, and to the firm moral principles which are instilled into this generation by nature and education, and supported by the influence of general moral opinions. Nor is it other than natural that under such circumstances many marriages are also unhappy, and that the number of divorces is large in a portion of the American States where the law does not lay any very momentous impediment in the way. The frequency of divorce here may also be caused by the circumstance of the Americans having less patience than other people with imperfection, and preferring to cut the Gordian knot asunder, than labor through a course of years in unloosening it. "Life is short!" say they.

Yet in the mean time have I nowhere seen more perfectly happy marriages than in America; *but* these were not entered into for the sake of money.

"What is there better here in the Western States than in those of the East that makes you prefer living here?" inquired I of my excellent hostess.

"More freedom and less prejudice," replied she; "more regard to the man than to his dress and his external circumstances; a freer scope for thought and enterprise, and more leisure for social life."

And yet I seem here to have remarked that shortness of temper, impatience, misunderstandings, and envyings, all the petty feuds of social life, no less take up their quarters here than in other great cities of the New World. The good seed and the tares spring up together every where in the fields of the earth, whether in the West or whether in the East.

The climate of Cincinnati is not good; the air is keen, and the rapid alternations in the weather may have some effect in producing that irritability of temperament which I seemed to observe.

It has been a pleasure to me while here to attend various lectures, and foremost among them I must mention Dr. Buchanan's animated and really intellectual extempore address in the Medical College on the activity of the brain and its relationship to human free-will. Another also, on Lord Bacon of Verulam, by the young Unitarian minister, Mr. Livermore, which was interesting from its impartiality and its profound pshychological glance. A third was by a planter and quondam slaveholder, Mr. Cassius M. Clay, of Kentucky, who emancipated the slaves upon his plantation, and now, having come forward as the opponent of slavery, a hostile feeling has been excited against him in the slave states. Hence it happened that during a public lecture given by him on the slavery question a year ago at a city of Kentucky (Louisville, I believe), he was attacked by a ferocious man and his adherents, who beat and cut him dreadfully, while he, unprepared for such an onslaught, had no weapon wherewith to defend himself. Already severely wounded by many bowie-knives, he would probably have perished had not his little son of thirteen bravely thrust his way through the crowd to his father, and given him a bowie-knife for his defense. Clay could now stand on the defensive, and he did that with so much effect that he gave his opponent his death-wound. He himself lay sick of the wounds which he had received for nearly twelve months, and this was now the first time after his recovery that he had given a public lecture, but not now in Kentucky, in Ohio.

The large hall in which he was to speak was full to overflowing. I had already become acquainted with him at the bridal party, and he had since then paid me a visit, and I was pleased with his manly, determined demeanor, and the deep gleam in his dark blue eye, as well as by the view he took of the necessarily rude and low condition of a state in which slavery is a "domestic institution," of its corrupting influence on the morals and tone of mind, and, as a consequence thereof, the dominion of the pistol and the bowie-knife. His belief was that negro slaves might and ought to be transformed into free laborers. I inquired from him how his own slaves conducted themselves as freemen.

"Excellently!" replied he; "but there were not many of them, and they had, by degrees, been prepared for freedom."

He inveighed boldly and earnestly in his speech this evening against an institution which loosened all family bonds and degraded women, and he uttered a violent tirade against the new Fugitive Slave Bill, as well as against Daniel Webster, who had supported it. He recalled to his recollection a painting, which he had seen as a child, in which the fires of Purgatory were represented. There might be seen various poor sinners who were endeavoring to come forth from the devouring flames, but a superintendent devil stood by with horns and claws, and a huge hay-fork in his hand, ever ready to seize each poor soul about to escape from the fire, to take him on the prongs of his fork and hurl him back again. This superintendent devil he recognized as Daniel Webster.

That was the brilliant point in the speech, which throughout was conventional, and which passed over from the Slave Bill and Webster to the Bible and Christianity. The clever combatant was not successful on this ground, and proved himself to be a poor theologian, inasmuch as he mistook Christianity for that contracted Church which lays sole claim to the appellation, and measured the words of the Bible according to their abuse or their irrational misapplication. But this abuse of Scripture is so common among the defenders of slavery, even among the clergy, that I am not surprised at many persons being provoked by it, and being led to suspect the wells of truth, from which men will draw up lies.

The numerous assembly, however, had a keen sense; they perceived the error and preserved silence. The speaker, who had been received with demonstrations of great enthusiasm, found his audience much cooled at the close.

Ohio is, as you know, a free state, and exactly on the opposite side of the beautiful river which bears its name lies the slave state of Kentucky, and slaves flying across the river to reach a free shore were heard of formerly as an every-day occurrence. Now such a flight avails nothing to the poor slaves. They are pursued and recaptured as well in a free as in a slave state.

I have heard histories of the flight of slaves which are full of the most intense interest, and I can not conceive why these incidents do not become the subjects of romances and novels in the literature of this country. I know no subject which could furnish opportunities for more heart-rending or more picturesque descriptions and scenes. The slaves, for example, who fly "the way of the North Star," as it is called, who know no other road to liberty than the road toward the North, who wander on by night when it shines, and conceal themselves by day in the deep forests, where sometimes gentle Friends (Quakers) carry out food to them, without which they would probably perish: this journey, with its dangers and its anticipations, its natural scenery and its nocturnal guiding star—what subjects are here for the pen of genius! Add to this the converse, the agony or the joy of warm, loving, suffering human hearts—in short, here are subjects of a higher romantic interest than are found in Chateaubriand's "Atala." I can not understand why, in particular, noble-minded American women, American mothers who have hearts and genius, do not take up the subject, and treat it with a power which should pierce through bone and marrow, should reduce all the prudential maxims of statesmen to dust and ashes, and produce a revolution even in the old widely-praised Constitution itself. It is the privilege of the woman and the mother which suffers most severely through slavery. And if the heart of the woman, and the woman would heave warmly and strongly with maternal life's blood, I am convinced that the earth, the spiritual earth of the United States, must quake thereby and overthrow slavery!

Often when I have heard the adventures of fugitive slaves, their successful escape or their destruction, and have thought of the natural scenery of America, and of those scenes which naturally suggest themselves on "the way of the North Star," I have had a wish and a longing desire to write the history of a fugitive pair, so as it seems to me it ought to be written, and I have been inclined to collect materials for that purpose. And if I lived by this river and amid these scenes, I know for what object I should then live. But as it is, I am deficient in local knowledge. I am not sufficiently acquainted with the particular detail of circumstances, which would be indispensable for such a delineation, which ought to be true, and to take a strong hold upon the reader. That office belongs to others besides myself. I will hope for and expect—the *American mother.*

Ohio is called "the Buckeye State," from the brown fruit of a kind of chestnut called the buckeye, which is very general throughout the state. The state is said to possess a fertile soil, good for grain and the rearing of cattle, and pastorally beautiful scenery, although not of a magnificent character. Both this state and Kentucky are renowned for their fine trees. I regret that the season of the year does not permit seeing more of their beauty and of the country; of that rich country which could maintain eight or ten millions of inhabitants beyond its present number.

All within doors is good, peaceful, and charming. A new guest, a friend of the family, has enlivened the social circle for the last few days. He is a Mr. D., from New England, but not at all a Yankee in disposition; on the contrary, he seems quite refined, very dapper, and highly perfumed, as if he had just stepped out of Madame De Sévigné's drawing-room circle into ours. He interests himself principally for social life and literature, for friends and acquaintance, for agreeable objects and the pleasures of the hour; is an amateur of handsome ladies, bonmots, and bonne chère; is acquainted with the minutest niceties of Shakspeare; and is able to see great things in a little billet of four lines written by a lady's hand; for the rest, he is an honorable man, a devoted friend, a good companion, and one who talks well on every-day subjects.

He has given a new turn to our observations of the Great West, regarding it from a mythological point of view, and as a new Jothunhun with Thor and Loke, the Krimthursar and Giants. And the comparisons which he makes between the Scandinavian Jothunhun, its heroes and their adventures, which he reads from a translation of Sturleson's Edda, by the poet Longfellow, and that of the New World's now existing Jothunhun and its giants, furnish occasion for many amusing narratives and relations. Thus the extreme West becomes the new Utgaerd, full of monsters and witches; the mammoth grotto is the glove of Skyenin; the divine hog, Schrimmer, lives here a thousand-fold, and the achievements of Thor and Starkotter are renewed in those of the giants of the giant river and the states of the Mississippi. Of these we have a great number of anecdotes, which season our meals, and our host, Mr. S. (whom Mr. D. and I call "the good Jothun," and who seems to like the title very well), contributes many a racy and amusing addition to this mythology of the West. See here two specimens.

A man, one of the men of the West, was standing on

the shore of the Mississippi, when a steamer blew up in the air, on which he exclaimed, "By God! the Americans are a great people!" A common exclamation in the Great West on every occasion.

Another man, a Viking on the Mississippi, struck his boat upon a snag in the river, and as he himself hung upon this, he exclaimed, while his boat was dashed to pieces,

"Hail, Columbia, happy land!
If I'm not lost, I'll be d——d!"

Another man, a passenger in one of the Mississippi steamers, lately got into a quarrel with another passenger. They went upon the upper deck and exchanged a few shots, and then came down again as if they had only been playing at ball. One of these gentlemen looked rather pale and went into his cabin, but came out morning, noon, and evening regularly to his meals for two days; on the third, however, he was found dead in his bed, with five bullets in his body.

One must confess that this was taking the matter coolly.

A certain humorous exaggeration seems to be characteristic of the inhabitants of the West, as well in their combatant disposition as in expression. Kentucky is particularly accused of this, and gives occasion for many amusing stories. Thus it is told of a Kentucky man that he boasted of the fertility of the soil of Kentucky in the following words: "If we manure well, and sow corn (maize), we shall get about one hundred and fifty grains for each one; if we sow without manure, we get one hundred; and if we neither manure nor sow, we get about fifty."

The Jothun histories belong now to our daily bread, and new ones come up every day. With Mr. S., the pale minister, I do not, however, talk about such things, but, on the contrary, of theology and Swedenborgology. We dispute a little; but I find so much to learn from the crystally-pure truth and beauty of his soul, that I have more pleasure in listening to its quiet expression than in maintaining my own arguments. He is one of the quiet in the land, whose lives are their best teaching. He still sorrows deeply for his departed wife.

"People do not know how sufficiently to value the blessings of matrimony," said he to me on one occasion. "We do not live in marriage up to the height of that happiness and that life which we, nevertheless, hold in our own hand."

Miss Harriet, the eldest sister of Mrs. S., an excellent, stout, grave, elderly lady, near upon sixty, does not make her appearance till dinner, and but very seldom in the drawing-room. On the contrary, I often found that she had some employment in my room, and in my drawers, and about my wash-stand, and that it was done stealthily, which appeared to me a little extraordinary, until I put in connection with it another extraordinary thing, and thus, by means of the latter, was able to explain the former. I discovered, namely, in my drawers, that a collar or a pair of muslin sleeves, which I had laid aside because they had become somewhat too gray for wear, had reassumed, by some inexplicable means, their pure white color, and lay there fresh washed and ironed as if of themselves. In the same way I found that the old collar had been mended, and still more, a new collar exhibited itself trimmed with real lace, and a new pair of muslin sleeves which had never been there before, but which were exactly of the kind that I wore—and for all that, Miss Harriet, when I met her, looked as grave as ever, and just as if she would say that she never concerned herself with other people's affairs, and wished that neither would others trouble themselves about hers. It was some time before I, in real earnest, began to suspect that Miss Harriet had taken upon herself the charge of the getting up and repairing of my fine linen, and supplying such new as I seemed to stand in need of. And when at length I charged her with it, she tried to look a little cross, but that good, roguish smile betrayed her; but the good, kind, sisterly soul has since then not been able to keep me at a distance by her somewhat harsh voice and grave manner. But that this voice never spoke other than in truth, and that under that apparently cold demeanor there dwelt a good, honest heart, a clear and sound understanding, a somewhat jocose and excellent temper and powers of conversation—all this I discovered by degrees, and this also had I been assured of by Mr. H.

And who is Mr. H.? He is one of the gentleman friends of the house, a man whom I would very gladly have for a friend. More of him you will probably know hereafter, as we are to be fellow-travelers to New Orleans.

Miss V., the second and younger friend and inmate of the family, is so silent and quiet, and it is merely from the lofty, intellectual forehead, and the repose of the whole noble figure, that one is led to suppose that she is the possessor of more than ordinary talent. True, however, it is, that now and then an observation is made, or some play of words is quietly and carelessly uttered, which makes one turn one's head, at once amused and surprised, toward the unpretending Miss V., because one seldom hears any where any thing so good as what she has said.

Thus, to-day at dinner, when they were talking of the excitement which Jenny Lind had produced in the United States, somebody said that they had seen an announcement offering "Jenny Lind herrings" for sale, and Miss V. immediately remarked that it was a *selfish idea*. And when we began to laugh, and some one said, "Oh, Miss V., do you make such puns?" our good Jothun returned, à la Kentuckian, "Yes, certainly—yes, certainly, she does nothing else. She it is who furnishes all our newspapers with puns."

But she does other things also for the pleasure of the family, and among these is the manipulation of delicate sponge-cake, the best cake which is made in this country, and of which I have here an abundance, as a reminder of the giant character of the Great West.

You thus may see a little of our every-day life; but the pearl of all to me in social life and conversation is my charming little, sensible, and kind hostess.

I have also here the pleasure of frequently hearing pieces by Beethoven played by a young girl, Miss K. G., one of the most intimate friends of the family; and played with so much fidelity, with such an inward comprehension, that not a tone nor intention of the great master is lost. This is a source to me of the greatest enjoyment. This young lady has in her appearance a great deal of that inward, beaming beauty, which I value beyond the mere exterior beauty, which is more common in the youthful countenances of this country. At my request she has carefully studied Beethoven's second adagio in the fourth symphony, which so much charmed me at Boston. Among the people who have given me pleasure here, I must mention a young poetess, Mrs. L., handsome, highly gifted, and amiable. It is a real musical delight to hear her read poetry.

Many Swedes are resident at this place, and among them several who, after having been unsuccessful in the Old World, have succeeded in the New, and are now in comfortable circumstances. One of these has made his fortune by exhibiting "Hell," a youthful production of the American sculptor, Hiram Powers, who was born in Cincinnati, worked here at a watchmaker's, and here commenced various works of art. Among these was a mechanical, moving representation of Hell. The Swede purchased it, set it up in a kind of museum, invited people to come and see how things went on in Hell, passed some violent electric shocks among them, accompanied by thunder and lightning, and is now a rich man, with wife, children, and country house, all acquired by his representation of Hell.

There are some American homes in Cincinnati into which I will introduce you. First to the home where a young widowed mother lives for the education and development of her five beautiful little boys into good Christians and fellow-citizens; then to the home where married couples without children make life rich to one another, through kindness and intelligence, dispelling ennui from their fireside, and causing sickness to become a means of deeper union between heart and heart, between heaven and earth. This is, in particular, a home where I know you would feel as I did; for it is beautiful to see people live well, but still more beautiful and still more rare to see them die so. And in this home there is one dying; quite a young girl, lovely as a rose-bud, and with such a fresh rose-tint on her cheek that no stranger could believe that death was at her heart. But she must die, and her mother knows it too. She suffers from a fatal disease of the heart; and the heart, which is becoming too large for the narrow chest, will cease to beat in a few weeks. Both mother and daughter know this, and prepare themselves, during the days and nights of suffering which they spend together, for their approaching separation, and this with heavenly light and calm. They speak of it to each other as of something beautiful for the younger one, and she prepares herself for the companionship of angels by becoming beneath the cross of suffering more patient, more affectionate to all—more like an angel still. There is nothing gloomy in this sick-room; friends come thither with presents and with love, still more to gladden the young girl while she lingers on the brink of the grave, and to obtain from her a word or a glance from that heaven with which she is already in communion.

This serenity as regards death, and this preparation for

its approach, are of more general occurrence among the people of England and North America than in any other country that I am acquainted with. People there regard it as one of their human privileges, that, as it must occur, to become acquainted with its state, and their own pilgrimage of death; to approach the hour of their change with an open glance and a vigilant mind, and with a full consciousness of the importance of their transit, to prepare themselves for it.

December 16th. A day of supreme life from a great number of living interests and thoughts. Thoughts regarding the human brain and the central point of view in which man stands with regard to the whole universe; glimpses of prevision from this sun and point of sight through an infinite expanse into the realms of all life, are predominant in my soul. Shall I ever be in full possession of myself, ever fully possess the world of thought which flashes through my soul?

I can not write much more to you to-day, because I must write many letters, and, above all, one to Böklin, which I shall inclose in this, and which you can read if you so incline. It will complete various things in my letter to you. Spite of all the interests which detain me here, and all the charms of my home, I long to proceed southward. I am afraid of the winter in the keen air of Cincinnati, and of the American mode of heating rooms, which is horrible. It is unquestionably the cause of much of that disease which seems more and more on the increase among the class of people who live most comfortably and most within doors. I long also to reach the South before Christmas, that I may, if possible, have an opportunity of seeing those dances and festivities of which I have heard are common among the negroes of the plantations at Christmas. I have heard much said about the happiness of the negroes in America, of their songs and dances, and I wish, therefore, for once to see this happiness and their festivals. In South Carolina and Georgia the preachers have done away with dancing and the singing of songs. In Louisiana there is no preaching to the slaves; perhaps they may there sing and dance.

17*th*. A large and excellent steamer leaves this evening for New Orleans, and with it I shall proceed thither with my cavalier, Mr. H.

I must still say a few words to you about two very pleasant parties which have been given by my friends. My objection to small familiar evening parties in America is that they occupy themselves so little by reading aloud, or by any other means of drawing the little circle toward one common point of interest.

In large parties, however, many of the elements are met with which make social intercourse perfect, among which may be reckoned as foremost that the two sexes are properly intermingled. One never sees the gentlemen here all crowding into one room, and the ladies into another, or the former in one corner of the drawing-room and the latter in another, just as if they were afraid of each other. The gentlemen who come into society—and they seem very fond of drawing-room society in an evening—consider it as a duty, and, as it seems to me, often also a pleasure, to entertain the ladies, and this evident good-will on their part awakes in them, perhaps, not a greater desire, but certainly a greater power of being agreeable and entertaining, more ability to impart to men of good taste and noble mind something much better than cigar smoke and punch. A gentleman will commonly occupy himself for a long time, frequently the whole evening, with one lady. People sit on lounges, or on small sofas of all sorts, in pairs, conversing together; or the gentleman gives the lady his arm, and they take a promenade through the room. Sometimes two ladies will sit conversing together for a long time; but the rule is for the two who associate together to be man and woman. Nor is it always the handsomest nor the most elegant lady who wins the most attention. I have seen Mr. H., a young and very agreeable man, occupy himself for whole hours in animated conversation with Miss Harriet. True it is that he has a great esteem for her, and in this he shows his good taste. I do not know that I have ever seen card-playing in any parties, large or small, in this country.

I shall always remember with feelings of affection some young girls with whom I have lately become acquainted, one among whom has lately met with a bitter trial; but, instead of allowing it to embitter her own heart, it has only the more caused it to expand with sympathy to all who suffer. God's peace rest upon that young girl! She would become very dear to me. Some sisters also there were, who in pleasure and in pain live together as sisters seldom do live. And that K. G., with her beaming soul and her music, she will always remain near my heart; but now I must proceed on my journey, and for this I must get ready.

"Belle Key," the steamer by which I shall travel, so called from the beautiful daughter of its proprietor, a belle of Louisville, is a sort of giant vessel, which, laded with every kind of product of the Great West, goes as a Christmas-envoy to New Orleans.

It is now cold at Cincinnati: the Queen of the West rains down soot and ashes, so that one becomes quite grimy. I long to be with that great Christmas-beast once more on the Mississippi.

P.S.—It is said that there is especially fine wooing in the Great West; a young girl has at least three or four suitors to choose from. Certainly, the number of men considerably predominates over that of women. In the Eastern States it seems to me that the women are in excess. The men go out thence into the West on the search for occupation and wealth. The preponderance of men over women increases the further you advance westward.

It was said at Cincinnati that at a ball at San Francisco there were fifty gentlemen for one lady. It is also said that in the gold district, where there are great numbers of men and no women, that they hung up in some kind of museum a lady's dress, which was contemplated as a sort of fabulous thing. But I suspect that this belongs to the mythological legends of the Great West.

In the same category may be placed that of the Garden of Eden near Cincinnati, which I am invited to visit. It is said to be a large vineyard; but the beauty of the views from the heights of the Ohio may justify the name.

LETTER XXX.

TO THE REV. P. J. BÖKLIN.

Cincinnati, November 27th.

I HAVE now spent more than a year in the New World without having fulfilled my promise of writing to you, my friend and teacher; without having told you what I think of it, and what I hope from it. And yet, at the same time, I knew that you wished to know it.

My good friend, I have not hitherto been able to write to you. I wished not to give you my crude thoughts and descriptions, and it was long before I could give other than such. The effect produced upon me, and the daily occurrences of my life in this country, were in the first instance overpowering, as well for soul as for body; and, to a certain degree, I was really borne down by them. The violent torrent of new, and, for the most part, rapturous impressions, the incessant labor with new objects, new people, together with the effects of a hot climate, and food to which I was unaccustomed, reduced me to that state of feverish, nervous excitement, that for months I was unable to read, or even to think on any subject which required the slightest exertion of mind.

The mercy of God, however, the care of good people, the healing powers of nature and of art, enabled me, by degrees, to rise above this state of weakness. I was able once more to live and learn.

But, during that daily labor, to make myself master of those subjects which pressed upon me on all sides during my wanderings, and the endeavor to arrange my thoughts, it became more and more clear to me that, in order to arrive at any just conclusion with regard to the moral, intellectual, and religious culture, as it existed in the states of North America, I must see more of its various forms and developments; I must become acquainted with life, as well in the Northeastern as in the Southern and the Western States of the Union; I must see the life of America, both where it had established and perfected itself, and where it was yet endeavoring to break the clod of the earth's surface, to build new homes, to conquer new life and new lands.

"When I shall have seen the Great West, the valley of the Mississippi, Cincinnati, the Queen of the West, I will write to Böklin. Then I shall better understand, shall be better able to speak of the New World, and of that future for humanity which it bears in its bosom!" Thus said I to myself.

Now I am at Cincinnati. I have seen and I see before me the Great West, the central region of North America. I have traveled through the valley of the Mississippi, the future home of more than two hundred and seventy-five millions of people; on the great river, the banks of which already swarm with multitudes of European people; from Minnesota, still the wild abode of the Indian tribes; from the Falls of St. Anthony, where commences the career of the river in the North, to its midmost region by the Missouri and the Ohio; and am now about to follow its course to its outlet into the Mexican Gulf, the realm of the sugar-cane and perpetual summer.

And while I am resting here on the banks of the beautiful River Ohio, like the wearied dove on the olive-branch, in one of those beautiful, peaceful homes which every where on my journeyings through America have opened themselves to me, and afforded me the repose of a mother's home—repose, peace, love, cheerfulness, and renewed strength—I will converse with you—you, my spirit's and my mind's best friend, found late but for eternity. Ah! but even now I can merely speak a few words to you, give you a few fragments of that which I have experienced and learned, and which I still experience and learn in this New World. But you will understand what I can merely imperfectly indicate; you will follow still further through the labyrinth the thread which I lay in your hand.

You know that I did not come to America to seek for a new object, but to establish a new hope. While one portion of the people of Europe, after a struggle for light and freedom, which in part mistook its own purpose, and not clearly knowing that which it desired, seemed (perhaps merely seemed) to sink back again under a despotism which knew better what it aimed at, obtaining for a time the power of might; in that gloomy season my soul raised itself in deep faith and love toward that distant land, where the people erected the banner of human freedom, declared the human right and ability to govern themselves, and on this right founded a monarchy of states—the commencement of the world's greatest governmental culture.

That which I sought for there was the new human being and his world; the new humanity and the sight of its future on the soil of the New World.

I will tell you what I have so far seen and found.

I spent the last autumn and winter in the northeastern states of the Union, New York, Massachusetts, Connecticut—the mother states from which the swarm of people have gone forth, and still go forth to populate the American continent, and to give it laws and manners. That which is most admirable in these mother states is the number of great institutions for the education of youth and in aid of the unfortunate, schools and asylums. These are the offspring of a large heart, and they have a broad basis. It is a joy to see and hear the children taught in these public schools, which are all free schools, in large and airy halls. One can see that they are all awake and full of life; one can hear that they understand that which they read and learn. The great reformation which has taken place in the conduct of schools, and the impulse which has been given toward a universal popular education in America, are the result, in great measure, of the enthusiasm, perseverance, and determined resolution of a single individual, Horace Mann; and this fact is, without question, one of the most beautiful and the most significant phenomena of this national cultivation, especially as it embraces woman as well as man, and places her side by side with him as the teachers of the rising generation.*

I have traced this from the East to the West, from those magnificent academies where five hundred students, boys or girls, study and take degrees preparatory to public life, as teachers and teacheresses, to the log-huts of the Western wilderness, where school-books lie open before the ragged children, which convey the mind over the whole world, and where the noblest pearls of American and English literature are to be found. I have talked with Horace Mann—the man of immeasurable hope, and I have thence derived great hope for the intellectual and moral perfecting of the human race, and for its future in this portion of the world; for that which *is* in the Northeastern States, in the oldest homes of the Pilgrims, the same *will be* soon-

* Young girls learn, in the high schools, Latin, Greek, mathematics, algebra, the physical sciences, and, it is said, have the greatest facility in acquiring a knowledge of these subjects, which are considered with us so difficult, if not incomprehensible, to the female intellect.

er or later in the South and the West. A great and living intelligence in the popular mind mixes itself up more and more in the great question of popular education, and goes onward conquering like a subtle power of nature, a stream of spiritual life forcing a way for itself through all impediment. Would you hear how it speaks through its most powerful representative in the New World? Thus writes Horace Mann in his invitation to the National Convention of the friends of Education, in August, 1850:

"A few considerations will serve to show that there never has been a period in the history of man when universal education was so imperative a duty as at the present moment. I mean education in its most comprehensive and philosophic sense, as including the education of the body, the education of the mind, and the education of the heart.

"In regard to the first topic, it is well known that physical qualities are hereditary. Disease and weakness descend from parent to offspring by a law of nature, as names descend by a law of custom. God still ordains that the bodily iniquities of the fathers shall be visited upon the children unto the third and fourth generation. When we look backward and see how the numbers of our ancestors is doubled at each remove in the ascending scale, it affrights us to reflect how many confluent streams from vicious fountains may have been poured into the physical system of a single individual. Where, for many generations, this horrid entailment of maladies has not been broken by a single obedient and virtuous life, who can conceive of the animal debasements and depravities that may centre in a single person? At every descent, the worst may become worse; and the possible series of deterioration is infinite. Before the human race, or any part of it, becomes more diseased, or physically more vile, is it not time to arrest and restore? This can be done through education or through miracles, and it would require more than three hundred and sixty-five miracles every year to preserve health and strength under our present vicious social habits. Those who do not expect the intervention of miracles are false to their families, to the community, and to God, if they do not urge forward the work of physical education as the only means of rescuing the race from an infinity of sicknesses, weaknesses, and pains. Public schools are the only instrumentality for inculcating upon the community at large a knowledge of the great laws of health and life.

"There never was such a necessity of imparting power to the human intellect, and of replenishing it with knowledge, as at the present time; and in no country is this necessity so imperative as in our own. The common affairs of life require a hundred times more knowledge now than they did a century ago. New forms, and kinds of business too, are daily emerging into practice, which must be conducted with intelligence and skill, or they will ruin their conductors. How much more knowledge and art are requisite to make a cotton or woolen factory, with all its nice and numerous appendages, than to manage a spinning-wheel or a distaff; to manage a locomotive on a railroad, than to drive a team on a highway; to manage a telegraph, than to send a courier, &c. The profoundest sciences are working their way into the every-day business of life, and carrying power, and beauty, and multiplication of products wherever they go, and whosoever can not rise upon the benefits they confer will be left in poverty, misery, and contempt.

"Not only in all the departments of business are there every where more life, energy, and compass, but the masses of the people are investing themselves, or are becoming invested, with new social and political prerogatives. The freeman, who may go where he pleases, and select whatever occupation he pleases, needs vastly more judgment and intelligence than the subject of a despotism who is born in some niche of labor, and must stay where he is born. The citizen, who manages not only his own personal affairs, but those of his municipality; who governs himself in all his political relations through representatives chosen by himself; whose vote may determine not only who shall be the rulers, but what measures of national or international policy shall be established or annulled, on whose will peace or war, national honor or national infamy may depend—such a citizen, in capacity, in knowledge, and in wisdom, should be as a god in comparison with a Russian serf or a Hindoo pariah. At this time, I say, there is vastly more for the mind of man to do and to understand than there ever was before, and therefore that mind must be proportionably strengthened and illumined.

"There never was a time when the moral nature of man needed culture and purification more than it needs them at the present hour. What we call civilization and progress have increased temptations a thousand-fold—in this country ten thousand-fold. The race for wealth, luxury, ambition, and pride is open to all. With our multiplied privileges have come not only multiplied obligations, which we may contemn, but multiplied dangers into which we may fall. Where oppression and despotism reign, all the nobler faculties of man are dwarfed, stunted, and shorn of their power. But oppression and despotism dwarfs and stunts, and despoils of their power, all the evil passions of men, not less than their nobler impulses. In this country, all that is base and depraved in the human heart has such full liberty and wide compass, and hot stimulus of action, as has never been known before. Wickedness not less than virtue—diabolism not less than utilitarianism, has its steam-engines, and its power-presses, and its lightning telegraphs. Those external restraints of blind reverence for authority, and superstitious dread of religious guides, and fiery penal codes, which once repressed the passions of man, and paralyzed all energy, are now lifted off. If internal and moral restraints be not substituted for the external and arbitrary ones that are removed, the people, instead of being conquerors and sovereigns over their passions, will be their victims and their slaves. Even the clearest revelations from heaven, and the sanctifying influences from God, unless vouchsafed to us so daily and momently as to supersede all volition and conscience of ours, would not preclude a virtuous training as an indispensable prerequisite to a happy and honorable life. He takes but a limited view of the influences and the efficacy of Christian ethics who does not strive to incorporate and mould them into the habits and sentiments of youth; who, as fast as the juvenile mind opens to the perception of wonder, and beauty, and of truth, has not exhaustless store of moral wonders, and beauties, and truths, ready for the transfusion into it."

Thus speaks the President of the National Convention of the Friends of Education, the man of Education *par excellence* in North America. He is a Massachusetts man, and is, at the present time, representative of the Pilgrim State in Congress.

You see the ground that he takes. The enlightenment of the moral and intellectual being by means of a school education, common to all, such is the foundation upon which the New World would erect its dominion, such the means by which the new human being is to be brought forth. Thus far has the popular consciousness advanced in the New World—*no further*, at least, with a perfect consciousness.

The consciousness has arisen most clearly and with most strength in the States of New England, the oldest home of the Pilgrims. Unwearied and fearless endeavors for the development of the life of the state, and the elevation of the more indigent classes of society, the endeavor to produce a perfectly harmonious human community, characterize the life of these states. The idea of a Christian state, a Christian community, evidently forms the basis of all this. The doctrines of Christ; the honor of labor; the right of all, and the well-being of all; every thing for all! are the battle-cries which one hears. The harps of the poets have called forth the moral ideal of man and of society!

From these states I proceeded in the month of March, while frost and snow covered the ground, to the Southern States of North America, and spent about three months in the Palmetto States, South Carolina and Georgia. There the sun was warm. And though I found slavery there, and saw its dark shadow on the sun-bright earth, saw its fetters contract the moral and political development of these states, I still enjoyed my life as I had not done in those intellectual, upward-striving, restlessly-laboring Northern States. I had more repose, and I was better in health. The soft beauty of the air and the climate at this season, the luxuriance of the vegetation, the beautiful new flowers, the odors, the fruits, the magnificence of the primeval forest along the banks of the Red River; the glow of the fire-flies in the dusk, warm nights; my rambles beneath the Gothic arcades of the live-oaks, hung with their long, swaying masses of moss, a spectacle at once novel and enchanting to a European eye; a certain romantic picturesqueness of life, caused by the contact of the black and the white races on this beautiful, fragrant soil; the peculiar life and temperament of the negroes, their songs, and religious festivals—will you forgive me for being enchanted with these, and for allowing myself to forget, or to see less strongly the darkness of slavery, than these images of light which the beauty of the South called forth in natural objects and individual man. No poet here has sung the moral ideal of society, but the hundred-tongued bird (*Turdus polyglottos*), the nightingale of North America, sings in those fragrant forests, and earth, with its human beings and its flowers, seems bathed in light. Yet, that I was not blinded to the night-side, and to the great lie in the life of the South, is proved by my letters home.

The most beautiful moral phenomenon which I saw, however, was the inbreaking light of Christianity among the children of Africa, the endeavors which true Christians, especially in Georgia, are making for the religious instruction of the slaves, and their emancipation and colonization in Liberia, on the African coast. A vessel goes annually from Savannah to Liberia, laden with emancipated slaves, together with the means for their establishment in that, the original mother country. But this phenomenon is no more than a little point of light in the gloomy picture of slavery in these states. It is a work of private individuals. The laws of the states are deficient in light and justice as regards the slave, and are unworthy of a free country and people!

In the month of May I hastened from the glowing South and traveled northward to Pennsylvania, and afterward to Delaware.

Amid the greatest heats of summer, I found myself in the hot cities of Philadelphia and Washington. I interested myself in Philadelphia by becoming acquainted with the Quakers, and the life of the inward light in good and benevolent institutions. I read the Declaration of Independence, the great charter of liberty of the American people, and proceeded onward to Washington, to watch the combat in Congress on the subject of the great contested question between the free and the slave states, between the North and the South, about the admission of California and New Mexico as free states into the Union. It was carried on with great violence, and the stability of the Union was threatened every day. You know already, through the newspapers, the compromise which was made, and which pacified the strife for a time; for the strife and the danger still exists, secretly or openly, so long as slavery and slaves are to be found within the American Union; and the stronger grows the human and the political consciousness of this country, the more keen will become the struggle to concentrate itself on this point, the fiercer will become the warfare.

I saw great statesmen and heard great speeches in Washington, and I believe that no country on earth can at this time present an assembly of greater talent or of more remarkable men than may be met with in the Senate of the United States. Political injustice and political bitterness I found here, as every where on the political battle-field.

That which struck me most in the Congress of the United States was the mode of representation. You know something of it from books and newspapers; each state, small or large, in the Union sends two senators to Congress. These constitute the Senate, or Upper House. The representatives, who constitute the second chamber, or Lower House, are sent by each separate state, according to the number of its population; the larger the population, the more representatives to Congress. Each individual state of the Union governs itself in the same manner by two chambers, a Senate and House of Representatives, the numbers of which are elected in the state by the citizens of the state; and each state has its own Capitol.

This mode of representation brings forth much nationality, and much that is picturesque in the living, peculiar life of each state. The Granite State and the Palmetto State, "Old Virginny" and new Wisconsin, Minnesota and Louisiana, each so separate and so peculiar in situation, scenery, climate, products, population, stand forth in Congress as individuals, and take part in the treatment of public questions, which are interesting to the whole human race, according to characteristics which are peculiar to themselves and common to all.

I could not help thinking, during all this, of the representation of Sweden, and its much-talked of construction. It occurred to me that there could not be any form more suitable or more calculated to awaken national life and consciousness than one resembling this of the United States. I saw Norrland and Scania, Dalecarlia and Bleking, East Göthland and West Göthland, and all our provinces, peculiar in people, scenery, products, stand forth in the Diet of Sweden, and by means of its senators cast new light upon the condition of the country, its wants, and its hitherto hidden or unavailing sources of prosperity. I saw the north, the south, and the central parts of Sweden, its east and its west, illumined by rays of light which till then had not penetrated them, and the popular consciousness and popular life under the guidance of representatives, worthy, through their knowledge and their personal character, to represent that individual province in its peculiarities and its life, as a portion of a great whole, of a country, a people with an inheritance as great as the former history of Sweden, a future which may emulate in human greatness that of the greatest people on the earth.

In the oldest times of Sweden, when the judges (Lagmüennen) of each province appeared at the Allshärjarthing, and there, as the wisest and best of the land, conveyed the speech of the common people to the King of Sweden (Svealand), the most ancient representation of our country was in idea similar to that now existing in North America.

Such a representation of country and of people seems to me in a high degree conformable to nature and nationality. And what a field is hereby opened to talent and to the orator!

President Taylor died during my stay at Washington, and I was present at the installation of his legal successor, President Fillmore, into his office—the highest in the United States. Nothing could be simpler, or more destitute of pomp and show, or more unlike our royal coronations. But—I have nothing to say against these. They present beautiful and picturesque spectacles; and without spectacle people can not very well live, not even in this country, as is seen by the eagerness with which they every where rush to see any thing new. What a beautiful spectacle did we not behold in Sweden on the coronation of King Carl Johan and King Oscar! I remember, in particular at the latter, those young princes, the three sons of Oscar, in their princely attire, when they came forward to take the oath to their royal father—no one could have seen more beautiful forms, hardly a more lovely sight!

After having bathed in the foaming sea on the eastern coast, I betook myself into the West. I had seen the North and the South of the Union, now I would see the Great West. I longed for it greatly. I had heard much in the Eastern States, and in the North and in the South also, of that *Great West*, of its wonderful growth and progress. In what did these consist? I had a great desire to know.

On my journey westward I made acquaintance with the giants of nature, Trenton and Niagara, sailed across the great lakes, Ontario, Erie, Michigan, to visit the Swedish and Norwegian settlements on the Mississippi, partook of Swedish hospitality, and saw Swedish roses bloom freshly in the new soil, and beheld a new Scandinavia arising in the wilderness of the West. After that I advanced up the Mississippi, to the region where lie the sources of the Great River, saw glorious mountainous scenery, ruin-like crags, ascending above oak-crowded hills, ruins of the primeval ages where the first-born Titans of nature, the Megatherium, the Mastodon, the Ichthyosaurian, wandered alone over the earth, and man as yet did not exist. And he is still an unfrequent guest in these immense wildernesses, where it is yet silent and desolate. It is true that here and there a little log-hut is erected at the foot of the hills on the banks of the Mississippi, and that beside it is seen a little field of Indian corn; that is the first trace of civilization in these regions. But it is like the print of the one human foot on Robinson Crusoe's uninhabited island. Close beside it are the primeval forests of the wilderness, where only the wild beasts and Indians, in perpetual warfare with each other, have their dwelling. Close beside it are those immense prairies, the flowery deserts of the Mississippi Valley, where the grass waves like heavy billows, far, far away toward the distant horizon, untouched by human hands, because here there are no human hands to mow, not one thousandth part. And that which made a deeper impression upon me than Niagara, than any thing which I have seen in this hemisphere or in Europe, are these immeasurable prairie views which belong to the valley of the Mississippi, and which increase in extent the nearer one approaches the Great River. It is glorious to behold these ocean-like views, with their waves of sunflowers, and their lofty, heaving billows of grass beneath the heaven of America, clear and resplendent with sunshine, or through bright expanses of which float masses of cloud. The soul expands itself, and, as it were, opens itself to the gentle, free wind which soughs over the plain, and sounding melodiously as it passes by the wires of the electric telegraph which are stretched across it. Each day of my journey westward was a festival, as I sped along on wings of steam over the plain, ever and ever toward the golden setting sun, as if speeding into his realms of light!

The valley of the Mississippi, from Minnesota in the north to Louisiana in the south, between the Alleghany Mountains on the east and the Rocky Mountains on the west, is throughout an immense "rolling prairie," with ridgy heights and hills of the most fertile soil, richly watered by rivers and lakes. This meadow-land, occupying a high level in the north, and producing northern pines and birches, gradually sinks lower and lower as it approaches the south, until in Louisiana it becomes a swampy morass, where the alligator paddles in the mud, but where also the sugar-cane and the palmetto spring up in the warm air, and orange-groves shed their perfume around. It embraces much variety in soil, climate, and production. But I will hear what a resident in this great valley, and one well acquainted with it, says of

"That great central valley of the continent of North America—a valley extending through twenty-one degrees of latitude and fifteen degrees of longitude—a valley just beginning to smile under the hand of cultivation, and which already invites to its large bosom those masses of people who are pouring out from the overstocked communities of the Old World, and which promises to requite the hand of cultivation by a provision for yet uncounted millions of the human race.

"Nature has gifted the soil in a remarkable degree with vegetable and mineral wealth, has bestowed upon it an exterior suited to every taste, and to the requirements of all, and has intersected it with rivers which are available to every species of industry, and for unlimited commercial transactions, embracing every production of the temperate zone within its northern and southern boundaries.

"This vast meadow, this rich and fertile valley, lying between the sources of the Mississippi on the north and the Gulf of Mexico in the south, the Rocky Mountains on the west, and the Alleghany chain on the east, although but a short time since a wilderness, embraces already eleven entire states, portions of two others, as well as two territories; it is full of the active spirit of labor, and is capable of sustaining half the population of the United States. Embracing within its limits 1,200,000 square miles, or 768,000,000 of acres, its importance and its power can as little be estimated as that of the Union itself. Its influence must become coextensive with that of the habitable globe, the garden and corn-magazine of which it will become; it must extend its dominion beyond that of the United States, and become the kernel of its empire, the source of its vital power, the diadem of its pride, the basis of the pyramid of its greatness. The Creator of the world has nowhere on the face of the earth diffused more affluent elements of human prosperity, nor more visibly made a beautiful and suitable provision for the requirements of humanity. Visit it not with the curse of a feeble government; do not throw impediments in the way of its improvement; keep not back the tide of emigration which is pouring into its bosom; let its broad arms receive the over-population which oppresses the fields of Europe, and the All-good Giver of every good gift will smile from his heaven upon a happy family of more than 275,000,000 of human beings."

If you should be tempted to smile at this specimen of the great views of the Great West as regards this great Mississippi Valley and its great future, still you will not fail to recognize in all a great mind—a great heart; and for the rest, that here the subject is not exactly a—small thing.

Mr. Allen, the senator of Missouri, from whose writings on the Trade and Navigation of the Mississippi Valley in the year 1850 I have extracted the above, proceeds to give the statistics of the various Mississippi States, and the trade and increase of their cities, a perfectly practical and statistical treatise, but which produces a certain poetical impression, not only by the wealth of the products which he enumerates, but also by the almost fairy-tale-like increase of cultivation and population of cities, and traffic on the rivers, by the wealth of the whole of this region.

The senator sent to Congress by Missouri, Colonel Benton, as well as Mr. Allen, who is eminently a practical man, becomes a poet when he glances at this subject, and exclaims, "The river navigation in the Great West is the most wonderful in the world, and possesses, by means of steam, all the properties of ocean navigation—rapidity, immense distance, low prices, and large freightage, all is there. The steam-boat is the ship of the river, and finds on the Mississippi and its tributaries the most perfect theatre for its application and its powers. Wonderful river! United to vast seas at its source and at its mouth—extending its arms toward the Atlantic and the Pacific Oceans—flowing through a stretch of valley which extends from the Mexican Gulf to Hudson's Bay, deriving its earliest waters, not from sterile mountains, but from a plateau of lakes in the centre of the continent, and in connection with the sources of the St. Lawrence, and those rivers which take their course northward to Hudson's Bay, flowing the greater part of its way through the richest meadow-land, conveying on its bosom the productions of every climate, even ice from the frigid zone, which it transports to the great market of the sunny South. Hither are brought the product of the whole world. Such is the Mississippi! And who can calculate the total of its advantages, and the greatness of its future commercial engagements!" But enough of Mississippi eloquence.

And now I must tell you of the growth and progress of the Great West, as they have appeared to me. This growth is principally *material* as yet, but the spiritual growth follows in its footsteps. Wherever Americans establish themselves, the first buildings that they erect, after their dwelling-houses and places of business, are schools and churches; then follow hotels and asylums. The West repeats the cities, the institutions, and the cultivation of the East, and their course is rapid and safe. First you see in the wilderness some log-houses, then neat frame and small stone houses, then elegant villas and cottages; and before many years are over, there stands, as if by magic, a town with its Capitol or State House, its handsome churches, splendid hotels, academies, and institutions of all kinds; and lectures are delivered, large newspapers printed, government-men are elected, public meetings are convened, and resolutions passed on the subject of popular education or intercourse with the whole world; their rail-roads are made, canals dug, ships built, rivers are traversed, forests are penetrated, mountains are leveled, and, amid all this, husbands build beautiful homes for their wives, plant trees and flowers around them, and woman rules as a monarch in the sacred world of home —thus does the country increase, thus is society arranged, and thus is a state prepared to take its place as an independent member of the great family-group of states. And although two thirds of the population of the Mississippi Valley consists of Scandinavians, Germans, Irish, and French, yet there too is the legislative and the formative spirit of the Anglo-Norman.

In certain respects, the character of the Western States is different from that of the Eastern. It has more breadth and cosmopolitanism; its people are a people of many nations, and it is asserted that this character betrays itself in a more liberal form of state government, as well as more unprejudiced views, and an easier mode of social life. The various religious sects become more and more amalgamated; the clergy prophesy the advent of a Millennian Church, which shall gather all sects into its embrace; and maintain the necessity of secular education, of science, and of polite literature, for the full development of the religious life.

The cities of the West are all of them pre-eminently cosmopolitan cities. The Germans have their quarters there—sometimes half the city, their newspapers, and their clubs; the Irish have theirs; and the French theirs. The Mississippi River is the great cosmopolitan which unites all people, which gives a definite purpose to their activity, and determines their abode, and which enables the life of every one, the inhabitants themselves and their products, to circulate from the one end to the other of this great central valley.

But here ends my admiration and my oration about greatness and growth, for the cities of the West appear to me in no respect larger or better than those of the East. St. Louis is only another New York placed on the western bank of the Mississippi; and San Francisco, on the shores of the Pacific Ocean, is merely a third repetition of the first city. The western state which glances forth beautifully in Wisconsin, sinks again in Missouri and Arkansas. The western portion of the American continent is no better than the eastern. Will it ever become so?

Will there be any thing different in development, in character—will it become higher and nobler, and more, will it approach somewhat nearer to perfection? That kingdom of the Millennium where the lion shall lie down with the lamb; where every man shall sit in the shadow of his own vine and fig-tree; where all people shall meet together in peace, and heaven shall smile over a happy family of 275,000,000 of human beings? is that kingdom of peace, and love, and prosperity to have its place here?

Ah! it has been very painful to me to give up that beautiful dream which gladdened me as I traveled westward, and saw the golden sun advance before me onward into that promised land of the West, into whose realms I seemed to be journeying. I no longer have any faith in it. It is gone!

The western land of the New World will not produce any thing essentially different from the eastern. The New Paradise is nowhere to be met with on earth. It will probably never be obtained in this world, and upon this earth!

There will, however, be no deficiency of enlightenment among the people of North America. But it will be merely obtained through the diffusion of general popular education, that great diffusion among all classes of cheap newspapers, in which all subjects are discussed, and which bring every vital question of life fully investigated, and all human thoughts, to the mind of every man. Life itself in this country, with its States' institutions, constitutes a great public educational establishment, demanding light and knowledge, and in the combat between light and darkness, between God and Mammon, which is going forward here, as well as in the great world's battle, the combat becomes more profound and more inward than it ever has been before on the earth; it concentrates itself more than ever upon the innermost ground of the will and the conscience, for no one can here henceforth excuse himself by saying

"*I did not know!*"

Hence it becomes to me more and more evident that that which we have to expect from this world's cultivation is not a Utopia, but—a judgment-day; that is to say, a more determined separation between the children of light and the children of darkness, between good and evil—a more rapid approach toward the last crisis.

The new man of the New World stands amid upon the line of separation between the powers of this world, but upon a higher platform, and with increased knowledge, and with a clearer consciousness he is again called upon to choose between them.

The whirl of life rolls with accelerated speed; all the powers of nature and of matter are made subservient to a mighty will. The roads to hell, as well as those to heaven, are now traveled with the speed of the rail-road and steam. The business of earthly life is hastening on to its close, and I seem to hear those prophetic words on the last page of the Book of Life,

"The time is at hand.

"He who is unjust, let him be unjust still; and he that is filthy, let him be filthy still; and he that is righteous, let him be righteous still; and he that is holy, let him be holy still.

"And behold, I come quickly; and my reward is with me, to give every man according as his work shall be."

What can give preponderance to the scale of the good, and double the number of the righteous and the holy?

In the salutation of that New Year which the hosts of heaven conveyed to earth, upon that great New Year's day from which the earth dates her centuries—it was sung,

"Good-will to man!"

What is it that can give force to this good-will to man?

The statesman of America has answered,

"The Constitution of the State; free political institutions."

But the Constitution of the United States has received slavery as a "domestic institution," and defends it on the ground of the right of these free states.

The learned men and the teachers of America have replied,

"Schools, and the education of the people in these schools."

But the popular education of schools speaks merely to the understanding, and can not do otherwise.

Both constitution and schools are alike perfect in their insufficiency.

They can not give new life to this good-will. They can not bring the kingdom of God into the innermost life of every human being.

The power to do this lies in an institution anterior on earth, and in human life, to constitutions or to schools.

Behold there on the banks of the river, amid that open field, or on that green hill, a small human habitation. It is neither large nor splendid, but its style of architecture is ornamental; it speaks of taste and convenience; a veranda or piazza formed of lovely trellis-work, up which clamber vines and the fragrant clematis, roses and honeysuckle, surround the house; beautiful trees, the natives of all zones, are planted around; you see the maple, the elm, and the linden-tree, the oak and the chestnut, the walnut and the robinia, the alanthus and the sycamore, the cedar and the magnolia, the cypress and the myrtle, and a great number of beautiful, odoriferous flowers: these are so grouped around the house as to give it a sheltered appearance, without impeding the views, which are always kept open to allow the inhabitants to behold a beautiful or extensive landscape.

You see *the home* of North America—the home, with its characteristic features, as it is found in all the states, as well on the heights of Massachusetts and Minnesota, as in the fragrant forest-meadows of South Carolina, and on the prairie-land of the Far West. And that home frequently deserved the appellation which the home obtained in our old North, the appellation of a *sacred room.* The fire of the domestic hearth burns in no country brighter, or is tended by purer hands than in the home of the United States. It is a pleasure to me to be able to say this with knowledge and conviction. Nor have I in any country seen the home so generally beautiful in its exterior, so guarded as the apple of the human eye. Neither have I ever seen people who know better how to follow the hint which the Creator gave, when he, having created Adam, placed him, not in a city, but in a garden. Even the American cities seem to have uneasy consciences when they begin to cluster themselves into closely-built masses of houses, and one might say that the houses there hastened to get apart from each other, and though they stand in rows forming streets and markets, they soon make open spaces, and surround themselves with a green-sward, and trees, and flowers. And the larger this verdant, shady, flowery plot, the more cheerful seems the American home. This is what it enjoys, but it likes to enjoy it in company, and wishes others to be as well off as itself. Order, comfort, embellishment, and an actual luxury of trees and flowers, distinguish the home of the New World. And this home is the earliest world of the child, of the new man.

It is to the home, it is to the heart of the home, to the guardian of the sacred fire upon its hearth, that I look for the entrance of the new man upon the theatre of the world, for the obtaining of the victory in the combat which is going on between the two powers of the world. The important thing is to obtain many and brave champions for the good cause; to win the heart, and to give the will a right and strong bias toward the good, that is the chief thing.

I have set my hope upon the weak, upon them who in their weakness are strong. I am certain that it depends upon them. And if they hesitate, or if they are not equal to the greatness of their vocation, then all is lost; for never was their influence of so much importance as in this land of free-will. See what Horace Mann says of the power of this influence on the unlimited development of the United States.

Can the home, can the American mother give the life, the power which is required?

I must answer the question with *No, they can not do so* in their present state of cultivation. And whatever value we may give to exceptional cases, still it is certain that the Home in the New World, as well as in the Old, has not yet come up to its requirements, and that woman still stands as hitherto almost isolated in the home and in social life, with no place in the life of fellow-citizenship, without any higher consciousness of the connection which exists between this and the life of home, or of the connection between moral and religious (or the higher political) questions, and social questions and political life; without consciousness of her own vocation, of her responsibility as a citizen of the great Christian Commonwealth. How, then, can she educate citizens; how can she kindle in the heart of the child a sacred zeal for the well-being of the native land; how so enlighten it that it may bring into exercise the same conscientious integrity, the same lofty piety for the conduct, worldly business, and political questions, as within the sacred world of home?

The women of the community of Quakers are the only women who are more generally alive to the consciousness of citizenship; but they are merely a small number.

How the great mass may ascend, and by that means enlighten the whole rising generation; how the home may become the greatest and the most beautiful school of society—life's high-school; of all this I have my own thoughts, but I shall not now give them utterance.

It is a joy to me to hear and to see that a presentiment of this is beginning to find its way into the universal mind of this country, both among men and women; and I expect that this higher development will be accomplished on American soil; and I will now conclude this subject with the words of an American author: "The darkness of the mothers casts its shadow over their children; and cloud and darkness must rest upon their descendants until their day begins to dawn over the hills."

And now let me speak of the American people. The traveler who finds in the United States a great uniformity and resemblance among the people there, has looked merely on the exterior. There is really a great, a too great uniformity in speech, manners, and dress (for a little costume, delicately expressive of individuality, belongs to a fully developed character); one travels from one end of the Union to the other, and hears the same questions about Jenny Lind; the same phraseology at the commencement of conversation; the same "last thoughts of Weber" on the piano. After this, however, an attentive observer soon remarks that there is no lack of character and individuality; and I have nowhere felt, as here, the distance between one human being and another, nor have seen any where so great a difference between man and man, wholly irrespective of caste, rank, uniform, outward circumstances. Here is the Transcendentalist, who treads the earth as though he were a god, who calls upon men to become gods, and from the beauty of his demeanor and his character, we are induced to think more highly of human nature; and here is the Clay-eater, who lives in the forest, without school or church, sometimes without a home, and who, impelled by a morbid appetite, eats clay until, demoniacally dragged downward by its oppressive power, he finds in it his grave; here is the Spiritualist, who lives on bread, and water, and fruit—who is nourished by the light, that he may preserve himself pure from the taint of any thing earthly—and who, not finding Christianity pure enough for his diluted moral atmosphere, adopts that noble socialism which exists merely to communicate benefits and blessings; and beside him is the worshiper of Mammon, who tramples every thing spiritual under his feet, and who acknowledges nothing holy, nothing which he can not and will not sacrifice to his idol—self. Every contrast of temperament, character, disposition, endeavor, which can be imagined to exist in human nature, may here be met with, and may here express itself with a more decided spiritual life.

I have frequently in the New World, and that in very various classes of society, heard it remarked of people that they belonged to "the best men" or "the best women;" and it has struck me how well people in general seem to understand the phrase, and how much they are agreed upon it. I have found also that these best men and women are commonly distinguished by intelligence, kindness, and active human-love; and I do not believe that so much is done in any country by private individuals for the public as in this, in particular in the free states. The feeling for the public weal, for the improvement of the country and the people at large, for the elevation of humanity, can scarcely be more living and active any where than it is here. The people of the United States have a warm heart, and that which gives this people their eternal prerogative of progress is their imitation of Christ —I say the *people of the United States*, and I maintain the assertion. Remove slavery from its Southern States (and it will be removed one of these days; already it is undermined by Christianity and by emigration from the North), and you will find there the same heart and the same spirit.

The right of the people of North America to be considered as one people, and as a peculiar people among the nations of the earth, is founded upon the character of its first emigrant colonies, they who were peculiarly the creators of the society of the New World, and who infused their spirit into it. They were in part heroes of the faith, as Puritans, Huguenots, and Hernhutters, in part warm-hearted souls, such as Fox, Penn, Oglethorpe, who had found their places in the Old World too circumscribed for them, and who passed over to the New World, there to establish their fraternal associations, and to create a more beautiful humanity. The first settlers of America belonged to the strongest and the best portions of the European population.

I will now tell you something about those best men and women of America with whom I have become acquainted during my pilgrimage through the land; about those men so simple, so gentle, but yet so strong without any pretension, so manly in their activity as citizens, husbands, fathers, friends; of those women, so kind, so motherly, so gentle in manner, so steadfast in principle, resting in the truth like flowers in the sunshine; of those homes, those happy, beautiful homes, in which I have been a happy guest for days, and weeks, and months; for my life in America has been, and is, a journey of familiar visits to homes which have opened themselves to me in every state throughout America, and where I have lived, not as a stranger, but as a sister with brothers and sisters, conversing openly with them on all subjects, as people may converse in heaven. I there met with more than I have words to tell, of true Christian life, of the love of truth, of kindness, of minds earnest for and receptive of every thing which is great and good in humanity; while my acquaintance with some beautiful, peculiar characters will serve as a guide to my soul forever. Nor have I any where met with more hospitality, or with a more abounding cordiality. And if I were to seek for one expression which would portray the peculiar character of the people of the New World, I could not find any other than that of *beautiful human beings.*

When I imagine to myself a Millennium in the valley of the Mississippi, a resting-point in the history of the earth, where Satan is bound, and love, beauty, and joy, and the fullness of love, becomes the portion of all, I then behold there men and women, such as my friends; homes such as their homes, and see these mighty rivers bearing from these flowery prairies, with their ocean-like views, and from these golden fields of maize, all the treasures of earth to all mankind, and mild, fresh winds blow over it, and the clear sun shines. Such were the glorious home of the Hesperides!

It is not at all difficult to predict that the valley of the Mississippi, in consequence of the variety of nations by which it is populated, and from the variety in its scenery and climate, will at a future time produce a popular life of a totally new kind, with infinite varieties of life and temperament, a wholly new aspect of human society on earth. But what appearance will the apex of the pyramid present, the basis of which is now being formed? One thing appears to me certain: the inhabitants of the Mississippi Valley must become citizens of the world—the universal mankind, *par excellence.*

Let me attempt to delineate some features of that common theatre of the great drama of which the performance has now commenced (a drama which embraces a thousand years in one act), and the dramatis personæ, the groups of which fill the stage; for they who in the life of the United States have seen merely uniformity or confusion, have not looked into it, or have seen it merely with a dull vision. Nothing strikes me so much in this world's and states' formation as its broad dramatic character.

First behold its theatre! You see two immense stretches of valley between three chains of mountains, running from the snowy North to the glowing South, the Alleghany, the Rocky Mountains, and Sierra Nevada, or the Snowy Mountains, which last chain is continued into Central America, and into the Cordilleras and Andes of South America; east and west of these the land descends toward the two great seas of the world.

The country lying between the mountains and toward the seas is every where remarkable for its fertility, and is intersected by navigable rivers and lakes. No country is so well watered as North America, or affords more available opportunity for the circulation of life; nor does any country afford such free access to the beauties, the climates, and productions of every zone.

I beheld advancing on this great stage various distinct groups of states, of various temperaments and conditions of life, united by community of customs, language, and states' government, as well as by outward and inward vital circulation. Here are the States of New England, with their Puritan descendants, legislating, educating, restless Vikings and heroes of peace. The natural scenery of these states reminds me of our Scandinavian north. Massachusetts has the romantic lakes and broken landscape of Sweden; New Hampshire, the rocky valley and White Mountains of Norway.

New York and Pennsylvania, the Empire and the Quaker States, with its milder climate, imitate each other in wealth of population and in beauties of nature. Rivers and valleys become wider; commercial life grows like a giant.

Virginia and the Carolinas, as well as Georgia and Florida, in the South, each form another group of states, peopled by the sons of the Cavaliers, with their planters and slaves, with a strong conservative life, and much peculiar beauty, but devoid of higher social aspiration. These Northern and Southern States lie between the Alleghany Mountains, which are contained within them, and the ocean on the east. On the other side of the mountains you find the valley of the Mississippi and the Mississippi States; to the north the young and vigorous Northwestern States, with free institutions, and an increasing population of Germans and Scandinavians, increasing still more in light and the life of freedom; to the south, the slave states, with two large cities, and in these a showy civilization, but for the rest much wilderness and much rudeness still, which all their cotton and all their sugar is not able to conceal. West of the Mississippi still is continued the distinction between the Northern and Southern States. The labor of the cultivator has here just commenced. You meet with the fires and the wigwams of the Indians still around the sources of the Mississippi in the North; and along the Red River in Arkansas and Louisiana, morasses and heathenism.

Westward of these Mississippi States is Texas, with the Rio Grande or Rio Bravo as its boundary on the west, and the Gulf of Mexico on the south, an immense territory, upon the fertile banks of whose rivers the flood of emigration is now beginning to settle. The upper portion of Texas elevates itself by degrees into a mountain range, and unites itself on the northeast to the latest conquest of the United States, New Mexico, which has beautiful terminal valleys on the east, but which extends itself westward into the Rocky Mountains, and becomes petrified in their arms.

Between these states and the Mississippi States lies the great hunting-ground of the Indians, that mystic Nebraska, a great portion of which, according to what I have heard, is a monotonous steppe-land, which extends northward as far as Canada. The wild Missouri whirls through it with a thousand angular windings; there are also great prairies and great rivers, herds of buffaloes, and tribes of warlike Indians. In one portion of this immense region, between Missouri and Texas, has sprung up a peaceful, flourishing Indian community, which ought at some future time to be admitted into the Great Union as an independent Christian Indian State. This would be a more beautiful conquest for the people of North America than their acquisition of New Mexico!

We have now reached the Rocky Mountains, an irregular, bold rock-formation, more remarkable for their fantastic shapes and masses than for their height. Westward of these extend the so-called Pacific States, Oregon, as yet merely an immense territory; and California, in the highest boundaries of which, or the Upper California, the Mormon State, Deseret or Utah, flourishes upon the fertile banks of the Great Salt Lake, Christian in faith and confession, hierarchical in their form of government, and in certain respects a mystery to their contemporaries.

These states, lying along the coast of the Pacific Ocean, and broken up by the Sierra Nevada Mountains, are possessed of every climate, and of every natural production which can be found from the region of snow to the heat of the tropics. Oregon, in particular, abounds in salmon and forests; California, as all the world knows, in gold.

And now we are on the shores of the Pacific Ocean, and here let us rest a while, for I confess to being weary with our long ramble. The North Americans will not rest till they have possessed themselves of the Southern portion of their hemisphere; already have they reached Panama with their rail-roads, canals, warehouses, homes, churches, and schools. And they say quite calmly, when speaking of the country between Panama and the Rio Grande, that is to say, the whole of Central Mexico, "When this is ours, then," &c.

I shall not tell you any thing about the Constitution of these states, nor of their institutions as individual, independent states, nor of their relation to one Federal government. You have long known, much better than I can describe it, that wonderful states' government, which affords such a boundless field and so strong an impulse to free competition and development, not merely for individuals, but for society and states. This constitutional form of government seems to me, more than any thing else, to prove that the destiny of a people is preordained by the hand of Providence before they themselves comprehend it. They must accomplish his plans, and the question as regards them is merely the doing it well or ill.

It is evident that the founders of the American republic, Washington and his men, did not take a philosophical review of the work which they had accomplished in it; that they had no presentiment of the future of which they had laid the foundation; they followed the beckoning hand of necessity; they did that which they must do; but they did not know what it was which they had done; and for a long time the states grew as the lilies of the field in God's sunshine, without knowing how or for what purpose!

It was not until long afterward that a portion of them awoke to a consciousness of the sublime mission which they are called upon to perform—the emancipation of humanity socially and politically.

The violent movement and rotation in public life, the perpetual appointment of officers to every department of government, and their deposition again in a short time, at most in four years, has made all Europe shake its head; and I suppose that all Asia would, if it could, shrug its shoulders in such a way as to cause the wall of China to quake. And it is not without reason that many wise men in this country have shook their heads thoughtfully at some application of the rotation principle which has occurred here and there: thus, for example, I heard serious complaints made in the young Mississippi States of the facility with which a right to vote was obtained by the emigrants who came there, even though they may be from the rudest and most ignorant population of Europe. A year's residence in a state gives a right to vote at the election of the officers of the state, which occurs annually; hence the election of low and truthless agitators, men every way unfit for their office; and the difficulty for the best men to get into the government, because the best men scorn to avail themselves of the means which men of low principles will condescend to in order to become the popular candidate, or to maintain themselves in a post which they have once obtained.

It is, however, difficult for me to regard this otherwise than as a transition-point in the great popular education which is now going on; and Wisconsin, in particular, seems to have dearly and strongly comprehended the right mode of meeting the danger, and by means of large and excellent educational institutions, both for boys and girls, to be preparing a bright future for the state.

I was traveling in the Northwestern Mississippi States just at the time when the annual election of state officers was going on. These elections, and the scenes to which they gave rise, struck me as a sort of political game or race; and the spirit which impels these gamblers and wrestlers on this scene of action is often little better than that of the ordinary gambling houses. The gambling and rival parties, Whigs and Democrats, are very little ashamed of puffing their candidate, or depreciating that of the opposite party. Newspapers are full of abuse and lies; outcries of treachery and of danger to the fatherland; flags are displayed, and great placards are posted in the streets with words of warning or exhortation, "Beware of the Whigs!" "The Democrats are Incendiaries!" "Vote for the Whigs, the true friends of our country!" "Vote for the Democrats, the preservers of popular rights!" and so on. The nearer the day of election approaches, the stronger becomes the agitation, the more violent the cry, the personal abuse, and the threats. One might imagine that the torch of discord was about to be lighted in every city, that the Union was at the point of being torn to shreds, and that every citizen was in danger of being attacked by his neighbor. During all this I could not but think of two men whom I had seen on the banks of the Hudson, each enlisting passengers for his steam-boat, and abusing that of his rival, hurling angry words and threatening glances at each other, while their lips often seemed to curl into a smile when they had said any thing magnificently bad of the other. I remember my asking Mr. Downing, as I witnessed this scene, what was the meaning of it? and he replied with a smile, "It means nothing. Here is an opposition between two steamers, and these men act this part every day."

Much of the great political agitation here, during the time of the elections, has much the same meaning; the candidates and their soldiers fix bayonets in their glances and their words; the ballot-box is put in motion; every thing becomes silent; the votes are thrown in amid the utmost order; a pause ensues; the ballot-box is emptied, the votes are read aloud and counted; the election is declared. The men of office are elected for one year or for two; the governor of some states is elected for four years, as is the case with the President of the United States; in others merely for two, in others again for one, and all is at an end; nobody makes any objection, but all go quietly to their own homes, ready to obey the new magistracy, and to console themselves, as Jacob Faithful did, with "better luck another time!" Rockets ascend in the quiet evening in honor of the successful candidate, and the whole city goes to bed and sleeps soundly.

It has occurred to me that this electioneering agitation, in which people exercise their minds and their oratorical powers—or, at all events, their ability to talk and to write, are like a safety-valve in the steam-boat, by which means any excess of steam may escape to fill the air with vapor; there is not a doubt, in the mean time, but that the steam-power within the state's machine might be applied to a better purpose; and it is difficult for me to believe that the people of the United States will not henceforth endeavor to obtain a little more stability in their mode of government, will not give their rulers a longer period, in which each can attend to his own business more thoroughly, and thus afford an ampler sphere for real talent and less for demagogues.

But even as it is, it will be seen that no talent or character of eminence runs any risk in the United States of not finding an opportunity for the exercise of all its powers. The best proof of this is, indeed, the number of distinguished statesmen, judges, or clergymen who year after year continue to adorn the Senate of the country, the judges' seat, and the pulpit, and of whom the people are as proud as monarchical realms of their kings and heroes. It is generally mediocre, or talent of an imperfect kind, which rushes into this violent rotation, and which goes up and down until it has acquired sufficient strength and completeness to remain stable at some one point.

There is one principle of movement in the United States which seems to me like a creative, or, at all events, a power of organization: this is the movement of association. The association, founded already in the Federal government of the states—an association of states, governed by a general principle or Constitution—exists as a fundamental feature of popular life. This people associate as easily as they breathe.

Whenever any subject or question of interest arises in society which demands public sympathy or co-operation, a "Convention" is immediately called to take it into consideration, and immediately, from all ends of the city or the state, or from every state in the Union, all who feel an interest in the subject or question fly upon the wings of steam to the appointed place of meeting and the appointed hour. The hotels and boarding-houses of the city are rapidly filled; they come together in the great hall of assembly, they shake hands, they become acquainted with one another, they make speeches, they vote, they carry their resolutions. And forth upon the wings of a thousand daily papers flies that which the meeting or the Convention has resolved. These resolutions may sometimes also be merely the expression of opinion—as, for example, they hold "Indignation meetings" on occasions when they wish to express their strong disapprobation either of public men or of public transactions. It is always admirable with what readiness, with what *savoir faire* this people advances onward in self-government, and how determinedly and rapidly it proceeds from "*proposed*" to "*resolved.*"*

In the populous free states, the meetings of the members of different trades and professions, as well as of agriculture, belong to the ordinary occurrences of the day. Thus one now hears of Industrial Congresses in New York State, where the trades-brethren of certain kindred

* A splendid proof of the *savoir faire* in self-government is given at this moment in the states' organization of California. During a couple of years have the wildest adventurers from all nations of the earth rushed thither in the delirium of the gold-fever. But the best of the people have banded together, organized, and maintained the observance of law and civil order, and California, rapidly advanced to a population of two hundred thousand souls, now takes its place as a fully competent state in the great circle of the free states of the Union. Even the Chinese, who hastened to California by thousands, settle themselves down and live in peaceful communion under the powerful hand of the Anglo-American.

occupations meet every month; and "agricultural fairs" are already held in the young states of Michigan and Illinois, where the agriculturists of the state exhibit the rich products of the country. Cincinnati as well as New York, and the great trading towns which lie between them, Pittsburg, Harrisburg, and many others, have their mechanical and mercantile associations, their meeting-houses, libraries, assembly-rooms, and guilds on a large scale. And these kindred associations are all in connection with each other. As, for instance, an artisan who can not get work in the Eastern States is passed on by means of these associations to their members in the Western States, where there is abundance of work for all hands.

Life in this country need never stand still or stagnate. The dangers lie in another direction. But this free association is evidently an organizing and conservative principle of life, called forth to give law and centralization to the floating atoms, to the disintegrated elements.

Among the various dramatic assemblies and scenes in which human nature and popular life exhibit themselves on the soil of the New World, I may mention those small communities of social wits who aim at producing a regenerated world (but who are all in a dwindling condition excepting the Shaker community, who have no children), those dancing Shakers, those silent Quaker meetings, those many-tongued anti-slavery meetings, those religious festivals, camp-meetings at night in the woods, and scenes of baptism by the rivers, beautiful and affecting, especially where they have reference to the children of Africa. At the Conventions for the Rights of Women, in which women as well as men stand forth and speak for the civil rights of woman, I have not as yet been present, but I intend to embrace the first opportunity of being so. These first originated in Ohio, but are just now being held in the States of New England—abused and calumniated by many, attended and supported by many also. These furnish and afford a striking scene in the great drama which is now being performed; for all that lives fettered in Europe is brought forward in America, acquires form, builds a church, combines in union, takes a name, speaks out, and obtains a hearing, a time of trial, an examination, and—judgment is passed, that is to say, time and opportunity to rise or to fall, according to its measure and its power.

Scenes also of the life of the Indians and the negroes in this country belong to the dramatic and picturesque life of America. The wild dances of the former on the prairies of the West, the gentle songs of the latter in the fragrant forests, belong to the theatre of the New World.

The government of America has not a little to reproach herself with as regards her treatment of the Indians. Latterly, however, this treatment has become more just and mild. The land is purchased from the Indians; they are subjected by gentle means and by money; prohibitions are made against the introduction of intoxicating liquors among them, and the missionary is encouraged in his labor of introducing Christianity and civilization. But this does not do much. The red men, who consider themselves the most successful creation of the Great Spirit, retire backward into the desert and die. Merely a small number of them have passed over to the faith, the manners, and the mode of government of the whites.

The progress of Christianity is much more considerable among the negro race. The doctrine of the Savior comes to the negro slaves as their most inward need, and as the accomplishment of the wishes of their souls. They themselves enunciate it with the purest joy. Their ardent, sensitive being obtains from this its most beautiful transfiguration. The ability of these people for prayer is something peculiar, and quite unusual. Their prayers burst forth into flame as they ascend to heaven. The children of the warm sun will yet teach us by their prayers the might of prayer.

During the conflict which is going forward in the free states for the abolition of slavery, the friends of the slave have divided themselves into two camps. The one demands immediate emancipation and their general education; the other, gradual emancipation and the colonization on the coast of Africa. The State of Ohio has adopted this latter mode, and has lately made an important purchase of land on the coast of Africa, in order to colonize there an African Ohio of free negroes.

Not a little is done in the free states for the instruction and elevation of the negroes; but still I can not convince myself that the Americans are doing this in the best way. They endeavor to form this human race so different to themselves, according to their own methods and institutions. When I see those frolicsome negro children in their school sit down like white children on benches and before desks, I am quite distressed. I am convinced that these children ought to learn their lessons standing, or dancing amid games and songs, and that their divine worship ought to be conducted with singing and dancing; and I will answer for it, that their songs and dances would have more life, beauty, and intelligence in them than those of the Shaker community. But who shall teach them thus? None but a negro can teach the negroes, and only one of their own people can become the deliverer of the people in the highest sense. But this captive Israel yet waits for its Moses.

That, however, which very much prevents the redemption of this people from captivity, is their own want of national spirit. Already split into tribes in Africa, where they were at war, and where they enslaved one another, it is difficult to take hold of any more widely extended interests than those of family and local society. I have spoken with many freemen of this people in good circumstances here, also with some young mulattoes who have studied and taken degrees at the Oberlin Institution in this state, and I have found them particularly lukewarm toward the interests of their captive brethren, and especially so as regards colonization in Liberia. Frederick Douglas is as yet the only strong champion among them for their own people.

But if any thing can awake within them a more comprehensive feeling for the whole people, it is assuredly that common slavery on the soil of America, and perhaps, more than any thing else at this moment, the bill which allows the recapture of fugitive slaves. I awoke to this thought to-day during a visit to a free negro church, where I had no occasion to lament any want of interest in the national affairs, either in the negro preacher or the congregation.

I had in the forenoon visited a negro Baptist Church belonging to the Episcopal creed. There were but few present, and they of the negro aristocracy of the city. The mode of conducting the divine service was quiet, very proper, and a little tedious. The hymns were beautifully and exquisitely sung. The sermon, which treated of "Love without dissimulation; how hard to win, how impossible without the influence of God and the communication of his power," was excellent. The preacher was a fair mulatto, with the features and demeanor of the white race, a man of very good intellect and conversational power, with whom I had become already acquainted in my Cincinnati home.

In the afternoon I went to the African Methodist Church in Cincinnati, which is situated in the African quarter. In this district live the greater number of the free colored people of the city; and the quarter bears the traces thereof. The streets and the houses have, it is true, the Anglo-American regularity; but broken windows and rags hanging from them, a certain neglected, disorderly aspect, both of houses and streets, testified of negro management. I found in the African Church African ardor and African life. The church was full to overflowing, and the congregation sang their own hymns. The singing ascended and poured forth like a melodious torrent, and the heads, feet, and elbows, of the congregation moved all in unison with it, amid evident enchantment and delight in the singing, which was in itself exquisitely pure and full of melodious life.

The hymns and psalms which the negroes have themselves composed have a peculiar *naïve* character, childlike, full of imagery and life. Here is a specimen of one of their popular church hymns:

"What ship is this that's landed at the shore?
Oh, glory halleluiah!
It's the old ship of Zion, halleluiah,
It's the old ship of Zion, halleluiah,
Is the mast all sure, and the timber all sound?
Oh, glory halleluiah!
She's built of gospel timber, halleluiah,
She's built, &c.

"What kind of men does she have on board?
Oh, glory halleluiah!
They're all true-hearted soldiers, halleluiah,
They're all, &c.

"What kind of Captain does she have on board?
Oh, glory halleluiah!
King Jesus is the Captain, halleluiah,
King Jesus, &c.

'Do you think she will be able to land us on the shore?
Oh, glory halleluiah!
I think she will be able, halleluiah,
I think, &c.

"She has landed over thousands, and can land as many more.
Oh, glory, halleluiah!" &c., &c.

After the singing of the hymns, which was not led by any organ or musical instrument whatever, but which arose like burning melodious sighs from the breasts of the congregation, the preacher mounted the pulpit. He was a very black negro, young, with a very retreating forehead, and the lower portion of the countenance protruding; upon the whole, not at all good-looking. But when he began to speak, the congregation hung upon his words, and I could not but admire his flowing eloquence. He admonished the assembly to reflect on the present need of their brethren; to pray for the fugitive slaves, who must now, in great multitudes, leave their acquired homes, and seek a shelter out of the country against legal violence and legal injustice. He exhorted them also to pray for that nation which, in its blindness, would pass such laws and oppress the innocent! This exhortation was received with deep groans and lamenting cries.

After this the preacher drew a picture of the death of "Sister Bryant," and related the history of her beautiful Christian devotion, and applied to her the words of the Book of Revelation, of those "who come out of great afflictions." The intention of suffering on earth, the glorious group of the children of suffering in their release, and thanksgiving-song as represented in so divine and grand a manner in the pages of Scripture, were placed by the negro preacher in the light as of noonday, and as I had never before heard from the lips of any ordinary ministers. After this the preacher nearly lost himself in the prayer for the sorrowing widower and his children, and their "little blossoming souls." Then came the sermon proper.

The preacher proposed to the congregation the question, "Is God with us?" "I speak of our nation, my brethren," said he; "I regard our nationality. Let us examine the matter." And with this he drew a very ingenious parallel between the captivity of the Israelites in Egypt and the negroes in America, and those trials by which Providence evinced His especial solicitude about the chosen people. After having represented the fate of the Israelites under Pharaoh and Moses, he went on to contemplate the fate of the negro people.

"How shall we know that God is with us? Let us look at the question thus."

He then boldly sketched out a picture of an enslaved people as oppressed in every way, but not the less "increasing in numbers and improving themselves, purchasing their own freedom from slavery (cries of 'Yes! yes!' 'Oh, glory!' throughout the church); purchasing land (shouts of joy); ever more and more land (increasing shouts); buying houses, large houses, larger and still larger houses (increasing jubilation and stamping of feet); building churches (still louder cries); still more and larger churches (louder and still louder cries, movement, stamping of feet, and clapping of hands); the people increasing still in number, in property, in prosperity, and in understanding, so that the rulers of the land began to be terrified, and to say, 'They are becoming too strong for us; let us send them over to Liberia!' (Violent fermentation and excitement.) This, then, will show us, my brethren, that God is with us. Let us not forsake Him; for He will lead us out of captivity, and make of us a great people!" (extreme delight and joy, with the cry of 'Amen!' 'Yes, yes!' 'Oh, glory!' and so on). The whole congregation was for several minutes like a stormy sea. The preacher's address had been a rushing tempest of natural eloquence. I doubt, however, whether his patriotism extended much beyond the moment of inspiration and of his pulpit; he was not a new Moses. Old Moses was slow of speech; he was a man of action.

This preacher was, however, the first negro from whom I had heard any distinct sentiment of nationality. The bill against fugitive slaves must mind what it is about, and what it may lead to.

With regard to the negro preacher's last outbreak against Liberia, it may be remarked, that the negroes of Ohio are in general opposed to colonization in Africa, and look with suspicion upon the endeavors of the whites in this direction. Unfortunately, the climate of Liberia is said to be so unhealthy from the constant rains that there seems to be some ground for the suspicion. It is a real misfortune for the youthful colony, which otherwise is favored by the unbounded fertility of the country around, and by its affluence in valuable tropical growth. The colony of Liberia, however, increases, although not rapidly, in population and trade, governed by rulers of its own election, and with churches, school-houses, printing-presses, warehouses, and shops. Three cities are already founded there.

Commodore Perry, in his account of the condition of the American-African colony, describes the settlement at Monrovia as especially promising for trade, and that at Cape Palmas for agriculture. For the rest, he describes the negroes of the colony as devoted to small trade rather than to agriculture. And this seems to be the bias of the negroes in all the native colonies along the coast. "Some of the colonists," says he, "have become wealthy through this small trade, while others, again, obtain merely a sufficient maintenance."

"But," adds the commodore, "it is pleasant to see the comforts with which a great number of these people have surrounded themselves; many of them enjoy conveniences of life which were unknown to the first settlers in North America. Want seems not to exist among them. If some of them suffer, it must be in consequence of their own laziness.

"I had at Cape Palmas an opportunity of seeing the small farms or clearings of the colonists. These exhibited considerable labor, and were beginning, by degrees, to assume the appearance of well-cultivated fields. The roads through the whole of this settlement were remarkably good, when the youth of the colony and its small means were taken into consideration.

"At all the various settlements the laws were faithfully observed; the morals of the people were good, and the community seemed to be animated by a strong religious sentiment.

"Governor Roberts, of Liberia, a fair mulatto, and Russwarm, of Cape Palmas, are clever and estimable men, and we have in these two men unanswerable proofs of the capacity of the colored people for self-government.

"The climate of Western Africa can not be considered as unwholesome to colored colonists. Every one must pass through the acclimating fever; but, now that more convenient dwellings are erected, so that the sick may be properly attended to, the mortality has considerably decreased. Once well through this sickness, the colonist finds the climate and the air suitable to his constitution; not so the white man. The residence of a few years on this coast is certain death to him.

"The experiment of the United States to found a colony upon this coast for the free colored people has succeeded beyond expectation, and I venture to predict that the descendants of the present colonists are destined to become a wise and powerful people."

A white American physician, who spent six years in Liberia, states that the imports of the young negro state amount to 120,000 dollars annually, and their exports to nearly the same sum. "The trade of our country with Africa," writes an American this year (1850), "is becoming daily of more importance."

The colony of Liberia is said to number at the present time upward of ten thousand persons. The English colony at Sierra Leone, older and more important, upward of forty thousand.

It thus appears as if Liberia and Sierra Leone would become the nurseries from which the new civilization and the more beautiful future of Africa would proceed: I can not believe but that these plants from a foreign land must before that time undergo a metamorphosis—must become more African.

If I had time and money enough, I would go over to Liberia for twelve months. But where would I not go to, and what would I not see, which is significant in nature or in popular life over the whole world? I would make the whole earth my own. Why is life so short?

Cincinnati, November 29th.

I yesterday celebrated Thanksgiving Day, one of the few national festivals of the New World, a festival which ought to be observed by all nations as one of the most worthy of a noble and clear-eyed humanity. The festival was celebrated on a week day, and converted it into a Sabbath. I attended in the forenoon in a Baptist church. The minister, a man of talent, took as the subject of his discourse, after thanksgiving for both public and private benefits which were enumerated, the subject of slavery in the United States. He had been upbraided as timid in expressing himself on this subject; he now, therefore, wished to clear himself from suspicion, and to show that he had no fear. He condemned slavery, and lamented its introduction into America, but he condemned also the proceedings of the Abolitionists. They had involved the affair, they had rendered emancipation impossible *in* America. The preacher considered that slavery in America had never less prospect of abolition than at the present time. "Never had the Southern States grasped the chain of slavery with a firmer hand. Threats and defiance have been the offspring of threats and defiance." The hope of the speaker lay in the devotion of the African people to America, and in the colonization of Christianized negro slaves on the coast of Africa, and these he considered to be the only available means for the gradual abolition of slavery. After some interesting statements regarding the products of Africa and the advantage which free African labor must have over slave labor, together with the increasing resources of Liberia, he presented a poetically beautiful view of the possible future of the Ethiopic race in its mother-country, this hot, mystic Africa.

I had followed the preacher with the deepest interest. His concluding remarks awoke a vision within my soul.

I believe that "hot, mystic Africa," with its Mountains of the Moon, its Nile, its pyramids, and its tropical forests swarming with animal life and the luxuriance of the vegetable kingdom, awake to a new existence. I beheld Asia, with its old, primeval wisdom, its old, half-petrified kingdoms; Europe, with its manifold kingdoms and people stamped with their living peculiarities of character; I beheld America, the youngest, but ere long the most powerful, of earth's own daughters, with her new men born from the morning dew of a new life; I beheld Australia, with its colonies of prodigal but forgiven sons again received into the father's house: I beheld them all raise themselves anew in the name of the Prince of Peace, and all unite as never before on the face of the earth, in songs of praise at the Divine Nativity, "Glory to God in the highest; on earth peace, and good-will to man!"

A stream of melodious sound burst through the church, bearing with it the words of the song of praise. I recognized that mighty, magnificent chorus. I had heard it before, but I knew not where. But it seemed to me that it was the soul of every song of praise on earth.

It was that Swedish Mass, "Praise and thank the Lord," &c., which is sung by the choir of the church. I had to thank a countryman of mine, the director of the choir of this church, for this pleasure. When the congregation arose and sang Halleluiah in the song of my native land, sang it for my people, and for all people on earth, it was glorious! But I then could not sing.

I can never celebrate a more beautiful thanksgiving festival; and never shall I forget this moment.

I must yet add a few words about the state and the

city in which I am a happy guest. The wealthy, beautiful Ohio is placed like the heart in that great group of states between the Eastern Ocean and the Mississippi. And although this state is one of the youngest in the Union, I feel that a more central life stirs here than in any of the states which I have hitherto visited. It seems to me as if people here wished with unprejudiced minds to do justice to all powers and tendencies of humanity, and to allow every one his proper share of the heart's life and blood. Among the facts of this class I place the Medical College here, under the direction of an intellectual young man, Dr. J. Buchanan, and in which Allopathy and Homeopathy, Hydropathy, and the so-called Botanical Medicine are admitted and studied as natural methods in nature's sanitary code, and all as serviceable in certain diseases and circumstances, all as necessary in a comprehensive system of study of health and disease. Buchanan makes man the measure of the universe and its centre. He sees the centre of man in the human brain, and from that point strikes out an infinite, glorious future, in which all those infinite possibilities now slumbering within it will develop themselves into life and harmony on earth and in the universe. Amid severe daily labor and many anxieties, he reposes in this view as in the Sabbath-festival of his spirit.

Among the facts of this class I place Oberlin College, where the youth of colored as well as white people, both boys and girls, study and take degrees in all those branches of knowledge which are taught in the American academies.

Among these I place the works and opinions of many distinguished men, who are occupied in organizing a more complete and comprehensive scheme of education for women as well as for men.

Cincinnati, the Queen of the West, which has her throne upon the banks of the beautiful river (Ohio), with a background of encircling hills, like a queen surrounded by her court ladies, is a cosmopolitan city, and embraces in her bosom peoples of all nations and all religious sects. Germans constitute a considerable portion of the population of the city, which now amounts to 120,000 souls. The Germans live here as in their old Germany. They are *gemüthlich*, drink beer, practice music, and still ponder here "*über die Weltgeschichte.*" I have lately read a little book with this title by a Dr. Patte, who resides here. The Queen of the West allows all her subjects to ponder, talk, and write as best pleases them. She is the most liberal queen in the world.

Schools, however, in Ohio are not equal to those of the Northeastern States; but there is an earnest endeavor at work for their improvement. When I visited one of the district boys' schools of Cincinnati, it was said to me, as I entered one of the halls of the school, "This is our best-regulated room; here it is never necessary to use corporal punishment."

I entered, and found a pale young woman, of a mild aspect, standing in the teacher's seat, controlling with gentle power from thirty to forty wild young republicans. The elementary schools for boys, as well as for girls, are under the management of women. They are considered as more skillful than men in the training of early youth. They receive a salary of from three to five hundred dollars annually, according to the ability which they show for employment. It was with great pleasure that I heard a lesson by which these lesser children were taught to treat animals with justice and kindness. They repeated from memory stories in which cruelty to animals had been punished in some striking manner. I am not aware whether we have such lessons in our schools, but I know well enough that they are needed.

Among the scientific institutions of Cincinnati, I perceive that the Observatory owes its existence to the genius and zeal of a private man, Professor O. M. Mitchell. The history of the origin of this beautiful observatory, which is one of the highest class, deserves to be known, in order to show in its true light what the determination and enthusiasm of an individual may achieve in the New World, and in what way he can interest the mass of the people for a science which he desires to make popular. It is the triumph of genius, and, at the same time, of patience and of persevering determination. It is a great commendation of the man, and of the masses also. But the history of all this would be too long.

The arts have also began to reveal themselves in Cincinnati; but, as yet, it is only a beginning. The city itself is hardly sixty years old. There is an Art Union here, the exhibition of which I visited twice. There were some good pictures. None, however, took so much hold on my memory as a humorous little painting representing three huge swine very naturally. They were sitting upon their hams, below a rock, on which was inscribed "lard oil;" and they were gazing very attentively at one of their brethren, who was attacking a dead whale, which had been cast upon the shore hard by. Beyond lay the great ocean. This little humorously-conceived and well-painted piece hung between two pictures, the subjects of which were the "Loves of the Angels"—ethereal figures floating forth over clear lakes, and meeting each other on verdant flowery shores. A greater contrast than between those poetical pictures and the prose of the former could scarcely have been imagined. Pity only that the execution of these did not equal that of the other. Our Södermark would have given the prize to the latter. So should I; but yet I would not have had the picture in my room, nor yet the angel-poems, with all their bright anticipations.

The fine arts have hitherto received but little attention in the United States; it may be that there is but little distinguished talent, or, which I suspect is the case, that

the people in general are deficient in artistic feeling. I have heard a deal said of an American painter named Alston, who is considered one of the greatest painters, and I have heard his works very highly praised and admired; yet, nevertheless, I read in one of the letters of the noble old Channing these words: "As long as I see such men as Alston in want of the necessaries of life, I feel that I have no right to possess its superfluities."

And I have heard my friends, the S.'s, of New York, speak of a young landscape painter of that city, who was possessed of unmistakable talent, and a man of estimable character, who, not long since, consulting with his young wife as to the best mode of managing for themselves and their two little ones, came to the agreement that the best mode of all would be for them to die! Good God! And this in this young, wealthy New World! And yet the pictures of this young artist are of the class which I would gladly see in every American home. And, thus encouraged, he would soon become for America what our Fahlkranz is to us, a poet in colors of the peculiar natural scenery of his country.

Sculpture has in the United States a much greater hope of successful progress; and in Hiram Powers they have produced an artist of the highest class, not so much as a creative genius as for feeling and execution. His Proserpine, his listening Fisher Boy, his Greek Slave, have been admired in old Italy. The expression, so refined and so full of soul, is as admirable in his works as the perfected beauty of the form. His creations seem to live.

Hiram Powers was born in Cincinnati, and worked there as a poor boy in the shop of a watchmaker. Here he even then showed his peculiar genius. Some of the affluent men of the city took charge of the promising boy, and furnished him with the means of studying and of traveling. Foremost among these was Mr. Longworth, and to him Powers sent, as a token of gratitude, his first

original creation in marble. I say *creation*, because there is nothing in this work which speaks of labor. It is a figure so complete, so living and beautiful, that it is not to be described. It is the bust of a woman the size of life. They have called it *Genevra*, but why I know not. It ought to be called *Galathea*, because Pygmalian Powers has infused into her a vitality which requires only a divine indication to breathe; or, rather, it ought to be called the *American*, because the peculiar beauty of the features, the form and action of the head and neck, are those of the American woman. There is none of the Greek stiffness in it; it is a regularity of beauty full of life and grace, and the expression—yes, thus ought she to look, the woman of the New World, she who, sustained by a public spirit full of benevolence, may without struggle and without protest develop the fullness and the earnestness of her being; thus ought she to smile, to glance, to move, reposing in this as in a world of truth, goodness, and beauty; thus ought she to be firm, and yet pleasing; thus divinely wise; thus angelically harmonious and kind; thus ought she to work! And then, then shall ascend the new day of the New World!

Mr. Longworth had jocularly prepared me, before he conducted me into his cabinet of art, where his bust stands, "for the rudeness of the first work of a young artist," and requested me to overlook this. I gazed at the figure, and contemplated it till my heart swelled with emotion and my eyes overflowed with tears. I wept before the ideal of the new beauty, not because I was myself so far removed from it—no, but in admiration, in joy, in hope, in the consciousness that I here beheld that woman of the New World, that Galathea, which now slumbers in marble, but who will one day receive life from the Divine touch. And have I not already seen her features, her life among some of the young women of this beautiful country? I see them, and I mention beloved names!

From this time forth I shall look for these features, this expression in the countenance of every young woman; she will become dear or indifferent to me according as she more or less resembles the image of the Galathea of the New World.

Casts of this bust ought to be in the possession of every American home, and every young girl should grow up under its observation, like as Hawthorn's youth grew up gazing upon that "great stone countenance," until his countenance acquired its beauty.

Have I told you that I here live in the vine-district of North America? The vine, which grows luxuriantly wild throughout the whole of North America, has been cultivated on the heights which border the Ohio River with great attention, principally by Mr. Longworth, and here is made American Sherry and Champagne. The Catawba and Isabella grapes are the kinds generally cultivated in this country, but they do not ripen here as regularly as on the Rhine and the Seine; the inequality of the climate is the cause of this.

Farewell! I must make an end. When I shall next converse with you I know not; but have we not commenced an intercourse and formed a friendship which esteems but lightly time and space, and the visible sign? Our place of communion is—Eternity. Yet, nevertheless, a visible sign is precious; and if you would give me one in this distant land, how welcome it would be!

Your words are ever with me like a silent communion: "I believe in a sun, an organizing power, of which every bright thought, all suggestive life, is an outpouring!" That was one of the first observations you made to me.

This sun has become my sun. In this light I go forth seeking and reflecting, and that which I see in this light you also shall see, for that which is mine is yours.

I embrace your wife, and kiss the little ones around her, and expect to be embraced and kissed by them again—in Sweden!

P.S.—My letter terrifies me; it has grown to such a length and breadth, that my friends in Cincinnati must regard it as one of the shapeless giant productions of the Great West, a sort of Rhine muse from the Mississippi Utgaerd. It strikes me like some sort of witch with many feet, and many eyes peeping out on all sides. And now it shall run off to Sweden! Off with it! and what the thing has of head and heart I will trust you for finding out.

In a few days I shall set off for New Orleans, and from thence to Cuba for the winter months. I wish to see the face of the earth under a tropical sun and under the dominion of the Spaniard. I wish to see the Southern Cross and the great star Argo in the heavens. Then I will turn back toward the Pole-star, and our silent North, my dear, quiet home!

LETTER XXXI.

Noah's Ark, on the Mississippi, Dec. 18th.

THE day before yesterday, the 16th, I left Cincinnati; my kind, excellent host and hostess accompanied me on board the steamer, and overwhelmed me at the last moment with proofs of their good-will, all light and agreeable to bear away with me, because they were bestowed with a warm heart, and they were to accompany me to Sweden, and there remind me of the beautiful Ohio and my Cincinnati home. The good Jothim, Mr. S., presented me with a collection of shells from the Ohio River, some of which are extremely beautiful.

It was a lovely sunny day, that on which I commenced my journey, and Cincinnati, its vine-covered hills, its lovely villas, and the River Ohio were brilliant in the sunshine. There was a sunny warmth in my soul likewise, and the proofs of kindness which I received from many friends in the city during the last few days were to me like the soft summer wind; but I was very weary after a violent headache and the excitement of departure. I longed for rest and silence.

The giant steamer Belle Key moved slowly along, thundering down the clear blue river, the lofty shores of which, with their ever-changing scenes, glided past cheerful and lovely. The river became broader, the hills sank lower, the villas disappeared, farm-houses and log-houses recurred at more and more distant intervals, the banks became more wooded and desolate. We approached the Mississippi.

What is going on? Why do the people rush out from the fields? A chase upon the water?

A stag with branching antlers swims across the river from the Kentucky to the Ohio shore. He is not far from the free shore; but two boats are after him from the slave shore. His proud antlers raise themselves high above the water. He swims rapidly; perhaps he may save himself! He is just at the shore. Ah! and now a boat puts out from the free shore toward him. Woe betide the poor fugitive! He turns round. The two boats from Kentucky meet him. Now he is surrounded. I see the oars lifted from all the three boats to give him his death-blow. That beautiful head is still seen above the water. Now fall the oars! I turn my head away. The steamer rounds a point. We have lost sight of the wild chase. The defenseless fugitive is in the power of his pursuers.

I am weary and dejected. The air is pleasant, the water bright and blue; heaven also is bright. Does the deer find no peaceful meadows beyond the river of death, where he may rest after the wild chase?

The steamer Belle Key is of the family of the river giants. I call it Noah's Ark, because it has more than a thousand animals on board, on the deck below us and above us. Immense oxen, really mammoth oxen, so fat that they can scarcely walk—cows, calves, horses, mules, sheep, pigs, whole herds of them, send forth the sound of their gruntings from the lower deck, and send up to us between times any thing but agreeable odors; and on the deck above us turkeys gobble—geese, ducks, hens, and cocks crow and fight, and little pigs go rushing wildly about, and among the poultry pens.

On the middle deck, where we, the sons and daughters of Adam are bestowed, every thing, in the mean time, is remarkably comfortable. The ladies' saloon is large and handsome, and the passengers few, and of an *excellent* class. I have my state-room to myself. I am like a princess in a fairy-tale. My cavalier for the journey, Mr. Lerner H., is one of that energetic and warm-hearted class of American men, and add to this a very agreeable fellow also, who in his behavior to "a lady intrusted to his care" has that blending of brotherly cordiality and chivalric politeness which makes the man of the New World the most agreeable companion that a lady can desire. No screaming children disturb the quietness on board; and the grunting of the swine and other animal sounds in our Noah's Ark we do not allow to trouble us. All these animals are destined to the Christmas market of New Orleans.

December 17th. The Mississippi-Missouri flows turbidly and broad with its increasing waters, full of drift-wood, trees, branches, and stumps, which give us sometimes no inconsiderable bumps. The shores are low and swampy, covered with the now leafless woods of a kind of poplar called cotton-wood. It is horribly monotonous. The weather is gray and cold, and every thing looks gray around us. We have now Missouri on our right, and Kentucky on our left. I am sorry not to have had time to see more of Kentucky and Kentucky people. They are peculiar in appearance and in disposition. They are tall, very limber in their joints, and dexterous, generous, free-spoken, good-natured, cordial, droll people, whom I should have become very fond of. And then "Skyrnir's Glove," the mammoth cave, and the little green river which flows there—I ought to have seen them! Lerner H. talks about that cave till I almost fany I have seen it.

I must tell you of a pleasure which he prepared for me one evening on the Ohio. He asked me whether I should like to hear the negroes of the ship sing, and led me for this purpose to the lowest deck, where I beheld a strange scene. The immense engine-fires are all on this deck, eight or nine apertures all in a row; they are like yawning fiery throats, and beside each throat stood a negro naked to his middle, who flung in fire-wood. Pieces of wood were passed onward to these feeders by other negroes, who stood up aloft on a large open place between them and a negro, who, standing on a lofty stack of fire-wood, threw down with vigorous arms food for the monsters on deck. Lerner H. encouraged the negroes to sing; and the negro up aloft on the pile of fire-wood began immediately an improvised song in stanzas, and at the close of each the negroes down below joined in vigorous chorus. It was a fantastic and grand sight to see these energetic black athletes lit up by the wildly flashing flames from the fiery throats, while they, amid their equally fantastic song, keeping time most exquisitely, hurled one piece of fire-wood after another into the yawning fiery gulf. Every thing went on with so much life, and so methodically, and the whole scene was so accordant and well arranged, that it would have produced a fine effect upon any theatre whatever. The improvisation was brought finally to a close with a hint that the singing would become doubly merry, and would sing twice as well, if they could have a little brandy when they reached Louisville, and that they could buy brandy if they could have a little money, and so on.

Nor did Mr. H. allow them to be mistaken in their anticipations.

We are still in the grain-district of the Mississippi, but we shall soon reach the region of cotton. We have now Arkansas on our right hand, and Tennessee on our left, slave states rich in natural beauty, but still rude in spiritual and material culture.

December 20th. We are now in the region of cotton. The shores on both sides are low and swampy, covered by forests of cotton-wood-trees, now leafless. Here and there, however, are interspersed cotton plantations, with the white slave villages and the habitations of the planters; and one sees swarthy figures moving about on the gray soil, gathering the cotton-pods that still remain upon the blackening shrubs. I went on shore to-day with Mr. H. at a cotton plantation, and broke off some branches, with tufts of cotton still hanging upon them, from shrubs which grew round a slave-hut. The tufts of cotton are extremely beautiful as they come forth from the opening capsules of the seed-pod. Every seed is imbedded in a pillow of cotton. Cotton is the envelope of the seed. You shall see it when I return.

We have now Arkansas on our right, and the State of Mississippi on our left. Along the river lie the cane-brake, thick reed-like canes, which stand up as impenetrable as a wall between the water and the land.

Thus far came Father Marquette upon his sun-bright Mississippi journey from the North; thus far, also, from the South advanced the first European discoverer, the Spaniard, Ferdinand de Soto.

The discovery of the Mississippi is two poems; the one beautiful and sun-bright as its idyllian islands and its clear waters in the North, the other as melancholy, as tragically gloomy as the tint and the scenery of the river in its southern portion, through which I am now journeying. The hero of the former is the mild, unpretending Father Marquette. The hero of the latter is the proud warrior, Ferdinand de Soto.

Soto had been the favorite companion of Pizarro in the conquest of Peru; he had distinguished himself at the storming of Cusco, and was favored by Charles V. in Spain, and rewarded both with honor and wealth, and finally appointed by him Governor of Cuba. But his proud, ambitious mind desired more. Fooled by false prophets, and most of all by his own heart, he desired to fit out an expedition at his own cost, which should advance from Florida into North America, and there conquer for the Spaniards richer treasures and more beautiful lands than those of Mexico and Peru; and his own belief possessed so great a power of influencing the mind of the Spaniards, that vast numbers of young men of noble birth and good fortune enlisted under his command. They sold their vineyards, their houses, and valuables to purchase expensive arms, equipments, and horses. Out of multitudes who offered themselves as volunteers on this new expedition of discovery, he selected six hundred young men, all adventurers, wealthy, and proud as himself.

A more magnificent spectacle was never beheld than that of the landing of these proud cavaliers on the shore of the New World; their banners and standards floating in the air, in the soft air of Florida, full, as it were, of youthful vitality, of the intoxicating elixir of life. Thus galloped they onward in burnished armor, "very gallant, with silk upon silk," along the shore between the sea and the unknown land which they believed to be full of gold and great cities.

Ferdinand de Soto, who wished to prevent all possibility, either for himself or his troop, of retreat, which might be desired by fickleness or by fear, sent back all his vessels to Cuba, and advanced with his warriors into the wildernesses of the New World. They took with them weapons of all kinds, work-tools, as well as chains and bloodhounds for the subjection of the natives.

It was in the month of May, 1539.

And ever as they advanced onward through the wilderness, mass was punctually performed by priests with all the pomp of Catholic observance, and ever as they advanced onward they practiced cruelty against the natives, while in their own camp they occupied themselves with the excitement of desperate gaming.

The wanderings of the first year were westward, thence into Georgia, which was then, like all the rest of the undetermined southeastern continent, called Florida. Their journeyings were difficult, and often dangerous, from the hostility of the Indians. They found abundance of maize, but no gold and no cities, only small Indian villages. Nor could the natives inform them of any land in which gold was to be found. Some of the adventurers now desired that their leader should turn back; but he replied,

"I will not turn back till I have seen the poverty of the country with my own eyes."

And he ordered the Indians to be burned or mutilated, whom he believed had intentionally misled him. Other captive Indians, alarmed at this, assured him that gold might be found further toward the northwest. And De Soto and his men journeyed on still further, plundering and desolating as they went.

The second year brought them into the highlands of Georgia, where they fell in with the peaceful and gentle Cherokee Indians. A number of De Soto's people wished to settle themselves down here in the midst of this beautiful region, to till the soil and enjoy the good things of the earth. But De Soto had promised Spain gold and great cities, and the proud Spaniard would not rest until he had found them. He was an obstinate man, of few words and strong will, and all his attendants yielded themselves to him.

They wandered still further; advanced into Alabama, where there was a large town called Mavilla (afterward Mobile). Here the Indians rose up against him. A battle ensued—the Spanish cavalry overcame the enemy: a more bloody Indian battle was never fought on American soil; the town was set on fire; two thousand five hundred Indians are said to have been slain, suffocated, or burned; the Spaniards lost a few of their number, and most of their baggage, which perished in the flames with the Indian town.

Spanish ships had, however, in the mean time, arrived from Cuba at Pensacola Bay, near Mavilla. But De Soto had not yet found either silver or gold; the flames of Mavilla had destroyed the curious collections which he had made, and, too proud to acknowledge his hopes defeated, he resolved to send no news of himself until he had obtained that for which he sought. He turned away from the sea-coast and proceeded northwestward, in the State of Mississippi. His little band was now diminished to five hundred men.

In the northern parts of Mississippi they were surprised by winter, with severe frost and snow. But maize was still standing in the fields, and the Spaniards were able to obtain a supply of food and shelter for the winter also in the deserted huts of the Chickasaw Indians. But they had not yet found gold; neither had the Indians golden ornaments. They were poor, but loved freedom. When spring came, and De Soto demanded from them an escort to carry the baggage of his soldiers, the Indians set fire to his camp, and their fierce war-whoop rang through the night and amid the flames.

The Spaniards lost here the clothing and the stores which had been saved from the fires of Mavilla. They were now as naked as their Indian enemies, and they suffered from cold and hunger; but with his difficulties increased the pride and obstinacy of De Soto. Was it for him, who had promised to conquer the treasures of the world, to return with half-naked men despoiled of their all?

He ordered the chains to be taken from the limbs of the captives, and new weapons to be forged; he clothed his troops in garments of skins and mats of ivy-leaves, and advanced still further west in search of the land of gold.

For seven days they wandered through a wilderness of forests and morasses. They then reached the Indian settlements on the banks of the Mississippi.

Ferdinand de Soto was the first European who beheld the mighty river.

The lapse of three centuries has not changed its character. It was then described as broad and turbid, flowing on with a powerful current, and with a quantity of trees and timber always floating on its stream.

In May, 1541, the Spaniards crossed the river in large boats which they themselves had built. De Soto proceeded into Arkansas. Here the Spaniards were saluted by the natives as children of the Sun, and the blind were brought to them that they might receive their sight from the children of the Light.

"Pray only to God who dwells in heaven," replied De Soto, "and He will give you what you need."

Following his dark impulse, De Soto advanced still further toward the northwest, and finally reached the highlands of the White River, two hundred miles from the Mississippi. But neither did these mountains yield gold nor precious stones!

De Soto and his people took up their winter quarters in an Indian town on the banks of the White River, Washita, among a peaceful Indian tribe, who were employed in agriculture, and who had fixed towns. The young cavaliers practiced upon the unoffending natives every cruelty which their unbridled caprice suggested. De Soto, it is said, had no pleasure in cruelty; but the lives and rights of the Indians were counted as nothing by him.

In the following spring De Soto determined to descend the Washita to its junction, and to obtain tidings of the sea. He bewildered himself among the morasses which border the Red River and its tributaries. In one province, called Guachoya, he inquired from the chief how far it was thence to the sea? The chief could not tell. Were there settlements through the country from that point to the junction of the river? He was told that the whole country there was an uninhabitable swamp. De Soto, unwilling to credit such discouraging intelligence, sent men on horseback to examine the land southward along the Mississippi. In eight days they were not able to advance further than thirty miles, they were so constantly impeded by morasses, by the denseness of the forests, and the impenetrable cane-brakes.

The governor heard their report in gloomy silence. Horses and men were dying around him, and the Indians were becoming more and more dangerous. He attempted to overawe a tribe of Indians near Natchez by saying that he was of supernatural descent, and therefore demanded of them obedience and tribute.

"You say that you are the child of the Sun," replied the chief: "dry up this river, and I will believe you!"

Ferdinand de Soto could no longer overawe or punish. His arrogance and his stubborn pride were now subdued by a gloomy melancholy, and his health began to decline under the conflict with adversity and suffering. He was attacked by a malignant fever, during which he was neither cared for nor visited as his state required. His little company had now melted away to three hundred men.

When he felt his death approach, he called around him the remnant of his faithful followers, who obeyed him to the last, and named his successor.

The following day he died. His soldiers pronounced his eulogy by sorrowing for his loss. The priests chanted over his body the first requiem which was ever heard by the waters of the Mississippi. In order to conceal his death, they wrapped his body in a mantle, and in the depth of night bore it out upon the Mississippi, and sank it silently in the middle of the stream.

It was now again May, and the spring burst forth glorious over the Mississippi, but De Soto rose up no more to meet it.

"The discoverer of the Mississippi," adds the historian, to whom I am much indebted for the above, "slept beneath its waters. For four years he had wandered to and fro over a great portion of the continent in search of gold, but had found nothing so remarkable as the place of his burial."

Father Marquette slumbered at the foot of the altar, without sickness and sorrow, after a life of peaceful conquest and uninterrupted success; and Ferdinand de Soto, slowly dying amid morasses and adversities, that proud heart the prey of anxiety and of humiliation—what pictures they present! Has poetry any thing brighter than the former, any thing more gloomy than the latter?

December 21st. The Mississippi flows gray, turbid, and broad; still broader and still more turbid it seems to me under this gray, chilly, wintery sky. Its waters become more and more swollen every day, and the shores become still more flat and swampy, bordered with cotton-wood and cane-brake. Great blocks of timber, trees, and all kind of things float along the Mississippi, all telling of wreck and desolation. This great river seems to me like the waters of the Deluge, and they bear along with them a vast register of sin. Our magnificent Noah's Ark, however, more cosmopolitan than its ancient predecessor, floats upon the great cosmopolitan waters with an easy conscience, and is such a capital place altogether, that, though I sometimes think of the Deluge and the Mississippi register of sin, and of De Soto's fate in these regions, and see the impression of his spirit stamped upon the gloomy landscape, upon the gray earth and sky yet so musing, I can not but feel cheerful of mood. I seem to see myself here, like a citizeness of the world, conveyed along by the great citizen of the world; and thus I know that I shall now become acquainted with its geographical history to its very close, and that I shall see that beautiful Cuba and the life of the tropics; and thus I think—many thoughts.

Every thing on board is quiet, and all goes on with order and propriety. I spend the forenoons by myself, read a little American history, and in Buchanan's "Journal of Man," and let my thoughts flow with the stream forth into the ocean. The afternoons and evenings are passed in company with some agreeable passengers on board. At meal-times Mr. H. always stands ready in the saloon to conduct me to table, and in the morning extends to me his hand with a brotherly salutation. He sits beside me at table, mentions the various dishes to me, and tells me what I may eat, and always is right; is charming and agreeable in every way; reminds me often in his manner of our Captain G., and resembles him also, inasmuch as he abuses his own head for being badly furnished, while he is possessed of a very excellent, acute, and sound intellect. How it may be with regard to his acquired knowledge I can not say, but this I know, that these strong practical characters, when they are united to a warm heart and a noble disposition, are to me at the same time especially a repose and a refreshment. A man who, from his own acquired property, purchases and furnishes a house for his father and sister, is one whom I should like to have for a brother; but not for the sake of the house.

The animals, who are both below us and above us, amuse me also, all except the pigs, which I would were all of them drowned together in the Mississippi, because they send such repulsive odors up to our piazza every now and then. The great variety of animal cries are not at all unpleasing to hear at a distance, and they all look in such good condition, and are so well off, that I generally once a day make a round of salutation among them. The oxen are so fat that they can hardly get up when they have laid themselves down; and they are obliged to be roused to that every morning by the keen caresses of the whip.

I must now tell you about some new acquaintance whom I have made on board. First, two young sisters from Vermont, real rose-buds in their exterior, and with souls of the purest crystal, genuine daughters of New England even in this, that though they might live in ease in their own home, they prefer as teachers to earn their own bread, and thus obtain an independent life for themselves. You would be as much fascinated with them as I am. The eldest sister is twenty-five, and is now on her way to undertake the management of a ladies' seminary in the State of Mississippi. The younger is only seventeen, and is going as a pupil in the school where her sister is teacher. Both are most charming girls, and both have each their favorite brother, of whom they can not say enough in praise, and whose portraits they have shown me. Their parents are dead. They are here quite alone on the vessel. Sometimes they stand together on the piazza, and sing duets together very sweetly.

The eldest is the loveliest type of the young teacher of the New World, that young woman, who, although delicate and slender in figure, and gifted with every feminine grace, stands more steadfastly upon her ground than the Alps or the pyramids of the earth; who understand Euclid and Algebra as well as any master of arts, and who understands better than any how to manage a school of unmanageable boys.

"I love to rule little boys," said Miss G., with a smile, which had a good deal of conscious power mingled with its amiability. And with this power of goodness and beautiful womanliness, she goes calmly to assume her vocation of teacher; but not merely as the teacher, but with the sentiment of being one of the young mothers of humanity.

And I do not know any image more beautiful. Such young women are the true heroines of romance of our day.

When I inquired whence that amiable young girl had derived both her strength and her gentle grace, her lofty view of the nobility of life, and the purpose of man, I was presented with a sweet and gravely beautiful image of her deceased mother.

"I remember," said she, as we sat together one evening in the twilight, "I remember how she used to go out with me in the morning when I was a little girl, and wander over the green hills while the dew was yet on the grass; and how she would show me the little clover-flowers on the field-turf which my foot trod, and let me see their perfect beauty, and taste how sweet they were with their honeyed juice!"

Bright tears shone in the beautiful eyes of the speaker. The little clover-flower has raised its head. It had become human.

I saw once more Hiram Powers' American, but not merely in marble, in living reality.

My other agreeable acquaintance on board is a gentleman between forty and fifty, with one of those pure, handsome countenances which one can not do otherwise than put one's entire trust in, and which remind me of that of our king, Gustavus Adolphus II., from its frankness and manliness, although it has less of the warlike in expression. My new friend is somewhat phlegmatic and contemplative. His conversation gives me especial pleasure. Do not be afraid if I tell you that he has lived long in the Southern States as a planter and a slave owner; you may see immediately, by his beautiful deep blue eyes, that he was the best of masters in the world. Are you afraid that I am in love with him, and in spirit do you see me give him my hand, and settle down on a cotton plantation on the Mississippi, in the midst of negro slaves?

Yes, if I were younger, and if my life's purpose were less decided than it now is, I confess that there is here and there one of these American gentlemen, with their energy, their cordiality, and chivalric spirit, who might be dangerous to my heart. But as it now is, I receive every sentiment of cordial liking which is evinced toward me, by man or by woman, with calm gratitude, as a cream on the good food of life, as the sunbeam and the spring-breeze, which makes the day beautiful. I seek not for them, but when they come, I enjoy them as flowers given by the hand of the all-good Father.

But now, as particularly regards this agreeable gentleman, he is already married, and is traveling with his family to Cuba, where, on account of the health of his wife, they will spend the winter, and after that to Europe. His wife is an invalid, but has the same character of seriousness and gentleness as himself. Both husband and wife appear to be sincerely attached to each other. Why should such people be slave-owners? or, rather, why could not all slave-owners be such people?

The planter's wife told me that her husband never was able to enjoy real peace of mind on the plantations, for that the thought of his slaves, and the wish to do them justice, and to treat them well, disturbed him day and night; he was always afraid of not doing enough for them.

We are now near Vicksburg, a city of bad reputation on the Mississippi, but a city also which shows the ability of the North Americans for self-government. A few years since a band of desperate gamblers and adventurers settled themselves down there. They set up a gambling-club, and decoyed young men thither, purposely excited quarrels, and fought with pistols in the streets, and even in houses, and committed every kind of outrage. The wise men of the city assembled, and announced to the gamblers that they must either vacate the city within eight days, or that they would be seized and hanged. The gamblers treated the announcement with scorn, and gambled and quarreled, and had their pistol-fights as before. When the eight days of grace were past, the friends of order in the city assembled, seized them, and hanged the one who was the worst of the set, and then, putting the rest in a boat, they turned them adrift on the Mississippi. Such summary treatment is called Lynch-law, and is the self-assumed administration of law, by a sense of justice, where there exists no ordinary executive power able to administer the law according to its usual forms. After this execution, which I believe occurred last year, Vicksburg became a creditable place.

We shall soon leave the region of cotton for that of sugar. But when shall we arrive at the region of summer? It is constantly cold and cheerless.

December 22d. Now we are there! Now we are there! and summer breezes and sunshine surround us! But— but I must tell you consecutively that which has formed a turning-point in my whole state of feeling.

This is the seventh day of my journey down the Mississippi. When I came out on the piazza in the morning, I felt as if I were in an enchanted world. The sweetest summer breezes caressed me; the softest blue heaven lay over the Mississippi, and airy, open, cultivated fields on its banks; snowy masses of summer-cloud were chased by the warm breeze; and upon the verdant meadows which covered the shores shone out lovely habitations, standing in groves of orange-trees, shrubberies of roses, cypresses, and cedars. An indescribably mild and delicious life of beauty breathed in every thing and over every thing. Every thing was changed. We had, below Memphis, entered the region of sugar, or the country in which the sugar-cane is cultivated, as well as cotton and maize. We had passed Natchez, where formerly a powerful Indian tribe had worshiped the sun, and maintained a perpetual fire, a place with bloody memories. We had left the city of the bloody memories behind us, we had left behind us the States of Mississippi and Arkansas. We were now in Louisiana, the limits of which embraced both shores of the river. We were speeding into the bosom of the South, and it received us with a warm heart. So I felt it, and my own heart expanded itself to every gentle power of life and of nature. I sat silently aft on the piazza the whole forenoon, in a sort of quiet intoxication of enjoyment, inhaling the delicious atmosphere and the southern landscape, thrilled with the enchanting aspect of heaven and earth, and the indescribable soft mild air which was diffused through the infinite between them.

It was noon. The air became more and more delicious, and more and more animated became the scenes on the river-banks. Caravans of black men and women were seen driving out from the planter's house to the fields. After them came one or two buggies or cabriolets, in which were probably the overseers or the masters themselves. I gazed on the whole scene in that spirit of human love, in which to keep one's self, one believes, in good humor, the best of all men, and in which one endeavors to see every thing and all circumstances on the sunny side.

Two hours later I still sat aft on the piazza, and inhaled the same mild, delicious atmosphere, still beheld the same scene of southern beauty, but gazed upon it with a heart full of bitterness. Yes, for a dark picture had been unfolded before my gaze—a picture which I never shall forget; which perpetually, like a spectre of the abyss, will step between me and the memory of that enchanting veil which one moment captivated and darkened my vision.

I sat and gazed upon that beautiful scene as one looks at the scene of a theatre. I enjoyed with childish delight the decorations. Then came my new friend, the planter, and seated himself in an arm-chair on the piazza. We spoke a few words about the deliciousness of the air, which he enjoyed as much as I did. Then we sat silently contemplating the scenery of the shores. We saw the caravans of slaves and their overseers proceeding over the fields. I said to my neighbor in that spirit of human love which I have mentioned,

"There is a great deal more happiness and comfort in this life (the slaves' life) than one commonly imagines."

The planter turned to me his beautiful head with a glance which I shall never forget; there was astonishment, almost reproach in it, and a profound melancholy.

"Oh!" said he, in a low voice, "you know nothing of that which occurs on these shores; if you did, you would not think so. Here is much violence and much suffering! At this season in particular, and from the time when the cotton is ready to pluck, a great deal of cruelty is practiced on the plantations around here. There are plantations here where the whip never rests during all these months. You can have no idea of such flogging."

I will not repeat those scenes which the planter related to me, scenes which he himself had witnessed of violence, cruelty, and suffering during more than fourteen years, abominations which finally drove him thence, which drove him to sell his plantation, and leave the slave states forever. I will merely introduce some of this excellent man's words.*

"I have known men and women who were actual devils toward their slaves—whose pleasure it was to torment them.

"People can flog a negro almost to death, and yet not let a drop of blood flow. The strip of cowhide which is

* I should not, however, now publish them if I did not know that *he* is now safe from all the unpleasantness which his integrity possibly might have drawn upon him, did I not consider that by communicating them I am performing his *last* will and—a higher will also.

used in doors can cause the most horrible torture without any mark being left.

"Women are not unfrequently the most horrible tormentors of the house-slaves, and I would rather be one of the field-hands than the house-slave of a passionate woman. The institution of slavery seems to change the very nature of woman.

"Slavery is destructive of the white. I have known young men and women, amiable in all respects, of the most attractive manners and dispositions, but toward their slaves they were unjust and severe.

"There are naturally exceptions. There are good and tender masters and mistresses, but they are few. The rule is, that slavery blinds and hardens the mind of the slave-owner from childhood upward.

"The state of things is considerably improved of late years, and still is improving. Light is beginning to enter this country; people are no longer afraid of speaking. A few years ago, if a person had published a seventh part of what I have now told you, he would have been shot without any further process. The slave-owner now acknowledges that the eye of the public is directed to him. It makes him more careful. Slaves, for the last ten or twelve years, have been better clothed and fed in this part of the country than they used to be; but sadly too much injustice and sadly too much cruelty exists still, and must always exist, so long as this institution lasts. And it is my conviction that it will soon become "*the question*"—the question of life and death within the American Union.

"Even now a man makes no demur about shooting down a negro whom he suspects of intending to run away, and the law is silent on all such acts of violence. I have seen many slaves severely wounded from having been shot at under such circumstances, but one only killed.

"Passion and insanity in the treatment of slaves are common.

"The law is no protection to the slave. It is nominally so, but it is not any actual defense. The slave suffers from his master; the lawyers shut their eyes to the affair as long as they can; and the negro can not be a witness in a court of justice.

"They talk of public opinion; but public opinion is here, as yet, for the most part the product of demagogues. And the cotton interest is the only conscience. Many people see all this as very wrong, and deplore it, but they are silent, from the fear of involving themselves in trouble.

"The festivals of the slaves are for the most part a fiction. On some plantations they are allowed to dance at Christmas, if the cotton is picked and the sugar is ground; but when the harvest is late, as it is this year, the festival is put off to eternity, and for the greater number it always remains there. If the harvest has been good and the work is done, then the negroes may sometimes dance.

"Hitherto no religious instruction has been allowed to the slave on the plantations, nor is it even to this hour. But God knows how it has happened, some of these poor creatures have, notwithstanding, got hold of some of the truths of the Gospel, and you can scarcely imagine the eagerness with which they listen to every word. I know two plantations where the slaves have regular Christian instruction, and it is very probable that this may spread and produce a change in the relationship between slave and master.

"The time is perhaps not far distant when public opinion will become a real defense to the slave, and more so than law can ever be.

"People are becoming compelled to more justice and gentleness toward their slaves, for their own safety. I have known times here when there was not a single planter who had a calm night's rest; at that time they never lay down to sleep without a brace of loaded pistols at their side.

"If people would only attempt to treat the slave with justice and with reason, they would be astonished at the results of these methods. The negro is in a high degree susceptible of kindness and justice. He is disposed to subordination under any real superior, and if the whites would avail themselves of such means, they would be able to govern the negro, or, at all events, he would work for him without the whip.

"I never allowed the whip to be used on my plantation to drive them to work; there was no need of it. Justice, regularity, reason, sufficed with them; and they worked well. I only allowed the whip to be used (and one can not, in the present uncultivated condition of the negroes, do without the whip on the plantations) as a punishment for theft and quarrels; but for driving them to their work it is not at all necessary.

"I am convinced that slaves might become free servants, and, as such, would work very well. All those dangers which are predicted in emancipation are, in my opinion, mere dreams. If emancipation were to take place gradually and wisely, it would then proceed without danger or difficulty. The experiments which some persons, and among these Mr. Macdonald and Mr. Henderson, have tried with their slaves has proved this.

"Education, accompanied by a prospect of emancipation, would be the right means.

"But a great many things must be changed here before such a thought as this becomes general. I know men of high religious professions who have been the most cruel of slave-owners.

"And if I were to divulge all that I have seen, and know has taken place, and still takes place in these states, it would be enough to make the hair stand on end on the head of every right-minded person.

"The histories of fugitive slaves, some of which I have read, are not always to be relied upon. I often see that they fabulate, and there is no need of fabulation to make the condition of the slave horrible. The reality is worse than any fiction. And if I were a slave, I should—oh, I should certainly—leap into the river, and put an end to my life!"

These words, and the narratives with which they were interspersed of fearful things which have occurred, and are still of daily occurrence on these shores, mingled themselves like a poisoned wind with the summer breezes which still caressed me. I beheld the old slave hunted to death because he dared to visit his wife—beheld him mangled, beaten, recaptured, fling himself into the water of the Black River, over which he was retaken into the power of his hard master. And the law was silent.

I beheld a young woman struck, for a hasty word, upon the temples, so that she dropped down dead! And the law was silent.

I heard the law, through its jury, adjudicate between a white man and a black, and sentence the latter to be flogged when the former only was guilty. And they who were honest among the jurymen in vain opposed the verdict!

I beheld here, on the shore of the Mississippi, only a few months since, a young negro girl fly from the maltreatment of her master, and he a professor of religion, and fling herself into the river.

I saw multitudes of captives, men and women, condemned to labor early and late, deprived of every ray of that light which could give hope to captivity, and prevented from hearing the voice of the Savior, which says, "Come unto me, all ye that labor and are heavy laden," debarred from all this by men who call themselves Christians. But forgive me, my Agatha! Why should your eyes be tormented with these gloomy pictures? I would that I could avoid seeing them. But the effect of them will never leave me. There was an end of all my enjoyment of the air and the beauty of the South. I seemed to hate my own kind who could perpetrate such cruelties and such injustice. I hated those who could gloss all this over for the interests of trade. I was indignant with myself for having wished to spare myself, to blind myself, to what I must have known would be the inevitable consequences of the institution of slavery. Yes, I ought to have known it; but I thought that it now no longer could be so!

Georgia and Carolina have, however, allowed the introduction of Christianity among the slaves. I had heard in Georgia and Carolina the children of Africa burst forth in songs of praise of their Redeemer!

But here, in the beautiful southern land of the Mississippi Valley, it was worse then heathenism! Mississippi, thou great Noah's flood, now do I know thy history to the end.

But in the midst of its darkest career, I have seen the conscience of the South glance brightly upward in a pure eye, directed toward heaven in a warm and honest heart; and this is my consolation and my hope. The sunshine on the Mississippi is no mere lie. "Darkness was upon the face of the deep, but the Spirit of God moved over the waters."

On the Mississippi

We have passed Baton Rouge, as the political capital of Louisiana is called, situated upon a high bluff, upon the lofty shore of the Mississippi. A fine Capitol commands the little city, and a magnificent state prison, just completed, stands with its foundations in the waters of the Noah's flood.

The Mississippi is at this point very broad. There are in the river sand-banks and verdant islands. Its waters are now clearer; the sun shines; the scenery of the shores is pleasing and quiet: plantations, orange groves, white slave villages amid the green fields, extensive views beneath the mild heavens of summer. The river is full of vessels, steamers, boats, and barges. We are approaching the gay city of New Orleans.

I had some conversation to-day with our stewardess, a pretty, well-disposed mulatto-girl. I found her in her little cabin busily studying a large alphabet. I had seen her twice before so employed. "The steward," she said, "had promised to teach her to read in secret. He could read, that he could." She longed so much to be able to read. I found her one day in our saloon, standing before the open Bible, which always lies upon the table there. I asked her what she was doing. "Oh, this book," said she; "I turn and I turn over its leaves, and wish I understood what is on them. I try and try; I should be so happy if I could read, but I can not."

We are approaching New Orleans, "that gay city." In a couple of hours we shall be there. All the animals in Noah's Ark make themselves heard.

New Orleans, La Fayette Square, Dec. 25th.

Far in the South, but without sun, at least for the present. But it shone brightly as we arrived at the Crescent City, which in the form of a half moon stands upon a broad tongue of land between the Mississippi and Lake Pontchartrain, into which great inland sea the waters of the Gulf of Mexico enter.

No less than three steamers had been blown up a short time before our arrival; one of them was quite new, and was out on an expedition of pleasure, with several of the most wealthy people of New Orleans on board. Many of these were very severely hurt, and two killed.

Our Noah's Ark, however, has borne us and all the animals safely to land.

The harbor which we entered was beautiful and inviting in its crescent form, but the roadstead was bad, and the quay of wood, and ill built.

On the arm of my faithful cavalier, Lerner H., I went on shore, and up to a magnificent building resembling the

Pantheon at Rome, shining out white with its splendid columns, not of marble, but of stucco. This was the Hotel St. Charles, and here we at first took up our quarters.

But when I found that for a cold little room, with an immense bed, up three flights of stairs, with the privilege of the great saloon, where I would not go if I could help it, and the privilege of eating a variety of meals, which I could not eat without making myself ill, and at hours that did not suit me—when I found that for all this magnificence I must pay three dollars per day, without being able with it all to enjoy one pleasant hour, I became anxious to find another home.

And another home I soon found, through the kind care of my kind countryman, Mr. Charles Schmidt, brother to the Justitierraed. And this morning Lerner H. brought me hither in a carriage, amid rain and cold. I am now living in a private boarding-house, with a respectable widow. I have a large, handsome room, carpeted, and with a fire-place, and two large windows looking out into a market-place planted with young trees still green, and with a grass-plot in the centre. This is La Fayette Square. It is a beautiful and very quiet place. I esteem myself quite happy in my dwelling, for which I pay, together with my board, only ten dollars per week, which is low for New Orleans.

I became acquainted in St. Charles's Hotel with two persons who may hereafter become more to me than mere acquaintance; these are Mr. and Mrs. G. They are from Cincinnati, but are residing, like Mr. H., through the winter in New Orleans, where both gentlemen have business. Lerner H. had prepared me to like Mrs. G. very much.

When, on the morning after my arrival, I went down to breakfast in the great eating-hall, no one was as yet there, and I set myself to guess my new friends' friend from those who entered.

I beheld ladies enter one after another, all with dresses

made high to the throat, little collars, without caps, and all dressed as much alike as if they had been modeled from one block; all were delicate, thin, or rather dried up, and looked, it seemed to me, dried up inwardly as well as outwardly. But in this I might be mistaken. Certain it is, I thirsted for a little life, a little individuality in the exterior as well as the interior. The Quakeresses are also all alike in costume. But what a clearly impressed individuality one reads in their countenances! Here, again, it was uniformity devoid of character; the simplicity was monotonous and tiresome. I had not discovered Mrs. G.

I said so to Lerner H. as he sat beside me at breakfast.

"Turn round," said he; "she sits at the table behind you!" (N.B.—We ate at long, narrow tables.)

I turned round, and met a gentle, oval, somewhat pale countenance, and a pair of deep, beautiful eyes, a clear forehead, over which the dark brown hair lay smooth on the temples in bands. That was Mrs. G. She was dressed like all the rest of the ladies, but in black silk; her hair was put up in the same style as the others, but still there was a great difference. She seemed to me a little stiff, but not dry; mild and noble.

I made a closer acquaintance with her on Christmas Eve, and on the afternoon of Christmas Day, which I spent in company in the great saloon with a portion of the population of St. Charles's Hotel, and she cordially pleased me. She has those refined, regular features which belong to American female beauty, and besides this, there is a quiet demeanor, that modest, dignified grace which one often does not meet with among the beauties of the New World. Mr. G., who is a good deal older than his handsome wife, has an animated, strongly-marked countenance; he is a warm Swedenborgian, and I foresee that we shall have some little contentions on this subject; but all in good part, for he is evidently a good Swedenborgian.

There was dancing in the great saloon. A young, handsome, and evidently consumptive girl waltzed with as much zeal as if she would make an end of herself; and her partner and lover helped her most loyally. I could not feel gay. I thought of Christmas in Sweden and at home. Here they did not understand how to celebrate Christmas. In Sweden, however, we do understand this festival.

I went to church on Christmas Day, to a grand church, the darkly-painted windows of which deprived it of all light, and heard a dry, soulless sermon. I was not edified, and felt as if New Orleans was a dry and wearisome place. I thought of the Christmas early morning service in our country churches, of the sledgings thither in the gay morning twilight, through pine woods, along the fresh snow; I thought of the little cottages in the woods, shining out with their Christmas candles; of the train of small peasant sledges, with their bells ringing merrily by the way; of the beautiful church, with its dark background of wood beaming with all its lighted meadows; of the cheerful scene of light and purple within it; those good country folk in their warm costume; I saw the representative of the Diet of Thyreste enter in his wolf-skin cloak at the church door; I saw the children with their beaming glances; I heard the animated, powerful hymn, "Hail to thee, lovely morning hour!" Yes, that was Christmas life and Christmas joy!

In New Orleans, Christmas is no Christmas. I felt as if I were in a heathen country.

On the evening of Christmas Day I was amused by a fine-speaking, original, elderly lady—a somewhat unusual personage among the women of the New World. Mrs. D. is worldly, but witty and peculiar with a vengeance; does not bend to the world, but has the courage to do what she likes even in dress. And her red velvet blowse, which, without a girdle, inwrapped her like a mantle, whether it is becoming or not in company, is very becoming to her tall, strong figure, which had quite a regal appearance, and was a refreshing sight to me. Thanks, Mrs. D.

If it clears up in the afternoon or in the morning, Mr. H. will take me to see the slave-market, which is one of the great sights of "the gay city." I begin now to have a presentiment of *why* I *must* go down the Mississippi, and why I must visit New Orleans.

December 27th. Three days' rain and bad weather in New Orleans—each day worse than the preceding, with sleet and cold. But I am quite well, my little heart, amuse myself in my excellent, cheerful room, and have to-day again one of those inward spring days which sometimes, in the midst of winter, astonish me with overflowing life, when every thing within my soul lives and grows in an infinite sunshine; when every thought bursts forth into blossom, and, as it were, produces abundant harvests, in a manner which astonishes and enchants me; when the head and breast feel too narrow for the emotions and the presentiments which are agitating within, and will, as it were, burst forth; when I feel myself to be a citizen of the world, and am ready to embrace the whole world; when I live—live—live! But enough of this. I can not, nevertheless, describe the animating impulse within me.

I embrace you and mamma in the fullness of my heart, and now close and send off this letter, for I believe it is long since I last wrote home.

P.S.—*December 28th.* At length a bright and beautiful day, after three days of incessant bad weather. And now one must be up and doing—visit asylums, schools, prisons, and drive out to plantations. I was yesterday, in the midst of the rain, surprised by a visit from unknown friends in New Orleans, warm, cordial people, so that it made me very happy. The heartfelt kindness of one young, amiable girl affected me to tears.

My new friends came with violets and invitations to go

out with them to a plantation up the Mississippi, where they would show me "what slavery really is;" thus speak they who merely see it, or choose to see it, as it is in one or two cases under good masters. But I now know enough not to let myself be beguiled even by good people to believe what a young, handsome gentleman (either stupid or false) assured me last evening, that the slaves in America are "as happy as can be!" My new friends were evidently kind and warm-hearted people, and forgot how often others are different.

When I write next I shall tell you more about the free people, and the slave people, and slavery in the gay city of New Orleans.

LETTER XXXI.

New Orleans, Louisiana, Jan. 1, 1851.

Good-morning! A good new year, my sweet sister, my sweet friend! May the morning of the new year shine brighter on you than it does on me, and the far North afford you a clear sun above the snowy, gleaming earth. Ah! a quiet sun-bright winter's day with us, when all the trees are white over with snow, and every thing shines and gleams kindly and cheerfully in that pure air—that air which is so light and invigorating to breathe—then to ramble forth, as I so often have done at this season, across the fiords and fields of the park, how glorious it was! But here, in this glorious South, it now rains and pours with rain incessantly! The beautiful day on which I last wrote had no successor. To-day we have sleet, and altogether bad weather. The young trees on the La Fayette Market look quite melancholy. The leaves hang on them like tatters. But I am very comfortable in my warm, light, excellent room, and there shines upon my chimney-piece a large bough full of the very sweetest—sweet in every way—little oranges; and beside them stand two large bottles of the genuine Louisiana grape-juice—New-year's gifts from kind new friends, who have brought summer and warmth into room and heart. I have sun enough on this new year, yes, and even a little more, to give away in case any body wanted it.

But I must tell you something about *Bushkiton!* Bushkiton is a festival which was celebrated annually by the Indians of the Mississippi in these southern regions, when the Europeans first intruded themselves here. It appears to me the most remarkable of all the festivals of the North American Indians, and some of its spiritual meaning might have been ingrafted beneficially upon the white race, which has now seized upon the soil of the red man.

This festival occurred at the close of the year, and continued eight days. Each day had its separate ceremony; but the principal features of the whole ceremonial were fasting, purification, and self-contemplation. It is said, in the narrative describing it, "that on these days (the third, fifth, and seventh, if I recollect right) the men sat silent in the market-place." Ashes played a principal part in the purifications; and it appears to me worthy of remark, that these ashes were to be conveyed to the warriors by young maidens who were still half children. The food, also, of which they partook during their fasts, was to be presented to them by these childish hands. The men—for the women are not mentioned at all—held also nocturnal dances by the light of the fire, during which they washed themselves with warm water, in which certain herbs and roots of a medicinal quality had been boiled. The seventh night's dance appears most symbolical and significant. On the seventh day the men again "sit silent in the market-place." The eighth is the last great day of purification. The men then ascend a bank by the river, and throw themselves headlong into it, diving down many times. After this they come out and reassume their every-day garments, manners, and occupations. It is remarkable, however, that after this time every thing which occurred before it is regarded as not having been. All neglect, all quarrels, great or small, between individuals of the nation, are to be forgotten, and life is regarded as if new born. Any one who, after this time, calls to remembrance any annoyance which occurred before it, or evinces any grudge, or cherishes ill will, must pay a fine. Bushkiton returns every year as a festival of reconciliation and renovation. How excellent, if all bitter memories whatever could be washed away by this Indian Lethe! And who shall deny but that Bushkiton, with its inward desire and outward labor, might not be a good help for such purpose.

We civilized people should do well by adopting the Bushkiton of the savages. And there is a custom in the United States, especially in their large cities, and it is said to flourish in New York and New Orleans, which probably may have its origin in the Indians' feast of reconciliation. In these cities, New-year's day is regarded, in some sort, as a day of renovation and reconciliation. New-year's visits are the means made use of. If any quarrel has arisen during the past year between two individuals or between two families, and if they have ceased to see one another or to speak to one another, a visit paid on New-year's day is sufficient, without any further explanation, to make all amicable again between them. And both sides are silently agreed to forget all that is past, and to let life begin anew.

The ladies of "*la haute volée*" do not go out on this day, but sit at home, splendidly dressed in their drawing-rooms, which are decorated for the occasion, to receive gentlemen, who pay complimentary visits; and I have heard it said that many a gentleman who is blessed with a numerous acquaintance in good families makes himself quite ill by incessantly driving about on this day from one house to another, rushing up steps and down steps many hundred times, from morning till late at night.

One kind family among my new friends at New Orleans invited me to spend this day with them, that I might see the cheerful scene. But it would have wearied me, without affording me what I need on New-year's day. If however, there were here any genuine Indian Bushkiton, then would I gladly be present, that I might endeavor to forget. For this I would willingly plunge into the Mississippi, if I could only be certain of—coming up again! God's deep mercy shall be my Bushkiton!

And now, while the weather is bad, and the great world is paying visits and compliments, and polite gentlemen are sunning themselves in the beautiful smiles of elegant ladies, in gas-lighted drawing-rooms, I will, at my ease, converse with you about the occurrences of the last few days, about the slave-market and a slave-auction at which I have been present.

I saw nothing especially repulsive in these places excepting the whole thing; and I can not help feeling a sort of astonishment that such a thing and such scenes are possible in a community calling itself Christian. It seems to me sometimes as if it could not be reality—as if it were a dream.

The great slave-market is held in several houses situated in a particular part of the city. One is soon aware of their neighborhood from the groups of colored men and women, of all shades between black and light yellow, which stand or sit unemployed at the doors. Accompanied by my kind doctor, I visited some of these houses. We saw at one of them the slave-keeper or owner—a kind, good-tempered man, who boasted of the good appearance of his people. The slaves were summoned into a large hall, and arranged in two rows. They were well fed and clothed, but I have heard it said by the people here that they have a very different appearance when they are brought hither, chained together two and two, in long rows, after many days' fatiguing marches.

I observed among the men some really athletic figures, with good countenances and remarkably good foreheads, broad and high. The slightest kind word or joke called forth a sunny smile, full of good humor, on their countenances, and revealed a shining row of beautiful pearl-like teeth. There was one negro in particular—his price was two thousand dollars—to whom I took a great fancy, and I said aloud that "I liked that boy, and I was sure we should be good friends."

"Oh yes, Missis!" with a good, cordial laugh.

Among the women, who were few in number in comparison with the men (there might be from seventy to eighty of them), there were some very pretty light mulattoes. A gentleman took one of the prettiest of them by the chin, and opened her mouth to see the state of her gums and teeth, with no more ceremony than if she had been a horse. Had I been in her place, I believe that I should have bitten his thumb, so much did I feel myself irritated by his behavior, in which he evidently, no more than she, found any thing offensive. Such is the custom of the place.

My inquiries from these poor human chattels confined themselves to the question of whence they came. Most of them came from Missouri and Kentucky. As I was constantly attended by the slave-keeper, I could not ask for any biographical information, nor could I, in any case, have been certain that what I here received was to be relied upon.

In another of these slave-houses I saw a gentleman whose exterior and expression I shall never forget. He seemed to be the owner of the slaves there, and my companion requested permission for himself and me to see them. He consented, but with an air, and a glance at me, as if he would annihilate me. He was a man of unusual size, and singularly handsome. His figure was Herculean, and the head had the features of a Jupiter; but majesty and gentleness were there converted into a hardness which was really horrible. One might just as well have talked about justice and humanity to a block of stone as to that man. One could see by the cold expression of that dark blue eye, by those firmly-closed lips, that he had set his foot upon his own conscience, made an end of all hesitation and doubt, and bade defiance both to heaven and hell. He *would* have *money*. If he could, by crushing the whole human race in his hand, have converted them into money, he would have done it with pleasure. The whole world was to him nothing excepting as a means of making money. The whole world might go to rack and ruin so that he could but rise above it—a rich man, as the only rich and powerful man in the world. If I wanted to portray the image of perfected, hardened selfishness, I would paint that beautiful head. That perfectly dark expression of countenance, the absence of light, life, joy, was only the more striking because the complexion was fair; and the cheeks, although somewhat sunken, had a beautiful bloom. He seemed to be about fifty.

After having visited three slave-houses or camps, and seen some of the rooms in which the slaves were lodged for the night, and which were great garrets without beds, chairs, or tables, I proceeded to the hospital of New Orleans. It is a large institution, and appears to me well managed. There were some cholera patients in it. One young man and a young girl lay dying. I laid my hand upon their foreheads, but they felt it not. They had already sunk into the last sleep.

I dined on this day, the 30th of December, at the house of my countryman, Mr. S., who wished to give me a real New Orleans dinner; and, in particular, a favorite soup in Louisiana, called gumbo, prepared from a kind of groat somewhat resembling sago.

Mr. S. is a lively little man, with a Creole grace of demeanor, very loquacious and kind. He is married—a second marriage—to a French Creole of New Orleans, and has by her several most beautiful little boys, with dark eyes, and dark, flowing locks, like little French children. The wife was also lovely, an excellent, simple creature, who never before had seen an authoress, and now seemed somewhat astonished to find her like other people, able to talk like them also. She seemed to have an idea that a person who wrote a book must talk like a book.

The New Orleans dinner was remarkably good, and gumbo is the crown of all the savory and remarkable soups in the world—a regular elixir of life of the substantial kind. He who has once eaten gumbo may look down disdainfully upon the most genuine turtle soup. After dinner, my hostess, her sister, and myself had a charming gossip over the fire. It was a real refreshment both for tongue and ear to listen to, and to talk French after that unmelodious and confused English language.

In the evening I drank tea with a family of the name of C., planters of Louisiana. Deep sorrow for the loss of two promising children seemed to have depressed the father, and almost crushed the heart of the mother. One daughter, Julia, still remains. When I behold the dance of the moon-beams on the waves; when I perceive the scent of violets and the glance of the mild forget-me-not; when I see any thing which is lovely and full of life, full of innocence and the joy of existence, but which, at the same time, looks as if it would not long linger on earth, I shall think, Julia, of thee, and long to clasp thee once more to my heart, thou pale, lovely, beaming child of the South, and to hold thee yet on earth, that thy mother's heart may not break, and that thy father and thy home may yet have some light!

On the 31st of December I went with my kind and estimable physician to witness a slave-auction, which took place not far from my abode. It was held at one of the small auction-rooms which are found in various parts of New Orleans. The principal scene of slave-auctions is a splendid rotunda, the magnificent dome of which is worthy to resound with songs of freedom. I once went there with Mr. Lerner H., to be present at a great slave-auction; but we arrived too late.

Dr. D. and I entered a large and somewhat cold and dirty hall, on the basement story of a house, and where a great number of people were assembled. About twenty gentlemenlike men stood in a half circle around a dirty wooden platform, which for the moment was unoccupied. On each side, by the wall, stood a number of black men and women, silent and serious. The whole assembly was silent, and it seemed to me as if a heavy gray cloud rested upon it. One heard through the open door the rain falling heavily in the street. The gentlemen looked askance at me with a gloomy expression, and probably wished that they could send me to the North Pole.

Two gentlemen hastily entered; one of them, a tall, stout man, with a gay and good-tempered aspect, evidently a *bon vivant*, ascended the auction platform. I was told that he was an Englishman, and I can believe it from his blooming complexion, which was not American. He came apparently from a good breakfast, and he seemed to be actively employed in swallowing his last mouthful. He took the auctioneer's hammer in his hand, and addressed the assembly much as follows:

" The slaves which I have now to sell, for what price I can get, are a few home-slaves, all the property of one master. This gentleman having given his bond for a friend who afterward became bankrupt, has been obliged to meet his responsibilities by parting with his faithful servants. These slaves are thus sold, not in consequence of any faults which they possess, or for any deficiencies. They are all faithful and excellent servants, and nothing but hard necessity would have compelled their master to part with them. They are worth the highest price, and he who purchases them may be sure that he increases the prosperity of his family."

After this he beckoned to a woman among the blacks to come forward, and he gave her his hand to mount upon the platform, where she remained standing beside him. She was a tall, well-grown mulatto, with a handsome but sorrowful countenance, and a remarkably modest, noble demeanor. She bore on her arm a young sleeping child, upon which, during the whole auction ceremonial, she kept her eyes immovably riveted, with her head cast down. She wore a gray dress made to the throat, and a pale yellow handkerchief, checked with brown, was tied round her head.

The auctioneer now began to laud this woman's good qualities, her skill, and her abilities, to the assembly. He praised her character, her good disposition, order, fidelity; her uncommon qualifications for taking care of a house; her piety, her talents, and remarked that the child which she bore at her breast, and which was to be sold with her, also increased her value. After this he shouted with a loud voice, "Now, gentlemen, how much for this very superior woman, this remarkable, &c., &c., and her child?"

He pointed with his outstretched arm and fore-finger from one to another of the gentlemen who stood around, and first one and then another replied to his appeal with a short silent nod, and all the while he continued in this style:

"Do you offer me five hundred dollars? Gentlemen, I am offered five hundred dollars for this superior woman and her child. It is a sum not to be thought of! She, with her child, is worth double that money. Five hundred and fifty, six hundred, six hundred and fifty, six hundred and sixty, six hundred and seventy. My good gentlemen, why do you not at once say seven hundred dollars for this uncommonly superior woman and her child? Seven hundred dollars—it is downright robbery! She would never have been sold at that price if her master had not been so unfortunate," &c., &c.

The hammer fell heavily; the woman and her child were sold for seven hundred dollars to one of those dark, silent figures before her. Who he was; whether he was good or bad; whether he would lead her into tolerable or intolerable slavery—of all this, the bought and sold woman and mother knew as little as I did, neither to what part of the world he would take her. And the father of her child—where was he?

With eyes still riveted upon that sleeping child, with dejected but yet submissive mien, the handsome mulatto stepped down from the auction-platform to take her stand beside the wall, but on the opposite side of the room.

Next, a very dark young negro girl stepped upon the platform. She wore a bright yellow handkerchief tied very daintily round her head, so that the two ends stood out like little wings, one on each side. Her figure was remarkably trim and neat, and her eyes glanced round the assembly both boldly and inquiringly.

The auctioneer exalted her merits likewise, and then exclaimed,

"How much for this very likely young girl?"

She was soon sold, and, if I recollect rightly, for three hundred and fifty dollars.

After her a young man took his place on the platform. "He was a mulatto, and had a remarkably good countenance, expressive of gentleness and refinement. He had been servant in his former master's family, had been brought up by him, was greatly beloved by him, and deserved to be so—a most excellent young man!"

He sold for six hundred dollars.

After this came an elderly woman, who had also one

of those good-natured, excellent countenances so common among the black population, and whose demeanor and general appearance showed that she too had been in the service of a good master, and, having been accustomed to gentle treatment, had become gentle and happy. All these slaves, as well as the young girl, who looked pert rather than good, bore the impression of having been accustomed to an affectionate family life.

And now, what was to be their future fate? How bitterly, if they fell into the hands of the wicked, would they feel the difference between then and now—how horrible would be their lot! The mother in particular, whose whole soul was centered in her child, and who, perhaps, would have soon to see that child sold away, far away from her—what would then be her state of mind!

No sermon, no anti-slavery oration could speak so powerfully against the institution of slavery as this slave-auction itself!

The master had been good, the servants good also, attached, and faithful, and yet they were sold to whoever would buy them—sold like brute beasts!

In the evening. New-year's day is at an end. I too have had visits from polite gentlemen, hitherto strangers to me. Among them I shall remember, with especial pleasure, two brothers of the name of D., bankers of the city, earnest and cordial men, who are said to be remarkable for their brotherly affection and public spirit. My countryman, Herr Charles S., has sat and talked with me this evening. He has lived long in New Orleans, and knows many circumstances of great interest; is frank and agreeable, so that his society is extremely pleasant to me.

I am as comfortable in this house as I can desire. I have even enjoyed the bad weather, because it has enabled me to read a little, and to draw, and the latter is a necessary repose and refreshment to me. I have sketched the portraits of some of my friends, and painted that of my little attendant here, a pretty dark mulatto, with lovely eyes, and a grand yellow handkerchief around her brow, tied in a manner peculiar to the negroes of Louisiana. She has hitherto been, comparatively speaking, a happy slave.

"Have your owners been kind to you?" inquired I.

"I have never had a bad word from them, Missis!" replied she.

But— there are slave-owners of another kind in New Orleans.

Sunday, January 5th. Hastily and shortly a few words about many things which have occupied me during the last few days, especially yesterday and to-day.

Yesterday forenoon I visited the prisons of the city, accompanied by the superintendents and two distinguished lawyers. The outward management of the prisons seems to me excellent. Order and cleanliness prevail throughout, as is always the case wherever the Anglo-American legislates. I preserve the following features of the internal management.

I visited some rooms where women accused of capital offenses were confined. Their dress spoke of circumstances far removed from poverty, but their countenances of the prevalence of violent and evil passion. Among them I remarked one in particular, a lady charged with the murder of her husband from jealousy, whose whole bearing denoted boldness and pride.

All these women declared their innocence, and complained of injustice. Each one had her own apartment, but might avail herself of companionship in the piazza which surrounded the building within a court. There sat under this piazza a group of negro women, apparently enjoying the sun, which was then shining warmly. They looked so good and quiet, and they all, especially two young girls, bore so evidently the stamp of innocence and of good disposition, that I asked, with no small degree of astonishment,

"Why are these here? What crimes have they committed?"

"They have committed no offense whatever," was the reply. "But their master having given security for a person who is now bankrupt, they are brought in here to prevent their being seized and sold by auction to cover the demand, and here they will remain till their master finds an opportunity of recovering them."

"You see," said one of the lawyers, "that it is to defend them; it is for their advantage that they are here."

"How long will they probably remain here?" inquired I, cogitating within myself as to what particular advantage could be derived by the innocent from that daily association with these white ladies accused of the darkest crimes.

"Oh, at furthest, two or three weeks—quite a short time," replied the lawyer.

One of the young negro girls smiled, half sadly, half bitterly. "Two weeks!" said she; "we have already been here two years!"

I looked at the lawyer. He seemed a little confounded.

"Ah!" said he, "it is extraordinary; something quite unusual—very unusual; altogether an exceptional case—very rare!" And he hurried away from the place.

Again, and always this injustice against human beings whose sole crime is—a dark skin.

Immediately after dinner I paid a visit to the Catholic Orphan Asylum, where two hundred little girls are placed under the care of fifteen Sisters of Mercy—a beautiful and well-managed institution.

Scarcely had I returned thence, when I was taken by some of my acquaintances to the French opera, where I saw "Jerusalem," by Verdi, which was very well given. The prima donna, Mademoiselle D., is a great favorite with the public, and deserves to be so, from her lovely figure, the nobility of her demeanor, and her exquisitely beautiful and melodious singing, although her voice in itself is not remarkable. Her hands and arms are of rare beauty, and their movement was in exquisite harmony with her singing.

The most interesting scene to me, however, was not on the stage, but in the theatre itself, where the ladies of New Orleans, seated in their boxes, presented the appearance of a parterre of white roses. They were all dressed in white, gauze-like dresses, with bare necks and arms, some of them very bare indeed, and some of them with flowers in their hair. All were very pale, but not unhealthy-looking; many of the young were quite pretty, with delicate features, and round, child-like countenances. Beauty is scarce here, as it is all over the world. The white pearl-powder, which the ladies here commonly use, gives to the complexion a great softness, in which, however, the art is too frequently apparent. I do not object to people in social life endeavoring to make themselves as beautiful as possible, but it should be done in the most delicate manner, and well done, otherwise the effect is coarse, and produces an unpleasing effect.

I sat in a box of the amphitheatre (which is divided into boxes) with an agreeable and musical gentleman, Mr. D., an acquaintance of my friend Lerner H.; and I had placed a beautiful white camellia which I received from him in Mrs. G.'s beautiful dark-brown hair, and had the pleasure of seeing it shining out on her beautiful noble head as she sat in her box in the front row. For the rest, I suffered from headache, owing to the heat and exertions of the day, but was so anxious to be quite well by the morrow, when I was to visit the French Market with Mr. Lerner H., that, by means of strong determination and strong coffee, I succeeded; and accordingly, at six o'clock in the early dawn, I and my cavalier took our way to the French portion of the city.

The French Market is in full bloom on Sunday morning each week, and this also shows the difference between the French popular feeling and that of the Anglo-Norman, who would regard such a circumstance as Sabbath-breaking.

The French Market is one of the most lively and picturesque scenes of New Orleans. One feels as if transported at once to a great Paris *marché*, with this difference, that one here meets with various races of people, hears many different languages spoken, and sees the productions of various zones. Here are English, Irish, Germans, French, Spaniards, Mexicans. Here are negroes and Indians. Most of those who offer articles for sale are black Creoles, or natives, who have the French animation and gayety, who speak French fluently, and "*Bon jour, madame! bon jour, madame!*" was addressed to me from many lips with the most cheerful smiles, revealing the whitest of teeth, as I wandered among the stalls, which were piled up with game, and fruit, and flowers, bread and confectionery, grain and vegetables, and innumerable good things all nicely arranged, and showing that abundance in the productions of the earth which involuntarily excited the feeling of a sheer impossibility that there could be any want on the earth, if all was as it should be. The fruit-stalls were really a magnificent sight; they were gorgeous with the splendid fruits of every zone, among which were many tropical ones quite new to me. Between two and three thousand persons, partly purchasers and partly sellers, were here in movement, but through all there prevailed so much good order and so much sunny, amiable vivacity, that one could not help being heartily amused. People breakfasted, and talked, and laughed just as in the markets at Paris, and were vociferous and jocular, especially the blacks—the children of the tropics beaming with life and mirth. The whole was a real sunny Southern scene, full of sunshine, cheerful life, and good humor.

On the outskirts of the market you found Indians. Little Indian girls were seated on the ground, wrapped in their blankets, with their serious, uniform, stiff countenances, and downcast eyes riveted upon an outspread cloth before them, on which were laid out wild roots and herbs which they had brought hither for sale. Behind them, and outside the market-place, Indian boys were shooting with bows and arrows to induce young white gentlemen to purchase their toy weapons. These red boys were adorned with some kind of brilliant ribbon round their brows, and with feathers, forming here also a strong contrast to those pale, modest, and unadorned girls. These Indians were of the Choctaw and Chickasaw tribes, many families of which may still be met with in Western Louisiana.

In the light of the ascending sun, for the sun was also at this market festival, and sucking the juice of delicious oranges, Lerner H. and I left the cheerful scene, and returned leisurely home by the harbor, where immense sugar hogsheads were stored.

Late in the forenoon I went to church. The minister, who is said to be "a genius," preached of human love in a heathenish way, by introducing the words of a celebrated romance:

"If a man does not trouble himself more about his neighbors than about his cattle and his slaves, he does not deserve the name of a good man."

This will suffice for the sermon and the preacher, who was not devoid of talent, especially in delivery, although that was accompanied by too much gesticulation.

Mr. G. took me in the afternoon to see the French burial-ground. It is really "a city of the dead;" whole streets and squares of tombs and graves, all standing above ground, from the fear of the waters below, as the whole ground here is very dropsical; and among these no trees, no grass-plots, nothing green, with the exception of two single graves; no flowers, nothing which testifies of life, of memory, or of love. All was dead; all stony, all desolate; for neither were there here any living beings beside ourselves. Wherever we walked, we walked between walled graves and tombs; wherever we turned, the eye encountered tombs and bare walls, with nothing over them, with no background except the clear blue heaven, for it was bright above the city of the dead. I thus wandered through these immense grave-yards: it was the greatest contrast which could be imagined to the scene of the morning.

To-morrow I shall accompany Mr. and Mrs. G. to Mobile in Alabama, whither I am invited by Mrs. W. le V., whom I have often heard spoken of as a very charming and much celebrated "belle" both in the North and South of the United States. We shall travel by steam-boat across Lake Pontchartrain and into the Gulf of Mexico, on the banks of which Mavilla, now Mobile, is situated.

Mobile, Alabama, Jan. 8th.

Summer, summer, perfect midsummer weather, my little Agatha! Oh! that I could by some magical power transport you to this air, or this air to you, for it would make you strong and happy, as happy as it has made me for the last few days. Ever since the 4th of January, when the weather changed from horrible to enchanting, and yet it had begun to clear up two days before, I have been in a sort of astonishment at such air, and such a delicious sensation as it occasions; and if I only had you here to enjoy it, I should want nothing more.

I left New Orleans on Monday afternoon, in company with the estimable Swedenborgian, Mr. G., and his amiable and truly agreeable lady. It was the most beautiful evening, and the sunset was glorious on Lake Pontchartrain, a large lake which empties itself into the Mexican Gulf, and upon the flat shores of which the planters of Louisiana have their beautiful, luxurious villas and gardens. The steam-boat "Florida," which conveyed us across the quiet, clear lake, was a flower among steam-boats, so ornamental and so pretty, and as yet in all its first freshness. Mr. G., one of the proprietors of the vessel, would not allow me to pay my passage. We inhaled the pleasant air, contemplated the magnificent evening sky, ate, drank, and slept well, and saw, the next morning, the sun rise bright above Mobile.

Mrs. Le V. came to meet me with her carriage. I found her a short, handsome lady, remarkably like Mrs. L. in appearance, bearing, and manner of speaking, but without her coldness of temperament. I had heard so much of Mrs. Le V.'s vivacity and grace that I was surprised to find evident traces of deep sorrow in her countenance. She had suffered, two years ago, blow after blow in the death of her brother and two of her children, since which she has altogether withdrawn herself from society, the ornament of which she had hitherto been. She shut herself within her own room for several months, which were spent in incessant weeping. The visit of Lady Emeline Stuart Wortley to Mobile, her intellectual society, and warm, womanly sympathy, drew the mourner somewhat out of her deep melancholy, and she is recovering by degrees. But all is still a burden to her, and she is, as it were, dead to the pleasures of the world. She believes that she can never overcome that sense of sorrow which seemed to have crushed her. Nevertheless, she is cheerful, and even sometimes laughs heartily—but her eyes show that they have shed many tears.

Yesterday she drove me to a beautiful promenade through a magnolia forest, along the shore of the Mexican Gulf. The magnolia is a laurel with evergreen foliage of a dark but clear color; it is irregular in its form, but tall, and its head, for the most part, round and rich. Thick masses of moss, the *Tillandsia usnoides*, hang like veils over its strong, knotted branches, amid alcoves of dark foliage. It is not a beautiful, but an extremely poetical tree, and when it shoots forth its snow-white fragrant flowers, it seems to recall some beautiful poem of Lord Byron's.

The air was pleasant. The waves of the Mexican Gulf broke softly and broadly against the shore, with a loud but soothing sound. The woods were silent, fresh, and green. I rested, breathed, enjoyed, in deep harmony with the scene around me and the young, amiable lady at my side.

In the evening I went to the theatre, to which I was invited by the theatrical manager, who had the politeness to place a box at my disposal during my stay in the city. I saw an amusing little piece called "Jenny Lind in Heidelberg," which was performed with much humor; and I was greatly pleased by another piece, "The Daughters of the Stars," in which a very young and highly gifted actress, Miss Julia D., caused me, to my surprise, to shed tears. I have never seen any acting in which so much pathos was combined with so much freshness and truth to nature since I saw Jenny Lind at the theatre in Stockholm.

From 7th to 12th July. Beautiful quiet days! I like Mobile, and the people of Mobile, and the weather of Mobile, and every thing in Mobile; I flourish in Mobile. My home here is with Mrs. W., the mother of Mr. Le V., a good old lady, the widow of the former Governor of Florida. The home is sunny and peaceful, and the appearance and demeanor of the negro slaves is sunny and peaceful also. I go out every morning to a camp of Choctaw Indians just outside the city, for it amuses me to see the life and manners of these wild people. In order to reach this camp, I must walk up Government Street, the principal street of the city, a broad, straight alley of beautiful villas, surrounded by trees and garden-plots; the most beautiful young orange-trees, covered with fruit, shine in the sun, and the sun, that beautiful, beneficent southern sun, shines here all day long!

The Indian camp consists of thirteen bark huts, something like our booths at fairs, but always open on one side, at least during the day. Within, the huts have a very poverty-stricken appearance. The whole business and anxiety of the inmates seem to be catering for the stomach. I have been there at various times of the day, and have found them always occupied in eating or in preparing food. This morning they breakfasted on oranges, which, piled up in great heaps, seemed to have been lately fetched to the camp. I suspect that they were not of the very best quality; but it was a very lively scene, those red people eating that splendid fruit on the edge of the splendid sunbright forest. Fire is always burning in front of the bark huts, and old, shriveled, gray-haired women sit by the fire, looking like real witches, sometimes stirring the contents of a kettle over the fire, and sometimes warming their skinny hands, and seeming as if they desired, as much as possible, to envelop themselves in the smoke. The children, who sit in groups around the fire, or leap about the green-sward playing at ball, are handsome, full of animation, and have beautiful dark eyes. The young women are sometimes very much ornamented with armlets and necklaces, and have a deal of painted finery on their cheeks. One meets continually Indian women on their way to the city, carrying on their backs large baskets of light-wood billets, which they are taking thither for sale. These baskets are supported by a broad belt, which they fasten round the forehead, like the Indian women of Minnesota. The men at this season are out hunting in the higher mountain district of Alabama. A couple of them, who are still lingering here, have made themselves a screen of boughs and leaves among the trees, behind which they dress, paint, and adorn themselves. They have rings in their noses, and they attire themselves very showily. One of these Indians is an unusually handsome young man, and wears his hair in long locks falling on his shoulders. I have sketched a couple of the young girls; they look very plump and merry, and in features are not unlike Jewesses, that is to say, such as have broad and flat noses.

These Indians are praised for their integrity, and the exactness with which they keep a promise. Further up the Alabama River, great numbers of Indians are still met with in a savage condition; but a great portion of the State of Alabama is still in a savage condition, not only as regards the country itself, but the manners of its white inhabitants. The state is young, having only obtained its Constitution in 1817, and it has the institution of slavery—the institution of all others least conducive to spiritual and temporal advancement. The fetters of slavery bind the white masters as well as the black servants.

Even Mobile has its slave-market, which I visited, but found there merely a few mulatto girls who remained unsold, and who looked stupid and indifferent, and who proposed to me that I should purchase them.

I have been repeatedly to the theatre, and always amused and interested by the young and promising actress, Miss D. I met her one evening, with a number of others of the theatrical company, at Mrs. Le V.'s. They all appeared agreeable and well-bred people, and young Miss D. was more beautiful in a room than on the stage, and as modest in dress and demeanor as any of the young Puritans of New England. She is accompanied by, or rather she accompanies, her father, who also is an actor of merit. It is evident that actors in the New World take a higher position in educated society than they have yet done in Europe. They do not here form a caste.

I have also seen at Mrs. Le V.'s a great number of the grandees of Mobile, and more lovely young ladies I have never met with. Some of these were from the Northern States, and exhibited that intelligence and life which especially belongs to these states. And again I am compelled to feel that any thing more agreeable than a lovely, refined American woman is scarcely to be found on the face of the earth.

Nor can I remember otherwise than with pleasure some elderly gentlemen, men of office in the states, who were wise and clear on all questions with the exception of slavery. And among the young men, I must have the pleasure of introducing to you, as my especial good friend, the young, gifted poet and dramatic author, Mr. Reynolds, who has accompanied me on many of my rambles, and who has afforded me many an agreeable hour by his excellent heart and genuine conversation. He has prepared for the stage some national historical pieces, and one of his dramas, "Alfred and Inez, or the Siege of St. Augustine," I shall take with me to read on my journey.

Lastly, I must tell you something of my little friend, Mrs. Le V. I mention her last, because she has nestled into the inmost of my heart.

How pleasant it is to be fond of and to love some one! That you know, my Agatha! And it is so strange that that little worldly lady, whom I had heard spoken of as a "belle," and as the most splendid ornament of society wherever she went, has yet become almost as dear to me as a young sister! But she has become so from being so very excellent, because she has suffered much, and because under a worldly exterior there is an unusually sound and pure intellect, and a heart full of affection, which can cast aside all the vanities of the world for the power of gratifying those whom she loves. And with this young lady have I conversed of Transcendentalists and practical Christians, of Mormonism and Christianity, and have found it a pleasure to converse with her, a pleasure to her also which I little expected. We have been involuntarily and naturally attracted to each other, so that we feel as if we had been always acquainted. She says that I have given to her that spiritual food of which she stood in need, and she has given me a pleasure, a gratification which is nourishing to my heart. Octavia le V. will be always united in my soul with the remembrance of the most delicious breezes and odors of the South, with the verdure of magnolia forests, with the fresh roar of the Mexican Gulf, with the sun and the song of birds in the orange groves of Mobile.

This fair daughter of beautiful Florida—for she was born in Florida, and there she spent her youth—is surrounded by a circle of relatives who seem to regard her as the apple of their eye; and if you would see the ideal of the relationship between a lady and her female slave, you should see Octavia le V. and her clever, handsome mulatto attendant, Betsy. Betsy seems really not to live for any thing else than for her Mistress Octavia; to dress her hair, *à la* Mary Stuart, every day, and to see her handsome, gay, and admired, that is Betsy's life and happiness. She has traveled with Octavia in the United States; and when she gets on this subject, and can tell how captivating, how much admired and worshiped was her lady, then is Betsy in her element.

"But ah!" said Betsy, "she is now no longer like herself. Formerly she had such beautiful roses—you should have seen her! No, she has never been like herself since her great sorrow!" And Betsy's eyes fill with tears.

Spite of Betsy's devoted affections—spite of Octavia's seeing in her own and her mother's house none but happy slaves, she still belongs to those whose excellent hearts and understandings do not confuse good and evil. Whenever an opportunity occurs, she simply and earnestly expresses her conviction that slavery is a curse, and on this subject we are perfectly harmonious.

Octavia le V. and I have agreed to go, together to Cuba. In the morning, therefore, we set off to New Orleans, in order early the following day, the 14th, to go on board the steamer "Pacific," which proceeds thither at that time.

The palms of Cuba shall fan Octavia's dejected countenance, and call fresh roses into her cheeks; her beautiful, kind eyes shall grow brighter as they raise themselves to that cloudless heaven; and there will I calmly talk to her of those subjects which can make her happy when I am no longer near her. Such is my dream and my hope.

And now, before I leave Alabama, and the pretty little city in which I have enjoyed so much kindness, I will merely tell you that Alabama is a cotton-growing state, and has in the south plantations, sandy tracts, and apparently thick forests, and in the north beautiful highlands; the Alleghany Mountains become more depressed, and cease, and the prairies also; the scenery along its navigable rivers is celebrated, in particular on the River Mobile, on which Montgomery, the capital of the state, is situated. I have been greatly tempted to make a journey thither. But time! time! Rail-roads, steam-boats, schools, academies have begun, during the later years, to diffuse light and vigorous life within the slave state, the white lady citizens of which, it is said, have, here and there, still a custom of seeking for a higher life's enjoyment by rubbing their gums with snuff, which produces a sort of intoxication very stimulating to the feelings, and to the conversation likewise.

The fascinating ladies of Mavilla must bear the same relation to the snuff-taking ones that the magnolia flower does to the flower of the henbane.

Adieu, beautiful, kind Mobile!

Adieu, my Agatha, my own sister friend. More from Cuba.

New Orleans, January 15th.

Ah no! there is no journey to Cuba this time! The journey from Mobile began under the most promising auspices. Octavia was gay and full of hope; she was now for the first time, after her sorrow, about to leave home and see new objects, and she was pleased to be with me, and I was pleased to be with her. The good Doctor Le V. had presented his little wife with a handsome sum of money, that she might be able thoroughly to enjoy herself in Cuba. Octavia's mother, and her two pretty little girls, had taken an affectionate leave of her, in the hope of seeing her return happy. Betsy was to travel with us, for Betsy spoke Spanish almost as well as Octavia; and Octavia could not dispense with Betsy, nor could Betsy live without Octavia; and Betsy was full of cheerful zeal, and managed cleverly and expeditiously all the business of the journey.

We went on board, and the morning sun arose gloriously over Lake Pontchartrain. We advanced the whole day calmly and in sunshine. We sat in Octavia's spacious cabin—I beg pardon, state-room—amid bouquets of flowers, inhaling the balmy atmosphere through the open window, and reading aloud, or conversing tranquilly with heartfelt, calm emotion. The moon shone gloriously in the evening. We sat on deck. Some gentlemen made our acquaintance; introduced themselves, or were introduced by others, and soon formed a circle around Octavia, whose naturally easy and agreeable style of conversation always exercises a captivating power. It was late when we retired to rest. I perceived in the middle of the night that our course was suddenly checked. I rose and looked out of the window; the moon shone bright over the mirror-like lake, and—we had run aground. It was about one in the morning. The next morning at six o'clock we were to have been at New Orleans, to go on board the "Pacific" at nine! Such had been our plan. But now we must remain where we were until one o'clock the next day, when high water would carry us off. We had run aground on a sand-bank.

The next day was as beautiful as its predecessor; and when certain dark presentiments of our not being able to have any dinner were dissipated by the endeavors of some of the gentlemen, who had themselves rowed to land and there purchased provisions, and a most delicate and abundant dinner was the result, there was nothing disagreeable in our little misadventure, except that the journey to Cuba was delayed to an indefinite time, and that I probably should have to make the journey by myself, as Octavia could not remain so long from home.

It was not until ten o'clock at night that we reached land, and no rail-road train was then running which would convey us to New Orleans. Betsy, who was never without resources, looked after our effects, and took charge of every thing; and two polite gentlemen, who in genuine Anglo-American fashion constituted themselves our cavaliers, conducted us to a country house near the rail-way, where, though the family was absent, a fire was soon lighted for us in a large drawing-room.

It was the most beautiful night. There was a large garden around, which was full of half-tropical plants, of a palm-like growth, such as I had never seen before. I spent a part of the night in wandering about among the beautiful rare plants, all the more rare and beautiful from the moonlight which threw over them its mystical romantic light.

Our polite gentlemen, who had ordered a carriage, finally conveyed us safe and sound to New Orleans. At half past twelve we were at St. Charles's Hotel. It was quite full, and it was with difficulty that we obtained rooms up four flights of stairs. When I entered Octavia's room, I found her bathed in tears, lying with her face downward on a chair, and Betsy standing in the middle of the room, in a state of consternation, with her eyes riveted on her mistress.

"It was here, in this very room," whispered Betsy to me, "that she (casting a glance on Octavia) lived two years ago, with those two little girls, and here she dressed them for a children's ball!"

I raised gently the head of the weeping Octavia. She said mildly,

"Will you change rooms with me?"

"Most willingly!" replied I.

Betsy and I removed Octavia into my room, nor did I leave her until I saw her somewhat calmer.

Our rooms were nearly under the roof, and I could not prevent myself measuring, with my eye, the distance from my window down to the court below, thinking what sort of leap I should have to make in case of fire breaking out in the hotel during the night—for people must always keep themselves prepared for such emergencies in the great cities of America. I started with the conviction that such a leap as that would be—my very last.

The next morning I was glad and thankful to find myself calmly in my bed. I found my poor Octavia still sadly out of spirits, but I was so tender of her in her sorrow that I succeeded in drawing her away from images of death and corruption.

I shall this afternoon leave this hotel and remove to a private family, to which I am invited by young Miss W., from Massachusetts, in the name of her cousin. There was something so agreeable to me in her whole person and manner, and even in her mode of inviting me, that I immediately felt an inclination to accept the invitation, and gave a half promise. I had done that before I came to Mobile, and now this forenoon Miss W. called on me, and said, with her refined and somewhat arch smile, and her calm, resolute bearing,

"I consider myself, Miss Bremer, to have a right to inquire why you are at this place?"

I could not do other than consent to be taken to Annunciation Street, and to the house of Mr. C., this very afternoon. Miss W. obviated all my *but*'s and *if*'s; she is a true descendant of the Pilgrims in her steadfastness of purpose, to which is added that charm which makes it irresistible.

I here find myself once more among friends, Mr. Lerner H., Mr. and Mrs. G., with whom I shall, in about an hour's time, drive out upon a road, about six miles long, made of cockle-shells, which runs along the shore. It is one of the remarkable things of New Orleans. Mr. G. resides at Cincinnati, but has business at New Orleans, and he and his wife will remain at an hotel here during the winter months, together with their two children, two magnificent boys, the youngest still quite young, and their nurse, a stout, capital negro woman, a free negro, but bound by the silken bonds of attachment, stronger than the iron fetters of slavery. Many families take up their abode thus at hotels for several months, and many young couples live in the same way also during the first months of their marriage. That, however, is not so much because they relish hotel life, as because it is very expensive to establish themselves in their own houses in America, and a family generally will have a house wholly to themselves. A young couple will frequently not wait to be married until they are wealthy enough "to keep house," as it is termed. That, however, in the mean time, is the object after which they strive. I have heard many ladies complain of the emptiness and weariness of life in an hotel, and deplore its influence on young girls, who have in it only too many temptations to live merely for pleasure, admiration, and vanity.

Later. I have seen Octavia once more the ornament of society, although still pale and her eyes red with weeping, dressed in grand costume, in a black satin dress, which, from its many points and adornments, I call *Yucca gloriosa*, surrounded by a little court of gentlemen, "*faire la belle conversation,*" in one of the splendid drawing-rooms of the hotel. Friends and admirers will soon make Octavia lively here, and I can now leave her comfortably, and go to a quieter home and to my amiable North Americans. Octavia is a rose, Anne W. is a diamond, Mrs. G. a genuine pearl, and you—you are my Agatha!

Annunciation Street, January 19th.

My dear Heart! * * * *

January 20th. I began to write, but was interrupted, on the second day after my removal to this good, quiet home, the home of a young couple, gentle and quiet people, who seem to live wholly and entirely for each other and their two little children, the youngest still a baby, just now beginning to open his little rosy mouth, and smile and coo. It was the most glorious weather on the afternoon and evening of the day on which I removed here; I can not describe the deliciousness of the air, the serenity of the heavens, the enchanting beauty of the sun, the clouds, the moon, and the stars on this day, when merely to live, to see, and to breathe sufficed to give a fullness to life. Miss W. and I sat out on the piazza with oleanders and magnolias around us, and enjoyed this affluence of nature. Tall aloes, the Yucca gloriosa, and many rare trees and plants, shone out verdantly from the little flower-beds of the garden which surround the lovely house. I enjoyed, besides this, her conversation, which is distinguished by its freshness and originality, its perfectly independent and earnest mode of feeling and judging. I again perceived that imprisoned fire which I had before seen glimmering in her clear, dark-brown eyes, diamond-like and still. It warmed me. We talked about Jane Eyre, and I for the first time heard any one openly express my own secret wishes with regard to Jane's behavior to Rochester. I love that virtue which is above conventional morality, and which knows something better than to be merely—free from blame.

But I ought to tell you the cause of the interruption in my letter yesterday. First it was the cold, and then it was the fire. I will explain. The day which succeeded that beautiful summer-day of which I have spoken was wretched weather, so cold that it shook both soul and body, and made me so irritable and so out of humor, that I thanked my good fortune not to have slaves, and that I thus should not be excited to wreak my bad temper on them. Never, until I came into America, had I any experience of the power which the feelings of the body can have over the soul. God help the slave-owner and the slave in this variable climate, the penetrative atmosphere of which causes both body and soul to vibrate according to its temperature.

Well, I was frozen, but I had a fire in my large, handsome room. Octavia le V. came, and Mrs. G., for I had begun to sketch their portraits in my album, and they were to sit to me.

I enjoyed the contemplation and the drawing of these two amiable ladies, the noble, earnest, regular profile of Mrs. G., and the round, child-like, piquant countenance of Octavia le V., with its little turned-up nose, which I imagine resembles Cleopatra's, and its fantastic arrangement of the hair, the artistic labor of Betsy's hands. We were very comfortable; Mrs. G. sat before the fire, Octavia before me, and we were talking earnestly and cheerfully about *love*, when a messenger came to Mrs. G. from her husband requesting her to send her keys. St. Charles's Hotel was on fire.

Mrs. G. could not be easy to remain; she knew that her husband and her children were at the burning hotel, and thither she hastened.

Octavia le V. had, before she came to me, given Betsy leave to go out, and had locked her room door. There was no one at the hotel who would take charge of her room or her effects. Her beautiful wardrobe, her casket containing several hundred dollars, destined to defray the expenses of her journey to Cuba, all would probably become the prey of the flames.

"Ah! it is quite certain every thing will be destroyed,"

said Octavia, and sat tranquilly before me, an image of unexampled equanimity. The heart which had bled with the deepest sorrow could not agitate itself by the loss of earthly possessions; the eye which had wept so long over a beloved brother and those dear children, had no tears for worldly adversity. I saw this evidently, while Octavia calmly reckoned up every thing which her room contained, and which would now be consumed. She said that early that morning she had seen a volume of black smoke issue from under her bed. She gave the alarm, and sent a message to the master of the hotel, who replied that there was no danger; that the smoke had merely found its way thither through a defect in one of the chimney-flues, and that all would soon be put to rights. An hour afterward smoke was again in the room; but it seemed perfectly to have subsided when she left the hotel.

I had seen so much of Betsy's precaution and alertness, as well as affection for her mistress, that I could not but hope for and rely upon her help on this occasion.

"She will soon," said I, "hear of the fire, and then she will immediately hasten to the place, and find some means of saving your property."

"She will not hear of it," said Octavia; "she has gone a long way out of the city. The hotel is built of wood, and the fire will consume it in a few hours; besides, I am certain that the fire has broke out near my room. Oh, no! all the things will be destroyed."

The loss seemed as nothing to Octavia. She was much more uneasy on account of the distress which her husband and her mother would feel if they should hear of the circumstance before she wrote.

In the mean time, as hour after hour went on, and we received no tidings either from Betsy or from St. Charles's, Octavia determined to go to one of her friends, who dwelt not far from the great hotel, that she might there gain some information, or even still go to the place itself.

When she had been gone about an hour, there was a hasty ring at the gate which leads from the garden into the street. I recognized Betsy, and rushed down to speak to her.

"How is it, Betsy?" cried I.

"All safe!" said she, so out of breath that she could hardly speak, but with a beaming countenance. "I have all the money with me!" and she laid her hand upon her breast. "Where is my Missis?"

"I believe that she is gone to St. Charles's," said I.

"There is no longer a St. Charles's," said Betsy. "It is burned to the ground!"

And so it was. In less than three hours' time that splendid building was a heap of ashes, and its population of nearly four hundred persons were houseless.

I went out with Betsy to seek for Mrs. Le V.

On our way, that faithful creature told me how the rumor of the fire had reached her, how she had hastened to the hotel, how one of the gentlemen there, a friend of Mrs. Le V., had broken open the door of her room, and how he and Betsy had saved all Octavia's property. Not an article was lost. Betsy told me still more as we went along, of how much she loved her mistress; of how she might have been married more than once, and how there was still a free man in the North who would gladly have her, but she could not think of leaving Mrs. Le V. "She was so fond of her, she should never leave her."

But who would not be fond of Octavia?

When we reached the residence of Mrs. Le V.'s friend, we found that she had been taken thence to a small hotel in the neighborhood of St. Charles, and thither Betsy hastened to seek for her.

With the thought of Mrs. G. I went to the scene of conflagration, in the hope of hearing some tidings of her there, and was fortunate enough, when near the place, to meet her eldest son, and to hear from him that she, his father, and little brother were all well lodged in the house of a friend at no great distance. I passed St. Charles's; merely a small number of people were now busied about the fire. It had done its work, and the flames were now consuming the lower portion of the beautiful colonnades, and ravaging the remains of the basement story. The burning ruins produced a very picturesque effect. Not a trace of tumult or disorder appeared on the open space in front. Every thing had been already disposed of and housed elsewhere; every thing was tranquil. It was now only about four hours from the outbreak of the fire, and I have heard to-day that a subscription is already on foot to erect another St. Charles's. American expedition!

A few persons have been injured by the fire, and many have lost their effects. The fire broke out just by Octavia's room, which was very near mine. How fortunate that it did not happen in the night!

I do not grieve about St. Charles's. It was, in my opinion, a dear, uncomfortable, splendid hotel, and worthy of such a death! I was obliged to pay four dollars and a quarter for a residence there of one night and half a day in a dark room, four stories high. But Louisiana is a very dear place, the dearest in the United States.

From 20th to 27th January. Quiet days, but disagreeable weather! Since the day when I last wrote, and when the weather had changed from warm to bitterly cold, it has rained incessantly, and been cold and cheerless with a perseverance such as I scarcely ever saw before. Not a blue speck in the heavens, not a sunbeam—perpetual fog, sleet, and gray cold. To-day, for the first time, it has cleared up, and seems as if it would again become pleasant. This weather has caused many excursions, both within and out of the city, to be deferred. But how thankful I am for my quiet and pleasant home during this time! Mr. and Mrs. C. are kind, gentle, and very quiet people, and that order and comfort, which is a distinguishing feature of American homes, prevails in their house. Anne W. is full of life and quiet fire, imprisoned within her, as in the diamond; she is an intellectual and interesting being, who affords me great pleasure, from the originality of her character, and her reading aloud in the evening. In this way she has made me acquainted with various English poets hitherto almost unknown to me. It has been a great pleasure to me to hear her read Shelley's magnificent poem, "Prometheus Unbound," which would be the most glorious poem of the age if its conclusion had been equal to its opening scenes. But this is stranded on a threadbare morality. I have also enjoyed the reading of Browning's poems and dramatic pieces, as well as some by Elizabeth Barrett, the wife of Browning. Browning does not appear to me great as an artist. There is a deficiency of strength and coherence in his compositions. But a something singularly grand and pure in feeling and tendency gladdens and warms the heart. A spirit of noble, self-sufficing heroism permeates his poems. One feels one's self refreshed as by the waftings of a something divinely great.

I spent one evening with Mr. and Mrs. D., friends of Mr. Lerner H., and heard good music, well played by amateur musicians, gentlemen and ladies of the Northern States. Another evening I attended the opera, where I heard Meyerbeer's "Prophète." The piece is unpoetical and meagre in its conception, but it affords grand spectacle, and the music of Meyerbeer has, in all cases, some dramatic, characteristically beautiful parts. Mrs. D., who performed the part of the mother of the prophet, played and sang nobly and well. The prophet was a wearisome person, so was his beloved. If the piece, instead of being founded on a poor love intrigue, had been sustained by religious fanaticism and spiritual pride, such as we meet with in the historical prophet, John of Leyden, the opera would have had a true interest. As it is, there is no food for thought, and it excited my nerves to that degree with its continual startling effects, that it was with difficulty I could keep my eyes open. The last scene was monstrously magnificent, and woke me up a little. The sight of the white-garmented, lovely young Creoles in the pit and boxes charmed my eyes as before. But I discovered some pearl-powdered noses on the faces of some of the elderly ladies.

I have also visited asylums and schools in consequence of invitations. New Orleans is divided into three municipalities; the schools are said to have greatly improved within the last few years. Teachers, both male and female, come hither from the Northern States, and wherever they come, they bring with them that energetic educational life which distinguishes those states. A female teacher in one of the schools of New Orleans can obtain a salary of one thousand dollars annually; but the living, on the other hand, costs three times as much as in the other states of the Union.

I heard the boys in the great boys' school singing boldly the praise of their native land, as

> The land of the brave and the land of the free!

This is sung in the slave states without any one perceiving the satire of the domestic institution which such praise implies.

Thus, from childhood upward, is the natural sense of right, and the pure glance of youth, falsified by the institution of slavery.

And it does not operate injuriously merely upon the upright mind of the child, so that it does not perceive the lie, but also upon its heart and its character. A noble lady of New Orleans, who has resided here some years, told me a great deal of the unhappy effects of slavery upon the education of the child, and its influence in making the young disposition stubborn and intractable. The child, surrounded by slaves from the cradle, accustoms himself to command them, to have all his caprices gratified, or to see the refusal punished, often with cruelty. Hence results that violence of temper, and those ferocious and bloody scenes which are of such frequent occurrence in the slave states. And how can it be otherwise? Even I have seen a few examples of the behavior of children to slaves, which has shown how much this institution tends to develop the naturally despotic disposition of the child.

I visited a school for young girls, where I could not but admire their capacity for making intellectual *salto mortales.*

During the examination which the superintendent caused them to pass through, and which they passed through with remarkable ability, the questions were proposed something in this style:

"What is snow? How large is the standing army of the Emperor of Russia? Where is Lapland? Who was Napoleon? What is saltpetre? How far is the earth from the sun? When did Shakspeare live? In what year did Washington die? What is the amount of the population of France? What is the moon?" and so on.

The girls answered in chorus, very quickly, and for the most part quite correctly. The whole examination was a succession of surprises to me, and I can not do other than admire the kind of order which must be obtained in those young souls, from their contact with snow, the standing army of Russia, Lapland, Napoleon, saltpetre, Washington, the population of France, and the moon!

I must now tell you about a real African tornado which Anne W. and I witnessed last Sunday afternoon. It was in the African Church, for even here, in this gay, light-hearted city of New Orleans, has Christianity commenced its work of renovated life; and they have Sunday-schools for negro children, where they receive instruction about the Savior; and the negro slaves are able to serve God in their own church.

We came too late to hear the sermon in this African Church, whither we had betaken ourselves. But at the close of the service, a so-called class-meeting was held. I do not know whether I have already said that the Methodists form, within their community, certain divisions or classes, which elect their own leaders or exhorters. These exhorters go round at the class-meeting to such of the members of their class as they deem to stand in need of consolation or encouragement, talk to them, aloud or in an under voice, receive their confessions, impart advice to them, and so on. I had seen such a class-meeting at Washington, and knew, therefore, what was the kind of scene which we might expect. But my expectations were quite exceeded here. Here we were nearer the tropical sun than at Washington.

The exhorters went round, and began to converse here and there with the people who sat on the benches. Scarcely, however, had they talked for a minute before the person addressed came into a state of exaltation, and began to speak and to perorate more loudly and more vehemently than the exhorter himself, and so to overpower him. There was one exhorter in particular, whose black, good-natured countenance was illumined by so great a degree of the inward light, by so much good-humor and joy, that it was a pleasure to see him, and to hear him too; for, although his phrases were pretty much the same, and the same over again, yet they were words full of Christian pith and marrow, and they were uttered with so much cordiality, that they could not do other than go straight to the heart with enlivening power. Sometimes his ideas seemed to come to an end, and he stood, as it were, seeking for a moment; but then he would begin again with what he had just now said, and his words always brought with them the same warmth and faithfulness, and he looked like a life-infusing sunbeam. And it was only as the messenger of the joy in Christ that he preached:

"Hold fast by Christ! He is the Lord! He is the mighty One! He will help! He will do every thing well! Trust in him, my sister, my brother. Call upon him. Yes. Yes. Hold fast by Christ! He is the Lord!" &c., &c.

By degrees the noise increased in the church, and became a storm of voices and cries. The words were heard, "Yes, come Lord Jesus! Come, oh come, oh glory!" and they who thus cried aloud began to leap—leaped aloft with a motion as of a cork flying out of a bottle, while they waved their arms and their handkerchiefs in the air, as if they were endeavoring to bring something down, and all the while crying aloud, "Come, oh come!" And as they leaped, they twisted their bodies round in a sort of cork-screw fashion, and were evidently in a state of convulsion; sometimes they fell down and rolled in the aisle, amid loud, lamenting cries and groans. I saw our tropical exhorter, the man with the sun-bright countenance, talking to a young negro with a crooked nose and eyes that squinted, and he too very soon began to talk and to preach, as he sprung high into the air, leaping up and down with incredible elasticity. Whichever way we looked in the church, we saw somebody leaping up and fanning the air; the whole church seemed transformed into a regular Bedlam, and the noise and the tumult was horrible. Still, however, the exhorters made their rounds with beaming countenances, as if they were in their right element, and as if every thing were going on as it ought to do. Presently we saw our hearty exhorter address a few words to a tall, handsome mulatto woman, who sat before us, and while he was preaching to her she began to preach to him; both talked for some time with evident enchantment, till she also got into motion, and sprang aloft with such vehemence, that three other women took hold of her by the skirts, as if to hold her still on the earth. Two of these laughed quietly, while they continued to hold her down, and she to leap up and throw her arms around. At length she fell and rolled about amid convulsive groans. After that she rose up and began to walk about, up and down the church, with outspread arms, ejaculating every now and then, "Halleluiah!" Her appearance was now calm, earnest, and really beautiful. Amid all the wild tumult of crying and leaping, on the right hand and the left, she continued to walk up and down the church, in all directions, with outspread arms, eyes cast upward, exclaiming, in a low voice, "Halleluiah! Halleluiah!" At length she sank down upon her knees on the platform by the altar, and there she became still.

After the crying and the leaping had continued for a good quarter of an hour longer, several negroes raised the mulatto woman, who was lying prostrate by the altar. She was now quite rigid. They bore her to a bench in front of us, and laid her down upon it.

"What has happened to her?" inquired Anne W. from a young negro girl whom she knew.

"Converted!" said she laconically, and joined those who were softly rubbing the pulses of the converted.

I laid my hand upon her brow. It was quite cold, so also were her hands.

When, by degrees, she had recovered consciousness, her glance was still fixed, but it seemed to me that it was directed rather inwardly than outwardly; she talked to herself in a low voice, and such a beautiful, blissful expression was portrayed in her countenance, that I would willingly experience that which she then experienced, saw, or perceived. It was no ordinary, no earthly scene. Her countenance was as it were transfigured. As soon as, after deep sighs, she had returned to her usual state, her appearance became usual also. But her demeanor was changed; she wept much, but calmly and silently.

The tornado gradually subsided in the church; shrieking and leaping, admonishing and preaching, all became hushed; and now people shook hands with each other, talked, laughed, congratulated one another so heartily, so cheerfully, with such cordial warmth and good-will, that it was a pleasure to behold. Of the whole raging, exciting scene there remained merely a feeling of satisfaction and pleasure, as if they had been together at some joyful feast.

I confess, however, to having been thoroughly amused by the frolic. Not so Anne W., who regarded that disorderly, wild worship with a feeling of astonishment, almost of indignation; and when our warm-hearted exhorter came up to us, and, turning especially to her, apologized for not having observed us before, that it was with no intention to neglect us, and so on, I saw her lovely coral-red upper lip curl with a bitter scorn as she replied, "I can not see in what respect you have neglected us." The man looked as if he would have been glad, with all his heart, to have preached to us, and, for my own part, I would gladly have listened to his Christian exhortation, given with its African ardor. We shook hands, however, in the name of our common Lord and Master.

And spite of all the irrationality and the want of good taste which may be felt in such scenes, I am certain that there is in them, although as yet in a chaotic state, the element of true African worship. Give only intelligence, order, system to this outbreak of the warm emotions, longings, and presentiments of life, and then that which now appears hideous will become beautiful, that which is discordant will become harmonious. The children of Africa may yet give us a form of divine worship in which invocation, supplication, and songs of praise may respond to the inner life of the fervent soul!

How many there are, even in our cold North, who in their youthful years have felt an Africa of religious life, and who might have produced glorious flowers and fruits if it only could have existed—if it had not been smothered by the snow and the gray coldness of conventionality—had not been imprisoned in the stone church of custom.

I have visited some other churches in New Orleans, a Unitarian, an Episcopalian, and a Catholic Church, the last with the name dear to me, that of St. Theresa. But the heavenly spirit of St. Theresa was not there. An Irishman jabbered an unintelligible jargon, and in not one of these houses of God could I observe or obtain that which I sought for—*edification.* There was, at all events, life and ardor in the church of the negro assembly.

What more have I to tell you about New Orleans? That it is a large city of one hundred thousand inhabitants, and the commercial capital of the southern portion of the Mississippi Valley, you can learn from books. The crescent-formed site of the city on the Mississippi is beautiful, and it has some handsome streets and markets, and splendid houses surrounded with trees and shrubs, like other American cities. The French and older portions of the city have a more bald and business-like character; but New Orleans is beyond every thing else a business and trading city, and it is far behind the other large cities of the United States as regards institutions for a higher intellectual and moral culture. It does not possess any means of artistic enjoyment, excepting at the theatres, and these, especially as regards dramatic scenes, do not take a very elevated stand.

At the present moment, people here are occupied with the prosecution of several of the gentlemen who accompanied Lopez as leaders on his robber expedition to Cuba. Lopez has been released on his finding surety to a considerable amount—15,000 dollars, I believe—but a certain Colonel Henderson, and others, have yet to be tried, and are to plead their own cause, as they are said to be possessed of great ability in—making speeches. The New Orleans gentlemen laugh, and call the whole thing "a farce," which will not result in any thing but—long speeches! There is no earnestness in the prosecution, and this gives rise to somewhat more than a suspicion that certain slave states have an interest in the expedition.

I have rambled about the city during the few fine days which have occurred while I have been here, but have found few objects of interest for the eye, excepting those lovely, colored Creole women, who, with their delicate features, fine eyes, and pretty heads, adorned with showy handkerchiefs, tastefully arranged, according to the custom of New Orleans, produce a very *piquante* appearance; and I have seen in the streets young servant-girls, quadroons, whose beauty was perfect. Their figures also are generally slender, and remarkably well-proportioned.

New Orleans has long been known as a "very gay city," but has not so good a reputation for its morality, into which French levity is strongly infused. This, however, it is said, decreases in proportion as the Anglo-American people obtain sway in the city. And their influence grows even here rapidly. The French population, on the contrary, does not increase, and their influence is on the decline. Nor have I heard the most favorable testimony given to the commercial morality of New Orleans. On one occasion I heard a merchant, a friend of mine, say, as he stood among the sugar-hogsheads on one of the great wharves of the city, "There has been more rascality practiced on this very place than would be sufficient to sink the whole city!"

Nevertheless, there is a good public spirit at work to make the city worthy to maintain its place on the earth. One excellent institution now in progress of erection here is a large sailors' home, in which it is intended to board and lodge in an excellent manner, and at a reasonable rate, sailors whose vessels are lying in the harbor either to land or to take in cargo. Hitherto, mariners arriving at the city have had no other abode than in ale-houses, which were regular nests of thieves. The large and magnificent house which is now being erected by good men of the city, will henceforth provide a comfortable and safe haven for the mariner. Two of my gentlemen friends, who are working for this cause, hope to interest Jenny Lind in it, who is shortly expected hither from Cuba; and as the house is intended for the benefit of the Swedish as well as any other seamen, it is probable that this patriotic and generous Swede will interest herself in its behalf.

I read to-day in a New Orleans paper, "The Daily Picayune" (picayune is the name of a little Spanish silver coin which is current here, value sixpence), a beautiful and earnest address to the inhabitants of New Orleans, beseeching them to leave the celebrated Swedish singer at full liberty in the exercise of her well-known beneficence, and not to fail in proper respect to a stranger by their obtrusiveness or exhortations, etc.

And it must be confessed, that although Jenny Lind has often had just cause to complain of the Americans' well-meant, but frequently thoughtless and childish obtrusiveness, yet I have often had opportunities of knowing and admiring the beautiful and magnanimous manner in which people here have felt for her. How many there are who have satisfied themselves by a silent benediction rather than cause her a moment's annoyance; how many who would not allow themselves to approach her, because they knew that they could not give her pleasure by so doing, nor would venture to invite her to their homes for the same reason.

I remember hearing an estimable old gentleman, a judge at Cincinnati—a magnificent old man he was!—say that he accompanied her, in the newspapers, every step of her journey, with that interest and solicitude which a father might have for his daughter; and that he felt real distress that she should, in any degree, compromise her beautiful reputation by any unadvised step. And I have heard so much said about Jenny Lind in America, that I know that while people love in her the singer and the giver of money, they love still more the young woman, in her beautiful *rôle* and reputation—the ideal Jenny Lind.

But I must now speak of Louisiana and New Orleans. Louisiana, as you know, was first discovered by the Spaniards and French. The French were the first who attempted to colonize Louisiana. They began and left off, and then began afresh. It would not succeed. But a great deal was said in France and England about Louisiana as a promised land, an El Dorado, with immeasurable internal wealth ready to be brought to light, and faith in this gave rise to the gigantic financial speculation of John Law, based upon the fabulous, delusive wealth of Louisiana, and afterward to the great bankruptcy of all who had taken part in that wild speculation. Louisiana, or that vast country embracing the southern part of the Mississippi, and which at that time included Arkansas, passed afterward from the dominion of the French to that of the Spaniards, then back to that of the French, until, in the year 1803, Louisiana was purchased by the government of the United States, and united to them as an independent state. In the mean time, Louisiana had been cultivated and peopled by the French, Spaniards, English, Germans, and other nations, and New Orleans had slowly grown up amid inundations and hurricanes, and with small prospect of ever becoming that "crescent city" which it now is.

The population of Louisiana did not exceed fifty thousand souls, not reckoning the Indians, when it was incorporated with the United States. Seven years later the amount of its population was three-fold. The new epoch, and new life, however, of both Louisiana and New Orleans, first commenced when, in the year 1812, the first steam-boat came thither upon the Great River. This was soon followed by hundreds of other steam-boats, and New Orleans rapidly increased to a city of the first rank among the cities of the South.

The whole of Louisiana is flat, in part swampy and under water, and in part rich and fertile country; sugar, cotton, maize, rice, indigo, are the products of Louisiana. In the northern portion, where the sand elevates itself into little hills, are forests, which abound in many kinds of trees—oak, chestnut, walnut, sassafras, magnolia, and poplar. In the south the palmetto, mulberry, live-oak, cedar, and pine, and every where an abundant growth of the wild vine. There are also many navigable rivers, tributaries of the Mississippi, which, as well as bogs and small lakes, abound in alligators. These alligators, though they do not venture to attack full-grown men, not unfrequently carry off little negro children. Louisiana is said to produce many poisonous plants, serpents, and other noxious creatures. It seems to me an undesirable place in every way. I would not live in it for all its sugar and cotton.

I must now tell something of the internal history of New Orleans, or, rather, a story which has struck me. That noble-minded Mr. Poinsett, the old ex-minister of South Carolina, told me that slavery seemed to operate still more prejudicially on women than on men, and that women not unfrequently were found to be the cruelest slave-owners. And, whether it was a mere accident or a confirmation of the truth of this assertion, the most terrible instances which I heard mentioned in South Carolina of the maltreatment of slaves were of women, and of women belonging to the higher grades of society. I believe I already have told you of the two ladies in Charleston who were publicly accused for the murder of their slaves, the one by hunger, the other by flogging, and who, although they were acquitted by cowardly laws and lawyers, yet fell under the ban of public opprobrium, and were left to a dishonorable solitude and to—the judgment of God.

My friend of the Mississippi, the pure conscience of

Louisiana, had asserted the same fact as Mr. Poinsett, and, as if it were in substantiation thereof, New Orleans has not in its chronicle of crime a more bloody or a more detested name than that of—a woman, Mrs. Lallorue, born Macarthy. It is to the honor of New Orleans that this wealthy lady has been obliged to fly from the fury of its hatred. But how long before that time had she tormented her victims?

It appears that the behavior of her brother to his mistresses of the colored race excited her hatred toward them. Other slave-owners maltreat their slaves in the irritation of the moment or the excess of temper, but Madamè Lallorue maltreated hers because she enjoyed and relished their sufferings. She was the possessor of a large plantation, and indulged upon it her arbitrary sway in such a manner as roused her neighbors in arms against her. They announced to her that they would no longer hear of such transactions; and that in case they did, she should become amenable to law.

On this, Madame Lallorue fled to New Orleans, where, less under observation, she could devote herself to her own private pleasure. She here derived an income by hiring out her slaves, who every week were compelled to bring home their earnings to her. If, however, they did not return to the time, or if their earnings were less than she thought proper—woe to them! Her own house-slaves had no better fate; on the slightest occasion—which never fails for those who desire it—she confined them in the cellar, fettered with iron chains, where she visited them only to practice her cruelty on them. I will not tell you the means which she used to indulge her lust of cruelty—the chronicles of heathenism and fanaticism know nothing worse. Enough—the doleful cries of her victims found their way above ground, through stone walls and bolted door, and made themselves heard. It was noised abroad in the city. The heart of the people swelled with indignation. They gathered in crowds round the house in which she lived; they vowed to release the victims, to pull down the house, and take vengeance on this monster in the shape of woman. The business was in rapid progress; the walls of the house were beginning to fall, when —the mayor appeared with an armed force. Madame Lallorue's house was preserved, and an opportunity was afforded her to escape through a back gate. She fled, half dressed, out of New Orleans; and, somewhat later, left America.

She afterward lived in Paris, and received there the income of an immense property acquired in Louisiana, by what means we know. She died, it is said, only a short time since. Who can doubt a hell after death when they see the life and pleasure of such persons on earth! Madame Lallorue's husband, a Frenchman, still resides in New Orleans, and is said to be a man of good character. He must at that time have lived separate from his wife.

This circumstance occurred ten or twelve years since.

If it really be true that women are the worst of slave-owners, it must proceed from their temperament being in general more excitable, and from the climate having an unusually irritating effect upon the nervous system by its stimulating character; besides which, women generally exceed men in their extremes either of good or evil; they are by nature more eccentric, more spiritual, nearer the spirits, whether they be angels or devils.

In Sweden also—in the highest circles of Stockholm—we have known ladies whose domestics bore bloody marks, and whom the police were obliged to take in charge. Countess L. was amiable, kind, agreeable to every body except her domestics, and she was not able to keep a servant in her house beyond six weeks. We have had the ladies of two foreign ministers—both English—both of whom, from their treatment of their servants, deserved the Christmas gift which one of them received from an acquaintance of the family—a bloody medal of bravery! A good thing is it that the servants of these ladies could leave them, thanks to the laws of a free country! But here, in this *free* country, people can, in the face of such facts, still defend slavery as a patriarchal institution, quite compatible with the laws of a free people, and with human rights and happiness!

I have had here several contests with a lady who defends these opinions, and who, in order to prove the justice and equity of slavery, and the happiness of the negro slaves under this excellent institution, avails herself of arguments and sophisms, backward and forward, with such an amazing contempt of logic and all sound reason, that I have sometimes become dumb from sheer astonishment.

I avoid, in a general way, as much as possible, conversation on this subject. The question of slavery is a sore eye which winches at the slightest touch. It is painful to the good, and it irritates those who are not good, while it serves no purpose one way or the other. I am therefore silent when I can be so with an easy conscience; but for all that, it is evident that the question can not rest; that the work of light has commenced for the release of the children of Africa, and that their condition, even here, is improving with every passing year.

I would gladly tell you of some good female slave-owner who might be placed as a counterbalance to Mrs. Lallorue, but—I do not know any; such, however, must exist. The very bad make a great noise, and the good but very little. But I must tell you of a gentleman, a slave-owner, who seems to me to stand in the slave states as an opened door to the house of bondage.

Two years ago there died in New Orleans a gentleman named Macdonald, who left behind him a property of many millions of dollars, the whole of which he bequeathed for purposes of public benevolence in Louisiana. This singular man, who lived in the most miserly manner, expended next to nothing upon himself, and never gave away any thing, not even to his near relatives, who were almost perishing of want; his one thought was how to save, to accumulate, and by the increase of each day to double his capital, and to this end all his activity and industry were applied, even in the smallest thing. He was parsimonious even of his words, and parted with nothing unnecessarily.

Nevertheless, he had great thoughts and plans. He considered himself as destined by Providence to acquire an immense property, by means of which to achieve great things for the good of the state of which he was a native. He regarded himself, therefore, as the steward of his wealth, and maintained that he had no right to give even the smallest portion thereof for the most trifling object. These, at least, were the pretexts with which he gilded his parsimony and his hardness of heart.

He said, "If I, year after year, double my capital in this (a certain given) proportion, I shall in the end become the richest man in Louisiana; I might, continuing in this way, ultimately purchase the whole of Louisiana, and then —" Then he would do great things, which would make Louisiana the finest and the happiest state in the Union. And Macdonald had views for this purpose, and plans which prove him to have been possessed of a deeply thinking mind. But the poor man forgot that he was mortal, and, although he attained to an extreme old age, yet he had not nearly acquired the wealth after which he strove when he was surprised by — death. His magnificent plans will die with him, and effect little or nothing for Louisiana, except possibly in one respect, and that is the one of which I spoke, as—the opening of the prison-door.

Macdonald was a planter and the owner of slaves. He determined to emancipate his slaves, and that in a mode by which they should gain, and he lose nothing.

He said to them,

"You shall work yourselves free, and purchase your own release from slavery for the same sum which I paid for you. I will give you the means of doing this. You shall work for me five days in each week, as heretofore, for food, clothing, and habitation; you shall work for me also on the sixth day, but I will pay you wages for that, and give you credit for the money thus earned, which I will employ for you. Thus the first year. During the second year you shall be paid for two days' labor in the week, provided that you work industriously and well; the following year three, and so on, till the sum is acquired which is requisite for my reimbursement, and for you to have a little over, so that you may possess enough to begin life with in Liberia, whither I shall send you when you are free."

The slaves knew that Macdonald would keep his word. They began to labor with new heart, because they now labored for their own freedom and their future well-being. Some accomplished it more rapidly, others more slowly, but within two years *all* the slaves on the plantation had worked themselves free. Macdonald fulfilled his part to them as he had promised, and they could now become free without detriment either to themselves or others. They had become accustomed to work, to forethought, and self-government, at least so far as regarded their own affairs. In the mean time, Macdonald's plantation had been unusually well cultivated, and the slaves had repaid their original purchase-money.

I do not know whether it was Macdonald's intention to have his plantation afterward cultivated by white laborers or by free blacks; but one thing appears to me certain, and that is, that Macdonald's mode of effecting the emancipation of slaves is deserving of consideration and imitation, as one of the wisest which can be devised for the gradual and general release of both the blacks and the whites of North America from the fetters of slavery.

I know many estimable and thinking men of New Orleans who consider that such a mode of emancipation, as would, by degrees, convert the negro slaves into free laborers, might be put into operation without much difficulty, and that all those dangerous results which people imagine are, in great measure, only fears and fancies.

I have been told that the severest slave-owners in this neighborhood are French, and I can credit it from the French popular temperament; the Scotch and the Dutch take the second place. Slaves of small and poor proprietors often suffer very much from hunger, as do also cattle. I heard to-day of one place where a considerable number of cattle had literally perished for want of food.

I have made inquiries after the Christmas dances and festivities of the negro slaves, of which I heard so much, but the sugar-harvest was late last year, and the sugar-grinding was not over till after New-year's day; the cotton is still being plucked on the plantations, and the dances are deferred. I have now traveled in search of these negro festivities from one end of the slave states to the other, without having been lucky enough to meet with, to see, nay, nor even to hear of one such occasion. I believe, nevertheless, that they do occur here and there on the plantations.

For the rest, I have experienced so much kindness, have met with so many good and warm-hearted friends, that I have been both astonished and affected. I had always heard New Orleans mentioned as a very lively but not very literary city, and Mr. Lerner H. had prepared me to find that the people of New Orleans liked to see that which was beautiful. It was clear, therefore, that for that very reason they would not like to look at me; and yet they have come and come again to me, have overwhelmed me with kindness and presents, as well men as women, and made my days pleasant in many ways. For my own part, I have no other memories of New Orleans but those of pleasure and gratitude.

Octavia le V. returned home a few days ago. Those eyes, which remained dry and bright when she was in danger of losing all her ornaments and her money, overflowed with tears when she had to part from her newly-found friend. I kissed away the tears from those pale cheeks. I feel that I am heartily attached to her.

Mrs. G. has been an incomparable friend to me at this time when I had to prepare my wardrobe for Cuba—somewhat elegant, and of a light summer texture at the same time—and when I had divers little misfortunes, partly caused by the dress-maker, but principally through my own blunders. You know how annoying all such business is to me; but you can scarcely imagine how I have felt it here, where weariness both of body and mind, as well as ignorance of prices and persons in the dress-making and millinery world, rendered all my difficulties tenfold. Neither can you at all imagine how kind and amiable Mrs. G. has been during all these great little troubles—her patience, her good temper; nor, lastly, how well she has helped me with every thing. Yes—I am ashamed when I compare myself with her; but then she is one of the most amiable people I ever met with.

In the evening. I have now had my last drive with Anne W. along the beautiful cockle-shell road to Lake Pontchartrain. The air was delicious, and the sky once more gazed upon us with blue eyes from between the clouds, which parted more and more. The road, for the most part, runs through flat and still unreclaimed forest-land. One does not here see our beautiful moss and lichen-covered mountains and hills, but thickets of the primeval forest, from which, on all sides, look forth those beautiful palmetto-trees, with their large, fan-like leaves waving in the air, and the regular and graceful form of many half-tropical plants, which, indicating a new phase of earth's vegetable productions, have a wonderful fascination for me.

In the morning, *in the morning*, my Agatha, I shall go on board the great steamer, "The Philadelphia," and in three days I shall be at Cuba. I shall be very glad to get there, both because I shall see some new beauties of nature, and because I shall breathe a milder air, and shall escape during the winter months this variable American climate, which is so trying to my strength both of body and mind. I have become physically ten years older during this twelve months' journey in North America.

But be not afraid for me, my dear heart, but trust, as I do, that my *traveling fairy*, your little friend, which has hitherto conducted me safely through all perils—which conducted me without any misadventure down the whole extent of the Mississippi to New Orleans, at the very time when four steamers, with their passengers, were blown into the air upon its waters, and caused me to remove from St. Charles's Hotel to this good home the day before the hotel became the prey of flames—the same will conduct me safe and sound once more to my own sister-friend, to YOU.

P.S.—I have been gladdened here by letters from my friends in the North, the Downings, the Springs, and the Lowells. These friends accompany me like good spirits, and I must tell you so, because you must love my friends. Maria Lowell writes, the little traveling companion who went with us every where, and to Niagara, and yet which never spoke, and remained so quiet, was—a little boy, who now, large, and stout, and rosy, is little Mabel's oracle. She listens to every sound he utters, and says to it all, "What does little brother mean?" Beloved, happy Maria!

Jenny Lind is now in Havana, and people speak differently of the success of her concerts. I believe, nevertheless, that she will gain the victory over her adversaries, who in reality belong to the French party in the country, and who contest her rank as a great singer. She will be received here in New Orleans with enthusiasm; every heart is warm, every ear open to her. She will leave Havana just when I am arriving, and it is doubtful whether I shall see her.

I am well, my beloved child, and in good spirits. God grant that you are so too! And you must be so, with the help of homeopathy. May Æsculapius enlighten you and those concerned.

I shall soon write again from Cuba!

LETTER XXXII.

Havana, Cuba, Feb. 5.

Sweet Child! I am sitting beneath the warm, bright heavens, and the beautiful palms of the tropics, and it is lovely and wonderful! The glorious, delicious air, the beautiful palm-trees are paradisaical; the rest, I suspect, affords pleasure rather through its novelty, its dissimilarity with any thing that I have already seen, than by its own great intrinsic beauty. But the unusual and the novel are amusing and full of refreshment; so I feel it in this case, and I am delighted to be here.

I left New Orleans early in the morning of the 28th of January. It was a beautiful, sunshiny morning, and as warm as summer. My friends accompanied me on board "The Philadelphia." Lerner H. came to take leave of me, and gave me a red camellia still in bud. His frank, cordial countenance, and that of Anne W., with its pure features, and the quiet fire in the dark eyes, were the last which I saw in the saloon below deck.

When I went on deck, the Crescent city stood bathed in morning sunlight, and the water of the harbor lay like a clear mirror in its light. I stood and enjoyed the delightful air and the expansive scene, but when the ladies came with their "How do you like America?" &c., my morning joy was disturbed; but I placed them among the goats.

We proceeded on our way, and I seated myself with a book in my hand on the piazza aft, and contemplated the shores and lived—high life. For there I could be alone, and the scenery of the shores was like a beautiful Southern fairy scene. We advanced down the Mississippi upon that arm which falls into Atchafalaya Bay, and thence into the Mexican Gulf. One plantation after another shone out upon the shore with its white houses inclosed in thickets of orange and cedar trees, flowering oleanders, aloes, and palmettoes. By degrees they were more scattered; the land descended more and more till it became one vast swamp, overgrown with grass and reeds, and without trees, shrubs, or human dwellings, yet still maintaining itself at a smooth level above the water, till finally it sunk below, but still forming within it that singular, uniform figure which is called the delta of the Mississippi, from its resemblance to the Greek letter of that name. Stems of grass still waved above the water, swayed to and fro by the waves and the wind. Then they too disappeared; the waves alone prevailed. And now the land, the vast continent of North America, lay behind me, and before me the great Gulf of Mexico, with its unfathomable depth, the Southern Sea, with its islands.

The dark blue, almost black blue color of the water struck me greatly. I was told that it is occasioned by the extreme depth. The heavens, with their soft white summer clouds, arched themselves light blue over the dark blue sea, which heaved and roared joyfully before the fresh, warm summer wind. Oh, how beautiful it was! I inhaled the breeze, and life, and rested from thought, and talk, and every thing which was not a portion of the beautiful life of the moment. The sea! the sea has in itself an inexpressibly rest-giving, healing, and regenerating power. If thou wilt commence within thyself and without a new life—cross the sea. Let the air and the life of the sea bathe thy soul for days and weeks. Every thing becomes new and fresh upon the sea.

Thus did I live the first day on the sea; thus did I live the second also. Now, however, I enjoyed a book at the same time, Browning's tragedy, "The Return of the Druses," the lofty thought and the life-warm spirit of which was in harmony with the spectacle around me; I inhaled from both the boundless, the great, and the profound; and if, during all this, there came one and another gentleman with the inquiry, "How do you like America?" or with a request for an autograph, it was only like a fly buzzing past ear and thought.

There was, however, one gentleman on board who was more agreeable and attentive to me than the others were disturbing. The same polite gentleman who had constituted himself my cavalier at the time of our disaster on Lake Pontchartrain, who conducted me to the beautiful garden at night, and afterward to New Orleans, was now on board on his way to Cuba, seeking for a milder climate than that of the United States during winter. This gentleman, Mr. V., is middle aged, with a noble and good countenance, refined and gentle manners, and during long journeys into the East and West he has become acquainted with many subjects of interest. Now, again, is he my cavalier; as a matter of course, gives me his arm to and from meals, sits at table beside me, and makes his attentions to me agreeable by his interesting and agreeable demeanor and conversation.

This vessel was not like the other splendid and convenient steamers to which I had become accustomed in America. All below deck was crowded and dark—cabins, passages, eating-rooms. In order to be alone, I had chosen my cabin quite aft, where the motion of the vessel was most perceptible; here, however, I could have a little solitary three-cornered cell, with a round window opening out on the sea. Of sea-sickness I was not afraid, and here I could be alone.

Among the passengers of interest on board was an elderly man, one of the richest planters of Louisiana, and his only child, a young girl. Her mother had died of consumption, and the father, ever since the childhood of his daughter, had endeavored so to bring her up that she might be preserved from the dangerous inheritance. She had lived in great freedom in the country, spent much of her time in the open air, and did not wear stays. Thus she grew up a handsome, blooming girl, and, as such, made her appearance in society. After merely one season of tight lacing and dancing in the social circles of New Orleans, the lovely flower was broken, and symptoms of the disease which had carried off the mother showed themselves in the daughter. The brightness of the eye, the flush of the cheek, its hollowness, the bearing of the tall, slender figure, all testified of danger.

It was affecting to see the old father stand and gaze silently at his daughter, with eyes that grew dim with tears—there was such a speechless sorrow, such a deep feeling of helplessness in his expression. Then she would look up at him and smile sweetly, like a sunbeam; but it was evident that the cloud was there—was in the ascendant, and that all the gold of the millionaire could not purchase life for his child and heiress.

The journey which they were now making was, however, an attempt at this; they were intending first to visit Cuba, and then Europe. A handsome and blooming young girl, a cousin of the invalid, was her companion.

There were two Swedes also on board, on their way to Chagres, whence they would proceed to California. One of them, named Hörlin, the nephew of Bishop H., was an agreeable-looking young man, of cultivated mind, and was now making his second journey to the land of gold, where he already, as a merchant, had made a considerable sum.

On the afternoon of the second day the sky became overcast, and the wind rose. I scarcely believed my eyes when I beheld, rising up to the clouds before us, lofty mountains and craggy peaks, not unlike a fortress with walls and towers, seen in the hazy distance, and was told that that was Cuba! And yet we could not arrive there before the morning of the following day. I had not yet seen such lofty and bold mountain peaks in this western land.

The night was stormy but very warm, and I opened my window for the admission of air. I could see from my bed, which was directly below the window, the cloudy sky and the stormy sea when the motion of the vessel sank it to the edge of the water on my side. The billows foamed and hissed close to my window, and soon came into my bed. But the water was so warm that I did not observe it at first; and afterward, when I had to choose between closing my window and breathing the suffocating air of the cabin, or to breathe the soft sea air, and now and then be embraced by the salt sea waves, I chose the latter. I only got a little wet, but was calm and happy; I felt on the most familiar and affectionate terms with the waves and the great sea. I lay there like a child in its comfortable cradle; it could not hurt me.

The following morning we were in Havana harbor.

The surf rose high, and broke with violence against the projecting rocky point on which stands the fortress of Moro, with its walls and towers, one of which is very lofty, to defend the narrow entrance of the harbor. But we lay tranquil in that beautiful almost circular harbor, as if in the stillest lake, and the sun shone upon a world of new objects around me.

There lay the large city, Hàvana, along the shore to the right of the entrance to the harbor, with its low houses of all colors, blue, yellow, green, orange, like an immense mass of showy articles of porcelain and glass on a stall of fancy-wares ; and no smoke, not the slightest column of smoke, to give any intimation of the atmosphere of a city with its cooking and manufacturing life, such as I had been accustomed to in the American cities. Groups of palm-trees rose up among the houses. One height to the left of us was covered by a great number of tall and extraordinary plants, resembling lofty green candelabra, with many pairs of arms. Between the verdant hills which surrounded the harbor stood groups of country houses and groves of cocoa palms and other palm-like trees, and over all this rested the clearest, softest heaven, and the most delicious air. The water of the harbor seemed as clear as crystal, and, above all, atmosphere and color seemed to be of the most diaphonous clearness and serenity. Among the objects which caught my sight were the fortress in which the state prisoners are kept, a second prison, and a—gallows. But those beautiful waving palms and those verdant hills enchanted my eyes.

Small, half-covered boats, rowed by men with Spanish physiognomies, surrounded our vessel, to convey the passengers on shore. But the passengers could not go on shore. News had reached the Spanish authorities of the island that a certain Colonel White, one of the leaders in Lopez's robber-expedition against Cuba, was on board our steamer, and a message now came from them to prohibit the landing of any of the passengers till further intimation was received from them. This was not quite right. Some of the gentlemen were greatly displeased, and wished any thing but good to Colonel White, who, big and bony, with a red face and an Irish nose, and an untroubled and careless expression, now made his appearance on deck, walking up and down, smoking a cigar, in the midst of the wrathful glances of the passengers. He merely intended, he said, to go to Chagres, on his way to California.

We lay for six hours in the harbor, awaiting our permission to land. For my part, it did not appear long, the view of the shores and the objects around were so enchanting to me. The weather was divine, and we had taken on board great clusters of beautiful golden bananas. They were presented by polite gentlemen, and I breakfasted with delight upon my favorite fruit, which is as delicious and beneficial to me as this tropical atmosphere. Sugar-cane was also added to the entertainment, and enjoyed by many. It was a regular tropical breakfast, eaten in the sunshine amid the harbor.

At length a boat approached, bearing the Spanish flag and several officers. They came on board our vessel. Colonel White was taken aside, and required to give his word of honor not to land on the island, but to proceed on his way to Chagres without leaving the vessel. I saw several of the officers (handsome men, with refined features) cast such glances at the robber leader! There were Spanish daggers in them!

The Spanish gentlemen retired, and after that, we innocent passengers prepared to go on shore. Polite gentlemen took charge of my landing, and it was necessary, for I have never experienced greater difficulty in landing than here. I was finally intrusted to an American hotel-keeper in Havana (a Mr. Woolcott), who conveyed me and my effects on shore, and then through the custom-house to his hotel, where he promised our respectable captain of "The Philadelphia" to make me comfortable. And before long I was seated in a large hall with a marble floor, and at a well-filled table, amid a numerous company, while the beautiful air and light poured in through the open doors and windows, for in Cuba people are not afraid of sunshine.

Here I ascertained that Jenny Lind was still at Havana, and would not yet leave for a couple of days. I wrote, therefore, a few lines to her, and dispatched them by our young countryman, Hörlin, who was glad to be the bearer of my letter. It was in the evening, and after that I took my light and went up stairs to my chamber to go to rest. But scarcely had I reached the top of the stairs, when I heard a voice below mention my name. I looked round astonished, and there, at the foot of the stairs, stood a lady holding by the balustrade, and looking up to me with a kind and beaming countenance. It was Jenny Lind—Jenny Lind here, and with that beaming, fresh, joyous expression of countenance which, when once seen, can never be forgotten! There is the whole Swedish spring in it. I was glad. All was forgotten in a moment which had formerly come between her and me. I could not but instantly go down, bend over the balustrade, and kiss her. That agreeable young man, Max Hjortsberg, was with her. I shook hands with him, but I took Jenny Lind with me into my chamber. We had never met since that time at Stockholm when I predicted for her an European reputation. She had now attained it in a higher degree than any other artist, because the praise and the laurels which she won every where had not reference alone to her gifts as a singer.

I spent with her the greater part of the two days while she yet remained in Havana, partly with her in her own apartments, and partly in driving with her on the beautiful promenades around the city, and partly in my own room, where I sketched her portrait; and I could not help once more loving her intensely. Beneath the palm-trees of Cuba we talked only of Sweden and our mutual friends there, and shed bitter tears together over the painful loss of others. We talked much about old friends and old connections in Sweden—nay, truly speaking, we talked of nothing else, because every thing else—honor, reputation, wealth, all which she had obtained out of Sweden—did not seem to have struck the least root in her soul. I should have liked to have heard something about them, but she had neither inclination nor pleasure in speaking of them. Sweden alone, and those old friends, as well as religious subjects, lay uppermost in her soul, and of these merely had she any wish to converse. In certain respects I could not entirely agree with her; but she was always an unusual and superior character, and so fresh, so Swedish! Jenny Lind is kindred with Trollhätan and Niagara, and with every vigorous and decided power of nature, and the effects which she produces resemble theirs.

The Americans are enchanted with her beneficence. I can not admire her for this; I can only congratulate her in being able to follow the impulse of her heart. But that Jenny Lind, with all the power she feels herself possessed of, with all the sway she exercises, amid all the praise and homage which is poured upon her, and the multitudes of people whom she sees at her feet, still looks up to something higher than all this, higher than herself, and in comparison with which she esteems herself and all this to be mean—that glance, that thirst after the holy and the highest, which during many changes always again returns and shows itself to be a dominant feature in Jenny Lind—this is, in my eyes, her most unusual and her noblest characteristic.

She was very amiable and affectionate to me; yes, so much so that it affected me. Little did I expect that beneath the palms of the tropics we should come so near to each other!

I met at dinner at her house the whole of her traveling party—Belletti, Mademoiselle Aehrström, Mr. Barnum and his daughter, and many others. The best understanding seems to prevail between her and them. She praised them all, and praised highly the behavior of Mr. Barnum to her. She was not now giving any concerts at Cuba, and was enjoying the repose, and the beautiful tropical scenery and air. She sang for me unasked (for I would not ask her to sing) one of Lindblad's songs—

"Talar jag sae hör du mig"—

and her voice seemed to me as fresh and youthful as ever.

One day she drove me to the Bishop's Garden, which was "beautiful, beautiful!" she said; beautiful park-like grounds, near Havana, where she was anxious to show me the bread-fruit-tree, and many other tropical plants, which proves her fresh taste for nature. In the evening we drove along the magnificent promenade, *el Passeo di Isabella seconda*, which extends for certainly upward of three English miles between broad avenues of palm and other tropical trees, beds of flowers, marble statues and fountains, and which is the finest promenade any one can imagine, to say nothing of its being under the clear heaven of Cuba. The moon was in her first quarter, and floated like a little boat above the western horizon. Jenny Lind made me observe its different position here to what it has with us, where the new moon is always upright, or merely in a slanting direction to the earth. The entire circle of the moon appeared unusually clear.

That soft young moonlight above the verdant, billowy fields, with their groups of palm-trees, was indescribably beautiful.

I fancied that Jenny Lind was tired of her wandering life and her *rôle* of singer. She evidently wished for a life of quieter and profounder character. We talked of—marriage and domestic life.

Of a certainty a change of this kind is approaching for Jenny Lind. But will it satisfy her soul, and be enough for her? I doubt.

She left that evening for New Orleans, out of spirits, and not happy in her own mind. The vessel by which she sailed was crowded with Californian adventurers, four hundred it was said, who were returning to New Orleans; and Jenny Lind had just heard a rumor that Captain West, who had brought her over from England to America, had perished in a disastrous voyage at sea. All this depressed her mind, and neither my encouragement—I went on board the vessel to take leave of her, to give her my good wishes and a bouquet of roses—nor the captain's offer of his cabin and saloon, where, above deck, she might have remained undisturbed by the Californians below, were able to cheer her. She was pale, and said little. She scarcely looked at my poor roses, although they were the most beautiful I could get in Havana; when, however, I again was seated in my little gondola, and was already at some distance from the vessel, I saw Jenny Lind lean over the railing toward me.

And all the beautiful, regular countenances of the West paled below the beaming, living beauty of expression in the countenance which I then saw, bathed in tears, kissing the roses, kissing her hands to me, glancing, beaming a whole summer of affluent, changing, enchanting, warm inward life. She felt that she had been cold to me, and she would now make amends for it.

And if I should never again see Jenny Lind, I shall always henceforth see her thus, as at this moment, always love her thus.

I have now been six days in this very good but very expensive hotel. I pay five dollars a day for a small chamber, which one can hardly imagine more scantily furnished, and in a couple more days shall be obliged to pay six dollars, or admit some unknown guest into my room; for in two more days a steam-boat comes in, and new guests from New Orleans. I have, therefore, been inquiring after a new lodging, but it is not here as in America. In the mean time, kind, amiable people, partly Germans, partly English and Americans, desirous of making the place as agreeable to me as possible, have interested themselves about my affairs, and, in consequence of their kindness, I shall to-morrow remove for a few days to a country house just by the Bishop's beautiful garden, where I can, in freedom, make acquaintance with the trees and flowers of Cuba. Is not that charming? Is not my little traveling fairy careful of me?

I have hitherto spent my day as follows. At half past seven in the morning Mrs. Mary enters my chamber with a cup of coffee and a little wheaten bread, which looks very enticing. And Mrs. Mary is an Irish woman, one of the most excellent, nicest, most thoughtful, and good-hearted beings one can imagine, and the greatest treasure of this hotel, to me at least. Mrs. Mary's good temper and kind solicitude give to this hotel a feeling of home, and I should get on infinitely well here if the place were not so terribly dear.

After I have drank my coffee and eaten my bread, I go out, first to *La Plaza des Armas*, where the governor, the intendant, and the great admiral, the three great dignitaries of the island, have their palaces, occupying three sides of the square, the fourth of which is an inclosed plantation, between the iron railing of which is seen a marble bust standing on its pedestal, and beyond this a chapel. This is the place where Catholic mass was first performed by order of Columbus. The bust is his, and it and the chapel have been erected there in memory of the first divine service on the island. A large white marble statue, that of Charles V., I believe, stands in the middle of the square, surrounded by lofty, magnificent king-palms, regular kings among trees, and around these small plantations of other trees and shrubs. Among these I have observed one tree, which has foliage and a head very like our lime-tree, although not so large, with fire-colored flowers not unlike our Indian cross-flower, but darker in color; and shrubs too, which have the same kind of flowers, and upon the stems of which small, splendid green lizards dart about and gaze quite calmly at me, while I gaze at them. A number of white marble seats are placed here, where people may rest in the shade of the palm-trees. But they do not cast much shade, and one has to keep watch for the moment, and for the spot where their proud crowns afford a shelter from the sun. But it is a pleasure to see their branches move, rustling in the wind, for their motion is majestic, and graceful at the same time!

Hence I go to an esplanade, or lofty terrace, called *La Cortine de Valdez*, raised along the harbor on the opposite side to the Moro. It is a short promenade, but has the most beautiful view. And here I wander, to inhale the sea air and to watch the waves, if it be calm, break in lofty white-crested surf against the rocks of the Moro, which exclude the tumult of the ocean, and leave the harbor calm; watch, through the mouth of the harbor, white sails skimming over the vast blue sea; watch little lizards dart out and in, or lie gently basking in the sun on the low walls which run along the esplanade, and white doves fly down to drink at a white marble basin below a lovely monument in honor of Valdez, which terminates the promenade. From the white wall of this monument a jet of clear water is thrown, which falls into a basin.

At ten o'clock I am again at home, and eating a second breakfast, with a large company, in the light marble hall, at an abundant table, but where I take merely coffee, my beloved Carolina rice, and an egg. After that I go to my room, write letters, and draw or paint till dinner. After dinner, one or another of my new friends here call in their *volante*, such being the name of the carriages of Cuba, to drive me out upon one of the beautiful and magnificent public roads beyond the city. In the evening, after tea, I go up to the roof of the house, which is flat, as are all the roofs here, and is called *azoteon*, surrounded by a low parapet, upon which stand urns, which are generally gray, with raised green ornaments, and little gilt flames at the top. Here I walk alone till late into the night, contemplating the starry heavens above me, and the city below my feet. The Moro-light, as the lofty beacon-fire in the Moro fortress is called, is kindled, and beams like a large, steadily-gleaming star, with the most resplendent light over the ocean and city. The air is delicious and calm, or breathes merely like a slumbering child; and around me I hear on all sides the sweetest, most serene little twitter, not unlike that of sparrows with us, but more serene, or with a softer sound. I am told that is the little lizards, which are here found in such abundance, and which have the gift of voice.

The city has a most peculiar aspect. The houses are low, and for the most part of but one story, never above two; the streets are narrow, so that in many cases the linen cloth, which serves as a shade to the shops, is stretched over the street from one side to the other. The walls of houses, palaces, or towers are colored blue, yellow, green, or orange, and frequently adorned with fresco-painting. The glare of the sunlight on white walls is feared, as injurious to the sight, and hence they are all tinted. No smoke is visible, nor yet a single chimney. Flat roofs are universal, with their parapets of stone or iron, and their urns with bronze flames. I can not understand where the fires are, nor what becomes of the smoke. The atmosphere of the city is as clear as crystal. The narrow streets are not paved, and when it rains, as it has done in torrents for a couple of days, immense puddles and holes are the consequence, and when it dries again, a great deal of dust. Narrow causeways, scarcely wide enough for two persons to pass, line each side of the street, and along the streets rush about in all directions, and wind in and out, a sort of huge insect, with immense hind legs and a long proboscis, upon which stands a tall black horn, or tower-like elevation—so at least appeared to me at first the Cuban equipages or volantes, which constitute the only kind of Havana carriage. If, however, you wish to take a clear survey, you will find that they resemble a species of cabriolet, but the two immense wheels are placed behind the body of the carriage, which rests upon springs between the wheels and the horses, and for the most part is supported by them. A postillion, who is always a negro in large, projecting riding-boots, is mounted upon the horse, which is considerably in advance of the carriage itself. This driver is called *calashero*, and both he and the horse are sometimes richly caparisoned with silver, often to the value of several thousand dollars. The whole equipage is of an unusual length, and reminds me of some queer kind of harry-long-legs.

When the volante is in great state, or prepared for a longer journey, it has two horses, or even three. The second horse is guided by the hand of the calashero, and runs a little ahead of the first.

When the volante is in great state, you will see two or three signoras seated in it, always without bonnets, and sometimes with flowers in their hair; bare arms and neck, and white dresses, as if attired for a ball. When they are three in number, the youngest sits in the middle, a little in advance of the other two. One sees such often on the public drives in the afternoon, or in the evening on *La Plaza des Armas*, where there is music and a great concourse. It is only seldom that a veil is seen worn over the head and shoulders, and scarcely ever a bonnet, which seems to belong to the foreigner.

When I first saw the rocking motion of the volante as it drove along the streets, I thought "that must be an extremely disagreeable carriage!" but when I was seated in one, I seemed to myself rocked on a cloud. I have never felt an easier motion.

The Creole ladies, that is, the native ladies of the island—do not make use of any defense from sun or wind, neither do they need it. After the hour of noon, when the breeze comes in from the sea, the air is not hot, neither does the sun burn here as on the Continent. The complexion of the Creoles is pale, but perfectly healthy, and has a soft, light olive tint, which, together with their beautiful dark, but, at the same time, soft eyes, gives a piquancy to their appearance. The priests, in their long cloaks and queer, large hats, go about on foot. The greater number of the people in the streets are negroes and mulattoes; even in the shops one sees mulattoes, especially in the cigar-shops. Cigars are smoked universally, especially a small kind called *cigaritos*. The colored population seem to intoxicate themselves with tobacco-smoke. I frequently see negroes and mulattoes sitting dozing before the shops with cigars in their mouths. The calashero, when he waits before a house, alights, seats himself by the carriage, smokes, and shuts his eyes in the sunshine. But where goes all the smoke? How can it be? It must be absorbed by the sea-air.

I must, however, make an end of my day. After I have walked about or sat upon the azoteon till toward midnight, enjoying the air, which, it seems to me, is possessed of a peculiarly sanative, beneficial life, and a banana, which has the same qualities, and my own solitary thoughts, I retire to my chamber, and go to rest in a bed without any bedding excepting a pillow and a coverlet, but on which I repose excellently, and sleep to the fanning of the wind, which enters playfully, as it were, through the iron grating of the door and window, to which there is neither glass nor shutter.

My chamber, and a row of the other chambers also, have each an outlet to the roof, which is very agreeable to me, as I can thus have air at any time, and I have, from my roof, merely to ascend a little flight of steps to arrive at the azoteon proper. The azoteon is the principal place of assembly for the Cuban families when in the evening they wish to enjoy *la brise*.

I must now tell you something about the family which has received me with so much kindness. They are, in the first place, an English family of the name of F., a highly-esteemed commercial house in the city, and a young married couple, Mr. and Mrs. S., the son-in-law and daughter of Mr. and Mrs. F. Mr. F. was formerly the agent in Cuba for the house of Rothschild in London, but he has resigned his business in favor of his son-in-law, Mr. S., who is a German.

Mr. F. is a young-elderly man, with a countenance and demeanor full of benevolence and good humor, lively and witty in society. His wife is of Danish descent, a native of the Danish island St. Croix, and has been a celebrated beauty, and even still, when about fifty, is a very handsome lady, with delicate features, and an expression of goodness which fascinates me. The house is full of handsome children, four sons and five daughters; the daughters, in particular, are handsome, and the two eldest married daughters are infinitely charming. The youngest of these is a blonde, and lovely, like a northern maiden of the old ballads. The eldest son of the family has returned home from England with his wife, a young beauty, with roses on her cheeks, such as only the daughters of Europe can show. The whole house is full of beauty, love, and gladness, with the newly-married, newly-betrothed, love-tokens, and glances in every corner. The family has, besides, a cheerful circle of acquaintance, where gentlemen from Europe, Germans, Englishmen, Scotch, or French, come with unstinted music and merriment.

Good Mrs. F. drove me last evening in her volante to the villa of her daughter and son-in-law, Mr. and Mrs. S., at a village two miles distant from Havana. There we found a company of handsome people assembled, not invited, but because it was the reception evening of the family. They amused themselves with *tableaux vivans*, music, and dancing. Those remarkably handsome ladies (regularly enchanting in the costumes of the *tableaux*), those well-bred, cheerful gentlemen, that excellent music —the young sisters F. sing extremely well—that Cuban contra-dance, and its music so peculiar, so delineative of the Creole temperament, inasmuch as it expresses an effeminate, playful, pleasure-loving, and yet half melancholy life, in which the breezes seem to waft, and the palm branches to rustle; that cheerful, free tone of social intercourse, the many languages which are spoken, the beautiful evenings, the soft winds and stars of night which glance in at open doors and windows—all these made this evening one of the most beautiful, the most perfectly festal occasions that I ever witnessed. Nothing was tiresome, nothing contracted; one rested, and enjoyed, and amused one's self at the same time.

I have seen mass performed twice in the early morning at the Cathedral church here; I have seen there such great priestly show and priestly magnificence in full bloom, that one might fancy one's self removed two or three centuries backward in time; I scarcely saw any praying in the church, and the priests marched hither and thither, and swung smoking censers, and lighted candles, and busied themselves with divers ecclesiastical ceremonies, evidently without any devotion at all. But there was supplication in the music; the music was beautiful, and replete with heartfelt prayer. A pious and inspired spirit had breathed its soul into it, and I prayed in unison with it. The Cathedral is handsome and light, although not large. It contains some pictures which gave me pleasure. One of these represents the spirits in Purgatory; above the flames float the Madonna and Child, glancing down with compassionate eyes. Some of the souls, becoming aware of them, are captivated by their beauty, and while they gaze upon them with involuntary prayer, they are raised out of the flames, without themselves being conscious of it.

Another picture represents the Holy Virgin standing upon the globe. Her glance is in heaven; her prayers, her whole soul lives there, and without apparent intention she treads upon the serpent, which glides away over the earth. These pictures are evidently the work of an age of profound spiritual inspiration.

The bones of Columbus rest in the Cathedral. A white marble tablet in the wall near the chancel points out the spot. This tablet presents also his head in bass-relief, below which are some symbols of a very common character, and below these, again, a poor, ill-constructed inscription, abounding in platitude, the purport of which is that his dust reposes here, but his fame shall live for many centuries.

One day, when I visited the church in company with Mr. V., we were attended by a youth who seemed to be one of the young neophytes. When he heard that Mr. V. had been at Jerusalem, he was delighted, and so anxious to hear about the holy grave and the holy places near the city, and then was so zealous to show us every remarkable thing about the church, that it was a pleasure to see him. This youth had evidently, as yet, an uncorrupted mind and a firm faith.

Yesterday, during a great procession in the church, and a great kissing of the hand of the bishop, who was a handsome prelate, with fat white hands, covered with sparkling jewels, I saw one of the great gentlemen—I fancy it was the Admiral—laugh as he knelt down before the holy father, and make pretense of kissing his hand; and, of a truth, the Bishop smiled too. They both knew that it was merely a great show. The costume of the priests and the official corps, as they sat together in arm-chairs in the church, produced as picturesque and imposing an effect as any costume can nowadays, and I am quite willing to feel its full effect, so long, at least, as I do not see a deceitful mask in it.

I have heard many complaints of the government of the island, complaints of monopolies, injustice, and official robbery of all kinds, as well among government officials as lawyers. They are said literally to devour the portions of the widow and the fatherless. I have heard almost incredible stories of this kind. People are now hoping great things from the new Governor-general Concha, who arrived here from Spain two months since. The last deposed governor distinguished himself by the peculation through which he became a rich man. The clergy are said to be quite unclerical, the greater number living in open defiance of their vows; and religion here is, I am told—dead. Traffic in slaves is also carried on in secret. The government is cognizant of the fact, but winks at it—nay, indeed, it is said that it derives a gain from it.

Ah! that this earthly paradise should be so poisoned by the old serpent!

Serro, Feb. 10th.

I have lived for the last three days at a rural abode in the little rural village, or small town of Serro, two miles from Havana, with a German-American family of the name of S., who have kindly invited me to spend a few days with them, to know something of life in the country, which I greatly wished, and to make a closer acquaintance with the Bishop's beautiful garden, which lies very near their home. I have a little newly-built house to myself, consisting of two airy rooms. Below the window of my sleeping-room stands a little clump of banana-trees laden with their beautiful fruit, and the light green ell-broad leaves, which are as soft as velvet, are wafted by the wind, and immediately beyond them roars a little mountain stream. Beyond our little garden, and just opposite to it, I see, within a blue-painted inclosure on a little hill, a group of glorious cocoa palms, poplars, and bamboo-trees, beneath which a fountain falls into a magnificent marble basin. The whole village is composed of gardens with their little dwellings, and beyond them the extensive plain is scattered over with king and cocoa palms, and trees, the names of which I am yet unacquainted with.

The first night that I slept here on my cool camp-bedstead, I heard the stream roaring along, and the banana leaves whispering outside my window, and felt the delicious night-winds around me like the wings of angels; it was to me enchantingly beautiful—so beautiful that I could scarcely sleep. I was obliged to get up many times to contemplate the heavens and the earth. I thus beheld a constellation of incomparable magnificence and brilliancy ascend above the hill of the cocoa palms. Could it be the ship Argo or the constellation Sagittarius? I do not as yet know. I am still ignorant what constellations of the southern hemisphere may be seen here. I have not yet met with any one who can tell me. People here think a deal more about trade and pleasure than about the stars. When the blush of morning appeared, amid beautiful gold and rosy clouds, I saw the morning star standing above the earth, wonderfully bright and large. I do not know why, but it produced in me a melancholy effect. It seemed to me like an eye full of a bright but sorrowful consciousness, gazing calmly, with deep earnestness, down upon earth, as if it knew of the sin and the sorrow of earth. That bright star stood above the beautiful island like its clear, accusing conscience.

There had been for the last two days cold weather, with rain in torrents; but the morning was bright and beautiful, and I wished after breakfast to visit the Bishop's garden, which lies only a few minutes' walk from our Serro. Mrs. S. said, "You will not be able to get there; you will stick fast in the mud after all this rain."

I would not believe her, and persisted in going. But she was right. I actually could not get along; at every step my feet stuck fast in the thick mud, the quality of which I had never before had any conception of. I was obliged to return, and wait till the sun had dried the earth, which it is not very long in doing. These torrents of rain which have met me in Cuba, and which are a little inconvenient to me, are, it is said, the parting salutations of the rainy season, which is now just at an end, and which gives place to the dry season, *la Secca*, which extends from the present time into May. Both yesterday and to-day there has been unremitting sunshine, so that I have to-day been to the Bishop's garden; and wandering under palms, bamboos, and many kinds of beautiful tropical trees, among splendid unusual flowers and butterflies, have celebrated alone the most glorious morning, a spirit of thanksgiving among the silent spirits of nature. Ah! when the Creator allows us here on earth to behold such beauty, allows us to experience such joy, what treasures of His kingdom has He not in store for His children, risen again and enfranchised from dust on the other side the grave!

The beauty of these trees and flowers, and of this air, give me a foretaste of a glory of creation, a fullness of existence in the consciousness of natural life, which exceeds all that I have hitherto imagined. When nature, in a perfected world, becomes a thanksgiving song of beauty, harmonious delight, and magnificence, what will not life become, what praises shall we not sing? We are not bold enough, we are not rich enough in imagination, as we glance toward the kingdom of heaven beyond the grave; we are too poor in faith to conceive of the power and affluence of the Creator.

Palms, laurel-trees, groves of bamboos, yellow jasmines, which fling their fragrant branches from stem to stem; the beautiful air filled with the purest life, all these whispered to me words and thoughts of that morning which is to be. And I walked alone through these magnificent avenues, amid those silent groves, where hundreds of splendid butterflies, all unknown to me, fluttered up out of the moist grasses, and I praised God in the name of all existence! How happy I was that morning!

"But the slaves—the slavery which surrounds this Eden!" you will say. Yes, I know; but slavery must cease, and the fetters of the slave fall from him; but the goodness and magnificence of God will remain forever. I lived here in the contemplation of this, and a day will come when the slave shall do so too.

The garden, or, more correctly speaking, the park, is much neglected since the death of the old bishop, and since a terrible hurricane in 1848, which entirely destroyed the house, of which merely a ruin now remains, and injured many trees and statues; but I am pleased with the less trim condition of the park, because it all the more resembles, from that very cause, a beautiful natural scene.

I dined yesterday at the villa of Mr. and Mrs. S. with a select party. The dinner was served in the veranda opening into the garden, which afforded us a glorious view beyond it over the island. This garden was, like other ornamental gardens which I have seen here, very ornamental, but stiff. Palms of many kinds, splendid flowers in beds, bordering well-graveled or flagged paths, marble basins with gold fish, &c. A beautiful little boy of two years old is the best treasure of the house.

In the evening I was once more with the F. family; saw amiable and cheerful young people dancing in the joy of their hearts, and heard again that enchanting Cuban dance-music. It has a broken, strange, but extremely animated movement. My kind, agreeable host, Mr. S., plays it on the piano-forte with the musical genius of a German.

Feb. 11th. Yesterday was Sunday, and although our little village of Serro did not go to church—because there is no church there—it still had quite a holiday appearance. At noon I heard from various distances the living cadence of the African drum, not unlike the sound of the flail in the barns around us at threshing time, only that here it has a much more animated life. This was the sign that the dances of the free negroes were now commencing at their assembling-places in the neighborhood. My host had the kindness to accompany me to one of these, very near our Serro. I found a large room, very like those of public houses among us, in which I saw these negroes naked to the waist, wild, energetic figures and countenances, who were beating drums with energetic animation. These drums were hollowed tree-stems, over the openings of which was stretched a parchment skin, on which the negroes drummed, in part with sticks and in part with their hands, with their thumbs, with their fists, with wonderful agility and skill, a wild, artistic perfection, or, I should rather say, a perfected natural art—they drummed as bees hum and beavers build. The time and measure, which sometimes varied, was exquisitely true; no one can imagine a more natural, perfect, lively precision in that irregular regular time. The drum was held between the knees; they held in their fists a large ball filled with stones or some other noisy things, and ornamented outside with a tuft of cock's feathers. They seem to me to create as much noise as possible. Some dancing couples assembled; ladies of various shades of color, dressed in ragged finery; men (negroes) without any finery, almost without any attire at all on the upper part of the body. A man took a woman by the hand, and then began to dance, she turning round on one spot with downcast eyes, he surrounding her with a vast many gambols, among which are most astounding summersets and leaps, remarkable for their boldness and agility. Other negroes, in the mean time, set up, every now and then, wild cries, and strike with sticks upon the walls and doors. The sweat pours from the drumming negroes, who look desperately in earnest. When the hall began to be crowded, I would not any longer detain my friend and his little daughter; but I shall do all in my power to witness again and again these African dances, with their peculiar wild life, at the same time so irregular and yet so rhythmical.

On our return we heard, both near and afar, the wild sound of the drums. It is only, however, the free negroes of the island who hold their dances at this season. During the whole time of *la Secca* the grinding of the sugar-cane is going forward on the plantations, and the negro slaves can not then dance, scarcely have time to sleep. There are, however, in Cuba a considerable number of free negroes.

As we entered the village, we met two young men who were playing a lively air on the guitar, and who were accompanied by several other young men. They were celebrating the birth or name-day of some of their friends—a beautiful poetical custom!

I have rambled about a good deal in this neighborhood, and have become acquainted with some of the beautiful trees of the island. Among these I must introduce to you the ceiba-tree, one of the loftiest and most lovely trees of Cuba. It shoots aloft, a strong and softly undulating stem, to a height exceeding that of the palm, and without any branches, until, all at once, it spreads out in a horizontal direction three or four arms, sinuous like those of the oak, but less abrupt; these subdivide themselves into lesser branches, and bear aloft the most beautiful crown of palmated rich green leaves. It is one of the most lovely trees I ever saw, and I know nothing to which I can compare it. But this beautiful tree has its grudging enemy, and upon the small, thorn-like excrescences with which its stem is covered a parasite is apt to fix itself, which by degrees embraces, and finally kills the tree. I observed also the beautiful dark green trees, Mamay Colorado and Mamay Santa Domingo, now covered with fruit, gray-brown outside, and within filled with a reddish-yellow flesh, very sweet, but to my taste insipid; and the sapota-tree, also with dark green leaves and brown fruit, about the size of small oranges, and, like these, consisting of juicy segments, very sweet, and extremely agreeable to my taste. The mango-tree has a thick, leafy head, which reminds me, both in form and compactness, of our chestnut-tree. The mango fruit is yet green, and hangs in long racemes, several upon a stalk, like colossal almonds in form. They are said to be of a beautiful golden yellow when ripe; they are called the apples of Cuba, and are much liked on the island. The mango-tree affords a thick, impenetrable shadow; the tamarind-tree, on the other hand, spreads out above your head like a fine, transparent, embroidered green veil, through which you see the blue sky. It bears pods with small beans in them, which have an acid, but very agreeable and fresh flavor.

The gourd, or calabash-tree—(N.B.—I tell you the names of the trees as I hear them called here, for I have no access to any botanical work)—resembles an apple-tree in its growth, has its branches overgrown with thick-set leaves, and bears fruit round as a ball, without any stem. This fruit, which will grow as large as a man's head, and which has a very hard rind, furnishes the poorer people with their most useful domestic utensils, and becomes, when cut in two, their bowl, dish, plate, drinking vessel, water cask, dipper, ladle, their all in all. The calabash, or gourd, is especially the negro's house furniture, and it is the calabash also which adorns his fists, and which occasions pleasure and noise at their dances. I might mention other trees, and many there are, of which as yet I do not know the names; but I must tell you how my beloved banana-tree blossoms and sets its fruit; for it is a peculiar story, which for a long time has puzzled me when I saw it from a distance, and now I have studied it near.

You see the banana-tree—you shall see it in my album—a tree of low growth, with a palm-like crown not much above your head in height. The stem shoots up straight, surrounded by leaves, which fall off as the stem increases in height, and which leave it somewhat rugged, and with rather a withered appearance. When the tree has attained the height of four or five ells, it ceases to grow, but unfolds and expands a crown of broad light green leaves, as soft as velvet, and from two to four ells long, and which bend and are swayed gracefully by the wind. The wind, however, is not quite gracious to them, but slits the leaves on each side of the strong leaf-fibre into many parts, so that it often looks tattered, but still preserves, even amid its tatters, its soft grace and its beautiful movement. From amid the crown of leaves shoots forth a bud upon a stalk, and resembling a large green flower-bud. This shoots up rapidly, and becomes as rapidly too heavy for its stalk, which bends under its weight. The bud now bends down to the stem, and grows as large probably as a cocoa-nut, its form being like that of a Provence rose-bud, and of a dark violet color. I saw upon almost all banana-trees, even on those which bore rich clusters of ripe fruit, this immense violet-colored bud hanging, and was not a little curious to know all about it. And now you shall know! One of the outer leaves or envelopments of the bud loosens itself, or opens itself gently at the top, and you now perceive that its innermost side glows with the most splendid vermilion red; and within its depth you see peeping forth, closely laid together side by side, six or seven little light yellow figures, not unlike little chickens, and very like the woolly seed-vessels in the single peony-flower. The leaf encasements open more and more to the light and the air, and those little light yellow fruit-chickens peep forth more and more. By degrees the leaf, with its little family, separates itself altogether from the bud, and a length of bare stem grows between them. The little chickens now gape with pale yellow flower-beaks, and put out their tongues (they are of the didynamia order) to drink in the sun and the air; but still the beautiful leaf bends itself over their heads like a screen, like a protecting wing, like a shadowy roof. The sun would as yet be too hot for the little ones. But they grow more and more. They begin to develop themselves, to plump out their breasts, and to raise their heads more and more. They will become independent; they will see the sun; they need no longer the old leaf. The leaf now disengages itself—the beautiful maternal leaf—and falls to the earth. I have frequently seen these leaf-screens lying on the ground beneath the tree, and taken them up and contemplated them with admiration, not only for the part they act, but for the rare beauty and clearness of the crimson color on their inner side; one might say that a warm drop of blood from a young mother's heart had infused itself there. The young chickens, which are cocks and hens at the same time, plume themselves now proudly, and with projecting breasts, and beautifully curved backs and heads, and beaks raised aloft, range themselves garland-like around the stem, and thus, in about two weeks' time, they ripen into delicious bananas, and are cut off in bunches.

The whole of that dark, purple-tinted bud-head is a thick cluster of such leaf-envelopes, each inclosing such an offspring. Thus releases itself one leaf after another, and falls off; thus grows to maturity one cluster of fruit after another, until the thick stalk is as full as it can hold of their garlands; but, nevertheless, there always remains a good deal of the bud-head, which is never able to develop the whole of its internal wealth during the year in which the banana-tree lives; for it lives and bears fruit only one year, and then dies. But, before that happens, it has given life to a large family of young descendants, who grow up at its feet, and the eldest of which are ready to blossom and bear fruit when the mother-tree dies.

Such is the history of the banana-tree, *Musa paradisiaca,* as it is called in the Tropical Flora. And of a certainty it was at home in the first paradise, where all was good.

One can scarcely imagine any thing prettier or more perfect than these young descendants, the banana children; they are the perfect image in miniature of the mother-tree, but the wind has no power upon their young leaves: they stand under the wing of the mother-tree in paradisiacal peace and beauty.

It has been attempted to transplant the banana-tree into the southern portion of North America, where so many trees from foreign climates flourish; but the banana-tree will not flourish there; its fruit will not ripen; it requires a more equal, more delicious warmth; it will not grow without the paradisiacal life of the tropics.

Roasted banana is as common a dish at the breakfasts of the Creoles as bread and coffee; but I like it only in its natural state.

The ladies in this country have very light house-keeping cares. The cook, always a negro woman, and if a man-cook, a negro also, receives a certain sum of money weekly with which to provide the family dinners. She goes to market and makes purchases, and selects that which seems best to her, or what she likes. The lady of the house frequently does not know what the family will have for dinner until it is on the table; and I can only wonder that the mistress can, with such perfect security, leave these matters to her cooks, and that all should succeed so well; but the faculty for, and the pleasure in all that concerns serving the table, is said to be universal among the negroes, and they compromise their honor if they do not serve up a good dinner.

Mrs. S. sits during the morning and reads with her two little girls in a hall, the doors of which open upon the piazza, and thence to the street or high road, and as the country people (*Monteros*, as they are here called, and who are always men) pass with their little horses heavily laden with vegetables, fruit, or poultry, now and then one of them will stop at the door and call to *la signora*, inquiring whether she will purchase this or that, and she says a couple of words in reply in that melodious Spanish tongue, and the whole is done in few words, without her needing to rise from her seat. Life might be very easy here. In the evening, after tea, we sit in rocking-chairs in the piazza, dressed as lightly as propriety will allow, and enjoy the air and the *dolce far niente.* All is then quiet in the little village; to breathe here is to live and enjoy!

My kind friends have taken me to the beautiful gardens of some of the aristocracy of the neighborhood—they are splendid, but formal. Every thing is set in rows along the graveled walks; and the tropical trees, the forms of which are regular by nature, add to the formality, when they are not grouped with some artistic and poetical feeling. In the lovely garden, for instance, of *El Conti Hernandinos*, it was this feeling which led to the planting of a circle of king-palms. In this way the most beautiful columned rotunda was formed which can be imagined; the crowns being all at the same height, locked their branches into each other, and formed a gigantic verdant garland, which waved and rustled in the wind, while the blue vault of heaven shone brightly through it.

I have taken a walk every morning into the Bishop's garden; but I was one morning persecuted there by a couple of half-naked, horrible-looking negroes, who probably said witty things while they begged, although I did not understand them, and they disturbed my comfort. Another morning I was so very unwell from something which I had taken, though I knew not what, that the joys of Paradise could not have pleased me; a third morning I was free and at peace, and again enjoyed life, but not as I did on the first morning. But neither was that needful; I was happy and thankful: *one* single morning such as that is enough for an immortal memory.

I have every night again saluted that large, magnificent constellation above the palm-tree mound, and have seen the quiet, melancholy, clear glance of the morning star over the earth. These nights, with the roar of the mountain stream and the rustling of the banana-trees, I shall never forget.

This morning Mrs. S. and myself went into the park. I observed some verses in Spanish inscribed upon a bamboo-tree, and asked her to read them to me. She could not do it, because their meaning was of the grossest kind. Again the old serpent!

One sees in the country around here small farms, on all of which are houses built of palm-trees, and thatched with tawny palm-leaves; the roofs are all pointed, and frequently taller than the cottages themselves. But all the dwelling-houses of the island are low, on account of the hurricanes, which otherwise would destroy them. Many small cottages are built of bark or of woven brushwood. The palm-tree, however, is the principal tree of the poor; it supplies them with material for their houses, and the calabash furnishes them with household wares. The little farms have a peculiar, although not ornamental appearance; still, they adorn the landscape with their own character.

I have heard a good deal of what occurred during the last hurricane. One spot was pointed out to me, near here, where stood a little peasant farm. The whole family were assembled in the house, twelve in number. The tempest shook the dwelling; the father admonished them all to pray; they threw themselves on their knees around him; he stood upright in the middle of the room, and prayed in the name of all. The tempest tore open a hole in the roof, and in the same moment overturned the house, leaving the father standing upright, but burying his wife, his children, and servants. Not a single one escaped excepting himself!

I shall, in the morning, return to Havana. If I could

but some time give pleasure to the excellent, kind people who have, by their hospitality, given so much to me! I am sorry to leave them, and, in particular, the youngest, most charming little girl, the dark-eyed little Ellen!

Havana, Feb. 15.

Again I am here! Heat is a good thing, but too much is—too much! And this heat is too stimulating both for soul and body. It may be possible to keep in health, but to keep in spirits is an impossibility; one becomes quite enervated. A fine sand-dust enters through the jalousies from the streets, and fills the air of the room, and covers every thing. Evening is the only time of the day in which one can breathe at all freely, partly in the open air, partly in the airy galleries within the house, opening into the court.

I am now staying with the F. family in *Calle* (street) *de Obra Pia.* Good Mrs. F. has arranged a room for my accommodation, and seems to have my comfort at heart in every possible way. She is one of those beautiful, maternal natures who make life so rich, and all in the house love her. I should love her if it were for no other reason than because she likes the negroes; is a motherly protector of the slaves; and openly takes the part of the negro character on all occasions, and can relate many beautiful traits of their nobility of mind, their faithfulness and good disposition. She spends one portion of the forenoon quite patriarchally in sitting and sewing among her female slaves, as well as in reading to the younger children in one of the long, open galleries, where she also receives visits, and gives orders for the business of the kitchen or the toilet. In the evening the large family party and their circle of friends gather around her in the galleries or the drawing-room. Then come the two young, lovely ladies, her daughters, with their husbands, both Germans, and one of whom is very musical; then come the English consul, Mr. C., with his lovely young wife, a daughter also of

Mrs. F., though by a former marriage; and there are the enamored pair, the eldest son of the house, and his blooming wife; and there are the betrothed couple, Louisa F., still almost a child, and her lover, a young Scotch gentleman, who is desperately in love, and very agreeable; there are the younger sons and daughters of the house, the youngest of these my grave little *Maestro* in the Spanish tongue, the thirteen-year-old Gulio and Emily, as pretty and graceful as one imagines a good fairy; then also come other friends of the family, and there is music, singing, and dancing; but the enamored bridegrooms, married or betrothed, sit beside their young brides and gaze at them, and will not let them dance or leave their sides.

The construction of houses in Havana is very peculiar, and one must get accustomed to them to like it. Every thing is arranged so as to produce as much air and as much circulation as possible. Long galleries, with wide semicircular arcades, open into the court (this house has them on four sides); in these galleries the whole household may be found, all busy, and leading a sort of public life; dinner is eaten, visits are received, the lady of the house sews surrounded by her female slaves, or instructs her children; her domestics wash, or perform their other respective household duties; every thing is done all in these open galleries, in which people and air circulate alike unimpeded. Within these galleries, which generally have marble floors, lie the sleeping rooms, separated from the gallery by Venetian shutters, the windows opening to the street, and which, in the upper story of the house, are inclosed in the same manner. On the ground floor, however, the windows have iron bars or gratings, and behind this grating a curtain which is drawn at night. During the day no curtain is seen, and these grated windows, with their upright iron bars, give a dismal, prison-like appearance to the story nearest to the street. In the more elegant houses, however, this window-grating is much ornamented, and frequently handsome ladies, rocking themselves in rocking-chairs, and fanning themselves with splendid fans, may be seen sitting behind the grating. Glass is never used. This construction of houses and arrangement of rooms gives free and general circulation to the air, and the air of Cuba can not be other than welcome, but with it comes, here in Havana, a vast deal of dust, which is detrimental both to neatness and comfort.

If one goes into the city—and I have rambled about a great deal by myself in the evening—one gets glimpses on all hands, through arcades and half-dusky passages, into homes and amid households, the figures of which are seen in a charming *clair-obscur*. They pass by and vanish into shade. On all sides you see new vistas open, new pictures in dusky arcades and beneath porticoes, ornamented with fresco-painting of fruits and flowers; but all is seen in a half light. Publicity has here a mystery, a shadowy depth; and in front of the open windows of the houses is iron grating. There is in the building of the city a great mixture of regularity and irregularity, of old and new, of the splendid and the dilapidated. Close beside the elegant arched arcade, with its gayly painted walls, stands a half-ruinous wall, the fresco-paintings of which are half obliterated or have pealed off with the mortar. And this old wall is not repaired, nor the old painting restored. All this—the countenances and life of the colored population; the silent, wedge-like way in which the volantes insinuate themselves between the rows of houses, give to Havana a peculiar character, and a romantic life which is unlike that of any other city which I have seen, and especially unlike those of England and North America.

We have now moonlight, and I can not but admire its brightness and transparency. Our moonlight in Sweden is tolerably bright, but has a colder, more blue tinge; here it is light yellow, and seems to me almost rose-tinted. Moonlight here is considered dangerous, and people do not venture into it with uncovered heads.

I have been two evenings to *La Plaza des Armas*, to hear the music, with my good friends Mr. and Mrs. F. Elegant signoras with light mantillas over their heads, which are adorned with flowers, walk about with polite caballeros under the magnificent king-palms, or sit on marble benches talking, while the music plays Cuban dances or marches, and pieces from favorite operas. A more beautiful festal hall than this place, with its palms and palaces, seen beneath the moonlight, and the beaming heaven of Cuba, can not be conceived. I have also seen here lovely poetical forms, and poetically lovely costumes. That transparent Spanish veil is like moonlight, a talisman which conceals deformity, and enhances beauty by its mystic, shadowy half light.

My amiable entertainers drove me one day to a village or small town, called Guanabacoa, which is said to be the oldest on the island, and which still preserves some memories of the aborigines, the mild, peaceful Indians who inhabited Cuba when the Spaniards discovered this beautiful island. And it is one of the peculiarities of Cuba that its aborigines were as mild as its climate, which even to this day exercises its delicious influence upon those who are born in the island. The Creoles are mild and of good disposition. There exist on the island neither poisonous plants nor venomous creatures. The native bee of Cuba has not even poison in its sting. The barbarities of the Spaniards in the island have not been able to poison its natural character; the blood of its massacred, inoffensive aborigines cries still from the earth, but its cry is a beautiful melody; it has baptized the most beautiful valley of Cuba with the name of *Yumori!*

Among the memories which the Indians have left in Guanabacoa is a kind of earthen vessel made from a sort of porous clay, peculiar to the place, and which is still made there. These earthen vessels are universal in Cuba for the keeping drinking-water cool in the house. The water evaporates through the porous vessel, around which a cloth is bound, which is thus always moist, and the water which is drawn off is fresh, if not always cool enough for my taste. The want of good drinking-water is a great want in Cuba. Ice is not as yet used there for the cooling of water, except in the large hotels of Havana.

The day was beautiful on which we drove to Guanabacoa, and the drive was beautiful also; but I was not able fully to enjoy it. I was worn out, from the want of rest for two nights, owing to the heat and the musquitoes, and I saw every thing in a half-slumbering state. The little town reminded me of a miniature picture of Havana, the houses built and painted in the same style, with the same flat roofs, and even ornamented azoteons, but all less and lower. The country exhibits still the same expanse of billowy plain scattered with palms and small farms, and with a background of that lofty mountain chain which runs from east to west, and which is every where a fine, prominent feature of its landscape. The highest peaks of these mountains, Patullo and Cobre, are said to be upward of 3000 feet.

The natural fortresses and strong-holds of the island have their own gloomy, romantic significance. Fugitive slaves live in these mountains, and have fortified themselves in their innumerable grottoes and caves, so that any pursuit of them is impossible. They have there built dwellings for themselves and obtained fire-arms, and at one time amounted to so large a number—it is said many thousands—that the government of Cuba entertained serious apprehensions from them. The difficulty, however, of obtaining food for themselves in these remote fastnesses have caused them of late greatly to decrease in number. Nevertheless, they prefer to live free, amid those free, stern mounttains, than to come down and live amid still sterner men.

The palm always constitutes an important feature in the landscape, especially when it stands singly or scattered in small groups. It strikes me as being the noblest and most human-like of all trees. On our homeward drive from Guanabacoa, I observed, in the clear moonlight, two palm-trees standing solitary in a large field. They stood a little apart, but the stems had more and more inclined toward each other, and their crowns met. Thus they stood, embracing each other with whispering branches, beneath that beautiful vault of heaven, themselves forming below it a lofty Gothic arch. Thus sometimes will two noble-minded adversaries approach each other and grow together the nearer they grow toward heaven.

Our road through the whole drive lay between quick hedges, consisting, for the most part, of immense aloes, the pointed, thorny leaves of which forbade any approach. I saw in the middle of these plants tall white and pink spikes of flowers not yet fully blown, and Mr. F. had the kindness to gather two of them for me. They resembled at a distance an immense hyacinth stem; they were the beautiful spikes of the aloe flower, and which afterward produce a pleasant juicy fruit, with a pine-apple flavor. Here and there an orange-tree shot up in the hedge, as well as that strange candelabra-like plant or tree which I had already observed on the heights around Havana harbor, but have not learned either its name or genus. Very unlike were these quick hedges to those of our country fields; they are, however, more odd-looking than really beautiful. We drove home in that clear, gold, and rose-tinted moonlight. I understand that there are many beautiful flowers which bloom only in this light, among which is the night-blowing cereus.

Among the miracles which the sun performs here, that which it performs in the depth of the sea is perhaps the most remarkable. The sun casts his prismatic bow into the deep, and colors the fish therewith. I yesterday paid a visit to the fish-market of Havana, and no stranger in Havana should fail of seeing this remarkable sight.

The fish glow with all the colors of the rainbow, with the most splendid clearness and distinctness; they are blue, yellow, red; they are edged with gold and violet, gold-tinted, and so on—it is the most magnificent fish-splendor that any one can imagine. The most beautiful algæ and corals are gathered from the sea around Cuba.

Good Mrs. F. has frequently invited me to accompany her to the opera, but I am so covetous of the air and the moonlight here, that I prefer spending my evenings on *La Plaza des Armas.* Nature here is to me No. 1; people and their fine shows, No. 2; I shall, however, go to-morrow to a large soirée at the house of the English consul, and see there the Spanish beauties. And then farewell to Havana for a time.

I have received two invitations which have greatly pleased me: the one to Matanzas, to the house of an American merchant there; the other to a plantation at a few miles' distance, from a Mrs. De C., whose friendly letter was a real refreshment to me; for there I shall be able to get out into the country, and to become acquainted with palms, and coffee-shrubs, and sugar-cane, and other tropical growths. I am greatly delighted. I wished to leave Havana, where the oppressive heat and the unusual mode of living have caused me to suffer from an intolerable headache, which I have now had for three days, and which I can not get rid of, although I am as much in the air as possible. To-morrow I shall go by rail-way to Matanzas, which is not quite a day's journey.

Before I close my letter, I must tell you the arrangement which the Swedish consul here, Mr. N., and Mr. S., wish to make for me. Mr. N. has a small country-house which he does not occupy, in the beautiful garden region close by the S.'s. This he wishes to furnish for me, and there I am to live in rural peace and freedom, attended by a respectable duenna, and to take my meals with the S.'s, who also invite me to take up my quarters with them as soon as their guest-chamber, which is now occupied, shall be at liberty. Is not this charming? I shall not probably avail myself of this proffered kindness, but I am grateful with all my heart for such hospitality. The good F.'s are, however, at the bottom of it all. God bless them!

You have now frost and snow, and cold, cold air, cold all around you! and here it is too hot for me; and heat is not much better than cold, particularly when one has a headache. But heart and soul are sound, and with them I embrace you in all love!

LETTER XXXIV.

Matanzas, Feb. 23d.

How beautiful it is here, my little heart; how good it is to be here! In this glorious air, fanned by balmy zephyrs, in this light, excellent, and, in every respect, comfortable home—the house of Mr. and Mrs. B.—where I am now staying, I feel myself, as it were, living anew. I have now been here for a whole week, which has passed like one bright, beautiful day.

It seemed to me pleasant to leave that hot, dusty Havana early on the morning of Monday the 16th, and there also I left my headache. I parted with it the night before, when I went to bed, and had a sound sleep. That kind, cordially good Mrs. F. was up with me at five o'clock the next morning, and had coffee brought for me and herself from a Restaurateur's, because she would not disturb her slaves so early; and after having taken a heartfelt leave of her and her husband, I seated myself in their volante, accompanied by one of the youngest sons of the house, and my favorite Frank. The calashero cracked his whip in the air, and we rapidly swung away to the rail-way station. I was glad when I, with the help of my young conductor, had got safely through all the difficulties and impediments of the rail-way, and was seated quietly in a spacious carriage. The carriages are built in the American fashion, because Americans constructed the rail-way and built the carriages at Cuba. All the windows were down, to allow the glorious morning air free ingress; and although all the gentlemen who were in the carriage—from forty to fifty in number—smoked cigars or cigaritos, there was no smell of smoke, and scarcely any to be perceived. The air of Cuba seems to have the power of annihilating smoke. I was the only lady in the carriage, and sat solitarily on my sofa, and nearly solitarily in my portion of the carriage; but all the more uninterruptedly could I see around me, and—ah! that morning, when I flew over the new earth, beautiful as a paradise, through a paradisiacal atmosphere, and saw around me new and enchanting scenes and objects—it was only by inward and deep thanksgiving that so much enjoyment could be sanctified.

There had been rain in the night, and splendid clouds piled themselves in masses along the horizon, and grouped themselves in fantastic shapes above the blue mountains. Now they lifted themselves in heavy draperies above them, to flee from the ascending sun; then formed a magnificent portal, with a frame of gold; and beyond it shone a sea of soft, rose-colored light; it lightened above the tops of the mountains, and—the sun rose. The fantastic little blue and yellow villas, with their splendid gardens full of splendid flowers and strange plants; the palm-thatched cottages in the fields, the lofty, green palm-trees above their yellow-gray roofs; groves of mango, plantain, orange, and cocoa-trees, the verdant hedges and fields, all shone fresh and beautiful amid the gushing sunshine in the moist, mild morning.

Along the whole course of the way new and lovely objects met my eye; flowers, plants, gardens, dwellings, all bade me good-morning as we sped past them. But a potato-field and a large cabbage-ground greeted me as fellow-countrymen and old friends. The whole country looked like an immense garden; beautiful palms presented themselves at all distances, waving their crowns in the morning wind, and along the edge of the horizon before me arose a chain of dark blue mountains, the heights of Camerioca.

I was quite well; no human being could be better; both body and soul had wings, and I flew over the beautiful, brilliant earth.

The villas disappeared by degrees, and plantations of sugar-cane, and other vegetable growths which were unknown to me, took their places. We traveled through whole forests of planted banana-trees. After that the landscape became wilder, and parasite plants showed themselves on tree and meadow. Presently those got the upper hand, and seemed to choke vegetation. The crowns of many trees bore whole gardens of orchids and aloes on their branches. The appearance was queer rather than beautiful, although various of these parasitic plants had very lovely flowers, but the whole looked heavy and unnatural. In one field not far from the road I noticed a lofty, half-dead ceiba-tree, around the gigantic stem of which the parasite *Yaguay embra*, a female fig-tree, had flung its hundred-fold arms in an immense embrace, entwining the tree from root to head, until it had nearly destroyed its life. This death-struggle between the ceiba-tree and the female parasite, which grows and nourishes itself with its life, and finally destroys it, is a frequent sight in Cuba, and it is a very remarkable and really unpleasant spectacle. There is a complete tragedy in the picture, which reminds one of Hercules and Dejanira, of King Agne and Aslög.

The first part of the day and the journey were full of

pleasures, among which I must reckon some excellent sandwiches and bananas which good Mrs. F. provided me with, and as I ate them I thought of her, so motherly, so kind, so thoughtful for me and for all who belong to her. Gratitude and joy in human beings is the best food of the soul. In a while the day became too warm, and the whole of nature too much overrun with parasitic growths. It oppressed me, and made me drowsy.

Some ladies with Spanish physiognomies entered the carriage at one of the rail-way stations. They seemed to be country people, but were well dressed, and wore no covering on the head. Two of them were very handsome, were stout, and bore themselves proudly and with great hauteur and ungraciousness to a couple of gentlemen, evidently their admirers, who attended them, and who, at the last moment, presented bouquets with an air which did not look despairing, but rather full of roguishness, as they withdrew, without obtaining a glance from the proud beauties. This woke me up a little. And I was wide awake when we, in the afternoon, left behind us that region of ensnarement, and the landscape suddenly expanding itself, the city of Matanzas was before us, its glorious bay now blue—clearly, brightly blue—and in the background the lofty mountain ridge, *Pan de Matanzas*, so called from its form, and the opening to Yumori Valley. The freshest, the most delicious breezes met us here; and at the rail-way station I was met by two gentlemen, with mild, agreeable countenances, who bade me welcome. It was my countryman, Mr. F., from Götheberg, now resident at Matanzas, and Mr. J. B., who conveyed me in his volante to his handsome house. Here I was received most kindly by his handsome young wife, a Creole, but with such a fair, fresh Northern appearance, that she needed merely a helmet on her brow to have served as a model for a Valkyria.

With this agreeable young couple I am spending my

time quietly and pleasantly, and invigorating myself, both soul and body, partly in their fresh pleasant home—(my young hostess is the daughter of an Anglo-American, and every thing in the house bears the impress of that cleanliness, order, and excellent management which distinguish the housewives of that race)—and partly by my solitary rambles in the neighborhood of the city, although it is so unusual for a lady out of doors—especially with a bonnet on her head—to make use of her own means of promenade, instead of those of the horse or volante, that little negro boys and girls run after me shouting and laughing, and grown-up people stand and stare, and horses and oxen are sometimes frightened. People are, however, beginning now to be used to me, and to seeing me go out; and I will not, without very good reasons, give up my solitary rambles of discovery.

Will you accompany me on one of them, the first, the most charming which I have yet made, and when I, early in the morning, visited alone the valley of Yumori? As a matter of course, you must understand that the morning was beautiful; but how beautiful nobody can understand who has not experienced the early morning hour, and the caresses of the spirit of the sea from Matanzas Bay. The valley of Yumori lies about two hundred paces from Matanzas. You see a gorge between two lofty crags, and through the gorge a bright little river, which flows between verdant banks to unite itself to the sea—I do not say throw itself into it, because it is too tranquil for that. It is clear and calm as a mirror. Let us follow the little stream through the rocky portals, outside of which is open meadow, and the broad blue Bay of Matanzas, with ships from all the nations of the world sailing in, or lying at anchor far, far into the distance.

We walk along the banks of the Yumori River, and pass the mountain portals; and within, a wonderfully beautiful valley expands, the green-sward overgrown with palms and verdurous shrubs, and inclosed on each side by lofty mountain ridges. The shadows of the hills lie cool and dusk upon that portion of the valley along which our path runs. How beautiful it is here in the cool shadow! On our left is the mirror-like river, which begins to withdraw, under our gaze, into a wood of mangrove—a species of shrub which grows in the water, and increases by throwing its twigs down to the bottom, where they take root and spring up afresh into green shrubs. On the opposite side of the river rises abruptly, but with a soft, waving outline, Pan de Matanzas, and on our side run sloping upward the heights of Combre. The rock shoots out on the hillsides in bold basaltic colonnades, scoops itself into grottoes, mysterious porticoes, and arches which are alone visited by the birds of heaven. The bold heights are here and there crested with palms, and heavy trails of creeping plants hang around them. Lower down, and at their feet, the vegetation becomes still more luxuriant; it is one rich mass of beautiful trees, shrubs, and flowers, among which I lost myself in delight and ignorance. I know the popular names, however, of some of the flowers. There glows the fever-flower, in gold and flame, indescribably brilliant; there is the wild heliotrope, luxuriant in growth, but as modest in color and form as our northern hot-house heliotrope; there is the beautiful white blossom of the mangrove, with a chalice half of the convolvulus and half of the lily form, and diffusing a delicious fragrance; and there, along our path, at our very feet, see that little shrub, full of small, splendidly crimson flowers, with hundreds of little mouths or bills gaping on its stalk, upward when they are young, and downward toward the earth, upon which they fall, still quite crimson and fresh, as they become older; and see how little velvet green humming-birds flutter around them—how enamored they are of them, how little afraid of us; how they dip, hovering on the wing, their long bills into the open bills of the flowers—animal life and vegetable life here meet and kiss—it is most beautiful! This plant, with its crimson, falling flowers, is Cupid's tears, *Lacrymos cupido.* But *Lacrymos cupido* are not the pale tears of sorrow. They are the glowing tears of an overflowing, blissful heart. They are wept by the heart of Nature, and winged lovers sip their sweetness.

The valley still lies before us, but its extent is hidden. The bend of the hills closes the view. Now, however, our path suddenly turns to the right, and the valley reveals itself. Before us on the right lies, in the bosom of the hills, and amid the most beautiful grove of palms, a little farm, a Cuban farm, with palm-leaf-thatched roof, and our path leads through groups of cocoa-palms, laden with fruit. Now we descend a little hill, and now on the right of the descent, at a short distance from the path, we find the ruins of a stone wall and a well. All around grow, in picturesque confusion, cocoa-palms, mamay, and mango-trees, cypresses, ceibas, and many other species of trees. We advance down the little hill, and toward the farm; but just below it the path winds round to the left, and now proceeds more straightforward up the valley. The valley opens to us like a vast and beautiful palm-grove, inclosed by an elliptical frame of hilltops. We still advance for a little distance; the valley becomes broader, with softly undulating ground; and, whichever way we turn, we see only palms—palms. Beneath such trees, such groves, beautiful, immortal beings might wander!

Here again lies a little farm not far from the path, with its straw-thatched house and brushwood cottage, between which shines out a large blossoming oleander. We enter to look around; we must beg a draught of water. *La fermière*, a thin, shriveled, brown-eyed woman, looks as if she would give us every thing which she possesses; but she does not understand us, and we do not understand her. But we obtain water for all that, and a great bunch of blossoming oleander, which she breaks off for us with a hearty good-will. The sun is now beginning to be hot, let us therefore return; we will come hither again, for we must become still better acquainted with the valley of Yumori.

And see, here come Monteros, with their heavily-laden horses, the packages being laid straight across their backs. They salute us kindly with melodious voices, halt, and inquire good-humoredly where goes *la signora*, and what she wants. La signora says that she comes from *Svecia.* The Monteros look at her perplexed, and then at one another. They do not know such a place as *Svecia*, and can not understand the wanderer. She tells them that she is from *un paeso sotto la estreja del Norte!* And now they believe she says that she comes from the *north star*, and they say, "Oh!" and look at one another, and smile significantly, and wrinkle their brows; they now comprehend that *la signora* is somewhat wrong in the head, and, compassionately shaking their heads, they drive on their horses. I can not tell you how gentle and good-hearted they seem; and, slowly following them, we pursue the road back to Matanzas. Still the lofty mountain wall casts its shadow over the cocoa palm grove by the well. We seat ourselves on the broken stone wall, and breakfast on bananas, which we have taken with us; an incomparable breakfast, in that delicious morning air, in that wonderfully beautiful valley! Gentle and happy people ought to live at the farm among the palm-trees, up among the hills. Amid such beautiful, joy-giving objects in that delicious air, human beings should become gentle and good.

The sun climbs over the hills, and it is quite hot before we reach Matanzas; but we have thus spent a beautiful morning in the valley of Yumori.

I have made some acquaintance in the city of Matanzas, and, through one of these, have been able to visit a large coffee and sugar plantation in the neighborhood of the city

N 2

There I saw avenues of many rare tropical trees and plants; a kind of palm-tree, which twists its gigantically strong branches like cork-screws, and bears gigantic fruit; a kind of citron-tree, which bears immense citron-like fruit, but which are not valued as such. I was most interested by making acquaintance with the sago and date palms, with arrow-root, with the guava-tree and its pleasant fruit, as well as with the wonderfully beautiful hibiscus flowers; and nothing delighted me more than to be surrounded with little fluttering humming-birds, which are, on the island, so remarkably fearless of man, and continually hover around the splendid red flowers with which Cuba seems to adorn herself rather than with flowers of any other color. Their rapid, arrow-like flight hither and thither, the fluttering movement of their wings while they are sipping from the flowers, are a perpetual astonishment and delight to me. They correspond with nothing which I have seen of animal or human life, and they seem to me not to be made of this earth's dust. A favorite place of resort for their building seems to be on the banks of lovely little purling brooks, shaded by thick masses of foliage, where the nests are concealed among the trees. Among the curiosities of the place, I observed many orchideous parasites hanging from the trees, as well as a large ceiba-tree, encircled by its hostile mistress, *Yaguay embra*, and killed by its dangerous embrace.

The plantation, for the rest, had a very forlorn appearance, in consequence of the two last tornadoes, which came in rapid succession, and left it in perfect desolation; besides which the cholera had carried off a great portion of the negro slaves.

"The Lord punishes our sins, punishes our sins!" said the owner of the plantation, with an expression half of levity, half of repentance and acknowledgment of the justice of the punishment. He was an elderly man, with French manners and nervous excitability, but a very polite host. I would very willingly be his guest, but not his slave. The slave-rooms, in a low wall or building, were no better than dark pig-styes with us. There was also a hospital. It was a large, dark room, in which stood some wooden bedsteads, but without coverlets or pillows, nor was there a ray of light in the room. He was himself, he said, the only physician of the sick: he could himself let blood, &c. I could not help shuddering. The plantation seemed almost a desert. I saw a shriveled old negro cripple steal past us, with a shy, submissive look. A little sharp lad waited at table with an unconcerned air, and who seemed not to trouble himself in the least about his master's violent exclamations and movements.

This gentleman was at one time very wealthy, but he has during the last few years suffered great losses, which he is said to bear with great equanimity.

Matanzas is built in the same style as Havana, but has a more open and cheerful appearance; the streets are considerably wider, although not paved. The house of my friends here is two stories high; a piazza runs round the upper story opening into the street, and here I walk in the evenings inhaling the air, while my hostess in the drawing-room plays Cuban contra-dances in exquisite time, and full of abounding life. One hears these dances ounding at all distances from the houses of the city. Wherever one may be, or wherever one goes in Matanzas, this dance-music may be heard. The time and measure are derived from the children of Africa, the peculiar music from the Spanish Creoles of Cuba, and one hears in it Spanish seguidillas, national songs, and marches. Both Mr. and Mrs. B. are musical, and it is a pleasure to me to hear him play, on the organ notes of the piano, the Catholic anthem, *Adeste Fideles*, and to hear him play the Spanish dances, *Hauta Arragonesa*, *El Sabbatheo*, &c. The most sparkling Champagne of life exists in these national dances. It is amusing to compare with these our polkas and other popular dances; they are not deficient in this abounding, sparkling life, but they want refinement and grace. These dissimilar national dances stand in the same relationship as Champagne, and ale, and mead.

Matanzas, March 1st.

If there be one place on earth where the spirit of life has a separate individual existence, as pure, as pleasant, as full of vitality as when it first was breathed forth by the Lord of life and love, it is—here. The atmosphere here has a kind of vitalizing life, which is a perpetual marvel to me and a perpetual delight. It is especially in the afternoons, after two or three o'clock, that this peculiar, wonderful life arises. It is one constant pleasant wafting, not from any particular distance, but every where, and from all points, which makes every light and movable thing around you waft, and, as it were, breathe and live. That indescribable, but, at the same time, pleasant and life-giving wafting caresses your brow, your cheek—lightly lifts your dress, your ribbons—surrounds you, goes through you, as it were, bathes you in an atmosphere of salutary, regenerating life. I feel its influence in both soul and body; I drink that wind, that air, as one might drink a renovating elixir of life, and I am ready to look round to see whether any angel is near, whether any heavenly presence sits on the crowns of the palms, which produces this wonderful life. I call it the breath of God, as I softly walk to and fro on the piazza, or lean over the iron railing and give myself up to its caresses, and until late at night inhale its salutary life. Oh my Agatha! it whispers to me wonderful emotions and anticipations of the Creator's wealth—of those hidden glories which "no eye hath seen, no ear heard, nor hath it entered into the heart of man to conceive, but which God hath prepared for those who love Him." This wonderful spirit of life is to me the greatest marvel of Cuba; and I can not describe how beneficial its influence seems to me.

Since I last wrote I have spent more deliciously tranquil days at Matanzas, the beautiful, healthy situation of which is not subject to oppressive heats, and where I feel so wonderfully well. Early in the mornings I set forth on my solitary expeditions of discovery, and in the afternoon drive out in a volante with my kind hostess, and breathe the soft sea-breeze as we drive along *la pleja*.

I have spent one whole day in Yumori Valley, partly to sketch some trees and cottages, and partly to see how the country people live here. For this purpose I determined to take up my quarters at the little peasant farm with the oleander-trees; and the good B.'s allowed me to drive there in their volante, and take with me one of their female negroes as a servant and interpreter. Cecilia, the negro woman, has the most beautiful dark eyes I ever saw in a dark countenance—although such have generally beautiful eyes—teeth like Oriental pearls, and a quiet, gentle, and unusually serious demeanor. My poor Cecilia is ill, and probably incurably so, of consumption, and Mrs. B. wishes her now to enjoy a little country air and life. Cecilia is only lately married to a young man of her own color; she is happy in her marriage, and happy as the slave of good owners, and would gladly live.

When we reached the peasant farm, Cecilia preferred my request to *la fermière*, who, with animated gestures, immediately declared that the whole house was at my *disposizion*. I installed myself in the most airy of the small houses, which was furnished likewise with a rustic piazza, shaded by the palm-leaf-thatched roof. The floors were of bare earth, but the rooms were in other respects comfortable, and had well-furnished beds, and were tolerably clean. A little colored picture on paper was pasted on the wall of the bed-room proper, representing the Virgin Mary and the child Jesus, with an inscription in Spanish. I inquired from the good housewife what was the purport of it, and she replied, with an aspect of devotion, that "it was written there that whoever bought such a picture obtained forgiveness of sin for forty days." It was also printed upon the picture that such an indulgence was granted *à todos los fideles*, as owned *una salve à nuestra Sennora del Rosario. C'est imprimé.*

Below the picture stood the following verse:

Fragranti rosa es Maria
En el jardin celestiel,
Y el amparo maternel
Del peccador cada die.

This indulgence for the sins of forty days might be bought for a quarter of a pesos (about a fourth of a dollar). It is remarkable that in a country where such permissions for sin are openly prepared, and bought and sold, that the people should still continue pious and inoffensive; but so it is. The poor country people of Cuba are said to be remarkable for their good and quiet disposition. It is certainly owing to the delicious air! The people of my rural abode were from the Canary Islands, where it is more difficult for the indigent to provide for themselves than in Cuba. For this reason, a great number of poor people, whose occupation is agriculture, come hither.

At about ten o'clock my hostess went up to some high ground, and blew upon a shell, which produced a shrill but not inharmonious sound, calculated to reach to a great distance. This was the signal for the men, who were out at work in the valley, to assemble for breakfast. The breakfast was prepared for seven or eight persons in the piazza under the straw roof of the little house which contained the kitchen. A parrot (*una cotorra*) sat below it also, in its cage of iron-wire. Violet-blue doves flew around us hither and thither, and cocks and hens promenaded round us with the queerest twisted necks, which gave them a deformed look. The men, both old and young, with gloomy, cheerless countenances, assembled for breakfast, which consisted of stock-fish and yams, maize-bread, roasted plantains (a coarse kind of bananas), and flesh-meat, besides which was a sort of light yellow meal, served in a large bowl, but the name of which I could not learn, because Cecilia spoke but imperfect English. The breakfast was abundant, but badly set out and badly cooked.

The dinner consisted of boiled meat, brown beans, and boiled rice; but all so insufficiently boiled, so hard and insipid, that I could not eat any thing which the kind-hearted *fermière* heaped up on a plate for me, and if Cecilia had not brought for herself some rice and potatoes (I would not bring more with us), which she cooked and she and I ate with fresh butter, also from my Matanzas home, I must have suffered that day from hunger. Now, however, I lived like a shepherdess in a story, and crowned my meal with bananas and delicate sugar-cake.

I talked about many things with my good Cecilia. She had been stolen as a child from Africa; she was only eight years old when she was taken from her mother, and this mother remained lovingly impressed on her memory. She remembered how her mother had loved her, how tender she had been toward her, and Cecilia wished to return to Africa that she might see her once more. She made no complaints of her master and mistress; they had always been kind to her, she said, and now especially was she happy in her situation; but she longed to see her mother once more.

And Cecilia will see her mother before long, but not on this earth.

Two little dark-eyed children, Joannito and Annita, were my play-fellows in the cottage, especially the little boy, who was full of merriment, and yet in a quiet and agreeable way.

I drew a little, sitting in the piazza, under the straw roof, and when the heat of the day was over I set out with Cecilia to explore the valley to its full extent. We did so, although the ramble was a long one, and Cecilia was so fatigued that I became very anxious about her. But, by resting at various places by the way, we at length reached the cottage in safety, though not until after the sun had set, when the stars shone brightly down into the valley. We did not meet with any one, excepting some Monteros in the twilight, who saluted us in their melodious voices with a "*Buona tardi*" or "*Adios!*"

The valley retained to its close very much the same features; a succession of beautiful palm-groves, here and there a little group of palm-leaf-thatched houses; and toward the end of the valley, which was there also inclosed by hills, although not equal in height to Pan de Matanzas and Combre, lay a sugar plantation, with a sugar-mill, negro slaves, a slave village, &c., belonging to it. The beautiful valley even has its share in the old curse. The crimson glow of sunset, seen above the verdant heights, and the calm splendor of heaven through the palm-trees, were indescribably beautiful, and when the stars shone forth they appeared to me larger and brighter than I had ever seen them before.

This beautiful valley has, however, no memories worthy of the pure glances of heaven. It derives its name, it is said, from the death-cry of its Indian aborigines, "*Io more*," when they, in order to escape being massacred by the Spaniards, flung themselves from the heights down into the river which divides one portion of the valley. And of the little farm in the palm-grove imbosomed in the hills, the loveliness of which enchanted me the first morning I was here, nothing is related excepting a bloody family-quarrel. A father dwelt there with several sons. They were to divide the farm, but a quarrel arose about the boundaries of the property, and every night one landmark or another was removed. One morning—one of those beautiful tropical mornings!—the brothers, who had quarreled about the landmarks, came to blows; other members of the family rushed in to take one side or the other, and the result of the combat was eleven dead bodies. Such is the story which was told me. It occurred not so long since, and the farm is now possessed by one of the sons who remained.

Such are the traditions of Yumori Valley; and Matanzas—Matanzas, where the wafting breath of life plays round you with such enchanting vitality—*Matanzas* is the name for "the field of blood," or "the battle-field," and is so called from a bloody battle which was fought here many hundred years ago by the Indian aborigines. It is sorrowful to think of it. It is not, however, without pleasure that I feel the breath of God in the wind pass over the formerly bloody field. It seems to say, when all scenes of murder and violence cease on the earth, He is still the same, and His life the same, eternally efficacious, eternally salutary, regenerating; and these beautiful palms, Cupid's tears, and humming-birds, and all the beautiful existences and shapes of life, shall appear with it, and—remain.

Mrs. B.'s volante came to fetch me and Cecilia in the deep twilight. We took with us sugar-cane from the plantation, which Cecilia desired for the little girls at home; and, as a token of her hearty good-will, my good *fermière* gave me as a parting gift her indulgence for forty days' sins, and which I shall take with me to Sweden and present to Bishop Fahlcrantz.

I returned home, half roasted in my rural abode, and for three days afterward had to work hard in freeing myself from swarms of fleas, which I brought back with me from my Arcadian excursion.

The number of small insects of various kinds is really one of the torments of this country, and I found this plague also in South Carolina and Georgia. If one left a little piece of cake or bread lying in the rooms, it was immediately surrounded by a swarm of little worms and creeping things. Here in Cuba it is the ants which are especially troublesome, one small kind of which will, it is said, undermine a large house.

During the days that I amused myself by drawing my little memorials of the valley of Yumori, and among other lovely things, the Cupid's tears kissed by the little humming-birds, I had laid some of those flowers upon the table beside me—that is to say, some of the small red blossoms which had fallen—that I might examine at my leisure their form and veining. To my surprise, however, I observed that one after another of these blossoms disappeared from the table. I laid some fresh ones there, but it was not long before they too had vanished. I could not understand how it was. By chance, however, casting my eyes toward one of the walls of the room, I there, to my astonishment, beheld my flowers advancing in a long row up it to the very ceiling. Very, very small light-colored ants were dragging them up, and had made a regular line from my table up to the ceiling, where they disappeared. They were so small and light that I at first had not noticed them. One single ant dragged in this way up the wall a blossom which was twelve times larger than itself.

I was one evening one of the spectators of a great ball given by the free negroes of Matanzas for *La Casa de Beneficienza* in the city, to which the white public were invited by the black. The ball took place in the theatre, and the gazing public occupied the boxes. Mr. B., and my young and agreeable countryman, Mr. F., accompanied me; and one of my unknown benefactors, who, I believe, was a Spaniard, hastened forward at the entrance to the theatre and paid the admission fee for the foreign *signora*. And speaking of this, I may as well mention what I have here heard of the politeness of Spaniards to ladies, which exceeds any thing that I have experienced among other nations; even the chivalry of the Americans is not to be compared to it. It is true, at times it seems to be more than necessary, and it may be mere sham and hollowness; but there is, nevertheless, something beautiful and noble at the bottom, in its usages and forms. As, for instance, ladies, and even gentlemen who are strangers, will not be allowed to pay for their own purchases at fancy-shops, in eating-houses, confectioners' shops, and such like, or for their tickets at the theatres; and yet neither the lady nor the stranger-gentleman will have any idea to whom it is that he is obliged for this politeness. Suppose, now, that you go to a perfumer's to purchase a bottle of *eau de rose*, or to a confectioner's for *un libro de dulces* (Cuba *dulces*, or sweetmeats, are very celebrated), and you are about to pay for them. You take out your *pesos*, but they are returned to you with a polite bow, and "It costs you nothing, *signora!*" And it will do no good though you should remonstrate, neither is it worth while. Some gentleman has been, or is then among the purchasers, perhaps unknown to you, but well known to the people of the shop, and he has given a secret sign or nod, which has expressed, "I shall pay for her!" and then has left the shop, or goes on reading his newspaper, and you never know to whom you are obliged for this polite attention. Two of my lady acquaintances at Havana told me that they were annoyed and distressed by continual politeness of this kind, and which laid them under silent obligations which they had no means of discharging; and I can very well understand that the thing may have its annoyances, but it is very polite nevertheless; and toward a foreigner and a stranger, it is a politeness which is both beautiful and noble, when it declines the possibility of thanks.

But to return to the negro banquet and ball.

A banquet, arranged with flowers, lamps, and ornaments, occupied the lower part of the dancing hall. The dancers amounted to between two and three hundred persons. The black ladies were, for the most part, well dressed, after the French mode, and many of them very fine. Some couples danced, with great dignity and precision, some exceedingly tiresome minuets. What a foolish dance it is when it is not danced with beauty by beautiful or charming people! The principal lady in this case was so ugly, spite of her really magnificent apparel and fine carriage, as to remind me of a dressed-up ape, and the movements of the cavaliers were deficient in natural elasticity, which the negroes in general seemed to want.

But the great dance of the ball, a kind of wreath-dance, in which the whole company took part, amid innumerable artistic entanglements and disentanglements—the grouping and inwreathing themselves, in an infinite variety of ways, with chains of artificial roses—all this was really lovely and picturesque, and was executed with exquisite precision; and if there had been a little less formality, and more natural animation, I could have believed that I beheld in it a type of civilized negro life. Those beautiful dark eyes, those splendid white teeth, in some pretty young girls especially, shone out joyously while they bent their heads and then rose from beneath the arches of rose-garlands.

Many of the negroes were wealthy, and one young negro was pointed out to me in the company as being possessed of property to the amount of 20,000 dollars.

The Spanish law for the West Indian colonies, *los lejes de los Indios,* has some excellent and just enactments, as regards the rights and the emancipation of negro slaves, which those of the American states are still deficient in, to their shame be it spoken! Their laws are purely opposed to the slave's acquisition of freedom and independence. The laws of the Spaniards favor the slaves in these respects. Here the slave is able to purchase his own freedom for the stipulated legal sum of five hundred dollars, and the judges (*syndics*) are commanded to watch over the rights of the slave. Here a mother may purchase the freedom of her child, before its birth, for fifteen dollars, and after its birth for double that sum. *She may emancipate her child.*

Slaves here, at all events in the cities, have a much better chance of acquiring money than in the American slave states; and, as free negroes, they are able to carry on trade, to rent land, to pursue agriculture and other occupations; and many free negroes have acquired property by trade. On the other hand, the condition of the slaves on the plantations here is, in general, much worse; they are worked much harder, and they lack all religious instruction. They are regarded altogether as cattle, and the slave-trade with Africa is still carried on actively, although privately. A few days ago a cargo of seven hundred negroes was secretly conveyed from Africa to Havana.* The government of the island received fifty dollars for each slave as "hush-money," and was silent. Pleasant and honorable!

The negroes in the cities look cheerful and healthy. One sees many handsome, well-grown, and not unfrequently splendidly dressed mulatto women on the promenades and in the churches. The fair mulattoes so nearly resemble the Spaniards in complexion and feature that it is difficult to distinguish them. The Spaniards are said to be, in general, very kind to their domestic slaves, and not unfrequently indulgent to their weaknesses.

March 2. Good-morning, my little heart! I have just returned from mass in Matanzas church, for Matanzas has only one church, although it has a population of above thirty thousand souls. I heard there thundering music from the Spanish soldiery of the city, which greatly resembled the music of the dance; saw great parade of those

* These poor creatures are not sold here publicly, but in secret. They are said to be emaciated in a high degree, and look miserable when they are first landed, after the voyage from Africa, which is a three weeks' martyrdom for them; and they require to be fed up and brought into condition before they can tempt purchasers.

occupying the centre aisle of the church; groups of ladies on their knees on splendid mats, many of them handsome, and all in grand array of silk and velvet, jewels or flowers, with bare necks and arms; all with transparent veils, black or white, thrown over the gayly-attired form, and evidently more occupied with their appearance than with their prayer-books; around them stood rows of well-dressed gentlemen, evidently more occupied with gazing at the ladies than with—any thing else; divine service and devotion existed not, excepting in the hearts of two persons—at least judging from appearance—the one an elderly man, and a Spaniard, the other a mulatto woman. The rest was a grand show of priests and ceremonial. The choir of the church was in a gallery near the roof, covered with palm-branches, banners, and holy pictures. Palm-leaves were blessed and distributed. The Spanish soldiers took part in the solemnity, standing in line in the church; most of them appeared to be young men of slender figure, and refined and handsome features. Slaves, both male and female, after they had rolled out the mats for their mistresses and their daughters, withdrew themselves into the background of the church, where they knelt upon the bare floor. A stranger and a Protestant knelt there among them and prayed—for them as well as for herself and her beloved ones. But her prayer here for herself is thanksgiving. She also received some of the blessed palm-leaves, and will convey them to her home in the remote North, in memory of this morning hour. It was a beautiful, warm, sunny morning. Life looked delicious and easy for all. Oh! if the inner life here only corresponded to the outer, how easy it would be to live and to crown one's self with garlands!

The costume of those beautiful ladies gave me pleasure, although I can not approve of it for a church, and that Spanish mantilla, which, however, is said to be going more and more out of use, produces an infinitely picturesque effect. The negro and mulatto women use it mostly as a long shawl and of thicker material, to screen them from the sun when they are out in the middle of the day. Sometimes, and even to-day, I have seen ladies, evidently not of the lower class, dressed in garments of coarse gray sackcloth, and with this scarf of the same cloth over the head. I have been told that this is in fulfillment of some vow or prayer, made in time of need, or of sickness for themselves or their friends.

I shall to-day leave Matanzas to accompany my kind friends to a sugar-plantation belonging to Mrs. B.'s parents, at a place called Limonar, about fifteen miles off. I shall there study trees and flowers, and the Lord knows what else. After a stay of a few days at Limonar, I shall go to Madame De C.'s, who resides on a large sugar-plantation situated between Matanzas and the city of Cardinas. Kind and hospitable people provide me here also with opportunities of seeing the country and the people, and I can not say how thankful I am for this kindness.

Ariadne Inhegno, March 7th.

I have now been here for more than a week in the very lap of slavery, and during the first few days of my visit I was so depressed that I was not able to do much. Close before my window—the residence of the planter is a large one-storied house—I could not avoid seeing the whole day a group of negro women working under the whip, the cracking of which (in the air, however) above their heads, and the driver's (a negro) impatiently-repeated cry of "*Arrea! Arrea!*" be quick! get on! kept them working on without any intermission. And through the night —the whole night—I heard their weary footsteps, as they spread out to dry upon the flagged pavement, outside my window, the crushed sugar-cane which they carried from the sugar-mill. In the daytime it is their work to rake up together the sun-dried canes, *la bagaza*, and carry them in baskets again to the sugar-mill, where they serve as fuel to heat the furnaces in which the sugar is boiled. The work on a sugar-plantation must go on incessantly, night and day, during the whole time of the sugar-harvest, which is, in Cuba, during the whole season called *la Secca*, which is probably half the year. It is true that I frequently heard the women chattering and laughing during their incessant labor, untroubled by the cracking of the whip, and that during the night I often heard African songs and merry shouts, but which—sounding from the sugar-mill—lacked all melody and music. I know also that the laborers on this plantation were changed every seven hours, so that they always have six hours in every four-and-twenty for rest and refreshment; and that during two nights in the week the sugar-mill rests, and they are able to sleep; but still I could not reconcile myself to it. Neither can I now, but I can bear it better, since I have seen the cheerfulness of the slaves at their work, and their good, pleasant, and even joyous appearance, as a general rule, on this plantation.

I have several times visited the Negro-Slaves' Bohea, which is a kind of low fortress-like wall, built on the four sides of a large, square court-yard, with a large gateway on one side, which is locked at night. The slaves' dwellings are within the wall—one room for each family—and open into the court. Nothing is to be seen on the outside of the wall but a row of small openings, secured with iron bars, one to each room, and so high in the wall that the slaves can not look out from within. In the middle of the large court-yard is a building which serves as a cooking-kitchen, wash-house, &c. I have been present in this bohea more than once at the slaves' meal-times, and seen them fetch their calabash bowls full of snow-white rice, which had been boiled for them in an immense kettle, and which the black cook dealt out with a ladle, and with what seemed to me unreserved liberality. I have seen the slaves' white teeth shine out, and heard them chattering and laughing as they devoured the white rice grains, of which they are very fond (many times helping themselves to them with their fingers). They have, besides, salt fish and smoked meat; I saw also, in some of their rooms, bunches of bananas and tomatoes. According to law, a planter must furnish each slave with a certain measure of dried fish or salted meat per week, together with a certain number of bananas. But the slave-master, of course, does just as he pleases, for what law will call him to account? The appearance, however, of the slaves on this plantation testifies evidently of their being well fed and well contented.

I often made the inquiry as I pointed to their food, *E buono?* and always received in reply the words *Si e buono!* with a contented and ready smile.

I have already heard it said in America that the French were considered the most judicious of slaveholders; and my host here, Mr. C., who is of French origin, born in St. Domingo, is a proof to me of the truth of this assertion. He works his slaves very hard; but he feeds them well, and takes good care of them, and they do their work cheerfully and quickly.

Mr. C. is a courteous, lively, and loquacious Frenchman, with a good deal of acuteness and sagacity of mind; and I have to thank him for much valuable information —among other things, on the various negro tribes of Africa, their character, life, and social state on the coast, from which the greater number of slaves are brought hither—for the most part purchased from African chiefs, according to agreement with the white slave-dealer—Mr. C. having himself been there, and being therefore good authority on the subject. I have also learned from him how to distinguish the different tribes by their characteristic features, and their various modes of tattooing themselves.

The Congo negroes, called the Frenchmen of Africa, are

a vivacious, gay, but vain people; they have depressed noses, wide mouths, thick lips, splendid teeth, and high cheek-bones; they are strong and broad built, but not tall of stature. The Gangas negroes are kindred to the Congoes. The Luccomées and Mandingoes, on the contrary, the noblest of these coast tribes, are tall of stature, with handsome and often remarkably regular, and even noble features, the expression of which is grave. The negro preachers and fortune-tellers are principally of the Mandingo tribes. The Luccomées are a proud and contentious people; they are difficult to manage in the commencement of their life of slavery; they are lovers of freedom, and easily excited to violence; but if they are well and justly treated—(such just treatment as they can receive when they are held as slaves!)—they become in a few years the best and the most confidential laborers on the plantation. The Callavalis, or Caraballis negroes, are also a good people, although more lazy and careless. I have seen among them some magnificent figures. They have flatter noses and broader countenances than the Luccomées, and the expression is not so grave. All the negroes here are tattooed in the face; some around the eyes, others on the cheek-bones, and so on, according to the custom of the nation to which they belong. The greater number—even of the men—wear necklaces of red or of blue beads—the red, the coral-like seed of a kind of tree on the island; and the greater number, men as well as women, wear striped cotton handkerchiefs bound around the head. There is here a negro of the Fellah tribe, a little man, with delicate features, and the long, black, shining hair which is said to be peculiar to this tribe.

Such are the principal of the negro tribes and characteristics with which I have become acquainted.

But I must tell you about one negro, whose history is closely connected with the family on this plantation, and which has been related to me. It is a beautiful instance of the peculiar nobility of the negro character when this approaches its proper development. This man is called Samedi, or Saturday, and was the servant of Mr. C.'s parents in St. Domingo when the celebrated massacre took place there, and from which he saved, at the peril of his own life, the two sons, then boys, of his master, my host being one of them. He carried them on his shoulders in the night, through all dangers, down to the harbor, where he had secured for himself and the boys a passage in a small vessel to Charleston, in South Carolina. Safely arrived here, he placed the two boys at school, and hired himself out as a servant. He and the boys also had lost every thing they possessed in the horrible night at St. Domingo. He had been alone able to save their lives. He now maintained and clothed them and himself by his labor. Each week he took to the boys each three dollars of his wages, and this he continued till the boys grew into young men, and he an old man.

My host went to sea, and acquired wealth by his ability and good fortune. Afterward, when he was possessed of a plantation in Cuba, and had married, he took old Saturday to live with him; and now he took care of him in his turn, and every week gave to him three dollars as pocket-money in return for those which he had received from this magnanimous negro in his boyish years. Old Saturday lived here long and happily, and free from care, beloved and esteemed by all. He died two years since in extreme old age. He was an upright Christian, and very pious. It was, therefore, a surprise to his master after his death to find that he wore upon his breast an African amulet, a piece of folded paper printed very small, with letters and words in an African tongue, and to which the negroes appear to ascribe a supernatural power. But good Christianity does not trouble herself about such little heathenish superstition, the remains of twilight after the old night. Our good Christian peasantry of Sweden can not help still believing in fairies and witchcraft, in wise men and women, and I myself believe in them to a certain degree. There is still witchcraft enough prevailing, but

> The good can say our dear Lord's prayer,
> And fear neither witch nor devil!

Still, nevertheless,

> It is so dark, far, far away in the forest!

What do you now say to this negro slave? Ought, indeed, a race of people which can show such heroes, ever to have been enslaved? But this conduct of Saturday's is by no means a solitary instance of its kind in that bloody night of St. Domingo. Many slaves saved, or endeavored to save, their masters or their children, and many lost their lives in the attempt.

My visit to the slaves' bohea was not so consolatory to me as two visits which I paid to the cottages of the free negroes in the village of Limonar, which is very near this plantation. Early one beautiful morning I set off thither on an expedition of discovery. The small houses there, some of bark, others of woven brushwood, were all built in the form of cones, with palm-leaf roofs, and surrounded with cocoa-nut, palm, and other tropical trees, so that the whole village had an African appearance, at least according to what I have read and heard of African huts and cities. There was a certain picturesque disorder in every thing—a beauty in the beautiful trees, which was refreshing after the Anglo-American regularity. The huts seemed built by guess, and with as little trouble as possible, and the trees had sprung up of themselves out of the warm earth to overshadow them. Each little homestead stood in the morning sun like an earthly paradise. And they were earthly paradises, these little farms with their bark huts and palms; they were, the greater number of them, the abodes of free negroes. I was not sure of this, as yet, this morning, but I had a presentiment of it as I wandered through the village. Some unusual-looking trees and fruit in a little inclosure to the right attracted me, and there I determined to make a morning visit. The little gate was the most rickety gate in the world, but the most willing to allow ingress. I passed through it, and, advancing along a little sanded path, which wound round to the left, arrived at a palm-thatched bark hut, under some cocoa palms. A little below lay a shadowy grove of banana and mango trees, and trees with a kind of white, round fruit hanging from their flexile branches; near the hut grew the tall trees, like some kind of palm, which had particularly attracted my attention; they were, I found, cactus plants and flowers. I was here struck, beyond every thing else, with a general appearance of order and attention, which it is very unusual to find in and about the houses of the children of Africa. The hut was well built and kept up, and the numerous tropical trees around it had evidently been planted *con amore*. The little hut had also its piazza under the palm-leaf roof, and some sugar-cane was lying on the table.

The door stood open; fire burned on the floor—a certain sign that it was inhabited by an African! The morning sun shone in through the door, and I also looked in. The interior was spacious, neat, and clean. On the left sat an old negro on his low bed, dressed in a blue shirt and woolen cap; he sat with his elbows propped on his knees, and his face resting on his hands, turned toward the fire, and evidently half asleep. He did not see me, and I therefore could look around me undisturbed. An iron pot with a plate over it stood on the fire, and before the fire sat a tortoise-shell cat, and by her, on one leg, stood a white chicken. Fire, iron pot, cat, and chicken, every thing seemed half asleep in the sunshine which streamed in upon them. The cat just looked at me, then winked her eyes again, and gazed at the fire. It was a picture of real tropical still-life. Golden ears of maize-corn, fruit, and dried meat, and garden-tools hung upon the brown walls of the cottage.

In a little while the old man rose up, and, without observing me, turned himself round and began to lay together his bed-clothes, very little of which, however, the bed possessed. He folded up sheets and coverlid, and finally rolled up a small, closely woven, and handsome mat, which served as a mattress. When he had laid them aside very carefully, he again seated himself on his little bedstead, which was merely a few boards, and gazed again sleepily at the fire. Presently, however, he looked up, and became aware of me. He gave me a friendly look, as if in salutation, and said "*Café!*" but I did not know whether he invited me to take coffee with him, or asked for some from me. The cat and the chicken seemed to smell breakfast, and began to move, and as I supposed that the breakfast hour might be at hand and the breakfast over the fire, I bade the old man, the cat, and the chicken "*Buon dios! Retornero!*" and leaving them to understand that as they might, I proceeded onward around the little plantation.

I found in the banana grove two little brushwood cottages, in each of which there dwelt a large pig, which was just now enjoying its breakfast of large banana leaves. Swine are the principal wealth of the negro husbandman, and even of the plantation-slaves. They are fattened without difficulty on banana leaves and the fruits of the earth, and are sold when fat for about fifteen dollars each. Beyond the fruit tree and swine grove lay a field in which maize and some kind of root were cultivated, but very indifferently. A negro man and woman were here at work, but the work was evidently *ad libitum*. We greeted one another, and made an attempt to converse, but it ended in laughter. They burst into peals of laughter at my words and at my want of understanding, and I laughed at their capital hearty laughter, really tropical, luxuriant laughter. It cheers the very soul to see negroes chattering and laughing.

This little homestead, which seemed to be about two acres, was inclosed with a fence, in part paling, in part a stone wall, and in part a quick hedge. After I had seen all there was to see, had laughed and shaken hands with the negroes, I returned to the sugar plantation to breakfast.

I learned from Mr. C. that the tall, palm-like trees, which were hung with bunches of fruit resembling small cocoa-nuts, are called *papaya*, and those which bear white fruits *caimetos;* that the old negro whom I visited is named Pedro; that he was born of a free mother, and has always been known as a remarkably good and honest man. He himself built his house and planted the trees on the little plot of ground, which he rented from the church for five pesos yearly. The village of Limonar was, as I imagined, principally built and inhabited by negro slaves who have purchased their own freedom, and who rent land in the village; many, however, he said, were not as creditable as old Pedro; many were lazy, and maintained themselves rather by stealing sugar-cane, fruit, &c., than by producing it.

At my request Mrs. C. accompanied me one afternoon on another visit to the negroes at Limonar, to act as interpreter in my conversation with them. This lady is as quiet and gentle in her demeanor as her husband is active and vivacious; she is musical, and has a voice which is real music to hear, in particular when she speaks the beautiful Spanish tongue. We visited various negro houses, most of which were inferior in all respects to that of Pedro. The negroes hold their plots of ground by the tenure of a small yearly payment, or by yielding up a portion of the produce to some Spanish Creole. I asked them if they wished to return to Africa; to which they replied, laughing, "No; they were very well off here!" Most of them had, nevertheless, been stolen from Africa after they had passed the years of childhood. We met with one woman whose arm had been injured, and on Mrs. C. asking her the cause of this, she related in Spanish, with animated gestures, the story of cruel treatment which she, the defenseless slave, had received at the hands of her master or his agent. Lastly, we went to old Pedro's. I had furnished myself with some coffee for him, and with some Spanish phrases for the people who had charge of him—the man and woman whom I had seen in the field. They were now in the cottage, and old Pedro was sitting there, just as before.

The man's right arm had been crushed in the sugar-mill, which had obliged it to be amputated above the elbow, after which he purchased his freedom for two hundred pesos; and the woman had also purchased her freedom for the same sum, if I remember correctly. I asked them whether they would like to return to Africa. They answered, with a merry laugh, "No; what should they do there? They were very happy here!" They were thoroughly contented and happy. I besought them to be kind to old Pedro, and God would recompense them! Again they laughed loudly, and replied, "Yes! yes!" Never before had I discovered how amusing I could be.

It had become dark while we were standing in the cottage under the cocoa and papaya trees; and the stars came forth, gleaming softly from the deep blue sky. We saw from the place where we stood, and which was considerably elevated ground, the red fires shining from the furnaces of Mr. C.'s sugar-mill, and heard the wild songs and shouts which proceeded thence. There was slave-labor; life without rest; the dominion of the whip; the glowing furnace of slavery; here freedom, peace, and rest beneath this beautiful tropical heaven, in the bosom of its affluent fruit-garden. The contrast was striking.

Cuba is at once the hell and the paradise of the negroes. The slave has severer labor on the plantation, but a better future, a better prospect of freedom and happiness than the slave of the United States. The slave standing by the hot furnace of the sugar-mill can look to those heights where the palm-trees are waving, and think to himself—"I too can take my rest beneath them one of these days!"

And when he does so, when he lives like old Pedro, or the man with only one arm and his wife, who can be happier than he? The sun gives him clothing, the earth yields him, with the least possible labor, abundant fare, the trees drop for him their beautiful fruits, and give him their leaves to roof his dwelling and to feed his creatures; each day, as it passes, is beautiful and free from care—each day, as it passes, affords him its enjoyment—sun, rest, fruits, existence in an atmosphere which, merely to breathe, is happiness; the negro desires nothing more. And when in the evening or the night he sees the red fires shining from the sugar-mill, and hears the cracking of the whip, and the shouts which resound thence, he can raise his eyes to the mild stars which glance through the palm-trees above his head, and bless the Lord of Heaven, who has prepared for the slave a way from captivity to paradise, even on earth. For he too was there by the blazing furnace, and beneath the lash of the driver, and now he is here in freedom and peace beneath his own palm-tree; and his heavily-laden brother may ere long be the same! What matters it to him that his arm was crushed; his heart is as sound as ever! He is free and happy, and none can take from him his freedom. The negro, under the dominion of the Spaniard, is possessed of a hope, and can lift up a song of thanksgiving which he can not do under the free Eagle of the American Union.

To-day is Sunday, and Mr. C. has done me the favor of allowing me to see the negroes of the plantation dance for an hour in the forenoon. In an ordinary way, they never dance during the dry season, *la Secca;* they are, however, very glad to do it, if they can only get the opportunity, spite of their laborious work both night and day. I already hear the African drum beating its peculiar, distinct, and lively measures, and after the baptism of a little negro child the dancing is to begin.

I enjoy myself very much with the kind family here, in which there seems to prevail a great deal of mutual affection, and somewhat of that cheerfulness which existed among us when we were so large a family altogether at home. Here are four sons and three daughters, who play and quarrel playfully one with another at all hours of the day, and the youngest, a pretty lad, is so childishly full of fun that he befools me to play with him.

In the morning and the evening I go out on my solitary rambles in the neighborhood, generally accompanied by three large blood-hounds, which I can not get rid of, but which are gentle as lambs, and lie down perfectly quiet around me whenever I sit down to sketch a tree or any remarkable object which takes my fancy; and it is perhaps as well for me that I have them with me, because there are said to be runaway negro slaves roving about on the island, and the dogs guard me from any surprise of this sort. These animals are so trained that, while they are perfectly gentle toward white people, they are dangerous to the blacks, and the blacks are afraid of them.

I have here sketched two remarkable trees, the one a beautiful ceiba in perfect health and magnificence, and a magnificent tree it really is; the other a ceiba in the arms of its terrible murderess or mistress, or both in one. In this tree one may see the parasite grasping the trunk with two gigantic hands, and, as it were, strangling it in its embrace. I have here also greatly enjoyed the balmy air, and the wonderful beauty and novelty of the vegetation. There are some beautiful avenues—*guadarajahs*, as they are called in Spanish—on this plantation, one of king-palms, another of mango-trees, and so on. In the evenings we have music—for the whole family is musical—and sit with open doors, while the delicious zephyrs sport round the room.

I could go through the whole process of sugar-making, from its very commencement to its close; that is to say, if I had sugar-cane and a sugar-mill. The process is so simple and so agreeable to witness, that I think you will not be displeased to see it here on paper as I have seen it in Mr. C.'s well-kept sugar-mill. We must first, however, see the cutting of the sugar-cane.

The sugar-cane is waving there in the field like a compact, tall green reed; the stems, about as thick as a stout walking-stick, are yellow, some with flame-colored stripes or spots, or with various characteristics of the cane, such as longer or shorter distances between the joints, each according to its species, for there are here many species of sugar-cane, as the Otaheitan-cane, ribbon-cane, and so on.

The cane is cut off near the root with a sharp reaping-hook, or short, crooked scythe, one or two canes at a time; the green top is cut off, and the cane cast to one side. The negroes perform this operation with great speed and dexterity, and, as it seems, *con amore*. It is said that they like to destroy, and I could almost believe that it was so; there is a crashing and crackling among the vigorous canes; it is cheerful work, and those black figures, with their broad chests and sinewy arms, look well so employed. The shorn canes are loaded upon wagons drawn by oxen and conveyed away to the sugar-mill, where, as soon as it reaches the open door, it is unloaded by women, who throw the canes into a broad, raised, long trough, which extends into the building, where upon an elevation are placed two broad mill-stones, turning in opposite directions, the one raised a little above the other. By the side of this trough stand women, who pass the canes onward and up to the grinding mill-stones (I have seen a couple of young women at work here who really were splendidly beautiful, with their dark glancing eyes, their white teeth, their coral necklaces round their throats, and the pink handkerchiefs bound round their heads), where stands a negro on a landing-place, who is called the feeder, his business being to see that all the canes pass regularly between the mill-stones. The juice is pressed out with every half revolution of the stones, and the canes which enter between them from above fall down, crushed dry, into another trough below, whence they are conveyed away by an opposite door, and then heaped up into another wagon drawn by oxen, which, as soon as it is loaded, moves off and gives place to another. This wagon, loaded with *la bagaza*, goes to the flagged pavement, where women unload it into baskets, and lay it out to dry, as we have already seen. On one side of the building in which the sugar-cane is ground stands a house containing the machinery which sets the wheels in motion, and which is worked principally by oxen, which are driven as the oxen with us in the operation of thrashing. There is a driver to each pair of oxen, and it is from these that the shouts and the kind of stamping sound proceed which are heard at night. A negro shouts aloud words which he invents for the occasion, and which are often entirely without meaning, and the others respond in chorus, repeating with some variation the given words. The shouts and the noises are unmelodious, but the negroes enliven themselves in this manner during their nocturnal labor.

The juice which flows from the crushed canes flows between the mill-stones into a porcelain trough, placed in a transverse direction to the great trough extending between the two doors, and through this it flows into a porcelain tank, where it is purified; after which it is again passed by another trough into the boiling-house, where it is boiled and skimmed in immense boilers or pans, fixed in the earth by masonry. By the side of each pan stands a negro, naked to the waist, who, with an immense ladle, as tall as himself, stirs and skims the boiling juice. The juice, when it flows from the cane, is a thin liquid, of a pale green color; it is now boiled in the pans to a thick sirup of a grayish tint; and this process being complete, it is allowed to flow into large, flat, long pans, where it is left to harden; after which it is broken up, packed into hogsheads, and sent out into the world.

Sugar is in no instance refined in Cuba; there is, therefore, no really white sugar there. The boilers are heated by furnaces, the mouths of which are in the walls, and which are continually fed by *la bagaza*, which, when dried, makes excellent fuel.

And this is the history of the sugar-cane before it comes into your coffee-cup.* Alas! that its sweetness can not, as yet, be obtained without much bitterness, and that human enjoyment costs so much human suffering; for I know very well that what I see at this place is not the darkest side of sugar cultivation. There is a far darker, of which I shall not now speak.

I will now go to the dance.

After the dance. There stands in the grass, at the back of the house, a large Otaheitan almond-tree, the leafy head of which casts a broad shadow. In the shade of this tree were assembled between forty and fifty negroes, men and women, all in clean attire, the men mostly in shirts or blouses, the women in long, plain dresses. I here saw representatives of the various African nations—Congoes, Mandingoes, Luccomées, Caraballis, and others dancing in the African fashion. Each nation has some variations of

* It is planted by placing the cane lengthwise in the ground, when it shoots up from the joints. The flower is not unlike that of the reed with us, and consists of a number of such minute florets that they can not be discerned by the naked eye. But it is extremely seldom that the sugar-cane is seen here to flower. Even Mr. C. has not yet seen it.

its own, but the principal features of the dance are in all essentially the same. The dance always requires a man and a woman, and always represents a series of courtship and coquetry; during which the lover expresses his feelings, partly by tremor in all his joints, so that he seems ready to fall to pieces as he turns round and round his fair one, like the planet around its sun, and partly by wonderful leaps and evolutions, often enfolding the lady with both his arms, but without touching her; yet still, as I said, this mode varied with the various nations. One negro, a Caraballis, threw one arm tenderly round the neck of his little lady during the dance, while with the other he placed a small silver coin in her mouth. And the black driver, an ugly little fellow (he under whose whip I saw the women at work), availed himself frequently of his rank, sometimes by kissing, during the dance, the prettiest of the girls that he danced with, and sometimes by interrupting the dancing of another man with a handsome young negro girl, or with one of the best dancers, and then taking his place; for it is the custom that if any one of the bystanders can thrust a stick or a hat between two dancers, they are parted, and he can take the man's place. In this manner a woman will sometimes have to dance with three or four partners without leaving her place. Women, also, may exclude each other from the dance, generally by throwing a handkerchief between the dancers, when they take the place of the other who retires, such interruptions being generally taken in very good part, the one who retires smiling and seeming well pleased to rest a little, only again to come forward, and the man laughing still more heartily to see himself the object of choice with so many. The dancing of the women always expresses a kind of bashfulness, mingled with a desire to charm, while, with downcast eyes, she turns herself round upon one spot with an air and grace very much resembling a turkey-hen, and with a neckerchief or colored handkerchief in her hand, sometimes one in each hand, she half drives away from her the advancing lover and half entices him to her —a mode of dancing which, in its symbolic intention, would suit all nations and all classes of people, though—Heaven be praised—not all the beloved. The spectators stood in a ring around the dancers, one or two couples accompanying the dance with singing, which consisted of the lively but monotonous repetition of a few words which were given out by one person in the circle, who seemed to be a sort of *improvisatore*, and who had been chosen as leader of the song. Each time that a fresh couple entered the dance they were greeted by shrill cries, and the words and tune of the song were changed; but both tune and voices were devoid of melody. It is difficult to imagine that these voices would develop that beauty, that incomparable, melodious purity, and this people that musical talent which they have attained to in the slave states of America. The wild African apple-tree has, when transplanted into American soil, ennobled both its nature and its fruit. The words of the singer were, I was told, insignificant, nor could I get any clew to their purport.

I have been told words used by French negro Creoles in their dances, which in their *patois* expressed a meaning which it seems to me would very well suit the negro dances here; they say,

Mal à tête, ce n'est pas maladie,
Mal aux dent, ce n'est pas maladie,
Mais l'amour, c'est maladie!

The dance has no distinct divisions, no development, no distinct termination, but appears to be continuous variations of one and the same theme improvised, according to the good-humor or inspiration of the dancers, but comprised within a very circumscribed sphere, and not advancing beyond the quiverings, the twirlings, and the evolutions of which I have spoken. If either man or woman wish to choose a partner, they go out of the circle and place their handkerchief on the shoulder of the desired partner, or put a hat upon his or her head, or an ornament of some kind upon them; and I saw, on this occasion, one young negro woman whirling round with a man's hat on her head, and hung all over with handkerchiefs. It is also a common custom, but not of the most refined kind, to place a small silver coin in the mouth of the dancing lady at the close of the dance. The music consisted, besides the singing, of drums. Three drummers stood beside the tree-trunk beating with their hands, their fists, their thumbs, and drumsticks upon skin stretched over hollowed tree-stems. They made as much noise as possible, but always keeping time and tune most correctly.

It was a very warm day, and I saw that the linen of the quivering and grimacing gentlemen was in a state as if it had just been taken out of the sea. Yet not the less danced they, evidently from the pleasure of their hearts, and seemed as if they would continue to dance to eternity; but a loud crack of the whip was heard not far from the dancing-ground, and immediately the dancing ceased, and the dancers hastened away obediently to labor. Sugar-grinding and boiling must again begin.

The slaves of Cuba have no holiday during *la Secca*, although on Mr. C.'s plantation labor has a pause for two hours on Sunday morning.

How much more lively and full of intelligence was this dance under the almond-tree than the greater number of our dances in society, at least if we except the waltz. Our dances have not enough of natural life; this dance has perhaps too much; but it is full of animation and straightforwardness, and has this good quality belonging to it, that every one in company may take part in it, either singing, or dancing, or applauding. Nobody is excluded; there is no need for any body to stand against the walls, for any body to be dull or have *ennui*. Long live the African dance!

I have made an interesting excursion with the family to one of those remarkable grottoes which abound in the mountains of Cuba. This is called *La Loma de Lorenzo de St. Domingo*, and is distant some miles from Limonar. Mrs. C. and I drove thither in their volante, the young ones riding the small Cuban horses, the most good-tempered, willing, and prettiest of all creatures of the horse-kind, and which carry the rider so lightly that he feels no fatigue: these horses are small; their action is a short and very even trot. John C., a cheerful, spirited, and very agreeable young man, ordered a couple of negroes to carry a quantity of straw and brushwood into various parts of the grotto, which was set fire to. This produced a splendid scene. Millions of terrified bats swarmed in the lofty and dark arches of the cavern; and what strange and wonderful shapes were revealed by the flames! It was a world of dreams, in which every form fashioned by nature, and of which the human heart has dreamed or had previsions, seemed to present itself in gloomy, chaotic outline. There seemed to be the human form wrapped as if in swaddling bands, awaiting patiently light and life; there were pulpits and thrones; wings which seemed about to loosen themselves from the walls; thousands of fantastic shapes, some lonely, some grotesque, some hideous. Ah! within these caverns of nature seem to be contained the whole of that dark world which the cavern of the human heart incloses, but the shapes of which we do not see, excepting when, in dark moments, a gloomy fire lights up its shadowy recesses. Every form which I beheld here I had seen long beforehand in—my own breast. And I know that they all exist there still, although God has allowed the sun to enter, and palms to spring up in those gloomy spaces. I know that beyond the light there still exist gloomy, night-like expanses unknown to myself, or, at all events, indistinctly known, and which will perhaps remain so through the whole of my earthly life.

But then—life's caverns are only imperfectly illumined on earth!

The most definite and the most beautiful formation in these grottoes are the pillars. A drop of water distilling from the roof of the cavern falls upon the earth, and petrifies; from these petrified water-drops grows up a conical elevation, from above also a similar cone is formed, depending from the roof, and slowly growing from petrifying water-drops; and in the course of centuries these two have met, and now form a column which seems to support the roof, and not unfrequently resembles a petrified palm-tree. Many such palm-trees stood in the vault of the grotto; many others were in process of formation. The power of a water-drop is great!

Monday morning. I have been wandering about in the inclosed pasture-ground, *el portrero*, contemplating parasitic growths and sketching trees. A wood in Cuba is a combined mass of tendriled and thorny vegetation which it is impossible to penetrate. I have seen in the inclosed pastures some beautiful tall trees, but many more deformed, from parasites and other causes; the beautiful and the unsightly stand there side by side. I saw to-day also a beautiful convolvulus, with large white flowers twining itself up to the very top of a dead tree, overhung with many heavy parasites. There are many kinds of the convolvulus here, which, with their beautiful flowers, constitute the principal ornament of the quick hedge, which they bind together into a dense mass and cover with lovely flowers. There are many species of wild passion-flower, some very large, which bear fruit, others very small. One of the most beautiful trees on this plantation is the *pomme-rosa* tree; it is just now in flower, and its blossom has an indescribably delicious fragrance.

I shall shortly leave the plantation of Ariadne, but shall return both from my own wishes and those of the family. I am anxious to leave with my kind entertainers, as a remembrance of me, a portrait of the youngest boy, my little playmate.

St. Amelia Inhegno, March 15th.

St. Amelia Inhegno is a large sugar plantation, and I am now sitting in the smoke of the sugar-mill, which enters through the open window into my room—a large, excellent room, with a regular glass window, from which I obtain a fine view of the hills of Camerisca, and the palm-groves and plantations at their feet. I have every thing here which I can wish for, only too much of the sugar manufacture, which is just opposite my one window, and which is on a much larger scale than on the plantation of Ariadne. Is it not singular that the word *Inhegno*, which here signifies an inclosed and cultivated place, and which is always used to indicate a plantation, so much resembles, both in sound and meaning, our Swedish word *Inhägnad?*

My hostess, Mrs. De C., is an agreeable and well-bred American lady, a widow with four children, three of whom are in the United States, and only one, a pretty girl of sixteen, remaining with her at home. She lives here with her father, an old officer of cheerful temperament, although lame, and confined for the most part to his arm-chair. A young American Creole, Mr. W., whose plantation adjoins, is a daily visitor in the family, and a most agreeable companion he is. He, like my hostess, is possessed of the gift of gay and easy conversation, below which lies a foundation of earnest integrity. Another young man belongs to the social circle of the evening and the dinner-table, and he is, under the old gentleman, overseer of the plantation. This young man is of great value to me, from the candor and readiness with which he communicates any information which I may desire to possess.

This plantation is much larger than the one I visited in Limonar, and a considerable portion of the slaves—two hundred in number—have lately been brought hither from

Africa, and have a much wilder appearance than those I saw at Ariadne. They are worked also with much more severity, because here they are allowed only four and a half hours out of the four-and-twenty for rest; that is to say, for their meals and sleep, and that during six or seven months of the year! Through the remaining portion of the twelve months, the "dead season," as it is called, the slaves are allowed to sleep the whole night. It is true, nevertheless, that even now, upon this plantation, they have *one night* a week for sleep, and a few hours in the forenoon of each alternate Sunday for rest. It is extraordinary how any human beings can sustain existence under such circumstances; and yet I see here powerful negroes who have been on the plantations for twenty or thirty years. When the negroes have once become accustomed to the labor and the life of the plantation, it seems to agree with them; but during the first years, when they are brought here free and wild from Africa, it is very hard to them, and many seek to free themselves from slavery by suicide. This is frequently the case among the Luccomées, who appear to be among the noblest tribes of Africa, and it is not long since eleven Luccomées were found hanging from the branches of a guasima-tree—a tree which has long, horizontal branches. They had each one bound his breakfast in a girdle around him; for the African believes that such as die here immediately arise again to new life in their native land. Many female slaves, therefore, will lay upon the corpse of the self-murdered the kerchief, or the head-gear, which she most admires, in the belief that it will thus be conveyed to those who are dear to her in the mother-country, and will bear to them a salutation from her. The corpse of a suicide-slave has been seen covered with hundreds of such tokens.

I am told here that nothing but severity will answer in the treatment of slaves; that they always must know that the whip is over them; that they are an ungrateful people; that in the disturbances of 1846 it was the kindest masters who were first massacred with their whole families, while, on the other hand, the severe masters were carried off by their slaves into the woods, there to be concealed during the disturbances. I am told that, in order for a man to be loved by his slaves, he must be feared. I do not believe it; such is not human nature; but there is a difference between fear and fear. There is one fear which does not exclude love, and one which produces hatred and revolution.

The slaves have here, in a general way, a dark and brooding appearance. They go to their work in the sugar-fields sleepy and weary. As they drive the oxen to and fro, I frequently see them sucking sugar-cane, which they are very fond of, and of which they seem allowed here to have as much as they like. This is, at all events, a refreshment. They are not fed here on rice, but principally upon a species of root called malanga, which, it is said, they like, but which seemed to me insipid. It is yellow, and something like the potato, but has a poor and somewhat bitter taste; each slave receives a portion of such root boiled for dinner, and eats it with his salt meat. They have for breakfast boiled maize, which they bruise and mix with wild tomatoes, the fruit of the plantain, or vegetables; for they are allowed a little land on the plantation where they may sow and reap for themselves, and besides this, each family has a pig, which they kill yearly and sell.

Sunday, March 17. It is the Sabbath, and forenoon; but the sugar-mill is still grinding, and the whip-lash sounds commanding labor. The slaves will continue to work the whole day as if it were a week-day. Next Sunday, they say, is the one on which the slaves will rest for some hours, and dance if they are inclined; but—they look so worn out!

There are in Cuba plantations where the slaves work twenty-one out of the four-and-twenty hours; plantations where there are only men who are driven like oxen to work, but with less mercy than oxen. The planter calculates that he is a gainer by so driving his slaves, that they may die within seven years, within which time he again supplies his plantation with fresh slaves, which are brought hither from Africa, and which he can purchase for two hundred dollars a head. The continuance of the slave-trade in Cuba keeps down the price of slaves. I have heard of "gangs" of male slaves, six hundred in each gang, who are treated as prisoners, and at night locked up in a jail; but this is on the plantations in the southern part of the island.

It is amid circumstances such as these that one may become enamored of the ideal communities of socialism, and when men such as Alcott seem like the saviors and high-priests of the earth. How beautiful appear to me associated brotherhoods on the earth, with all their extravagance of love, when compared with a social state in which human powers are so awfully abused, and human rights trampled under foot! Here I feel myself more ardent than ever for those social doctrines which are laboring to advance themselves in the free states of America; and when I return thither, I shall endeavor to become better acquainted with them and their leaders, and to do more justice to both.

Yet even here I have derived some little comfort with regard to the condition of the slaves on this plantation, at least from the visit which I have paid to their bohea. This is a large, square, but low fortress-like wall, in which the slaves live as at Ariadne plantation, and in which they are secured by bolts and bars during the night. I have often visited them here during meal-times, and have always felt it a refreshment to witness their vigorous life and their cheerfulness; nevertheless, I have seen countenances here steeped in such gloom, that not all the tropical sunshine would illumine, so hopeless, so bitter, so speechless were they—it was dreadful! The countenance of one young woman, in particular, I shall never forget!

I can not but often admire the Herculean frames among the men, the energetic countenances in which a savage power seems united to a manly good-heartedness, which last shows itself especially in their treatment of the children, and by the very manner in which they look at them. The little ones are not here familiar and merry as they are on the plantations in America; they do not stretch out their little hands for a friendly salutation; they look at the white man with suspicious glances—they are shy; but the very little Bambinos, which are quite naked, fat, and plump, as shiny as black, or black-brown silk, dance upon their mother's knees, generally with a blue or red string of beads around the loins, and another round the neck; they are the very prettiest little things one ever saw; and the mothers, with their strings of beads round their necks, their showy kerchiefs fastened, turban-wise, around the head, look very well too, especially when, with delighted glances, and shining, pearly teeth, they are laughing and dancing with their fat little ones. Such a young mother, with her child beneath a banana-tree, is a picture worthy the pencil of a good painter.

I saw in those dark little rooms—very like those at Ariadne plantation—more than one slave occupied during the short time allowed him for rest in weaving little baskets and hats of palm-leaves, and one of them had constructed a fine head-dress of showy patches and cock's feathers!

In other respects the slaves live in the bohea very much like cattle. Men and women live together, and part again according to fancy or whim. If a couple, after having lived together for some time, grow weary of each other, the one will give the other some cause of displeasure, and then they separate. In case of any noisy quarrel, the majoral is at hand with his whip to establish peace.

"Are there here no couples who live constantly together as in proper marriage; no men and women who love one another sufficiently well to be faithful to each other as husband and wife?" inquired I from my young, candid conductor.

"Yes," replied he, "there are really such couples who have always remained together since they have been upon this plantation."

"Lead me to one of these couples," said I.

It was just dinner-time. My companion led me to one of the rooms in the wall. The door stood open, as is commonly the case, to admit light and air. The man was out; the woman sat alone in the room; she might be about fifty, and was busy at some work. She had a round face, without beauty, but with a good and peaceful expression.

I asked her, through my interpreter, whether she was fond of her husband?

She replied cheerfully and without hesitation, "Yes; he is a good husband."

I inquired whether she had been attached to him in Africa?

"Yes, in Africa," she replied.

I asked how long she had been united to her husband—how many years?

This question seemed to trouble or perplex her; she smiled, and replied at length that she had had him *always!*

Always! She did not know how vast and profound that word was on her lips. It went to my heart. Weeks, months, seasons, years, youth, strength, many changes had passed by unnoted, unobserved; hemisphere had been changed for hemisphere, freedom for slavery, the palm-tree hut for the bohea, a life of liberty for a life of labor—every thing had changed; but one thing had remained steadfast, one thing had remained the same—her love—her fidelity! She had *always* had him, the husband whom she loved—

he had always had her. Of that which was variable and evanescent she knew not, made no account—she knew merely of time as regarded that which was eternal. She had had her husband *always;* she should have him always. That was evidently written in her calm countenance and in her calm voice. It could not be otherwise.

"Love requires to be sustained by duty!" said Geijer to me, on one occasion when he spoke of marriage. So it does; but it is beautiful to see that the natural marriage between two kindred souls can remain firm and strong merely through the law of love, amid the wild license of the bohea, and that in the case of two black people, two of the wild offspring of the desert!

Poets and philosophers have spoken of souls predestined for each other. Here I found two such. They had *always* belonged to each other. In the profound consciousness of God they had belonged to each other, and would belong to each other through all time—that is, in—eternity.

The man entered while I was still in the room. He seemed to be about the same age as the woman, and had the same good-hearted expression; but there was in his smile a sort of imprisoned sunshine, a cheerful beam of light, which, lit up from the heart itself, seemed as if it would gladly have free diffusion. I have often observed this imprisoned beam of light in the countenances of these children of bondage. They have brought it with them as an inheritance from their mother-country.

I went from this married pair to the prison cell, in which the slaves are placed after they have suffered punishment—women as well as men—and while the mind is still in a state of fermentation, after having endured bodily suffering. They are placed here in irons, made fast to a wooden frame, and here they sit, bound hands and feet—women as well as men—till their minds are again calm and their wounds healed, so that they can again go to their work. They are said to get fat while they remain here! The room was now empty, and inhabited merely by swarms of fleas.

I only wonder that suicide is not of more frequent occurrence among this people. How strong and tenacious the instinct of life must be!

The sugar-mill here affords, in its way, an interesting and picturesque scene. The athletic figures of those half-naked Africans who stand by the furnaces, or by the boiling sugar-pans, in those large, gloomy buildings, or who move about occupied in various ways, produce a singular effect. I can not behold without amazement and pleasure the savage but calm majesty of their bearing and movement, as well as the dark energy of their countenances. Sculptors ought to see and model from these African chests and shoulders. They seem made to sustain Atlas. And though the Atlas of slavery presses heavily upon them, they are still strong—terribly strong, if the hour of vengeance should ever come; now they are silent and gloomy. The Spanish majorals, in their white shirts and with their whips, or short, thin, square staves in their hands, stand or sit here and there on elevated platforms within the building, to overlook the work, and in the morning take the while their coffee and white bread. They seem to me, as far as form and appearance goes, to be much smaller and more insignificant than many of the black slaves. In the slave states of America no idea can be formed of the peculiar beauty of form of the African negro, especially those of certain tribes. The native slaves there are a weaker and gentler race. The wild raven has been tamed.

Many of the slaves, also, who are brought to Cuba have been princes and chiefs of their tribes, and such of their race as have accompanied them into slavery on the plantations always show them respect and obedience. A very young man, a prince of the Luccomées, with several of his nation, was taken to a plantation on which, from some cause or other, he was condemned to be flogged, and the others, as is customary in such cases, to witness the punishment. When the young prince laid himself down on the ground to receive the lashes, his attendants did the same likewise, requesting to be allowed to share his punishment. This affecting instance of loyalty produced merely the coarse assurance "that they should not fail of their full share of the whip when opportunity offered!"

This occurrence did not take place on this plantation.

There is more use made of machinery in this sugar-mill than in that at Ariadne. Instead of fixed troughs by which the sugar-cane is conveyed by human hands to and from the mill-stones, there are here carriages to convey the cane worked by machinery, and which run on many wheels in a long row, one after the other, from one door of the sugar-mill to the other, and it is merely at the entrance-gate that the cane is loaded by human hands.

And now you must have had enough of sugar-cane; but, before I leave the bohea, I must say a few words about the government of its population. This rests, after the master, upon an overseer, who is called the *majoral*, and below him is a *contra-majoral*, who sometimes is a negro. On large plantations, such as this, there are many white under-majorals. The condition of the slaves, and the prevailing state of feeling among them on a plantation, depends very much upon the ability, prudence, and humanity of the majorals. The savage murder of a majoral in Cuba not unfrequently bears witness to the despotism of their proceedings, and to the state of frenzied excitement into which cruel oppression may bring the naturally gentle and easily subjected negro-race.

However oppressive slavery may be to the inhabitants of the bohea, and though the planters quite naïvely ignore most of the Spanish laws for the emancipation of the slave, and though the justice of the law is also here nullified at pleasure, still the wafting breezes of the life of freedom can not be wholly excluded from the bohea. The slave knows, generally, that he can purchase his own freedom, and he knows also the means for the acquisition of money. The lottery is, in Cuba, one of the principal means for this purpose among the negro slaves, and they understand how to calculate their chances wisely. For instance, several individuals of a certain nation will unite for the purchase of a quantity of tickets, the numbers of which follow in close succession. Out of a total of consecutive numbers, one or two will commonly draw a prize, which, according to agreement, belongs to the nation, and is divided among all the members. In this way I have heard that the Luccomée nation lately obtained at Havana a prize of eleven thousand dollars, a portion of which, it is said, has been applied to purchase the freedom of slaves of their nation; and, if I mistake not, a Luccomée negro on this plantation has lately, with the consent of his owner, purchased his own freedom for two or three hundred dollars. Yes—some become free, but many, many never become so!

As far as concerns myself, my life here is as free and agreeable as I can desire. Mrs. De C. is a very charming and amiable person to associate with, and she allows me to have all the liberty I wish, and is infinitely agreeable to me. In the early mornings I go out alone; visit the slaves' bohea, or ramble about the plantation; I enjoy the air, and sketch trees and flowers. I have now become acquainted with that candelabra-like plant, which I have already mentioned. It is the flower-stalk of a plant of the aloe genus, called *Peta*, a shrub with stiff, thorny leaves, and this flower-stalk shoots up from the root every third year, and bears upon its branches bunches of yellowish flowers which produce fruit. It shoots up to a height of five or six ells, blossoms, and bears fruit all within the space of two months, after which it dies down. It has a singular but very ornamental appearance; I have made a drawing of it. Here, also, are a couple of remarkable ceiba-trees, the one on account of its beauty, the other for its deformity—its tragical combat with the parasite. The sugar-cane fields are inclosed with lofty, untrimmed hedges, in which grow wild orange and various tropical trees.

During the hottest part of the forenoon I sit quietly in my own light, excellent chamber, writing and drawing. Just before dinner I go out, look around me in the bohea, or seat myself under a mango-tree on a cross-road to catch a few breezes, if I can, in its shade. In the afternoon I generally drive out with Mrs. De C. in her volante, her daughter and Mr. W. accompanying us on horseback. To be rocked over the country in an open volante, in that heavenly, delicious air, is the most soothing, delightful enjoyment that any body can conceive.

The family assembles in the evening, and I then play American marches, "quick-steps," and other lively pieces, with Yankee Doodle for the old gentleman, who, with these, recalls his youthful achievements, and feels new life in his stiffened limbs. At a later hour I go out on the piazza to see the stars shining in the darkness of night, and to inhale the zephyrs which, though not so full of life as at Matanzas, are yet always full of delicious influence.

Among my pleasures, I must not forget the lovely humming-birds in the little garden. In the mornings, and directly after mid-day, one may be sure to see them hovering around the flowers, and around the red ones by preference. There are in the garden a couple of shrubs, which are now covered with most splendid red flowers; the shrub is called *La Coquette*, and over these the little humming-birds are always hovering, they too of a splendid red, like little flames of fire. They are the most gorgeous little creatures any body can imagine, as fat as little bull-finches, and like them, having plump, brilliant breasts.

They support themselves as if in the air, fluttering their wings for a considerable time about the red flowers, into which they then dip their bills, but how gracefully I can not describe. *La Coquette* and her winged wooers present the most lovely spectacle. I have here seen three kinds of humming-birds. The one with the crimson coloring of morning, of which I have just spoken; a little one of a smaragdus-green and more delicate form; and a third, green, with a crest of yellow rays on its head. They will sometimes all alight upon a bough, and as they fly away again, a soft, low twittering may be heard. They are quarrelsome, and pursue one another like little arrows through the air, while, as rivals, they approach the same flower.

Besides these most lovely little birds, I see here a black bird about as large as a jackdaw. It resembles the American blackbirds, and is called majitos or solibios (or solivios, for here there is a great confusion between "v" and "b," and "b" and "v;" thus Havana is frequently both written and pronounced Habana). I see these blackbirds often sitting upon the branches of the candelabra-like peta. These queer birds are said to be a species of communists, to live in communities, to lay their eggs together, to hatch them in common, and to feed the young in the same manner, without any difference of mine or thine. The humming-bird is evidently of a very different temperament, and is a violent anti-communist.

The heat is now becoming excessive, and I feel it so enervating that I think I shall leave Cuba on the 8th of April instead of the 28th, as I had intended. From Cuba I shall proceed to Charleston and Savannah, visit two plantations on the coast of Georgia, and so on to Virginia—the Old Dominion—which I must see, and where I shall probably spend the month of May; thence to Philadelphia and New York—to my dear home at Rose Cottage; then to the White Mountains in New Hampshire, pay a visit to

Maine and Vermont, and thence, in the month of July, to my first beautiful home on the banks of the Hudson; then to England, and then—home!

I am now going for a few days to Cardenas, a little city on the sea-coast; but I shall return hither. The kind Mrs. De C. will lend me her volante.

LETTER XXXIV.

Cardenas, March 19th.

It was at Cardenas that the first senseless robber-expedition against Cuba, under the conduct of Lopez, landed last year, and was repulsed by the bravery of the Spanish army. You are shown holes in the walls made by cannon-balls, and they are now living in daily expectation and fear of a new attack under the same leader, the news of which is just now in circulation, and people are on the alert in consequence, and the city under watch.

Cardenas is a small city, built in the same style as Havana, and carries on a brisk trade in sugar and treacle. It is situated by the sea, but lies so low that it can scarcely be seen from the sea; its harbor is very shallow, and will not admit vessels of large size. I am living in a small hotel kept by a Mrs. W., the widow of a Portuguese, and who has five daughters, which is nearly four too many! I should not be afraid of having ten daughters in the United States; I should be certain that they all, however poor they might be, would be able to attain to their proper human development, would gain consideration and a competence through their own merits and endeavors. But in Cuba, what could any one do with five daughters? Marriage is the only means there of obtaining for them respect and a living, and it is not so very easy to get married at Cuba, because it is not an easy thing to maintain yourself in an honorable way there. Two of these young girls are very pretty; the eldest, a perfect blonde, has the noblest profile. She is betrothed to a young officer; but it frequently happens that marriage does not follow love and betrothal.

Among the people who interest me here is a young lawyer, a Spaniard, more than ordinarily agreeable and lively in social intercourse. I have obtained a good deal of information from him respecting the administration of the laws of the island with regard to slaves and their treatment, of which I shall have more to say another time. In other respects Cardenas appears to me an uninteresting little city; but kind people here have afforded me an opportunity of seeing things in the neighborhood of the city which have great interest for me, one of which is a coffee plantation in full bloom. The coffee-plant flowers once a month, and the whole of the plantation is in blossom on one single day, and the flowers, which are in full bloom in the morning, wither in the evening. The earliest blossoming in the year is in February, the latest in November. The flowers, which are placed upon the twig in compact white racemes and bunches, produce small fruit-pods, which are first green, then red, and lastly of a dark brown, when they are gathered; these contain the coffee-beans. The harvest is, therefore, continually going on during three or four months of the year.

The coffee plantation which I visited was in full bloom, and the appearance was as of a shower of snow over the green shrubs. The coffee-shrub has beautiful rich green, smooth laurel-like leaves; the flowers resemble those of the single white hyacinth, and have a delicate, agreeable scent. This coffee plantation was remarkably lovely, with beautiful avenues of alternate orange-trees and sago-palms; the pine-apple grew there, and there were avenues and groves of bananas. The trees were full of blossoms and fruit. The people who lived here had never noticed the peculiar blossoming of the banana; people live amid the richest treasures of nature without paying attention to them.

Among the beautiful objects on this plantation, I must mention its proprietor, and her lovely young daughters especially. They presented me with flowers and fruit, and I have sketched a blossoming branch of the coffee-shrub for mamma.

The second object of interest to me was a little zoological garden, or museum, which a German collected in the neighborhood of Cardenas, of the birds and other animals of Cuba. Among the latter were a crocodile and an alligator together in the same tank. They were so alike, that to my ignorant eyes they seemed entirely so; but I was shown various distinctive markings. Their owner had made vain attempts to tame them. They seem to be the most devoid of intellect, as well as the ugliest of all animals, at least to my taste. Neither alligators nor crocodiles, however, are found in the rivers of Cuba; these have been brought hither as curiosities from America and Africa.

March 21st. There stands in the court into which my room looks a large hen-coop, containing many kinds of poultry for household use. The present cook of the family, a tall, handsome Spanish soldier, came this morning to fetch away a couple of the feathered company for dinner, for the family and guests. The first that he carried off was a large black turkey; and I could not but admire the manner in which he set about the business, it was so gentle, so humane, and wise. He stroked the turkey, in the first place, before he took it from the pen, and even this was done with so much suavity that the turkey, when he carried him off quite comfortably across the court, merely looked a little astonished, and uttered a few sounds in his throat, as if he would say, "Now what's going to be done?"

I have seen with us, when a hen was to be killed, the

whole poultry-yard in a state of uproar, and she herself breathless from terror before she gave up the ghost. Spaniards are not in a general way remarkable for humanity to animals; and the country people frequently come to market with turkeys and fowls hanging by the feet tied together across the horse's saddle, so that their heads hang down. This barbarity was forbidden by a Governor Tacon of Cuba, who is described as having been a severe man, but who abolished many abuses; this, however, is still continued, and I have frequently met monteros riding between clusters of poultry thus suspended, and sometimes half dead.

There is a district not far from Cardenas which is called Havanavana, which is almost entirely peopled by free negroes, the number of whom, I understand, amounts to twelve or thirteen hundred. They are mostly cultivators of land, on the half system, with Spanish Creoles. I should be extremely glad to see *how* these small farms are managed by them—to see with my own eyes how negroes manage when they are left to themselves; but I am advised not to go there, as I am not acquainted with the language of the country, and the government is very suspicious of strangers. The slave disturbances of 1846 are still fresh in the minds of people, and they originated in this part of the island. These disturbances, which gave rise to such cruel proceedings on the part of the Spanish government, have also caused severe restrictions to be laid upon the occupations and amusements of the free negroes. Formerly, it is said, might be heard every evening and night, both afar and near, the joyous sound of the African drum, as it was beaten at the negro dances. When, however, it was discovered that these dancing assemblies had been made use of for the organization of the disturbances which afterward took place, their liberty became very much circumscribed.

The free negroes of Havana have, each nation to itself,

their own halls of assembly and guilds, or, as they are called, *cabildos*, for which they elect queens, who again choose kings to assist them. I must see these *Cabildos de Negroes.*

St. Amelia Inhegno, March 23d.

Once more in my excellent room, with my charming Mrs. De C., for a couple of days. I came hither in a whirling cloud of hot, red dust. The soil of Cuba is as red as burned clay, and the dust is dreadful in windy weather. In rainy weather, again, it becomes a thick slime, which it is impossible to get through. This belongs to the obverse side of nature here. The volante, drawn by three horses abreast, flew like a whirlwind through the red dust, and our *calashero*, Patricio, seemed greatly to enjoy the wild career.

It is again Sunday, that Sunday upon which the slaves are to have a few leisure hours, and I have talked to both the old gentleman and the young one about it, and prayed that the slaves might have a dance; but we shall see how it will be. The sugar-mill is not at work, but I see the slaves going about, carrying *la bagaza*, and I hear the cracking of the whip keeping them to work. It is already late in the afternoon; I am waiting in expectation and impatience. Will there be a dance or no? I fear that some pretext will be found for changing the dance into labor. I confess that I shall be very much annoyed if it is so, for the dance has been promised me, and the poor people need enlivening; neither should I allow them to dance to no purpose. There—the African drum! There will be a dance. I hasten to witness it.

Later. The dance did not this time take place under a shady almond-tree, but in the hot court of the bohea. The musicians were stationed with their drums on the shady side of the kitchen. There was merely a small company of dancers, and the dance was of the same kind as that at Ariadne, and presented no new feature of interest, until an elderly Congo negro, called Carlo Congo, entered with his Herculean chest into the dance. He ordered the drummers to beat a new tune, and to this he performed a dance, which, with its bendings, its evolutions, and tremulosities, would have told well in a ballet of the Paris opera; that is to say, in the person of a satyr or faun, for the dance had no higher character; but it was admirable, from the power of the dancer, his agility, flexibility, bold transitions, and the wild, picturesque beauty of his evolutions. This was the Congo dance; but Carlo Congo could not execute it in its full perfection; wearied for four months' labor, day and night, his limbs were evidently deficient in the needful power; he was obliged to pause many times to rest, and, though he soon recommenced, he again came to a stand, shaking his head good-humoredly, as if he would say, "No! it will not do!" His countenance had that expression of power and sensibility which I have so often seen among the negroes; he wore a little cotton cap on his head, and a necklace of blue glass beads round his throat; the upper portion of the body and the muscular arms were bare; and their form, and the development of the muscles, during the dance, were worthy the study of a sculptor. The partner of this skillful dance was also more animated in her movements than any of the negro women whom I had yet seen, and swung round with great dexterity and art. Carlo placed a little sprig of myrtle in her mouth, after which she danced, holding it between her lips as a bird would have held it in his bill.

By degrees the dancers increased in number. The women also invited partners to dance, generally by giving a little blow with a handkerchief to the selected cavalier, who immediately showed himself ready and willing. Some of the men dropped on the knee during the dance; so true to nature does this movement appear to be, which of old obtained admission into the refined world of gallantry and chivalry.

There were others who danced solo to the beating of the drums, twirling round upon one spot, and waving the while up and down with the body; children also came, naked as God made them, and imitated, most excellently, the dancing of the elders. But others, both men and women, passed by, and cast gloomy, joyless glances on the dance; and the bitter expression of those dark, night-like countenances testified of the darkest night-life of slavery; countenances those were which I shall never forget—one especially, that of an elderly woman! Other negroes were passing through the gate of the bohea, laden with bunches of bananas and tomatoes (which here grow wild), or other green vegetables. The young overseer inquired whether they were from their own country, and they replied curtly, "Yes." They passed by the dancers, some with an indifferent glance, others with a half smile. The dancing in the mean time became more and more animated in that hot sun, and the numbers increased, both of men and women. Now, however, the loud crack of a whip was heard, and the dancing stopped at once. The dancers dispersed again to recommence work in the sugar-mill. I too left the bohea, but not without thanking the drummers, and, in particular, Carlo Congo, in the manner which I knew was most agreeable to them.

I am now again in my quiet chamber. The sugar-mill is clamoring and smoking, and the slaves are carrying *la bagaza*.

I see above the walls of the bohea, but far beyond them, the magnificent *guadarajah* of palms below the hills of Camerioca. These hills also have deep caverns and concealed tracts, which serve as the retreats of fugitive slaves. They dig pitfalls at the mouths of the caverns to preserve them from their pursuers. But the pursuit of them is now given up, as it is not only unavailing, but attended by great peril to the pursuers. Sometimes they will come down in the night-time to the plantations for sustenance, which they obtain from the negroes of the plantation, who never betray the fugitives of the mountains. The negroes, it is said, never betray one another except under the torture of the whip.

March 26th. I have visited with my kind hostess some of the plantations in the neighborhood. The most agreeable of these visits was to that of a handsome young couple, M. and Madame Belle C., French Creoles. An enchanting expression of human kindness was portrayed on their countenances. They are said to be very kind to their slaves, and I understand that M. Belle C. is thinking of taking a sugar plantation in Florida, on which he will employ only free negroes. May he succeed! One single successful experiment of this kind would effect a great change in American slavery. The man who does this may be reckoned as among the greatest benefactors of humanity.

I saw at M. and Madame Belle C.'s two of the sweetest little children, and a well-kept garden, in which were many beautiful plants. I saw some remarkably fine Provence roses, but without any sign of fragrance. The great heat, it is said, destroys the scent of this and many other flowers. This handsome young couple have invited me to spend some time with them, but I must decline the invitation.

The planters of Cuba are extremely hospitable, and as the life of the ladies is very monotonous, and increasingly so of late, for the hand of the Spanish government has rested heavily on the Spanish Creole since the late disturbances, compelling him to pay a tax, they are by no means unwilling to have the monotony of their every-day life diversified by the presence of a European stranger.

The character of the sugar plantation and the life upon it seems to me very much the same every where. The most beautiful features of these plantations are the great avenues, especially of palms; I can not walk through these *guadarajahs* without a sentiment of devotion, so beautiful and magnificent are they! The gardens are frequently quite small, and commonly but ill kept. The fields of sugar-cane encroach upon every thing else. The life of the ladies is not cheerful, and scarcely active at all. They seem to me to suffer from the condition of the plantation, which is never free from danger, and which does not allow them to develop at all their more beautiful activity—nay, which even checks their movements. They dare not go out alone—they are afraid of runaway slaves; besides, with all the beauty of trees and vegetation peculiar to the Cuban plantation, it still lacks that which constitutes one of the greatest delights of country life—when one looks at it merely from the pleasurable point of view—it lacks grass-sward—that soft, submissive, verdant sward, in which millions of small blades of grass and masses of little flowers are brought together, to prepare for human beings a fresh and soft couch on which to repose in the open air. It lacks those groves of shadowy trees and underwood, beneath and amid which we repose so pleasantly; and I soon observed that this paradisaical atmosphere and these guadarajahs could not compensate to the inhabitants of the island for the absence of those unpretending rural pleasures.

Besides, *we* behold no injustice around us in the country, no want which we can not in some degree lessen. They behold much daily which they can not do any thing to alleviate. Nay, the more noble a woman is in Cuba, the more unhappy must she become. And even if she be united to the best of husbands, who does all that lies in his power for her and for his slaves, she still can not close her eyes to that which occurs around her. The plantation is never many acres in extent, and it adjoins other plantations which are managed according to the disposition of their masters, and of what kind this sometimes is we know already. Add to this the state of the government of the island, the violence of government officials, slave-trade, slave tumults, the examinations of the Spanish government, and the punishments which it inflicts, one perpetual state of fear—no delicious waftings of the heavenly atmosphere of Cuba can give cheerfulness to life under such circumstances.

Last week a cargo of slaves from Africa arrived at Havana; they were no less than seven hundred in number, and all children, the eldest not eighteen, and the youngest under ten years of age. It was spoken of this evening in our circle.

"They who do this," said a mother of the party, bitterly, "ought to have some day the reward they deserve!"

And yet, if human beings are to be conveyed from their native country into foreign slavery, it is better that it should take place when they are children than when grown up; it is less bitter then. As children, they become accustomed to the bohea and to the whip, and have not the memory of a life of freedom, which drives them to despair and suicide.

Amid these gloomy thoughts and impressions, again and again the unspeakable beauty of the air and the vegetation presents itself, and affects my soul to thanksgiving, and shows me a future paradise.

It is again full moon, and the nights are indescribably beautiful. I returned home late last night from a visit with my hostess. We drove, with uncovered heads, in the open volante, through palm-groves, beneath the vault of heaven, which was flooded with light. The air was delicious and bland, as the purest human kindness.

There are two splendid palm avenues at the plantation of St. Amelia, a hundred trees in a row, I have no doubt. Many of them are just now in bloom. The luxuriant sprays of flowers shoot out like a garland of wings around the stem, a little below the palm-crown, in the most beautiful relationship both to it and the stem. There is another avenue of the tamarind (from the green heads of which the beans are now falling, and which the little negro children eagerly gather, to suck the agreeable acid fruit), and of mango-trees, and a species of acacia, with red berries, from which the negroes make necklaces. There are, in front of the house, many of those trees, with lime-tree-like heads, and dark, fiery-red flowers, such as I saw on *La Plaza des Armas* at Havana, the botanic name of which is *Hibiscus tiliacea.*

Cuba is an outer court of Paradise, worthy to be studied by the natural historian, the painter, and the poet. The forms and colors of the vegetation seem to typify a transition from earthly life to a freer and a loftier sphere of beauty.

Caffetal L'Industrie, April 1st.

Thank God that it is now the commencement of spring in Sweden, and that you can now begin to think about salt baths, summer, and convalescence, and that all around you can begin to live; way-side weeds, butterflies, the little yellow flowers, and larks—the cheerful larks, which warble and sing, "Now it is spring-time! now it is spring-time!" Ah! the diffusive joy which spring imparts among us, that—that is not known in this beautiful Cuba.

But—Cuba has beauty enough to make human life happy, if its beauty and its glorious atmosphere might only operate unimpededly.

I have now been for some days on a new plantation, both of sugar and coffee, with an American family of the name of P., consisting of an elderly gentleman, his wife, much younger than himself, two young sons, and two daughters. I have to thank the Swedish consul, Mr. Ninninger, for this invitation. Mr. P. is a warm republican, and courageous enough openly to express his republican sympathies in the very face of the Spanish authorities of the island. He would do it, he says, "at the mouth of a four-and-twenty pounder," and I believe him, the brave old gentleman, and I like him for it! Mrs. P. was born in England, and now, at near fifty, her countenance has still all the charm and sweetness of youth, combined with an expression of the greatest kindness. She reminds me of those springs of fresh water which God permits here and there to well up in the sandy deserts of the tropics for the invigoration of the desert pilgrim. Palm-trees grow around them, and the sward becomes verdant; the wanderer rests there, and drinks of the springs, and wishes only that he could linger there. When I meet with one of these characters of perfectly original goodness, I involuntarily ask myself why, when such might be created and given to the earth, we yet see so few of them. As it is, they seem like the spirit of the wind on this island, merely to reveal themselves on the earth, to remind us of a paradise which—is not to be found there.

There is a glorious view from the front of the house, across the country, and to the distant blue sea. I enjoy it, and the breezes from the sea, as I walk upon the broad piazza in the incomparably beautiful mornings and evenings. My charming little room adjoins the piazza, and from it also I have an extensive view; there, however, I am often disturbed by the little negro children, who climb up by the iron railing before my window, and peep in, exclaiming "*Buon dios, Signora,*" good-morning, missis! which, spite of their good-tempered, joyous countenances, splendid eyes and teeth, does not always amuse me, that is, when I wish to be quiet. But it is, after all, really a joy to see how fearless the negro children are on this plantation. The good, motherly lady and her daughters have produced this effect, and the children are evidently well cared for, and the elder ones well clad. They run about freely, and accompany us on our walks, sometimes in little troops. I frequently see the elder children carrying the younger ones, riding astride upon the left hip, while they hold them up with the left arm thrown round the bead-encircled bodies of the little creatures. I see them in this way move about, and even run, with great ease; the girls are particularly dexterous in this respect, and as I thus see them, I frequently can not help admiring their beautiful and perfectly developed frames.

The slaves on this plantation seem to me well fed and full of enjoyment. Neither is their bohea locked up and prison-like; it is left freely open, and I have seen dwelling-rooms there full of possessions like the dwellings of the slaves in America. The good lady of the plantation is fond of her people, and takes good care of the feeble and the sick.

From her gentle lips I have written down the following words:

"It is a great sin to call the slaves wicked; there are among them both bad and good, as among all people. It is rare to meet with such as are wicked, and many are very good!

"They who consider the whip necessary to drive the negroes to work, which they would do willingly with reasonable treatment, do not understand them, and frequently make them wicked. I can not tell you what I have suffered; nay, indeed, I have been ill for weeks from the grief occasioned by the sight of so much flogging, and of the many cruelties, which, in many cases, a kind and serious word might have prevented the necessity of! The negro nation is wonderfully susceptible to kindness and indulgence when they are judiciously used. They are capable of becoming the best and the most devoted of servants and friends."

The German overseer of a plantation, *La Sonona*, belonging also to Mr. P., made the following remarks regarding negro slaves:

"They are not at all difficult to manage, if they are treated, at the same time, with firmness and kindness

They love regularity and decision in their masters, and obey without difficulty when they are treated with equanimity and reason. It will not do to be remiss; neither is there any necessity for severity and cruelty."

This I believe to be the truth; and well would it be if many gentlemen would believe so too, and then treat them according to this belief; but a despotic temper and passion are often the masters' master, and the slaves suffer in consequence.

The most remarkable occurrence that has happened to me since I last wrote is my having seen the *Southern Cross*, and the *Cuculio*, or "the Cuban fire-fly," which now begins to make its appearance, but which is not a fly, but a beetle, which in form and appearance resembles our Thor-beetle, only somewhat longer and narrower. It flies in the same manner, but more slowly and much higher, and produces during its flight a still louder and more buzzing sound. It emits light in two ways, when it creeps along, or is still, from two round, small shining points immediately behind the eyes, and I read by the light thus produced with great ease last evening, by conducting the *cuculio* along the lines like a little lamp; and, secondly, when it flies, it emits from an opening in the stomach a strong clear light, now quickly shining out, and then extinguished, as is the case with the American fire-fly, but shining steadily as long as it remains on the wing: you can scarcely conceive how beautiful it is. Imagine now the planets Venus, Jupiter, Mars, and others as bright, coming down from above, and flying around through the air, over the roof, and among the trees and bushes, and you behold the *cuculio*: it has the loveliest, clear blue fire which you can imagine.

Fire-flies make their appearance at the commencement of the rainy season, and as we have now had a couple of small showers, to the great joy of the coffee-planters, the *cuculios* show themselves as soon as it begins to grow dark. They are not, however, numerous as yet; but I am told that when the rainy season sets in, in May, June, and July, they become so numerous that the heads of large trees are sometimes entirely covered with them, and gleam out as from millions of little tapers. It is not known here how and whence they come; it is maintained that during the dry season they conceal themselves in decayed trees; they now feed on sugar-cane, and I have a whole party in a glass in my room, where they suck pieces of sugar-cane. They seem to be very well off there, and think more about eating, apparently, than freedom; they sit quite still and suck the cane, and their light seems dimmed the while; but if I oblige them with a bath of fresh water, it becomes bright again, and the whole creature more lively. Sometimes, when I wake in the night, I hear a buzzing noise in my room, and see one or two *cuculios* flying about, and lighting up every part of the room which they approach.

I have to-day drawn a couple of them in my album. I have here a perfect phrensy, sketching and drawing people, birds, trees, flowers, dwellings, every thing which strikes me; and so much strikes me here, from its beauty or its novelty, that I am in a continual drawing fever. Many of my efforts are not wholly successful, both from want of time and artistic skill; but I shall carry home with me some small memories which it will be pleasant to possess.

I see in the evenings the Southern Cross slowly rising in a slanting direction with regard to the horizon; at midnight it stands perpendicularly above it. I went out last night to see it. This lovely constellation shone bright and beautiful amid the tranquil, beautiful night. The stars are of the second magnitude; one of them, however, is of the third; but the proportion between them is so perfect, that the whole figure is striking in the highest degree; besides which, the splendid Cross stands solitary in the southern heavens, with its foot almost touching the earth, and its arms extending over it. The whole figure produces a solemn but melancholy effect upon me. A glory is formed above the Cross by the stars of Centaur, and the two stars Circinus and Robur stand like sentinels, one on either side.

After midnight the Cross declines toward the right, and thus sinks, by degrees, once more beneath the orb of the earth. The nights are very dark, but the darkness is as if transparent; the air is not felt. There could not be more beautiful nights in Paradise. The beauty of our midsummer in the north of Sweden might emulate it, but in another way.

When I turn from the Southern Cross, and the palm-trees between which it shines, I see in the northern firmament, above a beautiful ceiba-tree in the court, the North Star and the Great Bear.

April 3d. I have spent this beautiful morning in the banana groves, which are always to be met with on coffee plantations, sketching the tree, with my favorite fruit and all its little upspringing family around its stem. I found here also flowering cotton-plants in a considerably wild state. The shrub has twisting, irregular stems, coarse lobed leaves of a dark dull green color. The flower resembles a double mallow, and is of a clear, light yellow color, and of the most delicate and graceful form. The manner in which the capsule opens, and throws out the bunches of cotton in which the seeds are imbedded, is wonderfully pretty. I must now paint this, as well as the Southern Cross above the palm-trees.

The palm-trees! I never grow weary of contemplating the waving of their heads in the wind, and the soft and majestic inclination of the branches. They are full of poetry and of symbolic beauty; they speak forcibly of the union of the noble in thought and deed, and the beautiful in expression; wherever I turn, they meet my eye with new aspects of beauty. The palm-tree's crown has generally from fourteen to sixteen branches. Every month, or every alternate month, one of the lower branches falls off. I have often seen such, six or seven ells long, lying across the path as I have been driving out, and every month a new one shoots forth. This always shoots up in the centre of the crown, like an upright sceptre ruling the tree; it unfolds itself first at the point, and the delicate leaves sport in the wind like a green flame, or flag, above the tree.

It is customary in this neighborhood to cut off the branches of the palm in the woods and fields for the purposes of thatching roofs, &c., and the tree is sometimes left with merely two or three branches, by which one might imagine that it was bereft of all its beauty; but no! the despoiled palm elevates its two remaining branches with a graceful bend toward the branches of another tree in the same condition, and you behold Gothic porticoes, and arches of the most beautiful proportions, arising in the fields, or in the depths of the forest: to deprive the palm of its nobility and its beauty requires the destruction of its life. The king-palm has always an upright column or stem; the cocoa-palm, on the contrary, has a curved, leaning stem, much thinner than that of the king-palm. I see the latter almost always heavily laden with fruit, which grows in clusters close to, or beneath the branches. People here are fond of the milk of the fruit, and consider it as a purifier of the blood; it has the appearance of whey, and one must be accustomed to its flavor before one can like it. The fruit of the king-palm is a berry, and is only used for fodder for cattle. The cabbage of the palm, as it is called—that is, the middle of the stem nearest to the crown—the very core, as it were, of the tree, is said to be a great delicacy, but it can not be removed without taking the life of the tree.

In the afternoons I have driven out with my kind hostess, in her volante, to visit some of the neighbors. Yesterday we called on an elderly French lady, who interested me by her strongly-marked individuality; it was a pleasure to hear her relate any thing, and to follow her expressions and gestures. In a general way, it seems to me that Europeans have far more accent and emphasis in their whole being than the Americans, or than those families of European origin which have been resident in America for any length of time. The former speak louder; emphasize the words more strongly; use more action; appear more forcible; make more demonstration: the latter move and speak with very little outward action; there is a something silent and without sound in their being; energy has a more inward, a more concentrated power. The great expression of the American seems to be properly, in his public institutions, in the development of the political life of the states, in the advancement of commerce, in the magnitude of his public undertakings. Individuality does not indeed vanish, but it seems to me to occupy itself in a higher species of manifestation.

The Spaniards present, in manners and appearance, the strongest contrast which can be conceived to the Anglo-American, and the melody and majesty of the Spanish language always enchants me—excepting, indeed, when I hear it spoken or screamed out by uneducated women. I visited a farm one afternoon, where we found an assembly of ten or twelve women belonging to the working-class, but not to the poorest. They were, the greater number of them, thin and very brown, and they screamed and made such a din, although it was all in kindness and cheerfulness, that it was almost deafening; one might have imagined one's self amid a flock of turkeys; and to all this noise was added a great deal of action, very energetic, but angular and quite devoid of grace. On the contrary, from the lips of educated and refined women, the Spanish language is the most beautiful music.

The beautiful cuculios are now my torment as well as my delight, because, oh! they are stupid; and when they fold together their wings, they are the most awkward and helpless of all creatures. During their flight they strike themselves against any thing that comes in their way, and then fall down, when they creep, or lie upon their backs as foolishly as our cock-chafers. They allow themselves to be caught with the greatest ease, and, once caught, they seem to forget that they have wings. The little negro children run after them, crying "*Cuccu! cuccu!*" catch them easily, and then torment them in many ways. And since the time when I purchased some of these poor, stupid creatures for a few *galietas*, to release them from the hands of their tormentors, dozens of these young negroes come crowding in the evening on the piazza, which lies on the same level with the great parlor, poke in their curly heads, and stretch out their hands, with the brilliant insects in them, shouting "*Cuccu! cuccu!*" One is obliged to purchase some of them out of captivity, but *all*—a whole pocket full of *galietas*, would not suffice for that! If one makes any demonstration of driving the children away, off they fly like a flock of sparrows, with a loud cry of exultation, for they are full of fun; but they are soon back again, shouting "*Cuccu! cuccu!*" If one takes no notice of them, they will steal into the room—that is to say, if no gentlemen are there—and come up to the piano when Miss P. is playing Cuban dances, or I Swedish polkas, and temptingly stretch out their hands full of "cuccus," merrily laughing. If I take up my handkerchief with a threatening gesture, away they scamper like the wind, but merely for a moment.

These beautiful cuculios are really the most tormenting of all creatures. The negroes place them in phials and bottles, and use them as lanterns and candles in their rooms. In this way they will live for a week, until finally they die of suffocation. If they were but as devoid of feeling as they are of sense! The children of the family and I amuse ourselves in the evenings by endeavoring to make the cuculios fly, which we have either picked up or purchased out of bondage. It is sometimes difficult to persuade them to it, but when one sets them on the point of one's finger, and holds it up in the air, one may often see them spread out their wings, and, making their droning sound, ascend aloft, giving forth their beautiful, incomparable light.

In the morning I return to Matanzas, and thence I shall proceed to Havana, and afterward to *San Antonio de los Bagnos*—a bathing-place, where the country is said to be magnificent, and thence to a plantation at some distance. A young planter here, a French Creole of the name of S., wishes me to become acquainted with his mother, a widow, after a second marriage with a Spanish marquis C., who resides there; and he has often spoken of her in such a manner as makes me wish to know her. Besides this, she is said to enjoy literature and art, and the company of people who are devoted to them. I shall thus remain longer in Cuba than I intended, but—I shall be at Cuba only once in my life; and Cuba is a home of beauty, and I am annoyed that it is so little known. Natural historians, architects, painters, and poets ought to come hither for new knowledge and new inspiration. Air and light, the vegetation above ground, and the caverns below it, are full of life and beauty! There is also a remarkable grotto not far from this plantation, which we, if possible, shall visit early in the morning.

We have now as visitor in the house a lively young girl, a French Creole, Eudoxia B., whose cheerful conversation, and natural, healthy, and graceful manners it is a pleasure both to hear and see. I hear from her that young girls have sometimes in Cuba, as well as in Sweden, certain Utopian dreams of a home (a kind of paradise for young girls) into which no man shall be allowed to enter. Eudoxia's only brother is said also to have similar dreams of a corresponding paradise for young men, from which all ladies are to be excluded. I am mistaken if these young exclusives will not, one fine day, exclude themselves from their paradise by entering the marriage state; I would not be surety for the pretty Eudoxia's vocation as a nun. I have drawn this charming young girl's portrait in my album. A little green lizard sat all the while, certainly for two hours, upon a vine-branch by the window, and peeped in; another lizard, its counterpart or spouse, sat a little higher up, just opposite, and seemed to watch its movements. The little creatures amuse me greatly, they look so wise and so reflective. When they would make themselves agreeable one to another, they open a kind of wing on one side, of the brightest red color, and wave it about like a fan.

I found this morning, to my astonishment, that all my cuculios had disappeared from the glass which always stands upon my toilet table. I could not comprehend how it could be, for I knew that they had not energy enough to leave the sugar-cane and fly away. Somewhat later in the forenoon, I beheld a huge coal-black spider—as large as a little child's hand—sitting upon the wall of my room with a cuculio in its mouth. I had already seen the ugly creature there several times. These spiders have a hideous appearance, but are said to be inoffensive to man. The multitudes of creeping things here are, nevertheless, a nuisance; in order to preserve eatables from them, they must be surrounded by water.

There is a general talk now of a fresh attack being made on Cuba, a new attempt at conquest which is said to originate with the Americans. It is said, also, that the expedition is arming at Yucatan, and consists of a number of people who were in the Mexican war; it is expected about Easter. Many families on the plantations hold themselves in readiness for flight from the island on the first outbreak of disturbances. The Creoles are bitterly displeased with the Spanish government, and they have reason for being so. They wish universally to be liberated from the Spanish yoke, but are themselves too weak to undertake their own liberation; and they fear the negroes, who, on the first occasion, would rise against them. The Spanish army is in active preparation to defend the island against the Americans. The American government has publicly declared itself opposed to these robber expeditions, and admonishes all good citizens of the United States to oppose them. The Spaniards, however, suspect the American slave states of being concerned in them, and of desiring their success, in order that, by the annexation of Cuba as a slave state, they might have a balance in the South, against the increase of the free states in the North. I shall hear the result of all this, however, in the United States.

On the 22d of April I shall bid farewell to this beautiful, but serpent-stung Cuba!

Matanzas, April 6th.

I am once more at the good and excellent house of Mr. and Mrs. B., happy to be with these young and handsome people inhaling the delicious air! No place has such air as Matanzas, so animating, and so charming; and nowhere does one hear so much music. The whole day through may be heard Cuban dances from four or five pianos in the neighborhood; and in the evening, a couple of gentlemen come out upon a piazza nearly opposite to ours, and sing Spanish songs, and accompany themselves on the guitar; a skillful harp-player goes about from door to door, twanging upon his harp-strings as he carries his harp on his back, and playing at the doors "*La Hauta Arragonesa*," that dance so full of quivering life, till my whole being quivers and dances as I listen to it—or *la Cachuca*, so full of grace; and during all this, the band is sounding from *La Plaza des Armas*, where the *beau monde* of Matanzas are walking about in the moonlight beneath the poplars; the ladies without bonnets, and with flowers or other ornaments in their hair, in their transparent veils and white dresses—and where I also walk during these pleasant evenings with my young hostess and the gentlemen of the house, or with my agreeable young countryman, Mr. F.; so that one hears music enough at Matanzas, that is, in the evenings especially, when there is a regular charivari of it, but which is by no means disagreeable, because the time and the spirit of the music is in all cases so very much alike. In all this there is a gay, sportive, care-free life; I give myself up to the influence of it, and bathe, as it were, in the softly floating atmosphere which dances around me, like playful zephyrs, as I pace the piazza till toward midnight, and see the Southern Cross gleaming as it ascends higher and higher in the heavens, above a row of dark-green, shadowy sapota-trees. Yes, this is indeed a peculiarly delicious, tranquil life; I wish that every body could thus enjoy it. On the prairies of America, and often in America, did I stretch out my arms and fly—fly over the whole earth. Here I wish merely to be quiet—to sit in the shade of the palms, and listen to the rustling of their branches, or on the piazza in a rocking-chair, soothed by music and the zephyrs of Paradise; thus could I sit, it seems to me, for an eternity, and feel nothing wanting!

Mrs. B. drove me last evening in her volante to the top of Combre. A pair of horses drew the volante rapidly up the hill, although it is a two hours' journey. The road lay between lofty candelabra-like aloe-plants; and when we had reached the summit or ridge of hills, we beheld the blue, vast sea stretching out on the right hand, scattered over with trading vessels and ships of war both large and small; all that great world's life and that boundless ocean of the world; and to the left, inclosed within mountains, Yumori Valley, with its green and lovely groves of palms, like a quiet, peaceful paradise—a greater or more beautiful contrast can not be imagined. Beautiful habitations, the country houses of the wealthy inhabitants of Matanzas, were scattered about this elevation, surrounded by trees and flowers. We saw the sun set and the moon rise in calm majesty. I could merely say, "God, how beautiful are thy works!"

Oh! I would bring to this height of Combre the woman wearied and imbittered by life—she who has seen into the darkened abysses of life; I would let her here see, breathe, and derive again courage and hope from these speaking symbols of the affluence and glory of the All-good! I would place her here, and say to her, "See, all this is thine—will be thine one day when thy desert-pilgrimage shall be ended, and thou shalt have won the victory—Trust and hope!"

We drove back through the clearest moonlight, with the view across the bay lying unbroken before us the whole way. But Mrs. B. and I had absorbed ourselves in a conversation upon quite another subject than the beauties of nature, and I gave to them merely a half attention, a preoccupied mind, and now feel a little reproach of conscience.

10*th*. Ah, how charming it was to receive a letter from you, and to know how every thing was at home. The letter was, it is true, somewhat old, for it was written in January, but it sounded deliciously fresh to me, poor West-Indian pilgrim! And nothing in it pleased me more than to know that you, on the first of June, will go with the Q.'s to Marstrand. Thoughtful, rational people, brother-in-law and sister!

I shall not, however, be at home in July, and perhaps not even in August; I have still so much to see and to consider thoroughly in the United States; but when colder weather comes, then, my dear child, I shall come and be with you and mamma. And how much of light, and warmth, and good, both in great and small, shall I not have gathered up in my wanderings—nor shall I keep them all to myself—of that you may be sure!

I have enjoyed, and still enjoy, much in Cuba, both in soul and body, and I have become really stout and young again there (N.B.—In comparison with what I was in the United States, where I grew both thin and old). I should have still further improved if I could only have rested somewhat. But my imagination has been so much invigorated—or, rather, so much excited here, that it has left me no repose, but has kept me in an almost continual fever. New objects and new combinations are continually presenting themselves, and exciting me to copy them or to avail myself of them, and urging me to undertake more than I can accomplish, both as regards time and ability. It is almost laughable, and sometimes also a little to be regretted, because I can get no rest. I am, however, more amused by my work than I have ever been, and I take portraits now better than I did formerly, but those which are most successful I generally leave at the homes where I am staying at the time. Yes, those good, beautiful homes! they have been as good to me at Cuba as in the United States; open, hospitable, they have afforded me rest and friends, and have enabled me to see and to know the inner life and condition of society, and have given me an opportunity of seeing people who will be united in my heart with the delicious air and the beautiful palms of Cuba. Among these is Mrs. P., one of the best hearts in the world—one of those gentle, motherly beings whom one must love and reverence with one's whole heart. It was a grief to me to part with her and her kind daughters, who overwhelmed me with kindnesses and gifts, even to the last moment.

I live with the young couple here as with a younger brother and sister, and am as happy as possible with them in their lovely home, and in the charming air of Matanzas.

I have again visited my beloved valley of Yumori, and made a drawing of its opening, as being most manageable from the azotea of the house, which commands a beautiful view of this point. I wished also to draw a Cuban house, and selected for this purpose a small, very pretty house on *La Plaza des Armas.* Very early in the morning, accordingly, I seated myself upon a bench, under the poplars there, with pencil and book, and thus hoped, quite unobserved, to place *Casa donna Fabriana Hernandez* in my album. The first morning, every thing succeeded to my wishes. One negro only looked out of the gate of the house and cast suspicious glances at me. The second morning, however, several heads peeped forth from the house, and a crowd of lads gathered round me, peeping into my album. On the third morning, the house was in evident inward uneasiness, and tall men came round me talking Spanish, not in any unfriendly manner, and with questions to which I could give no other reply than by showing them my drawing, and saying "*hermoso Casa in Matanzas.*" They laughed, but would see me at work, and there was no more tranquillity for me; I therefore left the place as soon as I had done sufficient of the house to enable me to finish the drawing at home. A handsome Cuban house, with its fresco-paintings, its handsome iron railing, parapet, and decorations, is a complete trinket from its ornament and loveliness. The gate of the house is, comparatively speaking, too large for the house, and there always stands the elegant volante, which may be regarded as the feet of the family, because these seldom move out of the house excepting to be conveyed by it. The gate is always kept fastened except when it is opened for the volante, and a little wicket in the gate serves for the ingress and egress of pedestrians.

I drive out in the afternoons with Mrs. B., sometimes to make purchases, and sometimes upon one of the beautiful promenades, *Paseo de Tacon* or *La Pleja;* this last, along the shore, where we breathe the fresh, delightful sea-air, while the waves dash and roar against the beach, is indescribably delightful. It is sometimes late before we return, and then it is beautiful to see the lights gleaming in Matanzas, in the shadow of the hills along the shore, in the dark but clear air.

Our shopping is managed in this way: the volante stops before a shop, when immediately one or two shopmen hasten out to the carriage, and inform themselves of what the signoras require. We mention what we wish, and immediately as great a choice of the particular article is brought out to us as we can desire, and our purchase is made without our leaving the volante. But, whether we purchase or not, the behavior of the young gentlemen of the shop is alike polite, attentive, and agreeable. Yes, one might fancy that a young page of the days of chivalry rather than a simple shopman was before one, so courteously and agreeably does he behave, that young Spaniard, to the purchasing *signoras* or *senoritas*, as he sometimes calls them in a flattering, melodious voice.

Many of these young tradesmen are sons of good families of the island, for the Creoles have not much higher prospect in life than trade or agriculture. Civil and military employment is generally given to Spaniards.

During these drives, my young hostess salutes the passers-by, or the people in their houses, with a gracious wave of the hand, and the word *adios!* as we proceed. Such is the custom here, and the salutation by a graceful and friendly movement of the hand, which has various degrees of expression and warmth, is universal both for ladies and gentlemen, and seems to me a graceful and becoming mode of salutation, in comparison with which our custom of a gentleman's taking off his hat seems very troublesome and unnecessary. The polite Spaniard adds to this salutation of a lady, "I kiss your hands!" which, of course, means nothing, but which sounds well, and the expression of his countenance is at the same time extremely charming. The Spaniards are certainly the most polite of all men, but it is asserted that they are just as fickle.

I yesterday afternoon saw the Spanish soldiers exercise. Their maneuvers were excellent; but they were very short men. Their discipline and conduct on the island is said to be very good.

With the evening comes music, both within and out of the house, and the play of the sea-breezes on the piazza. Mrs. B. plays the lively Cuban and Spanish dances remarkably well; and now also she plays Swedish polkas, which she has learned from me, and I play her dances. Sometimes there are visitors, both of the European settlers on the island and Spanish ladies, who always maneuver and flutter a great deal with their fans, for the weight and the splendor of the fan is the pride of the Spanish lady. I have seen here fans which have cost from twenty-five to one hundred dollars each. The most valuable are of ivory set with gold, and greatly ornamented, in part, with small oval mirrors on the outer sides. The maneuvering with the fan is quite a little science, in which the Spanish lady or Spanish Creole lady comprehends a whole language of signs, by which she converses when and how she will with the friend of her heart.

In the reception-rooms of Cuba stand two rows of rocking chairs, some of the Spanish and some of the American style—the Spanish being very much more magnificent and heavier—the one against the windows, and the other within the room. Here people sit and talk, rocking and fanning themselves while the wind sports in through the windows. They drink tea and eat preserves. The Creole ladies have fine, soft brown eyes; they are said to have good natural understanding and intelligence, but to be very ignorant. They are principally occupied within the house in sewing, dressing themselves, and receiving visitors.

I shall make one more excursion with my kind friends —that is to say, up the Canima, which is one of the most beautiful rivers of Cuba, and not far from this place; then I must say farewell to Matanzas.

April 13th, evening. Yesterday morning, before sunrise, we set out, Mrs. B., her brother Philip, and myself, and, just as the sun ascended in all his glory from the sea, we put off from the shore at Matanzas. An elderly, weather-beaten seaman from the Canary Isles, and his two young sons, were our boatmen. The sea was quite calm, or merely moved in long smooth waves without foam. This was all as it should be, for otherwise we could not have entered the Canima, which, in rough weather, is dangerous at its outlet into the sea. Cuba has many rivers flowing from the mountains, but none large, and none navigable to any great extent.

After a sail of about half an hour on the sea, we reached the outlet of the Canima, a clear little river flowing with a sweep into the sea, from between lofty, precipitous, rocky walls covered with tropical vegetation. Fan-palms waved on the heights in picturesque groups, and along the steep, rocky heights grew an infinite variety of trees and shrubs, amid which hung splendid orchids, with red, yellow, white, and purple flowers, around which hovered swarms of green humming-birds. Nearest to the river grew trees and shrubs of bamboo, bending down toward the water with a movement of such incomparable grace, that it enchanted me, and made me almost melancholy. The shadow of the hills fell over the river, which, perfectly calm, lay, with its tropical world, like a beautiful mystery before us. Thus advanced we onward hour after hour, and at every new bend of the river discovered new beauties, but all of the same character—palms, aloes, bamboos, orchids, humming-birds. A lovely white bird flew continually in advance of us for some time, alighting on the banks to rest, and then flying on again when we approached, only anew to show us the way; they called it the *gazza*. But the sun ascended, and there was not a breath of air in that deep glen. The boys who rowed us poured, every now and then, water down their throats from the spout of a clay vessel, in such a manner that the stream of water flowed straight into their stomachs without any appearance of swallowing. They held their heads slanting backward, their mouths wide open, and the clay spout at some distance from their mouths, and in this way the water flowed down their throats for several seconds, after which they cried or groaned out *Ave Maria!* laughed, and rowed on.

We landed at a little bend of the river, and ate our breakfast under some beautiful bamboo-trees, while the humming-birds danced over their red flowers around us.

I took a walk along the banks of the river, which is here very narrow. A couple of ruinous wooden houses stood upon the opposite bank; the most lovely groups of palms and bamboos were scattered beside the river. The whole scene had a luxuriant and paradisiacally wild appearance. Crabs, and that species of craw-fish which is called in America *the fiddler*, from its one large claw, swarmed on the shore, as they had done through the whole of our course. Spite of all the beauty of the vegetation, I felt that, in order for any one to live happily here in this narrow world, he must be either a crab or a humming-bird. I should have died here for want of fresh air.

We were surprised on our return by a thunder-storm of the wildest description, and, notwithstanding the arched sail-cloth covering of our boat, we were wet through, which made me very uneasy on account of Mrs. B., who was not well that day, and who is not strong. We were glad to reach home after a sail of ten hours. Our boatmen continued to pour water into themselves, and to sigh out their

Ave Maria! and were to the last in good humor, and apparently unwearied: I can not but admire their power of endurance.

We were very weary; but we had, however, seen the Canima, and I now can place the impression of its tropical scenery beside that of the Hudson, the Savannah, the Mississippi, the Ohio, and other rivers of the Western land which I traversed.

And now it is evening—my last evening at Matanzas; in the morning I shall set off to Havana. I have spent the evening alone with my young friends; I have for the last time heárd Mrs. B. play *La Hauta Arragonesa;* have heard for the last time *Adeste fideles* played by Mr. B. on the organ. I asked them for these pieces, that I might bear them away with me as my latest memories of the days spent in their home; and in the morning early I part from these estimable, kind people—from Matanzas and its beautiful neighborhood. It grieves me to leave them, but it can not be helped. Never more shall I feel such an atmosphere—such zephyrs; never again hear such a flood of joyous music; never again behold Yumori, Canima, and Combre!

LETTER XXXV.

Havana, April 15th.

Good-morning once more, my little heart, in Havana, where I am excellently lodged in Mr. Woolcott's good hotel, Havana House, and where I am now able to live cheaper than at first, because the flood of travelers has now somewhat withdrawn, and there is plenty of room. I have again my former little room, with its outlet on the roof, and the clever, good-tempered Mrs. Mary to look after me, and a black Rosetta, with splendid eyes and a cheerful smile, to wait upon me as a second servant. The good

F.'s have also again invited me to take up my former quarters in their house; but the house is full of children and guests, and I will not abuse their hospitality; besides, I so infinitely enjoy my solitude and my liberty.

This is Maunday-Thursday, a great holiday in the Christian Church, and I have this morning visited two churches in the city. There was great pomp in them. Ladies, dressed as for a ball, knelt upon splendid mats in silk attire, and satin shoes, jewels, gold ornaments, and flowers, with bare neck and arms, and every where the transparent black mantillas, and every where glittering, waving fans. Quite young girls, even, were so tricked out; and all around them stood gentlemen contemplating the ladies through their lorgnettes. The sight of all these adorned, only half-veiled women of all colors—for mulattoes also, very splendidly attired and with magnificent figures, were among them—prostrated in crowds on their knees in the centre aisle of the church, from the very end to the altar, is really beautiful, especially as the eyes and busts of the Spanish women are generally remarkably lovely. But the want of earnestness in every thing, excepting in vanity and the wish to be admired, was very striking, especially on a day such as this—the day of the Lord's Supper—that calm, unpretending, solemn day of initiation to the highest and holiest life of humanity. I called to remembrance a Maunday-Thursday in St. Jacob's Church at Stockholm; there simply called "Going to the Lord's Supper." Whole families assemble—father, mother, and children, assemble to drink together from the cup. I remembered the silence, the calm, deep devotion of all who filled that crowded church!

There is but one general voice in Cuba, among the strangers of various nations dwelling there, of the entire want of religious life on the island. The clergy live in open defiance of their vows; are respected by no one, nor deserve to be so; nor does morality stand any higher than religion.

"There is plenty of love and passion at Cuba," said a thoughtful young man, a resident there, to me, "but it is more frequently on the side of vice than of virtue."

The god of money is blindly worshiped. It is very seldom that a marriage takes place in which he has not been consulted before any other. Ladies who remain unmarried seldom continue blameless in their lives. Unmarried men never are so.

People come to this beautiful island, like parasites, merely to suck its life and live at its expense. But it avenges itself, flings around *them* its hundred-fold, oppressive, snake-like arms, drags them down, suffocates their higher life, and changes them into a corpse in its embrace.

In the evening. I have again visited three or four churches. They are splendidly illuminated this evening, especially the choirs and around the altar-pieces. They were less crowded than at morning mass, and now principally by a lower class of people. Several seemed to be kneeling and praying with devotion. There sat, one on each side the entrance of the Cathedral, two magnificent Spanish dames entirely covered with jewels, each with a table before her, upon which a collection was made for the poor. One single jewel from all their splendor would richly have outweighed all the offerings of those humble people. I passed in and out without impediment, mingled with the crowds in the churches, or with the crowds in the streets, and all was peaceable and quiet. The appearance was of a people going about to amuse themselves From this moment to Easter Sunday morning at about nine o'clock, a profound stillness prevails in Havana ; not a single volante is seen in the streets. To-morrow afternoon they will be occupied by a great procession.

Easter Sunday. I witnessed the procession the day before yesterday, with two American acquaintances, from the piazza of *La Plaza des Armas*. Ladies dressed as for a ball, white, yellow, brown, and black, attended by gentlemen, filled the square early in the afternoon, walking about, talking, and laughing. The mulatto ladies were particularly distinguishable by their showiness, brilliant flowers and ornaments in their hair and in their bosoms, and in these they flaunted about in the style of proud peacocks. It was evident that people were expecting a splendid show. In the twilight the procession approached with candles and blazing torches. The figure of the dead Christ is borne along lying upon a state-bed, beneath an immense chandelier, which lights up the pale, noble, wax countenance. Mary weeping is borne after in a gold-embroidered mantle, and with a golden crown on her head; and Mary Magdalene, and the other Mary, have also their magnificent garments. The procession was large, and not without a certain pomp and dignity. Among those who took part in the procession, I observed a number of negroes with large white scarfs bound across the breast and shoulders. I was told that they belonged to a kind of order of Freemasons, who attached themselves to the church by the exercise of deeds of mercy, taking care of hospitals, &c.

Thousands of people streamed gayly along the streets and squares, and the colored portion especially brilliant, in all the colors of the rainbow. It was a splendid spectacle, but not at all suitable for the occasion. Not a particle of seriousness was observable among the masses of people. It was very evident by this procession that religion was dead in Cuba!

Nevertheless, yesterday was a great fast, and a deep stillness prevailed throughout the lively Havana. This morning the image of the arisen Christ was borne in great procession from the Cathedral to the Church of St. Catalina; and from St. Catalina, in the mean time, another procession was advancing, the weeping Mary Magdalene seeking for Christ. When the processions meet, and it is proclaimed that Mary Magdalene has met Christ, a shot is fired, and all the bells of the churches begin to ring, flags to wave in the harbor and on the church towers, and trumpets to be blown. The fast is at an end. Volantes drive out of the gates, and negroes rush about also, shouting and laughing; a thoughtless, universal jubilation at once begins.

During all this I quietly betook myself to my favorite *Cortina de Valdez*. It was the loveliest morning that could be imagined. The bright blue sea, agitated by the wind, flung itself in lofty, silvery-crested waves around the feet of the rocks of the Moro, and the flags in the harbor fluttered cheerfully in the morning breeze. The atmosphere was full of regenerated life. White doves flew down to the white marble basin, and drank of its fresh spring waters; little green lizards darted about on the wall with love and delight; and as I walked along, my soul uttered these words:

She walks along lonely,
She comes from a foreign land;
She is distant from friends and from kindred;
She walks along lowly,
Lonely she walks among strangers;
They of her having no knowledge,
She not knowing them;
They look upon her
With cold and indifferent glances.
Yet still her spirit
O'erfloweth with joy,
With bliss gusheth over,
And bright are her eyes,
With warm tears of gladness.
She has *one friend*,
One friend who was dead,
And he has arisen,
And this is his day of arising,
The morning of Easter!
And fresh living breezes,
And the bright sun ascending,
And the ringing of church-bells,
And the fluttering of banners,
And flowers unfolding,

And twittering of lizards,
And the beating of drums,
And the blaring of trumpets,
And the great ocean,
And white doves which drink at the rim of the fountain;
They all speak of Him,
They all bear His name,
That name so beloved,
And His name by the whole world is borne!

April 20th. Your birth-day! Blessings on the day which gave me my dear friend! I can not to-day present you with flowers, but I can sit down in thought with you, and tell you the history of the day, which was to me party-colored, but amusing, and which will perhaps amuse you more than a bouquet.

Two American gentlemen, of the chivalric species, whom I hope our Lord will bless with man's best reward—good and beautiful wives—had taken charge of me and my effects when I came by rail-way from Matanzas to Havana, and conducted me and mine, safe and sound, to Havana House. One of them, who has resided much in Cuba, Texas, and Mexico, and who has, in consequence, a touch of the Spaniards' grace of speech and manner, has since that time been a very agreeable companion to me, and I have to thank him for presenting me, through conversation, with living pictures of the scenery, population, and manners of these Southern lands. The other, Mr. F., a merchant of New York, is grave and simple in his manners, one of those men with whom I always am at ease, and to whom I feel a sort of sisterly relationship.

This gentleman has accompanied me with noble American simplicity, and as kindly and with as little sense of impropriety as if he had been a brother, in various of my little excursions, making all the needful arrangements for me in the pleasantest manner. Thus we took a sail together to-day in the beautiful bay, crossed over to the heights *Casa Blanca*, which are covered with the wild candelabra-like aloes, and saw from thence a glorious sunset; after which we rowed round in the dark, clear shadows of the hills on the water, and saw it drip in gold and silver drops from the oars. It was a beautiful excursion, which had only one shadow; that was the company of a German gentleman, who had a great deal of that imperiousness which one frequently finds in European gentlemen, but seldom or never in Americans. His inflated manner formed on this occasion a great contrast to the single-mindedness of the American, who, in his simplicity, was so far his superior. But this is merely *en passant.*

I was, in reality, going to tell you of a visit which I and my two American gentlemen had made to the *Cabildos de Negros*, or to the assemblies of the free negroes of the city. It was not possible for me to go alone. These two gentlemen offered to escort me, and Mr. C., who spoke Spanish like a native, undertook to obtain admission for us, although the free negroes, in general, do not admit of the whites in their society, nor are they by any means so patient or so much under restraint as in the United States.

As these clubs generally meet in the afternoons and evenings of the Sunday, we set off in the afternoon to the street in which the *cabildos* are situated, for they occupy a whole street near one of the toll-gates of the city. The whole street swarmed with negroes, some decked out with ribbons and bells, some dancing, others standing in groups here and there. There prevailed a wild but not rude sort of lawlessness, and on all hands, near and afar off, was heard the gay, measured beat of the African drum. Round the gates of the different halls were collected groups of white people, most of them evidently sailors, who were endeavoring to get sight of what was passing inside; but a couple of negroes, stationed at each with sticks in their hands, kept the entrance closed with good-tempered determination, and did not allow the doors to open beyond half way.

By some means, however, Mr. C. succeeded in getting his head within the door of the Luccomées' *Cabildo*, and then requested permission for *la Signora* to enter. Some negro heads peeped out, and when they saw my white bonnet and veil, and the flowers which I wore—for I adorn myself more with flowers here than in Sweden—they looked kind, and granted permission *per la Signora*, and the gentlemen also who accompanied her were allowed to enter; but the door was immediately closed to various others who wished to thrust in after us.

Chairs were offered to us not far from the door; we were presented to the queen and the king of the assembly, who made demonstrations of good-will, and we were then left to look about us in quiet.

The room was tolerably large, and might contain about one hundred persons. On the wall just opposite to us was painted a crown, and a throne with a canopy over it. There stood the seats of the king and queen. The customary dancing was going forward in front of this seat. One woman danced alone, under a canopy supported by four people. Her dancing must have given great delight—though it was not very different from that of the negro ladies which I have already described—for all kinds of handkerchiefs were hanging about her, and a hat, even, had been placed upon her head. The women danced on this occasion with each other, and the men with the men; some struck the doors and benches with sticks, others rattled gourds filled with stones, and the drums thundered with deafening power. They were apparently endeavoring to make as much noise as possible. While this was going on, a figure was seen advancing with a scarlet hat upon his head, and with a great number of glittering strings of beads round his neck, arms, and body, which was naked to the waist, from which hung scarlet skirts. This figure, before which the people parted to each side, approached me, bowing all the time, and as he did so the whole upper portion of his body seemed to move in snake-like folds. Still making these serpentine movements, he stood before me with extended hands, I being not at all certain whether he was inviting me to dance, or what was the meaning of his apparently friendly grimaces, and his great, black, outstretched hands. At length he uttered, with other words, "*per la bonita!*" and I comprehended that all his bowings and bedizenment were intended as a compliment to me, and I made my reply by shaking one of the black hands, and placing within it a silver coin, after which we exchanged friendly gestures, and my friend made a serpentine retreat, and began to dance on his own account, receiving great applause from the by-standers. A great number of negroes were sitting on the benches, many of whose countenances were earnest, and remarkably agreeable. The Luccomées have, in general, beautiful oval countenances, good foreheads and noses, well-formed mouths, and the most beautiful teeth. They look less good-humored and gay than the other negro tribes, but have evidently more character and intelligence. The nation is regarded as rich, in consequence of the great prizes which it has won in the lottery, and this wealth it is said to apply to a good use—the purchasing the freedom of slaves of this tribe.

These cabildoes are governed, as I have already said, by queens, one or two, who decide upon the amusements, give tone to the society, and determine its extension. They possess the right of electing a king, who manages the pecuniary affairs of the society, and who has under him a secretary and master of the ceremonies. The latter presented me with a small printed card, which gave admission to the "*Cabildo de Señora Santa Barbara de la nacion Lucumi Alagua.*"*

* The Luccomée nation, like the other African tribes, Gangas, Congoes, &c., are divided into many subordinate tribes, with their various cognomens, and their various places of meeting.

After this, and when we had made a little offering to the treasury of the society, we took our departure, in order to visit other cabildoes. And in all cases they were so polite as to give free access to *la Signora, la bonita*, and her companions. I do not know whether this politeness is to be attributed to the negro character, or to the Spanish influence upon it, but am inclined to believe the latter.

I was received in the *Cabildo de Gangas* by the two queens, two young and very pretty black girls, dressed in perfectly good French taste, in pink gauze dresses, and beautiful bouquets of artificial roses in their bosoms and their hair: they both smoked cigarettes. They took me kindly each by the hand, seated me between them, and continued to smoke with Spanish gravity. One of them had the very loveliest eyes imaginable, both in form and expression. On the wall opposite to us was a large and well-painted leopard, probably the symbol of the nation. There were also some Catholic pictures and symbols in the hall. I here saw a whole group of women moving in a kind of dance, like galvanized frogs, but with slower action, bowing and twisting their bodies and all their joints without any meaning or purpose that I could discover. It seemed to be the expression of some kind of animal satisfaction; it had also the appearance as if they were seeking for something in the dark. And the poor benighted people may be said to be still seeking—their true life's joy, their life beyond that of Nature.

They seem, however, to have approached nearer to this in the States of North America. I thought of that nocturnal camp-meeting in the forest, by the light of the fire-altars, and of the melodious hymns which sounded from the camp of the negroes!

I saw in another *Cabildo de Gangas* that same irregular, serpentine dance, danced in circles and rows both by men and women around one another. I saw again, also, in a *Cabildo de Congos*, the Congo dance, as I had seen it in the bohea at St. Amelia, and another which seemed to be a mixture of the Spanish-Creole dance, Yuca and Congo dance. There is considerably more animation in the latter dances than in the former, as well as more art and poetical feeling. The symbol painted upon the wall of this room was a sun with a human face. Here also were several Christian symbols and pictures. But even here, also, the Christianized and truly Christian Africans retain somewhat of the superstition and idolatry of their native land. The Congo and Ganga nations seem to me born of a more careless temperament, and have a more animal appearance than the Luccomées.

I visited two other cabildoes, but did not find any new features of interest, and, finally, I was heartily wearied by the noise, and the rattling, and the bustle, and the dust, and the chaotic disorder in the dancing, and in the movements of their assemblies. I longed for pure air and clear water, and, to gratify my longing, Mr. F. drove me in his volante to Havana harbor.

It was sunset. We inquired for our friend, the boatman of the former evening, Rafael Hernandez, who soon made his appearance with his splendid boat, *La Leonora Rosita*, and rowed us out into the harbor.

Ah! how beautiful, in that tranquil, resplendent evening, to row softly along that palm-decorated shore, and silently to inhale the pure air, and to contemplate the soft, clear coloring of every object. The glowing blush of evening tinged all. Presently the lamps were lighted on the quay *la Alameda di Paula*, and other places along the harbor. These lit up the shore and the water with a wonderfully pure and clear splendor. It seems to me as if light and air here possessed sound and melody; I hear, as it were, their purity, while it strikes upon my eye. And now I felt as if I had come out of chaos into the world of pure light and harmony. But, of a truth, what ball-room would not have seemed to me dusty and stifling when compared with this rotunda of nature beneath the heaven of Cuba.

I asked our boatman—who spoke English as well as Spanish—whether he was satisfied with his condition in life. He shook his head: "Things were going dreadfully with him; he should find himself compelled some fine morning to run away from both boat and city."

"You smoke too many cigarettes, Hernandez!" said I.

"Only twenty a day, signora!" said he, and shrugged his shoulders.

April 22d. Good-morning, my beloved child: I get on charmingly now at the hotel. I have full freedom, have every thing excellent, and the good Mrs. Mary does not let me want for any thing. Early in the morning I go out to walk on my favorite *Cortina;* watch the waves breaking against the rocks of the Moro; inhale the sea-breezes; converse with the naiads; visit a church or two; look at the pomp there; listen to the music; then go home across *La Plaza des Armas*, where I linger a while to study the monument to Columbus, which I afterward at home sketch into my book; but I am obliged to make my observations very warily, for the military on the Square are already beginning to watch me. They suspect that I am plotting an invasion.

Late in the evening I walk about on the azotea among the urns, and watch the moon and the Moro light emulating each other in lighting up the city and the sea, and watch the Southern Cross rise in quiet majesty above the horizon, while toward the northern star, which shows out at sea, I always cast a friendly glance. The roar of the sea comes to me from the side of the Moro, and the gay sound of military music from *La Plaza des Armas.* Later in the night, the harmonious air and sounds are broken in upon by the *Serenos*, or fire-watchmen of Havana, who sing so—that it really would be deplorable if it were not so extremely ludicrous. I never before heard such a succession of false, jaw-breaking, inharmonious tones. I can not get angry with them for laughing.

I go to my friends, the F.'s, generally for an hour every morning, to paint the portrait of Mrs. F., which I wish to possess, in memory of one of the best, most motherly women in the world.

While I am thus occupied, she tells me the experience of her lifetime as regards the negro character. Her observations agree in the main with those of Mrs. P. Mrs. F. says, as she does, "that there is a great difference in the characters and tempers of the negroes, as is the case among the white races, but that they are, in general, more accessible than these to the sentiment of attachment, of tenderness, and gratitude. The whites make a great mistake when they accuse the negroes of ingratitude. They make them slaves, they demand incessant labor from them, and require after that that they should be *grateful*. Grateful for what? They who wish really to be the negro's friend will find him grateful and noble-minded. I have had both black and white nurses for my children, but with the black only have I been perfectly satisfied."

An affecting proof of love and strength of character among the negroes was related to me, in the history of a young negro couple who loved each other, without being able to marry, because the master of the young negro woman obstinately refused to consent to her marriage. Love, however, had had its way, and the young lovers had a child. The master of the negro woman, in a fury of anger at this discovery, forbade her again to see the young man, or he to see his child. The young negro was in service at Mrs. F.'s; he was an excellent young man, with one only fault—he loved liquor, and not unfrequently allowed himself to be overcome by it; and this propensity increased all the more, now that the sorrow of not being able to see his wife and little boy often almost drove him to despair. Mrs. F. said to him,

"If you will break yourself of this habit of strong drink, I will allow you a peso a week, and lay the money by for you, and with it you may, in time, buy the freedom of your child."

From this moment the man became perfectly sober, and persevered in being so for many months. After this time of trial, Mrs. F. paid him the money which she had promised, and added to it, in order, said she, to show him her esteem and satisfaction, as much more as was necessary to purchase the freedom of the child. He kissed her hand with joy and tears of gratitude; he was beside himself with happiness, and with the prospect which was afforded him of sometime being able to purchase the freedom of the child's mother also, and being united to her. This was now in progress of accomplishment. In the mean time, the parents and the child had secret meetings, and their love was as heartfelt, as romantically warm and steadfast as that which any novel-writer describes between his heroes and heroines.

Mrs. F. confirmed all that I had already heard of the kindness of the Spanish masters to their domestic slaves, and the care which they take of them in their old age.

But if the domestic slaves are commonly well treated, the slaves on the plantations are, in a general way, quite the reverse; they are looked upon, not as human beings, but as beasts of burden, and are treated with greater severity than these.

The house of the F.'s is now altogether full of love, music, and mirth. Young Louisa F. is married, and will, although still hardly more than a child, now become mistress of her own household.

I have been sorely tempted just now by a journey to Jamaica and thence to Mexico, which would have been by no means difficult of accomplishment. But time and

—besides, I should not in Jamaica, in Central America, nor yet in South America, see any thing essentially different in vegetation, population, manners, mode of building, or in any other way different to what I see in Cuba, under the tropical heavens and the dominion of the Spaniards. And this was essential to me for my picture of the New World. I have now received a clear impression of its southern hemisphere. Books and engravings will help me to see the difference.

And that they already do. I have seen at Mr. F.'s engravings of Mexico and other cities of Spanish America, which seem to me merely repetitions of Havana. And in Prescott's excellent history of the conquest of Mexico and Peru I have become acquainted with the highlands of these countries, as well as with the noble Aztecs who once dwelt there.

Christian Aztecs must one day rule over these glorious countries, and upon their noble heathen foundation erect a new temple, a new community, which shall, in spirit and in truth, make them the highlands of the world.

I have beheld the countenance of the earth beneath the sun's warmest beams, where they call forth palms and coffee-shrubs. I know the circumstances of every-day human life there, its pleasures and its miseries. I have comprehended this new page in the book of creation and the life of nature. I have enjoyed and been grateful. And after two weeks' longer stay in Cuba, to see Madame C. and the paradisiacal regions of the Caffetal to the east of Havana, I shall turn from the tropics and the palms once more toward the United States, and in the course of a few months hope to see again Sweden, you, and all my dear ones. Believe me, the home of the pine-tree is my home, dearer to me than the palm-groves here. Here I could not live, after all!

LETTER XXXVI.

San Antonio de los Bagnos, April 23.

Abroad on an adventure in foreign lands, my dear heart, and for the moment not of the most agreeable kind; I am here, all alone, in a little Spanish *posada* or *fonda* (a third-rate public house), as uncomfortable as possible, surrounded by people who do not understand me, and whom I do not understand either. I am here awaiting the arrival of a volante from Signora C., which is to take me to her plantation, about five English miles from this place. Possibly, however, she may not yet have received the letter which announced my arrival here, and the volante, in that case, may not come for a day or two, and I, in the mean time, shall have to stop here; but I am neither uneasy nor in want of food, for my little traveling fairy is with me, and keeps me in capital humor, and has enabled me to fall in with a little Spanish Don on the rail-way, who could speak a little French, and who was delighted to be of service to me. With his help, and my Spanish phrase-book and dictionary, I manage very well. And besides, I have sent off a letter of introduction, which I had with me, to Don Ildephonso Miranda, who lives not far from here, "*in su Caffetal en Alguizar*," and I expect to see him in the course of the day, and with his assistance I shall be able to get out of my *fonda*, for he speaks French like a native, I am told, and is, besides, a *caballero perfetto.*

I am now writing to you in a little room with bare whitewashed walls and earthen floor, the only furniture of which is one wooden chair and a wooden table, and with the wind blowing with all its might in through the window. But here it is the warm wind of Cuba, and one can not be angry with it.

My journey this morning by the rail-way was glorious, like another morning journey which I made some weeks since, and the palms and splendid flowers of the caffetals shone out the whole length of the way. The whole of this side of the island is celebrated for the beauty of its coffee plantations, the most splendid days of which are now over, as they are not able to produce coffee in the same quantity and of the same excellent quality as the more southern plantations of the island, and are, in consequence, somewhat on the decline. *San Antonio de los Bagnos* is a small city or town, celebrated for its baths, and for the beautiful mountain scenery of its neighborhood. Plantations lie scattered among these hills, where the heat is never extreme, where the sea-breezes continually blow, and the grass is green the year round; airy habitations are these, with splendid views over the vast sea. San Antonio is further celebrated for a subterranean river, which I shall go out and endeavor to discover for myself. I have dismissed the guide whom my friend Don Manuel obtained for me, saying that he was a *coquin*, and who appeared to me to be such in so high a degree, that I considered him quite capable of pitching me down into the subterranean river which I was going to see. I excused myself, therefore, on the plea of *el vento*. It blows so into my room that I can not write any more. The paper is in a perpetual flutter.

Caffetal la Concordia, April 27th.

I have had, since I last wrote, various small uneasinesses and misadventures, but all of which turned out for the best, and I now write to you from Madame C.'s beautiful coffee plantation, where I am staying amid the most delightful tranquillity and cheerfulness of her lovely family.

I spent the day quite alone at San Antonio in my little *posada*. My room, however, although naked and bare of furniture, was clean, and Raimund, the servant of the house, was very respectful and kind, and began by degrees, out of pure good-will, I believe, to understand me, and if I had not been left alone in this *posada* for a time;

and if these little adverse circumstances had not occurred, I should not have made acquaintance with *San Antonio de los Bagnos*, as I have now done, and that would have been a great pity.

When I had dined on some excellent boiled beef and yams, and the day began to grow cool, I set out on a solitary ramble, having long since become hardened against the wondering glances of the screaming and skipping negro children, who always follow me at first when I go out alone.

Some palm-thatched huts, standing in a plantation-grove at a little distance from the *posada*, attracted me, because I presumed them to be the dwellings of negroes; and I was not deceived in this respect. I soon found myself wandering in a small irregular town, through streets of birch-bark and brushwood cottages, surrounded with little gardens, and the beautiful trees and vegetation of the country. Cocoa-palms and bananas grow on all hands, and on all hands might be seen, beneath them, stark-naked negro children leaping and playing about; negro women were at work, or were standing at the doors of the cottages. I found myself evidently in an African region.

"*Bon jour*, *Madame*," sounded toward me from one of the huts, and, turning round, I beheld a stout and well-dressed negro woman standing at her door, who looked like a personified invitation. I accepted it, glad to have an opportunity of talking with some of the people; and on entering the cottage, which was spacious, I found her one of the very nicest, kindest, most cheerful old negro women that one can imagine. Every thing also in and about the cottage was clean and orderly, bed-room, kitchen, and garden, and the old woman took me to see everything, laughing with all her might at every question which I asked or observation which I made. She was born in St. Domingo, and had been servant in a

French family there before the revolution on the island. She expressed herself very imperfectly in French, but nevertheless gave me a deal of information regarding the condition of the negroes in the little town. They seemed to be happy and contented; supported themselves on their small allotments of land and by their animals, as well as by doing work of various kinds for the people of the city. She herself took in washing, and was well contented with her world. At the present moment she was enjoying a *dolce far niente*, and so also was her husband, who could not speak any other language than Spanish, and therefore did not take part in our conversation, but sat and smoked his cigar with an expression of the most cordial good-nature and contentment. When I saw some banana-trees in the garden (which was not remarkably well kept), I asked her whether she ate bananas at breakfast. This inquiry seemed to be inconceivably entertaining, and, almost choking with laughter, she said she must have roasted meat and coffee at breakfast, but that her husband ate roasted bananas.

Wishing that happy old couple a long life in their cottage, I went on my way, and every step increased my delight at the irregular, but poetical and picturesque scene which *San Antonio de los Bagnos* presented to my view.

Imagine ruins of old, lofty walls and porticoes covered with fresco-paintings, among small white or gayly tinted Cuban houses and small palm-thatched negro huts, all standing in picturesque confusion; a deep but narrow river, as clear as crystal, its banks overgrown with shadowy trees, among which stand negro huts, with their palm-leaf roofs, and over these, bending down from the sloping banks, bananas and bamboo-trees, and all around bushes covered with red and yellow flowers; in the river imagine boys bathing and gamboling about, and old stone and wooden bridges spanning it, with their pointed pillars and buttresses; and majorals riding over the bridges with pistols at their saddle-bows, and swords with silver hilts by their sides; and here and there, upon the verdant banks of the river, or beneath cocoa and bamboo trees, in gardens, or beside the old porticoes and the ruined walls, groups of olive-complexioned or white women, for the most part young and handsome, some smoking cigarettes, others with white flowers in their hair, commonly acknowledging the salutation of the passer-by with graceful inclinations of the head, and a melodious "*Buono tarde, Signora!*" and here and there groups of lightly-clad people, jolly negro men and women, and stark-naked negro children, carrying themselves like regular little savages; white men sitting on the stone walls, or wandering slowly along, smoking cigars; and over all this that mild tropical sky, that delicious air, a soft but joyous light—a slumberous, joy-giving, *far niente* life—and you see an outline of the panorama which I contemplated wandering hither and thither, until the shades of evening advanced, and stars came forth on the scene.

Again in my *fonda*, I prepared myself for the night. I had a neat little bed with clean sheets and a light coverlet. I obtained a cup of weak tea, some bread, and a night-lamp, my friend Raimund devoting himself to me with the utmost respect and gravity. I was now alone; and the sound of a guitar, accompanied by a tremulous, monotonous, but pleasingly melancholy song, similar in character to the Spanish seguidilla, reached me, and to the sound of this I fell asleep on my cool sacking bed, and passed an excellent night, undisturbed by the bloodthirsty robbers that I feared—gnats and fleas.

When I woke next morning, I saw the respectful face of my friend Raimund at my low window, come to inquire if I wished for any thing. I wished for coffee and an egg; and while I was thus breakfasting, *La Miranda* was announced in such a manner as showed that he was regarded as *a power* of the first rank.

And before long, I was prepared to receive Don Ildephonso Miranda, which I did in a room adjoining mine, and of the same unpretending character.

Don Ildephonso Miranda whistled to the people of the *posada*,* and they flew forward to receive his commands; he motioned with his hands, and they flew to all distances to fulfill them.

As for myself, La Miranda was really *en caballero perfetto*, infinitely polite in tone and mannner; he allowed me the use of his volante and his *calashero* to convey me to Madame C.'s; breakfasted with me; arranged every thing as I wished; and when I was about to set off, and inquired for my bill at the *posada*, it was already paid by La Miranda! It would have been no use protesting against it, neither would it have been becoming; I treated it, therefore, as unimportant, and thanked him, with a compliment on the politeness of the Spaniards. This politeness is really great toward ladies and foreigners, and must be founded on a certain national pride, which, at the bottom, is noble and beautiful.

I drove to the residence of Madame C., the Caffetal la Concordia, in Don Ildephonso's volante and in a tropical hot wind, which raised all the red dust on the road in a whirlwind; and in that flying career, and through the cloud of red dust, I could merely see, in passing, the beautiful palms and the brilliant flowers of the caffetals, gleaming above the stone walls which bounded either side of the way.

Madame C. was not at home on her plantation; she was away at the sea, on the southern side of the island, for the sake of bathing, together with her sons and grandchildren; and it was not until this morning that she would

* Whistling to people of the servant-class is customary in Cuba, and they make use of it also among themselves. The sound is, however, rather a hissing than a whistling sound, like a sharp " H!" and is audible at a considerable distance.

be able to receive mine and her son's letters. But the steward on the plantation, Don Felix, a polite, elderly gentleman, received me with Spanish courtesy, and said,

"*Toute la maison est à votre disposition! Vous êtes chez vous. Desposez de tout. La maison est à vous. Ce n'est pas un compliment!*"

We dined together, the polite old gentleman and myself. Don Felix spoke of Madame C. with an expression of worship.

"*Oh, c'est une dame, une dame, comme il y en a peu!*"

Trinidad, a kind negro woman with lovely eyes, and who speaks a little French, is my *femme de chambre*, and I slept that night at this place. The next morning brought a letter from Madame C., inviting me to join her at the sea-coast, arranging all for my coming, and appointing as my companion the very dearest of all handsome and graceful boys, Adolpho S., twelve years old, Madame C.'s eldest grandson.

We set off. It was an arduous journey in the commencement, through a perfect wilderness, over stocks and stones; then in a boat, drawn by men along a narrow stream, almost choked up with reeds and different kinds of water-plants. It was horribly wearisome and horribly hot. My little dark-eyed *cabellero*, the sweet lad, encouraged and comforted me: "It will soon be better," said he; "we have got over the worst now! We shall very soon come into more open water!" The amiable little fellow was really a refreshment to me on this part of the journey, which occupied three mortal hours; the water, after that, expanded into a little river, and we felt the breezes from the sea. At the outlet of the little river into the sea a few small birch-bark huts, regular fishers' huts, stood upon the bare turf; here dwelt the aristocratic family, and lived a kind of field-life for some weeks for the sake of the bathing.

Madame C. had just now returned from the bath. How

handsome and charming she appeared as she advanced toward me in her long white costume, with her mild, pale countenance, her noble bearing, her beautiful manner. She seemed to be between fifty and sixty, and the most refined womanly grace was impressed on face and form. Around the beautiful lady stood two young, tall, handsome men, her two youngest sons, Alfred and Sidney S., and a handsome Spanish lady, the wife of the eldest, and their six children, four boys and two girls, all handsome; and in the outskirts of this beautiful group, negro men, and women, and dogs.

A cottage on the other side of the little river, and opposite that of Madame C.'s, is prepared for me. I shall be there quite alone, and the excellent lady has made it as comfortable as it can be, with a bed, a chair, and a table. The wind blows straight through its walls of brushwood, on the side facing the sea, but then it is the wind of Cuba. There are no trees in the immediate neighborhood—nothing but swampy, low meadow, and beyond that the great sea, which extends, unbroken by rocks, into limitless distance. We are here on the southern side of the island, in a desolate region, inhabited alone by poor fishermen, for whom Madame C.'s residence among them makes the red-letter days of the year. The whole has the charm of novelty, and may do for a few days. I am almost sorry that I have come here, because I fear that I have caused a deal of inconvenience to the sea-bathing family. They are, however, too polite to wish me to perceive it, and I have determined to be contented with every thing; and that is not difficult in this air. We fared sumptuously at a small table on the piazza of Madame C.'s palm-hut, and afterward sat talking by star-light in the mild sea-wind, as I have not talked for a long time, on interesting periods in history—in Swedish history among the rest, for this intellectual lady and her well-educated sons are perfectly acquainted with its main features.

It was near midnight when, with the aid of a faithful old servant, I reached the other side of the river by means of a crazy old bridge; it blew strongly from the sea, and the waves roared very much. The Southern Cross, with its glory of Centaur's stars, and the magnificent star in the ship Argo, Canopus, stood bright above the sea in the southern heavens; I greeted them, and crept into my hut. The light was blown out; but the stars peeped in through the opening of the window which faced the sea. The curtain of the bed fanned and fluttered about in the wind; but it was the wind of Cuba. I lay down in my bed with it whistling round me, and though I did not sleep much, yet still enjoyed an unspeakable pleasure, as if borne upward by the wings of the wind, and by the fresh, gentle spirit of the sea. I did not seem to be conscious of my physical being; I felt, as it were, changed into spirit.

The next morning the scene presented a serious aspect. The heaven was clear; but the night-wind had driven the sea inland, and still continued to blow with the same force; the river swelled, and overflowed its banks and the land round our huts; one pool of water was brought into communication with another, and the pools all ran together into small lakes. It was no longer possible to walk from one hut to another; we paddled about like ducks in the water. The family began to be alarmed.

"If the wind continues in this direction, we shall be surrounded with water in the morning!"

The wind did blow from that quarter. It was now impossible to pass from one hut to another, excepting with boats; the water had risen as high as Madame C.'s piazza. We could no longer go out.

"*Ce n'est pas vivre ici.*"

And they came to the hasty resolution of leaving *La Pláya*, and returning every one of them to *La Concordia* next morning. The eldest son and all the children were ill. The remainder of the family and I sat and talked together cheerfully enough in the evening till half past ten, when I, in storm and darkness, partly splashing, and partly leaping through water, reached my cottage, where, with the storm roaring round me, and amid showers of rain, I still passed a very good night.

The next morning the camp broke up, and we returned to the caffetal by the same narrow brook which we had before traversed to reach *La Pláya.* In the crowded space, the heat and inconvenience of all kinds, I felt a sort of silent despair in being obliged to increase the general discomfort, though by only one individual additional presence; and I was at the same time filled with admiration of the amiable old lady, who, though herself very unwell, yet endeavored to shelter under her parasol as many of the young ones as she could from the heat, and to save my legs by theirs. The youngest Bambino screamed the whole half of the way. At length, wearied out, and in a very deplorable condition, we reached the caffetal.

But we recovered ourselves; and in the evening we sat out on the beautiful piazza, and saw the brilliant cuculios floating through the air, and listened to Spanish seguidillas, which Alfredo S., who is romantically handsome, sang to the guitar with a beautiful voice, and the utmost feeling and expression, so that it did one's soul good to hear him. How different is the same song when sung with or without soul! These Spanish seguidillas, the peculiar national songs of Spain, have also its peculiar national spirit, which breathes from them with indescribable freshness and nature. One recognizes in them the inspiration of a youthful primeval life. They have this in common with our popular songs, however different they may be from them in temperament and character. Our melodies are deeper and richer, but there is more sunshine in theirs, and a more joyous and a warmer life.

La Concordia, May 1st.

Again I bless God that he enables me in Madame C., the proprietor of this plantation, to be acquainted with and to love one of those beautiful maternal women, who are a blessing in all the countries of the world, and who are able, at least for a moment, to remove even from slavery its oppressive fetters, and to allow the slaves to forget them.

This was very soon evident to me from the apparent joy of the negro people in her return to the plantation, and from the beaming countenances which met her, and replied to her joyous, cordial salutation; and each passing day only makes this the more clear, as I silently observe the motherly spirit which induces her to visit the sick among the slaves herself, to send them the food, or allow them the little indulgence which they have wished for; as I have seen how, daily, on the piazza, her chair is surrounded by dozens of little negro children, who sit or creep at her feet, leap and play with one another around her, touching her white dress, coming and complaining to her just as familiarly as if they were her own children; seen the mutually joyful greetings between her and the negroes, both men and women, whom we meet in our walks; heard it also continually in her unpremeditated expressions, felt it in her heart, in the charm of the atmosphere which surrounds her beloved presence.

This evening, when she and I were returning in the twilight from a ramble in one of the woods of the plantation, we met a negro woman.

"Oh, Francisca, Francisca!" exclaimed Madame C., cordially, and inquired from her in Spanish how she was, &c.

Francisca replied, with a beaming expression, that she was well, was happy, and hoped soon to present *sua mercê* with a beautiful little *negrito.* She expected soon to become a mother. Mistress and servant could not have conversed more cordially in our own free country. The young anticipating mother was evidently certain that her child would, in the handsome white lady, meet with a motherly protector.

A little negro lad, who was one day playing with her youngest grandson, rushed up to her in a state of great excitement, complaining, "He calls me a negro without shame!" (*un negre sans honte*).

"Don't play any longer with him!" said Madame C., gravely. "Don't play with him now," continued she, addressing the other negro boys around them. And the handsome little Edwardo received a reproof, and was left alone and with downcast looks for some time.

I often admire the patience with which she allows herself to be surrounded and followed by the active little troop of black children, who kick up a cloud of dust on the roads around her white figure. I confess that I could not endure it as she does; but I shall often in memory hear her gentle voice say, as she frequently does, when I turn the conversation to this subject,

"These poor creatures, whose lot is so hard, who labor for us, and have so little prospect of freedom and happiness, ought we not to alleviate their fate, and sweeten their lives by all means in our power? I can not bear to see any thing suffer—not even an animal. It is a consolation to me to know that my negroes are fond of me. I am fond of them, and I have always found them devoted, and anxious to do all that I wish them to do. They are by no means difficult to manage when they once see that people really wish them well, and desire to be reasonable and just toward them.

"I never allow any flogging to take place on this plantation without my express permission. The majorals are rude, uneducated men, and often will strike a negro in passion and from ill humor. This ought not to be allowed. When a negro is guilty of any offense which deserves punishment, I am informed, and I determine the punishment. If the whip is to be used, it must be used without passion, and only when admonition and reprimand have proved themselves unavailing. My negroes are attached to me because they know that I will never allow them to be ill used."

"It is not, then, true," said I, triumphantly, "what I have been told of the ingratitude of the negroes, and that in the slave-disturbances in 1846 the kindest masters were those who were first murdered by their slaves?"

"Ah, no!" returned Madame C., "such conduct is not in accordance with human nature! It happened at that very time that I was quite alone among my negroes, and they it was who watched over my safety. My son was obliged to go to his plantation on the southern side of the island, where just then the tumult was in full force. The majoral was absent for a time. I summoned my contra-majorals, who were all negroes, and thus addressed them:

"'You know what is going forward at this time not far from this place—that the negroes have arisen, and that they murder and plunder their owners?'

"Yes, they knew of it.

"'Very well,' said I; 'I now place myself and my family under your protection. My son must leave me, and remain away for two or three weeks. There will not be a white man on the plantation; neither will I send for any. I depend upon you, and will confide myself to you. I shall consider you responsible for the behavior of the negroes. If you observe any disorder among them, let me be informed of it.'

"They promised me accordingly.

"I at that time, as now, and indeed ever since my husband's death, slept very badly, and often lay awake great part of the night. One night, therefore, being sleepless, I rose between two and three in the morning, and looked through the window, when I saw, to my astonishment, one of my majorals armed and walking sentry before my house. I called to him, and asked him if any thing were amiss.

"'No; all is tranquil,' replied he; 'but we fear, I and my comrades, that some of the negroes from —— might come here and disturb your grace, and therefore we determined to keep watch over your house in turn every night, so that your grace might be able to sleep quietly.'

"I thanked him for this proof of devotion, and inquired how the negroes were behaving, and whether they worked as usual.

"'Better than usual,' was the reply; 'they know that la Signora confides in them, and they wish to prove that they deserve her confidence. Your grace will be always safe.'"

After these proofs of the fidelity and worth of the negro character, the noble lady can not do other than suffer from the cruelty and the injustice which she sees practiced by so many of the slave-owners toward their slaves.

"Often," said she, on one occasion, "have I, in the bitterness which this has occasioned, wished that they all could be free!"

I often observe in her a shudder, as of anguish, and hear a sigh when the whip is heard to crack, which is the signal for the slaves to go to work; for here even she has not the power of having this abominable signal changed. Another more musical sound is heard daily, about eleven o'clock in the forenoon, when a long, melodious, far-resounding blast is blown on a shell, the summons from labor of such negro women as have infants at the breast, to go and suckle them, and rest before doing so.

So universally known is the kind disposition of Madame C. toward her negro slaves, that she is often besought by strange negroes who have displeased their masters to become their intercessors, and have them spared from punishment. It is not an unusual thing in Cuba for the offending slave to choose from among the white people a *Padrino* or a *Madrina* to intercede for them with their exasperated owner, who seldom or never refuses pardon which is thus asked. Madame C. has often been requested to become *Madrina*, and never in vain. Who, indeed, could refuse that noble, charming woman any thing which she might ask for? Wherever her white, beautiful form appears (she always is dressed in white), she seems to be a messenger of peace.

Madame C. was born in San Domingo, of French parents, who fled thither from France during the Reign of Terror. During the bloody tumults of San Domingo, she and her family were saved by the devoted zeal of faithful slaves. During the beautiful evenings of my stay in the house of this excellent woman, and which we spend on the piazza, or in quietly wandering in the palm-groves of the plantation, she has related to me many episodes from the romantic history of herself and her relatives; and she has no idea how much I am captivated by those traits of an unusually gifted and profoundly intelligent soul, which presented themselves the while, without herself understanding their beauty and their unusual character. We often converse, and her son Sidney with us, on more general topics, especially connected with history, and compare remarkable characters and incidents from the histories of different countries, and I do not make any bad figure in this way, with my Swedish men and women. We talk, we think, we paint together; we are very merry together; and I can not help grieving beforehand in having so soon to leave this place. Here I could live without suffering from what I see most nearly surrounding me, and here I could become so attached, and here I could draw and paint so much.

Madame C. draws and paints flowers, butterflies, and all natural objects remarkably well, because she maintains the utmost fidelity to nature, and draws with intelligence;

during her misfortunes (she lost her husband, Marqués C., and her youngest son by cholera, and suffered greatly in property by the late hurricanes), she lost her inclination for these cheerful occupations; but the delight I have in natural objects, and my fever for drawing, have revived it in her, and if I could remain here some months, we should make together a beautiful album of the flowers and fruits of Cuba, and it would be very agreeable, if greater and dearer vocations did not prevent me!

Many kinds of trees are blossoming now that the rainy season is at hand. Cuculios come out in great numbers, and constitute here, as at *L'Industrie*, my amusement and my torment. Madame C. can not, she declares, say sufficient about the splendor and the luxuriance of the vegetation during the rainy season, nor of the pomp and gorgeous coloring of the clouds. She would willingly tempt me to remain and see all this—with her!

We are now alone here, she, her youngest son, the young, giant-like Sidney S., and three of the second son's children, namely, my little *Cabellero* Adolpho; a most charming, pretty, and gracious little girl, Michaelita, the image of her grandmother; and a little boy, Edwardo, a living counterpart of Corregio's Amor. Madame C. reads with the children in the forenoon, while I draw and write in my own room. The afternoons and evenings we spend together. No one can live more agreeably than I do here, but the phrensy of drawing continues, and leaves me no peace. I am drawing Madame C.'s portrait, that I may carry home with me her gentle countenance, her beautiful, intelligent eyes, which so faithfully mirror her soul. I am taking a portrait of the poetically-beautiful head of Sidney S. for his mother. I am drawing a group of their sweet children, and while I paint them I am enchanted by the witchery of their countenances, the beauty of their eyes. I am drawing the trees, and flowers, and fruit, and birds which surround me, and I am continually in a state of half desperation that I can get so little done in the short time that I have to remain here. This *Caffetal* is the most beautiful and the best kept of any which I have yet seen. The whole of this district is full of coffee plantations, and in the time of their prosperity every one of these is said to have been a little paradise of beauty and luxury; their proprietors emulating each other in magnificence of life and lavish expenditure. Signor C., the husband of my beautiful friend, was one of the most distinguished planters for affluence, magnificent liberality, and beneficence. He was one day dining with a neighbor; the hour of his return arrived, and his volante, drawn by three magnificent horses, drove up to the house; the guests, on this, rose to the windows to see the horses of Signor C., which were celebrated for their beauty.

"Ah! how happy I should be if I were possessed of such horses," exclaimed one lady, as the splendid creatures advanced to the door at full trot.

"*Madame! ils sont à vous,*" said the polite Spaniard.

Terrified at the consequence of her thoughtless exclamation, the lady wished to refuse. It was of no use. Signor C. ordered the horses to be immediately taken out of the carriage, and, borrowing a pair from his friend, returned home. There was nothing for it but that the lady must retain the valuable gift. Such was the luxury and such the spirit which prevailed in the flourishing times of this coffee plantation. The depreciation of coffee as an article of commerce, and two hurricanes in succession, have changed the state of things in this part of the island. In the last which occurred, in the year 1848, the house of Madame C. was leveled to the ground, and books and pictures, which have since been dug out, were drenched and destroyed by salt water, which during the hurricane was driven upon the island. It is said that the ground is still sick from this dreadful tempest, and that the trees and plants have not yet recovered their former vigor. Many large trees, and among these a magnificent ceiba, lie still in the pasture meadows, prostrate on the ground. In the garden, however, all is again in the most beautiful luxuriance, and the lovely aviary contains a number of rare birds. The house, which was rebuilt by Sidney S. for his mother, by the help of the negroes alone, is one of the most lovely which I have seen in Cuba; so dexterous are negroes as handicraftsmen. The greater number of artisans in Cuba are negroes, and, as such, they gain so much that they can easily purchase their own freedom.

When at sunset I walk with Madame C., quietly conversing in some of the many alleys of the coffee plantation, I can not help stopping again and again, enraptured by the beauty and grace both in the form and movement of the young palm-trees which grow there. There is an incomparable grace about the branches of the cocoa-palm in its youth. Regularity and ease, precision and freedom, majesty and gentleness, reveal themselves here in living symbols. There is also among the beautiful features of this place a gigantic *berceau*, or lofty arcade of bamboo, called in Spanish *cagna brava*, which forms the termination of a magnificent *guadarajah* of king-palms. When I behold the setting sun through this light green temple arch, and see the delicate branches of bamboo forming lofty Gothic arcades—the grace of which is indescribable—against the pale red and golden clouds of the western heaven, I feel, with a mixture of melancholy and joy, that the creative artist must here drop his pen and pencil, and say, discouraged like Carlo Congo in the dance, "No! it is of no use!" No, it is not of any use to lift the hands to imitate, only to worship; but it is of use to see these fashionings of the greatest artist, to learn from them to worship, and that the mind, and art itself, may be ennobled and inspired by them!

I rise early in the mornings to draw, and to see from my window two large bushes of hybiscus, with their fiery red flowers, surrounded by a vast multitude of smaragdus-green humming-birds. There are also in the large plane-trees, which grow just by, a great many birds which are very amusing to me. Foremost of these are two long-legged, long-necked, pale red flamingoes, which were taken when young on the sea-shore, and which are now perfectly tame. They somewhat resemble swans in form, but have considerably longer and thinner legs, longer and thinner necks. They have small heads, and large, crooked bills, and make a noise like ducks, only much louder, and which becomes particularly audible when they do not receive their food at the accustomed time; and if they happen to see Madame C., they come walking after her screeching out their grievances, as if very anxious to complain to her of having been neglected. Their contempt for the hens and geese is indescribable, and the very important airs which they assume as they climb up and look down upon them, as if amazed at their presuming to come into their way, are really splendid. The hens, in the mean time, scuttle away from before them, as if humiliated by their transcendant greatness and by a conscious inferiority; but the fat and ponderous geese, who resemble city dames beside Austrian Archduchesses, avenge themselves sometimes by stretching out their necks after them, and uttering a derisive cackle, which the high-bred flamingoes do not think it worth their while to notice. Such are nature's democracy. The poor, high-bred flamingoes are, however, now nearly parched up with thirst; there is, it is true, a stone basin for them here which ought to contain water, but the continued drought has left it very nearly dry. Here, nevertheless, the flamingo pair take their morning bath with great ceremony, and when they perceive a little water on their wings, they go out upon the grass, and with great pomp and solemnity spread out their huge wings to dry in the wind and the ascending sun. After that they take a doze standing on one leg under a casuarina-tree, with long, outstretched branches, and turn their long necks in snake-like curves over their backs. It is most amusing to see them.

Here, as every where else in the world, people are never satisfied with the weather which God sends them. As people often in our country long for rain, so are they longing for it now in Cuba. And the hot air and the red dust causes the longing for rain here to be something burning and tormenting. I have said a great deal about the deliciousness of the air and the beauty of the vegetation of Cuba, and I have enjoyed both extremely; yet even here, in the midst of all this magnificence, I feel as if I had a sort of foreboding of what home-sickness must be. There are moments when I do not *dare* to think of our cool summer nights, and the white, soft mists which arise in the evening, and lie like white veils over the meadows below the house at Aersta, those mists beneath which the oxen lie so comfortably chewing their cuds and reposing! I know that if I should be ill here, I should, like the poor little Laplander, Tantas Potas, when he was dying in Italy, desire amid all the tropical magnificence that which I could not obtain—"a little snow to lay upon my head!"

May 3d. A shower! a shower! and the flamingoes have water to bathe in, and have had a great bathing, and the geese cackle, and vegetation shines out, and the animal creation raises its head. Now the coffee-shrubs will set their beans, and the Palma Christi* will stretch forth its green hands vigorously to the winds. The papaya-tree shakes the rain-drops from its crown, and cuculios come in swarms.

To-morrow, Sunday, the negroes will have a dance beneath the great almond-tree in front of the bohea. It will

* So called from the form of its leaves; the plant from which the castor-oil is extracted. Latterly, this plant has been much cultivated in Cuba and the southern states of America.

be my last day at La Concordia. The day after to-morrow I shall go to Havana, accompanied by Sidney S.

While I have it fresh in my memory, I must tell you a circumstance which has lately occurred not far from here, and which proves that, according to the treatment which he receives, the negro slave becomes either good or bad.

A French planter at Cuba, M. Chapeaud, went to Europe a few months since, and before his departure left the care of his plantation and his negro slaves to a majoral in whom he had confidence. He, however, was a stern and brutal-tempered man, who treated the slaves with severity and violence, and before a month had elapsed the whole working population of the plantation was in a state of complete tumult, and the life of the majoral was in danger. Madame Chapeaud—a lady whom I should like to be acquainted with—seeing this state of things, determined to dismiss the majoral and take upon herself his duties. Screened by an umbrella from the heat of the sun's rays, she herself went out with the negroes upon the sugar-cane fields, watched them at their work, attended them home, and looked after their food and their comfort, treating them all according to justice and reason. From this moment the most perfect order and obedience prevailed on the plantation. The slaves worked willingly, and were anxious to evince their devotion to the estimable lady, who continued to exercise the duty of a majoral on the plantation until a man was found capable of governing the plantation according to her views.

My last evening at La Concordia. Cuculios are shining beside me in the glass, and I could write by their light. I write, however, by one made by human hands, because the light, although not so beautiful, is yet stronger. It is my last evening at La Concordia. I have become acquainted with much that is beautiful in nature and in man at this place, for which I shall be eternally thankful. One thought makes me especially happy. I came hither unknown, even by literary reputation—because it is very seldom that European books reach Cuba—without any other recommendation than that of being a stranger from a far-distant land—the land of Gustavus Adolphus and Queen Christina—and, after a residence of little more than a week, I am become as a sister and a friend of the family. This relationship, which has renewed itself for me in various homes of Cuba, has given me the happy feeling of kindredship of soul, which, whenever it makes itself availing, becomes a much stronger bond of union than any mere outward ones. I have seldom ever felt myself more at home in a stranger's house than I have done in this. Madame C. is one of those persons to whom I could become cordially attached, and with whom I could live happily in daily and quiet communion. I could right earnestly quarrel with her son on certain subjects; but I should, nevertheless, become attached to him, and interested in him, as in a young giant character, richly gifted by nature, and capable of being kindled by great and noble thoughts. These sweet children, too—yes, I am fairly in love with them, especially with the youngest little *amor*, Edwardo. One can not imagine to one's self more beautiful or more graceful children! It is a grief to me to part from them all.

Flowers and fruits too, which are now beginning to come forth in yet greater abundance! I have here become acquainted with many which were hitherto unknown to me. These islands of the Southern Sea, favorites of the sun, abound in rich fruits and spices. None of the many savory dishes at Madame C.'s table have pleased me more than the favorite dish of the negro slaves, *foufou*, a kind of pulpy but very savory pudding, which is made of mashed bananas or plantains, and eaten with a sauce of tomatoes or other vegetables. It is a remarkably good and wholesome dish, which we have had many times at breakfast since I expressed my great liking for it; and next to our potatoes, which in Cuba are a rarity, I know no vegetable root so excellent, so savory and delicate at the same time, as that noble root *yuca*, which is eaten like potatoes with fresh butter, and which flourishes as well upon the poor land of the negroes as in the rich planters' well-manured caffetals. So good a mother is Nature, so good a Father is the Creator of Nature, that the most palatable and the most wholesome food of the earth is, in all countries, the most accessible to all. What have we in our country which for a continuance tastes so good and is so wholesome as potatoes and herring, milk and bread, and rye-meal hasty-pudding? "Even their excellences," I remember your saying, on one occasion, "may very well conclude with hasty-pudding!"—and water, clear, pure spring water, the first, best of all beverages of Nature, is the one which is given freely to all!

I must now say a few words about the last negro dance which I shall witness in Cuba.

It was in the afternoon of this day, under a large, shadowy almond-tree in front of the bohea, which here is not one of those castellated walls, with gates, and bolts, and bars, but a building lying open, and which reminds me of the large barns in our own country. It seems as if the coffee plantations were distinguished from sugar plantations by the style of the bohea.

The dance was altogether similar in character to the dances which I have already described. The negroes stood in a ring and sang, monotonously and inharmoniously, but with measured cadence, the words and the tune which a young negro gave out. In the centre of the ring two or three dancing couples flourished about, leaping and grimacing, the men with much animation, the women sheepishly. The dance was one continuous, monotonous improvisation. A number of little children joined in the ring, and among them stood the good white lady, *la dame blanche*, as I like to call her, gentle and motherly.

Again I asked and endeavored to ascertain the meaning of the words which were sung to the dance, and again I was told that these words were so insignificant, so completely *nothings*, that it was not worth while to attend to them. It may be that they frequently are so; but that this is not always the case, I know from many accounts which I have heard, and from many negro songs in the slave states of America. The faculty of the African for improvisation is a distinguishing feature of his life and temperament, and may, as we know, become the utterance of a higher degree of simple beauty in soul and action.

When the celebrated English traveler, Mungo Park, as he himself relates in the account of his travels, had lost his way in the African deserts, and was driven with abhorrence from the village where he had hoped to find a night's lodging, he seated himself under a tree, alone, hungry, wearied, dejected, with no other prospect before him than a miserable death, because a tempest threatened, and wild beasts roared around. Then came toward him in the twilight a woman returning from the field; she saw him, and had compassion upon him; took up the horse's saddle and bridle—for his horse had been stolen—and bade the unhappy traveler follow her.

She led him to her hut, lighted her lamp, spread out a mat upon the floor, and bade him rest upon it through the night. She then brought out a fine fish, which she roasted for him upon the coals, and gave it him for his supper.

During a great part of the night she spun cotton with other women in the hut, and as they spun they sang songs to enliven themselves, one of which was evidently improvised for the occasion. One woman sang it first alone, afterward the others joined in chorus. The air was soft and melancholy; the words were the following:

"The storm raged, and the rain fell; the poor white

man, weak and weary, sat beneath our tree. He has no mother to carry milk to him—no wife to grind his corn!

Chorus. "Have pity on the white man who has no mother," &c.

If the women of Africa, in America and the West Indies, sing less beautiful songs, it is no fault of theirs; if their improvisation is fettered like their bodies and souls, it is the fault of the white man.

It is his duty to emancipate them; to let them, by means of the sun of Christian love and education, shoot up like a palm-tree, like a bamboo-arcade from the sun-warmed earth; and then the people of the tropics, with their songs and dances, may one day correspond with the mild and beautiful scenery of the tropics. And that, too, is like the continued improvisation of a varied, luxuriant summer-life, which, amid its eternal blossoming, might make man almost forget that death is come into the world.

Later in this beautiful evening—one of the most beautiful which I have spent at *La Concordia*, for the atmosphere was refreshed by the rain, and the full moon ascended beautifully above the white dwelling-house—we sat out of doors, and saw the cuculios fluttering about in the air, and the fire shining out from the negroes' bohea. This people can not live without fire, even in the midst of the greatest heat, and they like to kindle it on the floor in the middle of their room; they contrive to make their beds—a wooden frame, with or without straw—by means of leafy branches and rags, as much like dens as possible, and in these they are fond of lying all in a heap.

Still later, I played with those sweet children on the piazza at "lend me your fire-stick," which is here changed into "*tu me da la candela*," which was a novelty to the children, and made them crazy with joy.

I shall set off early in the morning for Havana, whence, on the 8th of May, I proceed to Charleston by the "Isabel."

The dance under the almond-tree, and the beautiful

white lady there, like a mother among the black children, is a picture which I am glad to bear away with me.

But I bear away with me thence the memory of the words which the estimable Don Felix uttered one evening, and which in his mouth could not be questioned: "*Ah, c'est un malheur que d'être esclave!*"

That beautiful white lady can not, after all, protect the poor black slave!

Havana, May 7th.

Religion is not altogether dead in Cuba; it still exists there in some beautiful, charitable institutions for the benefit of orphan children and the unfortunate sick. It still exists there—more vital than in the United States of America *in one respect*, namely, that it acknowledges as worthy of its care the black as well as the white, and equally so as regards its hospital and benevolent institutions. I have seen this to-day, and have heard the same from the amiable Creole Alfredo S., with whom I visited the large infirmary of *St. Lazare*, of which he is *Intendente*. This great institution is appropriated to the unfortunates who are afflicted with the incurable diseases peculiar to the tropics, and in particular to the African race, leprosy, elephantiasis, in which the legs and feet swell to an unnatural size, and *la maladie de St. Antoine*, in which the hands and feet are contracted, and without apparent cause or sore, waste away to nothing. These unfortunates are here provided for in the most beautiful manner. The extensive building—built like an immense bohea around a square court, and with a grated door—is situated by the sea, which bathes with its roaring waves the rocky walls at its feet, and surrounds the home of the sick with its breezes, fraught with life and health. There were in the court beautiful shrubberies of oleanders, now in full bloom, and the beautiful pink flowers of which filled the air with a delicious fragrance. These beautiful shrubberies were the work of the young Intendant. Each unfortunate, whether black or white, who is afflicted with any one of these incurable maladies, has here his own separate convenient abode. Among those whom I visited was an old negro, who from his very youth had been afflicted with *la maladie de St. Antoine.* His hands were now merely finger-ends, and his feet knobs, upon which, nevertheless, he managed to move about by help of sticks, and contrived even with his poor finger-ends to perform his little household duties. His dwelling consisted of one little sitting-room, ditto chamber, a little kitchen, and a little garden besides, in which he cultivated bananas and various roots; every thing was small, but comfortable and neat. He looked good and contented. The other sick persons had all similar dwellings: nothing was wanting which might in any way alleviate their slowly-dying life. Christian love labored here for the most suffering of the children of men. The hopeless might here live for the most beautiful hope.

Another noble institution of mercy at Havana is *La Casa de Beneficenza.* This receives many hundreds of motherless children. Here they are educated, and each one, on leaving the establishment, receives a dower of five hundred pesos with which to commence his own career in life.

From *l'Infirmerie de St. Lazare*, Mr. S. conducted me to the great cemetery, *Campo Santo.* It is a large structure of white marble, in the lofty walls of which, within an immense sort of castle-court, each family has its little niche or ledge, that is to say, if the family is able to pay for it. Each such little niche was furnished with an inscription in gilt letters. The width and height of the walls made these grave-niches appear very small, but each is nevertheless capable of holding many coffins.

I had in the hospital beheld the spirit of Christianity; in the Campo Santo I again found that of heathenism. The bodies of the rich were interred in those lofty walls with their gilded inscriptions; those of the poor were buried in the earth without any token of memorial, without even a green sod over them, or a flower or shrub to speak of life above the grave; and there was one large quarter of the Campo Santo where the spectator beheld heaped-up mounds and walls of bones and skulls. This was the burial-place of the negro slave. It is forbidden to bury a negro here in a coffin; the bodies are therefore thrown either wholly or half naked into the ground, and lime, or some other kind of earth, which quickly consumes the flesh, is thrown upon them. In the course of from eight to fourteen days, the bodies are disinterred to make room for other corpses, and the bones are cast up in heaps to dry in the sun.

While we stood here we witnessed the interment of some humble person in the neighborhood of the negroes' quarter. I noticed that they laid cushions, coverlets, and articles of clothing with the dead in the grave.

During these, my last days at Havana, I have visited, in company with my good Mrs. F., several beautiful private gardens, in order to become acquainted with various flowers and fruits; I made the acquaintance, also, of Dr. Philippe Poé, the professor of botany, who has been so polite as to present me with some Cuban butterflies, among which is a specimen of the *urania*, the most beautiful butterfly of Cuba. It is of a splendid dark green color, and has a gloss as of velvet.

I regret not having earlier become acquainted with the interesting and kind Alfredo S., because I should have gained much knowledge from him in Havana which the shortness of time does not now admit of.

Many things even in Cuba seems to have greatly improved of late years; in particular, as regards police regulations and personal safety, as well in the whole island as in the city. Some years ago—I have been told this by various people—there would frequently be heard, late in the evening, the cry of "Assasino!" in the streets; but no one dared to go to the spot whence the cry proceeded, because the cry was not unfrequently a mere trick of the assassin himself. And if one person saw another lying murdered in the fields, he did not dare to render any assistance, because if the wounded man died, and there were not several witnesses to attest his innocence, he ran the risk of being himself accused of murder, and was sure to become involved in an endless legal prosecution. The present improved state of the public safety is attributed to the keen scrutiny and general reform of Governor Jacon. He was a stern man, whose despotic temper was beneficial to the public, while it made him hated by many private individuals.

Lawsuits and lawyers abound in Cuba, and the histories of the arbitrary power and venality of the law, and even of the judges' bench, as regards private individuals, and the difficulty which there is for any one to obtain justice, if he can not purchase it at a great price, are unprecedented. There requires, however, for the full reformation of all these abuses, a total reorganization, not only in the administration of justice, but in the government of the whole island.

During my rambles in Havana I have always observed the negro population there with great pleasure, because they appear to me freer and happier than in the cities of the United States. Certain it is that one here sees negroes and mulattoes much more frequently engaged in trade than there, and their wives are commonly very well, nay, even splendidly dressed. It is not unusual to see mulatto women, with flowers in their hair, walking with their families on the principal promenades in a manner which denotes freedom and prosperity. Mulattoes are generally to be found in the tobacco-shops, either as shopmen, or as the proprietors of the place. The black inhabitants emulate the white in cigar-smoking; many ladies of the second and third class are also fond of smoking their *cigaritos*, and it is asserted that, of the population of Cuba, one third is occupied in the preparation of the cigars, and that the other two thirds smoke them.

Two different styles of physiognomy are very evident among the population of the city. The one has refined features, an oval countenance, a proud and often gloomy expression: this belongs to those of Castilian descent. The second has a round countenance, flat, broad features, a jovial but plebeian expression: this marks the Catalonian. The former is spare in form, the latter stout. The Castilian is generally met with among the government officials, the Catalonian among the tradespeople. The latter form themselves into guilds and corporations, and are not on good terms either with Castilians or Creoles. The Creoles are good people, and seem to inherit from the delicious climate of the island a mild and inoffensive temperament.

I had wished to see in Jamaica the negroes who govern themselves as a Christian community; and though I have not been able to do so, I have obtained a tolerably clear idea of their condition from the elder Mr. F. and two of his acquaintance from that island. It appears that the Christianized negro remains very faithful to his African turn of mind. There have been built for them, in Jamaica, large houses, with convenient rooms, kitchens, and gardens, in which they might possess all the advantages of the domicile and the work-shop, private life and the life of association combined; but in vain! The large, convenient stone house stands empty. The negro likes neither stone nor association. The highest aim of the negro is to be able to purchase his own little plot of ground, a "*mountain*," as it is called, where he can erect for himself a birch-bark hut thatched with palm-leaves, plant his native trees, and grow sugar-cane, or maize and edible roots. He labors to gain for himself this earthly paradise. When he has obtained it, it is his pleasure to rest and enjoy himself as much as possible, and to labor as little. And why should he labor? That ambition, that lust of knowing and subduing the world, spiritually or physically, with which the Creator has endowed the Caucasian race, does not belong to him. He, on the contrary, is endowed with the power of care-free enjoyment, a gay temperament, and the ability for measured songs and dances. The climate under which he is born is propitious to the latter gifts, and opposed to the former.

Even in trade the negro evinces his bias toward the individuality of his own little world, and his disinclination or inability for association. Instead of one great trading house in sugar and coffee, the negroes open twenty small shops, where each one for himself sells sugar and coffee, without any connection with the rest.

In consequence of this tendency, they do not like to work for the larger planters, and require from such extravagant wages. If they can not obtain as much as they desire, they prefer not working at all. They can do without it; their wants are few, and the beautiful earth feeds them with small labor.

Hence it happens that all the great plantations in Jamaica have declined, and their owners are ruined. The greater number of the large plantations may now be purchased at very low prices. I have heard, nevertheless, of two great planters in Jamaica, the one an Englishman, the other a Spaniard, who have had no cause to complain, and who have always been able to obtain as much negro labor as they required; but I presume they did not require much, and that they were on good terms with the negroes.

And why should not labor be made cheerful to a cheerful people? The negroes themselves seem, by their songs in the sugar-mill at night, to show the way and the means by which they might work well. Let them go out to labor to the sound of music and singing, and perchance their labor may go on like a dance. The Europeans, however, believe generally that no labor can be carried on vigorously without day's wages, or—the whip!

Morning of May 8th. I had my last great view of Cuba from the azotea of Alfredo S.'s house last evening at sunset. For the last time have I seen its beautiful palm-groves, its gay, showy houses, its mild heaven, its bright blue sea. This afternoon I shall go on board the "Isabel," and bid farewell forever to the palms and ceibas of Cuba, to its cuculios and contra-dances, to its *guadarajahs* and constellations, to the African drums, songs, and dances, to its happy and its unhappy people, to its hell and its paradise!

I have taken leave of my good friends, have sketched the monument of Columbus on *La Plaza des Armas*, and this morning, for the last time, have I visited my beloved *Cortina de Valdez*, and seen the breakers dash around the rocks of the Moro. On my return, I called at a restaurateur's to purchase *des libros de dulces*, which I wished to give to the little girls. When, however, I was about to pay, I received back my money from the young man who stood behind the counter, with a polite "it costs nothing, Signora." I fancied I had misunderstood him, or that he had misunderstood me; I therefore again offered him the money, but received the same remark in return. I then recollected the Spanish and Cuban gallantry, and, looking round the shop, I observed Mr. S. at some distance, near the door, and now it was quite clear to me.

"Ah, this is one of your Spanish tricks!" said I to him. He smiled, but evidently did not wish to be thanked.

One day I by chance admired a little basket which his wife held in her hand, and immediately I was obliged to accept it. All my protests were in vain; I really became afraid of admiring any thing.

I must now bid adieu to the kind F.'s and S.'s, and then conclude some letters.

The next time I write it will be from the United States. I have inhaled new life in Cuba; but I could not live there. I could only live where a life of freedom exists and grows.

LETTER XXXVII.

LETTER TO HER MAJESTY, CAROLINA AMELIA, QUEEN DOWAGER OF DENMARK.

Cuba, West Indies, April.

YOUR MAJESTY—"Write to me from America!" were your majesty's last kind words to me at parting, when I had the pleasure of seeing your majesty at Sorgenfri. And these words have accompanied me on my long journey, as one of the beautiful and precious memories for which I have to thank good Denmark, because they remind me of the great kindness which the Queen of Denmark showed to me. I have wished to obey them by presenting to your majesty, from the soil of the New World, some very beautiful spiritual flowers, not unworthy of those roses which your majesty's own beautiful hand gave me, at the moment of parting, from your majesty's garden. But it was long before I found sufficient freedom of mind or tranquillity to be able to put together, from the rich Flora of America, any thing resembling a bouquet or a garland which it seemed to me could give pleasure to your majesty, and with less I would not be satisfied.

I now write, beautiful and good Queen of Denmark, from the Queen of the Antilles, from the beautiful tropical *Isla de Cuba.* And while a glowing sun ascends over groves of coffee and bananas on *Caffetal la Concordia,* my present home; while rose-colored flamingoes stretch out their wings to cool them in the morning wind, and little negro children, naked as God created them, leap and tumble about the green meadow, where smaragdus-green humming-birds flutter gayly around the hybiscus flowers, I wing my way, in spirit, to "the green islands," to the cool, shadowy dwelling where I heard the nightingales sing in the beech-woods around your majesty, and convey thither, in these lines, my tribute of respect and devotion.

I can from Cuba, better than from any other point on this side the globe, speak of the New World, because Cuba lies between North and South America: the Anglo-Norman and the Spanish races here meet, for good and for evil, secretly and openly combating for dominion; and in the midst of this wondrously beautiful scenery, which belongs to the tropics (beneath which the greater part of South America is situated), beneath the tropical sun, among palm-trees and coffee plantations, one sees already the homes of the North American, rail-roads, and shops. The Anglo-American "go-a-head" here comes in contact with the motto of the Spanish Creole, *poco-a-poco;* and—will run it down sooner or later, that is not difficult to foresee.

While the impression of the scenery of North America, its people, and states, was still clear in the soul, it was a great refreshment to receive in this beautiful island so strongly contrasting a picture as that of the scenery of South America, its people, and its states; for both belong essentially to the picture of the New World; and North America presents, in scenery, culture, and manners, merely one half thereof. That southern half, with its yet unorganized states, its chaotic popular life, its rich, grand scenery, its River Amazon, and its Andes, its palms, and its eternal summer, will still, in contact with the northern portion, develop a glorious life—not so strong, perhaps, but more gentle and beautiful. And both will become one in that great human kingdom which is growing up between the Atlantic and Pacific Oceans, between the North Sea and the South. For although South America does not as yet show either a people or character which demands esteem or admiration; although it as yet appears subject to nature instead of elevating itself above her, is enervated by the sun instead of being inspired by its glowing and pure light, yet we still know that it was in this climate, beneath this sun, these palms, that the worshipers of the sun, the Peruvians, and those noble Aztecs, lived; that it was in this climate, beneath this sun, and these palms in the East, that the most ancient wisdom, the most ancient poetry, was born on the earth; the Vedas of the Hindoos, their temples, the ruins of which still excite our admiration, their songs and poems, *Sakuntala Urvasi* and *Vikrama*, and many more, graceful and noble, such as only could be composed beneath palm-trees and in an atmosphere such as this; those intellectual legends, the game of chess, the airy dance of the Bayadere, and many another art and science for the beautifying of life, which could only have birth where the life of nature holds its holiday. And that which has once flourished may, under similar circumstances, again come forth in new, or still more elevated forms. The Oriental tropical zone has produced its bloom; that of the West will bring forth hers in the light of Christianity. As yet we can merely surmise what it will one day become—surmise that from the glorious natural life which now is its most beautiful production.

But it was about the people and the states of North America that your majesty wished to hear, and of these I will proceed to speak; for, however much your majesty loves the beautiful in nature, I know that your majesty loves still more that which gives to human weal and human happiness a still higher significance. Is not your majesty one of the mothers of humanity, one of the noble and the tender, who embrace the young generation in order to elevate them, and bring them nearer to the father of love and perfection? Was it not surrounded by fatherless and motherless children, who looked up to your majesty as to a mother, that I first saw your majesty, that Christmas-eve, when the Christmas candles burned in the Northern pine for the joy of the children and in honor of the heavenly friend of childhood! And have not I, more than once, heard your majesty express the wish and the hope for "a community on earth in which all the members should have equal opportunity for the attainment of virtue, knowledge, a life of activity and prosperity—a community in which goodness and capacity should constitute the highest aristocracy, and in which the highest rank should depend upon the highest human worth?"

And, however far the United States of America may be from having attained to this ideal of social life, still it can not be denied that it is at this that they are aiming, toward this to which they are daily more and more advancing—more, perhaps, than any other nation on the earth. This refers especially to the Northern and the free states of the Union, which are peopled principally by descendants of the oldest Pilgrims, and whence the Quaker State has every where sent abroad its messengers of "the inward light," of freedom, peace, and universal brotherhood. These Northern States are founded on enthusiasm for religion and human rights. And upon this foundation have they grown great and powerful, and still grow day by day, extending their dominion more and more.

The Southern States acknowledge, it is true, the same principles of freedom, human rights, and human well-being as their aim also, but they bear a fetter which impedes their progress on the path of human and social development, and which they in part will not, and in part *can not*, now throw off, namely, *the institution of slavery*. They have bound the negro as a slave, and the negro slave binds them; prevents them from developing education, industry, and every good social institution which gives strength and greatness to a nation.

It is a pure and noble joy to behold the development of the life of freedom in the Northern States; and in spite of various pernicious offshoots, which as yet run wild and produce disorder, the whole presents a glorious spectacle. For the whole movement of the social system tends upward; it is a growth of cultivation and improvement which embraces all classes, every branch of activity, and which extends to the most remote points, and includes the most humble individual. It corresponds with the glorious image of our mythological Ygdrasil, of which every single leaf derives vital aliment from the common root, and is watered by the Norna's hand from the renovating fountain of Urda.

Besides, the community has come clearly to feel within itself, and has clearly and forcibly expressed the same in word and deed, that *it is the duty of the state so to provide for every individual member that he may become a perfected human being.*

Hence the comprehensive and excellent system of popular education which commenced in the "pilgrim" State of Massachusetts, and which has since been adopted, and is being adopted, with modifications and improvements, in all the free states of the Union. On all hands have arisen free public schools, where children, boys and girls, in separate schools, receive free education to fifteen or sixteen years of age, when they may, from these schools, enter the high-schools and academies, unless they prefer to enter practical life with that amount of knowledge which the public schools have given them, and which does not appear to be so insignificant, as many of the "best men" and the first statesmen have not studied in any other schools than in these and—in that of life.

I would, before every thing else, present to the womanly and maternal mind of your majesty these great and increasingly developing institutions for the education of the rising generation, which are open to the younger members of the *entire* community, and which are advantageous to the children of the indigent still more than to the children of the wealthy, and, together with this picture, that of the increasing importance of the young woman in society as the teacher, and that not alone in families and homes. I would present to your majesty's view those large, cheerful school-rooms which are now to be met with in the public schools from Massachusetts to Wisconsin and Illinois, from New Hampshire to Ohio, where light and air obtain free access—school-rooms full of lovely children, with bright, animated glances, and where the young teachers, the daughters of New England, and the honor of New England, refined and graceful in manners and appearance, stand, at the same time, firmer to their principles than the earth's Alps and Andes on their foundations, and govern their troops of young republicans easier and better than any stern M. A. with thundering voice and ferule.

The youthful daughters of America in the free states of the Union are not kept in ignorance and inactivity, as are still the greater number of the young girls of Europe. They are early taught that they must rely upon God and themselves if they would win esteem and independent worth; they leave home early to enter the schools, where opportunity is afforded them to advance as far as young men in study and the sciences, and where they prove that the sciences, which have hitherto been considered as too difficult for them, are as easy for them to acquire as that superficial knowledge and accomplishment to which hitherto their education has been restricted. They distinguish themselves in mathematics, algebra, the physical sciences, the ancient languages, at least in Latin, and many other hitherto interdicted branches of learning; and their written compositions, in verse and prose, show an unusual purity of style, considering their age, clearness of thought, and expansion of mental horizon. It is evident that the spirit of the New World has unbound their intellectual wings, and permitted them a free flight over the fields of earth. The American woman is being formed for a citizen of the world; she is teaching herself to embrace the whole of humanity. Such is evidently the intention of her school education, even if an adequate system be yet wanting. Girls may from these schools also advance into the high-schools and ladies' academies, in which they can graduate and take diplomas, and, provided with these, go out as teachers over the whole Union.

Such are, in particular, the daughters of New England, who seem to have a peculiar vocation for the office of teacher, which they adopt most frequently from love rather than necessity. Every where throughout the United States, in the west as well as in the north and south of the Union, wherever schools are in operation, you meet with young teachers from the States of New England, that is to say, from those states which are peopled by the descendants of the Pilgrim Fathers. And the value of women as teachers of the young increases more and more in America.

But it is not merely as teachers that the spirit of the New World seeks to prepare for woman a freer development of her being, and a wider sphere of activity; it seeks to open for her free paths in arts and manufactures.

"If I must choose between giving education to the men or the women of a country, I would leave the men and begin with the women," said one of the legislators of this country to me one day.

And I believe that I do not say too much when I maintain that this mode of thinking is participated by the greater number of men in the United States; so strong is the conviction of the power of woman's influence on the rising generation.

The advancement of the higher development of woman, and her importance in society, is one of the most remarkable features of the New World's cultivation, its greatest merit and its principal labor for the future. All that is now wanting is merely that it does not stop half way. I do not believe that the right-mindedness and chivalry of the men will fail, if the women will, with discretion and noble earnestness, take the place which society here is willing to assign to them.

It is with justice that we are accustomed to estimate the measure of a nation's cultivation by the estimation in which woman is held, and the place which she occupies in society, because it requires no small degree of spiritual culture to value a being whose highest power is of a spiritual character. The people of America have shown themselves to be possessed of this, and it will increase in the same proportion as the women of the country make themselves deserving of it.

I mentioned a growth of cultivation and improvement which in the free states embraces the entire community, and spoke of popular education as its most essential power. This, and many institutions favorable to human development, belong to these states; but, besides these, there is a movement, a free development in popular life, which may be compared to the circulation of the sap in a vigorous, growing tree. Free associations now take the place of the old guilds and corporations as regulators and promoters of all the various interests and functions of the social system. Thus have religious, moral, and industrial corporations arisen within the great community, and in faithful adherence to it, at the same time that the good-will and the divers powers and talents of each individual are made available to its highest interests. The United States represent, at the same time, the highest development of the individual and the public at large. This internal, social movement of humanity is assisted from without, by the free circulation and communication which is afforded by the numerous navigable rivers of North America, upon which thousands of steam-boats go and come; and in still later years by the rail-roads and telegraphic lines which extend over all parts of America, from state to state, and from city to city. The great diffusion of newspapers within the country, of every book which wins the love of the popular heart, of that religious popular literature which, in millions of small works, "tracts," or tales, is poured forth over the nation like morning dew or a shower of manna—these all belong essentially to this life-giving circulation, and wherever the Anglo-American advances, the same cultivation, the same vitality arises. He accomplishes with astonishing certainty his mission as cultivator of the New World, and the framer of free, self-governing communities; and not even the institution of slavery is able to withstand the power of cultivation which advances with him over the earth.

Wherever the sons and daughters of the Pilgrims find their way, there are established homes, schools, and churches, shops, and legislative assemblies; the free press, hotels for strangers, and asylums for the unfortunate or the orphan; there is the prison converted into the reformatory institution—into a new school for the ignorant and depraved children of the earth. Wherever they come, they acknowledge aloud the name and doctrines of the Master who is "the way, the truth, and the life." The right of the Anglo-American people to become a great people consists in its Christianity. It is the spirit of the World's Redeemer which makes it the World's Conqueror.

When we leave the Northeastern States, where first the standards of religion and freedom were planted, and proceed westward to the limits of the wilderness beyond the Mississippi, where the Indian still hunts the deer, erects his wigwam, and kindles his nocturnal fires, then it is that we are at first aware of the advance and mode of this new cultivation.

Your majesty has certainly often read descriptions of the wonderful waterfall, Niagara; of the almost miraculous prairies of the West, where the sun mirrors his image in an ocean of sunflowers waving in the wind; of the rapid growth of states and cities in the Great West; of the great River Mississippi, and the gold mines of California, and many other lions of the Great West.

But less known are the first steps of cultivation, its first impress on the wilderness; and this it was, together with the great spectacle of Nature, which most attracted my earliest attention; for it is amusing to observe the first steps of the child, and how he advances and grows to man's estate. It is an image worthy the regards of a motherly queen.

The trees fall before the ax along the banks of the river—and rivers every where abound in North America—a little log-house is erected on the skirts of the forest and the banks of the river; a woman stands in the door-way with a little chubby child in her arms. The husband has dug up the earth around the house, and planted maize; beyond graze a couple of fat cows, and some sheep in the free, uninclosed meadow-land. The husband tills the land, and milks the cows, and performs the whole out-of-doors labor. The wife remains in the house, and takes care of child and home; nor can any woman do it better. The cleanliness and order of her person are reflected by every thing within the house. No neater nor more excellent home can be found on the face of the earth than that of the American woman, even of the poorest. No wonder that the husband is happy within it—that the American knows few other pleasures than those which he finds in his home, no other goal of bliss on earth than that of possessing a good wife—a good home!

The log-house has been erected in the forest, and not far from it are erected, in the same way, two or three other log-houses; they all are furnished with excellent beds, and there always lies on the shelf a Bible, a hymn-book, and some other religious books. A little further off stands a somewhat larger log-house, where a dozen or two children—the half-wild offspring of the wilderness—are assembled. This is the school. The room is poor, and without furniture; but the walls are covered with maps of all parts of the globe, and in the hands of the children are books which present them with views over the whole world, and reading-books which contain the noblest pearls of literature, in paragraphs, short essays, narratives, poems, &c. Anon other houses spring up; some of framed timber, some of stone; they become more and more ornamental; they surround themselves with fruit trees and flowers; you see a chapel of wood arising at the same time with the wooden houses; but when the stone houses come, there come also a stone church and a state-house. The fields around are covered with harvests; flocks and herds increase; and before long you behold one or two steam-boats advancing up the river; they lie-to at the new buildings; they purchase wares and cattle, and leave newspapers behind them. In two or three years there is here a little city of two thousand souls; motherly women institute Sunday-schools in the church, and assemble the little children to instruct them in Christianity, and establish an asylum for orphaned little ones. Shops spring up at the same time with the school and the church, and they constitute, together with the printing-press and the state-house, the ensign of the Anglo-American; and wherever he plants this, thence retreats the red man, now almost without resistance, with his wigwam and his subjected women, and goes to light his fires further off in the wilderness. He knows, by experience, that the new erections which he beholds will, within a quarter of a century, become a great city, with its fifty thousand inhabitants or more, and that the whole region round about will be full of a people alike potent in war as in peaceful civilization.

I have spoken of the progress of the new man in the West; but I must, for the sake of justice, also say a few words about the *old* man, for ah! the old progresses equally with the new, and he is here also, on the new earth, the same old sinner, and drinks, and quarrels, and gambles, and steals, and makes a fool of himself, and is puffed up with pride, *tout comme chez nous;* and in the Great West, on the Mississippi and the Pacific Ocean, perhaps a little more so, because many unconscientious adventurers are collected there, and the counteracting powers have not yet gained an ascendency. Freedom is still sowing its wild oats here. One great difficulty in the cultivation of the West is the great emigration thither of a large portion of the most rude and indigent population of Europe, as well as the unfortunate children of the Eastern American States. By degrees, however, this population becomes orderly under the influence of the New World's cultivation, and with every passing year the new Adam gains a greater ascendency over the old, in proportion as the better emigration from the Pilgrim States gains a firmer footing, and with this, schools, churches, and the better periodical press take their place.

The valley of the Mississippi has room for about two hundred millions of inhabitants, and the American Union has a heart large enough, and sufficient power to take under her charge all strangers, all neglected or unfortunate children of the earth, and to give them a portion of her earth and of her spiritual life.

This Mississippi Valley—the central region of North America—presents in its entire extent all the principal features which distinguish the great realm of North America, in which I also, as far as people and scenery are concerned, include the English colonies in the North. It includes, from the springs of the Mississippi, in the northern Minnesota, to the South, where the Great River empties itself into the Mexican Gulf, every climate, with the exception of the most northerly, all productions which this hemisphere brings forth, all people who inhabit her soil. The Indian is still found in prosperity at Minnesota; pine-forests are native there, and winter is vigorous as with us. There are glorious springs of water, rivers and lakes abounding in fish, rich hunting-ground, and good arable land, though as yet untilled. The Norwegian and the Dane have begun to turn it up; but the colonies proper of these nations and the Swedes are to the south of Minnesota, in the States of Wisconsin and Illinois, where the natural scenery is that of a grand and cheerful pastoral. A new Scandinavia is here growing up by degrees; and it is a joy to me to be able to testify that our countrymen are universally regarded as a valuable, industrious, and good people. They are obliged to work hard and to dispense with many comforts at the commencement; but the more the number of laborers increases, the lighter becomes labor, the richer the harvests which the universally productive soil yields to them. The Norwegians constitute the agricultural core of the Scandinavian population; the Danes, in comparison with these, are few in number, and I have found here that the Danes more generally devote themselves to trade than agriculture.

The great corn region proper of North America begins in Wisconsin and Illinois; and that immense corn district, which is continued on both sides of the Mississippi to the states of Kentucky and Missouri, is said to be capable of producing bread-stuffs for all the states of the Union, that is to say, when it becomes fully cultivated. One sees there indeed, at the present time, vast plains waving with golden maize, but still vaster upon which, as yet, only tall grass and wild flowers grow. Germans and the Irish flock to this region. Half the population of the larger cities consists of Germans; they have their concerts, their shooting-grounds, their dances, and they drink beer as in the Old World, while they participate in the legislative and commercial life of the New.

Lower down, in Kentucky and Missouri, commences the region of cotton. There cotton plantations and slave villages are to be seen. To this succeeds the region of the sugar-cane, with warm summer winds and the sun in the middle of winter, beautiful plantations, and groves of orange and magnolia trees. Here is Louisiana, the most southern of the Mississippi States.

Here we meet with the French and Spaniards, as well as people from all the countries of the world, all submitting to the laws and government of the Anglo-American.

These Southern States present, in their institution and scenery, a peculiar feature in the life of the United States. The traveler in these Southern States is not *edified;* no ideal of social life elevates here his mind and his glance; no public endeavor is made here, as in the individual and governmental life of the free states. But he is amused by the many novel and unusual objects which present themselves to his gaze; he meets many unusually cultivated and agreeable people, shining out like diamonds in the sand. A new world of nature full of treasures is opened to him—the enchantment of the peculiar scenery of the South, the delicious character of the atmosphere during the greater part of the year, the primeval forests along the banks of the red rivers, with their thousand varieties of trees, flowers, and creeping vegetation, the song of the hundred-tongued bird, the nightingale of America (*Turdus polyglottus*), and the pleasant but monotonous whistling "Whip-poor-will;" the many glorious trees, live-oaks, with their long, waving mosses, the magnolia, with its large, snow-white flowers, cypresses, tulip and amber trees, and fan-palms; the richness of sunshine, flower odors, birds' songs, and delicious fruits; and, in the midst of this beautiful natural scenery, the negro people, with their peculiar life, which slavery can not obliterate; their religious festivals, hymns, and cheerful songs —the traveler is not edified and animated, as in the North of the Union, by noble and magnificent efforts and institutions, but he rests and enjoys, when he is not disturbed by any new, bitter experience of that injustice which the laws here give rise to, or provoked by persons who, contrary to truth and sound reason, justify it as a good and allowable thing.

The contest respecting slavery is the great contested question of America, and will continue to be so, unless slavery ceases to exist there; because this institution is too evident a lie against the American social principle, too crying an outrage against justice and humanity.

Still it must be conceded that the social spirit of America has of late years tended greatly to ameliorate the condition of the slaves, and it may with truth be stated that this improves year by year. The nobler popular feeling in the Southern States is doing, at this moment, a great deal toward raising the condition of the black population, spiritually as well as temporally. The Gospel is preached more and more generally to the slaves—especially in those states where the religious life was strong of old, Georgia and Carolina—and wherever it is preached, there is the slave elevated ; there he forms religious communities, and there he himself preaches the Savior and redemption with joy and with power, and sings in honor of the Savior hymns, of the beauty and the harmony of which no idea can be formed by those who merely judge of the musical talent of the African from the songs and screeches of his wild condition. Yes, if the legislation of the Southern States would follow in the steps of the Gospel, a great work would then be accomplished, and they would prepare for themselves a great future.

If we contemplate the present condition of the slaves from its best side in the American States, we shall find it to be, under a good master, a tranquil life without a future, but not without its enjoyment. The slave on the plantation has his own neat little house, his own garden, and, besides this, his pig and his poultry. His labor is moderate, and he can make his days somewhat cheerful; his children are well fed, and he does not trouble himself about the morrow. The house-slaves, in good families, are still better off, still better cared for, as regards their dwelling and their old age, than free servants even are sometimes with us.

But it is not right to give one human being an irresponsible right over another. No human circumstances can be more horrible and more hopeless than those of the slave under a bad master, and proof enough of this is found in the every-day history of slavery in the United States. Besides this, the institution carries along with it unhappy and degrading results, both as regards the white and the black population, which not even the best master can obviate. Even the best master may die, or may fall into pecuniary difficulties, and his servants be sold to any who will purchase them. Slavery, to the really good and noble slave-owners in these states, is the source of anxiety and sorrow, and they regard it as a misfortune of which they would gladly be rid. And many of them are laboring silently for this purpose in their own immediate spheres.

In this rapid sketch of some of the principal features in the great community of the United States, I must of necessity pass over some of the lesser ones, which, nevertheless, like genre-pictures in a gallery of paintings, serve to give the whole a varied and more lively interest. I must, however, mention among these some small communities which exist independently in the great community, although they are separated from it by their modes and customs; as, for instance, the Quakers, with their simple costume, their *thee* and *thou* to all the world, their silent divine worship, their women, who are allowed to preach and participate in church and social government; the Shakers, with their dancing divine worship; and those small Socialist communities which seek in a spirit of love to make all true workers participate alike in the good gifts of the earth.

Among the peculiar, picturesque scenes of the American soil must be mentioned public baptisms on the banks of rivers and lakes, where both white and black neophytes are initiated into a life of holiness; and the religious festivals, called "camp-meetings," where, in the depth of night and the forest, by the flames of fire-altars, thousands of voices uniting in harmonious hymns, and souls trembling in religious ecstasy, are alternated with abundance both in eating and drinking. These festivals are the saturnalia of the negro slaves, and their prayers and songs are as ardent and living as the sun of the South.

When we leave the United States and betake ourselves to the southern hemisphere of America, we find that in three days' time we have removed into a new world. And this first meets us, as in Cuba. Heaven and earth, the people, language, laws, manners, style of building, every thing is new, and the refreshment produced by this rapid change of scene is indescribable, although, at the time, every thing in it is not good.

The scenery of South America, its dominant people and language, meet us in Cuba; we are in the region of the palm, of the tropical sun, of the language and rule of the Spaniard. One half of America belongs to the Germanic and Anglo-Norman race, the other half to the Roman. In the former Protestantism prevails, in the latter Catholicism. But in Cuba, that glorious island, situated between the two hemispheres, in the midst of the salt sea of the world, both races seem to have met—whether for war or for peaceful union, it is not yet possible to say.

Cuba is also at the present moment a field of combat for the powers of light and of darkness, and seldom, indeed, are they seen on earth to stand so close to each other, or in stronger contrast.

On the dark side stand the Church and the state; the state with its rule of violence and despotism (Spain blindly governing her distant colonies by deputies, over whom the mother-country can have no control, and who deny to the Creoles all right of self-government); the Church, which exists merely in pompous ceremonial, and is deficient in all spiritual life. On the night-side lies prominently slavery, which exists in Cuba in its worst form; and the slave-trade with Africa, which is said to be of daily occurrence, although not openly. The government of the island receives bribes from the slave-traders, and shuts its eyes to the thousands of slaves who are annually landed on the island. Nay, it is asserted that it is privately not unwilling to see the island filled with wild Africans, because the dread of the unrestrained power of these, if they should one day emancipate themselves, restrains the Creoles from rebellion against a government which they can not do other than hate. Government oppresses the slave-owner, the slave-owner oppresses the slave, and knows no other means of subjecting him but the whip and the chain. The sugar-planters not unfrequently work their slaves harder than beasts of burden, and require from them a greater amount of labor than human nature can sustain. In the prison walls of the bohea the slaves live like brute beasts; no Savior is preached to them, and the only pleasures which are allowed to them—and that often in the scantiest measure—are those of the animal. Wild tumults have been sometimes the evidence of the cruelty of oppression, and of the savage spirit and power of the negroes; more frequently, however, they die without venturing to utter a cry or to lift a hand in remonstrance or complaint; frequently, during the earlier period of their captivity, they themselves put an end to their days of misery, in the belief (which is current among them) that they will immediately after death rise again in their native land.

The government and condition of Cuba, from the governor's palace down to the bohea of the slave, is a government of violence and despotism. Justice and nobility of mind are, it is true, met with in individuals, but are not of general prevalence; and in the laws also there is some evidence of a magnanimous spirit, but it is nullified as much as possible.

Opposed to this dark side of life in Cuba stands the bright side in the most striking contrast. There is the tropical sky, as mild as an angel's glance, its sun as pure and clear as the purest tones of music; there is the wind, a spirit as gentle, as pure, as full of vitalizing life as if it came forth fresh from the fountain of life and love; there is the peculiar natural world of the tropics, full of marvelous plants and scenes; those palm-groves, where immortals might wander; those gardens, beautiful as that of Eden, where coffee-shrubs and bananas grow in beautiful plantations, one perpetual blossoming, one perpetual succession of fruit; those magnificent *guadarajahs* of king-palms, which seem planted as if for a triumphal procession of kings and queens; a beauty in atmosphere and life, in form and color, which involuntarily charms the senses, but which can not be described by words or by color, only by music. And Cuba, the Queen of the Antilles, is a Calypso, beautiful in her sins, who can so seduce the traveler that he, like Telemachus of old, would need, in order to resist her, a wise Mentor who should pitch him head-foremost into the sea. Thus did I feel as week after week I delayed my parting from the enchantress, captivated also by the amiable hospitality of the Creoles, and by the acquaintance of some of those noble beings who are the ornament of the earth, and who are able also to lift its curse even from slavery—at least for the moment. I must mention among these two ladies in particular—one of them born of Danish parents, whom I would introduce to the motherly Queen of Denmark, because they are mothers in the highest sense of the word—mothers of the motherless, of the stranger, of the slave, of all who are in need!

I have spoken of the night-side of the negroes' life in Cuba. Let me also speak of the bright side, because this belongs essentially to the day-side of Cuban life.

Cuba is at the same time the hell and the paradise of the slave. Spanish laws, as regard the slave, originating under the influence of men as mild and noble as Las Casas, are favorable also to their emancipation; and if they were adhered to, there would not be found under the Spanish dominion any wholly unfortunate slave, because there would be none without hope; but wherever the institution of slavery prevails, the law is unable to make itself availing. There are, however, in the mean time, some points in which the Spanish laws of manumission for the slave are really availing, and that because the Spaniard has established courts of justice, and judges who watch over them, and to whom the slaves can appeal.

According to these Spanish laws, a slave can purchase his freedom for the sum of five hundred dollars, which is the specified legal price; and no slave-owner has a right to refuse freedom to a slave who can pay down that sum. And it must be confessed that many slave-owners are kind and just enough to allow their slaves to purchase their freedom for considerably less. If a slave-owner should refuse freedom to his slave on those terms, he can appeal to the syndic of the city or district, who then selects one of three persons nominated by the slave and his master, and he decides the question.

According to the Spanish laws of freedom, a mother has a right to purchase the freedom of the child before its birth for fifteen dollars, and afterward for double that sum. This law, however, it is said, is not acted upon, excepting with the consent of kind-hearted masters.

The Spanish law of freedom allows the slave many opportunities of earning money, so that the moment of freedom can always shine like a star of Bethlehem upon his desert path. This, however, has reference more particularly to slaves in the cities. On the plantations and within the walls of the bohea, it is not an easy thing to hear of the star of freedom, still less to attain to it. Yet that happens sometimes even there.

These laws of emancipation have caused the negro population of Cuba to amount to nearly five hundred thousand souls ; about one half of the whole population of the island, and near one third free negroes. And the free negro of Cuba is the happiest of all created beings. He is protected by the laws of the country from that violence and those hostile attacks which continually threaten him in his own country from hostile tribes. He can for a small impost become the possessor of a couple of acres of land, on which he builds his hut of palm bark and palm leaves. Around this he plants the trees and edible roots of his native land, and the golden maize. The earth produces, at small expense of labor, all that he requires. He needs not to labor, and he can enjoy much, and rest the while. The sun gives him fire, and frees him from the necessity of clothing for the greater part of his body. The cocoa-palm gives him milk ; the plantain-tree bread ; the king-palm feeds his swine and his poultry ; the field gives him sugar-cane, and the wild trees of the forest drop for him their manifold fruits. The African drum with its cheerful life, the African dances and songs, are free to him here. He lives here a real life of Canaan, and will not on any account emigrate to Africa. He is happy, although his happiness is not of an elevated character.

I confess to your majesty that it has been astonishing to me, and distressing at the same time, to see the United States stand so far behind Spain in justice and sense of freedom in their legislation for the slave population, and it is difficult for me to explain how the noble-mindedness and national pride of a people can bear and allow themselves to be outdone in their laws regarding freedom by a nation which they consider far below themselves in humanity, and which is so, too, in many respects. The Spaniards of Cuba are not altogether wrong when they, on this subject, look down on the Americans, and call them, as I myself heard, "barbarians!"

There are in Cuba, probably, at this time, more happy black than white people. The slave-owner is not happy. For him wave no palm-trees; the delicious winds do not caress him; for him the mild, bright heavens shine not; between him and all the glory of nature stands the bohea and the sugar-mill, with their negro slaves, who dread him, and of whom he stands in dread. The mild heaven of Cuba gives him no peace; he sees the sword of Damocles hanging over his head, and the future is dark to him. Therefore his end and aim is merely to make as much money as he can, and then to—leave Cuba forever.

When I think of this beautiful island, of its glorious scenery, its rich resources, I can not avoid my imagination transforming it to what it ought to be, to what it seems intended to be by the mind of the Creator; yes, and not merely it, but all those beautiful islands which God has scattered with an affluent hand in the Southern sea, like jewels upon its billowy mantle.

Among these may be named, as representatives of all, three in particular, pre-eminent in beauty, grandeur, and wealth — Cuba, St. Domingo, and Jamaica. But I will now speak of Cuba, that beautiful Queen of the Antilles.

I behold her, then, freed from her fetters, and free from slaves; behold her crowned by her palms and her lofty mountain peaks, born again from the ocean waves, caressed by them and by immortal zephyrs, a new Eden, a home of perpetual spring, a golden chalice of health, to which all the sons and daughters of earth might make pilgrimages, and take draughts of new life, and receive new revelations of the Creator's wealth, and a foretaste of the abodes of the blessed in the great Father's house. There might they wander in banana and orange groves, enjoying the delicious fruits of Paradise, or sit in rocking-chairs on the hills where the palm-trees wave, and the breezes from the sea, full of renovating life, dance around them—sit thus and breathe, and behold, and think how beautiful is existence! The sun descends in mild glory; brilliant cuculios dart like stars through space, and cover the tree-tops with glittering jewels; the air is filled with the music of the Cuban contra-dances and the Spanish seguidillas; the cheerful measure of the African drums is heard in the background, and the Southern Cross rises slowly above the horizon in the growing darkness of night. It is night, but no one need dread the night here; it is not cold; it has no dew. The night of Paradise could not be more innocuous than that of Cuba. The weak and the suffering in body should come here and inhale invigorating life. The aged should come, to be reminded of an eternal youth; the dejected and the sorrowing, to gain new hope. The philosopher should come hither, that his glance might be extended over the infinite realm of man and his Creator; the poet and the artist, to study here new forms of beauty, new groupings of the noble and the lovely in coloring and in form. The statesman should come, to strengthen his faith in the ideal of life and the possibility of its realization. And this new realm of beauty and goodness on earth should be governed by a queen, a ruler of the heart as well as of the state, to whom all hearts and all people, black, and white, and red, and olive-complexioned, and yellow, should pay voluntary homage—a queen good and beautiful as your majesty!

Charleston, South Carolina, May 1st.

I conclude this letter to your majesty, which I commenced beneath the southern heavens, in the United States of North America. I no longer behold the infinitely mild skies of the South, and its waving palms, but I see before me a large and increasing popular life—a *guadarajah* of states growing aloft like palms. In the southern portion of North America nature is a great poet, in the northern a great human being.

It is still in this southern portion that I am now writing, and in one of the slave states of North America.

It is the month of May, and the luxuriant, but feeble, and almost diseased beauty of South Carolina is now in its fullest bloom. They are, however, glorious, these live-oaks, with their long, depending trails of moss, which convert the forest into a natural Gothic temple—these magnolia-trees, with their large, snow-white blossoms, and odors which fill the warm, soft air.

The songs of the negro slaves from the river, as they row home after having sold their wares in the city, reach me at this moment in the beautiful, homelike home from which I have now the happiness of writing to your majesty, and where I feel myself, as it were, nearer good Denmark, because its mistress, Mrs. William Howland, is a Dane, of the Danish line of Monefeldt, and well worthy to be introduced to the Queen of Denmark, both from the love which she bears to her mother-country, and for the beautiful, maternal feeling toward both blacks and whites which distinguish this noble Danish woman.

I have already spoken of slavery as the *misfortune* of the Southern States. I should at this moment be ready to call it their *good fortune*, that is to say, if at this moment they would take hold upon the misfortune, the curse, and convert it into a blessing. And there is no doubt but that they might do so. Charcoal, it is said, is the mother of the diamond. The states of the South possess in slavery the charcoal of a jewel; what do I say? of a diadem of jewels worthy of a new Queen of the South, more beautiful than she who came to Solomon!

Since I have seen in Cuba the negroes in their savage, original state—seen their dances, heard their songs, and am able to compare them with what they are at the best in the United States, there remains no longer a doubt in my mind as to the beneficial influence of Anglo-American culture on the negro, or of the great mission which America is called upon to accomplish with regard to the African race, precisely through the people who, having enslaved, they ought now, in a two-fold sense, to emancipate. The sour crab is not more unlike our noble, bright, Astrachan apple, than is the song of the wild African to the song of the Christian negro in the United States, whether it be hymns that he sings or gay negro songs that he has himself composed. And this comparison holds good through his whole being and world. There is a vast, vast difference between the screeching improvisation of the negroes in Cuba, and the inspired and inspiring preaching of the Savior, and his affluence of light and joy, which I have heard extemporized in South Carolina, Georgia, Maryland, and Louisiana. And low and sensual is that lawless life, and intoxication of the senses in those wild negro-dances, and those noisy festivities to the beat of the drum, compared with that life, and that spiritual intoxication in song and prayer, and religious joy, which is seen and heard at the religious festivals of the negro people here. Hard, and wild, and empty is the expression in the glances of the former, compared with that which I have seen beaming in those of the latter when the light-life of Christianity was preached to them with clearness and *naïveté.* And this is going on through wider and still wider circles, especially in the slave states of North America, in the south, from Virginia to South Carolina and Georgia; and this last-mentioned state, in particular, seemed to me to be animated by a noble, youthfully vigorous spirit of freedom. And it is becoming more and more general for the negroes themselves to stand forth as religious leaders of their people, and churches are erected for them. In the southwestern slave states, on the contrary, the religious life is but very little awakened, and the condition of the negroes on the plantations is, most frequently, alike gloomy with regard to the life both of soul and body. There is, however, no doubt but that light is breaking through; noble-minded Christians are opening a path for its rays, and the Gospel will soon be preached to the slaves, even among the swampy wildernesses of the Mississippi, and on the banks of the distant Red River, in Texas and Arkansas.

The Gospel advances, the Church of Christ unfolds its arms, and the gates of the slave prison-house burst open before it throughout the slave states of America! All that we have a right to demand from them as a Christian community is, that the Gospel should advance unimpeded, and that law should follow in the steps of the Gospel; that the slave legislation of the United States should adopt that law of emancipation which the Spanish legal code now possesses.

If the law of the Southern States, like that of the Spaniard, allowed the slaves, male or female, to purchase their own and their childrens' freedom by labor; if it would open to them a prospect of liberating themselves and their children for a reasonable and legally-fixed sum, and would appoint judges to watch over the rights of the black population; if it would, in addition to this, extend the system of popular education to the children of the blacks—even if they were in separate schools, and would fearlessly concede other consecutive means of moral and intellectual development, we might then confidently predict for the Southern States of America a great future. It would have accomplished a work which would entitle it to the gratitude of two hemispheres, and demand the admiration of the whole world—a work which evidently seems to lie in the plan of God's schemes, and which already the best and noblest citizens of the slave states speak of as American concession.

The Colonization and Christianization of Africa by means of the liberated negro slaves of America is this work, already commenced in the infant colony of Liberia, on the coast of Africa, and which annually increases by means of emigrants sent out by the southern as well as the northern free states, and through the generosity of private citizens.

Some of the slave states, and foremost among them the oldest, Virginia and Maryland, have appropriated a considerable amount of revenue to the colonization of the negroes in Africa, and two steamers annually proceed from Baltimore in Maryland, and from Savannah in Georgia, with black emigrants to Liberia, provided, both from public and private sources, with all that is requisite for their establishment in the old-new-country, each religious community providing separately for the members of their own body.

In the proposition and extension of this colony, the Northern and the Southern States have shown themselves to be a noble Union, with one heart and one soul. In this they extend their hands to each other for reconciliation in the great quarrel between them on the subject of slavery.

I must, however, confess that this work seems to me merely as a part of that which the Southern States ought to accomplish. These states would, without the negro population, lose much of their most picturesque, most peculiar life; besides which, they could not dispense with negro labor. It is declared that rice, cotton, and sugar could not be cultivated without the negro, who is habituated to the heat of the sun, and to whom it is a delight. The white man dies of the heat and the miasmas which are produced by the soil; the black man, on the contrary, flourishes there, increases and multiplies, or merely suffers slightly from climatic fevers. When the circumstances are favorable between the white and the black, it is evident that there exists no inimical relationship between them; they love each other, and are attracted to each other; equally unlike, their respective deficiencies perfect nature. The good-tempered, cheerful negro loves the grave, sensible white man, and allows himself to be guided by him, and he, in his turn, loves the good-hearted black man, and allows himself to be tended by him.

I say nothing but what noble and thinking men in the slave states consider to be possible when I state to your majesty the conviction that the noblest, because the most difficult, future endeavor of the slave states ought to be the converting of one portion of its slave population into free laborers. I say *one* portion, because it is clear that merely one portion thereof would be capable of remaining, as freemen, under American dominion. The portion of the slave population which longs to go to Africa should go there; and that portion which is attached to the soil and the people of America, and which is capable of acquiring its cultivation and its active, laborious spirit, should remain in its Southern States, where it has been brought up, to which it belongs, by nature, habitude, and affections, and where the coloring and the romantic life of these lands, beloved by the sun, would be greatly increased by their life of labor on the plantations and in the cities, by their religious festivities, and their songs and dances.

From what I have seen of the good understanding between the white man and the negro, I believe that many of the best heads and the ablest hands among the negro people would prefer remaining in America to emigrating from it.

The traveler may then visit these states with an admiration free from any depressing reservation, for they will then advance in moral beauty and political power, and the American Union will then, without an exception, become what it has already declared itself willing to become, a great asylum, diffusing the blessings of liberty to all the nations of the earth by both precept and example.

It is evident that such an emancipation can not take place at once, nay, perhaps not for several tens of years. It may be delayed for a century, if we can only see that it is approaching, if we can only see the commencement of its dawn, so that we may know that it will advance into the perfect day.

And it can not be otherwise; the streaks of dawn are

already, even at this moment, piercing the nocturnal shadows which the late political contests between the free states and the slave states called forth over the Union.

I have already mentioned to your majesty the labors of the Colonization Society, both in the Northern and the Southern States, as advancing the work of enfranchisement in Africa. I place among the movements, the aim of which is an emancipation of the black slave population of America, the scheme of a law, by that noble, patriotic statesman, Henry Clay, which should declare free all the children of the negro slave born after a certain year—1856, I believe—a scheme which, however, did not meet with the support of the less noble statesmen; and the endeavors of various noble private individuals for the education and liberation of their slaves.

There is, however, one among these efforts to which I desire pre-eminently to direct your majesty's eye, both because it proceeds from the womanly and maternal element in the community, and because it is the grain of mustard-seed, which, although a small seed, may yet grow into a large tree and spread its shadow far around.

I know in the slave states some young girls, the daughters and sisters of planters, who are not ashamed of keeping schools themselves for the children of the slaves on the plantation, and of teaching them to pray, to think, and work. They speak highly of the powers of mind, and the willingness to learn, of the negro children, especially when knowledge is presented to them in a living and pleasing form by means of narratives and pictures.

If the young daughters of the Southern States would generally imitate this good example, they would do more than any legislation to prepare the way for a happy emancipation; for emancipation might take place without any detriment either to the black or the white population, if the slave had been educated from his youth upward by love, and habituated to the fear of God, to order, and labor; and I participate fully in the views of an elderly man of the South, that the possibility of an approaching emancipation from slavery is much more in the hands of the women than of the men at the present moment.

I have spoken of the young teachers from the states of New England, the daughters of the Pilgrims, as "the young mothers of humanity." The young women of the Southern States have assigned to themselves a similar office, and that nearer home—yes, so near and so natural, that it seems to me assigned to them by God the Father himself.

It is a universal custom on the plantations of the South that while the slaves, men and women, are out at labor the children should all be collected at one place, under the care of one or two old women. I have sometimes seen as many as sixty or seventy, or even more together, and their guardians were a couple of old negro witches, who with a rod of reeds kept rule over these poor little black lambs, who with an unmistakable expression of fear and horror shrunk back in crowds whenever the threatening witches came forth, flourishing their rods. On smaller plantations, where the number of children is smaller, and the female guardians gentle, the scene, of course, is not so repulsive; nevertheless, it always reminded me of a flock of sheep or swine, which were fed merely to make them ready for eating. And yet these were *human beings*, capable of the noblest human development as regards sentiment and virtue—human beings with immortal souls!

Here are the subjects of Sunday-schools ready to hand. But where are the teachers, men—and women? The children are driven hither in the morning, are called over morning, noon, and night, and receive in the mean time threats and castigation, and then are driven back to their cottages in the evening; and thus it continues till they are old enough for labor, and can be brought under the law of the whip.

Would it be too much to demand from the wives, daughters, and sisters of the planters, too much to demand from Christian women, that they should once or twice in the week go down to this neglected crowd of children, and talk to them of their Father in heaven, and teach them to pray to "*Our* Father in heaven?"

How right and how beautiful it is to see a young white girl—an angel of light she appears, and really is, in such cases—standing amid the black little ones, teaching them to utter with knowledge this holy, universal prayer, "Our Father which art in heaven!"

First let this prayer be common to black and white, then will all the rest come in its time, and as the good and great Father wills it!

Good and beautiful would it also be if the young white woman would exercise the black children in singing and dancing, as they are practiced in their native land; those songs, for instance, with the chorus, which seems to be the heart of all songs among the natives of Africa, and which should contain some sensible meaning.

There is one song which might serve as a model for all such songs. It was sung by African women to a white traveler, to whom they gave shelter one stormy night in their hut, and its words are these:

> The storm roared, and the rain fell;
> The poor white man,
> Worn and weary in the dark night,
> Sat alone beneath our tree.
> He has no mother who can give him milk,
> No wife who can grind his corn!
> *Chorus.*—Have pity on the white man,
> He has no mother, &c.

This song from the mother-heart of Africa might show to America the best mode for the cultivation of the negro people. A popular mind which can produce such a song ought to be treated with respect. Such an occupation would be more beautiful, and more worthy of the young daughters of the South, than wasting their days in levity, or in paying visits, or in empty pastime, as most of them do now.

Yet I know some who have chosen the better part; many there ought to be. Blessings be upon them! May they become many! And the great work of emancipation will proceed in silence and in beauty, as if of itself.

It is very common in Europe to lay the blame of the institution of slavery on the United States of America, as a sin against the Holy Ghost, which takes away all truth and all value from their free estate. But people forget that it is only a part of these states which have slaves, and that it was Europe who first compelled them to have them! Many of the young colonies, in particular Virginia and Georgia, protested in the commencement, and that in the most strong and earnest manner, against the introduction of slavery. In vain. England was then the mother-country, and, carrying on the slave-trade, required a market for her cargoes of slaves, and commanded the young American colonies to become this market. The selfishness of the planters, the climate, and the productions of Southern North America, all assisted. Thus was slavery introduced into the United States. Climate, productions, and many other causes continue to maintain it there, until—something further.

England, during a period of newly-awakened national conscientiousness, and influenced by such men as Wilberforce, shook herself free from slavery, and liberated her slaves at the enormous sacrifice of twenty millions sterling. It is said that the whole thing might have been done more judiciously; it could scarcely have been done with more magnanimity. We yet look for the Wilberforce of America.

The people of the Southern States are greatly exasperated by Europe, and by the Northern States wishing to mix themselves up, as they say, in their own private affairs, and talking of and interfering with the institution of slavery and their established right to it, as if it was any thing to them.

Their excuse is that the American Union, and the great purpose which it declares itself called upon to accomplish, is of such vast importance, of such infinite significance in the eyes of all the free states, for the whole of humanity, and for all the nations of the world, that they could not allow themselves to be other than interested in its full accomplishment as in an affair that concerned themselves. And does it not in reality concern them?

The United States of America have declared the freedom and the rights of humanity. Every human being feels himself participant in this great charter of liberty.

"The Mayflower" was the name of the first ship which conveyed the first colony of free men and women from the Old to the New World, and who founded a new community on the soil of North America. "The Mayflower" was the symbol of the Old World's youngest anticipations. The community of the United States became the Mayflower of the human race. It will not tolerate that any worm should feed in its dewy chalice, that any Nidhögg should gnaw at its root. And it is right.

But I have too long detained the attention of your majesty by this side of the history of the United States, and I fear that in so doing my letter has extended itself to an undue length. I can not, however, close this account to your majesty of the life in the New World without saying a few words respecting the homes there.

During the whole period of my residence in this hemisphere, I have lived and been entertained in American homes, and it is in these homes and by familiar intercourse with their members that I have contemplated and reflected upon the social life of the New World; it is in them that I have loved and thought, reposed and enjoyed myself; it is the home of America which I have to thank pre-eminently for what I have here learned and experienced; it is the home of America which has conferred more upon me than the whole treasure of California—a new life both for heart and soul.

The home on the soil of the New World is that which the home was for our old North, and still is to this day —*a sacred room.* The American home, however, will be also a beautiful room. It loves to surround itself with green plots, with lovely trees and flowers. It is the same in the cities. More beautifully adorned homes are not to be met with in the world. Within the home, the fear of God, morality, and domestic love are met with. It is the American home which strengthens the American states, and makes them steadfast in the fear of God and a moral life. The best and the noblest men of America have every one of them, with Washington at their head, been brought up by pious mothers, in noble and moral homes.

Probably that which most distinguishes the home of the New World from that of the Old is the dominant sway which is assigned in it to woman. The rule of the American man is to allow the wife to establish the laws of home. He bows himself willingly to her sceptre, partly from affection, partly from the conviction that it is best and most just that it should be so, and from chivalric politeness to the sex; for the American believes that a something divine, a something of a higher and more refined nature, abides in woman. He loves to listen to it and to yield to it in all the questions of the inner life. He loves to place his partner in life higher than himself.

She is left to the free development of her world and her own being within the home, seldom contradicted, never compelled, is generally true to her nobler nature, and stands forth gentle, domestic, affectionate, and *God-fearing*. One of the most striking features in American women is their religious strength. Many American women, during the earliest periods of their wars with the Indians, like the mother of the Maccabees, strengthened their children under their martyrdom, admonishing them to hold fast by their God; many do the same at the present day during severe trials of sickness or misfortune. And from the Eastern Sea to the Mississippi, from the Northern Minnesota to the tropics, throughout the Western country, have I seen nothing more worthy of love, nothing more near to perfection, than the motherly woman.

Neither have I ever seen any where on the earth a being of more dew-like freshness, more beautiful, primevally vital life, than the young girl of America.

But beyond this group of beautiful womanhood I am obliged to confess that there are in the West many women who in no respects correspond to the ideal which the cultivation of the New World requires them to attain to —women whose thoughtlessness, insipidity, vanity, and pretension make the spectator pause and ask himself how far that great freedom, which is early permitted to young women, is in accordance with the higher development of her being.

The better class see this misdirection in a portion of their sex, and deplore it deeply. I would not, on their account, have this freedom circumscribed in the least degree—I would give merely a higher object and consciousness. That which woman requires is not a less, but, on the contrary, a higher esteem for home and her vocation—a higher comprehension of the human work and worth to which she is called. It is only a higher consciousness which can save her from her egotistical littleness.

As a general rule, it may be said that the citizeness is not as yet fully awakened within the community of the New World; as in the Old World, she still slumbers, lulled by the old cradle-song, and by *the little voice* which prevents her listening to *the great voice*, and by the liking which men have for the merely agreeable and outwardly attractive in the sex.

It is from this defective consciousness of a higher vocation that the influence of woman within the home, and on the education of the child, is still, in general, far from what it might be, and what it needs to be in this country, where the power of conscience and of the inner law ought to be strengthened ten-fold, in the same degree as the outward are less restrictive upon the wishes and the whims of the individual. The American woman is married young, and when she is scarcely past the years of childhood; she soon has children of her own, and shows her maternal love principally by spoiling them, by indulging all their whims and wishes, as she herself was indulged and spoiled in her paternal home. She leaves discipline and severity to the school, to which the child is sent early. And the school does what it can—gives style and grace to the outward being, but leaves the inward very much, probably, as it found it.

Hence, especially in the slave states, that unrestrained temper and mode of action—that want of a stricter moral law, of a keener conscientious perception, with which, and not without reason, the young men of America are reproached, and those disorderly occurrences in private life and in the community at large which are the consequent results.*

Strong, stern women, who would bring up republicans by severity and love—such women as Lycurgus would form to make his republic strong and great—are not to be met with here.

Neither is that Spartan type of physical strength the only necessary. The New World requires another. And if it should become more universal, if woman in the United States of America became that which she ought to be, and exercised that influence which it lies in her power to ex-

* I must, however, remark, that although such occurrences make a great noise here, they did not appear to me worse than such as take place more silently—and more numerously—in European countries.

ercise on the soul of the child and the man, on social life, on the great interests of the community, then would the United States become also the ideal states of the earth!

Many distinguished and amiable women in North America—Quaker women among these—have presented noble examples to their sex; and many movements in the States have latterly shown the dawn of public spirit among women. May it increase and strengthen; and I will venture to say that the American woman will then stand forward as the earth's most beautiful and most perfect woman.

If I were able to present to your majesty those American women who appear to me to be the purest representative type of the Eve of the New World, your majesty's glance would rest upon them with an expression of satisfaction, both as regards the sense of beauty and of moral feeling. I see your majesty's own gentle being thrilled by the recognition of a kindred being, and seem to hear from your majesty's lips this judgment.

"They resemble the most beloved women of our hemisphere; their grace of person is not less than their steadfastness in principle. But they have something more than the women of Europe. Their glance seems to me to embrace a larger world; their intelligence a larger activity; and their heart seems to me large enough to embrace and elevate the human community in all its spheres."

Probably it is only just to say that the *human being* of the New World is not *better* than he of the Old; but he stands on more advantageous ground, under more favorable circumstances as regards free and true development. Human nature, both in the individual and in the community at large, may become more perfected, because here every private advantage may become that of all; the circle of society is more complete.

But it is time for me to conclude, and I must already, I fear, have wearied your majesty by the length of my letter. The interest of the subjects, and the interest which your majesty expressed in them, must be my excuse.

I shall now very shortly leave the South. Its witchery is great, but my bias is now toward the North. The tree of freedom grows more vigorous amid its granite hills. And as it grows in the Northern States of America, grows it also in our Scandinavian North. But what this North possesses, and which America possesses not, is an antiquity full of song and saga, of glorious prophecy and symbolism, of gods and heroes who gave to Scandinavia so large, so peculiar, so romantic a life. It is this antiquity, its significance for the present time, its life in our scenery, and our every-day life, which attracts me once more to my native land, as powerfully as my mother's voice.

A visit to my beloved Copenhagen stands before me like a point of light on my return to Sweden, and I hope that this coming autumn will enable me to greet the cheerful capital of Denmark. I shall esteem myself fortunate if I see there once more the good and beautiful Queen of Denmark, and receive her bright image into the sanctuary of my heart, there to be preserved as one of its most precious treasures.

Your majesty's kindness makes me bold enough to hope it; and it is also in reliance upon that that I venture to solicit a place in your majesty's memory among the many who love your majesty, as does

Your majesty's humble and devoted servant,

FREDRIKA BREMER.

LETTER XXXVIII.

TO AGATHA.

Savannah, Georgia, May 13.

I HAVE left the island of the sun and of the palms, and am once more on the continent of America.

On the 3d I went on board the pretty but expensive steam-boat the "Isabel," where nothing was good excepting the captain and mate. My host at Havana, Mr. Woolcott had the politeness to see me on board himself, and to take charge of my luggage. He is a good and polite host, and understands perfectly every thing which a traveler requires, and his hotel in Havana is excellent, nor is it very dear, except during the so-called winter months, when the concourse of strangers to the city is extraordinarily great. Besides which, Havana is one of the dearest places in the world.

The last view I had of the Queen of the Antilles showed me her enveloped in dark clouds, the precursors of tempest. The sea rolled high, and the vessel rocked tremendously; and the Moro light was seen like a flambeau on its lofty rock, as the vessel rose on each ascending billow, to be again lost when it sunk into the abyss of the waves. That beautiful bright light, which so often gladdened me during the evenings and nights of Cuba, seemed to me now, in the rising tempest and darkening night, like some signal of misfortune flashing forth from the stormy horizon. On the day previous there had been an eclipse of the sun, and around the sun a vast black ring. This seemed to me a prophetic token; for the internal condition of Cuba, the despotism of the government, the prevailing venality and the thirst of gain, the bitter dissatisfaction of the Creoles, the state of the slaves, the continuance of the slave-trade, which annually peoples the island with thousands of wild Africans, the longing glances which America casts upon this new Helen, all forebode a stormy future, and, it may be, a terrible, bloody crisis! May I be an untrue diviner!

Ah! this beautiful island, with its delicious breezes, its glorious trees, its lovely evenings, its eternal summer—I shall always love it as one of God's most beautiful creations, and be thankful that I beheld it, and have learned from it the better to understand a new heaven and a new earth!

My secret wish and hope is, that Cuba may one day, by peaceful means, belong to the United States. When the United States shall comprehend within themselves the regions of the tropics, and shall thence extend their realm of states, then first will it become the universal realm which it ought to be. And Cuba in the hands of the Anglo-Americans would soon discontinue the slave-trade; the Gospel would be preached to the slaves; the fortress walls of the bohea would be converted into pretty American slave-villages; and perhaps the noble-minded laws of Cuba respecting the slave might be incorporated into the legislative code of the Union when Cuba itself became a part of the Union.

I arrived in Charleston on the morning of the 11th of May, and amid the brightest sunshine, which nevertheless seemed like moonlight, or like veiled sunshine, so gloomy and dim appeared to me the light on the walls and roofs of Charleston, or amid its shadowy trees, after the pomp and glory of sunshine to which I had become accustomed in Cuba. I could not help continually looking up to the sky, to see whether the sun were not obscured by cloud.

But what heartfelt pleasure it was to me to see Mrs. W. H. and her family once more, and to talk with them about Cuba, and to spend with them, in joy and tranquillity, one whole, beautiful day!

My thoughts, however, were not just now bent on tranquillity and quietness. I was about to undertake new journeys and new adventures. I desired to see Florida, and easily persuaded my good Mrs. W. H. to accompany me, being sure that the journey would give her pleasure, while it would be a great joy to me to make it in her company.

The determination must be quickly made. The following day a steamer left for Savannah, and there I was to meet with the Mac I. family, who, according to an agreement of a year's standing, were to make by it a journey to Florida, up the beautiful River St. John.

No sooner said than done. The next morning saw Mrs. W. H. and myself on board the steamer bound for Savannah. It was the most beautiful May morning, and just as we reached the shore, and were about to go on board, there was my friend from Belmont with a bouquet of flowers, and some other friends also. How kind and how delightful!

And now, after a day's pleasure-sail on the river, I am once more in this verdant city, once more among old friends, good, kind, and hospitable as formerly—Mr. and Mrs. T., Mrs. B., and many others.

I found the Mac I.'s in deep sorrow on account of the death of a beloved daughter and sister in the past autumn. The father, however, the estimable Colonel Mac I., and his youngest daughter, an intellectual and highly-cultivated young girl, were ready to accompany us to Florida, where we were to pay a visit to the eldest son of the family, who was married and lived there. On my return I shall visit the plantations of a Mr. C., where, I am told, I shall meet with the ideal of plantation-life in the slave states.

On the morning of the day after to-morrow we set off by a pretty little spick-and-span new steamer, "the Magnolia," and intend to go up the River St. John as far as steamers can go, that is to say, as far as Lake Monroe.

Miss Dix, who came by steamer to Savannah, has joined our little party, as she also wishes to visit Florida. The weather is glorious, the moon is at the full, and I am full of the desire for traveling, and the desire to see Florida, the flower of the Southern States, the land of which the delicious balmy odors made the Spaniards believe that the fountain of eternal youth was hidden there. And now—thither, thither, to taste its nectar!

The Magnolia, May 17.

Very seldom are letters written from a steamer which lies on a green meadow; it is from a steamer in that very predicament that I am now writing to you. And how long it and its passengers are so to lie, depends upon the moon and human kindness; but we have reason to suspect the good-will both of one and the other at this moment.

The first day of our voyage was a particularly merry one, and the ladies of our little party were very amusing to each other. Miss Mac I., now removed from an environment of sorrow, bloomed forth into such fresh life, and vivacity, and wit, as her earnest, classical countenance had not led me to expect from her. Mrs. W. H. has always a fund of calm, good-natured humor at hand, and the two together excited Miss Dix to a friendly quarrel. We had also a certain dominant and philanthropic lady on board, who would domineer over us all, and who made "mountains of mole-heaps." But we took it all in good part, and were very merry. Our pretty little Magnolia wedged its way gayly, in all sorts of curves and angles, through the swampy flats, where, among many currents, it had to find out its own. I could not help admiring its courage and its many expedients, only it seemed to me to have quite too great a fancy for the land, for we often struck against the banks while we swung between them, but there was often no space to take any free sweep.

"Beautiful evening, Missis!" said the black helmsman, looking out of his little house on deck with a good-homored countenance, and addressing one of the ladies of our party.

"Yes, but—shall we soon reach our quarters for the night?"

"Oh yes—oh yes, immediately! We shall soon get along. Don't be uneasy, Missis, Ma'am!"

Shortly after, when we were all sitting at tea, the vessel

was suddenly heaved up, as by a strong wave, and then—we stood still, although the engines kept working on for a moment. The captain, who was sitting at the table, and a couple of other gentlemen, sprang up and rushed out.

It was apparent that the ignorant extra-ordinary helmsman (the ordinary one lay sick at Savannah) had mistaken the channel of the stream, and had steered us directly upon a projecting point of land. It was overflowed with water, for the moon was that evening at her full, and it was high tide.

At ebb tide, therefore, the next morning, we found ourselves lying entirely on dry land, with green grass growing around us, and just by a grove of live-oaks and flowering magnolia-trees, which latter may have exercised some mysterious attractive power upon our poor little Magnolia, which now lies with its head turned toward the grove, just as if it would plow its way right into it.

We were quite fast. And we are still sticking quite fast now on the 17th, amid the green grass and the clay, saluted in the evenings by the whistling notes of the whippowil from the magnolia-grove, and in the morning by brilliant butterflies. A whole regiment of negro slaves are busied in digging around the keel of the vessel, to loosen it out of the sand and the clay, but thereby only to reveal the depth to which it is imbedded.

On the first day we said, "When the tide comes up in the evening, then—"

But when the tide came up it did not rise as high as on the preceding evening, and the moon, now past the full, looked down upon us coldly, and let us lie where we lay.

"In the morning, when the steam-boat, 'the Gaston,' passes by," we now said, "it will give us a pull, and help us off!" and Miss Mac I. proposed that all the ladies should, on the approach of the Gaston, come on deck, and show themselves with handkerchiefs to their eyes, and so move, by that means, the probably hard heart of the captain of the Gaston.

The morrow came, and the smoke of the Gaston was seen, and the smoke of hope ascended from our hearts.

The Gaston approached, paused, looked at us. The tide was in. We were full of anticipation of the Gaston's "pull." But the hard-hearted Gaston only looked at us and went on his way, and left us to our fate on dry land. (N.B.—The moving scene of the pocket-handkerchiefs was forgotten!)

Great indignation in the Magnolia. Our dominant lady vowed that she would draw up a declaration of indignation against the Gaston and put it in the newspapers. She proposed to the ladies on board a declaration of esteem for the captain of the Magnolia, and his gentlemanly conduct, which we applauded and signed.

Our hopes are now fixed on the steam-boat St. Matthew, which is expected to-morrow evening, and that it may show itself to be a good apostle, and take us on board, because it is clear that the Magnolia can not be released at present, as the moon decreases every day, and the tide is lower also, and the Magnolia sinks deeper every day, from its weight, in the sand.

We in the mean time console ourselves with good-humour, and a ramble every now and then on the shore, which we can do dry-shod from the vessel.

The ladies are especially good-tempered and merry. Good Mrs. W. H., who can not live without her housewifely activity, began to wash her muslins, and recommended herself as a laundress of fine linen to all whom it might concern, but got scolded for laziness and want of skill. Miss Dix, on the other hand, being suspected of theft, was threatened with the house of correction, and thus we laughed heartily and amused ourselves, especially Miss Mac I., in whose breast the fountain of youth seemed to well forth afresh, and who could not herself understand how she could be so lively; and in the evening we celebrated the birth-day of our captain's pretty little daughter. I wove a garland of wild flowers for her; the other ladies gave her little presents, and the little girl was very happy, and sprang forward to exhibit herself to her father.

There was in company a lady, not yet forty, handsome, tight laced, and well dressed, with light curls, and thoughts evidently directed to the world and its pleasures. This lady is, nevertheless, a widow after her third marriage, and the mother of twelve children, nine of whom are dead, and two married, and the grandmother of three grandchildren.

"And you got very well through all this?" said I, with some surprise.

"Yes, indeed," replied she, evidently well satisfied with herself and her own strength of mind.

"And you would not, perhaps, be unwilling to marry a fourth time?" said Mrs. W. H., a little curious as to the reply.

"Oh no!" replied she, calmly, "not if I could better myself by so doing."

Miss Mac I. was so indignant at this that she could hardly restrain herself from breaking out upon her.

Among the gentlemen was a young Californian adventurer, just returned from the land of gold, and on his way back to his wife and his home, with divers lumps of gold, melted and unmelted, Californian ducats, and a white China silk shawl for his wife. He was a handsome young man, more of a dandy, and more childish than is usual for an American, but all suitable for a Californian adventurer. I wanted to know something about the country, and the people, and the way of life in California; about the Chinese and their social state, their mode of worship, &c. But the young man merely knew that he had with him many nuggets of gold, and a Chinese silk shawl for his wife.

This afternoon we went a little way inland, and saw a fine cotton plantation, beautifully situated upon a lofty terrace by the river. It belonged, as we were told, to a Mr. Valburg. I was particularly pleased with some of the slave dwellings which I visited, and which bore evidence of a certain degree of prosperity, as did also the appearance of some of the slaves who had returned from labor.

There stood beside a well a very old negro woman, who was come hither to fetch water. I asked her how old she was.

"A little better than a hundred, ma'am!" was her reply.

The negroes have a great desire to be very old, and really do live to extreme old age when their life is easy.

I should have retained nothing but the most agreeable impression of this plantation had I not, in returning to the shore, met at a gate the overseer of the plantation (the owner and his family were abroad), and in him had seen a strong-limbed young man, with that fierce, lawless, wandering gaze which I have remarked in many overseers on the plantations, and which takes away all faith in the justice and integrity of their treatment of the slave. The slaves who are digging around our vessel are strong-built, and work hard, but as silently as if they were digging a grave. This is not natural for negroes, and is not a good sign.

There is the most beautiful moonlight in the evenings, and the melodious but monotonous cry of the whippowil resounds from the magnolia grove. In the daytime the heat is great, and—may St. Matthew only have mercy upon us!

Lake Monroe, Florida, May 20.

I now write to you from the heart of blooming Florida, reposing upon one of its lovely mirror-like lakes, with horrible alligators swimming around our little floating dwelling (a very rickety steam-boat named Sarah Spalding). A garland of dark green wood, resembling myrtle, surrounds the great lake, for at this distance we can not distinguish between groves of orange and palmetto and forests of cypress. The whole shore is low, and the lake as clear as a mirror, and every thing profoundly still around it. No cities and towns, no steam-boats, no boats of any kind, no human beings, excepting ourselves, the Florida travelers. Here is infant land, nay, almost wild land still. But how glad I am to be now in the poetical wilderness of Florida, to have seen something of its marvelous, natural poetry!

St. Matthew proved a good apostle to us, and on the afternoon of the 18th received us all into his bosom, poor, stranded sinners as we were, but who nevertheless did not experience any want, and were not much to be pitied, excepting that it was tiresome to lie quiet in a steamer on a neck of land, in the midst of the hot sunshine. Our captain, however, was mostly to be pitied; so were some of the men, who were already taken ill. Our deliverer, St. Matthew, did not come very near to us, but had us fetched off in a boat. Four negroes rowed us. I was thinking that they were rowing well, and with great precision, when our dominant lady, who is known to be very philanthropic to white sinners, and was keeping a sharp look-out on the blacks, said, the very next moment, in a stern voice,

"Why do you not row with more vigor?" and then turning to me, she added,

"One can see by their chests and their breathing whether they exert themselves as much as they are able."

The philanthropic lady thus sat and watched the respiration of the negroes, with her eyes riveted upon their bare chests, to ascertain whether they exerted themselves to the utmost to serve her and us. I am obliged to confess that this lady was from one of the states of New England. Such is the philanthropy of many American women.

Our dominant lady, in the mean time, did not get any one to concur in her remarks and admonitions. The negroes rowed calmly, but regularly and well, the heavily-loaded boat, and we all came happily on board the St. Matthew. And we soon found ourselves, to our great satisfaction, sweeping along the Altamaha River, whose waters here in the neighborhood of the sea are salt, and seemed in the evening twilight like a river of brightly-flowing silver, full of sparkling diamonds.

St. Matthew had already many passengers on board, and among them were three pair of turtle-doves of the human race. The first pair, physically handsome, but second-class people in cultivation and manners, were so in love with one another, and showed it to such a degree, that it was quite disgusting; the young man, with a huge breast-pin of sham diamonds in his shirt-frill, confessed to an acquaintance in the company that he considered himself to have married the most perfect woman in the world. But her perfectly handsome person did not appear to me to entertain much soul within it. Turtle-doves No. 2 were of a more refined character altogether, agreeable people, with the loving soul beaming from dark and beautiful eyes; she, very delicate in health, after only one year's marriage; he, very anxious about her. Turtle-doves No. 3 were neither of them any longer young or handsome, but they were of all the three pair the most interesting, and perhaps the most happy. It did one good to see them and to hear their history.

They belonged to the poorer class of white people, of Carolina and Georgia, living in the most sandy and sterile part of the country, without schools or any means of education. She married her husband without the consent of her relatives, and when, some time after their marriage, they fell into great poverty through some fault of her husband, her relatives gave her a home on the strict condition that she should never again see him. He, extremely angry at this prohibition, swore that they should never see him again until he came to fetch away his wife to her own home. He went away, and not a word was heard of him for seven years. She remained in the mean time with her parents, having her children with her, two boys and a girl, the youngest boy born just before the father left, and by degrees she lost almost all hope of ever again seeing her husband, whom she loved with all her heart. One day, however, the eldest boy exclaimed, "Here comes my father!" She could not believe him; she had so many years waited in vain to hear from him. She, however, went out of the house to see the approaching stranger, and when she at a distance recognized her husband, she sank fainting to the earth. He had, after persevering exertions, succeeded in securing a livelihood as a carpenter in Florida, where he had built himself a cottage, and to this home it was, in the land of eternal summer, that he was taking his wife and children. The family were now on their way thither.

This new home lay on the banks of Lake Monroe, and there it was that the married pair would begin a new life. In that moonlight evening they kissed and rested one against the other with the most heartfelt love and joy. He had a good and manly appearance. She had fine features, and had evidently been handsome, but seemed to have suffered from sorrow and hard labor. She could not be much above thirty, and he looked a few years younger than she. She rested her head upon his shoulder with an expression of deep confidence and peace. She needed no longer to labor alone for home and children, separated from her husband, and surrounded by relations who neither esteemed nor loved him. He was with her; she had him now again, and, what was still more, she had esteem for him as a man and a husband. He could and he would, from this time forward, provide for her and the children. He was taking her far, far away from the dreary sand-hills, where she had suffered so much misery, to the blooming Florida; orange-groves would overshadow her dwelling on the banks of the lake, and the summer winds of Florida call up fresh roses on her pale cheeks. All these delicious feelings and thoughts might clearly be read in the expression and demeanor of this husband and wife. They seemed to me the happiest of human beings, excepting—myself, who saw them, and to whom God has given so much enjoyment in the happiness of others.

The youngest child was a nice little lad, handsome and cheerful, with a smart little cap on his head; the oldest boy, fifteen years old, was not so nice; and the girl of fourteen, Molly by name, was a black line in the romance of the parents; for, although not ugly, and with the father's good looks in her round countenance, she was a genuine daughter of the sand-hills, and had grown up with her old grandmother, like a pine-tree in the sand, without any more trimming or training than it. Our dominant lady took this wild shoot of humanity under her charge, and her attempts to educate the young novice, and the girl's spirit and mode of behavior, furnished us with subjects for many a hearty laugh.

The first night on the St. Matthew was hot and oppressive in the crowded and narrow saloon. The floor was strewn over with outstretched ladies, some of whom were handsome, two quite young and with regularly classical features, very lovely in their sleep and their reposing position; and when I could not sleep, I amused myself by contemplating them with an artistic eye from my elevated berth.

By evening we had left the River Altamaha, and, after a few hours by sea, we found ourselves the next morning in the St. John's River, after having happily passed a dangerous sand-bank at its mouth without suffering more than a severe shock occasioned by a swell of the waves dashing us against the bank, and which made old St. Matthew creak in all his joints. But he did not go to pieces, which sometimes happens under such circumstances, in which case we should all infallibly have gone to the bottom, so that we had nothing to complain of.

Several of the passengers left the vessel at various colonies and plantations by the way, so that it became less crowded and more agreeable; and I enjoyed inexpressibly the glorious morning, and the journey up the river.

St. John's River—in the Indian language, Welaka, or the Lake-River—is like a chain of larger and smaller lakes, linked together by narrow but deep straits, which wind in innumerable sinuosities between shores, the wonderful scenery of which is scarcely to be imagined, if none similar to it have been seen before. Here is again primeval forest such as I saw on the Savannah River, but still richer in its productions, because Welaka flows, for the greater part, under a tropical sky, and below the boundary which frost approaches. We see here thick groves and belts of palmettoes; here are wild orange-groves laden with brilliant fruit which there are no hands to gather; masses of climbing plants, vanilla, wild vines, convolvuli, and many others, cover the shores in indescribable luxuriance, forming themselves into clumps and bushes as they grow over the trees, and cypresses, which present dark green pyramids, altars, perfect temples with columns, arches, porticoes, shadowy aisles, and, on all hands, the most beautiful, the most ornamental festoons flung along and over the clear river. From amid the masses of foliage towers upward the fan-palm, with its beautiful crown, free and fantastic; the magnolia stands full of snow-white flowers, and, pre-eminent amid that republic of plants, flowers, and multitudes of trees, stand the lofty cypresses like protecting, shadowy patriarchs, stretching out horizontally their light green heads, with long, waving mosses hanging down from their strong branches.

Here is the life of Nature in its luxuriance, but it is the realm and reign of the old pagan god of Nature, old Pan, which embraces both the good and the evil, life and death, with the same love, and which recognizes no law and no ordination but that of production and decay. Beneath these verdant, leafy arches which overshadow the water lie the peaceful tortoise, and the cruel alligator also, waiting for its prey. Elks inhabit these natural temples; also panthers, tigers, and black bears. Around these columns of leaves and flowers wind the rattlesnake and the poisonous moccasin, and that beautiful, romantic forest is full of small, poisonous, noxious creatures. But more dangerous than all is the pleasant air which comes laden, during the summer, with the miasmas of the primeval forests and the river, bringing to the colonist fever and slowly consuming diseases, and causing these wondrously beautiful shores still to lack human inhabitants. Small settlements have been commenced here and there on the river, but have, after a few years, been deserted and left to decay.

It is, however, precisely this primeval life in the wilderness, this wild, luxuriant beauty defying the power of man, and vigorous in its own affluence, which is so unspeakably interesting to me, and which supplies me with an incessant festival. And the air is so pleasant, and the magnolias so full of flower, the river so full of life, alligators and fishes splashing about, large and beautiful water-fowl on all hands—every thing is so luxuriant, so wonderfully rich, wild, and lovely, it is a never-ending fairy scene, especially in the evenings, when the moon rises and throws her mystic half light and half shadow into the arches and pillared aisles of these marvelous natural temples. I sit in silence on the piazza, and gaze upon it with devotion and rapture, as at every bend of the river new and striking scenes present themselves, happy when I can thus sit alone, or with my good Mrs. W. H. at my side, in company with whom I am always right.

But we are not without our little disturbing occurrences. On our first morning on the Welaka, St. Matthew, through carelessness, ran upon a snag, and this gave the dominant lady a deal to do in the way of reproof and command, and we had to lie still for a good hour to repair our damage. Molly of the sand-hills was always in our way, and when we by any chance stood in hers, we had nothing to expect but a good slap. Our dominant lady's educational management became more strict, but we began to lose all hope of the power of cultivation on this daughter of the wilderness. We had all sorts of droll scenes, and the gay young Miss Mac I. amused both herself and us by her observations on Molly and her ways.

The pair of turtle-doves No. 1 and No. 2 were landed at the little colony of Pilatka, which is in the midst of a hot, sandy plain, and which, probably, was on that account more healthy than other situations surrounded by luxuriant vegetation. The turtle-doves No. 3 would accompany us to Lake Monroe.

We refreshed ourselves at Pilatka by a grand washing and good milk. We are in Pilatka in the region where frost has power—where it is occasionally felt, though it does little damage. Somewhat more to the north, in the district of St. Augustine, a large plantation of sweet oranges was entirely destroyed about two years ago by frost, and the only wealth of several thousand persons thus perished. At Pilatka, however, I recognize the climate of that balmy atmosphere, and soft, fanning airs which I breathed in Cuba. This air can only exist where frost can not come.

Amid this enchanting air there lay at this time in Pilatka, far from his relations and friends, a youth who was dying of consumption. He was from Philadelphia, had journeyed to Florida for the recovery of his health; but the disease had overpowered him. The balmy winds of Florida sported in through the window of his room; a faithful negro sat and fanned the sick youth with a fan —in vain! Fever consumed him, and he could not have many days to live. He was handsome, with large blue eyes and fair hair. His grandmother was a Swede, and he bore her name of Rudolph. Feeble as he was, it yet seemed to give him pleasure to see his distant country-woman. He was now bent on returning to Philadelphia, and believed that he should be able to get there; but Miss Dix, always tenderly watchful over the sick, took the young man's address in Philadelphia in order to inform his relations of his danger.

We were at Pilatka delivered over by St. Matthew to the care of the little, ugly Sarah Spalding, which made me this evening almost repent of my undertaking, at least on account of my friends. Every thing was in the highest degree uncomfortable and poor, and our cabin swarmed with cockroaches. But I have scarcely ever laughed more than I did this evening. Miss Mac I. entered the cabin in a sort of merry rage against the disturbers of our peace, and pursued them with a comic fury; Mrs. W. H. too, like this splendid young girl, was so resolved to look at all our difficulties on the amusing side, that—every thing became a subject of mirth.

The moonlight nights were glorious, and we sat out till late on the little triangular piazza aft of the steamer, and two young sisters with sweet voices sang "Dearest May," and other delightful negro melodies; the scenery of the banks assumed more and more of a tropical character. We then slept a little, and I, for my part, soundly, spite of the cockroaches. Our dominant lady, however, who considered it her duty to watch over our comfort, and who was very uneasy all night, made horrible tigers out of little mice.

Early the next day we lay to land to take in fuel, and I went on shore to refresh myself after the uncomfortable night. The country seemed altogether uncultivated and wild. A little foot-path, however, wound into the woods, and along it I went, *à la bonne aventure*, on an expedition of discovery, and as I wandered alone here through the wilderness, my wings unfolded, and my whole being was full of joy. But then the morning and the wilderness too were so unspeakably beautiful! The live-oaks stood in their magnificence with their masses of hanging moss, their arcades penetrated by the beams of the ascending sun. The morning dew lay fresh and sparkling on the leaves of the amber-tree, on the innumerable small plants and bushes which bordered the path. The earth was full of fragrance. I kissed the dew from the leaves; I laid them upon my eyes, my brow, those fresh morning leaves of the young new earth; I wished to bathe anew in this Urda-fountain; I wept, half from pain, half from unspeakable gratitude and joy. Light as a bird I went onward, and sang a hymn of praise with the birds, for I had here indeed drank of the refreshing draught for which I had thirsted during a long pilgrimage in the desert; I had drank—I still drink the fullness of life from the fountains of God's abundance, and was sustained alone by His power, and by the wings which he had given me! Who was more free, who was more rich than I? What were the common joys and pleasures of life, those which I had childishly thirsted after, in comparison with those which now were mine; and not mine alone—might, would become those of many others, if the many only knew that—God gives them wings, and teaches them how to use them.

Thus rambled I onward, full of blissful emotions and thoughts, until I reached an open space in the forest, where man had been, where probably a settlement had formerly existed. But now the place was deserted. The lovely forest surrounded in silence the open, deserted spot. Neither man nor beast was to be seen. It was a profound, wild solitude. I so much enjoyed my morning ramble, that I wished Mrs. W. H. to participate it, and returned to seek for her. I found her sitting on the shore at the foot of some cypresses, but as she was not inclined for the walk, I seated myself by her, and noticed clusters of small white flowers, which, surrounded by a garland of leaves, floated on the water like little flowery islands. I did not know their name, but had before observed them as we came up the river. As they grew on the water close to the shore, I examined them, and found that the whole plant was fastened by merely one slender thread-like root to the soil at the bottom of the water. This was easily broken by wave and wind, and the plant, with its white flowers in the midst of its circlet of leaves, like the *Draba verna*, was now proceeding on its foreign travels, the sport of wave and wind.

Our state on board the "Sarah Spalding" was somewhat perturbed this morning. A couple of young and very pretty girls who are on board, without their mother or any older friend, had, by their giddiness and thoughtlessness, caused two gentlemen to pay them unbecoming attentions, which led to our dominant lady's very proper interference. The young girls received a very suitable admonition from two of the elder ladies, who, however, were strangers to them, and one of the faulty gentlemen was publicly reprimanded by the captain of the steamboat. He was an elderly man, and had such a good expression of countenance that I could scarcely believe that he deserved the rebuke which he received, and which affected him so much that he became ill.

It was with real pleasure that I heard the true and beautiful motherly reprimand which Mrs. W. H. gave the handsomest and, according to appearances, the most blamable of the young girls, and I saw with equal pleasure the manner in which the young girl received it. She stood silent before the elder lady, who had called her to her, and listened silently and respectfully; not a word, not a gesture, betrayed vexation or impatience; she seemed as if she would really let the good and wise words sink deep into her heart—as if a good seed for the future had been sown in her soul. I was the only one of the elder ladies who did not give the young girls a moral lecture. If the truth must be spoken, I had more inclination to address, as a sister, the sweet young girl who had received the motherly rebuke so beautifully. Perhaps she understood my good-will, for certain it is that during the day she seemed to wish to prove to me hers by various little agreeable services; and when we, in the evening, separated, she took leave of me in a manner which made me give her a cordial "God bless you!" Why were such young lambs sent out alone into the wilderness, among wolves and eagles, without any controlling or guiding friend? It is neither right nor well. My faith in the good and the pure in young girls is great, and has been strengthened even by this little occurrence; but people should not treat young children as if they had already cut their wise teeth.

Our journey was enchanting the whole day; we emerged from the narrow, winding river-passes into a large, clear lake, surrounded by luxuriant verdant banks. The affluence of vegetation and animal life seemed to increase with every hour; the Flora of the tropics and the atmosphere of the tropics seemed to approach; we advanced into the home of eternal summer. The wild sugar-cane, the maiden-cane grew along the banks, and showed that the soil was favorable for sugar cultivation. The temple of Nature became still richer. Beautiful, gorgeous flowers, red and blue, upon long stalks, white lilies, and gigantic water-plants, among which was the tall *Alisma plantago*, shone like stems of light beneath the dark green arches; flocks of little green parrots flew twittering over the wild sugar-cane and into the palm-groves; wild turkeys, larger than our tames ones, were seen on the shores; lovely, slender water-fowl fluttered fearlessly around us, and equally fearless, but much less lovely, thousands of alligators swam in front of and on each side of our vessel, and fish leaped and splashed about as if they were out of their senses, but whether from terror or from joy I know not. It was a grand spectacle the whole way.

We were also more comfortable on board, for our little *coterie* was now almost alone on the "Sarah Spalding," and there was added to it an enlightened and agreeable French Creole, Mr. Belle C., from Cuba, who, with a friend of his, were on a journey of discovery in Florida, to ascertain the availability of the soil for sugar cultivation. His society was a great pleasure and ornament to our little party. The captain was a polite and good-natured man, and the crew, who were all negroes, seemed to have very much their own way, but that was a good way; they were all agreeable and cheerful. The cook, a young man, who cooked very good dinners, was a really witty fellow, and said and did many very amusing things. But the pearl of the black company was our little waiter, the negro boy Sam, clever, intelligent, and willing, who attended to all our little wants, waited at table, and did every thing, and was always merry. We had no female attendant on board, which we found to be an advantage, because these ladies are, in the American steam-boats, not frequently patterns of their sex or of their race, whether they be white, black, brown, or yellow. We had, however, on the St. Matthew, a remarkable agreeable and also very handsome young negro woman as stewardess; she was a free woman, married to a free negro.

The only annoyance I experienced the whole way was the lust of shooting which possessed one of the passengers in particular, and who was not contented with shooting alligators right and left, but who even shot the lovely water-fowl, which, however, he could not make any use of, and it was distressing to me to see them fall down wounded, here and there, among the weeds. I took the liberty of speaking my mind to him about this needless shooting. He smiled, agreed with what I said, and continued to shoot. I wished him, *in petto*, bad digestion!

As regards the alligators, I could not have very much compassion on them. They are so hideous to behold, and are so terrible; for, though they do not attack grown people unless in self-defense, still they carry off the little negro children without ceremony. They swim, with the upper part of the body above the water, so that it is not difficult to hit them with a bullet in the body and the fore-legs. On this they dive down, or, if severely wounded, turn on one side; they are often seen like masses of living mud, rolling themselves on the shore to hide themselves among the water-reeds that grow there. Their number and their fearlessness here are amazing. It is said that even two years ago they were so numerous that it was difficult for boats to get along. They make a sort of grunting or bellowing sound, and it is said that early in the spring, at pairing-time, they make a horrible noise.

I spent the whole day on the piazza, dividing my attention between natural scenes and the perusal of Columbus's journal, which he kept during his first voyage of discovery among the enchanting islands of the New World. Molly of the sand-hills was troublesome all day, though she mostly kept out of the way of our dominant lady. In the afternoon we passed many wild orange-groves.

We reached Lake Monroe, the goal of our journey, last evening. Beyond this point there is neither steam-boat nor yet any carriage-road. Mr. Belle C. left us here, intending to continue his journey of discovery through the wilderness on horseback. We landed at Enterprise, a new settlement, with an hospital, in the neighborhood of Fort Melun, which also is situated near the lake, and is erected as a defense against the Indians. The house at

Enterprise stood in deep sand, and the rooms seemed so uncomfortable and the people so ill, that we determined to pass the night upon the lake in our little floating habitation, with which we are now become almost good friends. We put off, therefore, from the wretched, temporary quay at the unfortunate Enterprise, steered nearer to Fort Melun, and cast anchor at a short distance from it. At no great distance from the shore stood the home of the turtle-doves No. 3, and they were now about to leave the steamer. It was a beautiful sight, before they left, to see the husband and the wife sitting together on their baggage, quietly but joyfully awaiting the boat which would take them on shore. It was beautiful, also, to see them in the little boat, with their children and their effects, advancing toward the verdant shore, nodding a friendly farewell to us. If the daughter Molly had only been a little more charming! The last torment and the last memory of her was when she took hold of my shoulder, just as a man would take hold of a hedge-stake to help himself to climb up a bank, as her father's voice was heard calling her to the boat. No, no, amid the summer of Florida, she ought yet to bloom out like a rose, and be married to the commandant at Fort Melun, or to the owner of Enterprise.

We lost sight of the colonist family when they reached the shore, but a bright light was soon afterward seen glimmering in a house near the spot where they landed. It was now dusk, and twilight increased rapidly, although the sky was still clear. I sat for a long time on deck enjoying the quiet scene. The dark, low shore lay like a vast myrtle garland around the mirror-like lake. Fireflies glimmered here and there above it, and fishes, large and small, struck out their circles incessantly. The bird of evening, whippowil, whistled his pleasing note from the shore, and the alligators grunted in chorus. The negroes of our little vessel began to play duets upon the violin and the flageolet very sweetly, and with excellent musical skill and feeling, all of them gay and sportive melodies. They continued this toward midnight. From three places only on the shore were lights visible. The one was from an orange plantation belonging to a widow lady, the second from Enterprise, the third from the home of the colonist, the pair of turtle-doves No. 3, and this burned remarkably bright in the growing darkness of evening. The whole region was low; no single object stood forth pre-eminently. A few clouds floated, or rather lay, like small islands on the western horizon, and melted by degrees into evening glow. I endeavored in vain among them to discover some symbolic poetical shape; the highest that I could arrive at was a lady in a Quaker's bonnet, sitting on a haystack. She and all the other clouds changed themselves, finally, into a herd of little pigs, and then vanished. The lights at Enterprise, and at the widow lady's, were extinguished. Every breath of wind had laid itself to rest; every thing on the shore was dark; the light alone in the colonist's home still burned, but dimmer, and finally it also was extinguished. But I saw it burning in the house yet. Toward midnight the negroes' music was silent also, but the alligators and the whippowils continued their duet the whole night through.

I could sleep but very little, although I felt perfectly well. But the spirits of the air called me, and I was obliged to rise again and again, and go out upon our little piazza aft of the vessel, into which the doors of the saloon opened, and there, attired merely in my white night-dress, I contemplated again and again the tranquil scene. And still at early peep of dawn, when the stars grew dim, and only the morning star stood bright above the bright mirror of the lake, was continued the duet between the birds and the alligators. When the sun rose they became silent, and other birds then began to sing, and fishes to leap about; and the monsters of the river swam and swim still around us, pondering, as it seems, on our vessel and its provisions. The cruel sportsman is no longer with us, and we, in the Sarah Spalding, live at peace with the whole world, and merely, like the crocodiles, ponder about our breakfast.

Later. We were bent on having fresh fish for breakfast, and therefore our captain let a couple of negroes row out in a boat nearer to the shore, and throw out a couple of nets, which were thrown out and taken in again at once, and in ten minutes we were breakfasting on a most delicious fish, which resembled flounders in taste. No fishermen as yet dwell on these banks, and the river swarms with life.

In the afternoon we commenced our return. I shall not advance any further south in Florida, but I see here the character of the country and its scenery in this southern portion. The whole of this part of the country is low, and abounds in swampy ground and fogs, as well as in forests of fir-wood, called everglades, which are said to combine an amount of animal life which is truly astonishing. The natural historian, Agassiz, who saw these everglades for the first time this spring and summer, clasped his hands in admiration and devotion at the sight of these hitherto unknown riches of nature. Here, and yet further south toward the Mexican Gulf, the country becomes still more flat, and the vegetation is divided between the half tropical, which I had already seen, and vast forests of *Pinus Australis*, or light wood, in every-day language. Indians of the Seminole and Creek nations still live in these wild regions, and are dangerous to emigrants. In the most southern portion of Florida it is said that the cocoa-palm and the banana might be cultivated. What an empire, what a world is North America, embracing all climates, natural scenery, and productions. It is indeed an empire for all the nations of the earth.

Ortega Plantation, Florida, May 23.

Again, my child, on a bank, but not in a steam-boat (our poor little Magnolia is said to be lying there still, without any hope of getting off before the next full moon! melancholy!), but on a maize plantation belonging to relatives of the Mac I. family, where I am enjoying rest and refreshment with an amiable family, in a good and hospitable home. And very good it is to be able to rest after the fatigues and difficulties of the journey, which were not small by any means. There were indeed moments when I suspected that the first discoverers of these vast wildernesses could not have endured greater suffering than we did; baked as it were in an oven on our vessel by the burning sun, and without water fit to drink. With Mr. Belle C. disappeared all our good, ice-cold water, and we then only discovered that the polite Creole had allowed us ladies to enjoy the ice which he had brought from Cuba for his own use. There was now an end of that. Sarah Spalding had no supply of drinking water in her larder, and we were reduced to drink river-water, which was parboiled by the heat of the sun, and looked as if it were distilled from alligators. I could not drink it. But then the captain, at my request—a capital, good fellow was that captain!—landed myself and Co. in a wild orange-grove, and we there gathered whole sacks full of oranges, from which I brewed lemonade, and the whole company was refreshed thereby. That wild orange-grove was a wonderful sight. The captain and two of his men went on before with axes to cut a pathway from the shore. The wood itself was one wild tangle of thorny vegetation, fallen trees, and all kinds of bushes and plants. Within the orange-grove thousands of oranges lay on the ground, and on the slightest shaking of the trees showers of others came down upon us. Many of the oranges which grew here were as large as small infants' heads These oranges are sour, but very juicy, and of an agree able acid, and these golden chalices of the wilderness afforded us a real refreshment. The captain's store of sugar diminished rapidly, but the good, kind man said not a word, and so he had as much lemonade as he liked to drink. I had four of the huge projecting spines of the orange-tree, which are sometimes two ells long, hewn off for sticks for some gentlemen friends at home (brother-in-law Q. and Fabian W. are of the elect). These sticks are very handsome when they are stained; they are very strong, and greatly valued by the American gentlemen. As memories of the orange-grove, we took away with us, besides oranges and sticks, a multitude of small insects of the species here called *tick*, and with which we became personally acquainted at home, as small, ugly, flat creatures, which eat into the skin. I was particularly infested by these inhabitants of the orange-grove, and labored the whole day in getting rid of them. Among the adventures of our return was the taking fire of our sun-scorched vessel in one of the lakes, which gave our dominant lady a great deal to do with her tongue. She made the quarter of an ell long flames two ells long, and if it had not been for her there would have been an end to us all! The captain and his men, in the mean time, extinguished the fire so quickly and silently, that I did not know of the danger until it was over.

We suffered through the night from cockroaches and musquitoes, by day from the hot sun and suffocating fumes from the engine fire. Amid all these bitter moments came moments when the cool breezes enabled us to enjoy once more the invariably beautiful and fantastic scenery, and the intercourse and conversation of friends.

One afternoon we saw a large crane-roost, as it is called, that is, a republic of white cranes. It was upon an island, on which grew tall, shadowy trees. On the approach of the steamer, the republic rose into the air like a large cloud, then immediately after settled down again, and the island looked as if it were covered with snow.

We called, on our return, at two cities, Jacksonville and St. Mary's. Jacksonville is an increasing city, its situation being very favorable for trade; but it lies amid sand, and was a horribly hot, disagreeable place. We slept there one night, at a hotel which resembled a noisy wooden barrack. St. Mary's, which is some years older, is not so well situated for trade, and is on the decrease; it, however, was more agreeable than Jacksonville, from the beautiful, shady rows of trees in its streets. Wandering here, I saw a well-dressed negro, about fifty years old, who was tattooed like the Luccomées whom I had seen at Cuba. I addressed him, saying,

"You have come hither from Africa?" He replied, Yes; that he had been smuggled hither from Cuba many years ago. He was now overseer on a plantation, and was very well off. He was a Christian, and seemed pleased to be so. He spoke very sensibly and cheerfully, and had a good, open countenance.

"You do not wish to return to Africa?" said I.

"Oh yes, Missis; oh yes, that I do!" replied he; "there I should be still better off."

"But people often kill one another there," remonstrated I.

"Oh, but nobody troubles themselves about that. And there are a great many good people who live there at peace."

"But look here, my friend," said Colonel Mac I., who is a strong Calvinist; "if you had remained in Africa, you would not have become a Christian as you now are, and then the devil, in the end, would have had you!"

The negro laughed, looked down, shook his head, and twisted round his cap which he had in his hand, and at length exclaimed, again looking up with an expression of humor and inventive acuteness,

"Now, Massa, look'ee here! The Gospel is now being preached over the whole of Africa, and if I had remained there, what was to hinder me from being one who heard it as well there as here?"

To this there was no reply to be made, and the sensible, good-tempered negro had the last word.

One of our pleasant incidents was that our dominant lady left us by the way, to domineer, I should imagine, in some boarding-house of one of the cities in this part of Florida; and the atmosphere became much less oppressive in our little community in consequence. Miss Dix left us also to go to St. Augustine, the most southern city of the United States, the prisons and benevolent institutions of which place she wished to visit. Wherever she goes, she endeavors to do good to the sick, the neglected, or the criminal, and to scatter the seed of spiritual culture wherever she is able. She scatters about her, like morning dew, as she goes on her way, little miniature books called "Dewdrops," containing religious proverbs, and numbers of small tracts, with pretty wood-cuts and ditto stories. Molly of the sand-hills ought to derive nourishment from this manna which would suffice to make her a thinking and amiable woman.

St. Augustine was founded by the Spaniards, and is the oldest city in North America; the city still preserves the character and style of building which prove its origin, but of late years it has very much fallen into decay, and since the destruction by frost of the orange plantations, which constituted the principal branch of trade in the city, it has become still more deserted. It is now visited generally by invalids, who during the winter months come hither to breathe its pleasant atmosphere and invigorating sea-breezes. St. Augustine lies somewhat to the south of New Orleans, but has a far more salubrious climate.

It was not until the year 1819 that Florida passed from the dominion of the Spaniards to that of the United States, and it became united to these, as an independent state, in the year 1845, but is said not yet to contain a greater population than about 80,000 whites. The Indians and the insalubrity of the swampy soil have retarded, and still retard, the cultivation of the country. But in the northwestern portion of the state the land lies higher, and is more cultivated, and has two increasing cities; the political capital is Tallahassee, with beautiful plantations, villas, gardens, and, as I have been informed, pleasant domestic and social life amid that lovely summer-warm scenery. And where the Anglo-American comes, there always come at the same time happy domestic life, friendly social intercourse, and every comfort of life.

All these we enjoy also in this kind home, although joy is not properly at home here. The eldest daughter of the family, a beautiful, young, newly-married lady in the bloom of her life and her maternal joy, died lately in giving birth to her second child, and the grief of this weighs heavily on the mind of her mother. A splendid little grandson, very like his grandmother, and full of life, can not console her; and her husband and the other children participate in her sorrow. The whole family has an expression of so much good-heartedness and gentleness, that one sees plain enough that the slaves can not suffer. But the drought is fearful; the maize plants on this plantation are withered in the sand, of which this plantation has more than its ordinary share; and the harvest of this year wears a mournful appearance. It is now more than four months since I have seen a cloudy day. Even in this beautiful Florida, life is heavy and dry as regards the poor children of earth.

But when in the mornings early I wake and feel the balmy wind of Florida play through the white curtains round my bed, and hear the nightingale of America pouring forth, in its many tongues, its melodious inspirations in the trees before my window, then do I exalt the home of summer, and wonder not that Ferdinand de Soto and his young men were enchanted by it, and it seems to me almost unnatural that life here can be heavy or dark.

We remain here a couple of days in expectation of a good steam-boat which will take us to Mr. C.'s plantation at Darien, whence we return to Savannah.

This plantation lies in a sandy tract, and the sand considerably encroaches upon the charms of nature and country life. There is here, however, a foot-path by the river which follows a wild and woody shore, than which nothing more picturesque can be conceived, in particular the masses of trees and wild boscage which rise like a lofty wall between the shore and the sloping cultivated land. Splendid magnolias, covered with white flowers, lift aloft among these their dark, shady crowns. The magnolia is the most magnificent tree of the Southern States. I wander here alone in the afternoons, wondering sometimes whether I shall hear, from the dense thickets, the warning signal of the rattlesnake—for this serpent gives warning before he makes an attack or approaches near. But, although rattlesnakes are numerous in Florida, I have not yet happened either to see or to hear a living one. I however saw this afternoon one which the negroes had just killed on the plantation and brought to show the family. It might be about three yards long, and as thick as my arm. The head was much injured by the blows it had received, and the terrible poison-fangs were revealed. I have had the rattle, with its fourteen joints, given to me to take home with me to Sweden. A year ago a negro on the plantation was bitten on the leg by a rattlesnake; great endeavors were made to save the limb from amputation, but in vain; it was, in the end, obliged to be taken off, to put an end to the great and increasing suffering.

A pretty little village on the plantation is the home of the black nurse of the gentleman of the house, and there she rests from her labors, under circumstances which testify the tenderest care. She has her own neat little house, on a terrace by the river, and within it every convenience that an old person can desire; a comfortable rocking-chair is even among these, and children and children's children, whom she has faithfully nursed, visit her with love and presents. She has had many children of her own, but she acknowledged that the white children were dearest to her; and this affection of the black nurses, or foster-mothers, to the children of the whites is a well-known fact. Another fact also, which is often witnessed in the slave states, is the tender care which is bestowed upon these faithful black foster-mothers in their old age by the family, that is to say, when the families are able.

St. Simon's Island, May 27th.

In front of my window runs, broad and clear, the western arm of the Altamaha River, and beside it sits the undersigned upon an island on the coast of Georgia, between the river and the Atlantic Ocean. I am now at the house of Mr. J. C., a planter, in the midst of gardens and olive-groves, where the family seeks for its summer pleasure and the salubrious air of the sea when fevers begin to ravage the large plantation at Darien, the principal residence of the family.

Mr. C. is one of the greatest planters in the south of the United States, and owns about two thousand negro slaves, whom he employs on his rice and cotton plantations. He had been mentioned to me as a reformer, who had introduced trial by jury among his slaves, with many other educational institutions, to prepare them for a future life of liberty. And this created in me a desire to become acquainted with him and his plantations. But I did not find him a reformer, merely a disciplinarian, with great practical tact, and also some benevolence in the treatment of the negroes. In other respects I found him to be a true representative of the gentlemen of the Southern States—a very polite man, possessing as much knowledge as an encyclopedia, and interesting to me in a high degree through the wealth and fascination of his conversation. He is distinguished for his knowledge of natural history; he has a beautiful collection of the natural productions of America, and the lecture which I heard him read this morning, in the midst of these, on the geology and the rock formation of America, has given me a clearer knowledge of the geological structure of this portion of the world than I ever possessed before.

Mr. C. has an unusual faculty for systematization, and for demonstrating the characteristic points of a subject. A conversation with him on any subject can not fail of being interesting, even if one differs from him in opinion.

But as Mr. C., on the question of slavery, unites with the good party in the South, who regard the colonization of Africa by the liberated negro slaves as the final result and object of the institution of slavery, it was any thing but difficult for me to converse with him on this subject, and that which naturally belongs to it. Neither could I do other than agree with him in the views he expressed regarding the peculiar faculties of the negro race and their future destiny, because they accorded with my own observations. Among those views of his which I must adopt, I recall the following:

The tropical races can not attain to the development and intelligence of the native whites in the temperate zones. They are deficient in the power of abstract thought, of systematization, of pursuing strict laws of reason, and of uniting themselves on a basis of this kind. The tropical races typify the highest state of the life of feeling. Natural life imprisons them; released from this by religion, they would typify animal and vegetable life in their transfiguration. (N.B.—This idea, I believe, was presented to Mr. C. from my magazine.) They are receptive of culture, and may, during their subjection to a more developed race, develop a very respectable capacity for thought and artistic ability. They may arrive at a respectable degree of *semi-civilization*, interesting by the peculiar forms which it would assume from the peculiarity of the people themselves.

Mr. C. regards slavery in America as a school for the children of Africa, in which they may be educated for self-government on the soil of Africa. He was inclined to look at the institution of slavery as a benefit to them. And that it might be converted into a benefit is certain. But that it is the only means of imparting to Africa the blessings of Christianity and civilization may be safely denied, and I had here the pleasure of letting the wise negro from Florida preach to the wise white man.

In urbanity and grace of conversation Mr. C. reminds me of Waldo Emerson; but, in a general way, the Southern gentleman has too small a development of the organ of ideality, even as in the gentleman of the North it is too large. Mr. C. corroborated the facility with which the negroes acquire a knowledge of handcraft trades, and their dexterity as artisans. They have in Georgia begun to employ them advantageously in manufactures. I now remember having visited, last year, a cotton factory near Augusta, in which colored work-people were employed. It was not a sight which caused me pleasure, because I could not believe that the blacks would voluntarily choose this occupation, with its noise, difficulty, and dusty, unwholesome atmosphere—they who had been accustomed to the labor of the open fields.

I asked some women who were employed in winding how they liked it. Two of them replied that they liked it very well—as well as any other work. An elderly woman, however, with a good countenance, said, with an expression of deep dejection and weariness, No, she did not like this work; she would rather work out in the fields. I did not wonder at this, for the place was not like one of the Lowell Mills.

The home here is full of gay, youthful countenances, six boys and two girls, the youngest of which is the image and delight of her father; and Mrs. C. is a youthful, pretty, and happy mother of this handsome flock of children.

Not far from the house is a troop of little black children, seventy or eighty in number, whom I visited this evening, and who wanted mothers. A couple of witch-like negro women, with rods in their hands, governed the troop by fear and terror. I had been told that they also taught the children to pray. I gathered a little flock around me, and slowly repeated to them the Lord's Prayer, bidding them read the words after me. The children grinned, laughed, showed their white teeth, and evinced very plainly that none of them knew what that wonderful prayer meant, nor that they had a Father in heaven.

The children were well fed. They were kept here, separated from their parents, on account of fever raging on the plantations where they worked.

If I have not found here the reformer whom I expected, I have heard of two such planters, the one in Florida, the other in Georgia, who have established schools for the children of their negro slaves, with the intention of preparing them for good and free human beings. One of these gentlemen, Mr. N., is said to have the greatest hopes of the susceptibility for cultivation in the negro children, nay, even of its being greater than in the children of the whites.

Why have I not before heard of these Christian labors? I would have made every possible effort to have witnessed them, to have seen them with my own eyes. Such plantations in the slave states may be regarded as holy spots, to which pilgrimages would be made by those who seek for the soul's elevation, and for new power to hope and to believe. What, indeed, have I been so zealously seeking for, and inquiring after, in these Southern States, but for such places!

It is not natural to me to look out for subjects of blame. I do not recognize such excepting when they force themselves upon me. I do not avoid seeing darkness, but I seek for the light which can illumine the darkness, in all, and with all. In the darkness of slavery I have sought for the moment of freedom with faith and hope in the genius of America. It is no fault of mine that I have found the darkness so great, and the work of light as yet so feeble in the slave states.

Charleston, June 3d.

Again here in the good home of my good Mrs. W. H., a home which is at the same time one of the most peaceful and the most beautiful which I have found in the United States. It is an excellent thing to rest here a little while after the vagaries of the last three weeks, some of the fatigues of which were by no means small. But thus I have seen Florida, and have a better understanding of the nature and extent of that realm, that great home which is being prepared, in North America, for people of the whole world. From the home of eternal summer I now journey up toward the home of winter, the White Mountains, in the most northern states of New England, and thence home, because I shall then have seen all that I desire to see on this side the ocean.

Among the memorable events of the latter part of our journey, I must not omit our morning journey in large boats of hollowed cypress-trees from Ortega plantation to Jacksonville, where we took the steamer. The morning was glorious, and the negroes rowed vigorously and cheerfully. The gentlemen of the amiable family at Ortega accompanied us on board. They were of the good and the quiet of the land.

I parted from Mr. C. with sincere gratitude for his interesting society, and with a decided liking for one of the young sons of the plantation, whose broad forehead revealed a thoughtful, unprejudiced, and humorous turn of mind.

The place at which we were to take the steamer to Savannah was where the early city of Frederica had been founded by Oglethorpe, the first cultivator of Georgia. The situation appears to have been excellent, but of the city there now remains only two ruins, garlanded by green trees and bushes.

We arrived here in good time, but the steamer did not make its appearance for several hours. In the mean time it went on with us in a fairy tale. A most charming little old lady, just like a good little fairy, received us into her house, a regular little fairy palace for beauty, comfort, and attractiveness. Every thing was bright, and seemed to be alive from sheer cleanliness and care. The little lady—old in years, but full of youthfulness of mind, and with a pair of clear, lively blue eyes—gave me, as she made a playful demonstration round my head, a knock on my forehead, which might have cracked the skull if it had been less thick. She spread a table for us, brilliant with white linen, and china, and silver, and entertained us with tea and bread and butter, potatoes at my desire, eggs, and other good things. No, it would not have been possible for a meal spread by fairy hands to have been more delicate or more finely flavored. The clever and cheerful little lady and I drank together a toast, "Friendship and potatoes," as the chief indispensables of earthly happiness. After this we proceeded to Savannah.

I saw in Savannah, besides good old friends—always good and kind—a Seaman's Home, under the management of the ladies of the city. It was a simple, but well-ordered and successful institution, where the sailors, while in port at Savannah, may obtain at the lowest possible charges the best possible comforts in a large common hall, both food for the body and food for the soul—this latter consisting of good books and small tracts, containing treatises and narratives of a religious tendency. The lively, agreeable lady who conducted me thither—Mrs. B., the daughter of Judge Berrian—is one of the directresses, and, although a happy wife as well as mother of six boys and one girl, she finds time and heart to look after this home for the sons of Neptune, otherwise left to winds and waves more dangerous to them in the city than those out at sea. Wife, mother, citizen, are the titles of the woman of the New World.

In the evening at the hotel, Pulaski House, where I took up my quarters during the short time of my stay, that I might not be separated from Mrs. W. H., I made the acquaintance of a young lady, a planter, now come to the city with a family of seven boys, all in succession, with but one, or, at the most, two years between them. Both mother and children were full of the fresh spirit of life, the gay young mother's only anxiety being to keep the merry lads from running about in the city, as they were accustomed to do in the country. They were going to be placed in a school here.

Families in North America are very large, although not so large as in England. The largest family I heard spoken of here was twelve children by one father and mother, but this was considered unusual; seven seems to be, in a general way, the largest number of children in a family. Nor is it unusual to meet with married pairs without children at all.

But I must now tell you something about South Carolina, because South Carolina is resolved at this moment to be a state for itself, apart from the other states. It is, in fact, extremely incensed by the injustice which it considers that the Southern States suffered in the last Congress from the compromise between the free and the slave states on the Californian question; and a large Convention of the wise men of the state has just been held at Charleston, at which, after having eaten and drunk together, they with great enthusiasm took the heroic resolution of seceding from the Union, and assuming a hostile attitude against its Northern States. The Palmetto State seems to have calculated on meeting with co-operation from the other Southern States; but it appears that she is mistaken in this respect. Georgia, Alabama, and Louisiana, and several others, have openly declared themselves for the Union, and I have read in the Florida papers keen disapprobation of the proceedings of the Palmetto State. Mississippi is now the only one which seems to stand undetermined whether or not it shall declare itself for the Union, or against it and for South Carolina.

In the mean time, it seems as if South Carolina itself, like the great Emperor Philip of ancient memory, is of a different state of mind during the feast and after the feast, and that the good brothers who ate and drank together at Charleston, and there declared themselves for war, were, notwithstanding, much less inclined for hostilities when they had left Charleston and found themselves each one sitting quietly at home. Nor are there wanting wise and good citizens who openly declare themselves opposed to the heroic declarations of the great Convention, over which people now make themselves merry. In one of the newspapers of the city I read to-day the following quotation from a speech which is said to have been made by one of the warlike members of the great Convention:

"Yes, gentlemen, I protest that, when war breaks out, I shall be one of the first to run across my cotton field, exclaiming, like General Washington at the battle of Waterloo, 'A horse! a horse! my kingdom for a horse!'"

From the observations which I have heard made, and which I have read in the newspapers on this Convention and its consequences, one sees how vigorous and discreet is public opinion, and that it merely requires time.

And probably this declaration of secession on the part of South Carolina will merely be a proof of the internal strength of the Union to hold together, spite of the displeasure of individuals.

Mr. Poinsett's letter to the Convention (to which he was summoned, but could not attend) is spoken highly of, as being distinguished in a high degree for its nobility and statesmanlike wisdom. It counsels strongly to maintain the Union, and proves that South Carolina is wrong in her assertions.

I have received, also, a private letter from the noble old statesman, which has pleased me by the invitation which it contained for me again to visit him at his house, "that we might talk over together the present condition and future prospects of the United States." I should very much like such a conversation with him, but I have not the time to go as far as his hermitage.

Among the topics of conversation of the day is a scandalous paper war, which is being carried on in the New York newspapers between private individuals. One of the principal literary men of the city is involved in the contest, which has reference to the good name and fame of two respectable ladies. The warfare is carried on with great bitterness and unbridled license, and the good and thinking portion of the public look on with annoyance and disgust, and also censure severely that inclination for coarse personality which is one of the greatest sins of the American newspaper press. Generally, however, even this spares women, who always find powerful defenders. A man who in conversation or through the press should allow himself to attack a woman, or to express himself coarsely against her, would be condemned by the better portion of the people as a man of bad education and bad taste. A silent reprobation would exclude him from the better class of society. Thus noble and chivalric is the spirit of this country.

I shall now remain quietly here for about a week, partly because I find myself so comfortable here, and that I require rest, and partly to have my toilet refitted, under the advice and management of my good Mrs. W. H. I think more on this subject here than I did at home, because I must here appear as a Swede. I wish to do so with honor to my country, although with all becoming modesty. My costume, therefore, is always black silk, with a mantilla or light jacket, also of silk, trimmed with lace. You must fancy me when walking out in a white silk bonnet and veil, and black satin cloak or dress. I endeavor to combine gravity with a certain degree of elegance.

From this place I propose proceeding through the highlands of North Carolina and Georgia, the remarkable scenery of which I wish to become acquainted with, into the State of Tennessee, by the Tennessee River, and so into Virginia, the Old Dominion, where I think of remaining some time, to make myself familiar both with the people and the scenery. It is now terribly hot here, and one is as if in a constant bath. I ought to write many letters, and read various things; but, instead of doing so, I spend long hours in doing nothing but sitting in my rocking-chair and rocking to and fro.

"It is all very well as yet," says Mrs. W. H.; "but when this heat shall have continued four or five months, and seems as if it never would come to an end, then—"

No wonder that so many young ladies here seem pale and languishing.

Vegetation is in its highest glory, and the woods are splendidly in flower. The Indian-pride-tree, the French-tree, the tulip-tree, the magnolia, shoot forth their splendid fragrant flowers. In the gardens roses and orange-blossom fill the air with perfume; the fruit of the nectarine is set, and the fig-tree bears ripe fruit. People enjoy themselves, but with a languid animation. The evenings are the most beautiful part of the day, and my greatest enjoyment is to walk slowly backward and forward on the upper piazza, shaded by the trellised roses, and fanned by breezes from the river.

June 11*th*. In the morning I shall leave this good home and this amiable family forever. It is painful to me to say so, but so it is. I have spent delightful hours and days this time also with them and with some other friends in Charleston. I have again infinitely enjoyed the society of Mrs. H., wandering with her in the myrtle-groves at Belmont for one whole beautiful day, and in conversation on subjects which deepen and expand life at the same time. Mrs. H. has more imagination than I have, and her poetical feeling, united to an intellect of no ordinary grasp, which, taking its stand on the earth, comprehends the universal relationship of all things, and which, at the same time, derives its aliment from a religious centre based on Christianity, makes my intercouse with her highly enlivening and beneficial.

I have received from many kind friends renewed proofs of their steadfast warm-heartedness, and from the noble Unitarian minister, Mr. Gilman, a blessing which I have placed within my heart. When I was one day making a sketch of his pure, ascetic countenance, I asked him, "At what age have you felt yourself most happy ?"

"Between fifty and sixty," replied he.

I heard his reply with joy, because I am approaching that age, and I have hope in its tranquillizing power.

The young missionary, Miles, whose name and book you may remember as mentioned in my letter from this place last year, has had the pleasure of receiving some lines from the noble Neander in Berlin, containing these words: "The aged Neander extends his hand across the ocean, in brotherly union, to the young missionary in South Carolina, and in token of cordial acknowledgment." Such tokens are joyful signs of the times!

Among the remarkable things which I have seen of late, I must mention the Slaves' Fair last Saturday evening, that is to say, when the slaves resident on the plantations come to Charleston with their wares and small manufactured goods, woven baskets, mats, etc., and set them out publicly, cry them aloud, and sell them: the scene is lively, but it lasts only an evening; a visit which I made to two negro schools; the large, newly-laid-out cemetery of Charleston, the Magnolia, and a night on Sullivan's Island.

One of these negro schools was for the children of free negroes. It was kept by a white master, and with open doors. I saw here an assembly of colored children, of all shades between raven-black and almost perfect white. The school-books, which I desired to see, were the same as those in use in the American schools for the children of the whites.

This school is a good institution, but evidently a dangerous element in the slave states, unless it is kept in harmony by the instruction of the slaves, and the views which this will open to them.

I had also heard speak of secret schools for the children of slaves, but had extreme difficulty in discovering such an one, and when I had discovered one, to gain admittance into it, so great was the dread of the law's severity, which forbids, under a heavy punishment, the instruction of a slave in reading and writing. And when I did gain admittance into this secret chamber, I found in a wretched dark hole only half a dozen poor children, some with an aspect that testified the greatest stupidity and mere animal life. They had evidently been brought hither as an attempt to humanize them.

Magnolia Cemetery is a new, noble, and magnificent burial-place, and an honor to Charleston. It is situated by the sea, the pure, refreshing breezes of which blow over it with invigorating life. Three sides have a background of magnolia and cedar forest, and on the fourth lies the blue sea. The ground is flat, but not swampy, and canals have been dug to bring in the river and sea-water, so as to form small islands and promontories within the vast burial-ground. Beautiful groups of Southern trees stand here and there. The manner in which the people of America provide resting-places for their dead foretells for them a long life on earth.

I saw in this new burial-place only two monuments, but they had each of them so peculiar and so dissimilar a history that I must relate them to you in few words.

The one marks the grave of a young girl. She was her mother's only child. It one day happened that she touched her eye with her hand after having just gathered the poisonous flower called here Nightshade (*Solanun nigrum*), which has a pretty, pale yellow flower, in form like that of our potato blossom, and the eye became thereby poisoned. It became enlarged and deformed; and this enlargement, and the suffering which attended it, undermined the young girl's life. She withered away, but beautifully and piously. Her sufferings and her patience made her an object of general love. She and her mother converted the path to the grave, by the strength of religion, into a pathway of light; the *Nightshade* had no power over them. After two years of suffering, she died —if a good angel can die; and her grave is surrounded by memories of light.

The second belongs to the grave of a young man. He was an officer in the American army during the war in Texas or Mexico, I do not exactly remember which. One day, as he sat at the table with a comrade, he received an order to go to the commanding officer. In youthful insolence or pride, he said, "The deuce take me if I go!" or something of that kind. Nevertheless, he went. The thoughtless expression, which had been overheard, was reported to the superior officer, who commanded that, as a punishment, and for example's sake, he should be gagged for one or more days, I know not which. When the sentence was announced to the young man, he said, "From this time I will never eat any thing more. Nobody shall ever reproach me with having been gagged!"

And he refused to take food. The superior officer, informed of his words and his conduct on arrest, repented of his barbarous and hasty command, and went himself to the young man to induce him to give up his resolve. But in vain. The young, determined soldier died of a wounded heart, and of hunger, within a week, to the inexpressibly bitter grief of his family, who were withheld from prosecuting at law the inconsiderate commander merely by the mother of the dead, to whom the family of the other were nearly related, and by her saying, with truth,

"Revenge can not restore to me my son!"

Great sufferings have already consecrated Magnolia Cemetery as a resting-place.

Mrs. W. H. and myself made the journey to Sullivan's Island alone. It was pleasant to me to make this last excursion in South Carolina alone with her, and with her for the last time to feel the sea-breezes in the palmetto and myrtle groves of the island. A steam-boat conveyed us thither, and here we took a carriage to drive along the sands. Our driver was a Yankee of fifteen, good-natured and lively, who had come from Boston to Charleston to seek his fortune. The boy had gone to a common school, and was remarkably clever in his remarks and replies. We confided ourselves to his guidance, and, deeply engrossed in conversation, it was not until after half an hour's time that we observed that, instead of driving us on the firm sands, he was driving us quite into the water, and going in deeper and deeper. We called to the boy; he seemed to ponder about it, but said we should soon be right, and thus we drove on again for a while. The water, however, by this time was above half way up the wheels, and we were among deep holes; it was clear that we were not in the right road; and when we again spoke to our young driver, it appeared that, instead of driving on the usual and southern side of the island, he had driven on the northern shore, because he wished to ascertain whether it was possible to drive also on that side. He had chosen this occasion for the experiment.

Mrs. W. H. laughed so heartily at the idea of the lad's scheme of trying an experiment with us which might have cost us our lives, that her anger lost its power. The boy was a little frightened, but smiled nevertheless, and would willingly have continued his experiment to the end; but this we utterly forbade, as we none of us knew what ground we were upon, and each fresh step might be our last. We alighted, therefore, among the bushes of the shore, and left the boy to find his way across the island with the carriage and horses in the best way he was able.

We found our way through bushes and thickets, Mrs. W. H. laughing the whole way with incomparable good temper at the Yankee boy's characteristic scheme. After an hour's wandering, forcing our way through thick brushwood, and wading through sand, we found a foot-path and traces of a fence. From this point we looked around us, and saw, to our surprise, a carriage and horses standing on the top of the highest sand-hill in this part of the island. Was it? Yes, certainly it was our equipage, which had ascended this hill from the water, and there on the box sat quite tranquilly the Yankee boy, looking around him, and spying out the geography of the island.

When, in the course of about two hours, we had at length piloted ourselves to the southern side of the island, and down to the fortress, there we found our Yankee boy and his carriage waiting for us as tranquil and good-tempered as if every thing had gone on in the best manner possible.

We did not think that it had, and still less so when we saw, before we could reach the shore, the last steam-boat leave the island for the city. We should be obliged to remain over night in the island. But we found a good hotel, and we had the sea and the beautiful moonlight, and thus that night on Sullivan's Island, a great portion of which was spent awake, remains as one of the delightfully memorable nights which I spent beneath the heaven of South Carolina.

To-day, as we were driving out of the city in a carriage, I saw a man taking along a young negro lad, with his hands tied with a rope. The man was on horseback, and the lad, he might be about fourteen or fifteen, walked behind the horse. He had probably attempted to run away, and was now brought in this manner to the city to be flogged. The people looked with indifference, as on a very common sight. Beautiful manners!

On one of my walks in the city with my good Mrs. W. H., we saw an old, well-dressed negro sitting on a stone, bleeding at the nose. She stopped.

"Are you bleeding, daddy?" asked she.

"Yes, Missis, yes," replied he, very civilly; "it will not stop."

"You shall have my keys, daddy, to lay on your neck, and then it will stop," said Mrs. W. H., taking out her bunch of keys, and placing it on the neck of black daddy, and waiting a while until it had produced the desired effect. Daddy thanked her heartily, but not as if for any unusual mark of kindness. Neither is such behavior or such kindness shown by the whites to the blacks unusual either in the slave states. But the institution of slavery causes the good and the bad master to be placed under the ban of one hatred; and yet they are as unlike as day and night.

My proposed journey through the northern parts of Georgia and Tennessee, like that of last year, must be wholly given up. The heat is oppressive; Tennessee River is dried up, so that it is not navigable for a steamer; and there is no other mode of conveyance for me, while the fatigue of diligences upon those wretched roads would be greater than I could support. I shall, therefore, also this time confide myself to the sea, but merely for four-and-twenty hours, land in North Carolina, and proceed through that state to Virginia. I shall probably take the same steamer northward as Mr. and Mrs. H.

I am perfectly well, my little heart, and my friends in Savannah and Charleston flatter me with the assurance that I am grown younger in appearance—that I am wonderfully improved, and ascribe the change to the American climate (the worst climate under the sun for the renovating process). But I know better, and commend Cuba, and the good homes both here and there, before every thing else. Blessings be upon them! But I have nevertheless become old in exterior, that I see and feel, and must prepare you for. The exertion of traveling, and the climate of the West, have left visible traces on me. I might tell you of something, however, which is renewed in me, but I dare not now.

LETTER XXXIX.

Richmond, June 16th.

Good-morning, my beloved child, on this beautiful morning in the chief city of Virginia. I have just returned from a ramble in the park round the capital, from which I have seen the beautiful River St. James, in the Indian tongue Powkaton, with its foaming fall, and its calm water, bright as silver, winding on their way through verdant plains, and hills far, far away into the country. A glorious view from this magnificent capital. I wished that the intellectual and moral view from the States' seat of government corresponded with it. But Virginia is a slave state, and its views open, and its river of life flows, as in all other slave states, for one half of its population only. We are reminded of this the moment we reach the gate of the park of the capital, for on the pillars of the gate is placed the announcement in large letters, declaring that any slave who ventures within these gates shall be liable to a punishment of thirty-nine lashes! One can not enjoy or admire any thing in the slave states without having one's pleasure disturbed by these lashes!

But in a material respect, how well watered is North America! Throughout all its states flow these beautiful navigable rivers, which, like great arteries, receive into themselves innumerable lesser streams and brooks, and convey to all places the life and the fruits of civilization! I can not contemplate these beautiful rivers without the hope that they will prepare the way for the noblest of all.

I parted from my kind Mrs. W. H., who had become as dear to me as a sister, and from her family, with a pang which I endeavored to stifle, because parting is inevitable.

It was in the afternoon of the 12th of June that I left Charleston and South Carolina, where I had enjoyed so much kindness. The sea was rough, and the vessel so crowded with passengers that I regretted in silence that my wish to be with Mrs. H. had caused me to select this vessel, and not rather to have delayed my journey a couple of days longer. I feared now to incommode others, and to be incommoded myself. But Mrs. H. became my comfort and my help. As she was acquainted with the negro woman who waited in the ladies' saloon, she induced the old woman to make us up two beds on the soft sofas near the window, because all the cabins in the vessel were occupied, and by this means we escaped the heat of the cabins, and enjoyed during the night fresh air from the saloon window.

As night approached, the sea became rougher, and the clouds assumed a more stormy aspect; the air was op pressively hot, the passage was one of danger, and the vessel had not the best reputation.

But I consoled myself with thinking, "when the moon rises!" for I have an inborn faith in the moon as my friend. She attracted my glance to her when I was but a child, and before I could say any other word, before I could say father or mother, I said "Moon!" My first verses were dedicated to the Moon. They were poor enough; but the celestial presence which I saluted as the consoler of the fortunate and the unfortunate, has been, in her turn, equally propitious to me, and never yet, during my sea voyages, has she failed with her rising to dissipate the clouds, and to calm the restless winds and waves. I have always, therefore, endeavored to arrange my voyages that they should be during moonlight nights, and I had accordingly so arranged my present voyage, for the pleasure of which I had to thank both Mrs. H. and the moon. Neither of them deceived me.

Mrs. H. was somewhat sea-sick, but was still, amid the throng of the steam-boat, the same amiable, perfect lady as in the drawing-room and the myrtle-groves of Belmont; and the moon was, as soon as she arose on the sea, the same amiable planet as she had formerly shown herself to me. The clouds, it is true, did not vanish, but they stood, as it were, still, or withdrew in picturesque groups. The waves, it is true, still heaved, but not tempestuously; it lightened incessantly and splendidly amid the clouds, but there was no thunder. It was as if the severe countenance of the moon had stayed the tumult of the elements. I gazed at the moon, and enjoyed that grand, excited, but not stormy life in the heavens and on the sea amid the shadows of night.

The following day we went on shore, and proceeded by rail-road through North Carolina, which seemed to be one continued stretch of pine wood, with some open spaces for the cultivation of cotton and maize, a flat, uniform, and poor country, except as regards the sap of the pine forests, whence the state derives its popular name, "Old Tar and Turpentine." The northwestern portions of the state are hilly, and are possessed of much natural beauty. Mrs. H. told me that "Old Tar and Turpentine" was not renowned for any thing excepting for its politeness and simple manners. When other states in the Union refused to pay the debt to England which they had agreed to pay together (some loan affair, which was unsuccessful), "Old Tar and Turpentine" set them an example of punctuality and integrity, and paid its quota of the debt without any ado. North Carolina has been, although a slave state, one of the principal abodes of the Quaker sect in America, and has always been celebrated for its patriarchal life and manners.

Two places at which we stopped by the way were in the pine forest, and this was, as is usual in the Southern States, rich in many varieties of trees. I counted above fourteen in one of the forest woods.

Mrs. H. was to me on this journey, as she always is, a fountain of refreshment and delight. I have never met with any one, either man or woman, who possessed in so high a degree the power of calling others out in conversation. We accompany each other like two birds flying up and down, between heaven and earth, from star to star, from land to land, from tree to tree, from flower to flower. I learn much from her. She spends with her husband, the esteemed naturalist, Holbrook, her sister, Miss L., and her handsome old mother, a beautiful life, rich in domestic affection.

Toward the evening of this day we reached the little village of Weldon, on the boundaries between North Carolina and Virginia, and where the wild, foaming River Roanoke rolls along its waves, dividing the two states.

I went down to the falls in the evening twilight, and saw them foaming and rushing along. The fire-flies danced glimmering under the gloomy arch of the trees. Nature was here romantic, wild, and beautiful, and the whole district was as desolate and silent as if no human beings were to be found there.

We passed a comfortable night at the hotel, and although I was suffering from headache, yet, to my joy, I was well enough to proceed on my journey the next day by a slow accommodation rail-way train, which conveyed us very easily and excellently through the fields of Virginia to Richmond, the capital of the state, and which contains thirty thousand inhabitants, half of whom are blacks. Its situation is romantic, among hills and valleys, on the banks of the River St. James. And there am I now. I was obliged to take leave of my traveling companions last evening, as they continued their journey early this morning to Saratoga, whither they are going for the benefit of the water and the baths. Later in the summer I also intend to go thither myself, not to drink the medicinal waters, but to witness that scene of American social life which I am informed presents there its worst side—fashionable immorality and want of principle in their gala dress.

Later. Usch! such a sermon! Just the sermon, if such were the only means of divine knowledge, to make people either atheists or numskulls. It made me impatient and angry. The young preacher emptied with great self-complacency the vials of wrath, full of threatenings and penal judgments, into the contents of his Calvinistic sermon of wrath against the sinners who—were nowhere in the church, if I could judge from appearance. The church was thinly attended, and many people slept. A couple of very well fed and well dressed elderly gentlemen, who sat on a bench before me, took out their watches every now and then to see how the time went on, if it were near dinner-time, I presume; they were apparently not thinking about the last judgment, although the young preacher was thundering about it, and its advance upon a godless generation. True it is that the young preacher of condemnation dealt so much with abstract ideas and barren phraseology, that none of his descriptions of sin seemed to touch the heads of the people who sat on the benches. But I have heard other preachers besides this one who preach to an audience which evidently is not within the church.

I shall remain here for two days, and then pay a visit to our countryman, Professor Sheele de Vere, in Charlottesville, the University of Virginia, after which I shall return hither for a time.

June 18th. I have, both yesterday and to-day, received a great number of visits, and ditto invitations. Among the latter was one to a country-home near the city, which I immediately accepted on my return from Charlottesville, so greatly was I pleased with the persons who gave it, a Mrs. Van L., a widow and her daughter; intellect, kindness, and refinement of feeling were evident in their gentle countenances. The daughter, a pleasing, pale blonde, expressed so much compassion for the sufferings of the slave, that I was immediately attracted to her.

She drove me out yesterday to see the lovely environs of Richmond; the large, park-like church-yard, with its hills and dales, was among these. The whole country around Richmond is undulating, and every where is the River St. James a remarkable and refreshing feature in this landscape, through which it flows in manifold sinuosities. Although it is so near midsummer, it is cold, and I was really starved in the open carriage, and the air felt keen and ungenial.

We next drove to a large tobacco manufactory, as I wish to see one of the works in which this staple of Virginia was prepared. Here I heard the slaves, about a hundred in number, singing at their work in large rooms; they sung quartettes, choruses, and anthems, and that so purely, and in such perfect harmony, and with such exquisite feeling, that it was difficult to believe them self-taught. But so they were. God has given these poor creatures the gift of song for their consolation in the time of their probation. And their life in the tobacco manufactory is no life of Canaan. One part of their work, the rolling of the tobacco-leaf, in which they were at this moment employed, appears easy enough; but the packing of it in solid masses by means of screw machinery, which is turned by the hand and the chest, is so laborious that it not unfrequently produces diseases of the lungs, and costs the laborer his health and life. I suppose they become accustomed to the smell and the dirt which always prevails in a tobacco manufactory, and which to me seems murderous, as they are employed in it from their very childhood. As the work in the manufactory ceases, and the work-people are released for the rest of the day after six o'clock in the evening, and as that hour now approached, the beautiful song of the slaves, "Halleluiah, Amen!" did not sound like a burlesque; neither, however, did it sound cheerful, nor yet did the singers look cheerful. Good Miss Van L. could not refrain from weeping. The slaves were all Baptists, and sung only hymns. The gay, sunny negro songs are only heard here in the slave-selling houses, or the so-called negro jails. If these slaves had only any future, any thing to hope for, to strive for, to live for, any prospect before them, then I should not deplore their lot—but nothing, nothing!!! The extreme few who are released by the work of colonization can not be taken into consideration in comparison with the mass who have no hope at all!

I received, on leaving the manufactory, as a present from the proprietor (a stout, good kind of gentleman), guess what?—a large cake of chewing tobacco! The present was so characteristic both of the fabric and of Virginia, that I accepted it with great pleasure; and besides, it is of a very fine quality. I kept it, however, as far from my nose as possible on my drive home, but I know, nevertheless, mouths in Sweden that would set a high value on it.

In the evening I was invited to a large party, at which a thousand people, the *élite* of the society of Richmond, were to be present.

"He is the severest slave-owner in the whole neighborhood. One can tell his slaves when one meets them on the high road from their half-famished appearance!"

"Yes, he is a bad man, but he is very rich."

It was thus that I heard two people of my acquaintance, themselves slave-owners, talking to each other last evening.

"Who is so bad and so rich at the same time?" inquired I.

"That very gentleman, Mr. ——, to whose house you are invited to-morrow evening to the large party," was the reply.

I inquired still further from other persons, and found that these facts were universally acknowledged.

"And yet his house is frequented by the best society of the city," said I, astonished; "and yet you maintain that public opinion protects the slave and punishes the bad master."

"But then Mr. ——'s wife and daughters are so good and so amiable," argued they, "it is for their sake that people associate with Mr. ——."

But I suspect, in reality, that Mr. ——'s wealth has as much to do with their overlooking his offense as the goodness of his wife and daughter.

I returned my thanks for the invitation, but declined it.

In order for this much-praised public opinion to make a decided demonstration against the rich slave-owner, it is necessary that something very horrible and flagrant should be committed by him which can not be concealed. An instance of this kind has lately occurred in Virginia. A rich planter, not far from here, killed one of his house-slaves, one of his most confidential servants, by the most barbarous treatment, and that merely on suspicion. The fact was so horrible that it aroused the public indignation, and the murderer was brought before the court of justice.

I have heard slave-owners say, "If justice had been done, that man would have been hanged!" But he was rich; and on the sacrifice of a considerable amount of his property to the learned in the law, both the affair and the law were turned and twisted, and the sentence which has just been pronounced adjudges to the murderer five years' imprisonment in the House of Correction. Many right-minded people have declared it to be shameful, but the conscience of the slave state is enslaved.

An old free negro woman has just been sentenced to the same punishment because she endeavored to assist a young female slave to escape to the free states. The governor rejected the petition, which prayed for mercy in her case, on the plea "of the state of feeling between the free and the slave states at the present time."

Mammon and the fear of man!

I have to-day been present at a sitting of the great Convention in the Capitol, which has met there for the reconstruction, or rather extension, of the State Constitution. I had on this occasion the pleasure of seeing many well-formed heads and foreheads, and manly, vigorous forms among the one hundred and thirty legislators here assembled, and shook the friendly hands of divers of them. But a bill regarding general education was ordered to be laid on the table for some future time, without exciting much attention. The assembly occupied itself principally with the questions regarding an increase of judges in the country in accordance with the increased population. The purport of this Convention was similar to that in

Ohio, and was designed to place greater power than formerly in the hands of the people, by giving them a participation in the election of judges and other state officials, which formerly lay more immediately in the hands of the legislative power of the state. It delighted me to see America progress in its democratic tendencies, faithful to its fundamental principles; for if the new steps which are now taken in this direction do not produce an immediate advantage, still they have done much for the great popular education of a conscious public existence which is hereby asserted.

In the large rotunda-like entrance to the Capitol stands a statue of Washington, executed by the French sculptor Houdon. I do not know when I have seen a nobler work of art, or one which more perfectly represented the ideal human being in the every-day reality. It is Washington, the President, with the large chin, the somewhat stiff figure, in the old-fashioned costume; and yet it is, at the same time, the type of the man of the New World, with that noble, self-conscious, well-balanced mind which the Americans talk about as the highest excellence, in harmony with itself, certain of its own course and its own object, resolute in persevering to the end, asking advice from no one but the Divine Counselor. He has bound his sword to the column, and now stands by the plow, resting calmly with himself, without pride, but without hesitation or doubt; the grand, intellectual glance looking out into the future! In truth it is a glorious figure, a glorious statue, to which I shall gladly return when I return hither.

But I now leave the city for Charlottesville.

Charlottesville, June 20th.

I am at the beautiful home of Professor Sheele de V. The professor, since he was last in Sweden, has married the most charming wife, both pretty and good, and both he and she received me in the kindest manner.

I find myself here in a lovely mountain district, and within sight of what is called "The Blue Ridge," which is the boundary of the great Virginian Valley, which lies between this range of hill and the so-called "North Mountain Ridge," both portions of the Alleghany range. Around the University, which was built by the late President Jefferson, in a magnificent and regular style, lies a region of alternate hills and valleys, like a green carpet, bordered with lovely country houses and small farms, a beautiful, fertile landscape, in which nothing is wanting but water. Foremost among these elegant villas stands, upon a lofty hill, Jefferson's summer-delight, "Monticello," with its splendid trees, and an extensive view over the country, and the University, whose founder he was. I visited this place yesterday with my new friends. The house, now unoccupied, is very much neglected, and is evidently falling to decay. The internal decoration indicated a man who was not very much attached to republican simplicity in his own person. One saloon with an inlaid floor was a magnificent room. But I seemed to miss on all sides the appearance of comfort, the appearance of a light and pleasant home.

Jefferson was the friend of Thomas Paine, and, like him, was an Atheist, and his habits testified of a man of lax morality. His portraits and bust present the physiognomy of a man of an energetic but disquiet life; they express a combative character, obstinate, and extremely irritable if opposed; for the rest, active, cheerful, and communicative. The forehead is broad rather than lofty. There is none of Washington's calmness and nobility. Jefferson loved his country, and guided its efforts for freedom to its outbreak in that grand act, the Declaration of Independence, which was the product of the spirit of the time and the people rather than of his brain and pen.

From Monticello I saw the sun descend in beauty as it released itself from obscuring clouds—a sunset more like Washington's than Jefferson's evening of life.

Wandering in the park, I noticed that extremely delicious odor which filled the air, and which I have often perceived in America. I was told that it proceeded from the blossom of the wild vine, which grows luxuriantly here, as it does throughout the whole of the North American States. Nowhere so much as here does the prophecy seem to be fulfilled, of every man sitting under his own vine or fig-tree, and no one making him afraid.

Later in the evening I saw a considerable number of the teachers of the University and their wives, among whom were some very agreeable. The president, Mr. Harrison, with his beautiful meditative eyes, and a quiet, excellent manner, pleased me particularly. This University is celebrated for the solidity of the learning which it communicates, and the severity of its requirements as regards its students. Young men, therefore, who have obtained diplomas at the University, may be sure of situations and official appointments when they leave it. There is here a separate establishment, which affords indigent youths of good character, and who have the desire to learn, the opportunity of maintaining themselves at the academy free of cost.

When Jefferson founded the academy, he excluded from it any ecclesiastical establishment or clergy. Neither one nor the other found a place in his seat of learning. But so clear among this people is the conviction that social life requires religious life, and that the religious teacher must have his place in the community, that, soon after Jefferson's death, a room in one of the buildings of the University was fitted up for a place of worship, and the heads of the University agreed in summoning thither ministers of various religious persuasions, who should alternately perform divine service and give religious instruction, by which means the principal sects of the United States, Episcopalian, Calvinist, Methodist, and many others, might here be represented, so that none should have cause to complain of illiberal exclusion, and that the young students might have an opportunity of hearing all doctrines preached. The official period for each minister who is thus called to the academy is fixed to two years. The minister who is now the University preacher belongs to the Episcopalian Church. This excellent arrangement is so acceptable to the youthful students, that, although their participation in divine service, as well as the fees to the spiritual teacher, are left entirely to their own choice, yet they very rarely neglect the former—never morning and evening prayer—neither do they disregard the latter.

The room which is devoted to these religious services is in the highest degree unostentatious, and is low, as if it were afraid of raising itself too much, lest it should be observed by the spirit from Monticello: it seems afraid of something.

I intend remaining at Charlottesville over the approaching examination and distribution of prizes, that I may see something more of the young sons of Virginia and the flower of its beauty, which is expected to be here on this occasion. I shall, in the mean time, make an excursion across the Blue Mountains into Virginia Valley, and then visit a celebrated grotto called Wyer's Cave, after its discoverer. Perhaps I may extend my flight still further west into the hilly regions of Virginia, to see the natural bridge, and various other natural curiosities, which are very celebrated. My kind host and countryman, Professor De V., is a good friend and adviser. I set off from here in the afternoon by the diligence, under the escort of a fine old gentleman, both learned and good.

Charlottesville, June 26th.

I am just returned from my ramble across the Blue Mountains, but not in the diligence. I found that to be so thronged and so hot, that I merely got in to hurry out again; let it drive on, and then, with the help of my kind host, hired a private carriage with two horses, and a negro as driver; and now, my little heart, you must see me sitting there all alone, free and light as the bird on the bough, and very happy thus, in solitude and unimpeded, to travel through the grand, romantic scenery. And my negro Davis is the best, most cheerful negro in the world, drives well, knows every place we pass, is careful of his horses, and is careful of me. We did not this day get any further than the foot of the Blue Ridge, where we took up our quarters for the night.

The next morning, the 24th, I set out at sunrise to asscend the Blue Mountains, going the greater part of the way on foot, that I might the better witness that glorious spectacle of the sunrise over the stretches of valley of East and West Virginia on each side of the Blue Mountain Ridge. It was a beautiful, bright, but cold morning in the fresh mountain air The road was good, and rich masses of beautiful wood bounded its ascent up the mountain. My good negro followed me on foot, pointing out to me Albemarle and Nelson counties, and enjoying with unmistakable pleasure the grand, beautiful views, in which water merely was wanting.

Arrived at the summit of the Blue Ridge, I beheld rising before me another similar lofty blue mountain ridge, in a parallel direction to this—this was North Mountain Ridge. Between these two mountain ridges stretches itself Virginia Valley, east and west, a vast, fertile landscape, adorned with small, well-built farm-houses, cultivated fields, and pasture-land; a quiet, blooming country, from the excellent homes of which one would think that the Lord's Prayer must naturally arise, because all is pastoral, lovely, and peaceful; no proud mansions, no poor cottages; the lot of all seems to be alike good, and the house of God alone stands forth pre-eminently in the assembly.

We drove down into the valley, and I reached at noon the celebrated grotto, which is situated in a mountain on the banks of the lively River Shenandoah. Near to it is a hotel for strangers, whom the landlord, a stout, jolly man, conducts to the grotto. I was the only visitor there, and thus had the grotto all to myself. The landlord and Davis attended me with torches, and kindled fires here and there in the grotto.

The grotto is entered by a very small door on the mountain side, and some of its passages are narrow and difficult enough to creep through, but for this the stranger is rewarded by the sight of magnificent rocky halls and astonishing figures. It required about two hours to pass through the most remarkable portions of the grotto. The stalactite figures were similar to those which I had seen in the grottoes of Cuba, but certain forms occurred here more frequently. Among these were, in particular, fluted columns, organ-pipes, towers, cascades, as of frozen, foaming water; shields were reared against walls, which were hung with spears; immense depending draperies, often in the most soft and plastic folds, upon which, if one struck with a stick, a loud, clanging tone was returned, which resounded through the subterranean vaults. There were alcoves, in which were standing solitary figures resembling human masks; and between these figures, along the rock-walls, a confusion of fantastic forms of animals, flowers, wings, which seemed ready to fly away with the walls; cities, which stood forth in bold relief, with streets, and squares, and towers, and every thing which an active imagination could conceive. There is one crypt, in which the whole natural world is represented in stone masks—the dark dream of a mountain king about the life of the world of light, for even sun and moon are there represented by large round white dials shining forth from the deep, dusky vault. There are large halls, in the centre of which stand two or three solitary stone images, always in the semblance of man. Here are warriors about to draw the sword, there a philosopher deep in meditation, or a woman with a child wrapped in the folds of her robe; throughout the whole it is a mysterious world, where life seems petrified in the midst of its presentment. A clear little fountain, the musical dropping of whose water is heard at a considerable distance, furnishes a cool draught. But it was so very cool in that subterranean world, and I felt so ill there, both body and soul, that I was glad to leave it, and inhale God's warm air and sunshine.

It was an unimaginably beautiful evening, and the whole region was like the most lovely pastoral poem. I enjoyed it as I rambled alone beside the lively little, roaring, dancing River Shenandoah, and up among the fragrant fields, where the hay lay out in swathes, and where they were just beginning to cut the corn. The golden ears fell before large scythes, furnished with a sort of upper story of wooden spikes, which threw the corn aside in sheaves. It looked heavy work, but it succeeded perfectly. Men only, and no women, were at work in the fields. The men perform, in this country, all the out-of-doors labor, even to milking the cows. The women stay at home—the white women, I mean, for the black are not considered to belong to the weaker sex.

When I returned to my quarters for the night, I found a handsome old man sitting near the house, on the grass under the tree, reading in a thick book. Somewhat later I fell into discourse with him, and borrowed the book from him. It was a book published by the sect of United Brethren, and was a statement of their doctrines, accompanied by copper-plate engravings. Their peculiar doctrines seemed to me to consist in a more literal adherence to the usages of the early Christians than is now generally the case. Thus the sect practice feet-washing as a religious ceremony, give the salutation of the kiss when they meet, and adhere to many other ancient customs. This sect, called also "Dunkers," that is to say, *baptizers* or *dippers*, and which is very numerous in this part of the Virginia Valley, is said to have come hither origin ally from Holland, and to be distinguished by its religious narrowness and stagnation, but otherwise by great unanimity and brotherly love among themselves, as well as by great industry.

It is said that two years ago a deliberative council of the Dunkers was held at Wyer's Grotto, at which two hundred long-bearded and long-haired men were present, to consult upon the most important affairs of the sect. One of the principal questions which was brought forward was, as to how far it was sinful or not to place lightning-conductors against their houses. The resolution to which the assembly came, after an examination of the question, which continued for two days, was, "that the brethren who had already set up lightning-conductors against their houses should not be recommended to remove them, but that the brethren who had not yet set them up should be strongly recommended to do without them, and to trust in the Lord alone for the preservation of their houses." In consequence of this stagnating principle, the Dunkers allow their beards and their hair to grow in the most undisturbed repose, and by the same rule, they should not either cut their nails, if they would be perfectly consistent; but they admit of an exception when they find it for the best. They baptize each other in the river by immersing the whole body under water, whence probably their name, and they have meeting-houses, and meet together like the Quakers, with alternate preaching and silence, with occasional feet-washing. They practice agriculture, are generally in good circumstances, and, while they are friendly and communicative among themselves, are somewhat haughty and cold toward those whom they call the children of the world.

While the Dunkers stagnate in this manner in the Virginia Valley, rooted to the earth and the very letter of religion, a large colony is at this moment establishing itself in the most westerly portion of Virginia, under the name of *Egalitaires*, and which, headed by French Communists, have purchased large tracts of land for the establishment of a community, the tendency of which is considerably unlike that of the Dunkers. Fortunate country—where every thing can have a fair trial, and every bias of the human mind have its sphere and its place of action, to the benefit of the many-sided developments of the human spirit, without being detrimental to any!

During my journey from Wyer's Grotto the next morning, I visited a farm which belonged to a Dunker family. It was situated near the high road, and seemed to me the ideal of a little peasant farm, so neat and comfortable, so well built, so well kept, with its garden and fruit trees. The long-haired husband was out at work in the fields, but the wife, a stout old woman in a costume very like that of a Quakeress, was at home, and looked at me askance with suspicious glances. She had a strong Dutch accent, and could not be drawn into conversation; and when I had had the draught of water for which I asked, and had looked about me both within and without the house, I pursued my journey on that beautiful morning, between the mountain ridges to the right and to the left, to the little city of Staunton. Here I dined *en famille* with a very agreeable lawyer, Mr. B., whose conversation interested me much.

There are in Staunton some beautiful public institutions, among which is a large lunatic asylum, established on the same principles as those at Bloomingdale and in Philadelphia, and which produces the same results as regards the treatment of the insane. Cure is the rule—when the invalid is brought hither at the commencement of his malady—incurable cases are the exception.

I was very kindly invited to remain at Staunton, but I wished to continue my return, and at sunset I found myself once more on the summit of the Blue Mountains, quiet valleys lying east and west at my feet, with their quiet little farms in the midst of the golden corn-fields—a peaceful region to all appearance, but in which the strife about mine and thine is not the less hotly carried on at times, even to the separation of families.

As twilight came on, we stopped at a very pretty and excellent place at the foot of the mountain, where every thing was good, and the air so fresh that I was tempted to remain. But Davis and his horses were expensive luxuries, and therefore I drove to Charlottesville, to which place I had a pleasant journey through the quiet, fertile country.

I shall now remain quietly here till after the University examination, when I shall return to Richmond; and after two days' stay there, pay a visit to Harper's Ferry, one of the most romantic and beautiful tracts, it is said, in Virginia, at the union of the two rivers Potomac and Shenandoah—that lively little river which dances past Wyer's Grotto.

I intend to be ready to leave America by the end of August, and I must, therefore, give up the desire which I had to see more of the mountain districts of Virginia. Besides, the journey by diligence is too fatiguing for me, and by carriage too expensive. And, after all, Virginia has no mountains which can be compared in grandeur to the White Mountains, and those I shall visit.

While I linger in this beautiful and peaceful home—in which a good young couple make each other happy, and participate in the enjoyment of life's pleasures with a circle of friends—I read the early history of Virginia, and picture it to myself.

The earliest known history of Virginia is rendered remarkable by a poetical incident so beautiful and so affecting that I must transcribe it here for you, and copy for you also the portrait of its heroine, the young Indian girl Matoaka or Pocahontas.

The accounts which the early English navigators brought home of the beautiful and fertile country lying on the eastern shores of North America, which they were the first to examine during the reign of Queen Elizabeth, so enchanted that monarch, that she resolved to connect this new country more closely with herself, by giving to it the name which she herself loved to bear, that of *Virginia.* Virginia became the symbolic name of the new virgin-soil; and England first knew it under this name. Even the pilgrims from Leyden, who were borne by stress of wind and waves to the shore of Massachusetts, thought to sail "to the northern parts of Virginia, where they would found their colony."

Before this, English adventurers in the southern parts of Virginia had penetrated inland, seeking for gold. But the greater part of these had perished miserably, in consequence of their own excesses, and the diseases incident to the climate. One man, however, John Smith—an ambitious and bold adventurer, but equally prudent as courageous—succeeded by his personal influence in giving some stability to a small colony, which was planted by the James River, and where he founded a city called Jamestown.

Where Richmond now stands, and a little above the falls of the river, a powerful Indian Chief called Powhatan, styled also the emperor of the country, had his residence, and was obeyed by many smaller Indian tribes who were scattered over the surrounding country and cultivated the land. Smith advanced up the river, and endeavored to penetrate into the interior; but here, unfortunately, his men, disobeying his orders, were surprised by the Indians, put to death, and he himself taken prisoner. He had been a prisoner before; had been sold as a slave in Turkey, and, amid manifold adventures, which his restless spirit had impelled him to seek in Europe, Asia, and Africa, he had become well acquainted with dangers, and prepared for whatever might occur. Standing captive amid the Indians, whose hatred and cruelty he very well knew, he remained perfectly calm, and riveted the attention and interest of the Indians by showing them a compass, and exhibiting to them various proofs of his knowledge and his skill. This excited astonishment and admiration. He was conveyed from one tribe to another, like some wonderful animal or conjurer, and finally to the Emperor Powhatan, who was to decide upon his fate. While Powhatan and his chiefs were holding councils respecting the stranger, and to decide upon his fate, he employed himself in making battle-axes for the emperor, and necklaces of beads for his little daughter, the Princess Pocahontas, a girl of ten or twelve years old, who in appearance and expression greatly excelled all the Indian maidens, and who was called *nonpareille* among her people, from her intellect and her wit. The emperor and his chiefs condemned Smith to death. He was doomed to be sacrificed to the gods of the nation, and his head to be crushed by the blows of the tomahawk.

The Indians prepared themselves for a solemn festival. Fires were kindled before the images of their gods; Powhatan sat on his elevated seat; around him stood his warriors. Smith was brought forth and placed upon the ground, his head was laid upon a stone, and the tomahawks were lifted. But at once the little daughter of the emperor, Pocahontas, sprang forward, threw her arms around the captive's neck, and laid her head upon his. The tomahawks must fall upon her head before they reached his. Vain were threats, prayers, reasonings; the child remained resolute in still enfolding the victim in her protecting arms. This conduct at length moved the hearts of Powhatan and his savage warriors. Smith was pardoned for the sake of the little princess, and instead of his being treated as an enemy, the chief gave him their word of amity, and let him go to his own people.

The understanding, however, between the English and Indians continued to be one of mistrust and hostility; the Indians were continually on the look-out for opportunities to attack their enemies. Pocahontas proved, however, to be the good angel of the English; and on one occasion, when they were in great want, she brought them corn and provisions; on another, she came to their camp, alone, through the forest, in the dead of the night, pale, and with her hair flying in the wind, to warn them of an approaching attack.

The beauty and amiability of Pocahontas tempted, a few years later, an old, unprincipled adventurer, with the help of a set of lawless fellows like himself, to steal her from her father. But a noble, devout young Englishman, by name John Rolfe, an amiable enthusiast, became her protector. Daily, hourly, nay, in his very sleep, amid the forests of Virginia, had he heard a voice which seemed to bid him convert the Indian maiden to Christianity, and then marry her. And when the Holy Spirit asked him reproachfully (such are his own expressions) why he lived, the answer was given, "To lead the blind into the right way." He struggled for long against his inclination for the young pagan princess as against a dangerous temptation, but finally yielded to the admonishing voice. He won her confidence, and became her teacher, and she before long publicly received Christian baptism in the little church at Jamestown, the roof of which was supported by rough pine-tree stems from her father's forests, and where the font was a hollowed fir-tree. Here also, a short time afterward, was she married to Rolfe, stammering before the altar her marriage vows according to the rites of the English Church. All this, it is said, was done with the consent of the father and relatives, her uncle, the chief Opachisco himself, conducting her to the altar.

The marriage was universally approved, even by the English, and in the year 1616 Rolfe sailed to England with his Indian wife, who, under the name of Lady Rebecca, was presented at court, and was universally admired for her beauty and childlike *naïveté*. She was most admirable both as a wife and a young mother. But the young couple did not long enjoy their happiness; just as she was about preparing to return to America, she fell a victim to the English climate, at the age of twenty-two. She left one son, who became the ancestral head of many generations, who are to this day proud of tracing their descent from the Indian Pocahontas; and I do not wonder at it. Her memory remains in singular beauty and pure splendor. The race who produced such a daughter deserved a better treatment from the people whom she protected than it received.

The portrait of Pocahontas, which I have copied, represents her in the costume which was worn by the higher class of English in the time of Elizabeth; but the stiff Indian plaits of hair which hang down her cheeks from beneath her hat betray her descent. The countenance has an affecting expression of childlike goodness and innocence; the eyes have a melancholy charm, and the form of the countenance reminds me of the Feather-cloud woman in Minnesota. The portrait was taken in 1616, when she was twenty-one years old, and bears the inscription, *Matoaka als. Rebecca Filia potentiss. Princ. Powhatan Imp. Virginiæ.*

Smith's portrait, which I have also drawn, shows a resolute, but not handsome, and very bearded warrior. His history, also in Virginia, is a chain of contentions, of bold actions and misfortunes, by which he was finally subdued, without having left, of all his unquiet, combative life, any more beautiful memory than that which belongs to him from the childlike tenderness and attachment of the Indian girl. That which the strong arm of this ambitious man was not able to obtain, was obtained for him by two tender, childish arms which were wound round his neck.

My forenoons, as usual, I keep for myself, my afternoons are devoted to company, walking, &c. I have visited a few of the small farms in the neighborhood, which are cultivated by free negroes, and have found them to be as neat and comfortable as those which belong to the white farmer. I have also been with my charming hostess to see her parents, a planter's family not far from here—a family of good slaveholders, not rich enough to emancipate their slaves, but too good not to take care of and to make them happy. They belong to a considerable class in these middle slave states, who would willingly see slavery abolished, and have white laborers in the place of black to cultivate their maize and tobacco fields.

I like, in the twilight, to sit on the piazza under the beautiful trees with my amiable hostess, and decoy her on to tell me about her life in her father's house, of her first acquaintance with her husband, their courtship, and all that appertained thereto; of her happiness as a daughter, as a wife—a little romance as pure, as pleasant as the air and the perfume of flowers around us in these tranquil evening hours, while the fire-flies dance in the dark shadow of the trees. Her love for her father was her first love; that for her good husband was her second; and the third, for the child which she expects, is now awaking, yet with fear and trembling, in her young heart.

In the evenings I see company, either at home or at the houses of some of the professors. These good gentlemen have now a deal to do regarding the examination, and the preparation of testimonials and diplomas.

Two of the young students are to deliver farewell addresses before they leave the academy, where they have now finished their studies with honor, and I am invited to hear them.

28*th*. I heard one of them yesterday evening, and if the second, which I shall hear this evening, is of the same character, as I expect it will be, I shall not have much pleasure in it. It is amazing what an enslaving power the institution of slavery exercises over the minds of the young, and over intelligence in general; and the young speaker of yesterday evening belonged to this enslaved class. He was a young man of refined features, and a certain aristocratic expression of countenance, but without any peculiar nobility. He is celebrated for having passed through a splendid examination, and for possessing great talents as a speaker.

And his speech really flowed forth with a rushing rapidity; but such a shooting across the United States, such an ostentatious boast of the South, of the "Sons of the South, the flower and hope of the Union—nay, it was incomparable! *One* thing only impeded the grandeur and the growth of the United States, and its wonderful, mighty future, and this was—Abolitionism! It was this scorpion, this *hydra* in the social life of the United States, which ought to be crushed (and the speaker stamped vehemently and angrily on the floor) and annihilated! Then first only would the North and the South, like two mighty rivers, be united, and side by side start forth toward the same grand, honorable goal!"

What this honorable goal may be, I did not hear mentioned; but the students, who were present in great numbers, must have understood it, for they applauded tempestuously, and every heroic apostrophe to the heroism and nobility of the Sons of the South was followed by a salvo of clapping, which at the close of the speech was doubled and redoubled, and seemed as if it never would end. Thus delighted were the Sons of the South with the speaker, with each other, and with themselves.

I left the hall very much depressed. Shall I not then find within the slave states a noble, liberal youth, which is that upon which I most depend for the promise of approaching freedom? Must I again find among the young men that want of moral integrity, of courage and uprightness of mind? I have scarcely any desire to go and hear the speaker this evening, I am so weary of the old song.

29th. I have had a great and unexpected pleasure: I have heard "a new song sung," and—but I will tell you all in due course.

I again took my seat in the crowded, lamp-lighted hall, and the young man who was to speak sat alone on an elevated platform facing the assembly while the hall filled. This lasted for a good half hour, and it seemed to me that the young orator's situation could not be very pleasant, sitting there all alone, as he did, an object for all eyes; and I asked myself whether it could be this feeling which cast a certain shade, or a certain trance-like look, over his eyes. He was a tall young man, of handsome, strong proportions, who yet seemed to me not fully grown; the countenance was pure and good, not regularly handsome, but handsome nevertheless, with a youthfully fresh complexion, and clear, strongly-marked features. I endeavored inquisitively to guess from these the soul of the youth; but this lay, as it were, under a veil. The forehead was broad, the hair dark brown, and abundant.

At length the moment came when he must rise and speak. He did this with great simplicity, without grace, but without any awkwardness or confusion, and began his speech, without the facility of the former speaker, but with calmness and precision. In the first part of his speech he took a hasty review of the nations of antiquity, with regard to that which caused their greatness or their fall. He showed that in all countries where slavery had existed, it had degraded the people, and finally caused their downfall.

When I heard this, I confess that my heart beat high. "Is it possible," thought I, "that I shall really hear in this slave state, before this corporation of self-complacent advocates of slavery, a youth publicly, and like a man, raise his voice against slavery—the weak side of the South, and the nightshade of the New World?"

Yes, I shall! The youth continued boldly, and in the most logical manner, to apply to America those principles, the consequences of which he exhibited in the history of Europe and Asia. Without reservation, and with great beauty and decision of expression, he addressed his countrymen thus: "I accuse you not of any deficiency in courage, in nobility of mind, in feeling for the good and the beautiful, in enterprise, in piety. But of this I accuse you, that you do not give education to the poor of your country, that you do not labor for the elevation of the lower classes of your countrymen." And there is good reason for this accusation, for in Virginia, in consequence of the restrictive fetters of slavery, which prevent the increase of schools, there are upward of eighty thousand white people who can neither read nor write. The population of Virginia, whites and blacks taken together, amounts to about a million and a half.

The young orator declared the mission of America to be that of communicating the blessings of liberty and civilization to all nations. "If America fulfill her duty in this respect, she will become great and happy; if not, then she will fall, and the greatness of her fall will be commensurate with the greatness of her mission, and the intended future in which she has failed."

I can not tell you with what feelings of delight I listened to these large-minded and bold words from the pure soul of a youth, it was so unlike any thing which I had hitherto heard in the slave states. It was what I had been longing to hear. My tears flowed, and I did not trouble myself about them being seen. I was very happy.

But where now was the enthusiasm which on the former evening had animated the Sons of the South. They listened in silence, as it were, in amazement, and the applause which was given at the close of the speech was cold, and, as it were, forced.

The glorious youth looked as if applause or blame concerned him not. He had spoken from his own conviction; his youthfully fresh cheek glowed as with the crimson tinge of morning, and his dark eye and clear brow shone serenely as a cloudless heaven.

I could not have any conversation with him later in the evening, because he was summoned to his father, who was dangerously ill, and he was obliged to leave the place immediately. Nevertheless, I pressed his hand, and spoke my cordial thanks to him in the presence of his teachers and his companions.

The good professors were somewhat confounded by the unexpected character of the young man's speech, but full of admiration: Good heavens! they had not expected such a speech. Really an uncommon speech! Above the common average! and so on.

Alexander S. Brown (I write the name at full) was declared to be a fine fellow! a smart young man! The president even expressed himself very warmly in his praise. But the learned in law and books were nevertheless somewhat afraid of giving to Cæsar that which was due to Cæsar, and endeavored to indemnify themselves by certain depreciatory and apologistic concessions.

This was one of my happiest evenings in the Southern States, and I now looked with more cheerful, more loving glances upon this beautiful soil since it had produced such a youth. How noble and how happy ought not his mother to be!

Richmond, July 1st.

Again good-morning in the capital of Virginia; but not now in the city itself, but in one of its rural suburbs, where I am domiciled in a lovely country-house, beautifully situated upon a lofty terrace on the banks of the James River, surrounded by a park, with its lofty spreading trees. It is the residence of Mrs. Van S., a beautiful home, and I am infinitely well off here, in the midst of kind, well-wishing friends.

I left Professor S. de V. and his charming wife yesterday morning with mutual good wishes, and hope in a short time to have good tidings from them.

The business at Charlottesville on Saturday consisted for the most part of speeches and the distribution of diplomas. I could not hear much of the former, and my principal pleasure was the contemplation of the assembly of ladies, among whom I remarked a great number of very lovely and happy countenances. If the Juno style of beauty is not met with in America as it is in Europe, there are, on the contrary, a greater number of cheerful, lovely countenances, and scarcely any which can be called ugly. The men are not handsome, but have a manly appearance, and, in a general way, are well made and full of strength. This, I believe, I have said once or twice before, but I have not said, what nevertheless should be said, that among the Americans are not found that decided type of one distinct race as we find it among the English, Irish, French, Spaniards, Germans, &c. An American, male or female, might belong to any nation, in its beautiful human character, but divested of nationality; nay, even the Swedish, that is to say, when this is found in the most perfect faces, because a well-formed, fine nose, and an oval countenance, is almost universal among the ladies. Our full-moon countenances, and noses which come directly out of them like a handle, or a projecting point of rock, are not seen here; neither are potato-noses, like my own. Still, I have seen many a blooming young girl in the Northern States of America, many a handsome young man, more like Swedes than the English or the French. Nevertheless, light hair and light eyes are rare.

July 2d. How wearisome is this interrogative, this empty and thoughtless chatter of mere callers, especially ladies! Want of observation, want of an ear for life, is, after all, one of the greatest wants here, and the school which, before every other, is needed most in the New World, is the old Pythagorean.

Life, with its large, holy interests, its earnest scenes, passes by these childish, undeveloped beings without their either seeing or thinking about it. Dissipated by the outward and ordinary, they do not listen to the great still voice which calls to them every day from the midst of the life in which they live, like insects of a day.

July 3d. I have to-day, in company with an estimable German gentleman, resident at Richmond, visited some of the negro jails, that is, those places of imprisonment in which negroes are in part punished, and in part confined for sale. I saw in one of these jails a tall, strong-limbed negro, sitting silent and gloomy, with his right hand wrapped in a cloth. I asked if he were ill.

"No," replied his loquacious keeper, "but he is a very bad rascal. His master, who lives higher up the river, has parted him from his wife and children, to sell him down South, as he wanted to punish him, and now the scoundrel, to be revenged upon his master, and to make himself fetch a less sum of money, has cut off the fingers of his right hand! The rascal asked me to lend him an ax to knock the nails into his shoes with, and I lent it him without suspecting any bad intention, and now has the fellow gone and maimed himself for life!"

I went up to the negro, who certainly had not a good countenance, and asked him whether he were a Christian. He replied curtly "No!" Whether he ever had heard of Christ? He again replied "No!" I said to him, that if he had known him, he would not have done this act; but that even now he ought not to believe himself abandoned, because He who has said "Come unto me, all ye that are weary and heavy laden," had spoken also to him, and would console and recreate even him.

He listened to me at the commencement with a gloomy countenance, but by degrees he brightened up, and at the close looked quite melted. This imbittered soul was evidently still open and accessible to good. The sun shone into the prison-yard where he sat with his maimed hand, and the heavy irons on his feet, but no Christian had come hither to preach to him the Gospel of Mercy.

The door of the prison was opened to us by a negro, whose feet also were fettered by heavy irons. He looked so good-tempered and agreeable, that I asked, with some astonishment,

"But this man, what has he done that he should then be in irons?"

"Ah!" said the keeper, "just nothing but that his master had hired him out to work in the coal-pits, and something disagreeable happening to him there, the fellow after that would not work there, and refused to go; so his master wishes to sell him, to punish him; and he ordered that we should put him in irons, just to mortify him."

And this plan had succeeded completely. The poor fellow was so annoyed and ashamed that he did not seem to know which way to look while the keeper related his story; and besides that, he looked so good-tempered, so full of sensibility, that, strong fellow as he was, he seemed as if he would suffer rather from an injustice being done to him than be excited by it to defiance and revenge, as was the case with the other negro. He was evidently a good man, and deserved a better master.

In another prison we saw a pretty little white boy of about seven years of age sitting among some tall negro girls. The child had light hair, the most lovely light brown eyes, and cheeks as red as roses; he was, nevertheless, the child of a slave mother, and was to be sold as a slave. His price was three hundred and fifty dollars. The negro girls seemed very fond of the white boy, and he was left in their charge, but whether that was for his good or not is difficult to say. No motherly Christian mother visited either this innocent imprisoned boy or the negro girls. They were left to a heathenish life and the darkness of the prison.

In another "jail" were kept the so-called "fancy girls," for fancy purchasers. They were handsome fair mulattoes, some of them almost white girls.

We saw in one jail the room in which the slaves are flogged, both men and women. There were iron rings in the floor to which they are secured when they are laid down. I looked at the strip of cowhide, "the paddle," with which they are flogged, and remarked, "Blows from this could not, however, do very much harm."

"Oh, yes, yes; but," replied the keeper, grinning with a very significant glance, "it can cause as much torture as any other instrument, and even more, because one can give as many blows with this strip of hide without its leaving any outward sign; it does not cut into the flesh."

The slaves may remain many months in this prison before they are sold.

The Southern States are said to be remarkable for their strict attention to religious observances: they go regularly to church, they send out missionaries to China and to Africa, but they leave the innocent captive slave in their own prisons without instruction or consolation.

Yet once more—what might not women, what ought not women to do in this case!

I have heard young, beautiful girls declare themselves proud to be Americans, and, above every thing else, proud to be Virginians! I should like to have taken them to the jails, and have seen whether, in the face of all this injustice, they could have been proud of being Virginians, proud of the institutions of Virginia.

July 5th. Here also, as every where on my pilgrimage, have I become acquainted with good and thoughtful people, who form a perfect counterbalance to the unthinking and the bad, and who attach me to the place and the community where I am. Foremost among the good stands the family in which I am now a guest—yes, these are ladies so tender-hearted, especially toward the negroes, that I find myself standing upon the moderate and less liberal side, while I nevertheless inwardly enjoy the sight of warm hearts who only err through an excess of kindness to an oppressed people. Such a sight is very rare in a slave state. Agreeable and clever women, courteous and thinking men, have afforded me many a pleasant moment, and warmed my heart by their kindness and hospitality.

Among my gentlemen acquaintance who have contributed to my pleasure, I may mention an elderly clergyman, belonging, I believe, to the Episcopal Church, who has given me some interesting information respecting the religious life and songs of the negroes, and a Quaker, Mr. B., with a handsome, regular countenance, and a quiet, thoughtful turn of mind. He has told me much that is interesting regarding his own sect, and its form of internal government, and also that lately some Quaker women have been cited before a court of justice at New York, to given evidence in a complicated trial, and the clearness with which they did it was universally admired and commented upon by the newspapers. Mr. B. attributed this to the calmness and self-possession which distinguishes the Quaker women, and to their being early accustomed to self-government and public discussions in the part which they have to take in the business of their society.

Yesterday, the 4th of July, the great day of America, was celebrated, as usual, by speech-making and processions, and drinking of toasts, and publicly reading of the Declaration of Independence. It was read in the African church of the city; but why they selected the negro church of all others for the reading of the declaration of freedom, which is so diametrically opposed to the institution of slavery, I can not comprehend, when the burlesque of the whole thing must be so evident to every one.

I have been, with a kind and agreeable lady, Mrs. G.,

to visit the House of Correction here. The system which is pursued here has nothing new in it, and the polite old colonel who showed us the establishment looked like some formal relic of Washington's staff. It astonished me not to find here one single white prisoner. Of men there were about two hundred. There were some black women here, and among them that free negro woman who had endeavored to aid the young slave in making her escape. She had a very good and frank countenance, but was condemned to remain here for five years. The room in which these women were placed was large, light, and clean, and my companion, Mrs. G., was received by the black female prisoners with evident affection and joy. She belongs to a society of ladies, who here (as well as throughout the United States) are organized for the purpose of visiting the prisoners (but who, in the slave states, forget the innocent prisoner), and it was very apparent that the most cordial understanding existed between her and these black prisoners.

The rich planter who maltreated and killed his slave, and was therefore sentenced to five years' imprisonment in the House of Correction, ought to have been in it, but he was not yet brought hither, and probably he would purchase his exemption from the punishment. Mammon is mighty.

There exists in Virginia a growing feeling of the burden and the guilt of slavery, as is the case in all the middle slave states of America, which would be much more benefited by white than black labor, and which see their development, both physical and spiritual, restricted and hampered by the institution of slavery; and I believe, what I have been credibly informed is the case, that these states would have already shaken themselves from the yoke of slavery, and that Virginia indeed would have done so some years since, if they had not been withheld, and had not been irritated to antagonism by the unwise and unjust abolitionism of the North.

I do not say that this is high ground for them to take, because no injustice should prevent our doing that which is just and wise; but it is natural, and, to a certain extent, I myself can sympathize in it.

But now that the Northern States, for the preservation of peace, have conceded to the Southern the honorable and holy right of sanctuary which their states had afforded—now that they have given up the precious privilege of protecting the fugitive slave, out of regard to the constitutional rights of the Southern States—and now that violent abolitionism is more and more giving place to a nobler and calmer spirit, nothing, I think, ought any longer to prevent the middle slave states from carrying out such measures as would contribute to their highest interests.

The slave institution of Virginia has not merely permitted a vast amount of the white population to grow up —eighty thousand, I have understood—without being able either to read or write, and who are as low in morals as in education, but it has here, as well as elsewhere, prevented the development of industry and the extension of emigration, and has caused a want of enterprise in public works, and hence want of employment for an increasing poor population. The consequences of this have assumed every year a more threatening aspect. There is here no background of strong and noble popular life, as in the free states, in which the government of the states and the schools are filled as by a fresh germ of life. Immorality, ignorance, and poverty increase; and it can not be otherwise when one half of the people hold the other in slavery. The planters of Virginia, proud of their historic memories and of their slaves, among whom they fancy that they live like feudal princes of the Middle Ages, although this is a great mistake, intrenched behind their traditions and slave institutions, have styled themselves "high-blooded" and "high-minded," and other such terms, have sat still while the chariot of the age has passed by them. The rapidly-flourishing condition of the free states of the Union during a life full of great public undertakings, and the development of intelligence as well as of the industrial spirit, and the decline of Virginia, both in affluence and moral and intellectual culture, in comparison with the former, has begun to open the eyes of the people, and during the last few years a new life has shown itself through industrial undertakings which were formerly despised as mean and unnecessary. Rail-ways are beginning to be laid down, means of communication are required, and a more vigorous life is beginning to circulate in the material region of the state; and there is no fear of its stagnating.

The Convention which is now sitting at Richmond finds it has to deal with new difficulties, based on the institution of slavery. Eastern and Western Virginia are at this moment in open feud on the subject of voting at the elections. Eastern Virginia is possessed of plantations and slaves, and will, according to accepted usage, vote by its slaves, three slaves being considered equivalent to one freeman. Western Virginia, which is hilly country, has no plantations and very few slaves, and therefore opposes the right of Eastern Virginia to strengthen herself by the votes of her slaves. She has, therefore, sent to the Convention a powerful champion in a Mr. Weise, who, like a new Nimrod, has come forth from the forests in full hunter habiliments, and deals his blows around him with mighty hunter spirit, speaking in this style:

"What, you will let the voices of your slaves weigh against ours in elections? You have forgotten that you have declared the negro slave to have no soul. Come, don't contradict me! I tell you that you have declared that hundreds of times by your laws, by your customs, and by your statutes. Answer me—come forth and contradict me, if you can! Have you not bought and sold them like brute beasts? Have you not forbidden that they shall be educated—forbidden them to feel, to think, to speak like rational beings? I will give any one a hundred dollars who will prove me wrong. But it is much better that you keep your mouths shut and say nothing. It is the most sensible thing you can do, my friends. If any one murmurs, I will kill him with a word. I am a pro-slavery man, and I hate abolitionism. I will neither hear it spoken of nor the emancipation of the slaves. But when you come and assert that your slaves have souls, and that they are capable of voting against freemen — come, gentlemen, that is quite too foolish an idea, quite too irrational, because you have shown both by word and deed that negroes have no souls, and that they ought to be regarded as brute beasts. Talk here, talk there, talk as much as you like, nobody can talk me down!"

Thus does Mr. Weise talk and perorate the length and breadth of the Capitol at Richmond, with so much boldness and so much rude wit and jocularity, that he puts all opposition out of the question; and at the same time that he seems to favor slavery, he exhibits all the contradictions and the enormities to which it leads. This speech has caused great excitement at this moment, and the columns of the newspapers are full of it.

Through the newspapers is also made known at this time occurrences in Virginia which, more than any thing else, seem to speak powerfully against an institution which evidently undermines the morals and good sense of the white people, by allowing in their youth the indulgence of arbitrary and despotic passion. At Lynchburg, a large city in Virginia, two young men, both editors of newspapers, have just now shot each other with pistols in the open street. A little while ago they had a newspaper quarrel, in which they threatened each other. They met one morning accidentally, and, without agreement or preparation, at once fired at each other with an intent to kill. The one died the same day, the other is mortally wounded. Both were newly married, one only within a few weeks.

The second tragedy is a case of elopement. A young Dr. Williams loved a Miss Morris. Her father and family, planters of Virginia, opposed the union of the lovers, and he carried her off. Her father and brother pursued them, and overtook them in a small city. They came upon them as they sat at the *table d'hôte* of a hotel. Young Morris, Dr. Williams, and a young man, his friend, who had aided the lovers, fell into a dispute in the room, drew forth their pistols, exchanged shots, and the consequence of this scene was three corpses, two of which were Dr. Williams and young Morris. Old Mr. Morris returned home, taking with him the corpse of his son, and his daughter insane.

These occurrences are much talked of and deplored, but not as any thing very extraordinary.

The homes in the slave states can not possibly cultivate and guard the child as the homes of the free states can; they foster selfishness, and those dispositions which later in life disturb their peace.

In the good and affectionate home in which I am now a guest, I see nothing but the most beautiful relationship between white and black, and have occasion afresh to admire and marvel at the musical genius of the negro people. A young negro, who is house-servant and waits at table, sings songs as naturally as he breathes—sings even in the stomach, as a ventriloquist; and when he, during meal-times, brushes away the flies, as is usual here, with a large besom of feathers, he does it unconsciously to the tune of some melody which silently sounds in his memory.

I am now about to leave the slave states not to return to them, neither will I again return to the subject of slavery, but here give my parting words. I do this with the wish that the noble and right-thinking men and women, whom I know are to be met with in all the slave states of North America, would stand more determinedly forward and separate themselves from the mass, proving by word and deed that they have considered what belongs to the welfare of their people and state. I would have a Convention, a sort of high tribunal, formed of the best men both of the North and of the South, to deliberate on the question of slavery, and thus I believe that the friends of freedom and of the Union would alike have reason to rejoice in its results.*

The noblest of the slave states should take the lead of the rest by the adoption of those measures of legislative emancipation for the slave which at this moment make the Spanish monarchy in advance of the American republic.

No states appear to me more likely to take the lead in such a liberal movement than the youthful, liberal Georgia among the Southern States, and Virginia among the

* It was often assigned, as one reason for the impossibility of the emancipation of the negro slave, that he could not by any means be made participant of American civil rights, and the proposal which has been made in some of the free states to allow the free negroes the right of voting in the state has always been met by a strong public opposition. I believe that there may be justice in this. But what is there to prevent the negroes of the United States from forming themselves into small, free Christian communities for themselves, like the Shakers, Dunkers, &c., who live an independent life in the great community, without taking part in its affairs, and without disturbing them? It is not difficult to see from the negro character that they would trouble themselves very little about the government of the United States, if they could merely have their churches, their festivals, their songs and dances, their own independent ministers and chiefs. A *negro president* would always be a nullity. Let them have their chiefs or princes, and let the negro community become that picturesque and cheerful picture which God in his creation intended it to be, as he has evidently shown by the natural gifts which he has conferred upon them. The great realm of the United States would then present one natural family and one picturesque spectacle more—not by any means the least interesting which would be seen upon its soil.

Middle States; Virginia, one of the oldest of the American States, one of the foremost in civil liberty and in the war for independence; Virginia, the native land of Washington, Jefferson, and many other great men, and before all, of Washington, that true type of the man and the citizen of the New World, whose greatness was of that rare kind that it grows the nearer you approach it, and who, like every true American, did not allow himself to be ruled by time and by mankind, but who ruled them.

I rejoice in Washington's glorious statue in the capital of Virginia. I rejoice in that which I now read of him, sketched by Bancroft in the last pages of the third part of his "History of the United States."

"The treaties of Aix-la-Chapelle had been negotiated by the ablest statesmen of Europe, in the splendid forms of monarchical diplomacy. They believed themselves the arbiters of mankind, the pacificators of the world, reconstructing the colonial system on a basis which should endure for ages, confirming the peace of Europe by the mere adjustment of material forces. At the very time of the Congress of Aix-la-Chapelle, the woods of Virginia sheltered the youthful George Washington, the son of a widow. Born by the side of the Potomac, beneath the roof of a Westmoreland farmer, almost from infancy his lot had been the lot of an orphan. No academy had welcomed him to its shades; no college crowned him with its honors; to read, to write, to cipher—these had been his degrees in knowledge. And now, at sixteen years of age, in quest of an honest maintenance, encountering intolerable toil; cheered onward by being able to write to a school-boy friend—'Dear Richard, a doubloon is my constant gain every day, and sometimes six pistoles;' himself his own cook, having no spit but a forked stick, no plate but a large chip; 'roaming over spurs of the Alleghanies, and along the banks of the Shenandoah; alive to nature, and sometimes spending the best of the day in admiring the trees and the richness of the land;' among skin-clad savages with their scalps and rattles, or uncouth emigrants, that would never speak English; rarely sleeping in a bed, holding a bearskin a splendid couch; glad of a resting-place for the night on a little hay, straw, or fodder, and often camping in the forests, where the place nearest the fire was a happy luxury—this stripling surveyor in the woods, with no companion but his unlettered associates, and no implements of science but his compass and his chain, contrasted strongly with the imperial magnificence of the Congress of Aix-la-Chapelle. And yet God had selected, not Kaunitz nor Newcastle, not a monarch of the house of Hapsburg nor of Hanover, but the Virginian stripling, to give an impulse to human affairs, and, as far as events can depend on an individual, had placed the rights and destinies of countless millions in the keeping of the widow's son."

And after this truly great man had accomplished his important task, and achieved an independence for his native land, he crowned his life, rich in honor, by giving freedom to his slaves, after having faithfully provided for their future.

How long will Virginia remain behind her noblest son?

But, while we are earnest for the abolition of slavery and for the advancement of the honor of America, let us not forget what is the condition of the lower classes of our working-people in Europe, and even in our own country. Is not their life of labor too often like a hard slavery, especially as regards the women? Are not the daily wages of women in the country so miserably low, that, even if they work every day the whole year round, they can scarcely earn food and clothing for themselves and a couple of children. When a third child comes, then comes want necessarily with it. Is it not a common thing to hear the poor women on our country estates deplore, as even a punishment of God, when they are about to give birth to a poor child; to hear *mothers* thank God for having of his mercy taken away a child, that is to say, because it is dead? Of a truth, our own working-class *may* improve themselves, both intellectually and physically, and every one *may* be the artificer of his own fortune. And this is a great advantage. But circumstances are often so compulsory that even this liberty does not help much.

I leave Virginia grateful for the good which it has given me in beautiful scenery, amiable friends, for this home full of kindness, and for the memory of a youth, from whose pure soul I derive new hope for the future of America—hope and anticipation from the youthful generation whose representative I see in him!

LETTER XL.

Philadelphia, July 14th.

Since I last wrote, I have made some small excursions and had some small adventures.

I parted from my heartily kind entertainers at Richmond last Monday, and sailed down the St. James River to Baltimore in Maryland. The day was without a breath of air, and oppressively hot; and it became still more oppressive to me from a certain dogmatic rector, who took upon himself to be my spiritual cicerone, and as he instructed me in this, that, and the other, he stretched forth and made vehement demonstrations with his arms, as if he were preparing for a boxing-match or for some important operation, which threw me into such a fever of anxiety as destroyed the effect and the recollection of his teachings. A young, polite, and warm-hearted student of Charlottesville was my refreshment. He had the prejudices of the slave states in his head, but his heart was good and unspoiled, and I doubt not but that I shall find myself very well off at his father's plantation on the beautiful river. How amiable and refreshing is youth, when it will be so!

The banks of the river were romantically beautiful and exuberantly green; no wonder that the first white discoverers were so enchanted that they described the country as an earthly paradise.

The ruins of the first church in Jamestown were still standing, at least one wall, and shone out red brick from a bright green wood by the river.

At night on the sea it was also stifling hot. A good, kind negro woman was my attendant, and we talked of various things. She had been a slave in Baltimore, and her master's family had assisted her to obtain her freedom. I asked her if she was as well off now she was free, as when she was a slave in a good family.

"Better, ma'am, better," was her energetic reply; and added, "I do not believe that God intended any human being to be slave of another."

The woman was remarkably happy and contented with her present life.

There were very few passengers in the saloon. A couple of handsome elderly ladies sat and conversed together, in an under tone, about life and its incidents. They spoke of the fate of friends and acquaintances; they spoke of the death-bed of a Godless man, who had departed this life without one backward glance of regret for the past, without one glance of hope for the future; they made reflections on all this: their countenances were mild and serious.

Two young girls, from twelve to fifteen years of age, meantime rushed in and out of the room, like wild young colts or calves for the first time turned out into the pastures. I took care to keep out of their way. The elderly ladies looked at them.

"Wild young girls!" said one of them, mildly disapproving.

"Let them enjoy their freedom," said the other, yet more mildly, and with half a sigh; "it is now their time: life will tame them soon enough!"

But would it not, after all, be better if young girls were educated to meet the hand of the tamer with another spirit than the colt meets the bridle! The combat would then be less severe and more noble than after this freedom of the young colt.

The following morning I found myself at Baltimore, and set off thence immediately by rail-way to Harper's Ferry. I had heard so much of the beautiful scenery of this part of Virginia, that I determined to go there to enjoy the effect of "the most sublime scenery of Virginia," as it was called.

The rail-way train flew onward, making innumerable windings and turnings along the wooded and romantic banks of a little river, with such abruptness and irregularity as to remind me of a terrified cow, and to make me fear every moment lest it should be swung into the river. But we arrived, without let or hinderance, at the little hamlet at Harper's Ferry.

Here I remained for three days alone and unknown, enjoying greatly my solitary rambles over the hills, and in that romantic region. It reminded me of certain hilly districts of Dalecarlia, and still more of Münden Valley in Germany, where the Rivers Fulda and Verra meet, because the rock formation and the vegetation are similar in these two cases. Here it is that the lively, sportive Shenandoah and the grave Potomac meet and unite to form the great Potomac River. Shenandoah is a gay and good young maiden, dancing carelessly along between verdant banks—laughing, leaping in the innocent enjoyment of life. Potomac is a gentleman of much older years, who advances onward solemnly and silently from the forests of the West, with slow movement and shallow water. He meets the gay Shenandoah, and draws her silently to himself. She falls thoughtlessly into his bosom, and is swallowed up there. The rushing, dancing Shenandoah is no longer heard of, no longer seen ; it is all over with her gay temper; it is all over with herself; she has become Mrs. Potomac. Mr. Potomac, however, extends himself with increasing, swelling waters, and equally calmly, but more majestically, continues his course to Washington, and thence to the sea. Poor little Shenandoah! I am fond of her, and feel sympathy for her; and though I gladly saw from the heights the Potomac advancing onward in calm, profound sweeps through the western highlands, I yet preferred going down into the valley south of the mountain, where the Shenandoah, still a maiden, dances onward among the rocks which crowned her bacchante head with the most beautiful garlands and crowns of foliage, or beneath lofty trees, in which flocks of little yellow birds, like Canary birds, flew and twittered gayly. The country was here infinitely pretty and romantic, and the waters of the Shenandoah, although shallow, are as clear as crystal.

Lower down the river, on this same side, is a gun manufactory, which just at this moment is in a state of great activity. The houses of the work-people lie on the hillside—small houses, well built, all alike, and from which the views were very beautiful.

"We are all equal here," said a young woman to me in one of these dwellings, into which I had gone to rest; "our circumstances are all alike."

They were very good; and yet she did not look happy. We sat in a parlor where every thing was comfortable, and even elegant. The young woman had a little boy in her arms, and yet she was not happy; that was evident. Something in her mild, sorrowful expression told me that she was not happily married.

In another house I made the acquaintance of an older woman, whose countenance bore the impress of the deepest sorrow. She had lost her husband, and he had been the joy of her life. She spoke of him with words which made me mingle my tears with hers.

In the beautiful evenings the doors of the houses for the most part stood open, and women stood before them with their children, or sat outside and sewed. I made acquaintance first with the children, and then with the mothers.

All were similar in the lot of outward fortune, and yet with that eternal dissimilarity of the inner fortune of life! Thus will it always be. But yet this dissimilarity is borne more easily than that which is caused by the prejudices of caste. It causes less murmuring and less bitterness.

There was one evening a wedding down in the hamlet, and the wedding guests were seen in their gay wedding attire wandering down the foot-paths on the hill-side from the dwellings on the hill to the shore. They were dressed simply but tastefully, very much in the same style as the people dress themselves for company in the cities, but in less costly materials.

One evening, when somewhat late I was returning home over the hills, I saw, sitting on a style which I had to pass, a man in a blue artisan blouse, with his brow resting on his hand, in which he held a pocket-handkerchief. As I came nearer, he removed his hand and looked at me, and I saw an Irish nose in a good lively countenance, which seemed to be that of a man about thirty years of age.

"It's very warm!" said he, speaking English.

"Yes," said I, passing, "and you have worked hard, have you not?"

"Yes, my hands are quite spoiled!" and with that he exhibited a pair of coarse black hands.

I asked a little about his circumstances. He was an Irishman, named Jim, and had come hither to seek for work, which he had found at the manufactory, and by which he could earn twenty dollars a month. But still, he said, he loved the Old Country best, and he meant to return to it as soon as he could get together a thousand dollars.

I inquired if he were married.

No! he had thought it best to remain unmarried. And then he inquired if I were married.

I replied no; and added that, like him, I thought it best to remain unmarried, after which I bade him a friendly good-by.

But he rose up, and, following me, said,

"And you are wandering about here so alone, Miss! Don't you think it is wearisome to go wandering about by yourself?"

"No, Jim," said I; "I like to go by myself."

"Oh, but you would feel yourself so much better off," said he; "you would find yourself so much happier, if you had a young man to go about with you, and take care of you!"

"But I find myself very well off as I am, Jim," said I.

"Oh, but you'd find yourself much, much better off, if you had a young man, I assure you, a young man who was fond of you, and would go with you every where. It makes the greatest difference in the world to a lady, I do assure you!"

"But, Jim, I am an old lady now, and a young man would not trouble himself about me."

"You are not too old to be married, Miss," said he; "and then you are good-looking, Miss; you are very good-looking, Ma'am! and a nice young man would be very glad to have you, to go about every where with you."

"But, Jim, perhaps he would not like to go where I should like to go, and then how should we get on together?"

"Oh, yes, he would like, Ma'am, I assure you he would like it! And perhaps you have a thousand dollars on which you would maintain him, Ma'am."

"But, Jim, I should not like to have a husband who would merely have me for the sake of my dollars."

"You're right there, Miss, very right. But you would he so very much happier with a nice young man who would take care of you," &c.

"Look here, Jim," said I, finally; "up there, above the clouds, is a great big Gentleman who takes care of me, and if I have him, there is no need of any one else."

The thought struck my warm-hearted Irishman, who exclaimed,

"There you are right, Miss! Yes, He is the husband, after all! And if you have Him, you need not be afraid of any thing!"

"Nor am I afraid, Jim. But now," said I, "go ahead, for the path is too narrow for two."

And we separated. What now do you think of your proposed brother-in-law?

The third day of my stay, people began to have some knowledge of who was the solitary wanderer in the neighborhood, and kind visitors came with invitations, which I regretted not being able to receive and accept, in consequence of an attack of toothache. The heat, too, was again oppressive, and affected both soul and body.

From Harper's Ferry I proceeded to Philadelphia. The day was beautiful, but the journey was fatiguing, from the many changes which were requisite from steam-boat to rail-way and back again, and because I, being alone, without a gentleman friend, had to carry my own luggage, being unwilling to trouble any stranger. In my case, however, it mattered little, as I was strong and well; but I was really distressed for a lady, solitary like myself, but an invalid and suffering, who did not seem able to carry her carpet-bag herself. And when I saw tall, strong men, without any thing in their hands, passing by this lady, evidently a gentlewoman, who was so in need of help, without troubling themselves about her, I confess to my being somewhat surprised. Where was now that vaunted American politeness! I would have been very glad to have helped her myself, but that I had enough to do with my own effects, and there was so little time, because these changes were made very rapidly.

I dislike that woman should demand from men politeness and service, and I believe that women who have esteem for themselves are the very last who would make claims of this kind ; but yet it ought not to be forgotten that women within the house serve the men, and that they generally do so willingly and in the entire spirit of affection, and very few indeed are the men who do not, some time or other, experience the charm of this service, and still fewer are they who have not to thank the care and kindness of women for the care of their childhood and youth. It ought not, then, to be too much for them, on the highways of life, to extend to them, in passing by, a helping hand, especially when this can be done at the expense of very little time and no self-sacrifice. And in a general way there is no need to preach to American men about politeness. That which I saw on this and two other occasions in the United States were so very much opposed to the general politeness, and even kindness, that it merely proves the truth of the old proverb, "There is no rule without an exception."

And, now that I am speaking about rail-way traveling, I may mention that there is still a great want in America, where, however, so much is done for the convenience of the traveler, in there not being, as there are in England and other European countries, officials at the rail-way stations whose sole duty is to render any assistance to travelers which they may need. And in America, where ladies travel so much alone, it is more requisite than elsewhere, and would be to them the greatest comfort; for what woman of delicacy would ask for aid which it would be considered trouble to give her?

I spent the latter part of that beautiful day very pleasantly in quiet companionship with my new and only acquaintance on the journey, the already-mentioned and agreeable lady; watched the sun set, and the moon ascend in splendor!

In the evening I was at Philadelphia, excellently lodged in the handsome and comfortable dwelling of the kind Quaker couple, Mr. and Mrs. E. T.

The angelic young girl, Mary T. (the sister of Mrs. T.), whom I had seen this time last year lying in white garments on her bed, had now lain for two days in the earth beneath green trees. Her death was bright, as was her state in life, and she lies in her grave with her face turned to the rising sun. She who wrote of the insect's metamorphosis, and loved to converse of the moment when they freed their wings from their confinement, is now free and enfranchised as they.

I visited with her brother, last evening, her final resting-place on earth, a beautiful, peaceful spot.

July 15th. Ah, my child, how delighted I am with the drawing academy for young girls which I visited yesterday! It is an excellent institution, and will effect an infinite deal of good. Here genius and the impulse for cultivation in young women may receive nourishment and development, and patient industry and the power of labor have occupation and pecuniary profit in the most agreeable way. Young girls can receive instruction at this academy (the poor free of cost, the more wealthy on the payment of a small sum) in drawing, painting, composition; in the making of designs for woven fabrics, carpets, or paper-hangings; in wood engraving, lithography, &c.; and the establishment has already been so successful, and so great is the progress made by the pupils, so numerous are the orders for designs, wood engraving, &c., and so well paid is all, that the young girls are able already to make considerable earnings, and there is every prospect that the establishment will, within very few years, be able fully to support itself.

It is the same school which I saw last year in its infancy, with the warm-hearted Mrs. P., the wife of the British consul here, when it entirely depended on her support. Since then it has rapidly developed itself, has become incorporated with the excellent Franklin Institute here, and receives an annual stipend from its funds, and now grows from its own strength. Several of the young pupils gain already from ten to fifteen dollars per week. The publisher of "Sartain's Magazine" told me that the demand for such work in the United States; for newspapers, magazines, manufactures, &c., was so great, that all the women of the country, who had time to devote themselves to such occupation, might have full employment. And never have I seen, in any school whatever, so many cheerful, animated countenances. One of the most cheerful was that of a young girl who had hitherto maintained herself by dress-making, but who was found to possess so fine a talent for drawing, that she might now calculate with certainty on making by this means a respectable maintenance for her whole life.

The cheerful, agreeable superintendent, Mrs. Hill, told me that the young girls were so amused and interested by their work, that they sometimes remained in the school the whole day, instead of five hours, which constituted the proper school-time. I am enchanted with this institution, which reveals a bright future for so many young girls, otherwise unprovided for, and develops the feeling of beauty in their minds, while it opens a path for them in manifold ways. I am very much pleased with this academy also, because its design is applicable to Sweden, and may there open a prospect for many a one in the improvement of both soul and body. I have brought away with me many proofs and specimens, which have been kindly given to me, as well as all information which I could obtain.

Ah! let us, if possible, establish almshouses and asylums

for the old, the infirm, and the sick; but for the young, let us give *work*—free scope for emulation; let us unfold paths for their development, and noble objects for their lives. This is the only really good assistance which can be given to girls otherwise unprovided for, because it necessarily implies elevation, and secures happiness by self-acquired worth. More of this when we meet. I feel as if the time of our meeting were now so near, that it was hardly worth while to write long letters.

17*th*. The same excellent and agreeable gentleman (Dr. E.) who took me to the drawing academy, accompanied me to-day to the medical college for ladies, which was established here a year ago, and which will enable ladies to receive a scientific education as physicians. This institution has not been established without great opposition, but it has nevertheless come into operation, to the honor of the spirit and justice of the New World! To this ought also to be added the steadfastness and talent of a young American woman, and the reputation which she obtained abroad. Elizabeth Blackwell, after having for several years, by hard work, helped to educate and maintain several younger sisters, devoted herself to the profession of medicine, firmly resolved to open in this way a career for herself and other women. She was met by a thousand difficulties; prejudice and ill will threw impediments in every step; but she overcame all; and finally studied and graduated as physician at the city of Geneva, in Western New York. After this she went abroad, desirous of entering and passing the Medical College of Paris. The head of the college was shocked: "You must dress yourself as a man," said he, "otherwise it will be quite impossible."

"I shall not alter even a ribbon on my bonnet!" said she; "do as you will; but your conduct shall be made known. You have seen my certificate; you have no right to refuse me admission."

Mr. L. was obliged to comply. Elizabeth's womanly dignity and bearing, added to her remarkable knowledge, impressed the professors as well as students of the college. The young woman pursued her studies in peace, protected by her earnestness and scientific knowledge. Having greatly distinguished herself, and won the highest commendation, she left Paris for London, where she gathered fresh laurels, both in medical and chirurgical science. She is at this moment expected back in America, where she intends to be a practicing physician. Dr. E. wished me to become acquainted with this young woman—this vigorous soul in a slender and delicate frame—whom he cordially admires, and rejoices over as with paternal pride. He said, speaking of her to me,

"She is not taller than you, but she would take you under one arm and my daughter under the other, and run up stairs with you both."

I should like to see that.

It was now the time of vacation at this institution, which contains already upward of seventy female students; but the session will soon recommence, and the professor of anatomy, a handsome, agreeable man, was busied in the preparation of a human skeleton.

It seems to me very desirable that this establishment should direct the attention of the female students, or rather that they should themselves direct it, to that portion of medical science which pre-eminently belongs to them; for is there not here, as in all spheres of life, science, arts, and professions, one region which, beyond all others, belongs to woman, by reason of natural tendencies? In medicine, it is evidently partly the *preventive*—that is to say, by attention to health and diet, to effect the prevention of disease, especially in women and children—and partly, *par excellence*, *healing*, *curing*. Women have in all ages shown a remarkable talent for the healing art—have shown an ability, by herbs and the so-called domestic medicine, to cure or assuage human suffering. Their branch of medical art ought evidently to be that of the alleviation of pain; they should not be the instigators of suffering. In this they would make great progress. The instincts of the heart would be united in them with the knowledge of the head. Curative medicine would therefore be more adapted to them than surgery. And herbs, those beautiful healing herbs, which stand on the hilltops and amid the fields like beneficent angels beckoning in the summer winds, may be borne by the hands of the female physician into the dwellings of the sufferers, and, by means of miraculous powers called forth by love and art, may promulgate the Evangile of health more and more over the earth, and change, as much as is possible, even the so frequently terrible work of death into a peaceful transition state. Oh, to be young, to be able to devote a life to this glorious science!

Women, in all lands and in all ages, have practiced the art of the physician with this aim. The work which demands more prolonged study, a more vigorous resolution, a stronger, bolder hand, will in this profession, as in all others, always become the part of the man, because he is best fitted for it.

July 20th. Here I am, still detained by events in the family whose guest I am; for only one week after the death of Mary T., she was followed to the grave by her most beloved sister; and Mr. E. T., who was to accompany me to New York, is obliged to remain here yet a few days.

These two young sisters, who were both invalids, had vigorous, richly-endowed souls, and had always lived in a state of heartfelt friendship with each other, laboring together on literary subjects for the benefit of the young. Tenderly attached in life, it was well that they should accompany each other in death. But they have left a great vacuum in the home where there is now only one daughter remaining. She who last died lived during the last days of her earthly existence amid the most beautiful visions of her departed sister, and of their ascending together into a realm of glory.

The interment, at which I was present yesterday, took place according to Quaker custom, without any unnecessary pomp or parade, without any ceremony or show. It took place amid alternate short addresses both of men and women, and silence, all in accordance with the influence of the Spirit. It was really very affecting, when all the friends and relations were assembled in the house of the dead, and were sitting together in silence in one room, to hear the aged, deeply-afflicted mother lift up her trembling voice, and begin in these words:

"My heart has been severely tried, but God has seen me in his mercy!" All that she said came so purely from the depths of a Christian mother's heart, and was, at the same time, so tender in feeling, and so strong in faith and submission, that nothing could have been better. Most beautiful was the consolation which she derived from the knowledge of the purity of her departed daughters' views and objects in life, and the memory of her youngest daughter's last words shortly before her death.

When the mother ceased, amid the tears of all present, another elderly lady spoke and dried them again; for her speech was a cold and thin dilution of the words of the first. Then followed an elderly gentleman, who gave a third edition, but not improved. Nor indeed could it be.

We drove to the burial-place amid thunder and heavy rain. But just as we alighted from the carriages, and the coffin was lowered to the earth beneath the shadowy trees, the silvery sun burst forth from the clouds and illumined most splendidly the silent scene, the yet descending drops, the beautiful trees, and continued to shine the whole time during an address from one of the elders of the company (which was as dry and prosaic as the sunshine was warm and poetic), and until the coffin was laid in the earth.

It is very singular, but precisely the same occurrence is said to have taken place at Mary's interment; the same funeral procession amid the rain, the same splendid sunshine by the grave. Are such merely accidental? The two young sisters partake of the same grave beneath the same sheltering tree, as they partook of the same life, joys, and sorrows, and their poetical sister-in-law may sing of them,

> Lay them together side by side,
> To slumber most serenely, &c.

Mrs. E. T. has great poetical talent, especially for ballads and romances. Two of her small ballads are the prettiest I know. Her husband is an agreeable man, of very cultivated mind, with all that feeling for the public well-being which distinguishes the American. He himself is a celebrated dentist, and a member of an association of dentists, into which he is now endeavoring to introduce so liberal a spirit, that all beginners and imperfect practitioners may be admitted free of cost to the lectures and experiments of the association, and to the use of their instruments, so that the inferior members of the profession may be elevated by the influence and ready co-operation of the higher. Mr. T. delivers lectures every week gratis to young practitioners. "Leveling upward" is the impelling principle also with him, and he has written an excellent treatise upon the fundamental idea of this association. Association is the natural movement of life in the free states.

July 21st. I have happened during these last few days in Philadelphia to fall in love—yes, really to fall desperately in love—with a young girl, not so very handsome, but of a glorious young-womanly character richly endowed, both soul and body, with that spark of inspired life which is so enchanting and so infinitely revivifying; a girl fresh as morning dew, and who sings as I never have heard any one sing since *her* who has long since ceased to sing on earth, yet not in my soul. But true it is that she was Fanny Kemble's "pet," and had in her an incomparable instructress in declamation. And the girl, the glorious girl, the girl of the New World, whom I have for the first time seen since I had an idea of her: she is called—But no, I will not write her name; I feel as if that would desecrate it, and she is to me holy. I could weep when I think that such a girl should not have a different fate to quiet, ordinary girls. Such a young woman ought to be the priestess of a holy temple, and deliver oracles to the world. I will tell you more about her by word of mouth. She has called to life in my imagination a figure which has lain bound there for more than fifteen years.

I shall set off to-day to New York. It has been so oppressively hot this time in Philadelphia that I have not been able to accomplish much. To-day it is beautiful and fresh after yesterday's rain. N.B.—That was the first regular shower of rain which I had seen for five months, and through the whole of that time I had not seen one entire cloudy day.

I now cordially rejoice in the prospect of so soon seeing once more those good, excellent friends of mine at Rose Cottage.

Rose Cottage, July 24th.

And now I am with them, as happy as it is possible for me to be so far from my beloved; here I am with this beloved, *rose-colored* family, always alike good, alike *couleur de rose;* and all my friends from New York come to kiss me, to shake hands with me, and to say "How do you do?" Lively, cordial, fresh, impulsive people are these people of the New World; there is no denying that! And your letter, among dozens of others, to welcome me here! But ah! that it should be so cold and cheerless with you. It is very unworthy of Madame Svea to permit such weather in June! But now, now you must have sunshine enough, even in Sweden. I am preparing for my homeward journey, but am out of breath when I think of all I have yet to do before I can leave. I am now on my way to Boston, and thence to the White Mountains, to Maine, New Hampshire, Vermont, &c.

I commence my journey in the morning, going from one friend to another the whole length of the way. But it will not be before the commencement of September that I can be ready to leave America. But then I will leave it. Ah! I hardly dare to think about it, so painful will the parting be to me. When autumn comes in Sweden, then shall I be with my beloved! Mamma must propitiate St. Brigitta, that she give me a prosperous voyage over the great sea!

Great changes have taken place around Rose Cottage and its peaceful environs since I was last there, that is to say, since last year. Above a hundred houses, certainly, have sprung up around it in all directions, and a regular street runs now in front of its little park. When I first came to Rose Cottage, it stood in the country; now it lies in the very middle of the city. It is a good thing that there is yet a deal of space, and many trees around the house, to preserve free breathing-room.

LETTER XXXIX.

Nahant, Massachusetts, August 1st.

A GREETING and a kiss to you, my Agathina, on this cool, beautiful Sunday morning, which I am celebrating upon a rock in the midst of the sea, surrounded by glittering, dancing waves. I am with Mrs. B., in her cottage at Nahant, a little bathing-place a few miles north of Boston. The aristocracy of Boston have here their villas and cottages, where they, for a couple of months in the year, enjoy the sea air or bathing; and here, at the present moment, in these pretty dwellings, embowered by verdant, fragrant plants among the bare rocks, a select little party is assembled. Here is that splendid old Mrs. L. (the mother of Mrs. B.) in her cottage; here is Mr. Prescott, the excellent historian, with his family; the preacher Bellows, from New York; Mr. Longfellow, Mrs. S., with several other interesting persons, and the intercourse among them is easy and charming, with little dinner-parties or tea-suppers in the evenings. The Americans are in a high degree a social people, and they do not like to shut themselves up, or to shut their friends out.

I came hither that I might see Mrs. B. again, who was so infinitely kind to me—came hither from Boston, where I spent a week with my excellent friend, Dr. O., who, when he had made me strong as his patient, made me happy as his guest in his house, where I had merely one standing quarrel with him, and that was because he had not earlier made me acquainted with his wife, one of those happy, amiable characters, who are a fountain of joy and peace to all who surround them. Another singularly happy and affectionate married pair.

I made two small excursions from Boston, one of which was to Concord, because I wished to see Emerson and Elizabeth H. once more before leaving America forever. I can not exactly tell why I wished it, but my soul seemed to require it of me. I *must* see Emerson yet once more.

I reached Concord in the afternoon, and took up my quarters with Elizabeth H. We went together to Emerson's. They were both from home. I went for a moment into Emerson's study, a large room, in which every thing was simple, orderly, unstudied, comfortable. No refined feeling of beauty has, as is the case at the Downing's, converted the room into a temple, in which stand the forms of the heroes of science and literature. Ornament is banished from the sanctuary of the Stoic philosopher;

the furniture is comfortable, but of a grave character, merely as implements of usefulness; one large picture only is in the room, but this hangs there with a commanding power; it is a large oil painting, a copy of Michael Angelo's glorious "Parcæ;" the goddesses of fate, as there represented, are not horrible; they are too noble and beautiful for that, although inflexible. The one, in particular, who holds the thread of life in her hand, is beautiful; she who holds the shears to sever the thread, looks up to the former with a questioning, compassionate expression, and the other replies by a smile of the most beautiful assurance and trust. Mortal can not gaze upon it without resigning himself with confidence to the hands of the immortal maternal powers.

Upon the large table in the centre of the room, at which Emerson sits and writes, just opposite the picture, lay a number of papers, but all in perfect order. I stood silent for a moment in the room. Emerson's spirit seemed to pervade its calm, pure atmosphere.

In the evening I saw Emerson at Elizabeth H.'s. He was kind and bright, like himself in his most amiable mood. I was to leave the following morning. He opposed this, however, most decidedly.

"Oh no, no, you must not think of that!" said he, "I have been proposing to myself to drive you to one of our beautiful little forest lakes in the neighborhood, and then you must see my mother, and receive her blessing!"

I do not know whether I have told you that Emerson has a mother, in whose countenance may be seen many features resembling those of her son. The old mother was now confined to her bed in consequence of a fall, by which she had broken her leg.

I could not resist Emerson's kindness and these words.

The following day, therefore, he called for me in a cabriolet, which he himself drove, and took me by the loveliest forest road to a little lake which lay in the bosom of the forest, like a clear, oval mirror in a dark green frame. The place looked like a sanctuary of the kindly divinities of nature.

We talked a deal by the way; for I am always excited to conversation with Emerson in a calm and agreeable manner. The topic of conversation on this occasion arose principally from my asking Emerson whether he considered the intellectual culture of the New England States to have attained its acmé, and if we might not see in these a type of the perfected American community?"

"By no means," replied he; "there are at this time a number of Germanisms and other European ideas, nay, even ideas from Asia, which are now for the first time finding their way into the life of mind, and which will there produce new developments!"

Emerson evidently considers America intended to present under a higher metamorphosis those ideas, which during the course of ages have been prefigured in other parts of the world.

As regarded the late political concessions which the Northern States made to the slave states, the right of asylum to the fugitive slave, he expressed him in strong disapprobation, but still in his placid manner.

"Here is a spring famous for its excellent water," said Emerson, as he pulled up near some lofty trees by the road side. "May I give you a glass?"

I thanked him in the affirmative, and he alighted, fastened the reins to a tree, and soon returned with a glass of water clear as crystal from the spring.

A glass of water! How much may be comprised in this gift. Why this should become significant to me on this occasion I can not say, but so it was. I have silently within myself combated with Emerson from the first time that I became acquainted with him. I have questioned with myself in what consisted this power of the spirit over me, while I so much disapproved of his mode of thinking, when there was so much in him which was unsatisfactory to me; in what consisted his mysterious magical power —that invigorating, refreshing influence, which I always experience in his writings, or in intercourse with him? This cordial draught of clear water from the spring, given by his hand, I understood it. It is precisely this crystal, pure, fresh cold water in his individual character, in his writings, which has refreshed, and will again and yet again refresh me.

I have opposed Emerson in thought with myself, and in conversation with others who have blindly admired him. I shall oppose him also in public, from the conviction within my own soul of the highest justice and truth. But in long years to come, and when I am far from here, in my own native land, and when I am old and gray, yes, always, always will moments recur when I shall yearn toward Waldo Emerson, and long to receive from his hand that draught of fresh water. For wine, warmth-infusing, life-renovating wine, I would go to another.

Emerson baptizes in water; another there is who baptizes with the Spirit and with fire.

I left Emerson with an unmingled sentiment of gratitude for what he has been to me. I may perhaps see other more beautiful and more perfect forms, but never shall I see his equal again.

During my stay in Concord I again enjoyed my intercourse with the intellectual, profoundly thinking and feeling Elizabeth H. I also again saw Mrs. Channing, the younger sister of Margaret Fuller, now looking ten years older, so much had sorrow for the tragical fate of her highly-gifted sister weighed upon the young wife and mother.

I made another excursion from Boston, in company with the kind Miss P., to visit a seminary for teachers at West Newton, established by Horace Mann, as well as to greet once more and see Lydia Maria Child, who now resides in the neighborhood of the seminary. I was present at a lesson in the institution, at which from fifty to sixty young girls who are preparing themselves for instructors were present. One of them ascended the lecturer's chair, the others being seated on benches in the large, light, airy hall. The subject of the lesson was the form of government of the United States, in which she examined the others. The young teacher was handsome, with every appearance of a gentlewoman, and with an extremely agreeable deportment and manner. When she descended from her elevated seat, the others were encouraged to criticise her observations, or to point out any particulars in which she appeared to be in error. Several voices were raised in observation, one remarking that she had left the chair without any sign of acknowledgment to her audience. The young girl who took her place had a very different manner, was not so handsome, nor so much perhaps of the gentlewoman about her, but she was more ardent, more decided, and was evidently possessed of more than usual abilities. The subject of her lesson and examination was geographical statistics, and she gave it with a liveliness which gave animation to her whole audience. She too descended, and was criticised in her turn. In this way the young female teacher is early accustomed to the usual consequences of publicity, and is early accustomed to pay that attention to herself in all respects which is so important, especially for the school-teacher. The outward demeanor also, their movements, their gait, &c., all are subjects of observation and attention. Nothing must be allowed in the teacher which disgusts or excites ridicule in the scholar. Great numbers of young teachers are sent hence to the west and south of this vast country, where they are soon engaged by schools or—lovers.

After that I saw Horace Mann, the hopeful, meritorious man of education for the rising generation, and his agreeable young wife, at their cottage. I wished to have had with him some earnest conversation on the insufficiency of schools as educational institutions, but I forgot myself in Lydia Maria Child's home and company, until the railroad train was just about setting off, and I must return to Boston.

That noble and refined woman and gifted authoress lives here on a little farm, not much unlike a Swedish peasant's wife, and not in her proper element. A pretty little Spanish child, one of the many whom Lydia Maria Child had rescued from want, lives here with her and for her in heartfelt love. Friends surround her with affectionate solicitude. In North America, less than any where else, need people be solitary or neglected, unless they deserve to be so; and they who deserve many friends find them also.

During my stay in Boston I have been much interested by the new drawing-school for women, similar to that at Philadelphia, which is about to be established there by a Mr. Whiteacre, from London—a man with all the philanthropy of England in his eyes. Many respectable and wealthy men are ready to aid in this institution by every means in their power, from the interest they take in the future prospects of young women. I was present during a lesson given in the school, and rejoiced heartily in the prospects which these schools open for thousands of young women, and for the beautifying prospects of life in general. I think of Sweden and Swedish girls, Swedish drawing-schools, Swedish art and manufactures, and grow enthusiastic with many thoughts for the future.

It is now in Boston so cold and so cheerless with rain as I have not found it during the summer. Ever since the eclipse of the sun the other day, it has been as cloudy and cold as with us in October. This American climate leaps continually from one extreme to another. I am as cold as in winter. In other respects I am more vigorous than I have ever been since I left home, and I need be so to do all which I have now to do. Thus, for instance, I have been to-day in motion, and engaged in conversation from seven this morning till half past eleven at night, at five different places, some in and some out of Boston, with different persons, with whom I have to enter into interesting conversations on theology, art, politics, &c., with gentlemen at home, on all these subjects; but this amuses rather than wearies me. Among my more intimate acquaintance in Boston during the last winter, I have again met with an interesting lady, a Miss Parsons, of weak physical constitution, but of an unusually beautiful soul; that is to say, she is clairvoyant without sleeping, and can give the contents of a letter, or the character and state of the writer, merely by holding the letter closed in her hands, or pressing it upon her forehead. I would not believe in this species of clairvoyance at first, but have been obliged to believe in it after I had placed a letter from you in Swedish in her hand, without her having beforehand any knowledge of who had written the letter, or any thing about you. Besides which, her character is far above any thing of charlatanism. But this clear-sighted soul lives at the expense of the body, which becomes, as it were, more and more transparent and spirit-like.

At the house of my good doctor I have again seen many of my dear Boston friends, and made some new and interesting acquaintances, among whom is the Unitarian minister, Dr. Garratt.

Monday. I heard in Nahant church yesterday an excellent sermon by Mr. Bellows—one of those beautiful discourses from the very centre of Christianity—such a one as ought to be preached by the sea, the great sea in which all the individual waves rise and sink as in one general maternal bosom—as all separate Christian sects and creeds in the ocean of Christian love.

I had in the evening the great pleasure of conversing with two cultivated and thinking women of my acquaintance about the ladies of America—of that deficiency of many-sided development, that deficiency of instinct for the higher human interests, and of that want of the ability for conversation which is found in so great a number. These amiable ladies, themselves distinguished in all respects, agree with me in many of my observations, and, like myself, can not see any means of alleviating these deficiencies, excepting by a more thorough system of cultivation, a more broad and general development of mind; and many are the signs which will make this inevitable, if woman will maintain the esteem of their own sex as well as that of the men. Men have in general, at this time, more gallantry than actual esteem for women. They are polite to them, ready to comply with their wishes; but they regard them evidently more as pretty children than as their reasonable equals, and do not give them their society when they seek strengthening food for soul and thought. The many beautiful examples which one meets of an opposite, of a perfect relationship between the two sexes, can not be said to belong to the rule. Women are, it is true, rulers in the home and in social life, but that is frequently rather through their weaknesses than their virtues.

We spake of the signs which are indicative of the approach of a better state of things. We saw it by degrees gradually advancing in the public consciousness, and we marked also, as the forerunner of this, the Rights of Woman Conventions, which have now been held annually for some years in the Northern States. The holding of these Conventions is a movement of transition, which will cease of itself when the end is attained. Many true and profound thoughts were expressed in the last great Convention which was held last year in Massachusetts, and at which thousands of both men and women were present; excellent speeches were delivered, beautiful speeches, worthy of those distinguished speakers.

Among these thoughts I in particular remember what

was said on the life and culture of past ages in comparison with those of the present time.

Occupations and objects in life do not now separate the sexes, as was the case formerly. Man, except only in occasional instances, does not now live for the warlike profession; he does not now practice, above every thing else, strength of body and achievements of arms; the two sexes have, in a more spiritual sphere of life, come nearer to each other in the home and in social life. Woman becomes more and more the companion and helpmate of man; his powers of soul will be crippled or elevated in proportion as he finds in her that which retards or animates them. And the circumscribing of her development will operate unfavorably upon himself.

This was said, but far better than I have said it, by Mrs. Paulina Davis, the lovely president of the Convention, that pale lady with the noble features and expression of countenance, and the rich golden hair, whom I saw at my good female doctor's, Miss H.

The women of America have, as I have already said, their noblest types in the best of the American women. Nowhere can be found greater steadfastness to duty, or more energy of character united to greater gentleness and grace.

I have here greatly enjoyed the pure, fresh sea-air, amid quiet social intercourse with kind and cultivated people, under circumstances which combined enjoyment with all the charms and comforts of life. The "cottage" of the New World is a type of the pretty and the convenient united. Nature and art unite here to man. The veranda which runs round the house, with its leafy and flowery creepers, shadowy and fragrant, affords the most beautiful place for the quiet enjoyment, as well of nature as of society, during the most lovely weather.

I had imagined Prescott, the historian, to be an old man, bent down by study and labor, during which he had become almost blind. I could scarcely believe my eyes when, on the contrary, I found in him a tall and lively gentleman, with far more of the youth than of the aged thinker in his appearance and manner. His conversation and manners denote genius; they are full of life.

We have now moonlight, and our drives in the evenings along the sea-shore, while the waves are foaming and roaring, are a great enjoyment. Mrs. B. is one of the most delightful of hostesses, and with little Julia—ah! they who have such a little girl!

White Mountains, New Hampshire, August 10th.

Again several pleasant days have passed since I last wrote you from Nahant.

I went from Nahant to Salem on the 8th of this month, and at the house of the mayor there, Mr. S., was in company with, and shooks hands with between fifty and sixty Salemites, among whom were some very pretty young witches, and some very kind friends of mine.

The next morning, rush went we—my clever and agreeable hostess, Mr. S., and myself—from Salem to Boston, to see several persons; to be present at a lesson at Mr. Whiteacre's drawing-school, and at another at Mr. Barnard's phonographic school for little girls, who all conducted themselves like so many little miracles; to see Mrs. H., of Belmont, near Charlestown, yet once more, ah! for the last time; then back to the O.'s to write notes, see people, arrange meetings, take leave, and a deal more; then rushed back again by rail-way to Salem to dinner and evening parties; then one day to write, and, comparatively speaking, to rest, amid quiet calls, promenades, and conversation about the witch-trials at Salem in the year 1692, during which trials the same species of phenomena were exhibited as those which appeared among us in Dalecarlia a few years ago. Even in the free state of the Pilgrims a considerable number of innocent persons, especially women, were suspected of witchcraft, imprisoned, tortured, and several of them were put to death.

We are now, thank God! so far removed from such horrible scenes—more, however, by spirit than by time—that we speak of them as we speak of mad-house scenes, and make merry with them when we are in good-humor.

This was done last year in the city of Salem, on the great American day, the 4th of July. They celebrated it by a grand historical, humorous procession, in which also witch-trials, with their *dramatis personæ*, both witches and judges, were introduced, in grotesque, old-fashioned costume.

Among the historical *tableaux* of the procession was a series also which exhibited the progress made in the means of communication within the last fifty years. First came a horseman, riding slowly along, with the following inscription: "From Salem to Boston in forty-eight hours' time." Then came an old, heavy diligence, with the inscription, "From Salem to Boston in twelve hours' time." After them came a rail-way train, inscribed, "From Salem to Boston in half an hour;" and lastly an iron wire of the electric telegraph, inscribed, "From Salem to Boston in no time at all!" The whole of the historical procession seemed to me one of the cleverest, most ingenious, and amusing popular festivals which I ever heard of, and seemed to have caused the greatest delight. The New World, which is altogether deficient in traditional popular festivals (with the exception of the beautiful Thanksgiving festival), seems to have begun a new series of such, of a more rational purport, and with more food for sound thought and sentiment than the European popular amusements, which are often utterly devoid of meaning. Among the American festivals I have heard some very beautiful ones mentioned: the so-called Floral-feasts, in the months of May and June, which seem to me like lovely children of the spirit of the New World. But still, working-days are in this country so supreme, that people are hardly able to occupy themselves with festivals, at least the product of a self-conscious, developed popular life.

On the 7th of August I left Salem for the White Mountains, in company with Mrs. S. and her young son. Her voluntary offer to be my companion on this excursion was particularly agreeable to me, because I like her manners and her society, and I can, while I make this journey with her, avoid great parties and great companies, and can go about in freedom among the mountains, the waterfalls, and the forests, and see every thing as I wish to see it, in the quietest and the most agreeable manner in the world.

The first day's journey was to the Shaker community at Canterbury, by the Merrimac River in New Hampshire, which I wished to visit, that I might see its Botanic Garden, and become somewhat better acquainted with this remarkable sect. I had letters to the chief family of this Shaker community from my little ladies' doctor in Boston, Miss H., who was frequently called in here as physician. We went by rail-way into New Hampshire, but left it again in a forest, where we were to take a carriage which should convey us to the Shaker village at some miles' distance. After various small misadventures, we obtained a cart in which was a seat, on which Mrs. S. and I could sit, our driver sitting half on a little package and half on our knees. Thus proceeded we leisurely with a leisurely horse, along heavy, sandy roads, through the forest. It began to rain, first very small, then thicker and faster. We hoisted our umbrellas, and sat patiently for between two and three hours. Very glad, however, were we when at length we perceived through the vail of rain the cheerful, yellow, two-storied houses of the Shaker village shining out on the green hills through the rain, at some distance from us.

Pretty much like wet hens, we descended from our cart, and soon a hospitable door was opened to us, and two young sisters, with gentle, pale countenances, led us into a great chamber, where every thing was neat and delicate, and rubbed as bright as in a doll's house. I produced my letter, and immediately saw its good effect in an increased kindliness, and by the cordial manner in which Harriet H. was inquired after.

It was late when we arrived. The kind sisters gave us tea, with excellent bread and butter, preserves, &c., and at my request sang the while some of their spiritual songs. Their manner was tranquil, and, though not cheerful, had a heartfelt gentleness and serenity in it. After this evening meal we were conducted to our chambers, two large, light rooms, where nothing was unnecessarily ornamental, but where every thing was neat and convenient. Sister Lavinia took us particularly under her charge.

Some streaks of light in the west at sunset had led me to hope for a bright morrow, and they did not deceive me. The brightest of suns shone the next morning over the Shaker dwellings, and the pastoral, pleasing country which surrounded them, and a considerable portion of which belonged to their community. Not a single dwelling except their own was to be seen in that solitary region; and the whole scene which more immediately surrounded these was altogether as quiet and as orderly as if a life of labor did not exist there. It was altogether so calm and silent that it almost struck the mind as something spiritual.

After breakfast, which the sisters served in an excellent and bountiful manner, we were asked if we would like to see the school, and on answering in the affirmative, we were conducted into a spacious hall, in which about twenty little well-dressed girls were receiving instruction from a female teacher. This teacher, whom I will call Dora, was still quite young, and of singular beauty, neither had her complexion that paleness so common among women of this community; her cheeks were fresh as the blush of morning, and more beautiful eyes than hers I never beheld.

She allowed the little girls to show us one of their symbolic games. They placed themselves in a wide circle, each one standing at three or four paces distant from the other. They then began little verses, which, though I can not give literally accurate, were in substance as follows:

Must I here alone be standing,
Having none that I can love;
Having none my friend to be,
None who will grow fond of me?

On this each little girl approached the one nearest to her, and, taking each other's hands, they laid them upon their hearts and sung

Nay, my sister, come thou nearer,
And I will to thee be dearer,
Be to thee a faithful friend;
I will share with thee thy sadness;
Thou shalt share with me my gladness!

With this the children all took hold of hands, and slowly moving round in a circle, repeated the while these last words, or something like them; and in so doing, approached nearer and nearer together, wove their arms round each other like a garland of flowers, then sunk upon their knees, singing the while a hymn, the first verse of which was

Heavenly Father, look down in mercy
On this little flock,
United in thy name!
Give us of thy Holy Spirit, &c.

While singing this hymn, and while still upon their knees, the children all kissed each other, after which they rose up and separated. The beautiful symbolic meaning contained in the whole game, its simplicity, and the beautiful grace with which it was performed; the thought of the difference in the spirit of this game to the bitter reality of many a solitary existence in the great community of the world, affected me deeply; I could not refrain from weeping. Mrs. S. was also very much affected. From this moment the Shaker sisters were our friends and sisters, and embraced us with the greatest cordiality. Another beautiful song, worthy of serious attention, was sung very well by the children. It began, "Speak gently," and showed in several stanzas the effect of a gentle word. A song it was which all children ought to learn, and all grown people commit to memory.

It was an unexpected thing to me to meet with children here well practiced also in grammar, writing, arithmetic, geography, and other ordinary branches of learning. As a reward for, and an inducement to industry and good behavior, they receive small colored cards, printed with proverbs or exhortations, among which an occasional spur to a praiseworthy ambition was not wanting.

From the school we went to the room where the fine weaving was done, for which this Shaker community is celebrated.

We saw in one room a knitting-machine, which knit with its own hand woolen jackets, and could produce three in a shorter time than would be required for two pair of human hands to complete one. This machine, which seemed almost entirely to go on by itself, looked very curious, and almost like an enchanted thing.

We next paid a visit to the dairy, and to the room in which cheese-making was done, and which a number of fresh colossal cheeses testified of the good condition of the dairy-farm and all that appertained to it. The handsome, clever sister who managed this department was so fond of her employment, that, although she might have exchanged it for another, she had not done so, and had now been engaged in it for several years. From the dairy we proceeded to the kitchen, where I saw six blooming, handsome young girls employed as kitchen-maids; they were at this moment employed in baking large pies. These young girls were blooming as roses, and were ready to burst out into the gayest laughter when one gave them any occasion to do so.

"Look well after those sisters," said I, jokingly, to the Sister President. And the six handsome girls laughed so loudly and merrily that it was a pleasure to hear them.

From the medical garden, in which sarsaparilla and various other beneficial herbs are cultivated, we went to the house where they were picked and kept, and where rose-water was being just now distilled.

Finally, we were conducted into the sewing-room, and which is at the same time the apartment in which the aged sit together. Here, in this large, light, clean room, they sat in light-colored, and, for the most part, white clothing, and with bright, kindly countenances also. There now assembled a great number of the sisters round us, and we had conversation and singing, and I read aloud to the sisters, by their desire, a Swedish psalm. I selected the one beginning, "I will lift up mine eyes with the hills from whence cometh my help," which they thought sounded *quite proper*, and we joined them in singing various of their hymns, which were very beautiful, the time of which was marked, as is customary with them, by the waving of their hands. After that I made a sketch of Sister Dora, who consented on condition that I should not publish her name, "because," said the sister, mildly, "we are not accustomed to such things." Dora belongs to the Church-family of the community, and has had "inspiration," it is said. Of a truth, a more thankful, inspired glance than hers I never beheld. And her pure beauty charmed me still more as I sketched that noble, refined profile. I made a sketch also of Lavinia. She had not Dora's severe style of beauty, but, on the contrary, the gentlest grace.

I can not tell you how much I liked all that I saw of this little community during the whole of this day, or how admirable appeared to me the order and the neatness of every thing, from the sisters themselves to every thing which came under their hands. The male portion of the community were busied with the harvest, and I saw merely a few representatives of them. These seemed to me to have either a gloomy, almost fanatical expression, or to have very well-fed bodies without any spiritual expression at all. The good sisters, who now regarded us as their friends, gave us many presents from their stores of valuable wares, implements of the work-box, fragrant waters, cakes of maple-tree sugar, &c. And when, on the following day, we wished to pay for our entertainment, they replied, "We never take payment from our friends!" Nor would they receive the slightest sum.

A spacious traveling-carriage, with several seats, drawn by two fat horses, and driven by a stout Shaker brother, whom no Shaker dancing had been able to render less fat and jolly, made their appearance, and some of the sisters said that, as it was good for their health to take a little exercise in the open air, they would drive with us to the rail-way station. A politeness could not possibly have been done in a more delicate or handsome manner.

And now behold us seated on our buffalo skins, Mrs. S. between two Shaker sisters, and myself between two others, one of whom was the mild Lavinia, with two others seated behind us. We thus took our way through the forest, while the Shaker brother, a good-tempered, merry fellow, and the sisters sung spiritual songs, some of which were very characteristic, as, for instance,

> Ye trees and shrubs be dancing,
> Ye rivers rise on high,
> The Prince of Peace is advancing, &c.

In this style we drove seven English miles, and in this style we arrived at the rail-way station. And here the sisters remained with us till the train came, amused by looking over the portraits and sketches in my sketching books. As to paying any thing for our journey hither, that was not to be thought of; "the sisters required exercise, and it had been a pleasure for them to be with us," &c. It would not have been possible for people to behave with more naturally perfect politeness than the Shaker sisters behaved toward us. We separated with cordial shaking of hands. Many of these sisters evidently did not enjoy good health. I ascribe this less to their sedentary life than to their diet, which I do not believe to be wholesome. The eating of so much greasy pastry would be injurious to the soundest health in the country.

The Shaker community of Canterbury consists of about five hundred persons. There are here a vast many more fine and beautiful countenances among the young women than in the community of New Lebanon. The costume was the same, and the customs the same also. Among their customs is that of using the pronouns "*thee*" and "*thou*," as with the Quakers; and "*yea*" and "*nay*," instead of "*yes*" and "*no*." They lay great stress upon a friendly and kind behavior toward each other in word and deed. They endeavor in their large families to create that life of love which is the most beautiful flower of the lesser family. Work, and prayer, and mutual good offices are the business of their daily life.

I have already described to you the form of government which prevails in these small communities.

The Shaker community of Canterbury derives its principal income from its farming produce, its preparation of medicinal herbs for the pharmacopœia, and the weaving of woolen goods.

The Shaker communities are the most rational, and probably the happiest of all conventual institutions. I should be glad if similar ones were found in all countries. People may say what they will, and do the best they can in the great community, but there will always exist the need of places where the shipwrecked in life, the wearied of life, the solitary and feeble, may escape as to a refuge, and where their good-will and their powers of labor may, under a wise and affectionate management, be turned to account; where the children of misfortune or misery may be brought up in purity and love; where men and women may meet and associate as brethren and sisters in good-will and friendship, laboring all for the benefit and advantage of each other. And this is the case here. The Shaker community is—admitting some small, narrowed peculiarities—one of the best small communities in the world, and one of the most useful in the great community.

This sect is, in general, not understood. People consider its dancing mode of worship to be the main principle, when, in fact, that might just as well be away, though I, for my part, would willingly retain it for its symbolic meaning, like the heavenly child's-play which I saw this morning.

There are seventy or eighty Shaker communities in the free states of the Union, but that of Lebanon is the mother-community, and the others stand in a subordinate relationship to it The sect does not appear to have increased of late years—indeed, it has decreased. Every year solitary men or women, and even whole families, make their appearance to fill up the gaps which have occurred by death, or by members withdrawing from the association.

Toward the evening of this day we have a beautiful passage in the steamer across the large lake Winnipiseogee (the smile of the Great Spirit), which is scattered with small islands, and surrounded by broken mountain tops, and presents splendid views of the White Mountain, whose summits, Mount Washington, Mount Jefferson, Adams, La Fayette, and many other republican heroes, beckoned to us in Olympian majesty in the splendor of the brightest August sun. The sunset was most magnificent above that quiet, smiling lake. When the sun had sunk behind the mountains we had reached land, and found tolerably good quarters in the inn on the shore.

The evening was cool and bright, and it was a great happiness to me to find myself in a mountain district, and to be able to approach still nearer to the giants. Every thing was still and silent around us. Late, however, in the evening a "mammoth party" arrived, forty or fifty persons, ladies and gentlemen, who, like ourselves, were aiming at the White Mountains, and who took the hotel by storm. Mr. S. and I were a little out of humor with the company, partly on account of the noise they made, and partly because of their "staring," whenever we chanced to meet them. We, however, became thoroughly reconciled to them next morning, when they sent a greeting to me, and a request to sing to me on my departure.

Behold now, therefore, Mrs. E. and myself seated on our buffalo skins in the open traveling-wagon, and the company all assembled before the house, singing in quartette the touching and pretty song of "Sweet Home." The singers stood on the piazza, and around them and our wagon were probably a hundred persons assembled, all with friendly, earnest countenances. It was Sunday morning; the sky clear and dark blue, after thunder and rain yesterday; the atmosphere was fresh and pure as that of my own native land.

I looked up to the bright sky, and thought of my home, of my beloved ones; and listening to that melodious song, "Sweet home! sweet home!" my heart swelled, and my eyes were filled with tears. I never received a more beautiful morning salutation. With this in my heart, and amid the waving and kissing of hands, we drove off in our open wagon into the verdant mountain region.

A New Hampshire farmer, strong as a giant, drove us, his horses being brisk and gentle, and his wagon like one of our ordinary traveling-wagons, resting, unlike those, on easy springs, so that it was extremely comfortable. We drove on, and our being was full of gladness; the air was pure as crystal, the heat not extreme; there was no dust, and through the whole way our road was bordered with beautiful forest, now fresh green after the rain, and before us we had the great mountains, to which we were approaching nearer and nearer. There was now no snow upon their crowns, and they appeared rather green than white, and Mount Washington shrouded himself before long in a wreath of light cloud. The scenery around us resembled the central portion of the northern mountain districts of Sweden. The pine-tree and the birch are indigenous here, and beneath them grow the blueberry, the raspberry, the fern, &c. Nevertheless, here also grow maize, the sugar-maple, the walnut, and chestnut-trees, with many other plants and trees which belong to a more southern climate. I can not tell you how much I enjoyed this quiet, fresh journey in the open wagon, through a tranquil, summer-rejoicing mountain district, or how fresh and agreeable it seemed to me, in comparison with a journey in a covered vehicle or a rail-way carriage, which last, after the first two hours, becomes oppressively wearisome both to soul and body. But here we sat, awake and cheerful, the whole day through. Mount Washington stood before us the whole time like a landmark. This mountain, the largest and loftiest of the White Mountains, which is not more than three thousand feet above the level of the sea, has a very marked character. It is massive and pyramidal, but without an apex. The summit is a plateau, appearing at a distance like that which volcanoes present. But, unlike volcanoes, there is at the top of Mount Washington no crater, but a spring of fresh water. Deep furrows, as of mountain streams, plow the sides of the mountain. The other mountains, which link themselves in long array to this, bear a resemblance to it, but are less significant. All ascend in a gradual, pyramidal form, and have rounded tops or ridges.

The nearer we approached the great mountain, and the more the day declined, the cooler it became. The giants wrapped themselves in gray, misty mantles, and enfolded us in them also; they did not receive us kindly. Nevertheless, I felt kindly toward them, and, with a sort of pleasure, allowed myself to be inclosed in their cold breath. My friend, the moon, ascended, and combated for a while with the spirits of the mist, and looked down upon us from amid them with serene and kindly glances. My friend wished well to us, and that I knew perfectly well. She could not, however, perfectly penetrate those gray mantles.

We advanced deeper and deeper into the bosom of the mountains, by solitary roads, upon which we did not meet a single human being through the whole day. Already had the night set in. Whether it was the influence of the giants or not, I can not say, but I felt no sensation of weariness from the long day's journey—nay, indeed, I could very well have proceeded onward through the night. It was about midnight when we reached our quarters, and it was with the utmost difficulty, and by making a loud noise at the door, that we could wake the landlord of the little inn. At last, however, we succeeded, and the landlord, sleepy, but kind and hearty, made us a fire, and prepared all that we required for refreshment and our night's rest.

11*th*. A beautiful bright morning, an enchanting morning ramble, morning dew on the grass, in the soul, in life! The memory of the Vale Song, and its prophecy of the renovation of human beings born from dew! The heavens were a halleluiah—I have known such in the New World! They live in my soul, encave themselves into pictures of the imagination, long prefigured, but treasured in the silent work-shop of the soul. How strange! Beneath the wild heaven of South Carolina I would merely enjoy, and, enjoying, sing praises. Here I enjoy also, but in another manner. The soul is more powerful, more alive. It receives merely to give in return. It will produce—it will work. The dramatic life in the mountains, and in the mountain-streams, forests, clouds, and sunbeams, awaken the dramatic life within myself, and call to life pictures and scenes which have laid in swaddling-bands within my soul for fifteen or twenty years. They and I celebrate this morning as a festival of the resurrection. The roads are full of the songs of birds.

We shall, in the afternoon, proceed onward.

Franconia Notch, La Fayette House, August 15th.

I have lived in the bosom of the White Mountains since I last wrote, heartily enjoying the companionship of the giants, the fantastic gambols of the clouds around them, of the songs and the dances of the brooks in the deep glens, of the whole of this bold and strong scenery, which made me feel as if at home in Sweden, amid the glorious river-valleys of Dalecarlia or Norsland. Yet the scenery here is more picturesque, more playful and fantastic, has more cheerful diversity, and the affluence of wood and the beautiful foliage in the valleys is extraordinary; you walk or drive continually between the most lovely wild hedges of hazel, elm, sumach (a very beautiful shrub, which is general throughout America), sugar-maple, yellow birch, fir-trees, pines, and many other trees and shrubs; and on all sides is heard the singing and the roaring of the mountain streams, clear as silver, through the passes of the hills. It was so cold in certain parts of this mountain region that it was with difficulty that I could guide my pen, from the stiffness of my fingers. But both soul and body were hale, and Mrs. E. was equally vigorous and refreshing as the scenery itself, with all its heights and its singing brooks, its waving flowers and shrubs.

The peculiarity of these so-called White Mountains is the many gigantic human profiles which, in many places, look out from the mountains with a precision and perfect regularity of outline which is quite astonishing. They have very much amused me, and I have sketched several of them in my rambles. We have our quarters here very close to one of these countenances, which has long been known under the name of "the Old Man of the Mountain." It has not any nobility in its features, but resembles a very old man in a bad humor, and with a night-cap on his head, who is looking out from the mountain half inquisitive. Far below the old giant's face is an enchanting little lake, resembling a bright oval toilet glass, inclosed in a verdant frame of leafage. The Old Man of the Mountain looks out gloomily over this quiet lake, and the clouds float far below his chin.

Another head is that of a helmeted warrior, evidently one of Theo's good fellows. I flatter myself with having made the discovery of two faces. The one, which is seen in the distance against the blue sky, is the countenance of a beautiful woman, glancing upward with an expression of unspeakable melancholy. An old pine-tree stands like the sign of the cross above her head; the brow is surrounded as by a diadem of wavy hair. It is an extremely remarkable profile, especially for the soft beauty of the mouth and chin. Below this noble countenance, if you step back a few paces, another presents itself, ugly and cruel, with a great wart on its forehead. Evidently a wicked giant, who keeps a beautiful princess in captivity. I caught glimpses of several other countenances, and should certainly have traced them out if I had remained longer in company with the giants.

The Indians are said to have worshiped these faces, and to have offered sacrifices to them as to divinities; they are also said to have many legends concerning them. The conquerors and successors of the Indians have not left here any other traces than of some tragical events.

One place is called "Nanny Bridge," from a young girl who was found here frozen to death. She was the daughter of a farmer in the neighborhood, and had one evening a quarrel with her lover, in consequence of which he left her in anger. She followed him in a state of desperation, and was overtaken by night in a snow-storm. The next morning she was found frozen to death, and her lover became insane.

Not far from this place, in the valley, stands the now deserted "Wiley House," as it is called. A few years ago a large family dwelt here. One night they were aroused from sleep by a horrible noise and fall, and which was evidently the crash of an avalanche, which was descending from the mountain in the direction of the house, and would overwhelm it. The family rushed out in the dark night to find a place in which they believed they should escape the danger. But the avalanche took precisely that direction, and overwhelmed the whole fugitive family, consisting of nine persons. Hawthorne has taken this tragical incident as the subject of one of his household tales—"The Ambitious Guest."

It is now the custom to ascend the mountain from which the avalanche fell to obtain from its top a view of the valley. And just now has a trundling wagon, drawn by six horses, and conveying from twenty to thirty persons, driven at full speed from the hotel up the mountain. Mrs. S. and I declined to join the party, as I have also declined to ascend Mount Washington, which is done on horseback, and with incredible difficulty, in order to see—nothing under the most favorable circumstances, that is, if there are no clouds—a confused view of land and water.

The whole of this mountain district is very wild, and there is scarcely a dwelling to be seen excepting the hotels for travelers. It is, however, overflowing with noisy, unquiet company, who do not seem to understand any other mode of enjoying nature than in talking, laughing, eating, drinking, and by all kinds of noisy pleasures. They pass up the mountain laughing at full gallop, and come down again at full gallop. Champagne corks fly about at the hotels, gentlemen sit and play at cards in the middle of the day, and ladies talk about dress-makers and fashions. How unlike is this thoughtless life to that of nature, where the clouds come down as if to converse with the mountain, sometimes speeding over them like airy dragons, sometimes floating around them caressingly with garlands and light sylph-like forms, which moisten their forests with soft dewy vails; while in the valley below the little streams grow and sing, and trees and flowers waft over them their blessing as they speed along their way; and above all this, the play of light and shadow, sunbeams in the waterfalls which leap from the mountain, the mighty rock visages, the little twittering birds—that is life!

The senseless rioting of man in the midst of this grandeur of nature makes me almost sad for my kindred. And yet, when I was young, I did not understand how to enjoy life and nature in any other way. The inclination was not wanting, but there was want of education, and, amid all that noisy merriment, a vacuity was felt.

People seek for the spiritual Champagne, but they mistake what it is.

The true has the same relation to the ordinary that Bacchus Dithyrambus has to Silenus.

Yet there were also some true worshipers of the great goddess. One day we met a father and his little daughter. They had been botanizing in the woods, and showed us several beautiful *vacciniums*, as well as a *monotropa*, which has merely one single flower, and is here called the Indian pipes. The father and daughter looked gentle and happy. It was a beautiful and perfect little picture.

Mrs. S. and I are also of that class which silently receives the great spectacle into a thankful mind, now sitting beside the silver cascades for whole hours, now wandering on solitary rambles of discovery among the romantic mountain gorges.

We have this afternoon rambled up to the Thune. This is a narrow chasm between two lofty granite walls, through which a stream pours in almost a direct line upward of eight hundred feet, when it falls in a cascade from a height of six hundred feet. Along the front of one of the rock walls our host, in true Yankee fashion, had carried a pathway formed of pieces of timber, stones, branches which did not resemble any thing, but along which people, to their astonishment, could walk quite safely, and without the least difficulty, if they steadied themselves with one hand against the rock wall. Only a few days ago he had carried a path over the stream fifty feet higher up. At the point where it ceased we found ourselves near to an immense round block of stone, which had fallen into the chasm, and become fixed, so that it formed above it a kind of curtain. Beyond the gloomy gorge, which looked almost black, we saw up aloft the stream hurl itself from the left hand into the mountain chasm, in a strong stream, clear as crystal. Whence came it? That was impossible to say; but the sun shone brightly upon it, and over it a little birch-tree waved its soft, light green branches. The source of the dark river lay in light. It gladdened me, and all the way over that singing waterfall sang and sported within my soul scenes and conversations which I will relate to you at home.

All this scenery and this country are refreshing, wild, and picturesque. There are many "lions" among the mountains, and a printed card which I received from our host of La Fayette House promises

"An echo from the cannon every evening on the lake."

But I have already described sufficient.

We shall now proceed from the White Mountains of New Hampshire to the green hill, Vermont.

Burlington, on Lake Champlain, Vermont, August 19th.

I now write to you from a beautiful house on the shores of the Lake Champlain, which has one of the most glorious views over the water and the mountain region which I have ever seen since the Lake of Geneva, in Switzerland. Nature is on a grander scale there; nor the mountain of of Adirondack, now before me in Western New York, nor the Green Mountains of Vermont, aspire to the height of the Alps, but their forms are picturesque, combined with a certain degree of grandeur and boldness, and over the whole fine and cheerful district now shines a beautiful August sun, declining toward its setting, and filling the clouds with an indescribable golden splendor. The mountain called *Le lion couchant* seems possessed of life, and about to rise up in splendid glow of light—a magnificent giant form. And there are many other mountains in this neighborhood which possess strongly-marked symbolic shapes.

We, Mrs. S. and myself, are at the house of the ex-president of the academy, Mr. W., where I was kindly invited by both father and daughters. It is a noble and beautiful family, in which domestic devotion is practiced, and where a mother only is wanted. This mother has now been dead two years, and is yet tenderly sorrowed for by her children, three sons and three daughters, all agreeable and highly-gifted young people. The father of the family, a stately, elderly gentleman, and strict Puritan, nine feet in height, I fancy (and on whose arm, as we walked together, I hung like a swing in a tree), has a strongly-marked countenance, and keen, but kind eyes; is a firm Whig, and not favorable to the Democrats; in all other respects an extremely polite and agreeable gentleman, very entertaining to me in conversation, from his perfect knowledge of the ecclesiastical state of the country, from the clearness of all his views, though I could not accord with them all, and his agreeable manner of communication. The house is a villa near the city, and is possessed of all the charm and comfort of an Anglo-American home.

Yesterday we went on a pleasure party across the lake to Adirondack Mountain, on the New York shore. The day was beautiful, so also was the excursion; the scenery of the rapid, though shallow little river, Au Sable, where the rocks present the appearance of regularly built, inaccessible fortress walls of a most remarkable character, all of which I should have enjoyed much more if I had not been called upon to reply to so many useless questions. There was one lady in particular, with a sharp, shrill voice, who tormented me in this style: Where are you intending to go when you leave this? Whence did you come from hither? With whom did you stay there? Who did you see at their house? and so on.

Oh! that people were but a little more like the objects in nature, that they approached each other for some definite purpose, and had a pleasure in influencing each other by the silent communication of this; how much more would they then allure from us, how much more would they then know of us, than by these senseless, merely outward questionings, and which the better class in this country reprobate and ridicule as much as any foreigner whatever. Neither was there a want in this picnic of persons such as I have just wished for. There was, in particular, one charming young lady of very intellectual character, and as fresh as the singing brook or the waving tree. It was an agreeable invigoration to me to sit by her, to look at her, to listen to her conversation, which was overflowing with soul.

Whenever I take a fancy to a lady, and we are mutually attracted to each other, it generally happens that I very soon learn something of her biography. In that of this amiable young lady I was struck with the following:

She was overwhelmed by a severe and crushing affliction; she felt that she must either yield to it or—travel away from it—from it, from her own thoughts, from herself. Without any fixed plan or any other object than to get away, she seated herself in a rail-way carriage, and let the train convey her out into the wide world. The trees waved, and beckoned her on into the world; the clouds advanced before her, and she followed; and one new object exchanged itself for another; her spirits grew lighter, and the whole tone of her mind improved. She could think more freely; life and every thing assumed a brighter aspect. After a journey of merely a few days, she was able to return home to her parents with recovered self-possession and peace of mind. And now—two years later—she was amazed at the amount of happiness which she was capable of enjoying.

"The time of silent sighs is past," said Geijer, on one occasion. Ah! there is much yet wanted for that; but this is certain, that the facility there is for a change of scene, for the receiving of new impressions, and the ease with which they are imparted, approximates this time. In a country where rail-roads and steam-boats intersect the land in all directions, and enable people to fly through the world, there is no need for them to grow mouldy, as it were, or to grow sour from sitting still.

August 20th. Pity that three days of rest in this lovely home, among its kind inmates, are now drawing to a close. I have heartily enjoyed the glorious prospects, and the pomp of the sunsets which I have witnessed from my window. These lake districts are celebrated for their magnificent sunsets. Nor have I any where else seen such picturesque clouds, or such splendid transitions of color; there is in it a joyousness and a play of color altogether unlike the soft and mild splendor of the sky of the South. The peculiar outline of the mountains is also very attractive to me, and *Le lion couchant* becomes every day more animated to me. Lake Champlain has received its name from the brave and wise Frenchman, Champlain, who first discovered and then colonized this part of the country. Maine, New Hampshire, and Vermont were, at the commencement, peopled from France, and have to thank French missionaries and French colonists for their first cultivation. Of this but little now remains except the names of places and rivers, and some Catholic seminaries. Vast forests, large lakes and mountains, are the primeval features of these states; agriculture, the breeding of cattle, and the cutting of timber, are their principal occupations. One beautiful minor branch of trade is the preparation of maple-sugar, which is in considerable demand. The maple-tree is tapped for its sap, as the birch-tree with us, and the sugar is formed in small cakes of a brown color and very sweet flavor.

I saw yesterday evening at this house a great assembly of the society of Burlington; cheerful and agreeable countenances were there—many such among the young.

There was in the company a universally beloved and esteemed schoolmistress, who had, from her youth upward, labored alone for herself and her family. She had done this so successfully as to be able to educate several younger brothers and sisters; to pay the family debts; maintain her aged mother; and, finally, build her a dwelling-house. After having accomplished all this, she was now, at the age of thirty, about to be married herself to a man to whom she had long been engaged. She could now think about her own happiness, about her own house and home. The universal sympathy which seemed to have been excited, and the joy with which I heard all this related, speak highly for the rest of the community by whom the beautiful life and happiness of one humble individual is so much appreciated.

Saratoga, August 22d.

I have now come hither from the society of the White and Green Mountains, from the world-despising Shakers, to the most fashionable, the worst, and most worldly place in the United States, just to glance at and receive an impression of its life for my panorama of the New World.

We left Burlington yesterday. Many of my new friends accompanied us by steamer across the lake, and our polite host, the ex-president and his only daughter—a dearly beloved, but physically delicate young girl—came on hither, where they will remain a couple of days with us. The picture of that romantic lake, and of the colossal reposing granite lion, which in the setting sunlight seemed to increase in size, while it receded still further and further into the dim distance, is one which I shall ever retain in my mind among the most beautiful natural scenes of America. We reached Saratoga, in the western portion of New York, in the evening, and made that same evening our appearance in the public saloon.

Several couples, ladies and gentlemen, were promenading round and round in the middle of the room beneath the brilliant chandeliers. One couple, in particular, attracted our attention. It was a very handsome young girl, with very beautiful and quite bare shoulders, and a young man, elegant and handsome also. They were, it was said, the present season's pair of lovers. Among the elderly company was one handsome old lady, who was said to be very like Mrs. Martha Washington, and who was dressed in the same old-fashioned style, which was so very becoming to her that she looked in this costume both original and extremely well. I, who am very fond of a little costume, and who would like that every person should dress themselves according to their individuality, whether of figure or fancy, was greatly amused by the assembly, and as I chanced to meet there many new and old acquaintances, I was not only amused, but soon tired and was obliged to leave.

This evening, however, there is to be the great ball of the season, to which I am invited, and whither I shall go to see all that is to be seen. This season is said not to be very brilliant, owing to the weather having been cold and wet: It now rains.

23d. Now I have seen all that is to be seen, namely, the great ball, and that is not such a very great ball, after all. There were not many people, and among the people nothing remarkable, excepting some half dozen tasteful and lovely toilets. It would be impossible to conceive any thing more harmonious and elegant, without the slightest showiness or extravagance. The ladies who wore them were also handsome and agreeable, and had in their costume adopted the style which best suited them. I was much pleased with the principal belle and dancer of the ball, because she was so very singular in figure and style. Her dancing was so abrupt, and the wreath of red Provence roses which she wore was placed on her head with so little grace, that I only wondered at her. Neither did the gentlemen dance well; the polka was singularly ungraceful. It was painful to me to see some pale little girls tricked out like grown people, and old before their time. To take children out of their childhood is to destroy the whole of their future.

One of the gentlemen at the ball had taken it into his head that I did not properly appreciate Girard College at Philadelphia, and took upon himself to be my instructor on the subject of this college, which he maintained to be unparalleled in the whole world. I observed that such institutions were to be met with also in Switzerland and France. But no, not wholly such; there were no institutions in Europe which were altogether like this American one, which was vastly superior, as he would now show me.

I felt myself indescribably incapable of learning, and, sighing, bethought myself of Solomon's words, "That there was a time for all things." I wished to look quietly at the ball, and was very very glad when some new and agreeable acquaintance put an end to the lecture.

And it has often happened to me thus; just as I have had one instance of American assumption, the very next moment I meet with an American sense of forbearance.

An elderly gentleman at Saratoga, who appeared to be in ill health, but whose countenance was very agreeable, asked me, with a diffident expression, whether I really thought that the people of America were happier than those of Europe?

After so many self-conceited questions about America, it was a real refreshment to me, and I was glad that I could reply that I believed there was more hope here than elsewhere, and that in that alone consisted a greater happiness.

Spite of the many examples I have had of American criticism on Americans, I can not deny being sometimes reminded of the words of an Englishman: "I will not say that the Americans do not do many great things, but they are not done in a heroic way. And it has sometimes appeared to me, that that which this people need most to make them really great, is a high-minded dissatisfaction with themselves."

But is this to be found among Englishmen or Frenchmen? Is it possessed by any nation excepting in its noblest representatives? And such are not wanting here, as I know by frequent experience.

The illumination of the public buildings in the evening at Saratoga was tasteful. The supper and the arrangements of the ball showed care and good taste. Our sweet Vermont flower, Miss N., was unable—more was the pity—to be with us this evening. I took leave of her and her father with regret, very sorry not to be able to accept his invitation to be present with him at a grand synod of the Presbyterian Church, which will be held next month in Maine.

New York, September 4th.

Ah! my child, what a whirl of changing scenes, occupation, and engagements have not the latter few days been! I could scarcely collect my faculties, much less take pen quietly in hand, and even now I am writing on flying foot, like Mercury, if I may so say, ready to be carried off at a moment's warning, or by kind friends. Nevertheless, I must give you shortly, and in great haste, a little account of my proceedings.

From Saratoga we went to Lenox, in Massachusetts where, according to arrangement, I met my excellent friends the O.'s, from Boston. I here also parted with my agreeable traveling companion, Mrs. S. and her husband, who had kindly met us by the way.

The country around Lenox is romantically lovely, inspired with wood-covered hills, and the prettiest little lakes. Amid this scenery have Catharine Sedgwick and Nathaniel Hawthorne their rural homes. I had been invited to both, and I wished to see both. I spent four-and-twenty hours with the excellent and amiable Catharine Sedgwick and her family, enjoying her company and that of several agreeable ladies. There were no gentlemen—gentlemen, indeed, seemed to be rare in social circles of this neighborhood. But they were less missed here than is generally the case in society, because the women of this little circle are possessed of unusual intellectual cultivation—several of them endowed with genius and talent of a high order. Fanny Kemble has her home here when she resides in America; at the present time she is in England. The scenery is beautiful; these ladies enjoy it and each other's society, and life lacks nothing to the greater number.

I am, in a general way, struck with the number of ladies, and the scarcity of gentlemen in the homes of the lesser cities in the Eastern States. The gentlemen run over to the larger cities, or to the Great West, to carry on business, to construct rail-ways, or to acquire wealth in one way or another. Many solitary ladies are met with in these Eastern States, who are neither wanting in charms or endowments of soul, and yet who grow old unmarried. I have heard many of these wish for themselves a wider sphere of activity, the opportunity for leading a more cheerful and more generally useful life. The old lament over the stagnation and the heaviness of life, which I heard in Europe, is repeated here also. It ought not to be so here, in the young New World.

I spent an extremely agreeable day with Miss Sedgwick, and one evening with Hawthorne, in an endeavor in converse. But, whether it was his fault or mine, I can not say, but it did not succeed. I had to talk by myself, and at length became quite dejected, and felt I know not how. Nevertheless, Hawthorne was evidently kind, and wished to make me comfortable—but we could not get on together in conversation. It was, however, a pleasure to me to see his beautiful, significant, though not perfectly harmonious head. The forehead is capacious and serene as the arch of heaven, and a thick mass of soft dark brown hair beautifully clustered around it; the fine, deep-set eyes glance from beneath well-arched eyebrows like the dark but clear lakes of the neighborhood, lying in the sombre bosom of mountain and forest; the nose is refined and regular in form; the smile, like that of the sun smiling over the summer woods; nevertheless, it has a bitter expression. The whole upper part of the countenance is classically beautiful, but the lower part does not perfectly correspond, and is deficient in decided character.

Immediately in front of Hawthorne's house lies one of those small clear lakes, with its sombre margin of forest, which characterize this district, and Hawthorne seems greatly to enjoy the view of it, and the wildly wooded country. His amiable wife is inexpressibly happy to see him so happy here. A smile, a word from him conveys more to her than long speeches from other people. She reads his very soul, and—"he is the best of husbands." Rose, the youngest child, is still on the mother's breast. Hawthorne's house is a happy, quiet little abode, embracing a beautiful family life.

At the rural inn where I was staying with my friends, the O.'s, also resided as guests several young girls for the benefit of country air and life. There was also a handsome and still youthful mother, with five handsome daughters. I one morning asked every one of these what she wished for as her ultimatum in life. Every one replied by mentioning some tolerably indifferent occupation and condition of life. I reproached them with not being candid, and asked them whether in their conscience they would not reply, as an amiable young girl had done to whom I had once put the same question, "To be married, and to see all my friends happy around me?" The young girls laughed, and two of them said "Yes, if the right man came." And this reply is characteristic of the young American's state of life and feeling. These young girls, indulged by every one, enjoying their life and their liberty, without compulsion or restraint of any kind, are not likely to be anxious, or to trouble themselves about the circumstances of their lives: Yet they will not say "no" when "the right man comes." And for many young girls he comes quite too soon; at least, so it seems to me, in many cases where they are married as soon as they cease to be children. I have heard of a young girl who was married at fourteen, and then was sent by her husband to a girls' school.

I paid a visit with my friends on Sunday to the Shaker community at New Lebanon, which is merely a few miles distant from Lenox. We were again there in a great assembly; saw precisely the same figures in the dance, and heard the same kind of discourse and singing as I had heard a year before. The same friendly Shaker sisters brought forward benches for the spectators; the same elder Evans stood up and delivered the same kind of reproving sermon. Every thing had stood still; every thing stood exactly at the same point, or moved in the same circle.

During my stay in this part of the country it was very cold. The stalks of the potatoes in the potato-fields were quite destroyed by frost. The wind was keen, and full of a frosty feeling. I never remember in Sweden to have felt it so cold in the month of August.

I went with the O.'s from Lenox to New York through the beautiful Housatonic Valley, the wonderfully picturesque and sometimes splendidly gloomy scenery of which not all the rattle, and the dust, and the smoke of the railway could prevent me from seeing, though I can not say enjoying, so much does the mind become confounded by this mode of traveling.

Not far from New York we removed into another train, as long as a long street, and down which we wandered through lines of people, from one carriage to another, before we could find places. This moving street was a train conveying certainly a thousand persons. By this we arrived at New York; nor was I sorry, with it, to bid farewell to American rail-way trains. Excellent as they are in many respects, especially by the convenience they are to all, and by their low prices, equally reasonable to all, they are fatiguing in a high degree. After the first two hours, there is an end of all pleasure in traveling, and one sinks into a suffering and stupid state; one feels one's self not a human being, but a portmanteau, and I, for my part, can not conceive a less beneficial or pleasurable mode of traveling. One can not enjoy a mouthful of fresh air. If the quantity of smoke and dust could be diminished, it would be a great blessing to the travelers. The European rail-way trains, of which I have any experience, are all greatly superior to the American in this respect.

At New York I parted with the O.'s. Ah! it was painful for me to part with these friends, thinking, probably, that I might never see him more—my kind physician, my beloved Mary Anne, his wife! And to the last moment they overwhelmed me with proofs of love—I can not call them any thing else. Foremost among these I reckon the directions which he has given for the management of your health, according to the information I have given him of your state, and the ample supply of homeopathic medicines which he has provided both for you and me.

Thus he and she—ah! my Agatha, there are little affectionate motherly or sisterly attentions and kindnesses which are invaluable to the stranger in a foreign land, and which affect me more than large gifts, and I have to thank her for such services, as well as many other motherly-hearted women, not only in America, but in Cuba. When I think how their hands labored for me, how they cared for me to the most minute details, I feel that I must press those hands to my heart and to my lips. I shall always remember her kind, beautiful countenance, his grave eyes, with their glance so full of sentiment, and again I shall most certainly behold them at the resurrection. It can not be otherwise. The expression of such spirits can not die.

"There is a natural body, and there is a spiritual body," says St. Paul.

Among the friends who met me in New York was Professor De V., from Charlottesville. But no longer full of cheerfulness. His beautiful home was now a house of mourning. His young wife, my beloved hostess there, had died in giving birth to her first child. I was most sincerely grieved for him and his motherless child.

I spent some days at New York in making a closer acquaintance with that portion of the life of the great city which belongs to its night-side, to the dark realm of shadows and of hell, as it exists on the earth. I wandered through it, however, accompanied by an angel of light. I can not otherwise speak of the Quaker lady who accompanied me, for her countenance was bright and beautiful as the purest goodness, and above her mild blue eyes arched themselves brows as bright as those of the god

Balder must have been—they resembled merely a bright golden line.

Mrs. G. is the daughter of the celebrated old Quaker, Isaac Hopper. The daughter has inherited from the father that firm spirit of human love and that steadfastness of character which neither shrinks nor turns back from any impediment on the path which she has resolved to pursue. A great portion of her time is occupied in caring for the unfortunate, the guilty, and the prisoner; and so universally known and respected is her activity in these respects, that all prisons, all public benevolent institutions, are open to her, and whoever walks at her side through the abandoned haunts of New York may feel himself in safety. Her bright and mild countenance is known even in the darkest places as a messenger of light.

I went with her one day through that part of New York called the Five Points, because I wished to see this region, in which the rudest and the most degraded portion of the population of New York were thronged together, probably through the attraction which causes like to seek like. Not long ago it was unsafe for a stranger within these purlieus. But the Methodists of New York conceived the divinely bold idea of building a church to God in the heart of this central point of vice and misery. They hired a house, sent a minister to reside there, established schools, work-rooms, &c., which would give ample space for "the other master." The contest between good and evil has just begun in the Five Points, and already several signs betoken victory.

The Five Points is one of the oldest portions of New York, and received its name from five streets which open here into a large square. These streets, and especially the square, are the haunts of the extremest misery of that great city. Lower than to the Five Points it is not possible for fallen human nature to sink. Here are public dens of prostitution, where miserable women keep so-called "fancy-men" and "fancy-women." Quarrels and blows, theft and even murder, belong to the order of day and night. There is in the square, in particular, one large, yellow-colored, dilapidated old house, called "the Old Brewery," because formerly it was employed as such. This house is properly the head-quarters of vice and misery. And the old brewer of all the world's misery, the Evil One himself, has dominion there at this day.

We, Mrs. G. and myself, went alone through this house, where we visited many hidden dens, and conversed with their inhabitants. We considered it better and safer to go about here alone than in company with a gentleman. Neither did we meet any instance of rudeness or even incivility. We saw young lads sitting at the gaming-table with old ruffians; unfortunate women suffering from horrible diseases; sickly children; giddy young girls; ill-tempered women quarreling with the whole world; and some families also we saw, who seemed to me wretched rather through poverty than moral degradation. From unabashed, hardened crime, to those who, sinking under the consequences of vice, are passing down to death—without an ear to listen to their groans, without sympathy and without hope—is there, in every grade of moral corruption, festering and fermenting in the Old Brewery; filth, rags, pestilent air, every thing was in that Old Brewery; and yet there, after all, I did not see any thing worse than I had seen before in Paris, London, and Stockholm. Ah! in all large cities where human masses congregate, may be found the Old Brewery of vice and misery, and where the Old Brewer distills his poison. The offscouring of society flows hither, becomes still more corrupt, and will thence corrupt the atmosphere of society, until the fresh and better life obtains power over the old leaven—the new church over the Old Brewery. A great movement exists in this direction at the present time. The Church of Christ extends itself not merely to the soul, but is beginning to comprehend the whole human being; to develop itself in schols, in sanitary wardship, in every kind of institution which promotes the wholesome work of Christian love on earth, both for soul and body, and repeats the words of the Lord to the leper: "I will; be thou clean!"

From the Old Brewery and its horrible figures we went to the Mission House in the square directly opposite, and had a long conversation with the missionary, Mr. N., a man with a dark, bold eye, and that faith in God which can remove mountains, and with somewhat of that faith also in himself which may tend to self-deception, and to the belief that more is done than is actually the case. Certain it is, however, that hasty conversions of sinners, long accustomed to the indulgence of besetting vices, are rare, and not to be too much relied upon. Hypocrisy is also one scheme of the old serpent's.

In the middle of the square of the Five Points there is, as in many squares of New York, a little green inclosure of trees and bushes. It looks, however, dry and withered; no careful hands water the trees which attempt to put forth foliage, and on the fencing around it hang rags to dry.

It has often struck me how chance, or a mysterious foreknowledge, which, without human consciousness, concerns itself with human affairs, gives symbolic, or, as it were, prophetic appellations to things, places, or persons who afterward accomplish that which their appellations seem to have predestined them to. This I found to be the case with regard to the Five Points, the Old Brewery, and the prison which nearly abuts upon this region. The great prison of the city of New York is called *the Tombs*, from the massive, monumental style of building employed in it. The prison itself is of granite, and in the Egyptian style—heavy, but magnificent. A massive lofty granite wall, like the wall of a fortress, surrounds the court, in which stands the prison-house like a vast, regular, massive block of hewn granite. When one stands within the magnificent portals of this wall, one seems to stand within a gigantic tomb. And so it is. It gives admittance to the offscouring of the criminals of the great city. One portion condemned and executed here, another portion conveyed hence to Blackwell's Island, where is situated the House of Correction proper for New York. Few are they who leave this place free, who do not return hither to be more severely punished or to die. The Old Brewery furnishes unceasing food for the Tombs.

Before the door of the prison, in the interior court, sat a fine general, in a comfortable arm-chair, as keeper or orderly of the prison, with diamond rings on his fingers, and a diamond breast-pin in his shirt. Whether they were genuine, I can not say; they looked, however, as though they were; but that the man himself was not of genuine human worth was not difficult to see, neither that he was out of his place here. He was in a high degree haughty and self-sufficient, and did not even raise his hat to the noble, beautiful lady who addressed him, much less raise himself. She showed her card of introduction, and we were allowed to pass in, first into a room in which many of the officials of the prison were assembled. The person who was evidently the principal here, a fat man with a large face, sat with his hat on his head and one of his feet placed high against the wall, and one newspaper hanging over his leg, while he was busy reading another which he held in his hands. On Mrs. G. mildly and politely addressing him, he turned his head toward us slightly, but neither raised his hat nor his upraised foot from the wall, and then putting some question with as surly a mien as if he had been addressing some person in custody, let us wait a moment, after which we were allowed to enter, which probably would not have been the case if he dared to have hindered it. We could not avoid remarking that many of these jailers looked as if they ought to have been among the prisoners, nay, even looked much worse than many of them.

I could not but be greatly surprised at the disorder which prevailed in the great prison of the men, which is built of an elliptical form, with a gallery running in front of the cells. The prisoners were walking about, talking, smoking cigars, while dealers in cigars and other wares were wending about freely among them. Many of the cells were occupied by two prisoners. There were several condemned prisoners—two condemned to death. I asked one of these, who was a man of some little education, how he felt himself in prison? "Oh," replied he, with bitter irony, "as well as any one can do who has every moment of the twenty-four hours his sentence of death before his eyes;" and he showed me a paper pasted on the wall, on which might be read, badly written, the day and hour when he was to be hanged. The prisoners were much more polite and agreeable to us than the gentlemen on duty had been. Some of them seemed pleased by our visit, and thanked us, and talked in a cordial manner.

While we were there, a drunken old man was brought into the lower part of the prison. The manner in which he was carried in and thrown into the cell exhibited a high degree of coarseness. I was the whole time in one continued state of amazement that a prison in the United States—the prisons of which country have been so highly praised in Europe—should present such scenes and be in such a condition. But the city of New York, like the prisons of New York, are not the specimens by which American cities and prisons should be judged. The prison of Philadelphia was very unlike this.

We found the condition of the female portion of the Tombs very unlike that of the males. Here a woman had sway, and she was one of those genial, powerful characters which can create around them a new state of order, governed by wholesome influences. Her form, which indicated great cordiality and considerable physical power, seemed made, as it were, to sustain the children of the prison—to elevate, not to depress them. She was cheerful, and hearty, and good-tempered, yet nevertheless so resolute with the prisoners that none of them ventured to oppose her. Many seemed to look upon her as a mother, and she seemed to regard many of them as diseased children rather than as criminals; this was the case, in particular, with those who were imprisoned for drunkenness.

"Oh, Miss Foster! oh, Miss Foster!" lamented one scarcely half conscious woman, who was waking up in one cell from a fit of drunkenness, "I am now here again!"

"Yes, that you are, you poor thing!" said Miss Foster, and went compassionately to lift her head from the extremely uneasy position into which it had fallen in her drunken sleep.

When she entered the cells, the prisoners talked to her as to a guardian and a friend. One woman, who had been imprisoned many times, and brought hither for drunkenness, but who always, during the time of her imprisonment, had behaved in the most exemplary manner, had become so attached to Miss Foster that she begged to be allowed always to remain in prison, where she would assist Miss Foster. This had been permitted to her, and she was very useful to Miss Foster in the prison.

One room in the prison is called "The Five Days' Room," or "The Incurable's Room;" here women are taken who have been repeatedly found in a state of drunkenness. After five days' confinement they are dismissed. From the prisoners' room we went into the court where the five-days' prisoners sit during the day, after they have slept out their debauch. Here between forty and fifty women were assembled, many of whom were quite young, and some handsome. Among these women were also female vagrants, or such as had been taken up for quarreling and making disturbances in the streets during the night. One of these, a very young and pretty woman, wept bitterly. Mrs. G. spoke kindly to her, and asked her whether she would not come into *the Home* (meaning the Home in New York for fallen women), and there be well cared for, and receive instruction, and afterward be placed in service with some respectable family. She gratefully accepted the offer, and the whole thing was arranged. As soon as her five days of imprisonment had expired, she was to be received into *the Home*. Thus is the lost sheep sought for among the tombs, and brought again under the care of the Good Shepherd and his faithful servants.

The same question was put by Mrs. G. to another young woman, a handsome but wild Irish girl. She replied scornfully, "No! she would not go to such a place!" "Why not?" inquired Mrs. G., smiling kindly; "is it not a good place?" "Oh yes, ma'am, a very good place, very good, but—yet I won't go there."

That wild spirit evidently required a long trial yet before it would yield.

There also were two young negro women: I asked one if she were a Christian.

"No, ma'am," replied she.

"Have you not heard of Christ?"

"Yes, ma'am."

"Don't you love him?"

"Yes, oh yes, him, but—I have seen many things; I can not become a Christian."

"But why not, if you love Christ?"

"I have been servant with many Christians; I have seen many things: I can not turn to a Christian."

She would give no other reason.

During our conversation with these women, I could not but observe that they were attentive, and, as it were, struck by every rational word which was spoken to them in a calm and kind manner. Opposition and boldness of expression in all instances gave way, and a better, more thoughtful expression took its place. These souls were evidently not hardened, and would open themselves to receive the again and again recurring rays of light.

We found a great number of the prisoners out in the large court which surrounded the interior of the prison, and among them a boy of about ten years of age.

"What had he done, to be a prisoner here?"

"Nothing," was the reply; but he had been found at night in the streets, lying now here, now there, and could not give any account of a residence, and as they did not know what to do with him, they had brought him in hither, where he had been for a long time. While we talked with the little boy, many of the prisoners collected around us, all speaking kind words to the boy, and praising him greatly. I saw tears flow from the eyes of the motherly lady over the neglected motherless boy, and I heard her softly promise to take charge of him, and come and take him out.

While we were thus standing here, we perceived a movement in the court. The gates were heard to open, and the words "The Black Maria! the Black Maria!" passed through the crowd. And in came through the gates of the prison court a large sort of wooden chest, or caravan, painted red, and drawn by two horses. This was the vehicle which each day fetched from the various stations in the city such persons as have been found by the police out in the streets during the night, and had been conveyed to station-houses. They were carried to the Tombs to undergo examination and receive sentence. This red vehicle has received the name of the Black Maria from its having first driven a black woman of that name to the Tombs.

The red omnibus drew up before a gate of the prison, the door was opened, as in any other omnibus, and out came boys, and women, and men, many of them resembling the personages of the Old Brewery. They disappeared within the prison, and the vehicle was then immediately refilled with a new load, who were now to be conveyed from the Tombs to the House of Correction on Blackwell's Island.

We were shown within the court the place where criminals are executed.

Before I leave the Tombs, I must give a parting glance at Miss Foster—that living, genial, bright form among the Tombs; for her face, her cordiality, her patience, and good humor, the vigorous strength and perseverance with which she has lived for many years among the population of the Tombs, was a heart-strengthening sight. She had, within the court of the female prison, had a little flower-garden laid out and planted with flowers; and mignonette diffused its fragrance around, geraniums were in blossom, and Provence roses in bud: to such prisoners as behaved well, or were very much cast down, she gave some of these flowers. I received from her hand a Provence rose-bud, which I have kept in memory of her, and the hope of the Tombs; for within these Tombs I had beheld the work of resurrection.

Yet still I had received a gloomy impression from them. And I heard that in the great prison of Sing-Sing, dark scenes and abuse in the wardship of the prisoners have lately occurred. The society for the visiting of prisoners, of which Isaac Hopper is a member, has within a short period revealed several such facts. This society exercises a salutary control over the wardens of prisons, and their conduct and government, and it performs its work without hostility or opposition.

The following day, in company with Mrs. G., I visited the institution for poor or orphan children, on Randall's Island, a salubrious and excellent locale for the purpose. Here were large houses for the children, and a large hospital for the sick among them, and all was in the highest degree orderly, neat, and in good condition as regarded outward management; not so with regard to the inward. Among these ten or twelve hundred children, there lacked *mothers* or motherly women. The children were well kept, but like machines in a manufactory; they produced on my mind a sorrowful impression; although their spirit of life was not destroyed, they could be unruly enough sometimes. The superintendent, whom I saw sitting among brightly-scoured copper kettles, produced upon me herself the effect of a copper vessel, so hard and dismal did she look, not in the least like Miss Foster. And a Miss Foster, and many such as her, are so necessary for the mother warders and educators of such poor children as these! Here, it is true, there is one warm-hearted and benevolent woman; but age and increasing ill health have disabled her for activity. The copper-madam was also old and dried-up enough to have taken her leave, but she was retained, it was said, for "consideration' sake."

But a still sadder impression was produced upon me by the hospital for sick children, well kept and well managed as it seemed to be with regard to cleanliness and general convenience. A number of children, for instance, who are here for diseases of the eyes, were sitting in formal circles on the floor, without having any thing to do or any thing to play with. They sat silent and inanimate.

"Have these little ones no playthings?" asked I.

"They had had playthings given them by the ladies, but they only broke them," was the reply.

"But are they not allowed to employ themselves with any thing?"

"They must do nothing on account of their eyes."

Any one who knows how easily children will create for themselves a whole little world of living objects merely with little stones, pieces of wood, fir-cones, and such like trifles, and how happy they will be with them, must wonder to see these little creatures so devoid of all means of enjoyment and pastime, because "they break their playthings." And if they do, what is that in comparison with the blankness and deadness of life which they are now reduced to, and which must convert them into idiots if it is long continued thus?

There were at the Deaconess's institution at Kaiserswerth children also with diseases of the eye, but how cheerful and animated they were, each and all occupied with games or little playthings which did not require eyesight. All could sing cheerful and beautiful songs, and gentle sisters, the deaconesses, took motherly charge of them.

These institutions on Randall's Island as little corresponded with that which one has a right to expect from the Christian mind and power of the New World as the prison of New York. The mismanagement of the prisoners is chargeable upon the men, that of the children upon the women.

The Houses of Correction on Blackwell's Island are celebrated for being well managed, and for fully accomplishing their intention, and it was my intention to have visited them; but Marcus S. and W. H. Channing had invited me to a meeting of the North American Phalanstery, and this was what I could not by any means neglect. On the 29th, therefore, I left New York in company with Channing.

It was an indescribably beautiful day. The softest breezes wafted us from New York to the shore of New Jersey. Here we were met by the wagon of the Phalanstery, and joined by various persons from other places who were all bound on a visit to the Phalanstery.

Very different scenes, and very different faces to those I had just seen in New York met us here.

When we arrived at the little, dark wooded gorge which serves as a sort of portal to the territory of the harmonious association, we were surprised by the sight of Marcus S., who came driving along in his "buggy," drawn by Dolly —buggy, Dolly, and Marcus himself all garlanded with the blossoming wild clematis. I alighted from the wagon and seated myself beside Marcus, and thus we advanced slowly toward the Phalanstery, seated in a flowery, fragrant arbor. We were met in the park by the children and young people, and even by some elderly ones, all wearing green garlands and flowers. It was the most beautiful and the gayest procession which can be conceived. As we passed along we saw a group of agricultural laborers standing in the shade of a tree, busied in eating an immense water-melon. It was just now dinner-time.

Marcus S. had, during last year, built himself a lovely little house at the Phalanstery, in order to enjoy there, with his family, the good air and sea-bathing during the summer. The family lived here by themselves, but took their meals at the Phalanstery. I had here, as formerly at Rose Cottage, my own room in the house of my friends, and I now accompanied them to dinner at the Phalanstery.

Dinner was spread on small, separate tables, twelve or fourteen in number, in a very large, oblong hall, with windows in two sides: the freshest air was admitted by these lofty windows. At the bottom of the hall was placed a well-executed but somewhat fantastic painting of the Phalansterian Association in its perfected state on earth, and above this were the words, "The Great Joy," formed in evergreen leaves.

The tables, which would each conveniently accommodate from ten to twelve guests, were brilliant with white linen and porcelain. The group of waiters consisted of handsome youths and young girls, all with artistically formed wreaths of leaves around their heads. To these the good Marcus, also, now associated himself. A more beautiful group or a more gay dinner-scene it would not be easy to find. The dishes were simple, but remarkably excellent and well-served. There was neither wine, nor the drinking of toasts, nor yet songs, but a cheerful, soft murmur of kindly conversing voices was heard uninterruptedly during the whole meal, and mingled itself with the pleasantly fanning breezes, with the sight of all those cheerful, healthy countenances, and those lovely young people who floated round the tables like beautiful, beneficent ministering spirits, all united to make this meal-time more festal than any could be with sparkling Champagne and music.

A great improvement had taken place in the Phalanstery since I had been there two years before. A new house had been built, and besides the large hall they then had, another had been erected called "The Little Joy." The kitchen had been furnished with steam apparatus for cooking, which was a great saving not only of time and labor, but of expense, both in cooking and washing. Mr. Arnold, formerly the minister and farmer, was now the President of the Phalanstery, and his constructive brain had made itself useful as regarded the introduction of many excellent practical arrangements. The members of the association had now increased to one hundred persons, and many families had erected small dwellings around the principal buildings, where they lived, probably in the same relationship to the Phalanstery as the family of my friends, and watching with great interest the development of the institution.

After dinner the company assembled in the park, beneath some large, shadowy trees; large baskets of melons were carried thither, with which the people were splendidly regaled. I have never seen any where such an abundance of melons; they were here by hundreds; nor have I ever tasted any so good, sweet, juicy, and fine-flavored. The Canteloup-melons were especially remarkable. The soil in this part of the country, especially in New Jersey, is celebrated for the production of fine fruit.

I spent three days at the Phalanstery, amid a variety of scenes, many of which greatly interested me. Foremost among these I place a meeting, which was brought about by Channing, for the consideration of the social position of woman, and what it requires; her sufferings, their causes, and the means for averting them. The assembly consisted of about twenty women, and of those men whom they invited. It was an assembly of thoughtful, gentle countenances. The office of spokesman was unanimously assigned to Channing. He opened, therefore, the meeting with a representation of those sufferings which may befall a woman through the noblest and the best part of her nature, under the existing state of society. I listened to him with feelings which I have difficulty in describing.

"Is it possible," thought I, "is it really true, that I hear a man thus aware of, thus understand the sighs, the agony, the yearnings which I myself, during a greater portion of my life, experienced almost to despair—which many experience as I did, and under which many also sink? Is it a man whom I hear speaking for the captive, and demanding liberation? And do I hear through him really that a better time is approaching, a more just, more enlightened, more holy? Is it not a dream? Shall really the time of silent sighs cease upon earth? Shall there be light, and a path, and freedom, and a heaven opened to all?"

I looked around on the assembly. There were some beautiful women with thoughtful brows, whose remarkable destinies spoke powerfully for the reform which the speaker demanded; there were gentle, motherly women, such as Marcus's sisters, Mrs. A. and Rebecca, who, amid their own domestic happiness, had not lost the feeling of citizen-life, had not ceased to sympathize with their less fortunate sisters; there was Channing, with his noble and pure countenance glowing with inspiration; there was the earnest President of the Association, the good Marcus, and many others, in whom I recognized the representatives of the highest conscience of humanity.

As I cast my eyes around, they fell upon a picture, the only one in the room; it was a beautiful engraving, representing the dance of the hours around the flower-strewn car of Time. I thought of Geijer, in the prophetic visions and dreams in which this true seer beheld the advance of the new time, and hailed it with rejoicing shortly before he quitted this earthly scene. Oh! that he had been here; that he had heard and seen the time here arrived of which he had dreamed and spoken so rapturously, unintelligibly to many, yet not so to me, in his last moments. The memory of him—of the past; the impression of the present, of the future, took hold upon me with almost overwhelming power.

Excepting the speech of Channing, the meeting did not produce any thing which remained in my memory. The subjects which were here touched upon will be still further pursued and developed at the great Woman's Convention which will be held in the beginning of October, at Worcester, in Massachusetts, and which will be attended by many of the members now here present, my friends, Marcus and Rebecca, among the rest. They wish me also to be there, and I would very gladly, but on the 13th instant I must leave America for Europe. I must see England on my return, and I should, in that case, be too long detained from home.

While I am on the subject of woman's position in society, and Women's Rights' Conventions, I will say a few words about them. I am very glad of the latter, because they cause many facts, and many good thoughts to become public. I rejoice at the nobility and prudence with which many female speakers stand forth; at the profound truths, worthy of all consideration, which many of them utter; at the depth of woman's experience of life, her sufferings, and yearnings, which through them come to light; I rejoice and am amazed to see so many distinguished men sympathize in this movement, and support the women in their public appearance, often presenting the subject in language still stronger than they themselves use. I rejoice also that society, with decision peculiar to the Anglo-American spirit of association, has so rapidly advanced from talking to action—has divided into separate committees, for the development of the separate branches of the subject, preparatory to new social arrangements.

But I do not rejoice at some lesser, well-intentioned measures and steps which have been proposed; do not rejoice at the tone of accusation and bravado which has now and then been assumed in the Convention, and at several expressions less noble and beautiful.

It must, however, be confessed, that these clouds on the heaven of the new morning are few and fleeting in comparison with the vast and pure portions of light. Conventions are good, because they give emphasis to the great new moment of life in the community; they are good as a sifting wind separating the chaff from the wheat. They will, if rightly conducted, hasten on the approaching day; if otherwise, they will retard it. There are signs enough, both in Europe and in this country, which predict the approach of a time, of which Moses already prophesied in the words,

"The daughters enter in."

And if you should say, as you once said when we spoke on this subject,

"Then all the wrong-headed will rule, and the whole *corps* will be disgraced!"

To which I will reply, "I am not afraid of that, and less so now than ever. Look at the Society of Friends, and at the small Socialist community at this place. All the women in these have the right to speak in the public assemblies, but none avail themselves of the right but they who have talent for it, or who have something very good to say. All participate in the government, but it is done quietly, and evidently for the best interests of the community. Neither does one ever hear of quarrels between the men and women, of disunion and separation between married couples. With affectionately conceded privileges, the spirit of opposition and disquiet is generally appeased. The power of reason and affection obtain greater power. Thoughtfulness and gentleness are the distinguishing features of these free women."

A case of decision by general vote in the Phalanstery has just lately proved in a striking manner the good influence of the pure spirit and morals of home on the affairs of the community, through its direct influence from the heart and centre of the home.

"The Gauls," Tacitus tells us, "on important occasions summoned a select assembly of women into the councils, and their voice gave the final decision."

When the female consciousness of life becomes that which it may be in our time, its influence must be most beneficial in the councils of the community. As it is, this is now deprived of that fructifying life which belongs to the sphere of the mother, and the home does not now educate citizens and citizenesses.

Not that I imagine a new and better state of things would bring forth perfection. Ah! no one can have arrived at fifty without, both from one's own shortcomings and those of others, being too well acquainted with human imperfection to believe that every thing is to become perfect upon earth; but somewhat better they will be nevertheless, when they who are the mothers and foster-mothers of the human race become as good and as wise as the light of an extended sphere of life can make them—when that fountain of light with which the Creator has endowed their nature can flow forth unimpeded, and diffuse its living waters within the home and social life.

I can not see it otherwise. I believe that this development of liberty is the profoundest and the most vital principle upon which the regeneration of society depends, and upon which the greatness and the happiness of the New World depends.

"*The darkness of the mother casts its gloom over the child; the clearness of the mother casts its light over the child from generation to generation.*"

It is in this conviction that I will unite myself to the Convention, and say with it,

"Sing unto the Lord a new song; sing unto the Lord, all the earth."

And now again to the Phalanstery.

In the evening of the second day after our arrival, there was a little play and a ball. A lively little piece, but without any very profound meaning, was acted very well by a number of the young people. Many of the young ladies made their appearance at the ball in the so-called Bloomer costume, that is to say, short dresses made to the throat, and trowsers. This costume, which is, in reality, much more modest than that of the ordinary ball-room, and which looks extremely well on young ladies in their every-day occupations, is not advantageous for a ball-room, and is not at all becoming in the waltz, unless the skirts are very short, which was the case with two otherwise remarkably well-dressed and very pretty young girls. Some of them had really in their Bloomer costume a certain fantastic grace; but when I compared this with the true feminine grace which exhibited itself in some young girls with long dresses, and in other respects equally modest attire with the Bloomer ladies, I could not but give the palm to the long dresses. Among the most graceful of the dancers in long dresses was the lovely Abbie A., the daughter of the President of the Phalanstery.

The ball was in other respects far more beautiful (even if the toilets of the ladies were not so elegant), and the dancing in much better taste, than that which I saw at Saratoga.

When I was making a sketch in my room of the beautiful groups of waiters at the first day's dinner, I asked them, one after the other, if they were happy in their life at this place. They replied unanimously that they could not imagine themselves happy under other circumstances. Life appeared to them rich and beautiful. How many young people in the home of the Old World could give the same reply?

Among the ladies now members of the association was one still young, without beauty, but with a lofty, intellectual forehead. The mind had pondered within this forehead upon the unjust distribution of human lots—upon the disproportion between the longings which she felt within herself and that portion in life which was hers, as a young woman of weak health and small means. She dwelt on these thoughts and this state of life until she became also insane. Rigid, evangelical relations of hers counseled her "to bear her cross!" She came hither. Here she was received by love and freedom—the most invigorating atmosphere both for soul and body. Her being expanded and unfolded itself like a drooping flower. That life of social love, and that taste for fellow-citizenship which lay fettered within her, liberated itself, and she soon became one of the most active members of the little community, devoting herself to the cultivation of the garden, and to the care of its fruits and flowers. She is now a universal favorite in the little community, and is there only addressed by some appellation of endearment, expressive of the general love for her, and her affectionate activity for all.

I sat one evening in her little room, listening to the simple and affecting history of her former inward struggle and her present happiness. That little room was not larger than an ordinary prison cell; it had bare, whitewashed walls, but a large window which afforded light and air. We sat upon a very comfortable sofa, and the cornice and angles of the room were covered from floor to ceiling with rich sheaves of beautiful grasses, grouped with the most exquisite taste. The inmate of the room did not know their names; she had never had an opportunity of becoming acquainted with nature and its productions; but every one of these grasses had been gathered by her with love, had been contemplated with admiration, and bound together one with another, so that the peculiar beauty of each was made availing to the whole. That fantastic moulding of yellow grasses was richer than one of gilding.

My conversation in this little room was interrupted before I wished by my being called away to see one of the sweetest young girls dance the Scottish hornpipe.

On Sunday Channing gave a public discourse on the relationship of religion and the community, on the relationship between the inward and the outward laws, a discourse rich in Christian consciousness, and in which nothing was wanting but that prominence should have been given to the constant point of this consciousness, the need of mercy, and of the communication of the Divine Spirit, and of prayer, that wonderful speaking-tube between earth and heaven.

In the evening, which was beautiful, I ascended with Marcus and Eddy a green hill at some distance from the Phalanstery, which is called from its shape the Sugar-Loaf Hill. We had an extensive prospect from the summit, and saw in the golden light of the setting sun the whole fertile, cultivated region, full of small rural abodes embowered in their wooded parks, and among these the pale yellow-colored house of the Phalanstery looked like a large mansion. I gazed upon it with cheerful feelings, although I can not divest my mind of fears regarding its stability, more especially as some of its wisest members are not without anxieties regarding its pecuniary difficulties.

This community, and those which resemble it in this

country, aim at producing the model community on earth, a perfect state of social life. They call this community the Harmonians, and place it above the old one, in which the members graduate merely in artificial culture; their efforts are principally directed toward the spiritual, the natural, which, in its full state of culture, will lead to a perfect, and in all respects harmoniously developed social state.

Nevertheless, it seems to me that all the various talents and natural gifts, upon the development of which the full development of the community principally depends, can not here attain to the depth and fullness which is necessary for this purpose. A small community can scarcely furnish scope sufficient for the many dissimilar powers, and these—but I will not say more on this subject. I feel that I am not fully possessed of it, and that the objections which I might make could be met by the answer of the extended sphere of the nursery, which I have here seen. I will rather adhere to that portion of the subject which I understand with my whole heart, which makes the institution dear to me, and which, I am certain, forms a transition point in its life and activity as regards the life of humanity.

It is a work of Christian human love. It aims at preparing every man and every woman for a harmonious development, conformably to their innermost being, by means of a harmonious social life, in which all shall enjoy the fruits of the labor of all, and all enjoy the fruits of God's rich and beautiful earth. It enforces that object in individual activity at which it aims publicly in the great community. It is a forerunner and a prophet. The prophets of old were stoned, and are dead.

And their voices sound even now upon earth. The community of the Phalanstery, as I beheld it here, with its sound kernel of pious and earnest working members, with its surrounding garland of intellectual, devoted lookers-on, is a product of Christ's doctrine of love, and it aims at making this a vital principle of social life. *It is an upright and a noble endeavor.*

And the kingdom of God is extended by such endeavors. May one and all be faithful in their part. And should the Phalanstery, even in this its contracted form, become one of the earth's "*enfans perdus*," yet it will not be so in the history of the new community, neither in that of the house of God.

For my part, I feel convinced that these small socialist communities will not sustain themselves longer than they are sustained by the noble spirits who infuse into them their energetic life of love. Then probably their work will fall to pieces. But if they, during a short successful period, exhibit that which social humanity may become when all shall be influenced by a noble and beneficent spirit, and possessing all these material advantages which associated life affords, then they will not have flourished—will not have lived in vain.

And it can not be denied that the moral element which they adopt as the principle of association, and which constitutes their characteristic and recognizable feature, is also beginning to be valid in the great commercial, industrial, and scientific associations of North America. People are acknowledging more and more that man is more than meat, and "leveling upward" is the universal watchword in all associated life. Associations in all professions, and for all purposes, spring as the natural products of this soil, but only the more is it felt that the strongest bond of union is a supernatural one, and depends principally upon that which is highest and best in man. Associations become fraternities.

The last evening of my stay at the Phalanstery I conducted all its members through a grand Swedish *Nigarepolka*, which made a fervor. Seldom indeed had "the Great Joy" resounded with a more universal or hearty rejoicing.

The following morning Channing was to leave. After breakfast, therefore, we walked into the park for quiet conversation. We met several people who would gladly have exchanged a word with the beloved teacher, yet none interrupted us, none disturbed us. I saw a lady sitting reading under a shady tree; she sat as quietly there as in her own room: so much is the private circle respected by the members of the Phalanstery.

Among the varied scenes of these last few days was one of a somnambule, of that kind which is called *a medium*, *i. e.*, a person who, in the magnetic state, is, or believes himself to be, *en rapport* with a deceased friend or connection, and delivers communications from him. This medium was a pretty young girl (not a member of the Phalanstery), and the spirit that was said to converse with her was that of her father.

About twenty persons, myself being one of the number, sat round a table, all forming a chain by the contact of the hands; hymns were sung to cheerful tunes. Within a very short time the young girl became suddenly pale, her head sank, and her features grew livid and rigid almost as in death. This lasted for a few minutes, during which the singing was continued. The young girl then awoke with convulsive movements, and immediately afterward began, with convulsive rapidity, to pass her fingers over the letters of a large alphabet which lay before her, and in which she pointed out letters which were written down by other persons, and thus words and sentences were put together. Questions which were put to the somnambule were answered in the same manner, and I am convinced that there was no deception; nevertheless, the answers which she gave showed evidently that the spirit with which she stood *en rapport* was not very much wiser than we poor inquiring mortals. She had been extremely attached to the deceased father, and it was not until after his death that she fell into this singular condition. The answers showed indeed a pure spiritual life, but not any thing supernaturally so. The whole scene interested me, but produced a painful impression on Channing, whose pure, spiritual nature is displeased by these juggling or abnormal spiritual dealings.

There are in the United States at this time, especially in the North, a great number of clairvoyants of all grades; and mediums, "spiritual knockings," and many other dark spiritual phenomena belong to the order of the day. They are totally rejected by many, but earnestly accepted by others. I myself have seen sufficient of clairvoyant exhibitions to be convinced that they are by no means deficient of a light which exceeds that of the ordinary natural condition, at the same time that they are by no means infallible. The clairvoyant sees many things with wonderful clearness, but is mistaken in others. The clairvoyant is not a guide to be relied upon. Nevertheless, the certain result of the phenomenon of clairvoyance is infinitely precious, that is to say, the certainty it gives that the soul possesses organs and senses within the corporeal, and independent of them; that the spiritual body is superior to the natural; that the latter is merely the natural medium of the former.

After these cheerful, festal days at the Phalanstery, I returned to New York, where I am now, once more in my good Quaker-home, occupied in visiting the public institutions and making preparations for my journey. I am accompanied and assisted in all this by the eldest son of the family, an amiable youth of nineteen, beautiful in body and soul, one of those who make one think of the new human being of whom the song of Vala speaks, "fed with morning dew."

During my rambles hither and thither in New York, I have often met with large parties of military, and yesterday a large body of cavalry passed along the streets, both horses and men having a very martial and magnificent appearance. I have never seen in any of the capitals of Europe so much military movement as in New York. But the soldiers here are voluntary troops, and exercise themselves in military maneuvers for their own pleasure. Many times during the day gay military music may be heard on Broadway, and small detachments are seen marching along in splendid uniforms, and with fine military bearing, frequently with flowers stuck in their gun-barrels. These volunteer corps of young citizens have been exercising themselves beyond the city in firing and military exercises, and are now returning thence with bands of music, which are always good, and which play lively marches or "quick-steps." The peace-promulgating people are warlike by nature, and its spirit of conquest is double-faced, like the god Janus.

I have heard the Military Academy at West Point—the only establishment of this kind in the United States—praised by Europeans, who are authority on such subjects, as being very excellent, and that the officers who have been brought up there are as remarkable for their knowledge as for their bravery. During the Mexican war the number of killed and wounded of the officers greatly exceeded, in proportion, that of the common soldiers, and proved the courage with which they had led on their troops.

I have to-day engaged a cabin on board the large American steamer The Atlantic, which leaves New York for Liverpool on the 13th instant. The vessel and the captain, Mr. West, are both of the first class; with him I shall be quite safe.

I return this afternoon to my friends at Rose Cottage, and in the morning I shall be joined there by Mr. Downing, who is on his way from Washington, and who will take me with him to his beautiful home on the Hudson. There will be my last visit in America, where also was my first. Some other visits I shall be unable to pay, how ever much I desire it. But this is required from me, both from duty and from—love.

I spent last evening—my last evening at New York—with my amiable, kind hostess, Mrs. G., at the house of her father, the celebrated old Isaac Hopper. This magnificent old man, now eighty-five, is still as strong and ardent almost as a youth. In his strongly-marked, handsome countenance may be seen the ardor of the warlike spirit, combined with the steadfastness and wisdom of the peace-principle, relieved by a great deal of humor and shrewdness. His figure in his Quaker costume is not without a degree of chivalric stateliness. It is evident that Father Hopper, as he is commonly called, belongs to the Church militant, and all his life has borne testimony to this. He has, during his active life in the service of the oppressed, been the means of delivering more than a thousand fugitive slaves out of the hands of their pursuers, and in so doing has periled his own life, has been maltreated, has been hurled into the street, thrown out of windows—once out of the third story of a house—and always returned resolute, firm, cheerful, full of courage and resources to accomplish that which he had begun, with a good-humored obstinacy which finally conquered the malevolence of his adversaries. At the request of his daughter and myself, he related some of the occurrences of his life during his efforts to save fugitive slaves. I have seldom heard narratives more instructive, and seldom have I spent so rich and racy an evening.

Father Hopper has twelve children, and his handsome second wife sat at the table in her fine, white Quaker costume. A young unmarried daughter still beautified her old father's home.

Long life to Father Hopper and his family!

September 5th—10th. Days on the Hudson! The last days in my first beautiful home on its banks; beautiful days, but still sad. It is borne in upon my mind continually with a painful feeling, as of rending asunder, which I can not describe, that the time draws near for separation; that I actually and *forever* am leaving this grand, glorious country, in which I have lived so richly, which received me with such unexampled hospitality—these noble, amiable people, who are my friends, to whom I am so deeply attached, with whom I would then always live and associate. Nowhere have I found such friends. Do not imagine, my own Agatha, that I am less willing to return home; believe me, I could not love and work any where but in Sweden; but yet—it is bitter for me to tear myself away, and I sometimes believe that I can not—that it is not really possible! It seems to me so unreasonable!

What a pleasure it was to me to see once more Mr. Downing, Andrew Downing, my first friend on the soil of America, my young American brother, as I love to call him!

The good Marcus had driven me down to the steamer, and sat with me in the saloon, waiting till Downing, according to appointment, should come. He came from Washington, and Marcus left me in his charge. It was now more than a year and a half since I had last seen him. He seemed to me handsomer—more manly; it seemed to me as if he had grown, had developed himself; and so it was. He had spiritually developed himself and his world. His beautiful eyes beamed with a self-conscious power.

We advanced up the Hudson as we had done nearly two years before; he sat beside me, silent as usual, after we had exchanged the first natural communications between friends; neither did I feel it necessary to talk, for we understood one another. It was the most beautiful afternoon and evening. The wind was fresh and full of animation, although warm; the waves were agitated more than usual, and danced and sang around us; nature was full of cheerful and delicious life. No night-frosts as yet had breathed upon the verdant heights; the enchanting veil of the autumnal summer began to be unfolded over them.

The moon arose and mingled her waves of light with those of the wind and water. I sat silent, listening, and melancholy. I knew that the hour of parting drew nigh.

Caroline Downing met us, as on the former occasion. I found her also looking younger and more lovely. But I felt that I myself had become older, both body and soul. But then I had in these two years passed through more than in ten ordinary years, and much of this, which appertains to my innermost being, can only be imparted to you by word of mouth.

I rejoice to see the development of life and activity which has taken place in Downing. His outward sphere of activity is now very wide and effective. President Fillmore has it in contemplation to lay out extensive grounds around the Capitol at Washington, and there are here two young architects from England who, under Downing's direction, are preparing plans for houses which he is commissioned to erect for private persons, who in their villas and cottages desire to combine the beautiful with the useful. Downing's engagements and correspondence is at this time incredibly great, and extends over the whole Union; but then he does all so easily, so *con amore*, as Jenny Lind seems to sing. That, however, which pleases me in particular is the direction which his literary activity seems to take. I have sometimes, half in earnest and half in jest, reproached Downing with being more exclusive and aristocratic in his beautifying activity than became an honest, downright republican, and we have had, in consequence, various friendly little quarrels. It is very easy to see, from Downing's naturally refined manner, that it must be difficult for him to reconcile himself to a certain rudeness and unmannerliness which must exist among a people where all possess equal rights, and regard themselves as equally good, even before all have attained to that outward and inward degree of cultivation which can make equality natural, and the life of equality agreeable. He seemed to me also as if, in his feelings toward this class of people, he stood at too great a distance and was too indifferent. But so he ought not to be, it seemed to me, as a Christian republican. It is, therefore, with heartfelt joy that I have now read a leading article from his pen on the New York Park, in the last number of his monthly journal, "the Horticulturist," in which he takes a far higher stand than that which he was formerly accustomed to do.

You, my Agatha, must also write me a few words of this, because they deserve to be read, and they will be the last which I shall quote from the New World.

I will let Downing speak.

"We have said nothing of the *social* influence of such a great park* in New York. But this is really the most interesting phase of the whole matter. It is a fact not a little remarkable, that, ultra-democratic as are the political tendencies of America, its most intelligent social tendencies are almost wholly in a contrary direction. And among the topics discussed by the advocates and opponents of the new park, none seem so poorly understood as the social aspect of the thing. It is, indeed, both curious and amusing to see the stand taken on the one hand by the million, that the park is made for the "upper ten," who ride in fine carriages, and on the other hand, by the wealthy and refined, that a park in this country will be "usurped by rowdies and low people." Shame upon our republican compatriots, who so little understand the elevating influences of the beautiful in nature and art, when enjoyed in common by thousands and hundreds of thousands of all classes without distinction! They can never have seen how, all over France and Germany, the whole population of the cities pass their afternoons and evenings together in the beautiful public parks and gardens—how they enjoy together the same music, breathe the same atmosphere of

* Downing urges in his article that the park must be laid out on a much larger scale than had been contemplated.

art, enjoy the same scenery, and grow into social freedom by the very influences of easy intercourse, space, and beauty that surround them. In Germany, especially, they have never seen how the highest and the lowest partake alike of the common enjoyment—the prince seated beneath the trees on a rush-bottomed chair, before a little wooden table, sipping his coffee or his ice, with the same freedom from state and pretension as the simplest subject. Drawing-room conventionalities are too narrow for a mile or two of spacious garden landscape, and one can be happy with ten thousands in the social freedom of a community of genial influences, without the unutterable pang of not having been *introduced* to the company present.

"These social doubters, who thus intrench themselves in the sole citadel of *exclusiveness* in Republican America, mistake our people and their destiny. If we would but have listened to them, our magnificent river and lake steamers, those real palaces of the million, would have no velvet couches, no splendid mirrors, no luxurious carpets. Such costly and rare appliances of civilization, they would have told us, could only be rightly used by the privileged families of wealth, and would be trampled upon and utterly ruined by the democracy of the country, who travel one hundred miles for half a dollar. And yet these, our floating palaces and our monster hotels, with their purple and fine linen, are they not respected by the majority who use them, as truly as other palaces by their rightful sovereigns? Alas! for the faithlessness of the few who possess, regarding the capacity for culture of the many who are wanting. Even upon the lower platform of liberty and education that the masses stand in Europe, we see the elevating influences of a wide popular enjoyment of galleries of art, public libraries, parks and gardens, which have raised the people in *social* civilization and social culture to a far higher level than we have yet attained in Republican America. And yet this broad ground of popular refinement *must* be taken in Republican America, for it belongs of right more truly here than elsewhere. It is republican in its very idea and tendency. It takes up popular education where the common school and ballot-box leave it, and raises up the working-man to the same level of enjoyment with the man of leisure and accomplishment. The higher social and artistic elements of every man's nature lie dormant within him, and every laborer is a possible gentleman, not by the possession of money and fine clothes, but through the refining influence of intellectual and moral culture. Open wide, therefore, the doors of your libraries and picture galleries, all ye true republicans! Build halls, where knowledge shall be freely diffused among men, and not shut up within the narrow walls of narrow institutions. Place spacious parks in your cities, and unloose their gates as wide as the gates of the morning to the whole people. As there are no dark places at noonday, so education and culture, the true sunshine of the soul, will banish the plague-spots of democracy; and the dread of the ignorant exclusive, who has no faith in the refinement of a republic, will stand abashed in the next century before a whole people, whose system of voluntary education embraces, combined with perfect individual freedom, not only common schools of rudimentary knowledge, but common enjoyments for all classes in the higher realms of art, letters, science, social recreations, and enjoyments. Were our legislators but wise enough to understand to-day the destinies of the New World, the gentility of Sir Philip Sidney, made universal, would not be half so much a miracle fifty years hence in America, as the idea of a whole nation of laboring men reading and writing was in his day in England."

Thus my friend Downing, who has in this declared from his sphere the mission of the New World, and who has taken a position which is worthy a son of the new creation, that of Christian artist.

He has gone forth among the people to elevate them to his point of view; he has united himself with that great, true republican party in the country, all of whose endeavors tend to "*leveling upward*," and whose watch-word is "*all things for all*."

It is an especial source of joy to me to see how near Downing now approaches to that point of view taken by my friends the S.'s. Probably they will hereafter come into closer personal contact. Downing may visit the Phalanstery, and may perhaps give it the benefit of his knowledge and artistic genius in those building schemes which are under contemplation. Thus are fraternal chains formed, the first link of which rests in his hand who first declared on earth that all men are brethren. His power will permeate it to the very extremest link. Praise be unto him!

Evening. I can not write much more from this place; time fails me, my heart fails me. The writing of many letters and the duties of the present moment occupy the hours, and the thought of leaving this country, these friends, this people, is like a thorn in my heart. The weather also depresses me; the heat oppressive; not a breath of wind is stirring; the atmosphere is hot as if boiled. It is only beautiful in the evening, when the moon has risen, and pours her gushes of silver light among the shadows of the river and the shore.

Last evening I took a stroll through the park alone, and with an unspeakable melancholy in my soul.

"It is all past and gone, this beautiful time," thought I; "these bonds of friendship, these beautiful sights of a New World; these beautiful, animating circumstances; all past! past and gone!" And I wept bitterly.

But when I looked, the full moon was looking down upon me, large and splendid, and shone into my soul as she seemed to say,

"No, it is not all past and gone! Strengthen thy heart with the light which increases forever! That which the human being has thus found, thus acquired, is his forever, and can not die. It is an imperishable seed, which will renovate itself in new and abundant harvests in the kingdom of light! These friends, these memories, will not cease to live in thee. To each wane succeeds a new increase and a new fullness."

This was what the moon, my friend, seemed to say to me, and, comforted, I returned to the house, and was silent and thankful.

In the morning I go to New York, whither my friends accompany me.

My silent friend has let fall words full of important meaning to me during these last few days. He says but little, as formerly, but in that little—so much. He wishes me clearly to understand both good and evil in this country, and to express it without reserve, but he leaves it to my own mind to find out the way and the truth.

"That will all come clear to you," he says sometimes, "when you get home and are quiet."

His manner and his perfect confidence enchant me.

The interest he takes in the intellectual development of woman in America is one circumstance which particularly attaches me to him. This acute-minded observer sees clearly that which is still wanting in general. He has mentioned with great pleasure to me a work just published, entitled "Rural Hours," by Miss Cooper, the daughter of the novelist; a diary, in which she simply and faithfully chronicled, during a quiet residence in the country, all that occurred in the life of nature around her, so that the whole progress of the year is displayed—the grasses, the birds, the flowers come out and disappear, and beautiful drawings of the latter adorn the work.

Downing has spoken in high commendation of this work in his own journal, "The Horticulturist," both on account of its scientific worth, and for the example which it gives to female mind, directing its attention to the daily marvels of nature, and to that which is great even in the quiet every-day life of the country.

"Flowers, insects, and the biographies of birds ought especially to be drawn and studied by female students of Natural History."

Oh! that it is necessary to part from this friend; one of the best, and the most suitable for my character and turn of mind which can be imagined, or, rather, which the goodness of God can give me.

Rose Cottage, September 12th.

Yet a few more words, but merely a few, for I am overwhelmed by letters and objects which demand my attentions, and find that I am suffering from headache caused by over-excitement of mind and body.

Before I left the Downings we spent one day together at West Point. The view was glorious, but the day oppressively hot, and without any air. The vessels glided along the mirror-like Hudson, I know not by what power, for wind there was none.

At the *table d'hôte*, at dinner, there sat before us two meagre, sallow-complexioned, sickly-looking little girls, quite by themselves, who drank wine and ate all sorts of delicacies like grown-up people. This did not escape Downing's grave and disapproving glance. He said to me,

"This is one of the circumstances upon which I wish you to turn the general attention! There is so much done for children in this country—people look upon them as almost sacred beings, and yet children are spoiled by regular neglect!"

"You must take this as a present from me to your sister Agatha," said Downing, giving me a large, beautiful copper-plate engraving of the view from West Point.

His last gift to me was Bartlett's valuable work, "American Scenery," and Miss Cooper's "Rural Hours;" that was at New York. At the Astor House we parted, where we had first met; I felt that we parted forever on earth.

Marcus S., pale with the heat, always kind and attentive, came with his carriage to take me to his home.

It is now late in the evening, my last evening in the New World. The heat is horrible; the nights bring with them no refreshment. People look as if their faces were floured. All things seem to suffer and to pant.

I can not conceive how it is possible for me to be ready by morning. Good-night!

I shall soon behold Sweden once more! Ah, if then, when I come from Denmark, I could only see your sweet face on the shore—your blue eyes!

My dear heart, I have longed greatly to have received yet one letter more from you before I left America, which would tell me that you had become warm again—the two last were so very cold! But no warm summer letter has come, and I must leave in faith and in hope. And in love I embrace heartily mamma and you!

On the Sea, September, 1851.

P.S.—It is over. I have left them forever, that great country, those dear, precious friends! It was inevitable, and it is done; but I feel still stupefied, as it were, by it. Thank God, however, the severest moment is past.

And the morning on which I must go—it was a strange morning! I was almost bewildered by the multitude of small duties which I yet had to perform, and by a lingering headache; but all at once it went, and every thing brightened up. The good Marcus sat in my room, and sealed my letters as I wrote them, and received my commissions, saying calmly between whiles, "plenty of time"—"we are in good time." And it really seemed to me almost miraculous how the hours and the time spun themselves out; every thing disentangled itself; every thing became light and easy, so wonderfully calm and even pleasant—it was the influence of the gentle spirit that was near me.

In good time I was ready—every thing was ready. And I embraced my beloved Rebecca, kissed Jenny and the baby, and set off accompanied by Marcus and Eddy.

On board the "Atlantic" I found myself all at once in a regular whirlpool of old and new acquaintance; gentlemen who shook hands, and presented me with pamphlets which they had written; ladies who presented me with lovely gifts; acquaintance who introduced acquaintance; dear friends from the North, from the South, who astonished me here to say farewell, and whichever way I turned my head I was kissed by somebody. Ah! I was almost glad when the bell summoned my friends on shore, and I could hide myself in my berth.

The last faces I saw were those of the angelic Eddy and the good, brotherly Marcus.

After that I sat silent and immovable for hours. But Marcus had placed in my room a bouquet of evergreen plants, and the yellow and red everlastings from the garden at Rose Cottage, and hung to it a card on which were written a few words in pencil; and upon this bouquet I sat gazing immovably, until its rich green leaves were woven around my heart, and all my agitated feelings had subsided into calm.

It was at noon when we left the land. Toward evening I went on deck, to cast one more glance upon that great New World. There it lay on the western horizon, dark green upon the blue waters, in a grand half circle, like an open embrace, a calm and inviting harbor. Clouds of tender peach-colors, and from the darkest violet to the clearest gold, and the softest crimson, lay in picturesque masses above it—rain-showers and sunbeams were flung athwart it. The sun freed himself from the cloud, and shone all the brighter the lower he sank toward the horizon where the great land lay. And that was the last view I had of it; and thus shall I always behold it in the depth of my soul.

I now see it no longer with my eye—see only heaven and the ocean. I am now again passing through a pause between two periods of life, between two worlds. But my heart is full. And when people ask me what the people of the New World possess preferably to the Old, I reply, with the impression of that which I have seen and passed through in America fresh in my soul, a warmer heart's pulse—a more energetic, youthfully strong life.

Among the letters which I received shortly before coming on board is one which I shall always cherish. It is not signed by any name, but if its writer only knew (the style is that of a man) how much joy it gave me! I have sometimes complained bitterly of the want of a nice sense of delicacy; but I have not mentioned the many proofs I have received of the most charming delicate kindness, which approached merely to give me pleasure, and then withdrew to avoid thanks. This letter belongs to that class.

The weather is now stormy and the sea runs high. I keep quiet in my cabin. I look at the little bouquet of green leaves and splendid everlastings. They speak to me of America and the memories I carry thence. I shall not behold any dear object until I once more see the Swedish coast—and you.

She to whom these words were addressed I was never more to behold. On the threshold of my home I found her grave.

Had she lived, these letters certainly would have remained unpublished. Their contents would have undergone a change before they had been presented to the public, probably for the better; for then I should have had a friend at my side in whose pure soul I should have seen my faults as in a mirror. As it is, I have been alone, although I have sometimes believed that an angel was near me.

The letter to the distinguished Danish theologian, Professor H. Martinsen, which now follows, was thought over in America, but was written in Europe. I required quietness and the power of making a general review before writing it. I could not, while in the country, perfectly see the wood for trees, and from the great number of churches could not see *the church.*

Now, when the forests of the New World murmur in the distance, and the great picture of the New World's cultivation is seen in perspective beyond the agitated sea, am I able for the first time to trace the main features with greater clearness and precision. Some of these I have already presented. One of the most essential I have here endeavored to present to the noble and profound thinker whom I am still so happy to call my teacher and my friend.

LETTER XXXVIII.

TO THE PROFESSOR OF THEOLOGY, DR. H. MARTINSEN.

Stockholm, May, 1853.

Of the happy time during which I was able every week to enjoy your society and conversation, I retain in my soul two especial moments as focuses of that light which, through the mercy of God, flowed from your soul into mine. The one was that evening when, emboldened by the struggle of my spirit and by your goodness, I drew comparisons between the teachings of heathenism and Christianity, inquiring after the new life until I made you angry, but by so doing drew from your lips a word before which my spirit became silent, because it perceived therein the true answer to my inquiry, and the arising of the new life. The second moment was the completion of the first. Many questions had become entangled into one single knot. You disentangled them by a single blow of that spiritual sword, which is at the same time the sword of the Word and of discriminating reason, which the Eternal Word has placed in your hand, accompanied by a power but rarely given to mortals. The effect of these two words, which still resound in my inner being, was, that they reached the very core of the subject, and called forth within me that which was essential, that which was vital.

Would that I might do the same now, in giving you an account of that new life which, during the two years which have elapsed since we parted, I have contemplated in that great Western land, whither I went, as I had gone before to you, as an inquirer—a seeker.

This is my wish. And I can promise you one thing, I will not detain you by many words.

"For what purpose are you going to America—what do you desire to see there?" was the question which you and many other of my friends in Denmark put to me before I embarked. I desired to see—the approaching One.

For One there is who has silently advanced onward through time, from the beginning. Bloody ages, brilliantly splendid epochs, are merely dissimilar chambers through which he advances, silently, calmly, becoming more and more distinct, through the twilight vail, until he reaches that period on the threshold of which he now stands, contemplated by many with rapture, by many, too, with fear. And if it is asked whose is the form before which thrones totter, crowns fall off, and earthly purple grows pale, the reply is, MAN—*Man in his original truth, formed in the image of God.*

In all realms of Christendom, people are becoming aware of his presence—are speaking of him, combating for him, combating against him, and—preparing for him a way. For his day is at hand, and he will come with it.*

* As a beautiful proof of this may be instanced, it seems to me, that ready, cordial homage which free nations at the present time pay to noble and liberal-minded rulers, such as Leopold, Victoria, Oscar. What tri-

I wished to see humanity as she presented herself in the New World, now that she had cast off all dominion of courts, forms, and uniforms, which had become oppressive burdens in the Old World—now that she had there, on the new soil, erected for herself a kingdom and an asylum for all nations, according to no other law than that promulgated in the Christian revelation and within her own breast. That was the form of humanity which I desired to see and to comprehend, and with her the new community and life.

Contemplate with me, then, for a moment, this humanity as she emerges from the bosom of the Mayflower, and plants on the new soil the earliest legislative colony; behold her in the little company of the Pilgrim Fathers.

They have come hither from the Old World, because, in the midst of persecution for their faith and struggle for daily bread, they felt themselves called upon to extend the kingdom of Christ in the New World—yes, even though they should be, as it were, mere stepping-stones for others. They call themselves Independents, Non-conformists, and Puritans, because they have separated themselves from the outward Church and all worldly power, and demand their right to govern themselves conformably only to the Word of God and the light of their own conscience. The Bible and implements of labor were the principal effects which they conveyed with them to the New World.

They wished to establish on that new, virgin soil, a Church and a social state of the purest character, of the inner man enlightened by the Word of God.

Every individual of that little company is made free by God, and is a free fellow-citizen; and not fellow-citizen merely—ruler, priest, magistrate, public official of every kind, because he may and must also be all these, if he is

umphal procession of antiquity can indeed be compared to those noble human thanksgiving festivals which were this year celebrated, in Sweden and Norway, for the restored health of King Oscar—homage as much due to the man as to the monarch!

nominated to them by the community. Man bears within himself the ability for all. Each individual feels himself a man, and at the same time intimately bound up in consolidated union with the rest. The community governs itself by the appointment of its own governors. These are elected by vote. The majority of votes decides the election, all agreeing to respect rules and rulers which the majority have agreed to. The document of this agreement was signed by the emigrants before they left the Mayflower—before they had landed on the new soil. When the little community trod the shores of the New World, it had already perfected its essential, its formative principle. Within themselves were governors, priests, and magistrates, such as every human community would require, but they must all be chosen by the popular voice. Neither rank nor wealth availed any thing; nothing in that new community was of higher avail than those qualifications which made the fisherman Peter, and Paul the tentmaker, apostles in the kingdom of Christ. The human being made free through Christ holds the highest rank on earth; there can be none higher. Such rank and dignity are absolute; and the labor of this elevated and ennobled humanity becomes thereby of the highest value. Sanctity of life and the honor of labor are laws in the community of the Pilgrims; and the occupation of their lives during the earlier portion of their settlement in the New World was divine worship and labor.

Such was the little colony of the Mayflower. That was the seed. It fell in good soil, and bore fruit a hundred-fold. There was a creative power in that grain of corn; and we recognize the same to this day in all the social institutions and spiritual life of the United States, even where this is still cramped by accidental fetters, or darkened by the shades of the old night.

The humanity which became the lawgiver of this hemisphere stood forth there with a full consciousness of herself as the servant of God and a member of the social state. These two in her are one. This is her peculiarity or her peculiar perfection.

Many of our countrymen regard the United States merely as an aggregate of inharmonious parts, brought together by chance, and adhering together by chance, without any organized centre.

But no one who has lived for any length of time in the United States, with leisure to study their life, can fail to perceive that they are within themselves possessed of a common creative principle of life, which is vital in the highest degree, and this is their religious and civil consciousness.

It is this which every where erects churches, organizes social institutions, and those still more powerful free associations; this it is which gives the bent to education, which determines the character of the home; this which finds its way into literature, into all great social movements, the watch-word of which is every where that of the genuinely divine commandments, "Love God above all things, and thy neighbor as thyself." Nowhere, indeed, on the face of the earth has the Christian consciousness of true human freedom attained to so full a recognization as in the United States; nowhere has it expressed so universally, and still expresses, both by word and deed, the doctrine that pure religion is the foundation and fortress of sound morality; that the true worship of God is the true love of man; that the most acceptable sacrifice which can be presented to the Father of Nations is the sight of a free, pious, and happy people, all of whom have equal rights and equal opportunity to acquire the highest human worth, the highest human happiness.

This consciousness is the centre of gravity in the cultivation of the New World throughout the Northern States. Every thing else, whether it be statesmanship, material development, science, or art, are subordinate to this, and must voluntarily or involuntarily obey it. There are separate corps, and separate leaders, and many different names, but there is one Commander-in-chief, whom all must obey and follow, and this is *the great humanity*—humanity in its highest individual and social development. The leading principle of this idea is, that each and all must serve. This it is which must be realized in every individual human being, and in society at large.

The Pilgrims took with them the Bible and implements of labor from Europe to the New World, and it may be said with justice that these two are to this day great powers in the cultivation thereof. Religious and spiritual life develop themselves in proportion to physical improvement. The human being and humanity are regarded and advanced pre-eminently with reference to their heavenly and their merely earthly relationship; every thing else is secondary.

Spiritual life must be here regarded principally in its form as churches, and in the results thence accruing.

North America is usually upbraided, in Europe, with its many dissimilar religious sects, its many separated churches. Nevertheless, it may be perceived, at the same time, that they are possessed of an essential unity in doctrine and life, although each individual sect has, as its germ, gathered itself around some one individual truth which it elevates for its standard.*

* "What, even the Mormons?" you ask, suspiciously. Without being able to speak with precision of that which is distinctive in the doctrines of the Mormons, I must still say, on the ground of what I was able to collect in America regarding this sect—its leaders and doctrines—that I believe the accusations laid to their charge are for the greater part untrue. The Mormons acknowledge as theirs the revelation of Christ and the Bible. Their later prophets (as I myself had opportunity of ascertaining) have given merely more close and more special prophecies of Christ, but no new doctrines. I was assured by an intellectual man—not a Mormon—who had resided two years among the Mormons in Utah, that the morals of the people *were remarkably pure*, and that the Mormon women *were above all blame*.

This was its purpose, its mission, its necessity. "God would have it so!" I have been compelled to say many times to myself, as I contemplated the histories and the lives of the persons who founded the most remarkable sects of North America, Roger Williams, Anne Hutchinson, George Fox, Anne Lee, and others, were impelled by a spirit mightier than themselves. They began by opposing the inner voice (as Luther did), but in the end they were compelled to follow its commands. These persons, divinely possessed, were driven by their inward spirit from comfortable and cheerful homes out into the wilderness, into captivity and persecution, and amid manifold suffering, for the promulgation of that truth which they had received, to suffer, nay, even to die for the doctrines they proclaimed. They could not do otherwise—they ought not to do otherwise, if they were worthy to be the servants of God.

"Do not stand still with Luther and Calvin," exclaimed Robinson, the spiritual pastor of the Pilgrims, addressing them from the shores of the Old World; "they were great and shining lights in their time, but they penetrated not to the councils of God. I conjure you, bear this in your remembrance; it is an article of your Church communion that you hold yourselves in readiness to receive whatever

The founder of the sect, Joe Smith, was a man of simple education, but possessed of extraordinary natural gifts, even of that secondary prophetic kind which is known in Scotland under the name of "second-sight." He himself believed in his revelations—at least in a part of them. After his death, the Mormon community was governed by men whom Joe Smith appointed to be his successors. They rule, as Smith had done, according to the word of the Bible and the inspiration of the Spirit. The hierarchical character of the government, under prudent leaders, constitutes its present strength, and has caused its rapid prosperity, under the Anglo-American moral law and order—which even in the valley of the Salt Lake shows its formative powers—that very form of government constitutes its danger, and may probably one day bring about its fall. And that day will be whenever it violates the sanctity of private life. Should the *inspiration of the government* permit polygamy, the Anglo-American home will never allow it.

truth shall be revealed to you from the written word of God."

It was on the ground of this progressive, divine communication from God to man that Luther appealed from the Pope's bull to the Bible; it was on the ground of the same doctrine that the Puritans appealed from the state Church of England to the right of the human conscience, with the light of Scripture to decide, each man for himself, on his mode of faith and divine worship. It was also on the ground of the same doctrine that, still later, Anne Hutchinson and Henry Vane—in whom it was said that Calvinism went to seed—appealed from the dogmatic despotism of Calvinism to the judgment-seat of individual conscience, and the voice of God within it. God's light in the Scriptures, in connection with the revelation of God in the conscience of the searcher of the Scriptures, *could* and *should* alone decide. Persecution and banishment only served to strengthen the cry in the innermost of the soul.

Driven from home and country, deserted by all, accused by his friends, and reproached even by his wife, the gentle but steadfast Roger Williams was obliged to flee into the wilderness for the doctrines of the liberty of conscience. But God was with him, and there grew up around him the large city of Providence, and afterward a state, that of Rhode Island, the home of religious toleration and human love.

The principle of freedom which the Pilgrims first planted in the soil of the New World became more and more intrinsically inward, demanding for man that he should be left alone with God.

We know very well, my noble friend, to what dangers of self-delusion and arrogance the human mind is liable from this point of view. But—every point of view has its dangers when the eye is dark, and the human mind weak or inflated with pride; nevertheless, there is no higher or more inward point of view than this—Man alone with God. God spoke in the times of old with the great lawgivers, with Moses and the prophets. It is our Christian, our joy-giving belief, that God at this day speaks individually to all and each of his children, as He, through Christ, spoke to Peter and Mary; that all and each of us may, in our most sacred moments, perceive His voice, and become both ear and tongue for his truth. Every thing in this respect depends on purity and obedience in the individual man. It may be unpardonable audacity to stand forth in the pretension of a higher knowledge; it may be criminal cowardice to remain silent; God alone can be the judge of this. The human being always stands at the last alone with God, and no one can then come between them. The Church can teach much, society can give much culture, but at the last they are insufficient. The human soul must converse alone with God. In this lies a great danger, but great strength and consolation likewise. The founders of sects in America have known both.

If you should inquire in what way this division of the Church into so many sects exhibits itself in the New World, I would reply, firstly, in a large and universal love of the Church, and a powerful form of Church discipline. The number of churches—always well and handsomely built—in both the larger and smaller cities, must strike every traveler in the United States. Generally the churches are in proportion to the number of the inhabitants, one for each thousand persons, frequently each five hundred, sometimes for less. Each religious community governs itself, and takes cognizance of all its members, and of its poor, and exercises a salutary supervision of morals and general conduct. The minister is exclusively the shepherd of souls, and occupies himself with nothing excepting the care of souls, by public preaching and private admonition and sympathy. The community, which elects its own minister, is generally very much attached to him, and estimates him very highly if he deserves it. Much has been said in Europe on the fortune-hunting of the ministers in America; but I must say, that I found those ministers who were possessed of great Christian worth and great independence of character were always regarded with great affection by their congregations, supported by them, cared for and provided for as long as they lived. The ministers of religion constitute one portion of the aristocracy of America, and I have among them met with the most intelligent and interesting individuals.

The consequence of this liberty, which is extended to sects, exhibits itself still further by a large development of the religious mind. Each considerable sect has its own religious publication, in which its doctrines are developed by discussion with others, and the church relationship is contemplated in a many-sided manner. Hence the public mind is very much turned to these subjects, and a general comprehension of them is the result; and therefore it may be said of the American people, as Swedenborg, in his day, said of the English, in the "Vision of the Last Judgment,"

"The better portion of this nation are at the central point before all Christians, and the cause of their being at the centre is, that they have developed the intellectual light. This light proceeds from the freedom which they have enjoyed in thought, and consequently in speaking and writing. Among the people of other nations this intellectual light is concealed, because it has had no outlet."

You are of a certainty acquainted with a number of the more important religious sects in the United States. I will here, therefore, merely speak of that which distinguishes them in general, and is indicative of their inner congregational life. Some address themselves more immediately to the feelings, others to the intellect; all, however, lay the greatest importance on works of love. The Catholic and the Quaker, on this broad ground, extend to each other their hands. No sect, however, it seems to me, has attained to a universal church consciousness, proportioned to the political consciousness of the United States, excepting in some of their highest representatives. I have heard genial ministers among the Calvinists, the Unitarians, the Baptists, who all open the Church of Christ to the wide world. Especially so in the old Presbyterian Congregational Church, which I will also call the Church of the Pilgrims, and in which every layman takes part in the affairs of the Church. This Presbyterian Church seems to be possessed of a strong, growing, and expansive life, *i. e.*, in the free states; in the slave states that Church is in general enslaved and bigoted in character. In the free states it stands fixed on the Rock of Ages, but opens itself thence to embrace the whole world. Even nature, art, industry, and science are baptized to the service of God.

The so-called "Revivals" belong to the phenomena which are common to all the Protestant churches of the United States, and which are indications of their vitalizing principle. These revivals are times when persons, possessed of unusual gifts and impelled by burning zeal, go about as missionaries into the cities and the country, uttering afresh the cry of John the Baptist, "Be ye converted!" Such times and seasons permeate the life of the Church like deep, fresh respirations from the sphere of religious life, and thousands of individuals date from such their new and better life.

One of the most beautiful circumstances of the general Church in the United States appears to me to be the great institution for the diffusion of popular literature of a moral and religious tendency, but without any sectarian spirit, which was established in New York about twenty years ago, and to which the adherents of many different sects equally extended support, continuing to work amicably and powerfully together to the present time. Twenty steam-presses work off twenty-five thousand sheets daily, three thousand volumes, calculated to diffuse the knowledge of our Lord Jesus Christ as the redeemer of sinners, and to promote living piety and sound morality by the circulation of works which will meet the approval of all evangelical Christians.

The American Tract Society has thus made the press subserve for the evangelizing of America. The best of the religious and moral literature of England and America is collected in these popular works, which are handsomely printed, and furnished with beautiful wood-cuts. Many hundred colporteurs are sent out to diffuse these over the whole Union, over its most remote portions, among foreigners, and in the wildernesses, and thus the evangelical Church continues to the present day to scatter a gentle rain of manna over the land, as seed from the hand of the Great Sower, and the good which is thereby produced, and which springs up especially in the hearts of childhood and youth, is incalculable.

And if we turn from this great institution for the scattering of evangelical seed—which has now been imitated in many of the Northern States—to popular schools, to establishments for neglected humanity, for the criminal, for the sick, for the unfortunate of society, and, above all, to the increasing attention to these, and the labor which is bestowed upon them in the United States, it can not be denied that these, above all, deserve the name of Christian States.

But you will say that this is merely one side of the picture; that you know very well that another life increases also in these states, a worship and a Church which are not of God. I know it well also. The Old Serpent lives also on the soil of the New World. And call it Mammon-worship, slavery, despotism, mobocracy, or by whatever name you please, indicative of the principle of selfishness and lies, it lives, it grows there, as the tares among the wheat. Yes, it seems to me that the most essential impulses of the human spirit, for good as well as for evil, and which, during the ages of history, have sprung up and flourished in Asia and in Europe, have sprung up also in America, and will there ripen for harvest. Frequently, during my residence in America, was I reminded of your words, in your article on the coming of the Lord and the completion of all things, in which you say,

"The nearer history approaches to its close, the greater is the impetus attained by the wheel of time; the greater is the speed and the rapidity, the more quick the revolution of dissimilar conditions hurrying onward development; and he may greatly miscalculate who conceives that in the present condition of the world there still remains as much to do as may require the labor of centuries, and that the end may still be very distant; for, if the Lord so will, it may be done in an eventful day, and without such a one it never will be accomplished. Neither, therefore, is it opposed to the doctrine of Scripture, if we conceive of the Millennium as a very short period—as one day which concentrates in itself a fullness and a glory which otherwise would extend over a century."

The life of North America exhibits such a hurrying onward, such a concentration of the fullness of development in good and in evil. The vastness and comprehensiveness of this hemisphere, embracing the productions and peculiar beauties of every zone; the means of communication, their abundance and facility, which places them within the reach of every man; the extent of individual freedom, the unlimited scope for competition—nay, even the nervous temperament of the climate, and its stimulating effect upon a race whose inborn energy impels them onward, and, carrying all other people along with them, ever accelerates their speed with the force of the avalanche, onward to the goal, to the day of judgment; for, though I have already said it, I must repeat it here, we must not expect a Utopia from America, but rather a day of judgment; and to no nation so much as to this does the admonishing word of Christ seem so applicable—"Watch!"

Yet, nevertheless, when I look at that life, which is at this time most powerfully increasing—that which is in the ascendant and prevalent throughout the United States, I must confess that my heart is filled with hope; because, if the United States would—and I believe they will—remove from their present legislation its great anomaly—if they would introduce into slavery the right of liberation by labor, and establish a gradual emancipation according to law, then * * * * *

If I imagine to myself some great convulsion of nature, which should all at once annihilate this vast hemisphere—imagine it sunk in the twinkling of an eye into the depths of the sea, and there vanishing with its star-strewn banners, its fleets and rail-roads, its great cities and swarming human masses, its proud capitols and beautiful quiet homes—imagine to myself all this vanishing silently into the great deep, as into an immense grave, and the waves roaring over it, and the space being desolate and void, save for the angel of judgment, flying forth alone over the past world, with the record of its deeds in his hand, which he will place in the Book of Life before the throne of the Almighty Judge—then on this page we read,

"This people were in earnest to realize the kingdom of Christ on earth, for the honor of God the Father!"

Behold here, my precious friend and teacher, my confession of faith regarding the life of the New World. Let me hope that I may one day justify it to you, either in your home or in mine.

It was one of my most ardent wishes in the United States to make them acquainted with you and your theological opinions, and it lies very much at my heart to make you more intimately acquainted with them, being certain that the Christian mind of Scandinavia and the people of America are profoundly united by their labor in the service of the same Lord, and that they have much to say to each other.

Let me be included in your goodness, in your kind remembrance!

APPENDIX.

It was my intention, at the commencement of this work, to introduce in an Appendix at its close such of the scenes which I had witnessed, and my own experience in the slave states of America and in Cuba, as I considered necessary to be made known, but which I had not related in my letters, being unwilling to point out persons and places. The celebrated work, however, of Mrs. Harriet Beecher Stowe, "Uncle Tom's Cabin," and, still more, her lately published work, "A Key, &c.," have rendered this unpleasant duty unnecessary for me; for my narratives would not have presented any facts essentially different to those which she has introduced into her story, so that I need not further prolong this work, which is already too much extended, than by remarking that my proposed narration would have principally strengthened my often-repeated observation regarding the demoralizing effect of the institution of slavery on the white population.

When I saw a young man of almost angelic beauty, a noble by descent and appearance, sell his soul, with the full consciousness of doing so, to receive the wages of a slave-driver; heard him acknowledge that he did not dare to read the Bible; heard him say that he—at the beginning of his career—would not for any money have touched a negro with the whip, but that now he should be able, without hesitation, to have a negro flogged to death for "example's sake," and chase them with blood-hounds or any thing else; when I heard one of the richest planters of Louisiana, one of the politest of gentlemen, naïvely praise himself and the system on his plantation, without having the slightest idea of the miserable hypocrisy, and the despotism which the whole of his conduct on these plantations betrayed; when I saw a Christian woman and mother forbid her daughter to dance on a Sunday, yet perceive nothing offensive in compelling her slaves to work for her the whole of the Sunday to the music of the cracking whip; when I saw agreeable and amiable young people anxious one for another, yet witness with perfect indifference the brutal maltreatment of a young negro woman by her master for some trivial offense, I have been compelled to say with my friend, the planter on the Mississippi, "It is the system! it is the system which produced all this!"

Honor be to the noble, warm-hearted American woman, who has stood forth in our day—as no other woman in the realms of literature has yet done—for the cause of humanity and the honor of her native land, and that with a power which has won for her the whole ear of humanity. Honor and blessing be hers! What will not that people become who can produce such daughters!

I differ from the noble author of "Uncle Tom" in my convictions regarding the mode of emancipation from slavery. I am firmly persuaded that the slave states of America have really begun the work, inasmuch as they have begun to allow the negro slaves to form themselves into Christian communities, and by uniting emancipation with the colonization of Africa by free negroes. It is only by the establishment of Christian negro communities that a good emancipation can be effected. The condition of the negroes in Africa and Jamaica show what this people would become without a firm basis of Christian life and Christian teaching; it is nothing to praise, it has nothing inviting, I repeat it; a commencement is already made in several of the slave states to elevate the moral condition of the negro slaves, and my cordial wish and my hope is that still more will yet be done, as well by statutes of emancipation as by the instruction of negro children. The preachings of the slaves themselves, which I heard in many of the American slave states, are the best proof of the living and beneficial manner in which they receive Christianity. They have a peculiar capacity for the reception of its innermost life and understanding. God grant that they may come to hear the Gospel throughout the whole of the slave states! But as yet there is a great deal wanting for that—an unpardonably great deal!

My own hope rests still, however, as before, in the nobler South; my earnest wish is, that it may take the emancipation question into its own hand. It alone, and not England, nor yet the Northern States of America, can enter into the greatness of the question. The South alone knows the burden, the danger, the responsibility, all the great difficulties; it alone has the labor and the sorrows. If it succeed in unloosing the fetters of the slave, and freeing its glorious, grand country from slavery, it will achieve for itself unfading glory.

STOCKHOLM, May 1st, 1853.

THE END.

Letters, Conversations, and Recollections of S. T. Coleridge. 12mo, Muslin, 65 cents.

Specimens of the Table-talk of S. T. Coleridge. Edited by H. N. COLERIDGE. 12mo, Muslin, 70 cents.

Mardi: and a Voyage Thither. By HERMAN MELVILLE. 2 vols. 12mo, Muslin, $1 75.

Omoo; Or, a Narrative of Adventures in the South Seas. By HERMAN MELVILLE 12mo, Muslin, $1 25.

Montgomery's Lectures on General Literature, Poetry, &c., with a Retrospect of Literature, and a View of modern English Literature. 18mo, Muslin, 45 cents.

Boswell's Life of Dr. Johnson. Including a Journal of a Tour to the Hebrides. With numerous Additions and Notes, by J. W. CROKER, LL.D. A new Edition. Portraits. 2 vols. 8vo, Muslin, $2 75; Sheep extra, $3 00.

Dr. Samuel Johnson's complete Works. With an Essay on his Life and Genius, by A. MURPHY, Esq. Engravings. 2 vols. 8vo, Muslin, $2 75; Sheep extra, $3 00.

Cicero's Offices, Orations, &c. The Orations translated by DUNCAN; the Offices, by COCKMAN; and the Cato and Lælius, by MELMOTH. With a Portrait. 3 vols. 18mo, Muslin, $1 25.

Paley's Natural Theology. A new Edition, from large Type, edited by D. E. BARTLETT Copiously Illustrated, and a Life and Portrait of the Author. 2 vols. 12mo, Muslin, $1 50.

Paley's Natural Theology. With illustrative Notes, &c., by Lord BROUGHAM and Sir C. BELL, and preliminary Observations and Notes, by ALONZO POTTER, D.D. With Engravings. 2 vols. 18mo, Muslin, 90 cents.

The Orations of Demosthenes. Translated by Dr. LELAND. 2 vols. 18mo, Muslin, 85 cents.

Lamb's Works. Comprising his Letters, Poems, Essays of Elia, Essays upon Shakespeare, Hogarth, &c., and a Sketch of his Life, by T N. TALFOURD. Portrait 2 vols. royal 12mo, Muslin, $2 00.

Hoes and Way's Anecdotical Olio. Anecdotes, Literary Moral, Religious, and Miscellaneous. 8vo, Muslin, $1 00.

Dendy's Philosophy of Mystery. 12mo, Muslin, 50 cents.

www.ingramcontent.com/pod-product-compliance
Lightning Source LLC
LaVergne TN
LVHW021055110826
845150LV00001B/75

* 9 7 8 1 4 2 5 5 6 7 0 6 4 *